THE INSIDERS' GUIDE TO

W CALIFORNIA'S WINE COUNTRY

Including Napa, Sonoma, Mendocino and Lake Counties

by
Phil Barber
&
Ted Brock

The Insiders' Guide®
An imprint of Falcon® Publishing Inc.
A Landmark Communications company
P.O. Box 1718
Helena, MT 59624
(800) 582-2665
www.insiders.com

•

Sales and Marketing: Falcon Publishing, Inc.
P.O. Box 1718
Helena, MT 59624
(800) 582-2665
www.falcon.com

•

THIRD EDITION
1st printing

•

•

Printed in the United States of America

•

Cover photos of hot-air balloon and vineyards: Napa Valley Conference & Visitors Bureau

•

Publications from *The Insiders' Guide*® series are available at special discounts for bulk purchases for sales promotions, premiums or fundraisings. Special editions, including personalized covers, can be created in large quantities for special needs.
For more information, please contact Falcon Publishing.

ISBN 1-57380-167-4

Preface

WINE COUNTRY.

The very words inspire images of bucolic vineyards where grapes hang lush and heavy from the vines, of ancient stone wineries and cool cellars where Cabernet Sauvignon and Chablis mellow in rows of oaken casks. California's wine valleys do, indeed, contain all those things. But to the surprise of the first-time visitor and the constant delight of those familiar with the area, this wine-rich region offers a melange of other pleasures: historic towns that evoke the Spanish influence, quiet backcountry roads, redwoods, ocean vistas and air as clean and crisp as a good Chardonnay.

To be certain, there are other wine districts in California. But as the world is beginning to realize, it is this region north of San Francisco—the valleys of Napa, Sonoma, Mendocino and Lake counties—that visitors have in mind when they set out to visit the California Wine Country.

Its countryside is hard to match any time of year. From late autumn to early spring, the hills are as green as an Irishman's dream of home. Morning frosts spangle gnarled vines. In spring, the purple of wild lupine and the intense yellow of mustard accent the dark, twisted, dormant vines. In summer the hills turn to camel's-hair beige. In October, vines turn to velvet crimson and cadmium yellow. And on backcountry roads, where time moves at the pace of an aging Cabernet, a sudden flurry of activity heralds the time of the "crush." There's a frenzy of pickers at work and presses in motion, and the aroma of ripe fruit wafts over the valley.

If you've never seen the crush, you're in for a treat. Pickers head out in the cool of the morning to harvest grapes, load gondolas and tote their bounty to the wineries. There, the grapes are stemmed and crushed in high-tech machines before being siphoned off for fermentation. It's a fascinating process, and many wineries feature it on guided or self-guided tours.

Between tours and tastings you'll find myriad other things to do—hiking, biking, dining, horseback riding, hot-air ballooning, fishing, relaxing at a spa and more. The Sonoma Coast is one of the most intriguing along the Western seaboard. Nature lovers walk along the sand, leaving footprints soon to be erased by the tide. And from the headlands above, visitors gaze out on the Pacific for hours at a time, wrapped in the mystery of the ocean, nurturing their souls. Then, they set about finding a cozy seafood restaurant where they can satiate their hunger with crab and shrimp pulled fresh from the ocean.

Driving through the Napa-Sonoma countryside, you'll find the days are warm and golden, and the nights are made cool by the legendary Northern California fog as it creeps onto the coast from the ocean. The Mendocino Coast can often be cool and blustery when clouds cover the sun. When the sun finally burns through, it illuminates the most beautiful sights you'll ever see. Inland, along the valleys east of U.S. Highway 101, summer days and nights are brilliantly warm—ideal grape-growing weather for several varieties.

Grape-touring around the countryside, you'll also discover there's nothing the locals enjoy more than a picnic. Small shops specialize in picnic fixings and cater to those who mean it literally when they say they want to eat out. Even better, most wineries provide picnic facilities, and some have gourmet foods for you to purchase.

If Wine Country is a nice place to visit, it's also a nice place to live. Here is small-town tranquility with urban convenience, or at least highway proximity. Of all the visitors who come each year, there are always some who fall in love with Wine Country and decide to stay. In fact, it seems that most of the people who now call our area home first came to Napa, Sonoma, Mendocino or Lake County as visitors.

Whether you come as a tourist or a settler, we hope you will discover some intriguing stories, businesses and back roads and gain insight from this book.

We invite you to drop us a line and let us know how it worked out for you. And if you discovered something we missed, we'd like to know about that too. We update this guide annually, and we want it to be as accurate and helpful as possible.

Write to us at:

The Insiders' Guide to California's Wine Country
c/o Insiders' Guides
Falcon Publishing
P.O. Box 1718
Helena, MT 59624

You can also visit us on the Web at www.insiders.com.

About the Authors

Phil Barber

After splitting most of 32 years between the sleepy streets of Marysville and the multilingual din of Los Angeles, native Californian Phil Barber finally learned the career writer's most important lesson: If you're going to be penniless, you might as well do it in paradise. He has lived in Calistoga, in the upper corner of Napa Valley, for four years now.

Phil wishes he could make a living wage sipping wine and calling it research, but he can't. So he supplements this work with sports, travel and news features. He has written articles for the likes of *Sports Illustrated*, *The Sporting News*, the annual Super Bowl program, *California Homes*, the *Los Angeles Times* travel section and the *San Francisco Chronicle*. His wiseacre column, "Hot Water," appears in the *Napa Valley Register* each Wednesday. His book credits include co-authorship of *Football America*, a coffee-table edition published by Turner in 1996. He also is available for website text, advertising copy, and bar mitzvahs.

Even discounting the whole mustard-blooming-in-the-vineyards thing, Phil is surrounded by beauty—specifically his wife, Kara Brunzell, and his daughters—Ynez (5), Alice (3), and twins Simone and Nora (1). They all spend an inordinate amount of time watching the UCLA basketball team and listening to Johnny Cash.

Photo: Tina Luster-Hoban

The Napa County seal decorates the administration building in downtown Napa.

Ted Brock

With ex-wives in Napa and Sonoma and a home in Petaluma, Ted Brock was living proof that Wine Country is a place of peace and understanding. Then, toward the end of his work on the second edition of *The Insiders' Guide to California's Wine Country*, he made a logical move: to Modesto, 120 miles to the southeast, in the heart of California's other wine country. He works there as sports editor of *The Modesto Bee*, meanwhile returning on weekends to visit his 9-year-old son Bill. He often visits his 31-year-old daughter Molly too, though currently she's in Melbourne, Australia, training for the Olympic rowing trials for the lightweight double sculls event.

Ted is a native of Orinda, near Berkeley. Growing up, he spent summers in Inverness, a cozy Point Reyes Peninsula hamlet. Since 1971, Ted has contributed to numerous national and regional publications, including *Sport*, *Runner's World*, and books and magazines of the National Football League.

In the early nineties, Ted ghost-wrote "Ask Arnold," a fitness column by Arnold Schwarzenegger, which appeared every Sunday in *USA Weekend* magazine. Prior to his collaboration with Schwarzenegger, Ted was editor of *Simpsons Illustrated* magazine, working with Matt Groening and the rest of the Simpsons family. He also put in a stint as a freelance sports columnist for the *Los Angeles Times,* assembling the popular, nationally syndicated "Morning Briefing." In addition, Ted taught sportswriting at the University of Southern California from 1982 to 1991.

Ted met co-author Phil Barber in 1985 at National Football League Properties in Los Angeles, where Ted was finishing nine years as a staff writer and editor and Phil was beginning as an assistant librarian. Ted now visits the Sonoma County Library to check out books by Phil.

Acknowledgments

Phil Barber

Gratitude begins with a pair of engaging Northern California writers, Phyllis Zauner and Ted Brock, who have handled most of the Sonoma and Mendocino County listings to date. Phyllis composed the whole doggone History chapter. (Remember, if you don't like it, they wrote!)

I also must thank my primary Insiders' Guide editor, Carol Kopec, who is considerably milder and more forgiving than the Helena, Montana, winters. She would have paid me more if she could.

Here is a partial list of people who have helped me untangle various Wine Country subjects through the years: Deborah Russell of California Prudential Realty; Janice Maschek of Shore Line Realty and John Murdock of PNC Mortgage (Real Estate); Jim Swanson of the California Department of Fish and Game (Flora, Fauna and Climate); John Hoffman of the First United Methodist Church, Tony Carlin of St. John the Baptist Catholic Church, and Gary Shearer of Pacific Union College (Worship). Other acknowledgeable sources include Paul Franson, whose "What's Upvalley" column keeps *Napa Valley Register* readers up-to-date, and eternal Insider Cliff Morgan.

Most of all, thank you to my wife, the leggy Kara Brunzell, for being a remarkable chef and for forgiving the writer's vow of poverty, and to my daughters for barging into the office just often enough to make things interesting.

Ted Brock

Not long before wrapping up my contribution to *The Insiders' Guide to California's Wine Country*, I left Wine Country to take a job two hours away. There's irony in that, because thanks to the guide I was really getting to know the place. Chalk it up to the tug of purse strings. In a perfect world, I would have stuck around forever.

Having joined the project after the first edition was published, I needed support and direction. My friend and colleague Phil Barber supplied both in abundance. He'd been through the wars of cobbling together the thick, informative and entertaining first edition. Compared to his laying the book's considerable groundwork and building its frame, my contribution falls somewhere between census work and painting by numbers.

My son Bill deserves credit for his patience. Grudging thanks to the producers of Cartoon Network for supplying him with entertainment. High praise, though, to the makers of Lego, the world's greatest toy, for keeping Bill's imagination hopping while his dad talked with the innkeeper in Healdsburg or the bookstore owner in Ukiah.

Thanks to Falcon Publishing, especially associate editor Carol Kopec, for a trusting and gentle hand in the process. She kept the pace of the project at Wine Country tempo – relaxed, with just enough urgency. Where I'm coming from, that's the way to do it.

Editor's Note: A special thanks to Phil Barber for updating the complete text of *The Insiders' Guide to California's Wine Country* for this third edition.

Napa celebrated its 150th birthday in 1997.

Table of Contents

How to Use this Book 1
Area Overview 4
Getting Here, Getting Around 16
History 28
The Golden Gateway 45
Flora, Fauna and Climate 50
Hotels and Motels 56
Bed and Breakfast Inns 73
Spas and Resorts 97
Camping 105
Restaurants 113
Nightlife 141
Wineries 147
Attractions 194
Festivals and Annual Events 215
Shopping 236
Arts and Culture 260
Parks and Recreation 277
On the Water 298
Spectator Sports 307
Kidstuff 319
Daytrippin' 328
Real Estate 333
Retirement 346
Education and Child Care 357
Healthcare 372
Media 380
Worship 389
Index 400

Directory of Maps

Napa County Wine Trails x
Sonoma County Wine Trails xi
Mendocino County Wine Trails xii
Lake County Wine Trails xiii
California's Wine Country Overview Map xiv

Napa County Wine Trails

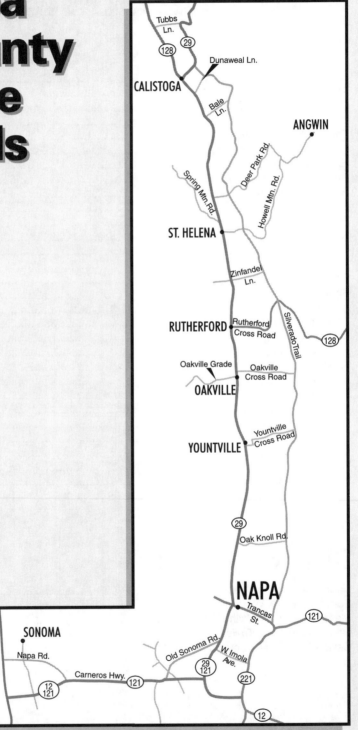

Sonoma County Wine Trails

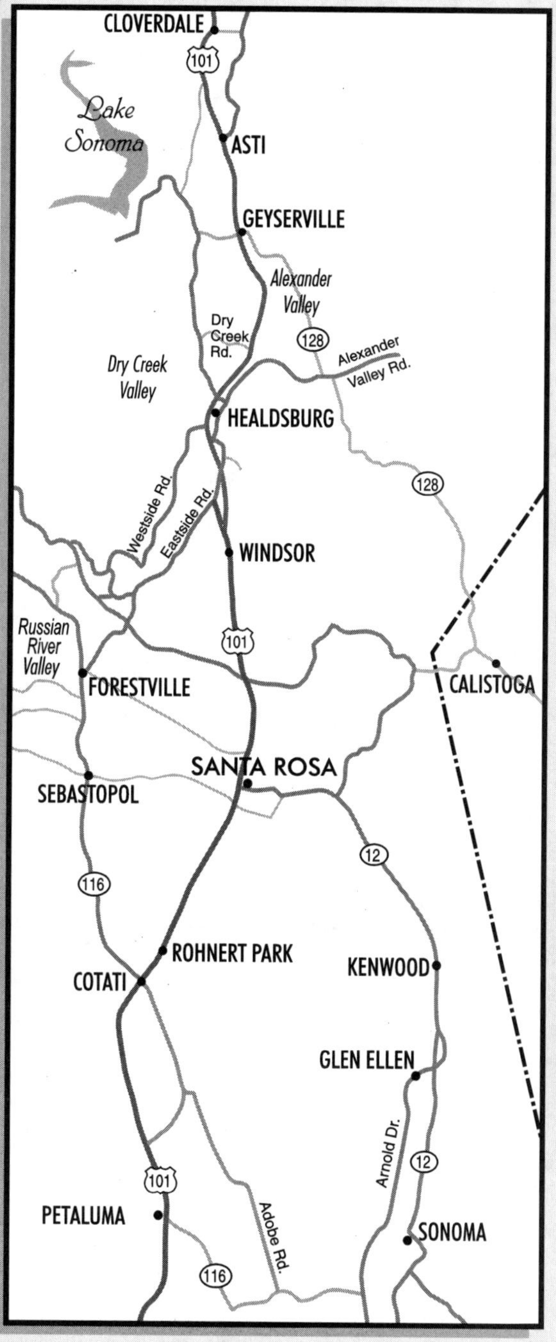

CLOVERDALE

101

Lake
Sonoma

ASTI

GEYSERVILLE

*Alexander
Valley*

Dry
Creek
Rd.

128

*Alexander
Valley Rd.*

*Dry Creek
Valley*

HEALDSBURG

128

Westside Rd.

Eastside Rd.

WINDSOR

101

*Russian
River
Valley*

FORESTVILLE

CALISTOGA

SANTA ROSA

SEBASTOPOL

12

116

ROHNERT PARK

KENWOOD

COTATI

GLEN ELLEN

Arnold Dr.

12

101

PETALUMA

Adobe Rd.

SONOMA

116

Mendocino County Wine Trails

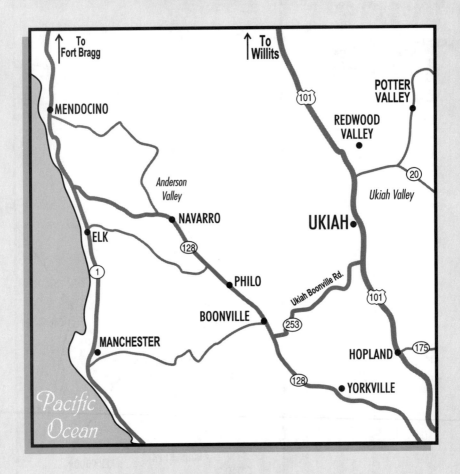

To Fort Bragg

To Willits

POTTER VALLEY

101

REDWOOD VALLEY

Anderson Valley

20

Ukiah Valley

MENDOCINO

NAVARRO

UKIAH

ELK

128

1

PHILO

Ukiah Boonville Rd.

101

BOONVILLE

253

MANCHESTER

HOPLAND

175

128

YORKVILLE

Pacific Ocean

Lake County
Wine Trails

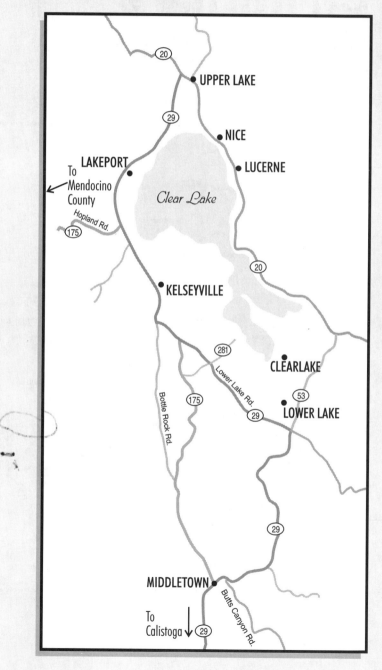

California's
Wine Country

Area of Detail

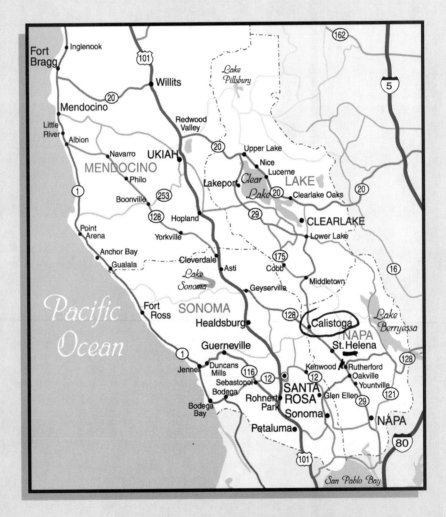

Fort Bragg
Inglenook
101
Willits
Lake Pillsbury
162
5

20
Mendocino
Redwood Valley

Little River
Albion
Navarro
UKIAH
20
Upper Lake
Nice
Lucerne

MENDOCINO
Philo
Lakeport
Clear Lake
LAKE
20

1
Boonville
253
Clearlake Oaks

128
Hopland
29
CLEARLAKE

Point Arena
Yorkville
Lower Lake

Anchor Bay
Gualala
Cloverdale
Asti
175
Cobb
Middletown
16

Lake Sonoma
Geyserville

Pacific Ocean
Fort Ross
SONOMA
Healdsburg
128
Calistoga
NAPA
St. Helena
Lake Berryessa

Guerneville
Kenwood
Rutherford
Oakville
128

Jenner
Duncans Mills
116
12
Sebastopol
Bodega
SANTA ROSA
Yountville
121

Bodega Bay
Rohnert Park
Glen Ellen
29

Sonoma
NAPA

Petaluma
80

101

San Pablo Bay

How To Use This Book

LOOK FOR:
- Napa County
- Sonoma County
- Mendocino County
- Lake County

First of all, here is how not to use *The Insiders' Guide to California's Wine Country*. Do not use it as a bath mat, a light snack or a tire block for changing your oil. And remember: Under no circumstances should this book be worn as protective headgear.

Now, how should you use it? Chances are, you already have thumbed through much of the book, tapping snippets of information about restaurants, wineries or real estate. That's all right. Data-heavy books such as this one are made for skimming. But at some point you will wish to find a particular "thing," and then it will help to understand how the book is structured.

Most of the chapter titles are self-explanatory, and if any questions remain, a quick peek at chapter introductions should answer them. But because the Wine Country is so expansive, in terms of both activity and physical space, the key to finding what you need is to know how the material is organized within chapters.

To deal with this massive chunk of Northern California, our decision was to follow a strict geographical order with the four counties that make up Wine Country. The sequence begins with entries in Napa County, followed by Sonoma, Mendocino and Lake counties. And we follow an equally rigid order within those counties, so that practically every town of consequence will have its place in line. The order is as follows. Learn it. Know it. Refer to it here when necessary.

Napa County

Napa, Yountville, Oakville, Rutherford, St. Helena, Angwin, Lake Berryessa, Calistoga

Sonoma County

Southern Sonoma
Sonoma, Glen Ellen, Kenwood, Petaluma, Cotati, Rohnert Park, Santa Rosa

Northern Sonoma
Windsor, Healdsburg, Geyserville, Cloverdale, Alexander Valley, Dry Creek Valley, Lake Sonoma, Westside Road

Sonoma Coast
Bodega, Bodega Bay, Jenner, Fort Ross

West County/Russian River
Sebastopol, Occidental, Forestville, Guerneville, Monte Rio, Cazadero, Duncans Mills

Mendocino County

U.S. Highway 101
Hopland, Ukiah, Willits

Calif. Highway 128
Yorkville, Boonville, Philo, Navarro

Mendocino Coast
Gualala, Point Arena, Albion, Little River, Mendocino, Fort Bragg

Lake County

Middletown, Cobb, Lower Lake, Clearlake, Clearlake Oaks, Kelseyville, Lakeport, Lucerne, Nice, Bartlett Springs, Upper Lake

The order will be clearer once you have used it to decode a chapter or two. As you might have noticed, the rotation generally follows a series of north-south corridors. We are not the ones who arbitrarily concocted those passages; it was the forces of volcanism and plate tectonics that have combined to form rows of longitudinal valleys in Northern California (see our Flora, Fauna and Climate chapter). Our order is intended to move south to north within those valleys, and from east to west between valleys.

Of course, it is not always so tidy. A few major roads defy the north-south standard, and some areas, such as west Sonoma County, are difficult to organize in any way. Also, some attractions—state parks and many wineries being perfect examples—don't reside within any city limits. Hence, we placed rural items with the municipalities closest to them or squeezed them between appropriate towns in the geographical breakdown. And we went south to north, east to west wherever we could.

Yes, there are a few exceptions. Destinations in the Golden Gateway (San Francisco) and Daytrippin' chapters lie outside the Wine Country. Likewise, the Spectator Sports chapter begins with a lineup of Bay Area and Sacramento professional teams. The Flora, Fauna and Climate chapter and, to some extent, the History one deal with phenomena that have no respect for county lines. And the Festivals and Annual Events chapter falls into a chronological order. Other than that, you can tie us down and pour second-rate white Zinfandel in our mouths if we fail to follow the basic geographic order.

And don't forget another important resource—the index. Many items are referenced several places in the book. Silverado Country Club, for instance, is mentioned in Spas and Resorts, Nightlife, Parks and Recreation and Spectator Sports. The index tells you that.

Lastly, you'll note that some material teeters on the fence that divides certain chapters. Take the annual Clear Lake Team Bass Tournament. Is it Sports? Is it an Event? Is it a Water activity? It's a little of all these, but we put it in the chapter called Festivals and Annual Events. Those issues arose constantly, and you might not always agree with our decisions. But the key is to cross-reference. We tried to briefly mention an event or activity or locale wherever appropriate and refer you to its primary description if that comes elsewhere.

We hope the book answers all your questions and raises a few you might not have considered. If you find anything you believe to be inaccurate or misleading, we urge you to let us know. You can send any pertinent notes to Insiders' Guides, Falcon Publishing, PO Box 1718, Helena, Montana 59624. Or contact us at www.insiders.com.

Happy hunting.

Photo: Napa Valley Conference & Visitors Bureau

They may be full of hot air, but balloons are a popular way to see Wine Country.

Area Overview

LOOK FOR:
• Napa County
• Sonoma County
• Mendocino County
• Lake County

Is the whole of the Wine Country greater than the sum of its parts? Being neither mathematicians nor philosophers, we'll leave that question unanswered. However, we would like to take a small amount of space to outline its municipal and county components.

Describing the towns of Napa, Sonoma, Mendocino and Lake counties collectively is a hopeless task. Excluding proximity to vineyards, Middletown has no more in common with Mendocino than Santa Fe has with Sheboygan. It's best to break down the outlook town by town, or at least by micro-region. That is what we will attempt to do here. Because we are dealing with close to 60 communities, the descriptions are not detailed accounts.

Napa County

Of the four counties profiled in this book, Napa is by far the most dependent on wine and tourism. Always rural in nature, Napa County has seen the rise and fall of wheat, cattle and prunes as the dominant product. Today it is grapes—and the visitors who love them—that drive the economy.

Sometimes it seems as though everyone in the valley works in some wine- or tourist-related capacity. And even those in the general service sector notice the great ebbs and flows of cash as the seasons change. Such homogeneity of industry tends to make folks nervous, but times are good for now: A 1998 report estimated Napa County's average household income at about $51,800. At the north end of the valley are two major bottlers of mineral water, Calistoga and Crystal Geyser.

The southern gateway to Napa Valley is the town of **Napa**, which, at about 62,000 people, makes up more than half of the county's population. Napa has several gracious, older districts—the lettered streets known as Old Town, the Fuller Park area south of downtown, and Alta Heights—connected by more down-to-earth neighborhoods. It also has outlying bedroom communities like American Canyon to the south and Browns Valley to the west. Napa is home to most of the budget- and family-oriented accommodations and eateries in the valley and some busy, densely commercial streets that don't reflect the charm that first-time visitors might expect here.

To the north, **Yountville**, named after Napa Valley pioneer George Yount (see our History chapter), is a small community that self-proclaims more fine restaurants per capita than any city in America. The town is dominated by two structures: the delightful Veterans Home complex (see our Attractions chapter) that watches over the proceedings from the hill west of Calif. Highway 29; and Vintage 1870, a historic winery rescued and converted into a warren of shops (see our Shopping chapter). **Oakville** and **Rutherford** appear frequently in addresses throughout the book, but usually the reference is to nearby, countryside locales. The towns themselves are minuscule; hardly more than bulges around Calif. 29. This is, however, an achingly beautiful part of Napa—a midway sector where the mountains begin to encroach upon the valley floor. Every experienced picnicker in the region knows the Oakville Grocery Company intimately. (Visitors from Southern California, as well as those who crave a good newspaper each morning, will note the *Los Angeles Times* is available from a rack outside the store.)

When most visitors close their eyes and imagine what they want a Wine Country town to look like, they envision **St. Helena**—the gingerbread cottages painted glistening white, the canopied sidewalks of a thriving-yet-nostalgic downtown, the pocket gardens with not a blade of grass out of place. Though it has its peripheral subdivisions and apartment complexes, the overall look of St. Helena is defined by high-priced neatness. The north end of town is dominated by the imposing structures of the Beringer and Charles Krug wineries and the Culinary Institute at Greystone (see our Education and Child Care chapter).

The hilltop community of **Angwin**, up Deer Park Road/Howell Mountain Road off the Silverado Trail, orbits around Pacific Union College. The town is so heavily Seventh-day Adventist that it's said to be one of only two in the nation where the post office delivers mail on Sunday rather than Saturday. Angwin's College Market is a richly stocked supermarket with dozens of bulk bins—but no meat or liquor section (yep, that includes wine). Man-made **Lake Berryessa** figures prominently in our On the Water chapter. The settlements thereof tend to lie on the western and southern shores of the lake, especially along Berryessa-Knoxville Road. The eastern perimeter is virtually inaccessible to any vehicle. Unlike Clear Lake in Lake County, Berryessa is not encircled with hotels and restaurants. There are a few, but it is known more as a spot for vacation homes. As such, it empties out a bit in the winter.

Calistoga, the northernmost town of Napa Valley, is an iconoclastic slice of California, a burg that sees itself as "real" and unadulterated even as it supports itself almost entirely through tourist dollars. It's a place where a prominent restaurateur in a restored Queen Anne can live between an elderly Russian woman in an unremarkable 1950s cottage and an apartment complex of mostly working-class Latino families. Calistoga's easygoing mood can crack when the locals feel threatened by rampant development. PepsiCo tried to open some fast-food franchises in town a few years ago, but the citizenry hastily mobilized and ran the scoundrels out of town. That led to a bold prohibition of all new "formula" businesses.

Sonoma County

Wine grapes are claiming an increasing share of the Sonoma County market, but they still are just one piece of a thriving agricultural picture that includes everything from apples to dairy products to plums and peaches.

Interestingly, the 1990 census indicated that Santa Rosa's mean household income ($35,000) was slightly lower than the countywide figure ($36,299), indicating healthy small-town economies. Santa Rosa's largest employers include Hewlett-Packard, the electronics giant, and Kaiser Permanente Medical Center. Like Napa County, Sonoma has a significant Hispanic population (about 11 percent here) but is pretty pale-faced beyond that.

For a description of **Sonoma**, the population-9,000 town that shares a name with the county, you would do well to turn to our History chapter. Sonoma is largely defined by its historic sites, especially those along the town's 8-acre central Plaza. There you'll find the Mission San Francisco de Solano, the Sonoma Barracks, the Swiss Hotel and more. The park in the middle of the square is a national historic landmark, and Sonoma's breezy climate makes it all a pleasant experience.

North of Sonoma are several enchanting hamlets, including **Glen Ellen** and **Kenwood**. Glen Ellen is especially enticing as a side trip, because it is tucked away from the traffic of Calif. Highway 12 on Arnold Drive. Main Street is only two blocks long, so you might have to invent an excuse to spend the whole day here. One possibility is Jack London State Historic Park, just west of town (see our Attractions chapter). Kenwood is even less substantial but equally beautiful. From the center of town (don't stand there; it's the middle of Calif. 12), you can see the forested crests of two state parks, Annadel and Sugarloaf Ridge (see our Parks and Recreation chapter).

Petaluma, the third-largest town in Wine Country with more than 43,000 people, is another nest of odd birds. The vague, down-and-out feeling of some sections is counterbalanced by the stately homes, art deco commercial palaces (like the McNear Building) and iron-front structures that proliferate downtown. For a short architectural walking tour, stroll down Sixth Street.

Petaluma became a pioneer in residential growth management in the early 1970s, adopting a resolution that regulates the number of residential allotments the City Council may grant in a given year. The resolution was challenged, but the Ninth Circuit Court of Appeals and the U.S. Supreme Court upheld the plan in 1975-76.

The Petaluma River isn't the important commercial route it once was (see our History chapter), but it still bears large cargo ships through a deep-water canal.

Heading north on U.S. Highway 101, the communities of **Cotati** and **Rohnert Park**, plus **Windsor** to the north of Santa Rosa, are primarily residential areas with a lot of new growth. Most tourists will end up using them—to stock up on food and gas, replace broken eyeglass frames and the like—rather than actually visiting them. **Santa Rosa**, meanwhile, will no doubt be the state capital of Winerfornia when the area wakes up and secedes from the union. It's not only far and away the largest city in Wine Country (with 123,000 people, its population is greater than that of any of the other three counties), but it's central to many of the region's tourist areas. Pointing to its many green spaces, it calls itself "The City Designed for Living." The most interesting part of Santa Rosa is downtown, on either side of U.S. 101. To the west are multiple antique shops and Railroad Square, made up of sturdy buildings constructed of locally quarried stone. To the east, especially along Fourth Street, are restaurants, coffee houses, music stores and similar hangouts—fun if you don't get run down by a skateboarder. The Luther Burbank Home and Gardens (see our Attractions chapter) are in the area, too.

Healdsburg is the Sonoma County version of St. Helena, lovely and self-aware, though perhaps a bit more affordable. (See our Real Estate chapter for more details.) Like Sonoma, it radiates outward from a delightful town square, where you can find good food and good books. Healdsburg is Antique Central in a region ga-ga over antiquities. **Geyserville** is named for The Geysers, the area of spectacular geothermal display northeast of the town. The fumaroles are visible from several points along epic Geyser Road, but are off-limits to the public at close range.

Still farther north on U.S. 101 is **Cloverdale**, a small, pleasant town at the headwaters of the Russian River. "Where the Vineyards Meet the Redwoods," the civic pamphlet says, and the characterization is valid. From this point north, the coast redwoods get bigger and more plentiful (see "The Big Trees" in our Daytrippin' chapter). The highway once ran through the middle of town; since a bypass was constructed, the streets of downtown Cloverdale are quieter than ever.

Alexander Valley, marked by Calif. Highway 128 as it heads southeast out of Geyserville, is a peaceful option to the relative bustle of Napa and Sonoma valleys. It doesn't have the sheer number of wineries, but it does have some good ones (see our Wineries chapter), and the traffic is comparatively light. It's quite pretty, too, especially in the spring when the hills are green. In the vineyards around Cloverdale, some of the older vines are still grown in the traditional style—spaced widely and allowed to spread freely, in contrast to the trellises you normally see today.

Where Alexander Valley parallels U.S. 101 to the east, **Dry Creek Valley** lies to the west. Viticultural space has been maximized here, with evenly spaced vineyards on the rich valley floor and terraces climbing the hillsides. Above the vines, thick forest overlooks the valley's western slope, while oak woodland makes up most of the sunnier eastern flank. Dry Creek Valley used to extend farther to the north, but much of it was submerged when Warm Springs Dam was built in 1982. That gave birth to Lake Sonoma, a recreational area profiled more thoroughly in our On The Water chapter. Next to the lake is a fish hatchery (see our Kidstuff chapter) where you can take a self-guided tour.

Moving to the southern Sonoma County coast, **Bodega** is the gateway to the Pacific. Much of *The Birds* was filmed here in 1963, but there haven't been any copycat avian attacks in the years since. The movie featured Potter School, built a century before Alfred Hitchcock's cameras moved in. **Bodega Bay** is where Calif. Highway 1 hits the coast and begins its precarious shuffle northward. The sleepy, sheltered harbor provides the largest fishing port between San Francisco and Eureka, and

INSIDERS' TIP

Robert L. Ripley, of "Believe It or Not" fame, was born in Santa Rosa, and Peanuts creator Charles Schulz calls the town his home. Schulz is a longtime regular at the Redwood Empire Ice Arena, which he gave to the town as a gift. His fellow cartoonist, Linus Maurer, whose first name Schulz made a household word, is a Sonoma Valley resident.

The Calistoga Police Department rarely handles anything more serious than barking dogs.

in September and October, the locals like to celebrate what they call "secret summer," when the thick morning fog disappears along with the tourists. The peninsula that pinches the harbor from the north is Bodega Head. A 4-mile drive from Calif. 1 on Westshore Road, it offers brilliant views and access to beaches and cliffs. Also on Bodega Head is the Bodega Marine Lab, a University of California field station that is open to the public every Friday from 2 to 4 PM.

About 7 miles north of Bodega Bay is **Jenner**, which occupies an exceptional position near the yawning mouth of the Russian River. Harbor seals seem to enjoy the scenery as much as camera-bearing humans—dozens of the pinnipeds can usually be spied basking in the sunlight. North of Jenner the coastal settlements are few and far between. Once the easternmost outpost of Czarist Russia, **Fort Ross** is now a state historic park (see our History and Attractions chapters). The fort, high on a promontory, was built as protection from Spanish troops but was never called into use.

If Gravenstein apples were suddenly discovered to have more saturated fat than buttered cinema popcorn, the whole town of **Sebastopol**, in the area known as West County, might just be nailed shut the next day. This place was paved with apple cores. Calif. Highway 116, which runs through the heart of town, is known as the Gravenstein Highway, and every summer Sebastopol throws a Gravenstein Apple Fair (see our Festivals and Annual Events chapter). The slow-paced town has some good antique shops, too, especially south of town along Calif. 116.

Occidental is a one-street town perched at the top of a hill in the middle of redwood country. It's a romantic setting, but what would you expect of a village connected to the Russian River by the Bohemian Highway? A lot of people know Occidental as the place where two Italian restaurants, Negri's Italian Dinners and the Union Hotel (see our Restaurants chapter), compete for customers with outlandishly proportioned dinners.

About halfway between Sebastopol and **Guerneville** on Calif. 116 is **Forestville**, a down-home farming town that seems barely to notice the traffic heading to and from the Russian River. The primary destination is Guerneville (pronounced GURN-ville), ground zero of a raucous, summer-long beach party. It's sometimes referred to as the Gay Riviera, with generations of San Francisco's gay professionals escaping that city's chilly fog by fleeing to the stilted houses that line the banks of the river. Guerneville, an old logging town, is pretty mainstream during the off-season, but it seems to have adopted a healthy tolerance when it comes to tourists.

Farther downstream is **Monte Rio** and, to the north, **Cazadero**. Both are unpretentious hamlets that catch some of the less flamboyant Russian River attention. And about 4 miles before Calif. 116 smacks into Calif. 1 is **Duncans Mills**, an old Victorian village restored to its appearance circa 1890, when it was a lumber center. The old railroad depot is now a museum (see our Attractions chapter), and the general store is a blast from a past that only your great-grandmother would remember.

Mendocino County

Tourism and now wine grapes have been something of a godsend to a county largely supported by lumber and fishing—two natural resources that are clearly not without limits. The Georgia-Pacific lumber company has 580 employees and vending and logging contracts with several hundred more people. It's estimated that the corporation annually contributes more than $60 million to the Fort Bragg-area economy. In inland areas such as the Yokayo Valley, agriculture is paramount. And because of the large holdings of public land in Mendocino County, the state parks system has become another important employer.

Hopland is a town that came by its name honestly. Awash in a field of hops in the early 1900s, it was the perfect choice as a home base for Mendocino Brewing Company, when in 1982 it became California's first brewery since Prohibition (see our Restaurants chapter). At the south end of Hopland is the Solar Living Center (see our Attractions chapter), a 12-acre site created by Real Goods, retailer of alternative energy products and services. Real Goods' 5,000-square-foot building is made of rice-straw bales, and all of its electrical needs are provided by wind generators and photovoltaic panels.

Ukiah is set in the Yokayo Valley between the Coast Range and Lake Mendocino. With 14,632 people, it is the largest town in Mendocino County. Lumber is the driving force here, as it has been for decades, but Ukiah also has become the financial, business, medical and service center not only for its county, but also for portions of Sonoma, Lake and Humboldt counties. Many descendants of the Pomo tribe still live and work in the area. Lake Mendocino, administered by the Army Corps of Engineers, is about 5 miles north of Ukiah (see our Parks and Recreation chapter).

Willits, to the north, also was kick-started during the 19th-century lumber boom, and most of the larger companies in the area are involved in manufacturing wood products. Driving along U.S. 101 6 miles south of town, look for a boulder directly across the highway from White Deer Lodge—it was a reputed hideout of Black Bart, the stagecoach robber who roamed the area more than 100 years ago. You probably won't catch a glimpse of Bart, but you might see a white fallow deer there on Ridgewood Summit. Herds of the deer were purchased from William Randolph Hearst's San Simeon Ranch in 1949.

The towns of Anderson Valley along Calif. 128—**Yorkville**, **Boonville**, **Philo** and **Navarro**—are too tiny to provide you with much more than pangs of envy toward the people who live there. The valley's northern latitude and salty breezes make it appropriate for growing cool-weather grapes such as Gewurztraminer and Riesling. Anderson Valley also brings forth a healthy supply of apples and sheep, and mushrooms are gathered in the soggy forests on either side of the valley. Boonville, as you'll see elsewhere in this book, is known for its unique language, called Boontling. Here's a poem a Boonie once recited on the *CBS Evening News*:

Cerk, Cerk, the Tooter's Tweed,
Strung a borp and shied.
They gormed the borp and dreeked wee Cerk,
And he piked plenty green-eyed!

We have no idea what it means, but it's probably off-color.

Gualala, pronounced "Wah-LA-la," is the southern gateway to the Mendocino Coast. Along with Anchor Bay, 4 miles to the north, it forms what locals call the Banana Belt, a relatively warm and fog-free pocket of coastline. Gualala was a thriving lumber town until the supply of unprotected trees dwindled in the 1960s, and you can still find the remains of some of the chutes and landings used to load redwood planks onto schooners years before. Today the town is something of an arts community, with resident painters, sculptors, photographers, writers and musicians (see our Arts and Culture chapter).

About 16 miles north of Gualala is **Point Arena**. With about 430 people, it's one of the smallest incorporated cities in the state. Once a lumber and fishing center, Point Arena now sticks mostly to the tourist trade. It needed the income in 1983, when a brutal winter storm splintered the town's century-old pier. The Point Arena Public Fishing Pier, a $2.2 million project, was completed seven years later. The new structure extends 330 feet into Arena Cove and is 25 feet above water level. Surfers say the harbor is one of the best surfing spots in Northern California. Point Arena Lighthouse, rebuilt after the 1906 earthquake, is a favorite stop for visitors.

Moving up the coast, **Albion** (between Whitesboro Cove and the Albion River) and **Little River** (near the waterway of the same name) are further possibilities for weary Calif. 1 drivers and white-knuckled passengers. Most people who stop there, other than those on their way to the Little River Inn (see our Spas and Resorts chapter), are heading for **Mendocino**, a village that has stood as a popular monument to social freedom since before the Sir Douglas Quintet sang about it in the late 1960s. It was little more than an economically depressed former lumber town when the Mendocino Art Center was founded in 1959, seeding an artists' colony that revitalized the community. The Art Center lives on, offering more than 200 classes, workshops and seminars each year (see our Attractions and Arts and Culture chapters).

What really draws the travelers is the integrated look of central Mendocino, a National Historic Preservation District. The gingerbread architecture, steep gables and white picket fences make it look like it was transported whole from the coast of New England—exactly the effect desired by the homesick sailors who built up the town in the mid-1800s. Some of the more outstanding architectural structures include the Mendocino Hotel, the Ford House and the Presbyterian Church of Mendocino, all on Main Street. The latter building is the oldest continuously used Presbyterian church in California.

Almost as charming, and more diversified economically, is **Fort Bragg**, originally established as a military outpost to help subdue the Mendocino Indian Reservation in 1857 (see our History chapter). Nearby beaches are prized for beachcombing, surf fishing and picnicking. Noyo Harbor, on the south end of town, is a bustle of activity as the fishing boats come and go, unload their hauls and clean up. It's the largest port between San Francisco and Eureka, and it is preferred by the vast majority of local seals and sea lions. The biggest industry in Fort Bragg, however, is lumber. You can get a map for a walking tour of the town from the Fort Bragg Chamber of Commerce at 332 N. Main Street.

Lake County

Lake County's mean household income—$22,869, according to the 1990 census—is the lowest among our four counties, and its cost of living is relatively high because of the area's isolation. The trade-off, of course, comes via bargain-basement housing prices.

Even more important than wine grapes and motel rooms to Lake County's economy is agriculture. Walnuts, kiwi fruit, wild rice and livestock are important commodities, but pears are royalty here—and the Bartlett is king. Farmers produced about 81,000 tons of Bartlett pears in 1991, and the pear harvest as a whole accounted for more than half of the county's $52 million in agricultural revenue. Other crucial Lake industries include gold mining and geothermal power, with Pacific Gas & Electric's Unit 13 at The Geysers steam field weighing in as the world's largest geothermal plant.

The first town you encounter in Lake County as you drive north on Calif. 29 is **Middletown**, a good, old-fashioned country town that hasn't quite discovered the tourist rush that is beginning to sweep over the area. Middletown has a couple of hearty cafes along its truncated Main Street. The Cobb Mountain resort area, north of Middletown via Calif. Highway 175, supports a series of tiny communities, with **Cobb** the foremost representative. The town sits at 2,500 feet, providing welcome breezes and pine-bough cover when the mercury rises during the summer.

Moving north you come to the many towns that ring Clear Lake like chairs arranged around a popular swimming

INSIDERS' TIP

Albion is tucked alongside the Albion River, and the bridge here, built in 1944, is the last wooden bridge remaining on Calif. Highway 1. The harbor at Albion is one of the locations thought likely to be the site of the fort of 16th-century explorer Francis Drake, used when he navigated the Pacific coast in 1579.

AREA OVERVIEW

Photo: Napa Valley Visitors Bureau

This welcome sign features Napa Valley's most famous attraction

pool. **Lower Lake**, where Calif. 29 splits off from Calif. Highway 53, is the southernmost locality. It has a quaint old downtown. Above that is **Clearlake**, the county's largest town (a whopping 11,804 people!). Clearlake used to be known as Clearlake Highlands before it incorporated in 1980. It's largely a collection of small motels and old-style resorts that cater to fishermen, boaters and overheated families. The town has the largest and newest library in the county and the Lake County campus of Yuba College (see our Education and Child Care chapter).

North of Clearlake, on Calif. Highway 20 and around a bend of the lake, is **Clearlake Oaks**. On the southwestern shore of Clear Lake, meanwhile, is **Kelseyville**, a tidy community with a rural economy at the base of Mt. Konocti. It's one of the few towns in the area that doesn't actually cozy up to the lake, though it's only about 3 miles away. Most famous for its Bartlett pears, Kelseyville also grows and packs walnuts and wine grapes in the agricultural area known as Big Valley. The town is the access point for Soda Bay, so called because of the tiny bubbles that naturally percolate in the cove.

Lakeport is a pleasant burg of about 5,000 on the westernmost bulge of the lake. It has been the Lake County seat since 1861, and the 1871 county courthouse is a modern-day link to the past. Library Park hugs the water and offers picnic tables and playgrounds. Lakeport is known as something of a retirement haven. **Lucerne** and **Nice** (pronounced like the French city, or your sibling's daughter, not the adjective) occupy the quieter, greener northern section of Clear Lake. The accommodations here tend to be family-oriented and rustic. Lucerne is called "Little Switzerland" by locals, and they have been known to don Alpine garb to prove the point. Finally comes **Upper Lake**, which is not on Clear Lake at all but about 3 miles due north of its uppermost shore. Upper Lake is a jumping-off point for Mendocino National Forest and the Blue Lakes, a more pristine alternative to their larger cousin to the south. It is also considered a must-hit spot for antique hunters.

INSIDERS' TIP

Petaluma's all-American appearance makes it ever popular with the film industry. *American Graffiti, Peggy Sue Got Married* and *Basic Instinct* are just a few of the movies shot there, and the commercials would be too numerous to mention.

Name Calling

OK, Hopland and Clearlake you can take a pretty safe stab at. But why Petaluma? What does Cazadero mean? What exactly is Middletown in the middle of? And if you take your nice niece to Nice, how will you pronounce your location?

Borrowing from the fourth edition of the delightful and copious *California Place Names*, written by Erwin G. Gudde in 1947 and still reprinted by the University of California Press, we have compiled a partial gazetteer of Wine Country locales, with emphasis on their christenings. Besides providing a few amusing tidbits, it might give you a sideways view of California history: the Native American tribes with their complex languages and straightforward place names; the Spanish missionaries who covered so much ground as they proselytized; the feudal land grants doled out by the Mexican government, most of them later recognized by the United States; the Russian exploration along the north coast in the first half of the 19th century; and the East Coast pioneers who eventually flooded the area in search of lumber, gold and cropland.

The whimsy we have lost over the years becomes apparent when you read Gudde's accounts of people like Dr. Edward Bale, the English surgeon who named his land grant *Rancho Carne Humana*. The translation is "Human Flesh Ranch," and it's now site of the Bale Grist Mill in Napa County.

Napa County

Napa: The name that eventually spread to a county, a city, a river, a creek, a slough and a junction first pops up in baptismal records printed in 1795. It derives from the indigenous cultures that once inhabited the area, though there has been endless debate about the exact meaning. Is it a southern Patwin word for "grizzly bear," a northern Patwin variation of "house" or "tribe," or a Suisun term that nearly translates to "motherland"? We can't say. The city was laid out by Nathan Coombs in 1848; the county was named in 1850.

Yountville: George C. Yount journeyed from North Carolina to California in 1831, and five years later he received a grant for Rancho Caymus. The name Yountville appears on an 1860 map of the grant.

St. Helena: The peak that marks the border between Napa, Lake and Sonoma counties was called Mount St. Helena at least as early as 1851, but no one is really sure why. Most assume it was Russian explorers who dubbed the mountain, perhaps J.G. Woznesenski, who bagged the summit and left a plaque in 1841. Helena was an empress of Czarist Russia, and Saint Helena was the name of a Russian ship that sailed to California. The town was christened in 1855.

Angwin: This hill town was named in 1874 for Edwin Angwin, who operated a summer resort on his property on Howell Mountain.

Berryessa: Berryessa Valley was named for Jose Jesus and Sisto Berryessa, brothers who were granted Rancho Las Putas in 1843. The lake created by Monticello Dam originally was known as Monticello Reservoir, but the U.S. Board on Geographic Names adopted Lake Berryessa in 1957.

Calistoga: Sam Brannan began this resort in 1859, and he explained the name this way, according to biographer Reva Scott: "'Someday I'll make this the Saratoga of California,' I started to say, but my tongue slipped and what I said was, 'I'll make this the Calistoga of Sarafornia.'" Brannan's moniker stuck.

Sonoma County

Sonoma: Some say the name came from the Wintun word for "nose," but it's unclear whether it was in reference to a geological or facial feature. Others say it was a

(Continued on next page)

Miyakmah word for "town," while still another translation is "many moons." The town was founded as Zanoma in 1835, and the present spelling appeared in 1844. The county, one of California's original 27, was named in 1850.

Petaluma: Consensus seems to be that it derives from two Coast Miwok words: "peta," meaning flat, and "luma," meaning back. The name was applied to a village and a low hill on the east side of what would be known as the Petaluma River. It later was given to a Mexican land grant (1834) and, of course, a city (1851).

Cotati: A land grant spelled Cotati or Cotate is dated 1844. The origin of the name is uncertain, though a Coast Miwok village north of the present town may have been called Kotati.

Rohnert Park: Incorporated in August 1962, this city was named after the Waldo Rohnert Seed Farm.

Santa Rosa: This is a popular place name throughout the state of California. Historian H.H. Bancroft lent this explanation to the naming of the creek (and later the city) in present-day Sonoma County: "the stream was named by a missionary priest who . . . captured and baptized in its waters an Indian girl, and gave her the name of Santa Rosa, in honor of the saint on whose day in the calendar this interesting ceremony was performed." The name first appears in a land grant document in 1831.

Healdsburg: The name was first applied to an outpost of the Post Office Department in 1857. It honored Harmon G. Heald, who established a trading post there in 1846.

Geyserville: Elisha Ely founded the town in 1851 and named it to advertise the nearby geothermal activity.

Bodega Bay: This long-established name is a tribute to captain Juan Francisco de Bodega, who sailed the *Sonora* into the bay in 1775. The town of Bodega was settled in 1853.

Fort Ross: Lots were drawn to choose the name of this outpost, which formed the nucleus of early 19th-century Russian activity in California. Ross is an obsolete poetic name for Russians, and its lot was selected from others placed at the base of an image of Christ.

Sebastopol: Sebastopol was the Russian city besieged by the English and French during the Crimean War in 1854. The highly publicized siege prompted no less than five California towns to adopt the name. This is the only one that bears it still. (Legend has it that when a local fight erupted, one group found itself under siege in the general store and the situation was likened to that of the famous city.)

Forestville: This town is at the edge of timber country, but it actually was named for its founder, Andrew Jackson Forrester, a Russian River saloonkeeper. The present spelling seems to have taken over by the late 1880s.

Cazadero: The terminus of the North Pacific Coast Railroad was named Cazadero in the late 1880s. It's a California Spanish word that means "hunting place."

Mendocino County

Hopland: When a toll road was built on the east side of the Russian River in 1874, the tiny town of Sanel packed up and moved across the river to meet the road. The name was changed to Hopland to acknowledge Stephen Knowles' successful experiment in growing the grain there. In 1890 the California Northwestern Railroad was extended to Ukiah, and tracks were laid on the west side of the river. Back came the town. The Post Office Department restored the name Sanel, but switched it to Hopland in 1891 or 1892.

Ukiah: Mendocino County's largest city was named for a Pomo Indian village that once existed nearby. It probably means "deep valley." The town was named in 1856.

Yorkville: When a post office was established here about 1870, the settlers could not decide which of two locally prominent families to honor: the Yorks or the Hiatts. The patriarchs of the two clans finally settled it with a contest. Unfortunately, we don't know what the test was, but Richard H. York won. The loser, Elijah M. Hiatt, received the postmastership as a consolation prize.

Boonville: In the mid-1860s W.W. Boone bought the Levi and Strauss store in Kendall's City and changed the name of the town to Booneville. The "e" was somehow misplaced when the post office was established in the 1880s.

Philo: Sometime after 1868 Cornelius Prather, landowner and postmaster, called this town after his favorite girl cousin, who (probably) was named Philomena.

Gualala: Here's a bone of contention. Most anthropologists familiar with the area insist the name is a corruption of Walali, a Pomo word meaning "where the waters meet." County histories and local tradition, on the other hand, claim it's a Spanish version of Walhalla, mythical abode of slain Teutonic heroes. In any case, when the town was named in 1862 (after the river), the namegiver applied the current spelling, mistakenly assuming it to be a Spanish word.

Point Arena: This cape on the Mendocino coast was sighted by Bartolome Ferrer in 1543 and called Cabo de Fortunas. By the late 18th century, the name had begun to give way to Barra de Arena, or "sand bar." The English-style Point Arena was in use by 1849.

Albion: New Albion was the name Sir Francis Drake bestowed upon northern California in the 16th century. Another Briton (and captain of the port of San Francisco), William A. Richardson, no doubt had that in mind when he named the river in 1844. The town was named in 1853.

Mendocino: This moniker is almost as old as Spanish exploration of the Pacific coast. In fact, no other name for a cape has survived as many phases of real or imagined California geography with the same spelling and in the same location.

The earliest known reference to Cabo Mendocino is on the maps of Ortelius in 1587. The only question is after which viceroy of New Spain the protrusion was named: Don Antonio de Mendoza or Lorenzo Suarez de Mendoza. (Mendocino would be an adjectival form of the name.) The county, one of California's original 27, was named in 1850, the town in 1852. Mendocino National Forest was created as Stony Creek Forest Reserve in 1907, renamed California National Forest in 1908 and given its current name in 1932.

Fort Bragg: The military post established in 1857 honored Lt. Col. Braxton Bragg, who had won some fame in the Mexican War. Bragg soon would become a Confederate general, and the town of Fort Bragg would be founded in 1885.

Lake County

Middletown: This small burg got its handle in the 1860s, when it was the stage stop halfway between Calistoga and Lower Lake.

Cobb: The town, the mountain, the valley and the creek are named for John Cobb, the Kentuckian who built a combination sawmill and gristmill in the valley in 1859.

Clear Lake: This name dates back at least to 1851, when it appeared in the journal of George Gibbs. Before that, the Spanish called it Laguna Grande (big lake), and the indigenous people called it Kah Shoh, the Clear Lake Valley Indians' word for lake. The towns of Lower Lake, Clearlake, Clearlake Oaks, Lakeport and Upper Lake all derive their names from their relationship to Clear Lake.

Kelseyville: When the town was established in the 1860s, it was called Kelsey Town in memory of Andrew Kelsey, the county's first white settler. Kelsey was a widely disliked character who was killed by a local tribe in 1849 in retaliation for years of mistreatment. The name was changed to Kelseyville around 1885.

Lucerne: Somebody evidently thought the shore of Clear Lake looked a lot like Switzerland's Lake Lucerne when the town (at that point, a hotel and a post office) was founded in 1926.

Nice: The community once known as Clear Lake Villas became Nice in 1927 or 1928, apparently because of the area's loose resemblance to the bluffs of the French Riviera.

Phone Numbers for Tourists

Napa County

Napa Valley Conference & Visitors Bureau
1310 Napa Town Center, Napa • (707) 226-7459
Napa Chamber of Commerce
1556 1st St., Napa • (707) 226-7455
Yountville Chamber of Commerce
6516 Yount St., Yountville • (707) 944-0904
St. Helena Chamber of Commerce
1020 Main St., St. Helena • (707) 963-4456
Calistoga Chamber of Commerce
1458 Lincoln Ave., Calistoga • (707) 942-6333

Sonoma County

Sonoma County Wine & Visitors Center
5000 Roberts Lake Rd., Rohnert Park • (707) 586-3795
Hispanic Chamber of Commerce of Sonoma County
2435 Professional Dr., Santa Rosa • (707) 526-7744
Sonoma Valley Visitors Bureau
453 1st St., Sonoma • (707) 996-1090
Sonoma Valley Chamber of Commerce
651 Broadway, Sonoma • (707) 996-1033
Petaluma Chamber of Commerce
799 Baywood Dr., Petaluma • (707) 762-2785
Petaluma Visitors Program
799 Baywood Dr., Petaluma • (707) 769-0429
Cotati Chamber of Commerce
7981 Old Redwood Hyw., Cotati • (707) 795-5508
Rohnert Park Chamber of Commerce
5000 Roberts Lake Rd., Rohnert Park • (707) 584-1415
Santa Rosa Covention & Visitors Bureau
9 4th St., Santa Rosa • (707) 577-8674
Santa Rosa Chamber of Commerce
637 1st St., Santa Rosa • (707) 545-1414
Sonoma County Tourism Information
401 College Ave., Santa Rosa • (707) 524-2589
Mark West Area Chamber of Commerce
4795 Old Redwood Hwy., Santa Rosa • (707) 578-7975
Windsor Chamber of Commerce
8499 Old Redwood Hwy., Windsor • (707) 838-7285
Healdsburg Chamber of Commerce
217 Healdsburg Ave., Healdsburg • (707) 433-6935
Geyserville Chamber of Commerce Information Center
21060 Geyserville Ave., Geyserville • (707) 857-3745
Cloverdale Chamber of Commerce
105 N. Cloverdale Blvd., Cloverdale • (707) 894-4470
Sonoma Coast Visitor Information/Bodega Bay Area Chamber of Commerce
850 Calif. Hwy. 1, Bodega Bay • (707) 875-3422
Jenner Visitors' Center
10439 Calif. Hwy. 1, Jenner • (707) 865-9433

Sebastopol Chamber of Commerce
265 S. Main St., Sebastopol • (707) 823-3032
Monte Rio Chamber of Commerce
(707) 865-1533
Forestville Chamber of Commerce and Visitors Center
6652 Front St., Forestville • (707) 887-1111
Russian River Region Visitors Bureau
14034 Armstrong Woods Rd., Guerneville • (707) 869-9212
Russian River Chamber of Commerce
16200 1st St., Guerneville • (707) 869-9000
Occidental Chamber of Commerce
(707) 874-3279

Mendocino County

Hopland Chamber of Commerce
(707) 744-1379
Ukiah Chamber of Commerce
200 S. School St., Ukiah • (707) 462-4705
Willits Chamber of Commerce
239 S. Main St., Willits • (707) 459-7910
Anderson Valley Chamber of Commerce
(707) 895-2379
Gualala Sea Ranch Coastal Chamber of Commerce
(707) 884-1182, (800) 778-5252
Fort Bragg-Mendocino Coast Chamber of Commerce
332 N. Main St., Fort Bragg • (707) 961-6300

Lake County

Lake County Visitor Information Center
875 Lakeport Blvd., Lakeport • (707) 263-9544, (800) 525-3743
Clear Lake Chamber of Commerce
4700 Golf Ave., Clearlake • (707) 994-3600
Lakeport Chamber of Commerce
290 S. Main St., Lakeport • (707) 263-5092

AREA OVERVIEW

Getting Here, Getting Around

LOOK FOR:
- **By Automobile**
- **By Air**
- **By Bus/Train**
- **By Limousine**
- **By Taxi**

It's about 142 miles from Sears Point Raceway at the southern tip of Sonoma County to the town of Piercy at the north end of Mendocino County. And that's as the crow flies; it is considerably farther as the tourist weaves. The point is this: The four counties that compose the Wine Country assume a massive chunk of California real estate.

And because the day's activity usually involves a steering wheel and a crumpled map of wineries, getting around is an essential part of enjoying yourself here. As explained in How to Use This Book, the major thoroughfares of the region run north-south, though they are periodically linked by horizontal or diagonal roads and highways. All the highways are covered here, starting with the four north-south routes. Due to space constraints the smaller routes are not, though they might be important links for locals. Some of those roads show up other places in the book. Unless otherwise stated, all roads mentioned are two-lane highways.

Following the route descriptions is information on public and private transportation, including airports, shuttle services, Amtrak and Greyhound, taxis, limousines and public buses.

This is as good a place as any to broach a serious subject—drunk driving. Wineries-plus-cars is a simple equation, and it can be a lethal one if you don't use some common sense. A full 38 percent of traffic fatalities in California involve intoxicated drivers. If you plan to drive to a series of tasting rooms, please designate one person to drink in moderation or, preferably, to guzzle nothing but Calistoga mineral water. And don't forget to eat. You can keep a couple of glasses of Cabernet from going straight to your head by bringing picnic fixings or stopping for lunch in town. Remember, the legal blood-alcohol threshold in California is .08 percent. That is lower than some visitors are accustomed to, and it is possible to be over this limit without feeling particularly buzzed. So play it safe. If you're not sure, you probably are drunk, at least by California Highway Patrol standards. Finally, even if you are white-eyed sober, others on the road might not be. As the old public-service ads used to say, drive defensively.

By Automobile

The Main North-South Arteries

Calif. Highway 29

This is the umbilical cord of Napa Valley, not to mention the perimeter route for half of Lake County's Clear Lake. The highway begins in Vallejo and, after passing through the city of Napa about 12 miles later, quickly becomes a ride in a wine-theme amusement park. It passes through some of the finest wine-grape country in America and connects the valley's towns: Napa, Yountville, Oakville, Rutherford, St. Helena and Calistoga. Its shoulders are weighed down by chateaux, fortresses, Victorians and renowned restaurants. Wine Country heavyweights such as Robert Mondavi and Domaine Chandon are here and so are great historic wineries like Beringer and Charles Krug (see our Wineries chapter).

Calif. 29 is four lanes from Vallejo to Yountville; two thereafter. The road makes a sharp right when it gets to Calistoga and proceeds through the mostly vintage downtown. It leaves Calistoga and heads due north, climbing the flank of Mt. St. Helena and dropping into the flats of Lake County. The highway then takes a serpentine path up to Lower Lake, where it veers sharply and heads northwest, skirting the southern and western shores of Clear Lake. Calif. 29 hits Kelseyville and Lakeport, then heads north and dies at the town of Upper Lake.

Calif. Highway 12

Calif. 12 is an east-west highway for most of its existence, but it garners acclaim for a relatively short north-south stretch that makes it the main artery of Sonoma County Wine Country. After gold field and Sacramento Delta meanderings, Calif. 12 joins with Calif. 29 below Napa. Four miles later it breaks west, joined by Calif. 121, then splits again, north into Sonoma. Here Calif. 12 slices through the postcard-perfect Valley of the Moon, past wineries and hot springs. It's a less-developed, more compact version of Napa Valley. Calif. 12 begins to veer west after Kenwood. It passes through the heart of Santa Rosa and continues to Sebastopol.

U.S. Highway 101

U.S. 101, also known as the Redwood Highway, doesn't have the good-life ring of Calif. 29 or 12, but it is the lifeline of the greater Wine Country population from commuters to truckers to farmers. It also is a classic California highway that runs from Hollywood into Oregon.

U.S. 101 enters Sonoma County about 5 miles south of Petaluma, and it holds few surprises. It is a left-leaning northward course that connects Rohnert Park, Santa Rosa, Healdsburg, Cloverdale, Ukiah, Willits, Laytonville and other, smaller towns, while offering constant views of big trees and ranch country. The southern Wine Country stretch of U.S. 101—from Petaluma to Windsor—is built up and populated, and traffic tends to bog down close to rush hour. In contrast, some of the northern stretches feel like a country lane. South of Cloverdale, U.S. 101 is four lanes; north of that it alternates between two lanes and four.

Calif. Highway 1

Calif. 1 isn't so much a link as a destination unto itself. This stretch is not as celebrated as the Big Sur-Carmel portion of Calif. 1, but it offers approximately 135 miles of breathtaking coastal highway—fabulous, shifting vistas of the craggy coastline to the west and, usually, stands of coastal live oak, pine, fir or coast redwoods to the east.

The highway intersects at least 24 state parks, state beaches, state reserves, regional parks and county parks on its ascent through the Wine Country (see our Parks and Recreation chapter). It also encounters towns such as Jenner, Gualala, Point Arena, Albion, Mendocino and Fort Bragg. If you've been there before, just the names are enough to make you smell salt air and clam chowder.

Northbound Calif. 1 cuts over to the ocean at Bodega Bay, about 8 miles after it enters Sonoma County. The highway leaves the sea again north of Rockport in the upper reaches of Mendocino County. You'll notice that between Bodega Bay and Fort Bragg in Mendocino County, the road is often designated as Coast Highway 1. And one note of realism: This is not 135 miles that you can drive in two hours. Even doing it in one full day will leave little time for beachcombing and otter spotting.

Other Wine Country Roadways

Calif. Highway 121

This highway joins Sonoma with the Lake Berryessa highlands, via Napa. The route is born at Sears Point, site of the famed motor raceway at the southern tip of Sonoma County (see our Spectator Sports chapter). It heads north, then makes a sharp right to join Calif. 12 on its way to Napa Valley.

A boat plies the waters of Fort Bragg Harbor.

Calif. 121 travels through the Carneros grape-growing region, which has only a few wineries but some of the most coveted vineyards in the state. The highway intersects Calif. 29 and is lured north, but it quickly departs with three sharp turns—right, left and right again—through the city of Napa. Calif. 121 then assumes a winding northeasterly course into the hills before it enters Calif. 128 not far from Lake Berryessa.

Calif. Highway 128

Calif. 128, best known as the path through the Alexander Valley wine region, is a rambling roadway that periodically hitches northward rides to augment its own northwesterly journey. It enters Napa County from the east, navigating the steep hills that hug Lake Berryessa. It sneaks around the southwest fingers of the lake, then follows Sage Creek west into Napa Valley. When it gets to Rutherford, Calif. 128 joins Calif. 29 on a northern jaunt through the vineyards. But when Calif. 29 makes a right turn into Calistoga, Calif. 128 continues northwest, into rustic Knights Valley and then lovely Alexander Valley with its first-rate wineries.

The road hits U.S. 101 just north of Geyserville and joins the bigger highway to Cloverdale. Then Calif. 128 breaks away again, heading northwest through Boonville and Philo on one of California's most unheralded scenic routes. Before it hits Calif. 1 near Navarro Point, Calif. 128 cuts into Navarro River Redwoods State Park, a skinny swath that basically straddles the highway.

Calif. Highway 20

If you want a detailed lesson in California geology, with a minor course in history, don't bother with a textbook. Just drive the length of Calif. 20, which begins high in the Sierra Nevada Mountains, descends through gold country and crosses the fertile Sacramento Valley on its search for the ocean. Calif. 20 enters the Wine Country in eastern Lake County and bears generally west along the northern edge of Clear Lake through towns such as Clearlake Oaks and Lucerne. The highway passes north of Lake Mendocino just before it hits U.S. Highway 101 at the town of Calpella. The two highways then merge on a northerly course. Calif. 20 breaks away from U.S. 101 at Willits, where it embarks on a jittery, handsome west-by-northwest track to the coast. It meets Calif. 1 just south of Fort Bragg.

Calif. Highway 116

Calif. 116 is the paved shadow of the Russian River. After connecting Sonoma and Petaluma in southern Sonoma County, it joins with U.S. 101 up to Cotati, then splits off and heads generally north through Sebastopol and Forestville. It's a perfectly nice highway during all of that, but Calif. 116 shines after it reaches Guerneville and follows the river to the coast. The water sparkles, the sunlight blinks through the trees, and the smooth, banking turns are tailor-made for four tires (or two).

The only drawback is that Calif. 116 is anything but a secret. The Russian River is densely packed with half-clothed human bodies in the summer, and if you make this drive on a weekend, one of the most memorable sights will be the rear end of the car in front of you.

Calif. Highway 253

This crooked highway connects Boonville and Ukiah in Mendocino County; in other words it connects U.S. 101 and seaward Calif. 128. If, by contrast, you want to go from Boonville to the coast, take Mountain View Road.

Calif. Highway 175

This is an alternative to Calif. 20 as a connection between Sonoma and Lake counties. It's also a pleasing drive, one of the roads less traveled in the Wine Country. Calif. 175 leaves Middletown in Lake County and proceeds north past the town of Cobb and Boggs Mountain State Forest. It joins Calif. 29 and goes almost to Lakeport before it breaks west. Calif. 175 then wiggles through the Mayacamas Mountains and ends up in Hopland at U.S. 101.

Calif. Highway 53

When Calif. 29 makes its impulsive left turn at Lower Lake in Lake County, Calif. 53 is there to pick up the northward trail. It skirts the east end of Clear Lake and connects drivers to Calif. 20.

Calif. Highway 162

This roadway leaves U.S. 101 at Longvale and winds northeast into the Round Valley Indian Reservation in Mendocino County. It's doubtful you will have any use for it unless you are visiting the reservation.

Calif. Highway 281

You can tell someone "I drove the length of California 281 without stopping to use a restroom," but it isn't as impressive as it sounds. Calif. 281 is about 2 miles long. It connects Calif. 29 with Clear Lake's Konocti Harbor.

By Air

The Wine Country is "serviced" by three major airports on its periphery—San Francisco, Oakland, and Sacramento—each of them as inconveniently located as the next. Of course, a lot of people think that being far from a major hub helps a destination in its pursuit of the pristine, which is why you don't hear many Wine Country citizens clamoring for an international terminal in downtown Healdsburg. The three airports are profiled below, as is the Sonoma County Airport, which is served by the United Express commuter line.

Among the big three, the airports in Oakland and Sacramento are slightly more efficient if you are entering the Wine Country through Napa or Sonoma, and Oakland gets the nod if the entry point is Petaluma. Figure on it taking 1¼ hours to drive from Oakland or Sacramento to Napa, 1½ hours from San Francisco to Santa Rosa. Of course, San Francisco welcomes a longer lineup of airlines. Six major

INSIDERS' TIP

If you are heading from San Francisco straight to Calistoga or lower Clear Lake, forget about going through Napa and up Calif. 29. Here's a way that will save you 15 to 30 minutes, and it is not as complicated as it sounds. Go north on U.S. 101, through Santa Rosa, to the Mark West Springs Road exit. Make a right and follow Mark West, which becomes Porter Creek Road and winds through the hills for about 10 miles until it hits a T intersection and a flashing red light. Make a left, which puts you onto Petrified Forest Road. After 5 miles you will hit Calif. 128. A right sends you into Calistoga. If you're proceeding to Clear Lake, make a left, then a right on Tubbs Lane. Make another left on Calif. 29 and you are on your way.

rental car companies—Hertz, Avis, Budget, Dollar, National and Alamo—serve all three airports with one exception: Dollar is not represented in Sacramento.

Major Airports

San Francisco International Airport
San Francisco
• **(650) 794-4000**
What started as Mills Field Municipal Airport in 1927 has burgeoned into a major Pacific Rim gateway and the fifth-busiest airport in the United States. With about 109,000 passengers a day, San Francisco International Airport (SFO) is something of a success story, a publicly owned and operated facility that receives no taxpayer support. It is 14 miles south of downtown San Francisco, in an unincorporated area of San Mateo County between the Bayshore Freeway and the San Francisco Bay. It is surrounded by more than 2,700 acres of undeveloped tidelands, its runways built upon land that was reclaimed from the bay.

Its amenities are impressive and locally flavored. There is the Crab Pot seafood restaurant and North Beach Deli. You can sip one of two coffee brands that San Franciscans swear by—Pasqua in the North Terminal and Spinelli in the International Terminal. (SFO has three main terminals, six sub-terminals and a total of 80 gates.) You can even pick up frozen seafood, a bouquet of flowers or a Jennifer Aniston cut at the hair salon. And if you have time to kill—and what else are airports for?—it has rotating art exhibitions, a permanent collection administered by the San Francisco Art Commission and a children's activity learning center in the International Terminal. In 2000 you can add to your itinerary an Aviation Library and Archival Research Center.

Every major airline carrier, and virtually every smaller carrier with any sort of presence in the western United States, touches down at SFO. If you're in doubt about service from a specific airline, contact the airport or your travel agent. There are outlets for all the expected rental car companies at the San Francisco airport. Here are the contact numbers you will need: Hertz, (800) 654-3131; Avis, (800) 331-1212; Budget, (800) 527-

0700; Dollar, (800) 800-4000; National, (415) 474-5300, (800) CAR-RENT; and Alamo, (415) 693-0191, (800) 327-9633.

The massive, central parking garage (6,379 spaces) is linked to the terminals by six pedestrian tunnels and two bridges. Rates in the garage begin at $1 for 20 minutes. It's $22 for the first full day, $35 for the second. In 2001 the powers-that-be hope to complete light-rail connections from metropolitan San Francisco to all terminals, plus rental car companies and long-term parking.

Oakland International Airport
Oakland • (510) 577-4021
Oakland's long-held inferiority complex regarding San Francisco gets no relief at the airport. (The East Bay can get just so much satisfaction from saying, "Oakland is the only Bay Area airport with nonstop service to Tahiti.")

The Oakland Airport (OAK) is smaller and less ambitious than its neighbor to the west, and that is exactly what makes it more attractive to many Wine Country visitors. With only two terminals and a dozen airlines, it can be a painless experience.

The Oakland Airport was established in 1927, the same year as SFO, and it, too, is municipally operated. South of downtown Oakland, take the Hegenberger Road exit from Interstate 880. Once inside there are 14 boarding gates at Terminal One and eight at Terminal Two, where no gate is farther than 400 feet from the curb. Terminal Two is devoted entirely to Southwest Airlines, which bases 300 of its pilots and nearly 500 flight attendants in Oakland.

Several major and regional airlines offer service at OAK. These include Alaska, American, America West, Corsair/New Frontier, Delta, Horizon, Southwest and United. Six major car rental companies operate at the Oakland airport. Note that the toll-free numbers listed for rental agencies at the San Francisco airport are the same ones used here. Local numbers are: Hertz, (510) 568-1177; Avis, (510) 636-4730; Budget, (510) 568-6442; Dollar, (510) 638-2750; National, (510) 632-2225; and Alamo, (510) 577-6360.

OAK, surprisingly, has more parking spaces than SFO. All the lots charge $1 for the first 30 minutes, but the rates vary for a day: It's $20 in the hourly lot, $10 in the daily lot and $8 in

INSIDERS' TIP

A first conviction for drunk driving in California brings a mandatory fine of $390 to $1,000. In addition, the judge may sentence you to six months in jail, suspend your license for up to six months and/or impound your vehicle for up to 30 days.

Photo: Ryan Lely

Sonoma Valley and most other areas of the Wine Country guide visitors to the local wineries by means of street signs.

of a thoroughly up-to-date food/retail mall. Still, SMF's scale makes it easy to get from car to gate if you make it your choice of port.

Nine major air carriers serve the Sacramento airport—Alaska, America West, American, Delta, Horizon, Northwest, Southwest, TWA and United. Several of the expected rental car agencies can provide you with wheels at SMF. Again, the toll-free numbers included with the San Francisco airport information will also work for Sacramento. Local numbers are: Hertz, (916) 927-3882; Avis, (916) 922-5601; Budget, (916) 922-7317; National, (916) 568-2415; and Alamo, (916) 646-6020. Parking is $1 for the first hour, $2 per hour thereafter in the hourly lot, with a maximum of $20 a day. The daily lots charge $7 per day.

Sonoma County Airport
2200 Airport Blvd., Santa Rosa
• **(707) 524-7240**

This is one of the Wine Country's best-kept secrets. Even some experienced residents don't know that United Express serves Sonoma County. But it does, making this the only commercial service airport between Oakland and Arcata (about 100 miles south of the Oregon border). You can fly to San Francisco on United Express, then branch out to a practically unlimited web of flight paths. Sonoma County Airport also welcomes private planes. There are no landing fees, though the overnight rate is $6 to $17, and the monthly rate can be anywhere from $36 to $109 (depending on wingspan). The airport is about 7 miles north of downtown Santa Rosa, 2.2 miles west of U.S. 101 on Airport Boulevard. Hertz, (800) 654-3131 or (707) 528-0834, and Avis, (800) 331-1212 or (707) 571-0465, both offer rental car services at the Sonoma County Airport.

economy. The Black Muslim Bakery is there in Terminal One to remind you that you're not in Kansas anymore.

Sacramento International Airport
Sacramento
• **(916) 929-5411**

It used to be that politicians shuttling back and forth between their constituents and the State Capitol created most of the traffic at Sacramento Airport (SMF), about 10 miles north of downtown Sacramento (and accessible from Interstate 5). But this is now the 46th busiest airport in the nation, and a new terminal that opened in October 1998 effectively doubled the size of the facility. It also harkened the arrival

Smaller Wine Country Airports

The four-county area includes at least a dozen smaller airports open to private planes. Here is a listing of the most accessible, with numbers you can call for details. Unless otherwise stated, figure on no landing fees and an overnight charge of $4 or $5.

Napa County Airport
2030 Airport Rd., Napa
• (707) 253-4300

Perhaps the most elaborate of the small airports, Napa County offers Bridgeford Flying Service and Jonesy's Famous Steakhouse. Japan Air Lines maintains a multimillion-dollar pilot training facility on the grounds. The airport is 1 mile west of the intersection of Calif. 12 and 29. There is no landing fee for private planes. The overnight fee is $4 for a single-engine plane, $5 for a double-engine and $15 for a commercial plane

Boonville Airport
Airport Rd., Boonville • (707) 895-9918

The airport is northwest of town, off Ornbaun Road.

Cloverdale Municipal Airport
220 Airport Rd., Cloverdale
• (707) 894-1895

The airport is south of town, off Asti Road.

Healdsburg Municipal Airport
1500 Lytton Springs Rd., Healdsburg
• (707) 433-8540

The airport is north of town, accessible from U.S. 101 or Dry Creek Road.

Lampson Field
4745 Highland Springs Rd., Finley
• (707) 263-2341

Finley is situated halfway between Kelseyville and Lakeport, off Calif. 29. The overnight fee is $5 for one engine, $7.50 for two.

Little River Airport
43001 Airport Rd., Little River
• (707) 937-5129

The airport is east of town, off Little River Airport Road. The overnight fee is $7 for a single-engine plane, $8 for a double-engine.

Parrett Field
100 Angwin Ave., Angwin
• (707) 965-6219

The airport is off College Avenue, behind Pacific Union College. The overnight fee is $5 (single engine) or $7 (double).

Petaluma Municipal Airport
601 Sky Ranch Rd., Petaluma
• (707) 778-4404

The airport is on the east end of town, off Washington Street.

Sonoma Sky Park
21870 Eighth St. E., Sonoma
• (707) 996-2100

This is another airport just south of Sonoma, near the community of Schellville.

Sonoma Valley Airport
23980 Arnold Dr., Sonoma
• (707) 938-5382

The airport is just south of Sonoma, near the junction of Calif. 116 and 121.

Ukiah Municipal Airport
1411 S. State St., Ukiah
• (707) 467-2817

The airport is on the south end of town, off S. State Street. For commercial aircraft greater than 12,500 pounds, the landing fee is $1.75 per 1,000 pounds.

Airport Shuttles

If you enter the Wine Country via San Francisco, Oakland or Sonoma County Airport, you don't have to be stranded at the baggage carousel. The following carriers specialize in airport transportation. Take note: Most do not operate on Christmas and, in some cases, other major holidays.

Evans Airport Service
4075 Solano Ave., Napa
• (707) 255-1559, (707) 944-2025

Evans Airport Service, long the prime mode of getting to SFO from Napa (or vice-versa), now goes to OAK, too. Evans has 11 daily departures on weekdays, nine Saturday and 10 Sunday to San Francisco; and eight on weekdays, seven on weekends to Oakland. The buses are full-size and comfortable. The fare is $18 one-way from Evans' large, pa-

Photo: Tina Luster-Hoban

The Napa Valley Wine Train is a popular attraction among locals and visitors. It's a first-class ticket through Wine Country.

trolled lot, but children younger than 13 ride for half price. The office is open from 5 AM to midnight, and you can leave a reservation with the answering service if no one is home. To get to Evans take Calif. 29 to Trower Avenue and go west one mini-block to Solano Avenue, the frontage road. Turn right and look for the first building past the fire station. Parking is $2 per day.

Santa Rosa Airporter
175 Railroad St., Santa Rosa
• (707) 545-8015

The Airporter delivers to and from both San Francisco and Oakland, and offers six Wine Country pickup spots—at the Sonoma County Airport, Santa Rosa, Rohnert Park, and Petaluma—and another in Marin County. Call for exact locations. The Airporter offers a comprehensive schedule of 19 departures every hour on the half-hour from 3:30 AM to 9:30 PM. You can park for $3 a day at the Ramada Limited in Rohnert Park (6278 Redwood Drive) or for $4 a day at the Sun Plaza Resort in Santa Rosa (3345 Santa Rosa Ave.) or the Petaluma Fairgrounds (East Washington and Payvan Streets. The cost from Sonoma County is $18 one way or $30 roundtrip. There are discounts for children (3-11), seniors, members of the military and airline employees. Check out the July/Au-

gust special: Kids 11 and under ride free with a paid adult.

Sonoma County Airport Express
4246 Petaluma Blvd. N., Petaluma
• (707) 837-8700

The Airport Express makes 26 daily runs from the Sonoma County Airport to San Francisco International, with three stops in between. In effect, it provides Greyhound-sized buses to and from two different airports. The intermediate stops are at the Hotel La Rose, Wilson and 5th streets in Santa Rosa; the Doubletree Hotel at 1 Doubletree Drive in Rohnert Park; and the company's office in Petaluma. The cost is $18 one-way, $30 round trip. Those rates are $15 and $25, respectively, for seniors (55 and older) and $10 and $15 for children 3 to 11. There is free, unsecured parking at Sonoma County Airport and the Doubletree (72 hours maximum) and secured parking at the Express lot for $4 a day.

Sonoma Airporter
524 W. Napa St., Sonoma
• (707) 938-4246, (800) 611-4246

The Airporter makes six daily runs (five on Saturday) from Sonoma Valley to SFO, with a connection in San Rafael. The nine-passenger vans will pick you up practically anywhere in

Sonoma, Boyes Hot Springs, Glen Ellen, Kenwood or Oakmont, and deposit you at your terminal about an hour and 40 minutes later. The fare is $25 for adults, $15 for children 2-11 (free for infants with an adult chaperone), but it's $5 less if you pick up the bus at Sonoma City Hall.

By Bus/Train

Amtrak
1275 McKinstry St., Napa
• (800) 872-7245

The only viable railroad lines in the Wine Country are tourist-oriented puffers described in the Attractions chapter. There are no Amtrak stations, but the company has contracted Amador Stage Lines to run buses from Napa, Petaluma, Rohnert Park, Santa Rosa, Cloverdale, Ukiah and Willits. These buses will drop you off at an Amtrak station, or deliver you from a station. The fee varies with destination but generally is quite reasonable. For examples, Napa to Martinez is $4 and Santa Rosa to Martinez is $6. From Martinez the rail line can take you to Sacramento or Stockton and on to practically anywhere in the country. Call Amtrak for details.

INSIDERS' TIP

Napa Valley Insiders have a two-word mantra when they get behind the wheel: "Silverado Trail." The Trail is a gently winding, eastward road parallel to California 29 that avoids towns and sees about a tenth of Calif. 29's traffic during peak periods. Silverado has plenty of roadside wineries, too, though they tend to be small, family-run establishments. If you are bogged down on Calif. 29, cut over to the Trail at your first chance. (Look for the crossroads — Yountville Cross Road, Rutherford Cross Road, etc.)

Greyhound Bus Lines
3854 Santa Rosa Ave., Santa Rosa
• (707) 545-6495, (800) 231-2222

Greyhound's only true Wine Country station is in downtown Santa Rosa. Other towns—Napa, Petaluma, Sonoma, and Ukiah included—are "flagstop" stations. That means they have infrequent but regular pickups at specific corners and parking lots. Call for details.

Public Transportation

Public buses and vans might not be a viable option for a week of exploring and winetasting, but they are handy for specific errands. And for those of you who live here or stay with friends for any significant time, they can be a blessing. The Wine Country has an extensive network of inter- and intracity public vehicles, many of which are connected by a transfer system. Only basic information is provided below; please call for more details.

Napa County

Napa Valley Transit (Vallejo to Calistoga)
1151 Pearl St., Napa
• (800) 696-6443, (707) 226-9722 (TDD),

Napa Valley Transit is a great way to view the sights on Calif. 29 if you are making one great leap rather than a bunch of small hops. Seven buses run between Napa and Calistoga every weekday, six on Saturday but none on Sunday. Stops include Bothe-Napa State Park (see our Parks and Recreation chapter) and the Veteran's Home near Yountville (see our Attractions chapter).

There also are 13 buses on weekdays and eight on Saturday to Vallejo, if you have any reason to go there. The fare varies with distance. Calistoga to St. Helena is $1, while Calistoga to American Canyon, just south of Napa, is $2.50. Students get about a 25 percent discount; seniors 50 percent. All NVT buses are accessible to wheelchairs and bicycles.

The VINE
1151 Pearl St., Napa
• (707) 255-7631, (800) 696-6443, (707) 226-9722 (TDD)

The VINE is a five-line municipal bus service within the Napa city limits. The basic fare is $1 for adults, 75 cents for students and 50 cents for seniors and the disabled, with transfers available to Napa Valley Transit. Buses run about every half-hour on weekdays, starting at 6:45 AM and ending at 6 PM. They show up about once an hour on Saturday; the service does not run at all on Sunday. All VINE buses can accommodate wheelchairs and bicycles. The main VINE terminal is downtown, at 1151 Pearl Street.

Sonoma County

Golden Gate Transit (Santa Rosa to San Francisco)
Pioneer Way and Industrial Dr.
• **(707) 541-2000, (415) 257-4554 (TDD)**

Golden Gate Transit (GGT) is a comprehensive network that connects San Francisco with that amorphous region known as the North Bay. Most of the routes end in Marin County, but several continue north into the Wine Country. There are service points in the Valley of the Moon, Petaluma, Cotati, Rohnert Park, Santa Rosa and Sebastopol. The basic adult fare is $4 or $4.50 to San Francisco, depending on where you embark. There are discounts for kids, seniors and the disabled. Once in the city you get transfer privileges for the Bay Area Rapid Transit system (BART) and the San Francisco Municipal Railway (Muni). Call for schedule information and locations of GGT's 11 park-and-ride lots in the Wine Country.

Healdsburg Municipal Transit
401 Grove St., Healdsburg
• **(707) 431-3309**

This in-city bus has only one route, but it tries its damnedest to hit every corner in town, making almost 60 stops. The busier pickup points get hourly service between 8:30 AM and 4:30 PM. The standard adult fare is $1, falling to 75 cents for students and 60 cents for seniors and the disabled.

Petaluma Transit
482 Kenilworth Dr., Petaluma
• **(707) 778-4460**

Three routes serve downtown Petaluma and its surroundings. Buses generally run every hour between 6:30 AM and 6 PM with a condensed schedule on Saturday and no service on Sunday. Adults and students ride for 75 cents, seniors and the disabled for 35 cents and children 5 or younger for free. Discounted monthly and multi-ride passes are available.

Santa Rosa CityBus
Second and B Sts., Santa Rosa
• **(707) 543-3333, (707) 543-3926 (TDD)**

This network offers 13 convenient routes within the Santa Rosa city limits plus free transfers to Golden Gate Transit or Sonoma County Transit. Most CityBuses operate from 6 AM to 8 PM Monday through Friday, 8 AM to 5:30 PM on Saturday and 10 AM to 5 PM on Sunday. The fares are $1 for adults, 75 cents for students, 50 cents for seniors and free for children 5 or younger. Monthly passes are available.

Sonoma County Transit (Petaluma to Cloverdale)
335 W. Robles Ave., Santa Rosa
• **(707) 576-RIDE, (800) 345-7433**

Sonoma County Transit (SCT) serves an area bounded by Petaluma to the south, Sonoma to the east, Cloverdale to the north and Occidental to the west, with most of the action in the vicinity of U.S. 101. Basic adult fares run from $1.05 to $3.15, depending on distance. Kids get a small discount, while seniors and the disabled get a larger one. SCT offers transfers to Santa Rosa CityBus, Golden Gate Transit and the Sonoma County municipal transit systems that lie within a designated area. Most buses run from 5 AM to 10:30 PM during the work week and 7 AM to 7 PM on weekends.

Volunteer Wheels
1041 Fourth St., Santa Rosa
• **(707) 573-3377, (800) 992-1006**

Volunteer Wheels, a door-to-door service in Sonoma County, is part of the Americans with Disabilities Act program, administered locally as a nonprofit organization. As its name implies, all drivers work on a volunteer basis. The one-way fare is $2 within the Santa Rosa city limits and between $1.70 and $4.20 elsewhere in Sonoma County.

Mendocino County

Mendocino County Dial-a-Ride
241 Plant Rd., Ukiah
• **(707) 462-3881 (Ukiah), (707) 459-9038 (Willits), (707) 964-1800 (Fort Bragg)**

Though the phone numbers are different, these three lines are coordinated by the same office. Service is door-to-door, with customers sharing vans. The fare is $2.50 within the respective city limits, and rates climb as you travel through concentric, mapped-out zones. The high end is about $12.50. Seniors and kids get discounts.

Mendocino Transit Authority (Santa Rosa to Fort Bragg)
241 Plant Rd., Ukiah
• **(707) 462-1422, (800) 696-4MTA**

MTA has four lines in Sonoma and Mendocino counties. Taken as a whole, they form a long rectangle with U.S. 101 (Santa Rosa to Willits) on the east, Calif. 20 (Willits to Fort

Bragg) on the north, coastal Calif. 1 (Bodega to Fort Bragg) on the west and Bodega Highway (Santa Rosa to Bodega) on the south. One other route cuts across the rectangle from Ukiah to Albion, on Calif. 253/Calif. 128. The MTA buses run only once or twice a day, so don't miss the one you're after. Fares vary wildly according to distance. Fort Bragg to Albion is 65 cents, Bodega Bay to Point Arena is $4.50 and Santa Rosa to Mendocino is $16. Call for specifics. Seniors and the disabled ride for half-price, and children younger than 6 ride for free.

Lake County

Lake County Dial-a-Ride
2222 Park Pl., Clearlake
• (707) 994-3334

This private operation is based in the town of Clearlake, but the vans circumnavigate the water. The basic, one-way fare is $2, but seniors receive a discount and children younger than 5 ride for free. The service is door-to-door.

By Limousine

You see so many stretch limos during summer in the Wine Country that you'll swear the Academy Awards are at the next intersection. And it makes sense when you think about it. If no one in your group is selfless enough to volunteer for designated-driver duties, a limousine will escort you from tasting room to tasting room, freeing you up to daydream and act silly.

Many of the limo services provide drivers who are knowledgeable about the region and its vintages. But we must draw a distinction. Companies offering something that clearly goes beyond transportation—lunch at an exclusive winery or unscheduled informational tours— are included in the Attractions chapter, under the subheading "Tours." If transportation is the primary service, then the companies are listed here regardless of how far they go to help you plan your itinerary. Most limousine businesses prefer not to quote rates because the variables— type of car, size of party, distance, etc.—are multiple. If they do offer basic rates, we report them here.

Napa County

Pure Luxury
Napa • (707) 253-0296, (800) 626-LIMO

Pure Luxury will take you anywhere in the Wine Country, for any reason: wine tours, weddings, airport transportation—you name it. Call to customize a tour.

Antique Tours
Napa • (707) 226-9227

This company stands out for one simply luxurious reason: its small fleet of restored 1947 Packard convertible limos (and one 1948 hardtop). Little did you know that post-war Packards were equipped with AM/FM stereo cassette players, ice drawers and air conditioning. The Packards accommodate up to seven passengers, and the charge is $70 per hour on weekdays, $90 on weekends; there is a three-hour minimum. Wine tours booked for six hours or more receive a free gourmet picnic lunch.

Executive Limousine
Napa • (707) 257-2949

Executive generally operates within a 50- to-70-mile radius around Napa, but show 'em the money and they'll go anywhere. They have a range of vehicles from short to long (10 passenger), and they usually charge by the hour, though rates vary.

Napa Valley Crown Limousine
Napa • (707) 257-0879, (800) 286-8228

The proprietors of this service have plenty of experience in the tourist biz. Before getting behind the wheel they ran a bed and breakfast inn and a tourist information office, and they still get many recommendations from wedding planners and tourist bureaus. They go anywhere (even to Mexico once!), and their winery knowledge is superior. And now you have the option of riding in a Phantom Excalibur, styled to look like a classic Deusenberg. The cost for that is $65 an hour during the week, $75 an hour on weekends.

Royal Coach Limousine Service
Napa • (800) 995-7692

Take your choice of six- or eight-passenger cars and a range of itineraries. Ask for Matt if you want to customize something special.

Sonoma County

California Wine Tours
Sonoma • (707) 939-7225, (800) 294-6386

These operators deserve mention for their extensive wine knowledge and detailed suggestions. They offer a standard, five-hour tasting tour for $39 per person. Customized tours begin at $55 per hour, with a four-hour minimum on weekends.

Pacific Limousine
Rohnert Park • (707) 792-1500

Pacific has been operating since 1990. They charge $45 per hour on weekdays, $50 per hour on weekends. (That is for a carload of tourists.) The flat rate to either San Francisco International or Oakland International Airport is $115 for a town car, $125 for a stretch limo.

A Touch of Class Limousine Service
Santa Rosa • (707) 539-0945

With additional cars operating under the banners of Lap of Luxury and Style & Comfort (companies it recently acquired), Touch of Class has the largest fleet (and, they swear, the newest cars) in Santa Rosa. It has served the Wine Country since 1988.

Just D-Vine Limousine Service
Santa Rosa • (707) 576-1725

This owner-operated company (established 1985) prefers to stay within Sonoma County but, hey, if the meter's running they'll take you to Peoria. They offer a four person, six-hour tour for $199.

Heaven on Wheels
Windsor • (707) 838-7778

Greg Baker, the 12-year-old company's owner/operator, checks out all wineries before suggesting them for tours. His basic package is four hours. Rates are customized, and the cars go anywhere in Northern California.

Odyssey Limousine
Windsor • (707) 836-0672, (800) 544-1929

This is another service that customizes by car and number of people. Odyssey has been gliding around Napa and Sonoma counties since 1988.

Mendocino County

Fort Bragg Door to Door
Ft. Bragg • (707) 964-8294

Stephen Seago, Sr. has run this limo service for 8 years. "This is my life," he says, and he makes the most of it. Seago covers all of Mendocino and Lake counties, occasionally venturing to Sea Ranch or making Bay Area airport runs. Door to Door comprises a seven-passenger luxury van (basic rate: $50 an hour) and a Lincoln Town Car stretch limo ($63 an hour).

By Taxi

Your chances of flagging down a taxi on the roads of the Wine Country are statistically smaller than your odds of being trampled by a cow. Here, "hailing a cab" means saluting a robust Cabernet Sauvignon. But there are plenty of companies to get you from curb to curb. The standard rate is a $2 baseline and $2 per mile.

In Napa County, you'll find Napa Valley Cab, Napa, (707) 257-6444; or Taxi Cabernet, St. Helena, (707) 963-2620 or (707) 942-2226.

In Sonoma County, there's A-1 Taxi of Petaluma, (707) 763-3393; A-C Taxi, Santa Rosa, (707) 526-4888; Bear Flag Taxi, Sonoma, (707) 996-6733; Bill's Taxi Service, Guerneville, (707) 869-2177; George's Taxi/Yellow Cab, Santa Rosa, (707) 546-3322 or (707) 544-4444; or Santa Rosa Taxi Cab, (707) 579-8601 or (877) 333-5000.

Mendocino cab services are provided by Fort Bragg Door to Door, Fort Bragg, (707) 964-TAXI or (888) 961-TAXI.

The lone taxi service in Lake County is Clearlake Cab Company, Lower Lake, (707) 994-TAXI.

History

In the annals of Northern California history, the most sharply defined point of reference is the Gold Rush of 1849. The accidental discovery of one tiny nugget in 1848 by James Marshall, a moody carpenter working a sawmill in the Sierra foothills, set off one of the greatest mass migrations of human beings ever known.

LOOK FOR:
- Napa County—
  City on the River,
  Those Amazing
  Hot Springs,
  The Silver
  Commotion,
  The Emergence of
  Fine Wine
- Sonoma County—
  The Bear Flag
  Rebellion,
  The New State of
  California,
  Santa Rosa,
  Petaluma,
  Jack London in
  Glen Ellen,
  Northern Somona
  County,
  Russian River and
  West County,
  The Sonoma Coast
- Mendocino County—
  Anderson Valley,
  The Mendocino
  Coast,
  The City of
  Mendocino,
  Fort Bragg
- Lake County—
  Lillie Langtry in the
  Vineyards

California was then a part of Mexico—a remote, sparsely populated region cut off from the United States by 1,800 miles of broiling desert and impassable mountains between Missouri and the Pacific Ocean. Gold changed that, triggering an inundation of scrambling fortune seekers. They crossed the Great American Desert (now Nevada) without seeing water for 20 days; they sailed from America's East Coast around South America's Cape Horn; they came from Germany, from England and Wales, from Ireland. By the summer of 1849, more than 100 abandoned sailing vessels clogged San Francisco Bay, with passengers and crew headed off to the gold fields.

Before 1848, Northern California was a sleepy, languid land where fiestas were frequent. To assure the territory remained settled (and others didn't move in), the Mexican government generously handed out immense tracts of land, most of which were close to the coastline. Gen. Mariano Vallejo, as commandant of the Sonoma area, had several.

The inland areas were the wilder domain of various Indian tribes. Covered with wild grasses, rich in forests, the countryside teemed with wildlife, notably bear and herds of elk. Deer were everywhere and ducks by the thousands wintered in the marshes. This land ultimately would become home to vineyards stretching in neat rows to the horizons. Its wineries would achieve worldwide fame. Labels of vintners from Napa, Sonoma, Mendocino and Lake counties would be recognized in the finest restaurants. And the countryside itself would gain fame as Wine Country.

Napa County

For 10,000 years or more, the Pomos had been the undisputed occupants of the lands of the upper Sonoma and Napa valleys, on up to Clear Lake and the surrounding lands. It was their custom to settle into smaller groups, each of which spoke a different dialect of the same language. They lived an orderly life, with the men carrying on the outdoor work and often specializing in fishing or crafting arrowheads. Marriage was conducted in traditional fashion, and babies were the domain of the women—mothers, grandmothers, aunts and cousins.

The Pomos lived peacefully and enjoyed a relatively easy existence compared to tribes in other regions of California. The climate was mild; the streams abounded with fish. The Pomos were the first to discover the value of the mineral and hot springs south of Clear Lake. They were also on friendly terms with the Nappa tribe to the south near the Napa River.

The first white settler in the Napa Valley was George Yount—frontiersman, hunter, trapper and mountain man. He had left his wife and three children in Missouri in 1832 to take a job driving mules with a pack train to Santa Fe. The job fizzled, but Yount never saw reason to return to Missouri. Instead, his restless feet took him to California's coast where he trapped beaver for a while and eventually made his way north in the summer of 1834 to the mission in Sonoma.

There he was welcomed with considerable enthusiasm by Padre Jose Quijas, who had been praying for someone to repair the mission buildings. In Yount he found a resourceful man who could do almost anything.

In time Yount became acquainted with the Mexican commandant Vallejo, who, it turned out, also needed work done—a new roof for his hacienda. Soon Yount was turning out 1,000 shingles a day and training the mission workers to help. Yount's payment likely came via a 12,000-acre Napa Valley land grant he received, with Vallejo's help. Land was seldom given to outsiders unless they were converted to Catholicism and married into a Mexican family. Indeed, Padre Quijas did baptize Yount. But it's certain that, with a wife in Missouri, Yount couldn't marry the daughter of a Mexican landowner. Yount was content never to see his wife again. He learned years later from a passing stranger that she had divorced him.

Upon Yount's arrival in Napa Valley he hiked up an old Indian trail leading to the top of Mount St. Helena. From there he could look across the entire valley, and he was ready to settle down. In 1836 he set about building a Kentucky-style blockhouse for himself. He got on well with the Pomos and Nappas and taught them how to help. Then he erected a flour mill and sawmill, planted wheat and potatoes and started a small vineyard. But like most God-fearing Missourians who made their way to Napa, he knew grapes were for eating, not for making wine. Yount's name would eventually live on into future generations—the town of Yountville was named in his honor (see our "Name Calling" Close-up in the Area Overview chapter).

Soon another settler appeared on the scene—Dr. Edward Bale, a young English surgeon. His marriage to a niece of Gen. Vallejo made him a Mexican citizen, and as such he was given a land grant north of Yount's. Bale established a sawmill to cut timber, and a grist mill (still extant and known as Bale Mill) to grind the settlers' grain. The mills became centers of great activity and supplied work for new settlers, but the best was yet to come for Bale. When gold diggers poured into the state, flour became a premium product, and Bale's mill was a gold mine in its own right.

Between 1836 and 1846, most Napa County land had been given away in the form of grants to citizens who had proven their loyalty to Mexico. That left little territory for overland immigrants. Sometimes the grantees sold small parcels of their land to settlers, but that was later outlawed by Mexico. The legal descriptions in some of these deeds were quite primitive and sometimes took years to untangle. Typical was the following: "Bounded on the northwest by the spring on which the grist mill stands, as far as its waters run, easterly to the main creek, thence to a high bluff on which there are two dead trees one of which has its top broken off. . . ."

Validation of the land grants was guaranteed by a treaty between Mexico and the United States, but long after the U.S. acquired California in 1850, tricky court cases raged on. The near-wilderness aspect of the Napa Valley changed dramatically after gold was discovered in the Sierra foothills, 100 miles east of San Francisco, in 1848. The city by the bay, which boasted a population of less than 450, was virtually abandoned in the rush to the gold fields. And although Napa was 40 miles to the north—not exactly on the direct route to the foothills—large numbers of gold seekers did wander off course and find their way into the valley, on foot or on horseback. If anyone in town had a horse for sale, the sale was quickly made. Sometimes the horse was simply stolen.

Miners also found the valley a popular wintering place when rains drowned the mines. Some stayed in the area. In two years Napa's population tripled to 450. A census two years later showed a jump to 2,116 (including 252 women). In just one decade, wilderness had transformed to populace.

City on the River

The first town in the valley, founded in 1836, was Napa City—not that it amounted to much. Until the Gold Rush there was not one house in town, only a handful of adobe huts. There were no roads, no bridges. Hides and tallow served as the media of exchange.

But soon after the discovery of gold, prosperity set in. The chief places of business were saloons, and the method of payment was likely to be gold dust. It was amazing what a difference the gold brought about. The main artery into town was the Napa River. In fact, it was the only way, since there were no bridges.

The first steamboat to make a regular run between Napa and San Francisco was the *Dolphin*, a tiny ship no larger than a whaleboat. It was a harbinger of things to come. The channel was deep, so before long bigger steamers were plying the river, transporting passengers to San Francisco and Sacramento for a $1 fare, lunch included. But the river's main value was for moving freight. The valley's fertile soil was producing such a profusion of fruits and vegetables that ships lined up daily at the Napa docks to load up for the San Francisco market.

In the outlying Berryessa Valley, some 30 miles inland, wheat grew so abundantly it became an international product. Ships from foreign ports arrived regularly at the Napa Embarcadero to load Napa County wheat. The river brought in industry that would last until the end of the century. Lined up along its shores were potteries, iron works, tile factories and tanneries. The term "Napa leather" was listed in Webster's dictionary as "a type of leather resembling the original glove leather made in Napa by tanning sheepskins with a soap and oil mixture."

Many residents prospered beyond their wildest dreams, and by the 1880s Napa had achieved a fame for both charm and wealth. That reputation brought in the bankers, who were by no means above ostentation in the building of their great Victorian mansions. Some of those homes still stand today as an architectural reminder of other times. With all this commerce and commotion, the river became a sort of freeway, replete with snarled traffic. One wild day in January 1880, some 50 ships clogged the river channel.

But it came to an abrupt end. Napa's river traffic was killed by a single structure—a bridge built across the Carquinez Straits between Martinez and Vallejo. That allowed trucks to come into Napa Valley for the first time.

Those Amazing Hot Springs

During the 1860s it became fashionable all over the country to "take the waters." Soaking in hot mineral baths or mineral-rich mud was touted to cure virtually every known ailment. The first entrepreneur to capitalize on these bubbling springs was Sam Brannan, who had become a millionaire selling shovels and picks to miners.

Some of that wealth was spent acquiring 1 square mile of land in the northern valley. It was Brannan's vision to build an extravagant resort spa that would become a holiday retreat for San Francisco's shamefully rich. He called the place Calistoga—a combination of his fondness for Saratoga Springs and the word California. On the grounds there soon appeared a lavish hotel, 25 gingerbread cottages, an observatory tower, large stables with many fine horses, a winery and distillery. Brannan imported great herds of merino sheep from England and silkworms and mulberry trees from China. The benefits of the hot springs, of course, were obvious and needed no further publicity.

Not one to do things in a niggardly way, Brannan first revealed his outrageously opulent Calistoga resort to San Francisco society with a gala opening. He chartered a ship to carry his guests from San Francisco to Vallejo, where they were met by a fleet of coaches that brought them to Calistoga. For the feast, roast fowl and champagne were served indoors; outdoors was a bountiful barbecue with beer by the barrel. The guests frolicked the night away, presumably soaking away their ills the next morning in the healing waters of the spa.

INSIDERS' TIP

The smallest jail in the United States is in Lower Lake on the south shore of Clear Lake, built in 1876 by Theodore and John Copsey. The Copseys celebrated its completion so much that they became drunk and disorderly, thereby becoming the jail's first occupants.

But success slipped away from Sam Brannan. His flair for moneymaking deserted him in Calistoga, in San Francisco, in the gold country in general. His beautiful Calistoga hotel burned. He was shot in the back by a disgruntled mill hand and harassed by his creditors. Sick and discouraged, he left Calistoga. Brannan never recovered the promise of his early youth, but he wrote a fantastic chapter in the history of Napa Valley. He died in Southern California in 1889, practically alone and quite poor.

In time another hot springs resort, Napa Soda Springs, was developed 5 miles east of Napa City and took the place of Calistoga in the fickle favor of San Franciscans accustomed to lavish living. Banked against a flower-carpeted hillside, it presented an unequaled view of Napa Valley and San Pablo Bay. A good deal of faith was put in the healing pow-

Photo: Ryan Lely

Buena Vista Winery was established 140 years ago by Count Agoston Haraszthy.

ers of "a course at the springs." According to the report of a Dr. Anderson, the waters were beneficial "in the treatment of chronic metritis and ovaritis, for Bright's disease, acid blood and dyspepsia."

The popularity of Wine Country's hot springs and spas has endured, with a number of accommodations and other businesses still built around mineral baths, mud packs, massages and other forms of relaxation and body therapy. See our Spas and Resorts chapter for lodging options (from world-class resorts to more modest, old-fashioned choices) and our Attractions chapter for businesses that offer walk-in spa services.

The Silver Commotion

In the winter of 1858, rumors started percolating that silver had been discovered in the mountains. In no time at all, every unemployed man had turned prospector. Most of those wielding a pick knew nothing of the characteristics of silver ledges, and outcrops of barren rock of any description were equally valued to their ignorant eyes. The commotion continued for several weeks. A local assay office was even opened. The assayer was a competent man but gave such discouraging reports that nobody believed him. So miners instead hauled their rocks to San Francisco, where reports came back "no silver at all" or "a trace." Bonanza quickly turned to *borrasco*, and tons of shiny rocks were unloaded by the disenchanted miners to make paving material for the streets of Napa.

Of more serious import were the quicksilver mines that developed in the 1860s in the Mayacamas Mountains that separate the Napa and Sonoma valleys. Mining quicksilver, or mercury, was a hazardous process, and newspapers of the day were filled with accident stories. A typical one involved a foreman: "While inspecting a piece of ground there fell without warning a mass of rock weighing half a ton, rendering him insensible for nearly an hour." (One would certainly think so!)

In the 1870s, silver fever struck again. A vein of silver was discovered in the Calistoga hills, and a new town sprang up around the diggings—Silverado City. The hillsides soon were pocked with mining claims, and the city prospered briefly. The vein was short-lived, but the town's hotel and mining office became famous, for it was here that Robert Louis Stevenson brought his bride on a honeymoon.

It was a strange entourage that straggled into the Napa Valley on a warm May day in 1880—gaunt, ailing Robert Louis Stevenson; his new bride, Fanny; her 12-year-old son and a setter-spaniel named Chuchu. They had decided to honeymoon in Calistoga, hoping to cure the Scottish author's lung problems. They arrived at the Springs Hotel, where they lived a short time in a "cottage on the green," but after a couple of weeks they located cheaper quarters. They moved into the assayer's office and bunkhouse of an abandoned silver mine as squatters, paying no rent.

With a secondhand cookstove and a few household effects pulled up the mountain by a new neighbor who was also a squatter, they settled down for the summer, living the free life of gypsies. Here Stevenson wrote in his journal the notes that became his first literary success, *The Silverado Squatters*.

The Emergence of Fine Wine

Although Yount and Bale were the first to raise grapes in Napa Valley, it seems doubtful either had the inclination to cultivate fine wines. That distinction came to several German immigrants who arrived in the 1870s: Jacob Schram (who barbered by day and planted vines by moonlight), Charles Krug (known as the father of Napa viniculture), Jacob and Frederick Beringer (Jacob was Krug's winemaker until he built his own winery) and Gottlieb Groezinger (his winery stands as Yountville's Vintage 1870).

The 1870s marked tremendous growth in the Napa Valley wine industry. Local viticulture clubs began organizing in 1875, with Charles Krug chosen president of the largest. (A note that will come in handy: Generally speaking, we use "viticulture" when talking specifically about the science and practice of growing grapes, and "viniculture" to discuss the process of making wines.) About the same time, the Beringer brothers established their winery, complete with a cellar dug into a hillside by Chinese laborers and reinforced with stone—a feat of advanced architecture as well as masonry. Adding to the growth of the industry was an outbreak of phylloxera (a ravenous louse that eats the plant's roots) in French vineyards. Napa wineries continued to expand.

Unfortunately, this led to overproduction. In the late 1880s growers were all feeling the pinch, and Charles Krug's vineyards and cellar went into receivership. More bad times loomed in the form of a general nationwide depression in 1890. But the blow that brought valley growers to their knees was the discovery that the dreaded, grapevine-ravaging phylloxera—for which there was no cure—had infected the vineyards of the entire area. By the turn of the century, almost every vineyard had been ruined.

Plantings of resistant varieties brought fresh hope. Viticulture looked to be getting back on track. But those bright hopes were dashed by a new cataclysm. It was called Prohibition. For the Old World grape growers, who considered wine the elixir of life, the law was inexplicable madness. One Italian immigrant in Pope Valley continued selling his wine because he believed wine to be "a natural way of life." He was arrested, naturally.

Fourteen years it lasted, from 1920 to 1933. Some vintners survived Prohibition by making sacramental or pharmaceutical wines. But for others it would take years to build back their businesses. Still, one thing was clear: There would be no returning to wheat or cattle raising. Napa County was on its way to becoming America's premier wine region.

By 1966 wine was becoming fashionable, not only in California, but across the nation. Between 1966 and 1972 wine consumption doubled. Visitors started pouring into the area to look, sample and buy. By the mid-'70s, there were again more than 50 wineries in operation in Napa Valley, and a new promotional technique had been developed—winetastings. In order to let the public see how great the product was, vintners opened their doors and uncorked their bottles for sampling. Many opened their cellars for touring. Add to it all an outstanding showing by Napa County wines in a 1976 blind taste test with some of the most prestigious wineries in France, and the worldwide wine community was beginning to take notice (see our Close-up, "The Discovery of California," in our Wineries chapter).

In the 1980s viticulture became a sort of dream occupation—a creative endeavor that could be both financially rewarding and personally satisfying. New wineries popped up almost over-night, many operated by individuals drawn into the field because they savored living close to the soil. Wineries started gaining public acceptance by offering extra attractions—Shakespearean plays and readings in the caves, Mozart played at eventide on expansive green lawns. Wine

Country golf courses and croquet courts drew international competition. Cooking classes featured famous chefs. It all drew attention to the work of the winemaker. And along the path of progress, the city of Napa became a bedroom community for San Francisco. (Commuting isn't all bad when you have a scenic home to return to.)

Sonoma County

Before there were towns and vineyards in the southern end of Sonoma Valley, its hills and valleys were home to elk, deer, cougars and bears, and to the golden poppies that grew wild in the spring.

To this unsettled land came a zealous young Spanish priest, Father Jose Altimira, to establish in 1823 the Mission San Francisco de Solano, northernmost in a chain of missions spaced a day's journey apart along California's coast. This mission was the only one to be dedicated after Mexico overthrew Spanish rule earlier that year. In fact, not everyone in the mission hierarchy thought it was a good idea. But Altimira was nothing if not enthusiastic, and he convinced his colleagues it would be a better climate than San Francisco for the Native American converts.

Compared to other, grander missions, Altimira's was unimpressive—a flimsy wooden structure that was swept twice by fire before achieving its present, fireproof adobe state. Within six years, Altimira claimed 1,000 converts (some may have been transfers). An adobe chapel had been added, as had a number of small shops where converts could learn weaving and agricultural skills.

But the mission was doomed from the start. A decree was passed down from the Mexican government that all church properties would be "secularized" (that is, confiscated). In 1834 a young lieutenant, the aforementioned Mariano Vallejo, was sent from Monterey to carry out that order—to seize all mission property and dispose of grain fields and thousands of head of cattle, sheep and horses. It was scarcely less than outright thievery.

The converts were turned loose to fend for themselves, and in truth, they may have been grateful. They didn't much like Altimira, a cold and impersonal man, and they didn't care for the Spanish or the Mexicans, who were sometimes oppressive. In any case, the Mexican government at this time had another, more serious reason to send an emissary into the territory—to discourage foreign invaders. Trappers were arriving in ever-increasing poaching forays over the Sierra Nevada Mountains, and some were staying on as settlers. On the north coast there was another serious threat from Russia, which had established Fort Ross as a base for pursuing sea otter herds. Their stockade enclosed a roomy, well-furnished commandant's house, barracks and a chapel, and outside the palisade were houses for 60 Russian colonists. Fort Ross lasted three decades before the sea otter had been hunted to near-extinction. Having little more reason to stay, the Russians departed in 1841, leaving Mexico feeling a little more secure.

Meanwhile, young Lt. Vallejo moved his beautiful, cultured wife, Francisca Benicia, to this rough, untamed land and set up house in the abandoned mission. In one of its 37 rooms, their first daughter was born. In time, Vallejo set about creating the town of Sonoma. Using a pocket compass, he laid out an 8-acre plaza around which the town would rise. The plaza would serve as a promenade area for the populace as well as a parade ground where young soldiers could drill and practice their horsemanship skills. At the same time, Vallejo was preoccupied with developing a 66,000-acre ranch in the grasslands of Petaluma Valley, some 10 miles away. Also built as a defense against intruders, its walls were 3 feet thick, braced by redwood beams. It became a second home for the growing Vallejo family (eventually numbering 15 children). Mexican cowhands rode through the big courtyard scattering chickens and scaring sheep. Their women wove fabrics, made candles and patted tortillas in the many work rooms.

Some 2,000 American Indians (most of them transfers from the mission ranks) answered roll call daily in the courtyard before going to work making saddles and boots. These products were marketed to settlers or shipped to coastal communities as far south as San Blas, Mexico. It all had a ring of permanence about it, but trouble was brewing. On a Sunday morning in June 1846, Vallejo was awakened by a group of 33 ragtag settlers and squatters who had marched

HISTORY

INSIDERS' TIP

In a quiet corner of Yountville's Pioneer Cemetery lie the mortal remains of George Yount, the first American given a land grant in the Napa Valley.

from Sutter's Fort (now the town of Sacramento) with plans to overthrow the Mexican government, arrest Vallejo and set up their own republic.

The Bear Flag Rebellion

"About half past five in the morning of Sunday, June 14, a group of desperados surrounded the house of General Vallejo and arrested him," wrote his sister. "Vallejo, dressed in the uniform of a General, was the prisoner of this group of rough-looking men, some wearing on their heads caps made with the skins of coyotes or wolves. . . . Shoes were to be seen on the feet of 15 or 20 among the whole lot."

The grievance that incited these men to rebellion involved the luring of wagonloads of settlers to the Sonoma and Napa valleys by reports of fertile soil, pleasant climate and land for the taking. When they found a Mexican decree barred them from buying land, they became squatters, raising crops and cattle on land they didn't own. As a consequence, Governor Pio Pico issued a decree that the lot of them were to be deported, and they were thoroughly alarmed.

With that, the renegade malcontents decided to go to Sonoma to get the land they wanted. Along the way they hastily fashioned a flag for the new republic, made of a woman's red flannel petticoat and a length of unbleached muslin. For their emblem they used berry juice to paint on it the picture of a bear (it looked more like a pig) and the words California Republic. The ever cordial Vallejo, not fully aware of the situation, brought up some wine for those who had entered his home while others waited outside, and they spent some time in convivial conversation. But in the end he was carried off to Sutter's Fort in Sacramento, where Vallejo's friend John Sutter reluctantly jailed him.

The California Republic lasted 26 days. On July 9, 1846, U.S. Navy Lt. Joseph Revere lowered the bear flag and replaced it with the American stars and stripes. Vallejo was released from jail August 6. He had been away no more than a month, but in that time his horses and cattle had been stolen, his fields stripped of grain.

The New State of California

The months that followed brought mass confusion. Nobody knew who was in charge. A group of military volunteers known as Company C from New York City's Bowery arrived. But since there wasn't much for the soldiers to do (unless they wanted to stoop to manual labor), they improved their leisure by riding spirited horses, hunting waterfowl and staging cruel bear-and-bull fights in a makeshift stadium behind their barracks.

The event that interrupted this tumultuous period was the discovery of gold. Settler and soldier alike stocked up on provisions and left Sonoma to be run by the womenfolk. The village sank into stagnation. Vallejo, on the other hand, wasn't too bad off. He had seen what was coming and had hedged his bets. While serving Mexico loyally (virtually without pay), he had also taken steps to ingratiate himself to the United States. In time he actually became a California senator.

But Vallejo's plans of becoming a prominent American somehow went astray. One by one his dreams vanished. Lawsuit after lawsuit went against him, and his land empire disappeared. He slipped deeper into debt. He did manage to hold onto his Sonoma home, Lachryma Montis, and here his wife, once pampered, sold dried fruit and chili peppers for the San Francisco market. In old age, Vallejo became a symbol of the link between an idealized Mexican era and the Yankee-dominated present. In his unfailing dignity and hospitality, he seemed to personify all that was best about the past.

By the mid-1860s, Sonoma had become almost totally neglected. There were no trees, and the plaza had degenerated. A fire in 1866 destroyed much of what the early settlers had built. Facing up to this depressing situation, some of the early pioneers took action, organizing a Pioneer Society of 340 members to revitalize the town. They planted trees, built fences and cleaned up the plaza (appointing one member to be in charge of keeping livestock out of that area of town). Gradually the town took on a more respectable look, though the Society itself fizzled out.

About 1888, many Italian workmen, newly arrived from Italy and Switzerland, came to quarry cobblestones for the streets of San Francisco. At the same time, Samuele Sebastiani arrived from Italy and quickly recognized the possibilities for growing wine grapes, due to the valley's soil and climate. In no time at all he was supplying the demand of the Italian workmen for wine—and making a name for his winery. Today the strong Italian influence remains, easily detected in the lifestyle of Sonoma, where Italian restaurants line the streets around the plaza.

One of Vallejo's mandates when he took over as commandant was to see to it the lands north of San Francisco were settled. At the time this northern frontier was a lonesome wilderness, and Vallejo had some trouble convincing any of his fellow Californians to apply for grants. But he had plenty of relatives, so most of them fell heir to large tracts. In 1837 he convinced his widowed mother to leave her San Diego adobe and travel 700 miles to an area near Santa Rosa Creek. She packed up her nine children and seven-trunk wardrobe and built the Cabrillo adobe, the first bona fide home in the Santa Rosa Valley. In time it became the nucleus of a settlement.

Santa Rosa

By 1854 the developing town of Santa Rosa could be claimed as little more than a trading post. A few small businesses and houses had sprung up along the creek, and the town had a representative in the state senate. That man was William Bennett, another former Missourian, and it was his ambition to capture the county seat away from Sonoma. To help voters make up their minds on the issue, a big Fourth of July barbecue was held, attended, according to one historian, "by the lame, the halt and blind if they could influence a vote." Not surprisingly the vote went in favor of Santa Rosa. The following daybreak a group of Santa Rosans, fearing Sonoma wouldn't release the county records, hired a wagon and raced to Sonoma, grabbed the records and raced back to Santa Rosa.

Reporting the hijacking, the *Sonoma Bulletin* editor wrote, "We are only sorry they did not take the adobe courthouse too . . . its removal would have embellished our plaza." Within three years, according to the newly launched *Sonoma Democrat*, Santa Rosa had grown to 100 buildings. After the arrival of the railroad in 1870, the town's population exploded to 6,000.

About this time a shy, trim New Englander named Luther Burbank opened a nursery in the town and began experimenting on flowers, fruits and vegetables. His uncanny talent for interpreting the results of his experiments earned him the lasting title of "plant wizard." A wizard of a different sort next appeared in town—spiritualist-sage Thomas Harris, a man of magnetic personality and piercing eyes "like revolving lights." In the outlying area called Fountain Grove, Harris established the esoteric Brotherhood of New Life, a colony of communal living that separated its members from their spouses (and their cash) to await their celestial mates in another world revealed to Harris in his conversations with the angels. It was left to a lady reporter to provide the impetus to drive Holy Harris from the gates of his Eden. She joined the group long enough to write a lurid expose that sent Harris packing.

The 1906 earthquake that shook San Francisco also rattled Santa Rosa. The courthouse collapsed, and downtown buildings were destroyed. Nearly 100 people died. One of the strongest influences on Santa Rosa was the completion of the Golden Gate Bridge in 1937. Previously the only passage across the Golden Gate was by ferry. With a bridge that linked to Highway 101, Santa Rosa started a new life as a community for commuters.

Petaluma

Rivers were the highways of the mid-1800s until railroads took over. In the Petaluma River, steamboats, introduced to California during the Gold Rush, operated regularly in the 1850s, hauling wool, butter, cream, eggs and live chicks down the twisting tidal river to San Francisco Bay. By the 1890s Petaluma was the third-busiest waterway in the state.

But it was neither the river nor steamboats that gave Petaluma its enduring fame. In the 1880s it became known as the "Egg Basket of the World" when the first practical chicken incubator was invented there and marketed on a mass scale. Immigrants from Europe thronged to Petaluma to set up hundreds of hatcheries and thousands of chicken-feed mills. As many as 600 million eggs per year were shipped to worldwide points. Scientific discoveries were made, and a chicken pharmacy was opened. But chicken-related prosperity declined in the 1930s due to high feed costs. Leghorn hens were replaced by Holstein cows. Today the Petaluma countryside is California's dairyland.

The Father of California Viticulture

Although both Father Jose Altimira and General Mariano Vallejo planted wine grapes when they came to Sonoma, the first one to recognize the untapped potential for fine wine grapes was Count Agoston Haraszthy, a flamboyant aristocrat who had fled political turmoil in his native Hungary to seek his fortunes in America.

A man of enormous energy, Haraszthy had first stopped in Wisconsin long enough to found Sauk City — to build homes, mills and stores, plant hops and start a vineyard. The town remains to this day.

Having wearied of that project, he headed down the Santa Fe Trail to California and arrived at the gold fields on horseback, an Argonaut in silken shirt, red sash and velour hat, seeking whatever opportunities might exist. He was working as an assayer at the San Francisco mint when Gen. Vallejo heard of the man's interest in viticulture and invited him to Sonoma in 1856.

Haraszthy was entranced by the prospects in Sonoma's soil. Convinced that grapes could prosper without irrigation, he sailed for Europe and returned with 300 varieties of grape cuttings, the basis for his 6,000-acre vineyards.

The winery he built was of massive stones, with cellars dug into the hillsides. For himself, he built a grand Pompeian-style villa next to his vineyards. His fame spread quickly, and vintners from other parts of California, as well as those newly arrived from Europe, came to him for advice and for cuttings. It created something of a "grape rush" in the Sonoma and Napa valleys.

But by 1868 the count was again restless and decided to turn his enthusiasm to raising sugar in Nicaragua. He left his two sons (who had married Vallejo daughters) to run the winery business. They never saw their father again, for he vanished mysteriously in the jungle. According to legend, he fell from a tree into a river he was trying to cross and was devoured by crocodiles.

The villa he built in Sonoma was destroyed by the passage of time, but in the 1980s, townsfolk rebuilt a replica next to the first vineyards he planted. Both are there to see today.

Photo: Lou Zauner

This is a modern replica of Agoston Haraszthy's Sonoma home.

Jack London in Glen Ellen

Glen Ellen, 9 miles north of Sonoma, lies in an area forested with oak, madrone, redwood and buckeye trees. Author Jack London came to this countryside in 1903 at the invitation of friends who owned a ranch, and here, at age 30, he met their vivacious daughter, Charmian. Instantly attracted to one another, they spent their days riding horseback and having sprightly conversations. They were perfectly matched, adventurous individuals, and he stayed on to marry Charmian.

At first they lived at her family's ranch, but London fell in love with the land the Indians called "Valley of the Moon." He started accumulating land until he had a 1,500-acre tract, and here the Londons lived in a simple white house. He called the place Beauty Ranch, and it was there he produced most of his prodigious output of books. London's success as an author was initially spurred by the appearance of a Yukon story in *Atlantic Monthly* magazine, and confirmed by publication of *The Call of the Wild* when he was 22.

Within eight years, he was America's highest paid author. In his short lifetime he wrote 54 books, 1,300 articles and 188 short stories, some translated into 30 languages. His house overflowed with guests—scientists, actresses, writers, socialists. He was of a restless nature—there was a stint as a war correspondent and a long sea voyage with Charmian on a ship he designed himself. Exuberance marked everything he did. He took up scientific farming and designed a pigpen that gave each pig family an apartment.

But London's most wondrous dream was Wolf House, his 26-room mansion, an imposing affair of redwood and huge stone blocks, with arched windows opening onto forest slopes and the entire valley. London wrote, "It will last one-thousand years, God willing." But one midnight in August 1913, billows of black smoke filled the sky as a raging fire burned out of control. The author watched silently from a nearby hill as his dream crumbled to the earth. London never quite recovered from the calamity. Three years later he died at age 40. Official cause was uremic poisoning, but rumors persisted it was suicide. The magnificent ruins of Wolf House, as well as all of Beauty Ranch, live on as a California state park.

Northern Sonoma County

For the Pomo tribe that lived for centuries in what is now northern Sonoma County, life was good—game was plentiful, streams were filled with trout and the climate was favorable.

In 1841, a portion of this Pomo domain was granted by Mexico to a New England sea captain, Henry Fitch (nobody consulted the Pomos, of course), who had eloped with General Vallejo's sister. But Fitch, having received such an excellent dowry, saw no reason to live out his life in such a lonely land. He hired Cyrus Alexander to manage a ranch there with immense herds of cattle. The names of both men live on as landmarks—Fitch Mountain hovers over Healdsburg, and to the east lies Alexander Valley, Cyrus's payment for his work on the ranch.

The town that grew up in the northern part of today's Sonoma County, though, was named for Harmon Heald, a disenchanted '49er who arrived on the scene in 1852 and claimed land for a townsite. He surveyed the town and sold lots for $15 apiece around a central plaza. By the end of the decade, Healdsburg had a population of 500.

The town acquired a newspaper, the *Review*, after the editor of the newspaper in Sonoma, A. J. Cox, advised his readers, "the old blunderbuss has dried up," shut down the presses and moved north to publish the paper in Healdsburg. The town's main attraction was that it lay on the road to the geysers, a tourist attraction considered "the greatest of curiosities in the state next to Yosemite Valley." To get there, tourists clung in awestruck terror within Charlie Foss's stagecoach as he careened over narrow roads and rattled over Hog's Back Ridge.

Russian River and West County

The Russian River, which runs east to west between Healdsburg and the Pacific, was initially explored by otter hunters from Fort Ross who wandered in from the sea. But homesteaders from Missouri were the first to be awestruck by the mammoth redwoods and the run of salmon, which you could take with pitchforks. The legendary forests brought in loggers from Canada and Scandinavia who could see the financial possibilities. They began felling trees as though there could be no end. One ancient redwood measured 23 feet in diameter. But inevitably the trees were nearly gone, and most lumber mills closed in the early 1900s.

The area gained a new influx of visitors during the Roaring '20s, when weekenders discovered it as a destination. Roadhouses sprang up, and revelers danced and drank booze from backcountry stills. It was a brief boom before the Russian River went into a phase of quiet sleep. The 1970s brought a renaissance, as families rediscovered it as a place to canoe, camp and swim. Today it's a popular destination, with resorts along its length and a number of elegant B&Bs. (See our On The Water and Bed and Breakfast Inns chapters.)

Joaquin Carillo, another Vallejo relative with the standard family land grant (this one of 13,000 acres), was the first Sebastopol resident. After American settlers overran his lands, he turned his house into a hotel.

The town acquired its name in a strange way. A fist-fight had erupted in front of Dougherty's store, and the man who was getting the worst of it retreated into the store, where Dougherty prevented the attacker from advancing. The Crimean War was then in progress and onlookers compared this encounter with the fight going on in the village of Sebastopol in the Russian Crimea.

The forests of West County gave way to orchards, and in 1883 Nathaniel Griffin, aided by the young naturalist Luther Burbank, developed a new strain of apple. The advantage of this Gravenstein apple was that it ripened earlier. Today, 90 percent of Gravenstein apples grow in this countryside, and Calif. Highway 116 running through it is called the Gravenstein Highway.

Other towns in the West County are farm communities: Valley Ford, Bloomfield, Forestville. Occidental was first settled by Bill Howard, who had survived a shipwreck off New York, a fever in Africa and a revolution in Brazil. He and a sawmill operator lured a railroad into the territory, and after that success built the whole town of Occidental in four months. Italian woodcutters were brought in from Tuscany to work in the forests, but a few opened restaurants where a big meal of pasta could be had for two bits. A tradition was established, and today Occidental is the place to go for oversized Italian dinners.

The Sonoma Coast

For almost 60 miles along the jagged coastline, Sonoma County's Calif. Highway 1 (called "Coast Highway 1" in many locales) twists and turns on a ledge between the Coast Range and the Pacific, passing through countryside as lonely and peaceful as the pale mists that creep over its capes and slip into its coves. The ocean, sometimes tempestuous, flings itself against the crags and sea stacks with a mighty roar. Then the sun burns through, the sky turns blue and the landscape comes to life in brilliant color.

Centuries ago the Miwok and Pomo tribes fished these coastal waters. They were still there in the early 1820s, when Russian fur traders came down from Fort Ross and established ranches at Bodega Bay and inland Bodega village, where they remained for three decades. When Russia abandoned California, Mexico was delighted to move in, granting lands extending from Bodega to the Russian River. One of the grantees, a Capt. Smith, acquired a steam sawmill and soon transformed the peaceful fishing port into a shipping point for timber and agricultural products. But it wasn't until Calif. 1 was opened to auto traffic that Bodega Bay reached the public eye (giving fishermen and vacationers access).

This was the setting for Alfred Hitchcock's classic thriller, *The Birds*, the filming of which is now commemorated by a wall-size photo at Bay View Restaurant at the popular Inn at the Tides (see our Restaurants and Hotels and Motels chapters). Almost all the land between Bodega Bay and Fort Ross is government-owned and accessible to the public,

INSIDERS' TIP

The Chinese were among the most coveted of mining employees during the Gold Rush. They were reliable because they tended to drink less, and they were healthier because they boiled their water for tea.

including Fort Ross, which is now a state historic park. Were the Russian settlers interested only in otters? Or did they hope to make a niche for Russia in the new land? The passing years have erased any urgency to answer the question. The sheep pass in and out of the fortress, caring little if they munch Russian, American or Spanish grass. North from Fort Ross to the Mendocino County border, the Sonoma coast remains one of California's few undeveloped coastal regions.

This is the house that Lillie Langtry built when she came to Lake County.

Photo: Lou Zauner

Mendocino County

In the language of the Pomo tribe, Ukiah means "deep valley." The surrounding hills rise rather sharply, particularly in the east, where roads struggle to find a way across the rugged terrain to neighboring Lake County. There is a certain wildness to these hills, as if civilization were still waiting to invade the isolation.

The first adventuring white pioneers to disturb this primitive life arrived in the 1840s, drawn there by rumors of gold discoveries. The rumors were false and no gold was to be found, but the land itself was pleasant—a good place to settle down and raise sheep, plant fruit trees and grow hops. Among the early arrivals was Sam Orr, a Kentuckian who brought his wife in 1857 along with a quantity of grape cuttings to start a vineyard. Soon another American wandered in, a prospector from the gold country named Seward. He bought some of Orr's cuttings and also started a vineyard. Apparently he had found success in his mining venture, as he built an imposing Colonial-style house, several outbuildings and a winery. Still, the valley's greatest fame rested not with grapes but with hops.

Hop trellises became a sort of adjunct to the scenery, and the center of the district was Hopland. By the 1890s the Ukiah Valley had achieved modest fame for its vast hop fields, and there was an air of prosperity. The town of Ukiah had two hotels, three livery stables and 10 saloons. Its dirt streets were the horror of everyone, dusty in summer, muddy in winter. One especially wet year a two-horse wagon sank hub-deep in the middle of Main Street.

Most incoming travelers arrived by way of Fort Bragg on a stagecoach that left at 7 AM and made a loading stop at Mendocino before rumbling over twisty, dusty, uphill roads to Ukiah. Along the route the stage stopped for a meal and change of horses, with passengers arriving in Ukiah well-shaken about dinnertime. Plain to many, what was needed was a railroad. A.T. Perkins, owner of the local newspaper, grumbled in a wry editorial, "Rumors of a railroad are floating around, although there is not enough money in the county to build a decent dirt road." (Later a street was named after him.)

Perkins' predictions notwithstanding, the railroad did come through with service from San Francisco, and it started a tourist boom. Passengers caught a ferry to Tiburon, a train to Ukiah and from there a hack to anywhere they wanted to go. By then the hop fields had achieved notoriety, and travelers came from hundreds of miles away just to spend a weekend in the country watching the hop pickers. Some even came to join in the fun. A magazine travel article of the day made Hopland sound as romantic as a trip down the Rhine: "If your nerves have become super-sensitive from the corrosions of city life . . . take a vacation among the hop fields in the gilded autumn area of California. A few hours' travel north from San Francisco and one looms upon acres of trellised hop vines and graceful, luxurious beauty delighting the eye at every turn. Pickers are at work by the hundreds."

For the hundreds of hop pickers, those trellised vines were less romantic. In an oral history of Mendocino County, pioneer Hazel Pittman recalled those days: "It was awfully hard work. We wore gauntlet gloves and still the hops would cut through with the stickers on them. You would perspire from the terrible heat and itch. But we made a penny a pound, and if you could pick a hundred pounds a day there was a whole dollar."

Other attractions arose to bring tourists. This was the age of the curative mineral bath, and the area boasted several. Most elegant was Vichy Springs, an upscale resort featuring such niceties as croquet, horseback rides, hunting safaris and dancing under the stars. The water in the swimming pool was claimed to be "charged with electricity and gas, a real Champagne Bath." Vichy Springs had a long fallow period, but in the late 1980s it was revived, reconstructed and rejuvenated, and is once again an elegant resort spa (see our Spas and Resorts chapter).

Meanwhile, in the early 1900s, grape growing and winemaking were becoming serious business. Dozens of small operations were producing wine in light volume. Zinfandel was the main product. Hard-working Italians planted grapes on the hillsides. For the most part, however, the wine industry in Mendocino County at this time involved growers shipping their fruit to other wine-producing regions for blending. Typical of early growers were the Malone family, who sold their grapes as reds and whites, with no varietal distinction.

In 1910, a census counted 5,800 Mendocino County acres in grape production, with 90,000 gallons of wine produced. Much of the activity stemmed from the arrival of the railroad, which opened up new markets. But for Mendocino County, as for the nation, wine production came to a halt when Prohibition became the law of the land. Today's wine industry is based not so much on quantity as on quality. Mendocino wine is now recognized worldwide as premier.

Anderson Valley

Walter Anderson came here in 1851 with his wife, who may have been the first white woman in these parts. Early accounts describe Anderson as a man who chose to forsake civilization and pitch his tent where the foot of man had never trod. Yet in time he became a wealthy man with broad acres of land and large herds of cattle. Eventually Anderson was joined by others like himself—farmers or cattlemen living on spreads that were remote from the trappings and amenities of city life. A few enterprising homesteaders tried planting grapes, but the valley's proximity to ocean temperatures 10 degrees cooler than in Ukiah meant it was not only Prohibition that killed the wine industry here, but also adverse weather.

Not until the 1960s did anyone get serious about vineyards. In 1964, Dr. Donald Edmeades, against all sensible advice, planted 24 acres of grapes. He hung out a sign, "Edmeades' Folly." Today there are a dozen small wineries in the area, mostly growing cooler-climate grapes such as Chardonnay and Pinot Noir.

The Mendocino Coast

The jagged Mendocino Coast bears little resemblance to its southern relative, that stretch of beach that's lined with sunbathers from Santa Barbara to San Diego. Here the fog-festooned sand dunes are spotted with wild grasses, overwhelming in their lonely beauty. In springtime the hills are golden with Scotch broom, and in summer rhododendrons grow wild. Nowhere is nature more glorious.

It's a rugged coast, dotted with doghole ports that prospered as busy lumber towns for two decades in the rush for building materials following the 1906 San Francisco earthquake. Many of these burgs have vanished or are greatly diminished. For some years, Point Arena was the largest, most active lumber port between San Francisco and Eureka. It was also a whaling station and regular port of call for passenger steamers. Today, its most impressive feature is its classic, soaring lighthouse, 115 feet up from the tip of a narrow, bleak, eroding rockbound point. It's the closest point to Hawaii on the west coast. The light tower was built in 1870, then rebuilt after the devastating 1906 earthquake. For 36 years, it faithfully guided ships through the treacherous rocks, but today's visitors will see only seals, migrating gray whales and cavorting sea lions.

The settlement called Elk, 18 miles north of the Point Arena light tower, used to be a lively port. The cove is heavily studded with craggy islets and tall, dome-shaped sea stacks. Steam schooners used to brave this navigator's nightmare to load lumber among the rocks.

The single event that turned the Mendocino Coast into a lumberjack's paradise was the Gold Rush. San Francisco burgeoned into a bustling city in urgent need of lumber to build houses. At the time, the only lumber available came from the Sandwich Islands (now known as Hawaii) and was very costly. When news of the great redwood forest on the north coast trickled down, there was no holding back the tide. The history of the coast changed overnight.

Along a 20-mile stretch of coast south of Mendocino city are a handful of country inns with colorful histories, some perched on bluffs, others snuggled into the foothills (see our Bed and Breakfast Inns chapter). Several of the fine old structures date back to the mid-1800s. Logging had been booming in Little River for 10 years when Silas Coombs selected it as one of the best-weather ports on the coast to build a mill. The mill wasn't memorable (it burned in 1910), but the mansion Coombs built lives on as Little River Inn, one of the coast's loveliest, with gabled windows and eaves festooned with wooden scrollwork. From the porch where Silas once spotted ship arrivals, visitors now can watch the annual migration of gray whales from cold Alaska to warm mating areas in Baja California (see our Spas and Resorts chapter).

There's another historic inn nearby. Heritage House is an old Victorian farmhouse dating to the 1850s. It was an early base for smuggling both liquor and foreign laborers and once was a hideout for 1930s gangster "Baby Face" Nelson. Today, it's a leisurely retreat with a commanding view of the craggy coast.

The City of Mendocino

This antique settlement was among the largest and most cosmopolitan of the old lumber ports. Nearly everything in Mendocino is built of wood, including the sidewalks and the water towers that stand on the skyline. The settlement was first known as Meiggsville, for "Honest Harry" Meiggs, a San Francisco politician and wharf owner with a weakness for speculation. The town name was changed in 1854 after Meiggs got into financial hot water and had to flee the country. He recouped by building the first railroad over the Andes in South America, but his partners in Mendocino were left facing bankruptcy.

The incident that brought Meiggs hot-footing to Mendocino in the first place was the wrecking of a Chilean barque bound for San Francisco loaded with silks and spices. When Meiggs sent a salvage party, they found no silks but instead great forests of redwood. Meiggs, a born promoter, rounded up a schooner, some mill equipment and some partners and headed for the forested coast. In no time mills sprung up in every gulch. Prosperity followed—mansions with leaded-glass windows were perched on hillsides, and fine furnishings were shipped around Cape Horn to this remote outpost. Breweries, churches and schools followed. On Steamer Day, when passengers came into port, carriages from eight hotels met ships from all over the globe.

But all this feverish activity had its effect on the forests, which had seemed so unlimited. There was little left to cut down. Mills closed one by one, and Mendocino fell asleep and snoozed for a long while. The city was fading fast in the 1960s, when it suddenly blossomed as a center for artists and bohemians seeking freedom of style and life on the cheap. William Zacha came up from the Bay Area to open an art gallery, then conceived the Mendocino Art Center, a rambling collection of buildings on a rise at the edge of town (see our Shopping and Arts and Culture chapters).

It was this art colony that first attracted a more affluent breed of visitor seeking escape from urban living. They came to stroll boardwalks and wander back streets occupied mainly by dogs and kids on bikes. While looking for a simpler life, they inadvertently gave the town a cachet of chic, inspiring the rise of gourmet restaurants and some uncommonly civilized inns. It is this ambience that sets Mendocino apart from other north coast villages. The fact that Mendocino looks a lot like the coast of Maine has not escaped the notice of filmmakers. Devotees of the television series *Murder, She Wrote* will recognize some "Cabot Cove" settings.

Fort Bragg

Fort Bragg is only 8 miles north, but far different in mood from Mendocino. There's the smell of sawdust, and local talk is about lumber. One of the most spectacular scenes in Fort Bragg is Noyo Harbor, a snug refuge along the Noyo River that protects commercial fishing boats. In the predawn you can see the parade of boats heading down the river to the sea, their lights making an attractive scene.

But Fort Bragg's greatest fame derives from the California Western Railroad's Skunk, an old-time logging train that rattles through 40 miles of dense redwood forest, over 31 bridges and trestles, through two deep mountain tunnels and around sinuous switchbacks. It was a nightmare to build. The inland end of the Skunk's line is Willits.

Beyond Fort Bragg, Calif. 1 clings to the ocean, passing through ghost-filled lumbering villages once peopled with thousands but now inhabited by only a few. The foamy green surf bangs against a thousand rocky coves and doghole ports, where schooners came crashing to grief in lumber heydays.

Lake County

For centuries Pomo tribes lived around Clear Lake, fishing in canoes of willow poles interwoven with tules, while their women made baskets so fine they could hold water. There was plenty of obsidian for spears and tools. The Pomo bathed in the hot springs and played games on the small islands that dot the lake. Volcanic Mt. Konocti, with its eerie caves, was considered sacred ground.

The first white men at Clear Lake were probably Russian fur trappers from Fort Ross. They were followed by French-Canadian fur trappers and American mountain men. Then in 1836 General Vallejo's brother, Salvador, brought cattle and horses onto a newly acquired land grant. For the most part, Salvador ran the ranch from Sonoma headquarters, and the Pomo lifestyle was not interrupted.

But in 1847, Salvador sold out to two Americans, Andrew Kelsey and Charles Stone. They enslaved the natives, oppressed them, starved them. In desperation two of the Pomos were hired to steal a steer, but they bungled the job. Fearing a cruel reprisal they decided to kill Stone and Kelsey. Stone died from an arrow, Kelsey at the hands of a Pomo woman whose son had been tortured. Frightened settlers called in the military from Benicia. A battle ensued and the frightened Pomos, holed up on a Clear Lake island, were massacred, giving the name Bloody Island to the site.

The island is no more, as farmers reclaimed the marshes around it. But the name of Andrew Kelsey lives on in Kelseyville. In the early 1850s, wagon trains began arriving and settlers started raising cattle and planting fields. John Cobb, one of the first, had come from Kentucky by way of the Wabash, Tippecanoe, Quincy and the gold mines of Placerville before finally settling down in what is now known as Cobb Valley.

By 1857, a county government had been set up in a tiny wooden courthouse, and Lakeport was on its way to being the county seat. It was assumed the key to growth was a railroad to market products elsewhere but Lake County did grow, albeit slowly, despite the handicap of having no railroad. A number of vineyards and wineries appeared, most of them clinging to the valleys around Clear Lake, since the rest of the county was quite rugged.

But wine would not be the real attraction in the area. That would turn out to be the hot springs that bubbled up everywhere. By 1880, 100,000 people had traveled to Lake County to partake of the beneficial waters and luxuriate in the elegant hotels adjacent to the mineral springs. Posh casinos, music halls redolent with gold leaf and formal dining rooms gleaming with silver and crystal were just some of the luxuries offered during leisure hours, while the more energetic indulged in bowling, croquet, lawn tennis and riding.

As the fame of the resorts grew, so did the services. Hundreds were employed as servants and culinary workers, hundreds more in riding stables and on vegetable farms. Bartlett Springs could accommodate 5,000 guests, and some

INSIDERS' TIP

Calistoga today retains its fame as a health resort with natural hot-water geysers, mineral springs and mineralized mud baths.

Photo: Tina Luster-Hoban

Silverado Country Club in Napa was originally a private mansion built in 1889.

were notable. One year, Queen Marie of Romania sojourned for a while. Nearby Harbin Springs boasted two large hotels, 15 cottages and springs of hot arsenic, hot iron and sulphur with a temperature of 120 degrees. (See Harbin Hot Springs in our Spas and Resorts chapter.)

For generations, many faithfully vacationed at these spas not only for health benefits, but also as a gathering place for the socially elite. The undoing of this salubrious way of life was the invention of the combustion engine. With the advent of the automobile, people no longer lingered for weeks. Instead, they came for a few days and moved on to another spot. The fine old hotels degenerated, and most of them burned. It was the end of a gracious era that lasted a half-century.

Lillie Langtry in the Vineyards

Of all the rich and famous who made their way to Lake County, none was more illustrious than the vibrant, graceful Lillie Langtry—famed actress and vivacious mistress of Britain's Prince of Wales, later King Edward VII. She came to Guenoc Valley in 1887, weary of the acting circuit and trying to get a divorce from her English husband. She bought a 4,000-acre ranch and intended to raise grapes and thoroughbred horses. With her was her celebrated lover, Freddie Gebhart, a wealthy horseman who had bought an adjoining 3,200 acres.

Langtry was enchanted with Lake County from the moment she came via jostling stage-coach from St. Helena at the end of the railroad line. She was intrigued by the ways of the Wild West. "We all took part in the process of corralling the different herds of cattle and the roundup of horses," she wrote. "We counted about 80 horses. My manager was in his glory and stabled about 20." Langtry had other plans for Guenoc Ranch as well. She wanted to produce wine from her own grapes and winery. She decided that no one but a Frenchman could cope with this challenge, and she engaged a capable man from Bordeaux.

The vintage that resulted never reached market. "A new law putting liquor into bond for a period spoiled the sale of those bottles with a picture of myself on the label," she complained, "and I suppose now that the country is dry my portrait still adorns the Customs." Langtry stayed at the ranch a fortnight and eagerly looked to return after completing her committed engagements. However, she never saw the ranch again, though she owned it 18 years.

When Prohibition dealt its death blow to winemaking, Lake County turned its land over to pears, walnuts and grazing pasture. Not until the 1960s did the vineyards reappear. Now there are several top-rated wineries in operation, and one of them is Guenoc.

When Orville Magoon bought and revived the vineyards of Lillie Langtry's beloved Guenoc Ranch, he discovered old agricultural records stating that Langtry Farms had produced 50 tons of Burgundy wine in 1891. The area where Lillie's grapes grew has now been replanted and, with some additional acreage, stretches out along Butts Canyon Road. From the winery's tasting rooms that rise above a small lake, one can see in the distance the house where Langtry lived, looking almost exactly as it did when she was there. And once again the wines of Guenoc are bottled with her portrait on the label (see our Wineries chapter).

The centerpiece of Lake County has always been Clear Lake, the largest natural lake in California that is completely contained within the state borders. But the abundance of Clear Lake had its limits. Land clearing and farming gradually released silt and nutrients into the lake, eventually causing the once-blue waters to cloud with dirt and algae. In the 1940s, gnats swarmed and had to be sprayed with DDT—the results were that fish and fish-eating birds and animals began to die off. Today the ecological balance has been largely restored. Clear Lake is especially popular with fishermen and campers.

HISTORY

The Golden Gateway

It's a fact: Many visitors to Wine Country arrive via San Francisco, where they will snag a rental car for their trek to the luscious country to the north. Another fact: Just about everyone who encounters this most intriguing, craziest of municipal quilts knows that "just passing through" San Francisco usually (hopefully!) means staying at least a couple of days and nights. If you're stopping over in the city and staring straight at one of those "so much to do and so little time" quandaries, here are some handy suggestions for seeing San Francisco on the fly.

Those who do arrive in Wine Country by way of the Bay Area will quickly discover that The City (always capitalized by locals, many of whom have heard of New York) really is everything it claims to be. The little cable cars really do climb halfway to the stars (or at least as far as Nob Hill). The golden fog does swirl around the Golden Gate Bridge, leaving its ramparts floating like an orange gateway to nirvana. At eventide the golden glow of the setting sun glints from the windows of Alcatraz Island, making the old prison seem somehow romantic. And errant sailors tack home against the late and misty sky.

Enchanting? Yes!

So . . . if you had only two days in San Francisco, what places would you feel terrible if you missed? Everyone's tastes are different, but here are some of the best.

Nob Hill, at the top of California and Sacramento streets, with its posh hotels, private clubs and smart addresses, retains much of the glamour and gentility it possessed at the end of the 19th century, when men who had made fortunes in silver erected grand mansions for the world to envy on these unobstructed, commanding heights.

From this corner you can catch a cable car for a dashing ride down to Fisherman's Wharf. Clickety-clacking down the California hill, you can see straight across the bay. The ride is particularly intriguing at night. And incidentally, it's no accident that all three cable car lines cross Nob Hill. When it was invented in 1873, the cable car made Nob Hill readily accessible for the first time.

Fisherman's Wharf, with its picturesque views and pungent aromas, is where the sea's bounty is collected and sold from steaming crab pots and in fine restaurants. West Coast Dungeness crab is considered by local gourmets (and commoners alike) to be the best seafood in the world. Fishing boats bob alongside the wharf, while seagulls watch the passing parade with haughty disdain from the wharf pilings. Walkaway shrimp cocktails are sold from the sidewalk, along with clam chowder and sourdough bread, and it's pleasant to walk out on the wharf and scarf up a little seafood while watching the fishing boats come in. Parking is available in public lots along Beach and North Point streets. (If you crave the best seafood in town and would rather avoid the touristy Fisherman's Wharf crowds, get on Geary Street and drive west until you're near the ocean. Your destination is the **Pacific Café** at 7000 Geary. They don't take reservations, but you can sip a glass of wine on the sidewalk while you wait. You won't be disappointed.)

While in the neighborhood, you might want to walk down to the **Hyde Street Pier** and look at the tall 19th-century ships permanently berthed there. **Ghirardelli Square**, a short walk uphill on Hyde Street, is one of San Francisco's most successful attempts to hang onto the transient past. Until 1964 it was a crumbling, abandoned factory that had once turned out Civil War uniforms and later served as a chocolate factory where Domingo Ghirardelli made cocoa. It was steamship magnate William Matson Roth who saved the old beauty from the wrecker's ball and made it a showcase—one of the most pleasurable places in the city. Within the rambling complex are a dozen fine restaurants, snug cafes and almost 100 shops and galleries.

The Cannery, just down the street on Leavenworth, is where Del Monte once tinned fruit. Now it's a delightful and original collection of sprightly shops, art galleries and restaurants; a place to buy French lingerie, English antiques, primitive art and the newest in contemporary furniture. Often there's entertainment in the courtyard—small combo bands, magicians and jugglers.

From a high vantage point you can look out on **Alcatraz Island**, once the end of the line and the beginning of hopelessness for federal prisoners. Now it's part of a national park and can be reached by boats that leave several times a day from Pier 41 at Fisherman's Wharf. A cellblock tour gives some insight into life behind bars for men like Al Capone and Machine Gun Kelly, who lived out their days here without visitors.

> **INSIDERS' TIP**
>
> Gray Line offers a selection of full- and half-day excursions in San Francisco departing from Trans-Bay Terminal at First and Mission streets. Night tours depart from Union Square at Powell and Geary streets. The 3½-hour tour departs daily at 9, 10 and 11 AM and at 1:30, 2:30 and 3:30 PM.

Those who are curious (and not claustrophobic) are allowed to spend 60 seconds in the "dark hole," where the recalcitrant spent some days and nights on the damp cement floors. An excellent audio tour narrated by former guards and inmates is full of fascinating anecdotes about day-to-day life on Alcatraz, some of the more notorious criminals, escape attempts and the prison riot of 1946. Same-day tickets are available at Pier 41 (you'll run into long lines in summer), or you can get them one month in advance by calling (415) 546-2628.

The central point of San Francisco is **Union Square**, the only green area laid out by early city planners. With its flower stands, it's the heart of the city's downtown shopping district, bounded by Powell, Geary, Post and Stockton streets. Posh shops extend a few blocks down each street as well as around the square: Neiman Marcus, Saks Fifth Avenue, Gucci and Hermes. Also there is Gump's, famed for its collection of jade as well as fine china and crystal. In years to come, look for even more commercial activity, as a Union Square building boom attracts even more retail giants.

Chinatown is just a short walk up Grant Avenue from Union Square. This "city within a city" is home to more Chinese than any other place outside of Asia. Some 80,000 San Franciscans live, work, shop, worship and play in Chinatown. It's packed with open-air markets, a variety of bakeries, restaurants, temples, souvenir shops and, yes, people. Grant Avenue is touristy, but Stockton Street, a block up from Grant, is where you'll get a real taste of Chinatown. Streets are lined with tearooms, temples, Chinese schools and shops that offer exotic produce and delicacies like yellow croaker salted fish, dried papaw, dried fish peel and dried black fungus.

For a rare treat, stop for a dim sum lunch at one of the restaurants showing dim sum signboards. You order from one of the carts being wheeled around by waitresses who call out their particular specialty in Chinese. Every specialty is good!

One way to get a real Insider's view of Chinatown is to take a walking tour. One of the best is **Wok Wiz**, operated by a woman who grew up in Chinatown and knows its history, culture and food customs. Call (415) 355-9657 for more information.

Between Chinatown and Fisherman's Wharf is **North Beach**, the Italian district of the city. The soul of North Beach is pasta and provolone, boccie and cappuccino, and you'll find many restaurants to sample some of each. The birthplace of the Beat movement, North Beach is the

This shot from high above the Golden Gate Bridge offers a bird's-eye view of the city.

home of bookstores, cafes, galleries, small theatres and nightclubs. **City Lights Books** at 261 Columbus Avenue still thrives as a gathering place of writers.

Early in the city's history, both Chinatown and North Beach were actually under bay water. Landfill has put the waterfront far away now. Still, the ocean has always been the main draw for San Franciscans. The real place to get the feel of the Pacific today is along the **Great Highway**. If you start at Point Lobos Avenue and the Great Highway, you can visit Cliff House, a once-famous resort area that overlooks the ocean and nearby Seal Rock, habitat of noisy sea lions. From here the long windswept strand of Ocean Beach stretches to the great sand dunes to the south. Leave your bathing suit at the hotel, and stay out of the roiling surf, where the south-bound tidal currents traveling at 12 mph have a habit of swallowing swimmers and surfers alike.

Along this highway you'll discover an entrance to **Golden Gate Park**, the city's great green retreat, bordered by the Great Highway, Lincoln Way, Stanyan and Fulton streets. In 1887 when the park was built, it comprised 730 acres of dunes and 270 acres of arable land. Today its 1,000 acres are lush with meadows, lakes and 5,000 varieties of shrubs, flowers and trees. Within its borders you can visit two art museums, an aquarium, a planetarium and a plant conservatory that looks a lot like Kew Gardens in London. You can watch a polo game, gaze at buffaloes grazing, rent a bike, hear a Sunday band concert or stop for lunch at the beautifully landscaped Japanese Tea Garden. The park also includes a nifty nine-hole pitch-and-putt golf course, possibly the best-kept golf facility in town.

INSIDERS' TIP

Perhaps the best bet for parking in downtown San Francisco is the Union Square Garage, with an entrance on Geary Street. It's within walking distance of the hotels and department stores surrounding Union Square, as well as Chinatown. You can pick up a cable car at the corner of Powell and Geary streets.

San Francisco is also a great place to spend an evening. Ease into a silky-smooth night of jazz at the New Orleans room at the **Fairmont Hotel**, California and Mason streets, and also inquire as to who's playing at the velvet-gloved and sedate Venetian room there. Give an amen for some soulful gospel music at **Biscuits and Blues**, 401 Mason Street, or enjoy an evening of comedy at **Punch Line**, 444 Battery Street. One of the best comedy shows in town is the long-running **Beach Blanket Babylon** at Club Fugazi, 678 Green Street. It's wacky and it's fun.

Of course, this listing of attractions only scratches the surface. It is said that everyone who visits San Francisco wants to come back again, and our tour leaves plenty more to see on a return trip. It would be nice, for instance, to take in the **Cable Car Barn and Museum** on Washington and Mason streets to see the historic old paraphernalia and glimpse the innards of these machines in action. (Just how does that cable car work anyway?) Kids and parents alike should see the **Exploratorium**, Marina Boulevard and Lyon Street, which contains more than 600 interactive science exhibits.

Fort Mason is where a million good-byes were said during World War II. Now it's a regional cultural center with workshops and studios. A local delight is to walk across the Golden Gate Bridge on a Sunday and tarry on the far side for a magnificent view of San Francisco.

The city's Victorian architecture is almost as famous as its cable cars. Handsome and slightly irrational, painted brightly in all combinations of colors, these structures are certainly unique. Some of the best can be seen on **Pacific Heights**, particularly on these streets: Vallejo, Broadway, Pacific, Jackson, Washington, Pierce and Scott, generally in blocks between 1600 and 3000.

Another distinctive neighborhood you might want to see is **Cole Valley**. This is a recently semi-gentrified annex to the Haight-Ashbury district, that place once filled with disaffected youth and made famous during the "summer of love" in 1967. Cole Valley is home to one of San Francisco's best but least-publicized cafes, **Zazie**, at 941 Cole Street.

Of course there are other restaurants you may want to try during your short San Francisco visit. **Pane e Vino** is a well-camouflaged eating spot, tucked just below the trendy Union Street shopping zone at 3011 Steiner Street. This is a simple, well-attended Italian café within walking distance of **Perry's**, at 1944 Union Street. More than just a sports bar or watering hole, Perry's is one of San Francisco's see-and-be-seen hangouts in the same genre as North Beach's **Washington Square Bar and Grill** at 1707 Powell Street and **Moose's**, across Washington Square at 1652 Stockton Street. Between these last two landmarks stands the cherished Italian restaurant,

Fior d'Italia, at 601 Union Street and the city's definitive espresso bar, **Mario's Bohemian Cigar Store**, at 566 Columbus Avenue.

After your double espresso, you might get an urge to walk four or five blocks north to the corner of Columbus and Bay Street for a museum-like tour of another cathedral of sorts, **Tower Records**. Careful observers on this route will note they've come full circle to the end of the Powell Street Cable Car line, hard by Fisherman's Wharf.

After walking this far, we hope you're still warm. One thing visitors should keep in mind is that San Francisco weather is, well, unpredictable. True, temperatures don't often vary outside a range of 50 to 70 degrees, summer or winter. But sometimes January and February can be the sunniest, most glorious months. On the other hand, summer can be so cold that tourists who mistakenly thought California called for shorts huddle in downtown doorways to keep warm. Mark Twain reportedly once said, "The coldest winter I ever spent was a summer in San Francisco." Locals generally dress as though it were perpetually December, and they can tell you the two most pleasant months of the year are September and October. So you may want to have that sweater or jacket handy if you're walking.

If you're driving you have other things to prepare for, namely San Francisco's traffic idiosyncrasies. In negotiating the city by automobile, keep in mind the red-light-running fools, and expect traffic jams at any hour. On-street parking is virtually nonexistent—at best scarce—and those who overstay their legal welcome are subject to heavy fines and might even be clamped with "the boot," which immobilizes the vehicle. An impounded car is endless trouble to retrieve.

Fortunately there are a number of public parking facilities, one of the handiest offering underground parking at Union Square. In hilly San Francisco, it is illegal to park a car on a grade exceeding 3 percent without setting your parking brake and turning the wheels into the curb. When parking uphill the wheels must be "heeled," with the inside front tire resting securely against the curb. Parking downhill, tires must be "toed"—turned in.

San Francisco has an irrepressible spirit, unshaken and resilient after the terrible earthquake of 1906 and the more recent Loma Prieta quake of 1989, which interrupted that year's World Series. It remains intact and strong, a grand dame waiting at the edge of the continent, where the West comes to an end by the sea.

It's still a sightseer's paradise, where enjoying yourself comes easy. It costs nothing to breathe the fragrance of a vendor's flowers on Union Square; to hike up Telegraph Hill, where houses clutch onto steep hills, then take in the breathtaking view from Coit Tower at the crest; to stroll through Chinatown or Little Italy; or to photograph the busy fleet at Fisherman's Wharf.

In fact, the best way to get the feeling that will ultimately instill the most devotion to San Francisco is to simply walk its streets and back roads.

Flora, Fauna and Climate

LOOK FOR:
- Geology
- Soil
- Climate
- Flora
- Fauna

No matter how impressive those modern-day stone chateaux may be, few Wine Country visitors plan to spend the bulk of their time in tasting rooms and wine caves. Picnicking is just as entrenched here as fine dining, and the bicycle is a common mode of sightseeing. The hiking trails are full of boot prints, the skies are full of hot-air balloons, and the reason is simple: This is, with no room for sensible rebuttal, one of the most beautiful parcels of real estate you will ever see.

From the marshes of San Pablo Bay to the mountains of Mendocino National Forest, and from the roaring Pacific to shimmering Clear Lake, the terrain is rarely less than wondrous. In spring the wildflowers color-code the roadsides. In summer the grapevines practically glow with verdant life. In fall the vineyards are a patchwork of red and orange. And even winter, wet but not harsh, is a misty and mysteriously beautiful time to visit. Following, herein, is a brief and incomplete introduction to the natural world of the Wine Country—the grape outdoors, if you will.

Geology

A hundred million years ago, the Wine Country area was exceptionally poor as a grape-growing region. In fact, all of it was under water. It took a lot of tectonic activity—movement of the massive plates that together form the earth's crust—to swing Napa, Sonoma and environs eastward onto dry land. It was all part of the succession of north-south "island arcs" that violently, if patiently, crashed into the North American continent and sent California on the way to its modern-day topography.

Of course, the movement hasn't exactly come to a standstill. The San Andreas system, a massive network of strike-slip faults that forms the border between the Pacific and North American tectonic plates, runs the length of coastline in Sonoma and Mendocino counties. Several smaller, generally north-south faults lurk beneath the Wine Country, including the Rodgers Creek Fault, which caused some destruction in Santa Rosa with a 1969 quake that measured 5.7 on the Richter scale.

Things could be worse. In fact, they used to be. Much of the current four-county area was the scene of frightful volcanic activity 3 to 4 million years ago. Those eruptions, combined with the unrelenting seismic activity, have given the valleys of California's North Coast ranges a highly complex geologic profile. And this is of more than theoretical interest, for two of the lures that historically have drawn people to the region are direct results of geology.

The most obvious of these is geothermal activity. Sonoma and Napa counties are pierced by fault "pipelines" that send water—heated by magma 8 miles below the earth's surface—percolating upward. In the Calistoga area you can pay to gawk at a burst of hot water (at the Old

Faithful Geyser) or to soak in the stuff (at the many spas). And around one section of the Sonoma-Lake border, geothermal sites are even used to generate electricity. In fact, Pacific Gas & Electric's Unit 13 at The Geysers steam field weighs in as the world's largest geothermal plant.

But the peculiar North Coast geology has spawned a lot more than mud baths. The second regional drawing card with its roots in plate tectonics is the mighty grapevine.

Soil

Soils reflect the rocks they used to be, so it makes sense that an area of convoluted geology will contain many types of soil. And because soil composition greatly affects the chemistry of a growing grape, it follows that precisely where you plant your vines has a lot to do with the quality of your wine.

The soil within a single vineyard can vary substantially. Red soil tends to produce soft wine; light, "fluffy" soils are known for hard, austere wines; and gravelly ground, which has a hard time holding water, tends to result in earthy wines. Moreover, wine made from hillside grapes usually is riskier and more robust than valley wine, because the grapes are smaller and therefore have a higher skin-to-pulp ratio. (The intense flavor is in the skin.) And some of the best vineyard soil in Napa Valley is found on the Oakville and Rutherford "benches"—broad, nutrient-rich alluvial fans that have been washed from the Mayacamas Mountains.

Of course, all of this is gross oversimplification. We provide more information on the whole business of "appellations"—slightly varied microclimates that produce grapes and yield wines with specific, refined characteristics—in our Wineries chapter, but sorting out the details is what separates a successful vintner from the rest of us guzzlers. The point is that, in a manner of speaking, the Merlot you're savoring today has been in the works for about 100 million years.

Climate

Geology also helps determine climate, and, excluding coastal fog and a few 100-degree days in some parts of Wine Country, our weather happens to be blissful. Yes, it varies dramatically throughout the four counties, but certain rules apply.

First, think of the Pacific Ocean as a giant climate-control device, set on MILD. In general, the farther you stray from salt water, the hotter your summers will be and the colder your winters. The temperature variations along the coast are minuscule, and towns such as Guerneville and Napa, just upriver, also are fairly mild. There's only about a 5-degree differential in the usual maximum winter high temperature on the Mendocino Coast (56 degrees) and the average summer high (the low 60s). Though coastal winter nights are cooler, they don't often see temps drop lower than 40. There is morning summer fog, and evening sea breezes.

That is in stark contrast to places such as Ukiah, Calistoga and Middletown, where hilly terrain has formed a barrier to ocean influences. Each of these towns can be uncomfortably still and hot in August. Inland Lake County gets upwards of 100 degrees regularly in summer, and its susceptibility to colder winters will see some days at or below the freezing mark. On the other hand, when it's hot, it qualifies as "dry heat." Californians tend to consider that phrase a meaningless cliche, but long-suffering Midwesterners and Easterners can immediately feel the difference. A 100-degree day is a test no matter how you look at it, but the night air has a chance to cool considerably when humidity is low.

Rainfall, too, varies across the Wine Country. Cobb Mountain, in southwest Lake County, receives about 60 inches of rain a year. The Mendocino Coast gets about 39 inches, St. Helena about 34 and the Clear Lake Basin about 25. Regardless of volume, however, you can expect most of the rain between December and February, with residual storms in March and April. Summer and fall downpours are rare here.

We would be remiss if we failed to mention winter flooding in the Wine Country. Most areas are nothing worse than soggy, but the Russian and Napa rivers have overflowed their banks several times in recent years. The Guerneville area, in particular, seems to be vulnerable to flooding (hundreds were evacuated in January 1997).

In general, spring and autumn are the best months to visit. The weather is mild, and there is added color from wildflowers or turning leaves. And if spring and autumn lasted, say, five months each, you would be able to visit about half the places that are nicest during those times

Our Offensive Feathered Friends

It happens all the time. You'll be lounging on the patio of some hillside B&B, watching the birds describe their lazy circles.

"Hawks," you might say.

But the size, the shadowy hue, and the tilting imperfection in the animal's dihedral glide give it away.

"Actually they're vultures," someone will reply, and it may be disappointment that you feel. Hawks and eagles and falcons are the sort of animal you add to your mental checklist. Turkey vultures? They're wild animals, all right, but they're so…common.

You might see 100 vultures for every hawk in some parts of Wine Country. You almost don't see them at all after a while. They're like telephone lines, visual debris your mind begins to filter out in self-defense.

But it isn't just their ubiquity that makes turkey vultures so decidedly unhip. Using almost any standard of human judgment, these are distasteful creatures. They are homely, from their bald red heads to their scruffy feathers to their gnarled feet. They don't sing sweetly like other birds, nor even screech or whistle. Vultures lack a syrinx, the avian voice box; the only sounds they are capable of making are hisses and raspy grunts. They are prone to biting, often infecting would-be human handlers. They smell bad, we are told. Their breath is atrocious. Their favorite defense mechanism is projectile vomiting.

Even their role in the natural order is detestable. They eat dead things — smashed things, maggoty things, putrid things.

Perhaps it is all this unpleasantness that has discouraged thorough academic study. As professional and amateur ornithologists took to surveying various species, they began with the majestic and the beautiful, the exotic and the melodic. Only recently have they gotten around to the scavengers.

Hence, there is much we don't know about turkey vultures. What we *do* know is fascinating, sometimes perplexing, occasionally disgusting, says Dr. Stephen Laymon, adjunct professor of biology at San Francisco State University. Laymon, who lives in Weldon, California, was patient enough to give *The Insiders' Guide* a quick correspondence course in vultures.

Lesson 1: There is no such thing as a California Turkey Vulture. You often hear the reference, but really what you see as you drive the back roads and front roads of Wine Country is the Western Turkey Vulture (*Cathartes aura teter*), whose vast range stretches from southern British Columbia to Costa Rica. *C.a. teter* is one of three North American subspecies, none of which is even remotely related to "buzzards," the British term for buteos (hawks of the *Buteo* genus), or even to Old World vultures. Though the latter look very much like turkey vultures, it seems to be a case of convergent evolution. Old Worlders are related to hawks, while New Worlders reside in the stork family.

Turkey vultures, unlike most birds, have a keen sense of smell. They live 20 to 30 years. An adult has a wingspan of 6 feet, though an ancestor dredged out of La Brea Tar Pit in Southern California had a 12-foot reach. They average about 3.3 pounds. That doesn't seem like much, but a recent U.S. Air Force paper labeled turkey vultures a serious threat to safety. The space shuttle rarely lands at Kennedy Space Center in Florida, in fact, because the risk of colliding with one of the critters is so high. "Turkey vultures cause more damage to military aircraft — we're talking millions of dollars — than all other species of birds put together," Laymon says.

A lot of things about old *C.a. teter* might surprise you. Contrary to popular belief, vultures do not survive on road kill alone. They have been known to attack young and helpless, though otherwise healthy animals. And a recent analysis of almost 400 pellets collected in the Castro Valley and Livermore areas just east of the Bay Area (positions undoubtedly are available if such work appeals to you) revealed that plant matter, mostly grass and leaves, made up about a quarter of the total dried weight. (Other yummy food items included shrew, mole, squirrel, gopher, mouse, rat, rabbit, bird, reptile, insect, muskrat, opossum, raccoon, skunk, badger, coyote, deer, cow, sheep and, yes, little Ranger and Snowball.)

Photo: Dan Sullivan

Turkey Vulture

Did you know turkey vultures migrate? They do, in vast numbers and over tremendous distances. The annual autumn count in Kernville, California, which happens to be directly under the flight path, turned up 27,000 birds last year. A vulture can literally stay aloft all day, riding the thermals much like a glider plane. (Flapping only consumes energy, though the birds are able to do this, too.) Even after unpacking their bags they are apt to travel at least 50 miles, and possibly more than 100 miles, from the roosts they make in cliff hollows, logs or rock piles.

Or bathrooms. Not long ago, a woman in Pennsylvania returned from a three-day trip to find that a turkey vulture had settled in her loo. When a friend entered the bathroom to set down food and water and open the window wider, the bird deliberately turned to face the opposite direction. A newsletter distributed by the Turkey Vulture Society (yes, there is such a thing) characterized the response as, "If I can't see you, then you can't see me."

It's a contract most humans are perfectly happy to honor.

of year. Summer temperatures in Sonoma County usually edge into the mid-80s, but the nights are still comfortable (chilly even), with the mercury falling into the 50s.

Flora

A flora list from the Covelo Ranger District in Mendocino National Forest alone refers to 18 different coniferous trees, 13 varieties of oak, six types of willow and six species of manzanita. So we won't try to construct any sort of comprehensive list here—it would be voluminous. We can, however, state a few generalities.

The valley floors of the Wine Country were covered by native bunch grasses before the arrival of European settlers, but they proved to be especially sensitive to trampling by livestock. Spanish explorers (see our History chapter), who carried feed grain for their horses and mules, were among the first Europeans to introduce "exotic" grasses: ryegrass, bromes, foxtail, wild oats and the like.

The rolling hills of Napa and Sonoma counties are dominated by two types of ecosystem: oak woodland and chaparral. It's impossible to drive along U.S. Highway 101 or Calif. Highway

Photo: Tina Luster-Hoban

Bodega Bay, made famous by Alfred Hitchcock's The Birds, *continues to attract the feathered creatures.*

29 without noticing the stolid oak trees, but the collection includes many varieties. Coast live oaks are perhaps the most impressive, with a single tree able to spread its branches up to 130 feet. These trees prefer moist locations, such as creek bottoms and north slopes. Canyon live oaks, with their exceptionally hard wood, thrive on steep hillsides. Blue oaks like hot, dry slopes, and California black oaks pop up on mesas with deep soil and gentle slopes.

Chaparral, made up of shrubs such as manzanita, ceanothus and toyon, is more closely associated with the hills of Southern California, but it is prevalent here too. It is an inhospitable environment for humans: It's made to burn—many of its plant species have highly flammable oils in their bark—and the underbrush can be thorny and impenetrable.

While most of the grapes are grown at lower elevation, the Wine Country counties include a lot of mountainous, forested topography. That's especially true in the upper half of Lake County and the northeast corner of Mendocino County, which form part of Mendocino National Forest.

The standout citizen of the damp, misty Coast Range forests is the coast redwood, the tallest tree in the world. The biggest of all are found in Humboldt County (see "The Big Trees" section of our Daytrippin' chapter), including the 368-foot champion, but Mendocino and Sonoma also have several preserves devoted to redwoods (see our Parks and Recreation chapter). You might also stumble on a redwood in steep, darker canyons along Wine Country streams. Other dominant trees include the ponderosa pine, with its arrow-straight trunk; the Pacific madrone, whose gnarled trunk will creep 50 feet horizontally to find sunlight; and the Douglas fir, the Western Hemisphere's premier lumber tree.

No matter which Wine Country microclimate you're in, you are likely to see wildflowers if your timing is sound. Somewhere between February and June, depending on elevation and intensity of sunlight, literally hundreds of shrubs and herbs burst into bloom. The most eye-catching include the California poppy—the bright orange state flower that pops up

INSIDERS' TIP

The first fall rain usually entices a wide range of edible mushrooms in the coastal areas of Sonoma and Mendocino counties, including porcinis, chanterelles and oysters. But do not, under any circumstances, attempt to gather the little butter-sponges if you are inexperienced in the field. Risk of fatality is high. (Sam Sebastiani Jr., member of the famed wine family, died after eating poisonous mushrooms in January 1997.)

FLORA, FAUNA, AND CLIMATE

just about anywhere—and mustard, which lays a breathtaking yellow carpet in the vineyards (and inspires all sorts of reverent celebrations—see our Festivals and Events chapter) upon the year's first solid week of sunshine. Other native wildflowers to look for include orchids, irises, monkey flowers, Indian paintbrushes, golden bushes, wild roses, lupines, violets, shooting stars, fiddlenecks, lilies, wild onions and buttercups.

Fauna

It isn't exactly a jungle out here, but keen observers will spy a wide range of furry, feathered or fishy creatures in the Wine Country.

Drive the scenic routes at dusk in summer and fall, and you are likely to see the omnipresent black-tailed deer nibbling scrub oak or buckbrush in the meadows. You are even more likely to see skunks, raccoons and opossums, though it might be in the form of roadkill. They are among the most common of the region's mammals, especially in semi-developed areas. The more mountainous areas are home to all sorts of animals, including black bears, mountain lions and bobcats, coyotes, bats, diminutive gray foxes, porcupines, badgers, feral pigs, and even the occasional ring-tailed cat or tule elk. Many of them are nocturnal and all are elusive, but they are out there, trying to stay downwind of the humans.

The rugged coastal areas have their own communities: seals and sea lions on the rocks; river otters in the estuaries; and gray whales offshore, migrating southward from the Bering Sea to Baja California between December and April. River otters are found in much of the Wine Country's freshwater. The reptile and amphibian crowd includes alligator lizards, pond turtles, king snakes, rubber boas, skinks and the ones you need to watch out for—western rattlesnakes.

The local waterways are dominated by anadromous fish—that is, by species that travel from the sea to spawn in fresh water—primarily in the Napa, Eel and Russian rivers. The three big fish in the Wine Country (as in most of northern California) are Chinook salmon, coho salmon and steelhead, which are basically rainbow trout that have learned to migrate. Most of the good lake fishing is for bass (smallmouth and largemouth) and catfish, though none of them are native sons. (See more on fishing in our On The Water chapter.)

Audubon Society chapters are active throughout the four-county region, and they have plenty to catalogue. There are swallows and swifts, American robins and northern mocking-birds, woodpeckers and warblers, finches and flycatchers. There are at least six species of hawk and seven species of owl—including the northern spotted, that rather harmless old-growth percher despised by a generation of loggers.

Golden eagles (the nation's largest raptor, with a wingspan of up to 7 feet), ospreys, kestrels and peregrine falcons ride the thermals along high bluffs and cliff faces. Peregrines, with a maximum flight speed of up to 275 mph, have been known to overtake small airplanes. Herons and egrets poke about in swampy spots, such as the Napa-Sonoma Marshes Wildlife Area, south of those two towns, and we've got a varied collection of ducks and geese. And if jet lag and ambitious winetasting have you feeling dehydrated and fatigued, don't fret too much about those California turkey vultures circling overhead. It's nothing personal—the hefty, red-faced scavengers are quite populous in the Wine Country (see Close-up).

Hotels and Motels

LOOK FOR:
- Napa County
- Sonoma County
- Mendocino County
- Lake County
- Vacation Rentals

Price Code

The schedule of dollar-sign symbols shown below indicates the approximate price range for a one-night, weekend, double-occupancy stay, not including tax, gratuities or other add-on amenities such as room service or premium movie channels.

$	$70 or less
$$	$71 to $110
$$$	$111 to $150
$$$$	$151 to $200
$$$$$	$201 and more

Those of us who live in Wine Country are continually amazed at the beauty of this place. There is a sense of strength in the surrounding mountains…the countryside is combed in vineyards.

We realize full well we are not metropolitan. Cosmopolitan, yes. Metropolitan, no. The largest city in all four counties, Santa Rosa, has a modest population of about 123,000.

Our hotels reflect this dichotomy. Business people who come for conferences and meetings find themselves bedded down not in structures of glass and steel but in low-lying resort hotels with golf, tennis, swimming, horseback riding and winery tours serving as relaxing options at day's end. Facilities may be ultramodern and services may match any big-city hotel, but the nation's business travelers share these accommodations with plain old tourists from across America and a few foreign countries.

Other hotels in smaller towns are built to appeal to the thousands of visitors who swarm to vine land in summer and on weekends to bask in the rural atmosphere and savor the hospitality of the wineries.

Such hotels are often tucked right in the midst of vineyards. Some have a small-town, homey aura; others are posh and extravagant—and expensive.

In this atmosphere of country living, bed and breakfast inns flourish. Most developed out of love for a handsome historic home that was crying out for restoration. Others began there, then continued expanding into extensive hostelries with luxuries befitting the finest hotels.

So, contemplating this mixture of rural life and cosmopolitan airs, how do we define a hotel or motel? When is a hotel a resort? What's a country inn? How big can a bed and breakfast be before it becomes a hostelry?

For this chapter we have decided, in our limited wisdom, to define hotels and motels as structures that were built for the express purpose of providing lodging. For our purposes, bed and breakfast inns should make you feel as though you are sleeping over at someone's house. They are places with few guest rooms, places that may have started out as someone's residence. Everything else, especially anything with a staff and a dining room, is rated as a hotel or motel.

Unless we state otherwise, assume that hotels and motels take major credit cards (check when you call to see if your plastic of choice is included) and that pets are not welcome. Although California smoking laws are extremely stringent, all hotels listed do provide rooms for their guests who smoke. Expect that all entries will have color TV.

Hotels and motels are listed using the geographical sequence explained in our How to Use This Book chapter. We start with the Napa County accommodations, followed by those in Sonoma, Mendocino and Lake counties. Afterwards we give agencies specializing in vacation rentals.

Napa County

Embassy Suites Napa Valley
$$$$$ • 1075 California Blvd., Napa
• (707) 253-9540, (800) 433-4600

In a valley where "business" usually takes the form of buying wine by the bottle and drinking it for lunch, this is as close as it comes to a high-end business traveler's hotel. A group of three-story, canary-and-burgundy buildings, the Embassy Suites offers a nice combination of corporate know-how and Wine Country charm. There are indoor and outdoor pools, wet and dry saunas, swans in the koi pond and a soaring lobby with terra cotta tiles and parlor chairs. Every guest unit is a two-room suite with extra pullout sofa, wet bar and microwave. The tariff includes a full, cooked-to-order breakfast and an afternoon Manager's Reception with complimentary drinks. And if you really are here on business, Embassy Suites boasts eight meeting rooms (arranged around the Fountain Court), full conference facilities and two-line phones with modem access in each room.

Napa Valley Marriott
$$$$ • 3425 Solano Ave., Napa
• (707) 253-7433, (800) 228-9290

If you have come to rely on the Marriott chain for its dependable accommodations, you are not without recourse in Napa Valley. The 191-room hotel (including four suites) is just off Calif. Highway 29, north of the Trancas Street/Redwood Road exit. Each room has individual climate control, in-room pay movies, iron and ironing board, a work desk and voice mail. The Harvest Cafe, specializing in steaks and California vegetables, serves breakfast and dinner; Character's Sports Bar & Grill serves lunch and dinner. For $10 extra, you can get breakfast along with your room. The Marriott also has a heated outdoor pool and Jacuzzi, lighted tennis courts and a fitness center. And one entire level of the hotel gets down to business, with 8,500 square feet of flexible meeting space that can handle groups of 15 to 500.

Wine Valley Lodge
$$$$ • 200 S. Coombs St., Napa
• (707) 224-7911, (800) 696-7911

South of downtown Napa, close to Calif. Highway 121, the Mission-style Lodge has 53 guest rooms. There is a heated pool in the motor court, and you get complimentary continental breakfast on summer weekends. Ask about the Elvis Presley and Marilyn Monroe suites, which are not haunted by self-destructive stars but do sleep four and six people, respectively.

Best Western Inn at the Vines
$$$ • 100 Soscol Ave., Napa
• (707) 257-1930

Best Western offers few surprises, which is probably why it's one of America's most popular chains. The Napa version has 68 rooms, including eight suites. Two of the suites are loft-style, with a bed upstairs and living room below; others are one-level units with sitting rooms. All rooms have cable TV and refrigerators. There is a heated pool and spa, a meeting room for up to 50 people and a 24-hour Denny's restaurant on the property.

Napa Country Inn
$ • 314 Soscol Ave., Napa
• (707) 226-1878

There is nothing fancy about this motel, but it is clean and well-maintained. The 29 rooms all have air conditioning, phones and cable TV. The inn is across the street from a shopping plaza.

Napa Valley Travelodge
$$$ • 853 Coombs St., Napa
• (707) 226-1871

If location is everything, the Travelodge has it all. The downtown Napa locale puts you two blocks from Riverwalk, four blocks from the Wine Train depot (see our Attractions chapter) and a few steps away from shops and cafes. The 40-room motel has a heated pool. Each unit comes with a two-line phone with a fax port, individual air conditioning and a big-screen TV with VCR. Movie rentals are available through the motel.

Chardonnay Lodge
$ • 2640 Jefferson St., Napa
• (707) 224-0789

The lodge offers convenient Napa centrality and beds of various proportions. The 20 rooms are air-conditioned, and they have phones and cable TV.

The Chateau
$$$ • 4195 Solano Ave., Napa
• (707) 253-9300

Somewhere between a budget motel and a major corporate hotel, The Chateau offers comfort and reliability, if not luxury. The 115 rooms are sizable, and each has a separate vanity dressing area and individual climate control. The two-story motel has six spacious suites too, with wet bars and fold-out couches. Also on the grounds are two conference centers that hold 75 and 25 people, respectively, and a swimming pool and spa. Kids 12 and younger stay free in the same room as their guardians. The Wine Country Bistro is just across the parking lot, and guests of the motel get $3 bistro coupons each day of their stay.

The John Muir Inn
$$$ • 1998 Trower Ave., Napa
• (707) 257-7220, (800) 522-8999

Somehow we can't imagine John Muir, the naturalist who wandered through the Sierra Nevada Mountains stocked with nothing more than a pocket full of biscuits, staying here at the intersection of Trower Avenue and Calif. 29. But, hey, the inn that bears his name is very environmentally conscious. Anyway, Muir might have gone for the cable TV with Showtime. The hotel is a solid mid-priced choice with a courtyard swimming pool and whirlpool spa, a 36-person conference room, a 24-hour front desk and free continental breakfast. About one-quarter of the 60 rooms have kitchenettes, and some have wet bars or private spas. Children 14 and younger stay free. There is no restaurant at the inn, but Marie Callendar's is within shouting distance.

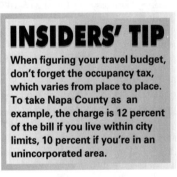

INSIDERS' TIP

When figuring your travel budget, don't forget the occupancy tax, which varies from place to place. To take Napa County as an example, the charge is 12 percent of the bill if you live within city limits, 10 percent if you're in an unincorporated area.

Yountville Inn
$$$$$ • 6462 Washington St., Yountville
• (707) 944-5600, (800) 972-2293

One of the mid-valley's newest options is Yountville Inn, nestled against Hopper Creek. The rambling hotel has seven buildings and 51 bright and spacious rooms. Each unit boasts a fieldstone fireplace, French doors leading to a patio, a wood-beamed ceiling and a refrigerator. All guests receive free continental breakfast. The inn also has a heated pool and spa, and is right next door to the new Yountville Golf Course. Should you be mixing business with pleasure, the elegantly comfortable Club Room facilitates groups of up to 60 people.

Napa Valley Railway Inn
$$$ • 6503 Washington St., Yountville
• (707) 944-2000

If the kids have earned suffrage, you'll probably be staying here, just south of Vintage 1870. The rooms are restored cabooses and boxcars, nine in all, sitting on original track from the defunct Napa Valley Railroad. Being train cars, the living space tends to be l-o-n-g and narrow, perhaps 8-by-40 feet. Each room has a queen bed, air conditioning and a private, tiled bathroom. The cars are arranged along two sides of a wooden platform, adding to the whole locomotive picture. And if you have a phobia of rectangular spaces, you can stay in the square Station House Room.

Vintage Inn
$$$$$ • 6541 Washington St., Yountville
• (707) 944-1112, (800) 351-1133 in Calif.,
(800) 351-1133 elsewhere

This elegant, country-style inn is spread out on a large, landscaped lot. It has 80 units—basic rooms, mini-suites and villas—divided between the outer court and the more protected inner court. Most have patios or balconies. All of them have fireplaces and come with a complimentary continental breakfast buffet, including California champagne. Vintage Inn offers room service, a 60-foot lap pool and hot tub, tennis courts, bike rentals in the summer and a private limousine service. About 15 percent of the rooms are smoker-friendly, and you can even bring your dog if you don't mind plunking down the $25 cleaning fee. The inn also has executive conference facilities that can handle 20 to 200 people.

Napa Valley Lodge
$$$$$ • 2230 Madison St., Yountville
• (707) 944-2468, (800) 368-2468

If you've ever stayed at one of Woodside Hotels' Northern California establishments, you'll be keen to reserve a spot at this 55-room, hacienda-style hotel at the north end of Yountville. Woodside is known for its gracious service and amenities, and Napa Valley Lodge is right in step—from the 400-book lending library and hearth in the lobby to the free champagne buffet breakfast to the Spanish-tile double vanities, duvet bed coverings and reproduced vintage tapestries in the rooms. About three-fourths of the units have fireplaces, and all feature a balcony or terrace with views to vineyard or pool and gardens.

Besides the pool, the hotel has a spa, a redwood sauna and a small exercise room, and if they get your blood pumping, you can head to Chardonnay Golf Club (see our Parks and Recreation chapter), where guests receive a weekday discount on greens fees. Napa Valley Lodge does brisk corporate business—not surprising when you note the hotel's two warm, well-appointed conference rooms.

Rancho Caymus
$$$$$ • 1140 Rutherford Cross Rd., Rutherford • (707) 963-1777, (800) 845-1777

If Father Junipero Serra had built a really fancy mission to impress the folks back home in Spain, it might have looked like this. Rancho Caymus, a couple of blocks east of Calif. 29 on Rutherford Cross Road (a.k.a. Calif. 128), carries off the hacienda motif flawlessly, from the adobe-looking stucco to the tile roof. The rough-hewn white oak and pine beams are salvaged from an 80-year-old barn in Ohio; the parota wood chairs, tables and dressers are from Guadalajara; and the wool rugs and wall hangings are made by indigenous Ecuadorians. A central, tiled courtyard brims with flowers and small trees.

Most of the 26 units have fireplaces and a split-level layout. Five of them have kitchenettes, and about 65 percent are smoking rooms. Continental breakfast is included, and the site now includes fine dining at chef Ken Frank's La Toque restaurant.

El Bonita Motel
$$$$ • 195 Main St., St. Helena • (707) 963-3216, (800) 541-3284

All right, you grammarians de español, forget the article-noun gender disagreement. El Bonita gets most everything else right. The old neon sign and poolside layout point to the motel's roots as a classic 1950s roadside motor hotel, but there have been upgrades galore since then. The 42 rooms are nicely furnished and painted in subdued gray-green tones. About two-thirds have microwaves and refrigerators. Some allow pets. There is a fireplace in the recently remodeled lobby, and each guest receives continental breakfast. Flowers and fountains proliferate in the lawn areas, while the pool is complemented by a sauna and a Jacuzzi.

Harvest Inn
$$$$$ • 1 Main St., St. Helena • (707) 963-WINE, (800) 950-8466

The Inn's reception building, the Harvest Centre, is built to evoke the English countryside, with its corkscrewed brick chimneys and oak-paneled great room. But "rustic" this place isn't. It is a sprawling, manicured complex that specializes in (but isn't limited to) corporate functions, with conference facilities accommodating as many as 60 captains of industry. On-site catering is available through Pinot Blanc (see our Restaurants chapter). Set between Sutter Home Winery and Sulphur Springs Avenue on the southern fringe of St. Helena, and bordering a 14-acre vineyard, Harvest Inn has 54 rooms. Most of them have king beds, brick fireplaces, wet bars and dressing vanities, and some have patio balconies. There are two heated pools and Whirlpool spas on the grounds, and all guests are served continental breakfast. Most units allow smokers, and some (the ones with hardwood floors) take pets. The rates are too wide-ranging to properly classify—they go from $149 for a small room in winter to $649 for an "imperial suite" on a high-season weekend. Most run just more than $200.

The Wine Country Inn
$$$$ • 1152 Lodi Ln., St. Helena • (707) 963-7077

This hard-to-categorize accommodation does a good job of blending the comforts of a bed and breakfast with the convenience of a small hotel. The Wine Country Inn offers a full buffet breakfast, afternoon appetizers and winetasting, distinctive rooms filled with hand-picked antiques, a large pool and Jacuzzi, a well-trained staff and easy parking. No matter how the inn is defined, Lodi Lane, about 2 miles north of St. Helena, is hard to beat for serenity. Immediately to the east is a working vineyard; almost all of the 24 rooms have private patios or balconies that practically sit on the trellises. Most units have fireplaces, and some even have private hot tubs. The Wine Country Inn is still a family operation, founded by Ned Smith in 1975. Son Jim Smith runs the place now. Ned's widow, Marge, did most of the quilt work, and his daughter, Kate, did much of the decorative painting. The hotel, popular with honeymooners, caters to adults rather than to families with children.

The Inn at Southbridge
$$$$$ • 1020 Main St., St. Helena • (707) 967-9400, (800) 520-6800

This upscale St. Helena hotel, which opened in November 1995, looks something like a winery with its earth tones and creeping vines. The resemblance is no coincidence, as archi-

This charming painting by Barbara Beavers portrays the Spanish hacienda-style architecture of Rancho Caymus.

tect William Turnbull Jr. is known for his winery design. The Inn at Southbridge has 21 ample rooms (only two smoking units), each with a vaulted ceiling, fireplace, sisal-style carpets and down comforter. French doors open onto a private balcony overlooking the courtyard. The rooms are set up for corporate clients, each having dual phone lines and a fax/modem port. The inn has a lap pool and a full-service health club with steam, weights and stationary bikes. Guests also enjoy (paid) access to Meadowood resort's recreational facilities—the establishments are co-owned (see our Spas and Resorts chapter for more on Meadowood). The restaurant Tomatina shares space with The Inn at Southbridge (they'll provide room service), and Merryvale Winery is just across the parking lot (see our Wineries chapter).

Hotel St. Helena
$$$$ • 1309 Main St., St. Helena
• (707) 963-4388

This restored hotel in the heart of downtown is quintessential St. Helena: immaculate, charming and not cheap. It was an upscale hotel when it was built back in 1881, but soon deteriorated into a second-floor flophouse over the local Montgomery Ward. Now it has recaptured and redefined its glory. At ground level

are shops and a flowery arcade, plus a wine and coffee bar in the lobby. Upstairs are 18 antique-filled rooms painted in combinations of subdued tones: burgundy, mauve, chocolate, dark tan and pale gold. Four of the rooms share two baths; the rest have private bathrooms, some with old clawfoot tubs. There is a sitting room at the top of the stairs and a TV-equipped solarium overlooking the arcade. A large continental breakfast is included in the price. Occupancy is restricted to two guests unless you rent the spacious Lillie Langtry Suite for $325 per night. In some rooms a temporary bed for a third person can be added for $20.

Calistoga Inn
$ • 1250 Lincoln Ave., Calistoga
• (707) 942-4101

For a no-frills (OK, maybe a couple of frills), ambiance-thick stay in Calistoga, try the Inn, an old Western-style hotel that dates back to 1882. The 18 second-floor rooms, connected by a creaking wood-floored hallway, sit over a restaurant and microbrewery/bar (see our Restaurants and Nightlife chapters). Each room has a sink and a queen or king bed, but there are central, shared bathrooms and showers and no in-room TVs. At $55 (midweek) and $70 (weekends), including continental breakfast, these are the cheapest tourist digs in town. What's more, the Inn never has more than a one-night minimum stay, a rarity in these parts.

Mount View Hotel
$$$$ • 1457 Lincoln Ave., Calistoga
• (707) 942-6877

This is the closest Calistoga comes to the Ritz-Carlton. The Mission Revival building was constructed in 1919 and served the area for years as the European Hotel, haunt of literary bigwigs and first ladies. (It is said that Mrs. Herbert Hoover planted the roses in the garden.) An elegant lobby takes you to either the hotel, Mount View Spa or Catahoula Restaurant; all three are run separately and catalogued separately in this book. Mount View Hotel has 32 rooms, suites and cottages, the latter being detached units (with private Jacuzzis) out by the pool. The other rooms are on the second floor, and some have antique furnishings. Continental breakfast is delivered to your room. The wide range of tariffs runs from $130 to $230, so inquire about specifics.

Hotel D'Amici
$$$$ • 1436 Lincoln Ave., Calistoga
• (707) 942-1007

If Calistoga had luxury apartment suites, they'd look something like this. Hotel D'Amici is downtown, perched on the second floor of a 1936 building once known as Green Hotel. (The "secret door" is just to the right of the restaurant entrance.) The hotel has four spacious, well-appointed rooms, two of which share a balcony over Lincoln Avenue, making them coveted spaces during the Fourth of July and its Silverado Parade (see our Festivals and Annual Events chapter). All have private baths and kitchenettes. For now, children are welcome, but you might call ahead to make sure. The owners are the Pestonis, who run Rutherford Grove winery. You pick up your keys there (1673 Calif. Hwy. 29 in Rutherford) and get a complimentary winetasting. You also get a bottle of Rutherford Grove Chardonnay in your fridge at the D'Amici.

Comfort Inn
$$$ • 1865 Lincoln Ave., Calistoga
• (707) 942-9400, (800) 228-5150

Only in Calistoga would the Comfort Inn have a mineral water swimming pool and whirlpool tub. It also has a sauna and steam room. Each of the 55 rooms (including a two-room suite) features HBO and individual temperature control; most are in the functional style

Comfort Inn is known for. Continental breakfast is included in the price.

Stevenson Manor Inn
$$$$ • 1830 Lincoln Ave., Calistoga
• (707) 942-1112

This motel is affiliated with Best Western. Stevenson Manor has a pool, a sauna and a gazebo-sheltered central courtyard. The 34 rooms are done in subdued shades of green and burgundy. Four of them have private whirlpool baths, and seven are warmed by fireplaces; all of them are equipped with refrigerators and coffee makers. Guests of the inn receive a 10 percent discount at the nearby Calistoga Village Inn & Spa (see our Spas and Resorts chapter).

Triple-S-Ranch
$ • 4600 Mountain Home Ranch Rd., Calistoga • (707) 942-6730

The ranch's proprietors say no one is lukewarm about their stay here. Ranch life is the thing for you, or it ain't. The Schellenger family bought the property in 1958, turned the 1920s-era barn into a restaurant, added four cabins to the two that already existed for farm workers and *voila*: a rustic retreat was born. The one-room cabins have private bathrooms but little else (no phones or TVs), and breakfast is not included. All sleep from one to six people, with the price climbing in increments of $6 to $8. It's a quiet, pine-speckled spot off Petrified Forest Road, about a five-minute drive from Calistoga. Children and pets are welcome, and you can smoke in your room if you promise not to burn down the cabin. Hiking, horseshoes and bocce ball are other options. The Triple-S is closed from January 1 through March 31. (See our Restaurants chapter for information about the on-site steak house.)

Mountain Home Ranch
$$ • 3400 Mountain Home Ranch Rd., Calistoga • (707) 942-6616

Down the road from the Triple-S-Ranch are accommodations unlike any you're likely to find in the Wine Country. You want seclusion? Mountain Home is about 2½ miles out of town, then another 2 miles off Petrified Forest Road in a setting that is more campground than estate. Opened for "boarders" in 1915, it's a third-generation tourist bed-down that boasts third-generation clientele. The ranch is set on 260 acres of mixed oak and pine forest. There are miles of hiking trails, two swimming pools, a natural sulphur spring, a tennis court, a fishing lake and rows of picnic tables set under a grapevine arbor. The grounds are strewn with old wooden wagons and Adirondack chairs. Mountain Home has three types of rooms: seven rustic cabins with toilets but no hot water, seven private-bath hotel rooms in the rambling farmhouse and eight prim cabanas with kitchens. Complimentary breakfast is served in a spacious dining room. Pets are allowed in the cabins.

Sonoma County

Southern Sonoma

El Dorado Hotel
$$$$ • 405 First St. W., Sonoma
• (707) 996-3030

On the northwest corner of Sonoma Plaza, the El Dorado has had a checkered history as a government office, college, winery and hotel. Salvador Vallejo built the adobe between 1836 and 1846; subsequently, it was occupied by Bear Flag Party members (see our History chapter) as well as Gen. John C. Fremont during the opening days of the Mexican War. Today its 26 rooms have an Old World aura of casual elegance. It's definitely the right choice for those who really want to revel in the plaza's historical ambiance. Some rooms face the plaza with balconies that give a view of the city below. Other rooms face onto a garden courtyard and overlook flowers and trees. Continental breakfast is included in the room rate.

El Pueblo Inn
$$ • 896 W. Napa St., Sonoma
• (707) 996-3651

Built of adobe brick, it is the classic L-shaped motel of the 1950s. El Pueblo has been in the same family since it was built in 1959 and is now run by the original owners' daughters. With a large, heated swimming pool, a new spa and a grassy, shaded garden area around the 38-room complex, it is an excellent location for either families or singles. Cribs are available, and there's a coffee maker in each room, plus cocoa for the kids.

Sonoma Hotel
$$$$ • 110 W. Spain St., Sonoma
• (707) 996-2996

Situated on the northwest corner of Sonoma Plaza, this fine old hotel was originally a town hall built in the 1880s. Rooms are furnished with antique furniture and one, the Vallejo

Room, has a bedroom suite of carved rosewood once owned by Gen. Mariano Vallejo's family (see our History chapter). All rooms are furnished in keeping with the 19th century, and all have been given names to match their decor—Bear Flag room, Yerba Buena, Italian Suite. In one of the rooms, author/poet/actress Maya Angelou holed up to write her third novel. All 16 rooms have private baths and air conditioning. Breakfast of fresh pastries, coffee and juices is served in a quaint foyer that retains the original fireplace and stained glass windows.

Best Western Sonoma Valley Inn
$$$$$ • 550 Second St. W., Sonoma
• (707) 938-9200, (800) 334-5784

This hotel is of recent origin (built in 1987), but it has been designed in California mission-style architecture to match the ambiance of the town's early Mexican heritage. One of its great assets is its location: It's only two blocks from the city's plaza (see our Shopping chapter), yet away from city hubbub with rooms that face onto an inner courtyard. You park your car outside your room, motel-style, yet your view is of the swimming pool, spa, gazebo and fountain. Most rooms have patios or decks for outdoor privacy. The spacious rooms feature either a fireplace or a Jacuzzi bath. Open the refrigerator in your room, and you'll find a complimentary bottle of wine. Coffee and biscotti are served in the afternoon. Children 12 and younger can stay in the room with the grown-ups without charge. A laundry room is available. A continental breakfast is delivered to your room.

Best Western Petaluma Inn
$$ • 200 S. McDowell Blvd., Petaluma
• (707) 763-0994

Plopped in the midst of Victorian homes, beautiful parks and grand old buildings from Gold Rush days, the Petaluma Inn's 75 rooms are convenient to downtown. In keeping with the style of its Victorian neighbors, the lobby and rooms are decorated with lush fabrics, artwork and vases of silk flowers. A large swimming pool is appealing for summer days.

Quality Inn
$$ • 5100 Montero Way, Petaluma
• (707) 664-1155

Built in 1985, the hotel comprises seven clustered Cape Cod-style buildings nestled amid landscaped grounds and redwood arbors planted with grapes. Its 111 rooms include 36 with in-room spas and four two-room suites

Stunning architecture characterizes the Fountaingrove Inn in Santa Rosa.

with private spas. The outdoor pool is surrounded by a large sundeck with a sauna adjacent. Its location near Adobe Creek Golf Club and its Robert Trent Jones-designed track makes it appealing to golfers (see the Golf section of our Parks and Recreation chapter), and shoppers will be glad to know it's the closest inn to Petaluma Village Factory Outlet Mall (see our Shopping chapter). A full continental breakfast is served. Special offers include a three-day Wine & Woods package; call for details.

Doubletree Hotel
$$ • 1 Doubletree Dr., Rohnert Park • (707) 584-5466

Set on attractively landscaped grounds between two golf courses, the hotel's tiled roofs and arched windows evoke Sonoma County's Spanish heritage. For business travelers, the hotel offers every convenience and amenity necessary for successful meetings and full conferences, including 11,000 square feet of conference space. But those on business will also find, as do great numbers of tourists, that it's a very enjoyable resort, with 245 luxurious guest rooms and suites, a restaurant, a pool and Jacuzzi and live entertainment. At the adjacent Sonoma County Wine and Visitors Center, there's ample opportunity to sample the best of Sonoma County's wines and learn about a part of California that is like no other.

Flamingo Resort Hotel & Fitness Center
$$$ • 2777 Fourth St., Santa Rosa • (707) 545-8530

Lush landscaping makes this resort hotel very appealing, both as a vacation spot and as a business center offering conference facilities for 600 people. For both the harried executive and the tourist, there's plenty of physical activity available, including a heated Olympic-size pool, Jacuzzi, tennis courts, a lighted jogging path, basketball and volleyball courts and table tennis. Also available for a modest fee is the Montecito Heights Health & Racquet Club. The Flamingo's golf package makes good use of the nearby Fountaingrove course, as well as other top Wine Country tracks.

The 170 rooms are luxuriously appointed with top-of-the-line furniture that comple-

ments the carpeting and draperies. Tables and chairs are provided for guests who choose to "dine in" in a different way. Some rooms also have copy machines and refrigerators.

Fountaingrove Inn
$$$$ • 101 Fountaingrove Pkwy., Santa Rosa • (707) 578-6101

The architecture of this inn is stunning. Redwood and stone buildings sweep low across historic Fountaingrove Ranch, the estate of famed Japanese wine baron Kanaye Nagasawa, affording an unobstructed view of the landmark Round Barn, which sits atop a small hill. The lobby, too, is far from ordinary, dominated by a large redwood sculpture of the legendary horse, Equus. Utmost restraint and understated elegance mark the inn's 125 rooms, which are almost Oriental in their simplicity. All rooms have separate dressing alcoves, double closets and work spaces with modern dataports for traveling executives. The inn's pool, waterfall and spa offer a breathtaking view of the landscape and historic Round Barn. Guests gather in the restaurant each morning for a generous buffet breakfast. The inn's restaurant, not surprisingly called Equus, carries out the theme, with the legendary horse etched in glass and redwood carvings (see our Restaurants chapter).

Sonoma County Hilton
$$$$ • 3555 Round Barn Blvd., Santa Rosa • (707) 523-7555

Just off U.S. Highway 101 north of downtown Santa Rosa on 13 acres of Fountaingrove Ranch, this hotel has let stand the historic landmark known as the Round Barn to mark its entrance. This chalet-style hotel has 246 rooms and suites and boasts many amenities including a state-of-the-art in-room phone system, business center, the award-winning Harvest Grill restaurant serving fresh Sonoma cuisine, an outdoor patio with a panoramic view of the Santa Rosa valley, a Junior Olympic-size swimming pool and an on-site workout facility.

Best Western Garden Inn
$$ • 1500 Santa Rosa Ave., Santa Rosa • (707) 546-4031, (800) 929-2771

It's a Best Western—a name you've learned to

> **INSIDERS' TIP**
>
> Need help locating accommodations? Call Napa Valley Reservations Unlimited at (800) 251-NAPA or, within the area, at (707) 252-1985 or (707) 944-0709. They will assist you in selecting a hotel, motel, bed and breakfast inn, resort or condo, and they won't charge you a cent.

count on—and it's also very attractive in a garden setting, shaded by trees. With its mountain views, the place has the feel of country living, but it is still close to Santa Rosa business, shopping and museums. The 78 rooms are spacious, with typical Best Western decor, and you can enjoy breakfast from 6:30 to 11 AM in a cheerful cafe overlooking the garden. A meeting room seats 10 to 12. At the end of the workday or a round of shopping, you can drop into one of the inn's two unheated swimming pools.

Vintners Inn
$$$ • 4350 Barnes Rd., Santa Rosa
• (707) 575-7350

Your first vision at Vintners Inn may make you feel as if you've dropped in on a French village. A group of three red-roofed buildings is arranged around a plaza and fountain, surrounded by 45 acres of vineyards. It's a European-style hotel with an Old World atmosphere—from its French country decor to the arched windows and wrought-iron railings. Many of the oversized rooms in this Provence-inspired inn have fireplaces, exposed-beam ceilings and pine furniture, some of which dates back to the turn of the century. Ground- floor rooms have patios; second-floor suites have balconies with vineyard or courtyard views. On the premises is John Ash & Company, a nationally acclaimed restaurant serving some of the best cuisine in Sonoma County. Its wine list won the Sonoma Harvest Fair Sweepstakes Award for three years running (see our Restaurants chapter).

Santa Rosa Courtyard by Marriott
$$$ •175 Railroad St., Santa Rosa
• (707) 573-9000

Right on the edge of historic Railroad Square, this Days Inn has close access to enough antique shops to delight any collector looking for bargains or the unusual. All the standard amenities are available in this 138-room inn. Kids will love the swimming pool, spa and in-room movies, and adults may wander down for cocktails between 5 and 10. Kids younger than 12 stay free. There are wheelchair accessible rooms.

Hotel La Rose
$$$$ • 308 Wilson St., Santa Rosa
• (707) 579-3200

A quaint and romantic hotel in Santa Rosa's historic Railroad Square, Hotel La Rose was reconstructed in 1985 and designated a National Historic Landmark. The hotel is graced with a charming English Country interior decor that belies the fact that this is a very modern hotel. The four-story hotel has elevator access to its 29 nonsmoking rooms, and the carriage house, added in 1985, has 20 additional guest rooms (seven are designated for smokers) built around a lovely courtyard. A 1998 remodel included marbled bathrooms and a spa. One of the hotel's great assets is its proximity to the restaurants in Railroad Square.

Northern Sonoma

Best Western Dry Creek Inn
$$$ • 198 Dry Creek Rd., Healdsburg
• (707) 433-0300

The distinguishing factor here is this motel's outstanding location for wine touring in the beautiful Dry Creek Valley. The 102 rooms (including some "executive" rooms) are pleasant, in the standard motel style, but the bonus is a spectacular view of the valley's vineyards from most of the units. A continental breakfast is included. There's a pool, whirlpool and exercise room.

Travelodge/Vineyard Valley Inn Motel
$$ • 178 Dry Creek Rd., Healdsburg
• (707) 433-0101, (800) 499-0103

Built in 1992, this is not your ordinary Travelodge, though it is part of the chain. The Vineyard Valley Inn Motel has 23 rooms and suites that blend into the Wine Country setting while still providing all the modern amenities that seasoned travelers have come to expect. Rooms are furnished with two double beds or one queen. A two-room suite is available with wet bar, refrigerator and entertainment area.

Geyserville Inn
$$$ • 21714 Geyserville Ave., Geyserville
• (707) 857-4343

This is a new hotel, situated at the north end of the town of Geyserville and surrounded by vineyards. The location is ideal for visiting any number of wineries, as well as hitting the bike trails that crisscross this rural countryside. It's also close to Lake Sonoma (see our On The Water chapter). The 38 rooms are furnished with a Wine Country feel, decorated under the direction of a local interior decorator in shades of vineyard green and the russet colors of autumn. Rooms are graced with various amenities—for example, patios or balconies and fireplaces—and guests can enjoy the swimming pool and spa. A continental breakfast is served each morning.

Sonoma Coast

Bodega Bay Lodge Resort
$$$$$ • 103 Coast Hwy. 1, Bodega Bay
• (707) 875-3525, (800) 368-2468

Luxurious and intimate, the Lodge overlooks wildflower-covered dunes and protected marshlands, the Pacific Ocean and the gentle surf of Doran Beach. While it's close enough to enjoy the sound of the surf, the wood-shingled lodge is sheltered from coastal winds. All 84 spacious guest rooms have fireplaces and private balconies. Many feature vaulted ceilings, spa baths, refrigerators, wet bars and coffee makers. Original artwork and bronze sculptures grace the rooms and 8 acres of landscaped grounds. The 5,000-square-foot conference center is impressive, with high, arched ceilings braced by thick beams of polished oak. The Duck Club Restaurant can be counted on for imaginative cuisine (see our Restaurants chapter). Complimentary wine is served in the late afternoon. An 18-hole Robert Trent Jones-designed golf course is next door at Bodega Harbour Golf Links (see our Parks and Recreation chapter).

Inn at the Tides
$$$$ • 800 Coast Hwy. 1, Bodega Bay
• (707) 875-2751, (800) 541-7788

Six coastal acres with natural landscaping surround this inn, which is actually an enclave of 12 separate lodges that appear to be part of the rumpled hills and tawny headlands. It presides over Bodega Bay, home port for one of the coast's most productive fishing fleets. Each of the 86 guest quarters keep watch over this busy harbor. Amenities include a heated indoor-outdoor pool, spacious spa and soothing sauna. In your room you'll find luxurious logo robes emblazoned with the Inn's logo. A continental breakfast is served, and gourmet cuisine is featured in the Bay View Restaurant & Lounge (see our Restaurants chapter).

INSIDERS' TIP

Just about every Wine Country inn has its summer high season, but note the Napa Valley Marriott's "super high season," between mid-July and mid-August. That's when the Oakland Raiders occupy the premises for training camp. Rates go up $10 per room, and all the garden-view units are taken. Of course, it might be a small price to pay for a chance to see Steve Wisniewski sitting by the pool.

Fort Ross Lodge
$$$ • 20706 Coast Hwy. 1, Jenner
• (707) 847-3333

Just north of the historic Fort Ross Russian settlement (see our History and Attractions chapters), there's a sheltered cove where seals lounge on rocky outcroppings. This is the setting of Fort Ross Lodge. There's plenty of space in the guest rooms to stretch out and relax, or you can unwind in the hot tub and sauna. The 22 rooms are decorated in natural tones and hues. Each is cozy and as individual as a friend's guest room. There's a barbecue on your deck, and a country store across the street. Children younger than 12 are free. At the top of the hill are secluded, intimate suites for adults only. And the lodge now offers a private two-bedroom home at $220 per night; add a separate-entry suite and it's $300.

Salt Point Lodge
$$ • 23255 Calif. Hwy. 1, Timber Cove
• (707) 847-3234

This is a well-maintained, older motor lodge, with 16 rooms. Situated on a knoll overlooking the ocean, Salt Point Lodge includes a restaurant with a full bar. Lovely gardens surround the place, and it's open year-round. There are TVs and VCRs in the rooms, but no phones. Besides the nearby beaches, there are miles of hiking trails to explore.

Sea Ranch Lodge
$$$ • 60 Sea Wall Dr., Sea Ranch
• (707) 785-2371

On bluffs above the Pacific Ocean, this lodge has one of the best vistas in Wine Country. All but one of its 20 rooms face the sea, and cozy window seats offer front-row viewing for spectacular sunsets. The location is remote, but if you're in need of a peaceful getaway, this is the place. Not far south of the Mendocino county line on Calif. Highway 1, Sea Ranch appears like a full-blown city of vacation homes and permanent residences in the city of Gualala. Rooms are walled in knotty pine, and the aura is rustic. Hiking trails along the bluffs are well-marked but bring a windbreaker—the fog does creep in. A challenging golf course (soon to be enlarged to 18 holes) is available, and there's a restaurant. Some units have fireplaces, and family units are available. All are luxuriously appointed.

West County/Russian River

Cazanoma Lodge
$$ • 1000 Kidd Creek Rd., Cazadero
• (707) 632-5255

A beautiful Old World lodge spectacularly situated on 147 acres of giant redwoods in western Sonoma County, Cazanoma Lodge is a charming vacation retreat nestled between two creeks. Two spacious, comfortable cabins have wood-burning fireplaces, contemporary kitchens and baths. Three suites and one room in the main lodge overlook the lodge's cascading waterfall, trout pond and creeks. A bottle of wine or champagne plus brie and crackers and fresh fruit await guests at check-in. The restaurant features Bavarian specialties (sauerbraten, hasenpfeffer and roast duck) and American cuisine. The lodge is open March through November.

Mendocino County

U.S. Highway 101

Days Inn
$ • 950 N. State St., Ukiah
• (707) 462-7584

Yes, it's a chain, but the rooms are spacious and luxuriously decorated, the inn is comfortable and convenient, and the staff is professional. This Days Inn has 54 units, a swimming pool and a restaurant. It offers free local calls, and pets are welcome. Breakfast is included in the nightly rate.

Discovery Inn
$$ • 1340 N. State St., Ukiah • (707) 462-8873

This is the largest of Ukiah's motels, with 177 units, two heated pools, four indoor spas and a conference room. A workout room is a recent addition, and guest laundry facilities are available. Complimentary breakfast is included.

An unusual attraction is a small park filled with carved redwood figures—a bear, a shark, a man—surrounding an attractive fountain.

Baechtel Creek Inn
$ • 101 Gregory Ln., Willits
• (707) 459-9063

An attractive two-story hotel built in 1992, Baechtel Creek Inn has 46 rooms, a heated swimming pool and spa and conference rooms. Baechtel Creek runs right past the inn, providing considerable entertainment for kids and grown-ups alike by attracting such wild creatures as rabbits, squirrels, deer and an occasional turtle. This is a nice, clean place to stay in a town that doesn't see all that many visitors.

Mendocino Coast

Breakers Inn
$$$$ • 39300 Coast Hwy. 1 S., Gualala
• (707) 884-3200, (800) BREAKER

The 24 oceanfront rooms at the Breakers are designed to offer spectacular panoramic views of the dramatic coast through large picture windows and spacious decks. Your stay will be punctuated by incredible ocean sunsets and the sound of waves crashing on the shore. In winter and spring, the deck provides a front-row seat to the migration of gray whales. Each room is individually decorated in the theme of a country or state in a seacoast region, highlighting locations such as Cape Cod, Ireland and Japan. All rooms except the three garden rooms feature decks, fireplaces, wet bars and ocean views, and deluxe continental breakfast is included each morning. The Luxury Spa Room is near a picture window so you can soak and enjoy the view.

Albion River Inn
$$$$ • 3790 N. Coast Hwy. 1, Albion
• (707) 937-1919, (800) 479-7944

Six miles south of Mendocino, Albion River Inn occupies a prime oceanfront spot on 10 secluded acres of gardens and ocean bluffs. Guests are quartered in 20 cliff-side, New England-style rooms for two, most in duplex arrangements and all with spectacular ocean views. All

INSIDERS' TIP

The round barn on a hill above Fountaingrove Inn dates from the late 19th century when Thomas Harris, spiritual leader of the commune Brotherhood of New Life, came to gather converts. He was later exposed as a fraud by a lady reporter (see our History chapter), but one of his followers, a Japanese nobleman, stayed on to develop some of the finest vineyards in the county.

have fireplaces and private decks, and many have a spa tub or tub for two. A full breakfast is included in the adjoining restaurant, which shares the view.

Hill House of Mendocino
$$$$ • 10701 Palette Dr., Mendocino • (707) 937-0554

You'd swear you were on the New England coast. The recently constructed Hill House Inn captures the essence of the coast of Maine in the spectacular and unspoiled land and sea along California's scenic Highway 1. Forty-four guest rooms feature brass beds with comforters, lace curtains, elegant wooden furnishings and the convenience of private baths. Hill House not only attracts vacationers but also caters to seminars and small conferences, with rooms designed to accommodate up to 100 people. A chapel is available for wedding ceremonies.

Mendocino Hotel
$$$$ • 45080 Main St., Mendocino • (707) 937-0511, (800) 548-0513

The venerable, 121-year-old Mendocino Hotel is an opulent Victorian jewel named "best small hotel in Northern California" by *Focus* magazine. Guests register at a teller's cage from an old Kansas bank and congregate for drinks in a front parlor replete with antiques, leaded windows and Oriental rugs. The historic section offers suites with balconies overlooking the Pacific as well as rooms with shared baths in the European style. The garden suites, across the courtyard, are fully modern but still maintain the Victorian decor. Look for lots of solid wood paneling, leaded glass, brass and walls papered in period fabrics. Fifty-one rooms fill the main hotel and the garden suites. An elegant dining room features California cuisine and an extensive wine list. The Garden Café is open in the daytime, as is the Garden Bar. The Lobby Bar operates in the evening. Advance reservations are almost mandatory during the summer months.

Sweetwater Spa & Inn
$$$ • 955 Ukiah St. (spa), 44840 Main St. (inn), Mendocino • (707) 937-4140

The Sweetwater complex takes up most of the two blocks between Ukiah and Main streets in the village of Mendocino, and that's not all. Besides the 10 units downtown, the company has six more in Little River and two separate houses elsewhere. One of the homes, Redwood Cottage, is a popular lodging about five minutes east of Mendocino. The other is Sweetwater Cove, a three-bedroom, two-bath structure on a spectacular stretch of coastline between Caspar and Fort Bragg. (The Cove goes for upwards of $200 per night.)

The spa offers a variety of massage options, including the ever-popular Sweetheart Special—stay two nights in any room, book two massages and receive a $15 discount. Sweetwater also has hot tubs and sauna, with prices that vary according to privacy and tub size. Kids are welcome in all units.

Anchor Lodge Motel
$$ • 32260 N. Harbor Dr., Fort Bragg • (707) 964-4283

Located in the heart of Noyo Fishing Village, Anchor Lodge has been a focal point for visitors and locals for more than 40 years. You can't get much closer to the water without being in it. There are 18 rooms here, and guests have their pick of four options: economy (two persons), waterfront (two persons) or an apartment with kitchen for two or four persons.

Anchor Lodge operates in conjunction with The Wharf Restaurant and Lodge, which features fresh fish, steak and prime rib.

INSIDERS' TIP

Organizing an informal summer getaway for a group? Here's an idea: Book the house that complements Bell Haven Resort's nine cabins on Soda Bay. Built in the 1920s, Heron House has a stone fireplace and views of Clear Lake. It costs $255 a night and sleeps up to 18 people.

Harbor Lite Lodge
$$ • 120 N. Harbor Dr., Fort Bragg • (707) 964-0221, (800) 643-2700

One of the attractive features of this rustic redwood motel is that its balconies overlook Noyo River and its fishing fleet. If you're awake in the early dawn, you can see the lights of the fleet as boats head out for the day's fishing, stretching in a colorful parade out to sea. In late afternoon the parade returns in reverse. The lodge has 79 comfortable rooms, some with wood-burning stoves. A meeting center for business or educational conferences has two large rooms accommodating 30 and 50 people, respectively. Complimentary coffee, tea and cocoa are served in the lobby each morning.

Hi-Seas Inn
$$ • 1201 N. Main St., Fort Bragg
• (707) 964-5929

All 15 of the rooms here have a full ocean view. Just slide back the big glass door that leads to the deck with tables and chairs. Between the deck and the ocean is a two-acre lawn. And right behind the Inn is a 10-mile hiking trail that goes through Fort Bragg and back into the nearby hills. Each room has a coffeemaker, and the Inn has a microwave everyone can use.

Pine Beach Inn & Suites
$$ • 16801 N. Calif. Hwy. 1, Fort Bragg
• (707) 964-5603

You can walk to a beach and cove from this 50-room hotel, which is on 12 acres of landscaped grounds in a majestic setting of redwoods. The beach is secluded, the private path is paved, and you'll enjoy breathtaking views all the way down to the mighty Pacific as it thunders in against the high rocks and cliffs. The rooms (nine are suites) are large, decorated with fine furniture, and comforters and pillow shams adorn the beds; 24 of the units have ocean views. If you're in the mood for tennis, championship courts await, offering the chance to lob into the clear blue skies. From April through October the on-site restaurant features broiled steaks and fresh local seafood. When the restaurant is closed during the off-season, a continental breakfast is served.

Seabird Lodge
$$ •191 South St., Fort Bragg
• (707) 964-4731, (800) 345-0022

One of the best-known features of this 65-room motel is a continuing package special that includes passage on the Skunk Train. The train, of course, travels between Fort Bragg and Willits (see our Attractions chapter), and most visitors find an overnight stay in Fort Bragg to be a favorable option. The package deal may vary (it seldom does), but it usually includes two nights lodging, two Skunk Train tickets, breakfast each morning and dinner one evening at your choice of three restaurants.

The Seabird will also shuttle you to and from the depot. The lodge has an indoor pool and hot tub, and there is a restaurant right next door.

INSIDERS' TIP
Motorists heading up Calif. Highway 1 will notice that from Bodega Bay north to Fort Bragg in Mendocino County, this highway is often designated as Coast Highway 1. This is used as the address for homes and businesses along this section of the road.

Surrey Inn
$ • 888 S. Main St., Fort Bragg
• (707) 964-4003, (800) 206-9833

This inn, run by longtime local residents, offers affordable accommodations, a convenient location and old-fashioned hospitality. The 53 rooms have cable TV and private phones, and there is a full-service restaurant on the premises. Staff will be delighted to give a rundown on all the unique natural wonders to be explored in the vicinity—Mackerricher State Park, for instance, or Glass Beach or Pudding Creek headlands—as well as family activities available on sea and on land.

Vista Manor Inn
$$ • 1100 N. Main St., Fort Bragg
• (707) 964-4776, (800) 821-9498

This Best Western motel includes 55 units and is located at the north end of Fort Bragg, about a mile from downtown. There's an indoor heated pool, complimentary continental breakfast and a coffeemaker in every room. Other amenities? How about the world's largest body of water? All rooms have ocean views, and a nearby tunnel dips beneath Highway 1, giving you about five minutes to walk to the beach.

Lake County

Cobb Village Inn Motel
$ • 16595 Calif. Hwy. 175, Cobb
• (707) 928-5242, (800) COBB-MTN

Tucked into the pines at about 3,000 feet, this quiet motel starts to look pretty good in the wilting days of August. Cobb Village has 19 rooms, five of them with kitchenettes and three with Whirlpool tubs, feather beds and VCRs. The office, a rich source of local information, is open from 9 AM to 9 PM. The motel is across the road from Hobergs-Forest Lake Golf Course (see our Parks and Recreation chapter) and within walking distance of a pizza parlor, a fish-and-chips pub and a breakfast cafe. Don't bother looking for the address—Cobb Village is at the intersection of Calif. 175 and Golf Road.

Travelodge
$ • 4775 Old Calif. Hwy. 53, Clearlake
• (707) 994-1499

Calif. Highway 53 used to meander through downtown Clearlake be-

Hill House is one of Wine Country's picturesque lodgings found near or along California's scenic Highway 1.

fore they built a bypass to the east; the old route is still called Old Highway 53. Where it intersects Lakeshore Drive, about a block and a half from Redbud Park, you'll find the Travelodge. It has 31 rooms, all of which come with cable TV and air conditioning. There is a swimming pool, a spa, and individual power hook-ups for boats. Ask about their commercial and senior rates.

Days Inn
$$ • 13865 Lakeshore Dr., Clearlake • (707) 994-8982, (800) 300-8982

Days Inn is right on the water in the northwest section of town, with a 200-foot dock that juts into Clear Lake. The motel has 20 guest units, in-room coffee makers and a swimming pool if you prefer smaller bodies of water.

Best Western El Grande
$$ • 15135 Lakeshore Dr., Clearlake • (707) 994-2000, (800) 528-1234

One of the biggest motels in Lake County, El Grande has 68 rooms, including 24 suites. Each of the suites comes with a refrigerator, and in the sitting room there's a second TV and phone—even a hide-a-bed. Inside you'll find an atrium and a full-service restaurant and bar, not to men-

tion a sitting pool. Outside are a hot tub and spa. It's only 1-½ blocks from the lake.

Lake Point Lodge
$ • 13440 E. Calif. Hwy. 20, Clearlake Oaks • (707) 998-4350

You get a lot for your dollar at this 40-unit motel in Clearlake Oaks. Half the rooms have king beds, half have two queens, and all come with cable TV and continental breakfast. The lodge also has four suites with whirlpool tubs and microwave ovens. There is a swimming pool in back.

Bell Haven Resort
$$ • 3415 White Oak Way, Kelseyville • (707) 279-4329

If the perimeter of Clear Lake is getting too commercial for you—it does start to feel like a sandy circus midway sometimes—it may be time for Bell Haven. The Woosters offer the sort of doting attention you expect at a bed and breakfast inn. Their woodsy resort has 9 cabins; size varies, but all have kitchens. It also offers a hot tub, free kayaks and, in the summer, free El Toro sailboats. Within walking distance are a hamburger joint and a market with full deli. Call to ask about weekly vacation rates.

Kelseyville Motel
$ • 5575 Seventh St., Kelseyville
• (707) 279-1874, (800) KV-MOTEL

Just blocks from either Calif. 29 or Kelseyville's Main Street, this cozy motel is a convenient choice. Each of the 16 rooms has individual heat and air, color TV with cable and a refrigerator. Three rooms have kitchenettes, and you might talk them into accepting your beloved pet.

Anchorage Inn
$ • 950 N. Main St., Lakeport
• (707) 263-5417

Right on the lake and just a few blocks from Library Park, the Anchorage has 34 air-conditioned rooms with cable color TV. The motel has a pool, a sauna, a Jacuzzi, a barbecue area, and a pier and boat-docking facilities in a sheltered cove. In addition to the standard rooms, the inn has apartment-like one-bedroom suites and sizable two-bedroom suites with grand living rooms and writing tables. The suites range from $64 to $115.

Starlite Motel
$ • 5960 E. Calif. Hwy. 20, Lucerne
• (707) 274-5515

If you wind up on the less populated side of Clear Lake, the Starlite has 22 rooms, a swimming pool and picnic area. Each room comes with air conditioning, cable TV and a small refrigerator. Pets are sometimes accommodated. The motel is just across the highway from the water.

Super 8 Motel
$$ • 450 E. Calif. Hwy. 20, Upper Lake
• (707) 275-0888, (800) 800-8000

You get what you pay for at the Super 8, and that's enough to convince some weary travelers. Four of the 34 rooms come with spa tubs. A restaurant, Judy's Junction, is just across the street. There is a swimming pool and hot tub on the premises.

Pine Acres Resort
$$ • 5328 Blue Lakes Rd., Upper Lake
• (707) 275-2811

Just off Calif. 20, about halfway between where it leaves the shore of Clear Lake and where it meets U.S. 101 to the west, are the Blue Lakes, two skinny, steep-sided troughs fed by natural springs. Pine Acres is on Upper Blue Lake. It offers 11 rooms and cabins, some with two double beds and a full kitchen, some with queen beds and a small refrigerator. It also has roomy deluxe units that go for $90 to $120 a

night. Smoking is allowed in most of the cabins, and pets are allowed everywhere for a $7 fee. Babies stay free, while children ages 2 through 10 incur a $2 per night charge. The resort has a private beach, a fishing dock, a small store (including a bait-and-tackle shop) and boat rentals.

Vacation Rentals

Sonoma County

Russian River Vacation Homes
14080 Mill St., Guerneville
• (707) 869-9030,
(800) 310-0804 (in California),
(800) 997-3312

Since 1975 this firm has provided a large selection of vacation rental homes throughout western Sonoma County at nightly rates ranging from $135 to $450; weekly rates from $550 to $1,600.

Russian River Getaways
16201 First St., Guerneville
• (707) 869-4560

This friendly rental company would like you to "experience getaway heaven in your very own home away from home." All the homes they offer are first-class, with many choices in size, location and amenities. Picture yourself in a cozy hideaway for two in the redwoods or rendezvous with your family or co-workers in a beach house that sleeps 18. Or you might prefer an elegant lodge with a dramatic river view in the wine-tasting region. Many houses are dog-friendly, and there's only a two-night minimum. Prices range from $125 to $750 per night, $600 to $4,500 per week.

Sea Coast Hide-a-Ways
21350 North Coast Hwy. 1, Jenner
• (707) 847-3278

You have a choice here of oceanside vistas or seclusion among the redwoods. Hot tubs and fireplaces are featured, with boat rentals available at Sea Coast's Timber Cove boat landing. Prices range from $195 to $650 for two nights and $545 to $1,900 weekly, with midweek discounts available.

Rams Head Realty
1000 Annapolis Rd., Sea Ranch
• (707) 785-2427, (800) 785-3455

More than 120 vacation rentals are offered

from two-night stays to multiple weeks at a rate of $100 to $300 per night. Sites are available in the meadows, in the forest or on the oceanfront. The most desirable oceanfront sites offer grand vistas and the dramatic crashing of the waves.

Mendocino County

Pacific Resorts Realty
7675 Calif. Hwy. 1, Little River
• (707) 937-3000

Owner Jim Robichaud offers luxury vacation rentals all along the Pacific coastline from Albion to Fort Bragg. These are homes owned by buyers who plan to some day retire on the coast, but meanwhile elect to rent until that retirement day comes. Homes all have ocean views, full kitchens and hot tubs. Rentals cost $200 to $300 a day or $1,000 to $1,500 a week, depending on size and amenities.

Mendocino Coast Reservations
1000 Main St., Mendocino
• (707) 937-5033

Here you'll find listings of the finest in weekend and vacation lodging, from cozy cottages to oceanfront estates. Some are right in the village of Mendocino, some on the coast, some in the forest. In July and August, a three-day minimum is imposed. A wide range of rental fees varies due to weekly or weekend occupancy, time of year, size and property amenities. A three-day, two-night visit during high season ranges from $328 for a studio in the village to $1,080 for a house with an ocean view and a hot tub.

Bed and Breakfast Inns

LOOK FOR:
• Napa County
• Sonoma County
• Mendocino County
• Lake County

Spying the hand-carved wooden sign, you pull your Ford Explorer down a long driveway. Immediately you are cooled by the airy shade of a 200-year-old oak tree, a pine or a redwood. The front door has a brass knocker and a leaded-glass window, and when it opens, a woman you've never met before greets you like a former neighbor.

Signing the guest book, you catch a subtle whiff of furniture polish. The parlor brims with pristine antiques—an oak secretary, a walnut roll-top desk, a marble fireplace. The only sound is the tock-tock-tock of a grandfather clock. You carry your bag up the stairs (they creak slightly and melodically) and find your bedroom. It has a name. Inside is a four-poster bed and other furnishings much nicer than any you would put in your own house. A gentle breeze ruffles the lace curtain; drawing it aside you look out to the private rose garden and its grapevine arbor. Later you'll have wine and cheese in the parlor, and tomorrow you will enjoy a big breakfast while chatting with an unwinding lawyer from Los Angeles and a history professor from Toronto. Right now, however, all you want to do is sit in your stuffed Louis the Something-or-Other chair and eat one of the chocolate-chip cookies left on your nightstand.

We've just described exactly what some people don't want in an accommodation. But for others this is the perfect vacation lodging. If you place yourself in the latter category, have we got a place for you. Actually, make that a few dozen places. The California Wine Country has made something of a cottage industry out of cottages. If you take Napa Valley north of Napa as an example, there are far more bed and breakfast inns than motels. People come here to be charmed—swept off their feet—and staying in an 1890s Victorian or restored country farmhouse fits into the plan.

The only problem is deciding exactly what is a bed and breakfast, and what is a hotel or a resort. Usually it is obvious. Sometimes you feel like a video store employee trying to figure out if that Coen Brothers video should be shelved under comedy, drama or crime. Life doesn't always provide a miscellaneous category. One criterion we didn't want to use was whether the establishment serves breakfast. The Comfort Inn in Calistoga provides continental breakfast. Does that make it a B&B? The cozy Hideaway Cottages a few blocks away does not. Does that make it a hotel? No, twice.

The standard we used was this: Does staying at a particular inn make you feel as though you are sleeping over at someone's home, or at least in their separate guest quarters? It's admittedly subjective, but we figure that's what travelers are looking for in a bed and breakfast inn. Some folks seek out the arms-length anonymity of a motel. Others want to feel at home. They want to sit in the living room and read the morning paper; they want help in selecting and reserving a restaurant; they want that chocolate-chip cookie. (Go ahead, say it: "I want that chocolate-chip cookie.")

Price Code

Please refer to the dollar-sign code laid out below for tariffs. Rates are for double occupancy on a weekend in high season (generally, May through October). Most inns offer significant discounts for off-season or midweek stays. Note that prices do not include taxes or gratuities, or services that are considered "extra."

$	**$90 or lower**
$$	**$91 to $120**
$$$	**$121 to $150**
$$$$	**$151 to $180**
$$$$$	**$181 or higher**

You will find that practically all the B&Bs were converted from private residences and workplaces, while practically all of the hotels, motels and spas were constructed as just that. Unless you read otherwise in this chapter, you can expect a few things about each of the listed inns. They have rooms with private bathrooms but no television sets; the bedrooms have lovely full- or queen-size beds; they do not allow pets or any indoor smoking; they accept MasterCard and Visa, and quite possibly other major credit cards; and they serve full breakfast.

The issue of issue (that is, children) is hazier. Most places do not want to forbid kids. In fact, current California law apparently won't let them make any such prohibition. However, the innkeepers acknowledge that many of their guests are attempting, above all else, to get away from children for a couple days. Also, a house of steep, hardwood staircases and fragile antiques might not be the best place for your toddler. So unless we tell you different, assume that kids are strongly discouraged in the bed and breakfasts. Most parents agree that it's better to know such a policy up front than to be told that children are welcome, only to sense disapproval and have it spoil the entire stay.

Napa County

The Blue Violet Mansion
$$$$$ • 443 Brown St., Napa
• (707) 253-2583, (800) 959-2583

The Blue Violet Mansion won the Reader's Choice Award in 1996, outdistancing inns from all over North America. It isn't hard to imagine why. Every detail is celebrated with a flourish here, from the in-room port (complimentary) and rack full of wine (pay as you go) to the brass door frame salvaged from the Bank of Italy, to the iron front gate reproduced to match the original. The Queen Anne Victorian home was built in 1886 by Emanuel Manasse, executive at Sawyer Tannery and pioneer of patent leather production. Manasse's trade is evident in a most distinctive feature—embossed leather wainscotting that runs through much of the house.

The Blue Violet Mansion has 17 rooms on three floors. Each of them has a king or queen bed and a modem jack. Two ground-floor rooms are equipped with Murphy beds, making them ideal for upscale corporate meetings. And upstairs is the Camelot Floor, four rooms painstakingly hand-painted in tromp l'oeuil fashion. Book the Royal Suite and sip your wine from Arthur and Guinevere silver goblets. On the one-acre grounds you'll find a heated swimming pool, a spa, an herb garden and roses. And at the back of the mansion is Violette's, a French restaurant serving a seven-course prix fixe dinner for $75 per person. Extra guests are welcome—for an additional $75 ($50 for children 5 and under).

Churchill Manor Bed & Breakfast Inn
$$$$ • 485 Brown St., Napa
• (707) 253-7733

In the heart of the Fuller Park Historic District is a grandiose, three-story Second Empire mansion built in 1889 for local banker Edward Churchill. With close to 10,000 square feet of space (and that doesn't even include the full basement or the pillar-supported, three-sided verandah), it was said to be the largest domicile in Napa Valley for decades. The interior is essentially unaltered. There are four grand parlor rooms with beveled and leaded glass, and redwood moldings and fireplace frames. Old political cartoons and Victorian prints line the hallways.

The 10 guest rooms, nine of which are on the second and third floors, don't exactly look like a college dormitory, either. They're filled with massive cherry armoires and desks, and some of the claw-foot tubs are "in the European style"—they sit fetchingly in a corner of the bedroom. Other units have oversized tubs with two-person showers. You get a full breakfast in the dining room, plus complimentary wine and cheese (and fresh-baked cookies) in the afternoon. Play croquet in the side garden, borrow a tandem bicycle or just stroll around the acre of grounds and toast the fat wallet of Edward Churchill.

Cedar Gables Inn
$$$$ • 486 Coombs St., Napa
• (707) 224-7969, (800) 309-7969

Chances are, you've never seen a house like this one. Designed by British architect Ernest Coxhead in 1892, it's an immense, brown-shingled home that you might expect to find on an estate in England's Cotswolds. In fact, the feeling here is decidedly masculine, making it a logical choice for not-better halves who reflexively scratch themselves when they hear the phrase "bed and breakfast." Cedar Gables' guest rooms—six going on nine—are sizable and brimming with period antiques. The Churchill Chamber, originally the master bedroom used by Edward and Alice Churchill, has a walnut-encased whirlpool tub to match the fireplace. Several of the rooms have old coal-burning fireplaces, converted to gas. Breakfast is served either at the long, formal dining room table or cafe-style in the adjacent sun room. Cedars, palm trees and a cork oak shade the house in the summer.

Inn on Randolph
$$$$ • 411 Randolph St., Napa
• (707) 257-2886

This modest, tasteful inn is on a quiet street in a neighborhood of historic homes. The main house, an 1860 Gothic Revival Victorian, has five rooms with seasonal themes (the fifth is called Equinox). Spring, for example, has hand-painted flowers on the walls and ceiling, and Autumn features a handcrafted bent-willow canopy bed. Five more expensive rooms ($244 to $259) are in the newly refurbished 1930s cottages. All of the cottages and some of the main-house rooms have gas fireplaces and two-person whirlpool tubs; some have private decks. Roses line the front walk, and the gardens are flanked by a common deck, a gazebo and hammocks. The Inn on Randolph serves a full breakfast, and in-room massage can be arranged upon request.

The Beazley House
$$$$ • 1910 First St., Napa
• (707) 257-1649, (800) 559-1649

The checkered past of this house took a happy turn in 1981 when Jim and Carol Beazley turned it into Napa's first bed and breakfast inn. On a row of rambling turn-of-the-century mansions, it was originally built for local surgeon and politician Adolph Kahn in 1902, but he and his wife divorced and left the area seven years later. Subsequent owners included the Hanna Boys Center and San Francisco jet setter Joan Hitchcock, who reputedly had an affair with JFK and certainly had seven husbands.

The Beazley now has 11 rooms, six in the main house and five in the Carriage house. The latter are large units, each with a fireplace and two-person spa tub. Our vote for best room (and, without question, best value) is the Sun Room, a bright and nostalgic corner with a two-sided balcony and a 6-foot soaking tub.

Full breakfast is served in the formal dining room. Children are permitted, and pets are assessed on a case-by-case basis.

The Hennessey House
$$$$ • 1727 Main St., Napa
• (707) 226-3774

Adjacent to the Jarvis Conservatory on the fringe of Napa's turn-of-the-century downtown, The Hennessey House is an Eastlake-style Queen Anne built for Dr. Edwin Hennessey, one-time mayor of the town, in 1889. The 10 rooms (six in the main residence, four in the carriage house) are air-conditioned, and most have canopy, brass or feather beds. Some have claw-foot or two-person whirlpool tubs in the bathroom, and the carriage-house rooms have fireplaces. The tariff ranges from $145 to $230, so ask for details.

Breakfast has been known to feature delights such as blueberry-stuffed French toast or basil-cheese strata. A hand-painted, stamped tin ceiling shelters the dining room. In the evening you can enjoy wine and cheese by the garden fountain. Hennessey House offers discounts on the Wine Train, golf, hot-air balloon rides and in-room massage.

Arbor Guest House
$$$$ • 1436 G St., Napa
• (707) 252-8144

In the Napa neighborhood appropriately known as Old Town, the Arbor Guest House is a pretty, whitewashed Colonial with a porch swing in front and a shady garden in back. The house is compact, but the rooms—three units upstairs, two more in the original Carriage house—manage to be ample. Two of them have spa tubs, three have fireplaces, and the main-house rooms are cooled by a reliable cross-breeze (and air conditioning, if things get serious). Breakfast is served in the dining room or the garden or, if you're staying in the carriage house, it is brought to your door with prior notice.

La Belle Epoque
$$$$$ • 1386 Calistoga Ave., Napa
• (707) 257-2161, (800) 238-8070

In 1893 Napa's leading hardware dealer built this splendid Queen Anne for his infant daugh-

> **INSIDERS' TIP**
> If you can't decide between two or three bed and breakfast inns, call each and ask a few questions. Make a difficult request. Tell them you're coming from Oakland and your car can't make left-hand turns. In short, quickly try to gauge their friendliness and helpfulness. After all, those two measures are likely to mean the difference between a happy stay and a mixed one.

Joshua Grindle came from Maine to Mendocino, where in 1879 he built the home that bears his name today.

ter, who died shortly thereafter. Tragic origins aside, La Belle Epoque beams with class: multi-gabled dormers, Oriental carpets, divans, marble-topped dressers and radiant stained glass, much of it transplanted from an old church. The inn has six rooms, with all the cozy alcoves and claw-foot tubs you would expect. You get your full breakfast in the formal dining room or on the garden patio. Innkeeper Georgia Jump serves evening wine and appetizers in the wine cellar.

The Old World Inn
**$$$$ • 1301 Jefferson St., Napa
• (707) 257-0112, (800) 966-6624**

This 1906 Victorian isn't as noisy as you might think, despite being situated on busy Jefferson Street (where it meets Calistoga Avenue). The inn is touched up in mellow pastel blue, rose, peach and mint—colors inspired by Swedish artist Carl Larsson—and the interior walls bear hand-lettered quotations, most of which could be filed under the heading "Be Kind to Strangers." And they do practice what they preach.

You'll receive a complimentary carafe of local wine upon arrival, evening hors d'oeuvres such as smoked salmon or Moroccan eggplant on sourdough bread, and a late-night buffet of chocolate treats. Of course, you get a full, hot breakfast in the dining room. Some rooms have canopied beds; some have claw-foot tubs. Others have fireplaces and private Jacuzzis. There is also an outdoor Jacuzzi shared by all guests of the Old World Inn.

Brookside Vineyard Bed & Breakfast
$$, no credit cards • 3194 Redwood Rd., Napa • (707) 944-1661

There isn't much traffic on shady Redwood Road other than the folks trekking back and forth to the Hess Collection Winery. Anyway, with 7 acres of land, Brookside offers plenty of room for sequestering. Tom and Susan Ridley's homey spot is full of images and relics true to the house's Mission style, including a long, pew-style bench in the entranceway. The three ground-floor guest rooms are off a long hallway, and each opens onto the garden. About half the acreage is devoted to vineyard, and visitors have been known to join the autumn crush. Elsewhere, fruit trees, California poppies and Douglas fir Christmas trees abound, and a path descends to a creekside clearing. (At least it's creekside when Redwood Creek is flowing.) Brookside has a swimming pool, and the largest bedroom has a dry sauna. The Ridleys accept personal checks.

La Residence

$$$$$ • 4066 St. Helena Hwy. N., Napa
• (707) 253-0337

Is it a hotel disguised as a bed and breakfast inn, or a B&B masquerading as a hotel? Does it matter when you're sitting in the elegant, sun-infused dining room at a table for two, eating a three-course breakfast from the fixed but ever-changing menu? La Res, as it is called, is a nice surprise within shouting distance of Calif. 29. The 16 rooms and four suites, divided between the 1870 Gothic Revival mansion and the newer French Barn, are decorated in French-Provincial style. Most include working fireplaces and patios or verandas. The inn sits on 2-½ acres of heritage oaks, pines and fledgling vines. There is a swimming pool, a separate Jacuzzi and a small meeting room for up to 15 people. Smoking is prohibited in all rooms, and the place isn't really set up for children.

> ## INSIDERS' TIP
>
> **Maison Fleurie in Yountville is part of the Four Sisters Inns group. If you stay four nights at three of their inns within a two-week period, your last evening is 50 percent off. If you stay six nights, the seventh is free. Call (800) 234-1425 for details.**

Oak Knoll Inn

$$$$$ • 2200 E. Oak Knoll Ave., Napa
• (707) 255-2200

The land around Oak Knoll Inn is part of Napa County's agricultural preserve. Businesses such as this are not allowed. Fortunately for its guests, the inn was here in 1984, before the prohibition. In effect, it has a virtual monopoly on 360-degree vineyard views. There is a big wooden deck outside the rooms, so you can spend all day looking at the Chardonnay and Merlot grapes before they head to Rutherford Hill, Beaulieu or Trefethen, which is just down the road. Oak Knoll Inn has four units, each with a fireplace and private entrance. There is a heated pool and spa for common use. The place is known for its breakfasts; on one recent morning it included baked pears in cognac sauce, baked herbed eggs and fresh muffins. But mostly the inn is renowned for the incredibly detailed itineraries that owner Barbara Bassino customizes and prints out for guests. This is not a good option for couples with children.

Trubody Ranch

$$$$ • 5444 St. Helena Hwy., Napa
• (707) 255-5907

It feels like the end of the earth, but really it's just the end of Trubody Lane, a peaceful road that departs Washington Street, the eastside frontage road to Calif. 29, about 2 miles south of Yountville. (Ignore the doubly misleading address in the header.) A working ranch since 1872, the property was deeded by the Trubodys to their friends and fellow Missouri-to-California pioneers, the Pages, in the late 1960s. The Victorian home and farm buildings are now surrounded by vineyard, and Jeff and Mary Page have done such an admirable job with the restoration that Napa County Landmarks gave them an award of merit.

There are only three rooms here: two in the perfectly restored water tower (Jeff is a carpenter) and another, larger unit in a detached cottage. The upper tower room has two lounging lofts, and the cottage has a living room with a walnut fireplace and a private patio with a hammock. All the quarters are furnished largely with antiques original to the farmhouse. Breakfast is served in the cheery dining room of the main house, with views onto the gardens of flowers and herbs. Call for prices, as the cottage is substantially more expensive than the other rooms.

Maison Fleurie

$$$$ • 6529 Yount St., Yountville
• (707) 944-2056, (800) 788-0369

In the middle of Yountville (but a block away from most of the traffic) is this French-style country inn. The 100-year-old main building has 2-foot-thick stone walls, terra cotta tile and a gas fireplace in the brick parlor. Two other structures—the Old Bakery (a working bakery in the 1970s) and the Carriage house—bring the total number of rooms to 13. Units range from $115 to $245 per night. You get a gourmet breakfast (or breakfast in bed if you'd rather) and a jar of homemade cookies in the lobby. There is a swimming pool, spa tub and mountain bikes for guest use. Maison Fleurie is part of Four Sisters Inns, a group of nine bed and breakfast establishments, most of them on the California coast.

Burgundy House Inn

$$$ • 6711 Washington St., Yountville
• (707) 944-0889

Yountville's main drag may not be the place you'd expect to find an Old World country inn, but Burgundy House has the requisites. It's a durable cube with 22-inch-thick walls, hand-hewn posts and lintels and lace curtains. Built as a brandy distillery in the 1890s from local fieldstone and river rock, it has also been a winery, a hotel, an antique warehouse and, now, a five-room inn. Buffet breakfast is served in the "distillery" or outside on the rose garden patio. Children older than 12 are permitted.

The Ink House
$$$$ • 1575 St. Helena Hwy. S., St. Helena • (707) 963-3890

If you have driven the length of Calif. Highway 29 a few times, you have no doubt taken notice of this remarkable house, a wedding-cake Italianate Victorian with a wraparound porch and third-floor crow's nest. Built by Theron H. Ink in 1884, it's now a seven-room bed and breakfast inn where the highway meets Whitehall Lane. The Ink House has a formal parlor and dining room for guests. You get a full breakfast in the morning, appetizers and wine, usually poured by a local winery, in the afternoon. Tapestries and polished antiques abound, and paintings are hung with brocade.

The rooms are lovely but not huge—five have private baths; the two that share a bath are only $100 apiece. The observatory serves as the TV room. While taking advantage of the 360-degree panorama, you might pop in a video of *Wild in the Country*, an Elvis Presley romp filmed at the Ink House in 1960. The inn also offers 18-speed bicycles, and an antique pool table in the basement. A steep staircase makes this an iffy choice for families with kids.

Shady Oaks Country Inn
$$$$ • 399 Zinfandel Ln., St. Helena • (707) 963-1190

The buildings are full of history at Shady Oaks, but it's the two acres of outdoor space that really sell the inn. The towering oaks are indeed shady. On one side of the house is a working walnut orchard; on the other are grapevines. And in back, a twisted 100-year-old wisteria vine protects the patio. Shady Oaks offers two suites (each with private entrance) in a two-story, stone structure that operated as a winery from 1883 to 1887. Three more rooms are found in John and Lisa Runnells' 1920s, craftsman-style home. Each unit features its own small collection of antiques; particularly lovely are the beds, such as the brass and ivory king-size in the Winery Retreat. Three of the rooms have fireplaces, and the Sunny Retreat has an adjoining second bedroom.

Afternoon wine is served on the patio. Champagne breakfast, meanwhile, is a splendid affair likely to entail eggs Benedict or Belgian waffles served in elegant style. Besides advice on restaurants and attractions, they can usually set up private tours at lesser-known wineries. Please note that children are not recommended here.

La Fleur Bed and Breakfast Inn
$$$$, no credit cards • 1475 Inglewood Ave., St. Helena • (707) 963-0233

This is a classic Wine Country inn—an 1882 Queen Anne Victorian with vineyard views, on a quiet road in the heart of Napa Valley. Up a steep, curving staircase you'll find the guest units. All have private bathrooms. Four have old-fashioned tubs; four have fireplaces. The wonderfully bright Vineyard Room has a big balcony hanging over the vines. (La Fleur actually owns a vineyard and makes two Petite Sirahs, a dry and a port.) The inn is across the highway from V. Sattui (see our Wineries chapter) and next door to Villa Helena Winery, where guests are accompanied for special tours. A large buffet breakfast is served in the solarium or outside on the porch, depending on the weather.

Glass Mountain Inn
$$$$$ • 3100 Silverado Tr., St. Helena • (707) 968-9400

Glass Mountain was named for its large deposits of obsidian, also known as "black glass." That obsidian is evident in the dining room of the Glass Mountain Inn, where guests can peer into a wine cave dug by Chinese laborers (originally for perishables, not Pinots) in the late 1800s. The house, with its wood shingles and steepled roof, isn't nearly as old as the cave. The inn has three large rooms with private baths, each room with individual strengths—the queen bed in the Mountain View Suite is framed by five arched windows; the Garden Suite has an oversized, oval whirlpool tub; and the Treetops Suite has a claw-foot tub and a private deck. Guests are greeted with a full breakfast each morning. Children are permitted.

Cinnamon Bear Bed & Breakfast
$$$$ • 1407 Kearney St., St. Helena • (707) 963-4653, (888) 963-4600

The name accurately describes this inn at the corner of Kearney and Adams streets in bucolic St. Helena. From the handmade quilts and floral wallpaper to the braided rugs to the army of antique teddy bears, it all adds up to cuteness. The ample, shingled craftsman bungalow was built in 1904, a wedding gift for Susan Smith from her father. The man Susan married, Walter Metzner, later was mayor of St. Helena for 20 years. His former abode has been fabulously restored. The inn has three second-floor guest rooms, two with queen beds and one with a king. Proprietor Cathye Ranieri is a chef, so you can expect a complete and well-executed breakfast (on the porch if the weather is nice). Children 10 and older are welcome.

The Ambrose Bierce House
$$$$ • 1515 Main St., St. Helena • (707) 963-3003

Ambrose Bierce was a novelist, a poet, an essayist, a cartoonist and a noted misanthrope. He wrote *The Devil's Dictionary* before disappearing in Mexico in 1913. The 1872 Victorian home he left behind in St. Helena bears his name and offers visitors three lovely rooms and a covered balcony tucked next to a grand redwood tree. The Ambrose Bierce suite, secluded on the second floor, has a private sitting room (with a television) that can be converted into a second bedroom. The Lillie Langtry Room is painted in lavender and white, while the Eadweard Muybridge Room is awash in deep blue and white. All three have plush, raised beds; stools are provided to help you make your way up under the covers.

Like its sister bed and breakfast, Shady Oaks Country Inn (see write-up above), Ambrose Bierce House is guided by the Runnells family. John and Lisa serve a full champagne breakfast in the morning, premium wine and cheese in the evening. Each guestroom is equipped with a crystal decanter of Port. Relax to classical music in the parlor, or soak in the home's new hot tub. Parents, please note that children are not recommended here.

Scarlett's Country Inn
$$$, no credit cards • 3918 Silverado Trail, Calistoga • (707) 942-6669

A "country inn" can sometimes mean a suburban cul-de-sac and a large rose garden. But Scarlett's is the real thing, a bucolic acre midway between Calistoga and St. Helena, where guests share space with friendly dogs and chickens. Scarlett Dwyer has lived on the property since 1965, and has run the inn since 1981. Her house is a former chicken processing building. The early-century farmhouse, meanwhile, now holds two of the three guest units—the Gamay Suite and the Camellia Suite, which actually can be opened into a full house for larger parties. Each room boasts a separate entrance, a queen bed, a TV, a microwave and a fridge. But the outdoor space is the big selling point here: a hammock, a tree swing, an aviary with finches and canaries, a lush fig tree, a pine-protected swimming pool and spa. Guests can choose the time and place for their full breakfast—and you know where the eggs are from. Note that Scarlett's does not accept credit cards, though personal checks are all right. The inn is just south of Wermuth Winery.

Christopher's Inn
$$$$$ • 1010 Foothill Blvd., Calistoga • (707) 942-5755

This inn proves the old adage that you can't judge a booking by its cover. The owner, an architect, joined an 80-year-old house with two cottages to make one large building. It's nice enough from the outside, but doesn't hint at the luxury held within the 22 rooms. Laura Ashley prints, exquisite antique desks, fresh flowers and high, open ceilings—it's a tasteful experience. Some newly added rooms have private Jacuzzis. Breakfast—yogurt, baked cobbler, etc.—is delivered to your door.

Christopher's also has two voluminous flats in back, facing onto Myrtle Street. They cost $365 but sleep as many as five people. Children are allowed at the inn.

Wine Way Inn
$$$ • 1019 Foothill Blvd., Calistoga • (707) 942-0680, (800) 572-0679

This bed and breakfast inn, opened in 1979, was the first in Calistoga. It's right next to Calistoga's busiest intersection, and owners Cecile and Moye Stephens want you to know up front that there is some street noise. Not that the Stephenses haven't managed to create a pleasant environment in their circa 1915 home. From the solid oak front door with

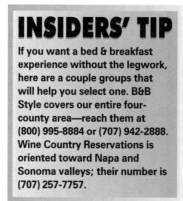

INSIDERS' TIP

If you want a bed & breakfast experience without the legwork, here are a couple groups that will help you select one. B&B Style covers our entire four-county area—reach them at (800) 995-8884 or (707) 942-2888. Wine Country Reservations is oriented toward Napa and Sonoma valleys; their number is (707) 257-7757.

etched glass to the patchwork quilts in each second-story room, they've taken care of the details. In addition to the five interior rooms, the Calistoga Room is a detached unit—it's out by the multi-tiered deck that backs up to a wooded hillside. The breakfasts alternate daily between sweet and savory, with specialties such as frittata and tomato omelettes. And for no extra charge, George the dog will perform stupid pet tricks (including the critically acclaimed "Burning Building") while you enjoy your complimentary wine and snacks in the afternoon.

The Elms
$$$$ • 1300 Cedar St., Calistoga
• (707) 942-9476, (800) 235-4316

A.C. Palmer, the first circuit judge of Napa and Sonoma counties, went to France for his honeymoon sometime around 1870, and he and his bride returned to Calistoga with two important items: designs for a new home, and a small number of elm seedlings. The house lives as The Elms, shaded by the now-towering trees. Without a doubt, it is one of the most impressive homes in the valley. Palmer ran a lumber yard just across the Napa River, and The Elms is full of richly detailed, hand-hewn wood. It's also brimming with antiques—mostly French—thanks to the current owners.

The inn has four rooms in the main house. Two of them face Cedar Street, while another (the one in which Audrey Hepburn once slept) gazes upon pretty Pioneer Park. At the rear of the property are three rooms in the refurbished Carriage House, including the Honeymoon Cottage, a large unit with a two-person shower and views to the river. Five of the rooms have fireplaces, and all seven come with a TV, plus port and chocolate. The Elms is not a good choice for those with children.

La Chaumiere
$$$$ • 1301 Cedar St., Calistoga
• (707) 942-5139

What grabs you first is the garden, an explosion of ferns and flowers surrounding a tall pine in front of the house. La Chaumiere is a small, picturesque house with a pitched roof and an arched window that looks across the street to Pioneer Park. There are two well-appointed rooms in the house (one has a sitting room in addition to the bedroom), plus a detached cabin in the rear. The bathrooms are part of the attraction—one has antique lavender-and-black tile work, the other has a mirror framed by an old billiards cue-rack.

The log cabin, built in 1932, isn't exactly

the kind Abe Lincoln grew up in. The whole-timber redwood uprights and crossbeams are complemented by touches of comfort, including a wood stove, a fireplace built of petrified wood and a large kitchen. The outdoor common areas include a flowery patio and a treehouse built around the trunk of a redwood. You get a full breakfast in the AM, plus wine and cheese in the afternoon and port in your room. La Chaumiere is just a block off Lincoln Avenue.

Scott Courtyard
$$$ • 1443 Second St., Calistoga
• (707) 942-0948, (800) 942-1515

This small, six-suite bed and breakfast on the corner of Fair Way and Second Street tries for neither Victorian splendor nor designer finery. The hallmarks at Scott are service, comfortable outdoor space and, if you want it, privacy. Each unit has a sitting room, bedroom and private bath; some have kitchen facilities. Children are allowed in some rooms, but are not really encouraged. There is a latticed courtyard, a pool and hot tub, a small aviary full of flitting finches and an artist's studio that inspired guests are allowed to use. (Local artists sometimes lead seminars there.) Breakfast, served in the bistro-style dining room or on the patio, tends to get rave reviews, with dishes such as banana-walnut pancakes and Thai chicken sausage.

Hideaway Cottages
$$$ • 1412 Fair Way, Calistoga
• (707) 942-4108

If you want a classic bed-and-breakfast experience without the breakfast, try this establishment on peaceful Fair Way. Look for the hedges and palm trees in front of a two-story gingerbread house. In back are 17 recently renovated cottages facing onto a landscaped courtyard. Many of the rooms have full kitchens. Hideaway, an affiliate of Dr. Wilkinson's Hot Springs (see our Spas and Resorts chapter), has a large mineral pool and Spa Jet tub. Most of the rooms go for $89 to $155 in high season, but the large Genoa cottage sleeps six and costs $160-$190 per night.

Wisteria Garden Bed & Breakfast
$$$ • 1508 Fair Way, Calistoga
• (707) 942-5358

This circa 1910 Colonial Revival cottage, about halfway between Lincoln Avenue and the fairgrounds, takes its name from the 100-year-old wisteria vines that drape over the

This elegantly appointed parlor beckons guests of the Gables Inn in Santa Rosa.

carport. Behind the house is an old valley oak that shades the two guest rooms. Both units have private baths, gas fireplaces, air conditioning, refrigerators and microwaves, cable TV and VCRs. Continental breakfast is served on weekends, and while Wisteria Garden does not have an on-site pool, guests receive complimentary passes to the plunge at a local spa. Children are permitted and pets might be, too—state your case to Carmen Maib, the innkeeper. The inn offers substantial, even negotiable, savings for midweek stays.

Brannan Cottage Inn
$$$$ • 109 Wapoo Ave., Calistoga
• (707) 942-4200

About 130 years ago, this spot had row upon row of one-story white bungalows, all with five-arched fronts, intricate gingerbread gable boards, wraparound porches and scalloped cresting. Now only one of them remains on its original site, and it's a six-room inn. (Two of the rooms are out back in the carriage house.) The look of the place—the 11-foot ceilings, oak floors and ceiling fans—whisks you right back to the days of Sam Brannan and his stay-rich schemes (see our History chapter). Each unit has a queen bed and a refrigerator. Full buffet breakfast is served in the dining room or on the patio. Children 10 and older are accepted, but the inn won't take credit card reservations over the phone.

Cottage Grove Inn
$$$$$ • 1711 Lincoln Ave., Calistoga
• (707) 942-8400, (800) 799-2284

In stark contrast to the trailer park that occupied this space for many years, the Cottage Grove is decidedly high-end. That's appropriate, because long before the trailer park this was the promenade area of Brannan's Hot Springs Resort, the spa that gave birth to Calistoga (see our History chapter). The grove of Siberian elms was planted by Brannan in the 1850s, and today they form an effective visual barrier to the traffic of Lincoln Avenue.

Each of Cottage Grove's 16 private cottages has a wood-burning fireplace (and a basket of wood on the porch), a CD stereo system, TV and VCR, air conditioner, private bath with two-person Jacuzzi tub, Egyptian cotton towels and an ironing board. Each has a theme, too, like the Music Cottage, the Audubon Cottage and the Fly Fishing Cottage. Continental breakfast and evening wine and appetizers are served in the common room. The owners allow children aged 12 and older.

The Wayside Inn
$$$ • 1523 Foothill Blvd., Calistoga
• (707) 942-0645

This split-level, Spanish-style home, built in the 1920s, is more like something you would expect to see in an older Los Angeles neighborhood, but it seems right at home in Napa Valley. The living room has rough beams and a wood fireplace. The back yard is densely shaded by trees—a dogwood, English walnut, a loquat and at least a dozen others. The three guest rooms are distinctly furnished and cooled by ceiling fans. One of them, the Camellia Room, has sole use of the home's original master bathroom; some people don't like having to step out into the hallway, but the impeccable seagreen tile work makes it worth the three extra strides. If you are journeying at night, look for the oversized wreath, twinkling with white lights, in the arched window of the front room.

Bear Flag Inn
$$$$ • 2653 Foothill Blvd., Calistoga
• (707) 942-5534

Just northwest of the intersection of Calif. 128 and Petrified Forest Road, this five-room bed and breakfast is a renovated farmhouse built in the 1930s. Purportedly, it was on this very site that Peter Storm constructed one of the flags used for the Bear Flag Revolt in 1846. The Bear Flag Inn sits on three acres, surrounded by vineyard and meadowed hillside. Four rooms are in the two-story house; the cottage is a detached unit with a sitting room. All have private baths. There is a swimming pool and an outdoor hot tub for guests.

Foothill House
$$$$$ • 3037 Foothill Blvd., Calistoga
• (707) 942-6933, (800) 942-6933

One of Calistoga's most renowned B&Bs sits in a woodsy setting on the northwest outskirts of town. Fountains and cascades lend a soothing air, and views to Mount St. Helena help to keep you oriented as you sit in the arbor or Jacuzzi. The interiors are impeccable—with hand-picked antiques and handmade quilts complementing the Laura Ashley designs—and as expansive as you are likely to find. Each room includes TV and VCR, CD player, refrigerator and fireplace or wood stove. Three of the four have whirlpool tubs. Each has its strengths, but the Quails Roost, a detached cottage just up the hillside, is clearly the palatial unit. The owners, Gus and Doris Beckert, call this their "event room." Quiet and private, the Quails Roost has a full kitchen and a washer/dryer setup; guests have been known to book it for a week and go into hiding. (If you are bringing children, please book the Foothill Cottage.) Doris, trained as a chef, oversees breakfast and the afternoon "wine appreciation hour."

Hillcrest B&B
$$$, no credit cards • 3225 Lake Co. Hwy., Calistoga • (707) 942-6334

From Calif. 29 (a.k.a. Lake County Highway) as it begins to wind up Mt. St. Helena, look for the twin stone pillars and drive to the end of the rutted quarter-mile driveway. The owner, Debbie O'Gorman, is the great-great-granddaughter of Senator Tubbs, who constructed Chateau Montelena on the valley floor (see our Wineries chapter), and this property has been in her family since 1860. Views from the house, especially from the big-paned windows of the living room, are superb. Be apprised that the mood here is *extremely* casual. Guests come and go as they please and are often left with a free run of the premises. Hillcrest has a fishing pond, hiking paths, a swimming pool and outdoor Jacuzzi, and a barbecue area. There are six rooms—three have private bathrooms and balconies, one has a bathroom but no balcony and two share both bath and balcony. All of them have fireplaces. Children and dogs are accepted. Credit cards are not, but you can write a personal check.

Sonoma County

Southern Sonoma

The Cottage
$$$$ • 302 First St. E., Sonoma • (707) 996-5220

Located on a quiet street a block off the Plaza, The Cottage invites visitors into its courtyards, which include fountains and a seating area. A nearby six-person hot tub is available to all guests. But we're getting ahead of ourselves. Five of the rooms open onto the courtyards, and five have their own private outdoor spaces. The Cottage offers one studio and two suites. The studio has a cathedral ceiling, and five of the units include fireplaces.

Thistle Dew Inn
$$$$ • 171 W. Spain St., Sonoma • (707) 938-2909

This is a prime location for Wine Country visitors. Just a half-block off the Sonoma Plaza, the Thistle Dew puts guests within walking distance (or biking distance, if you want to borrow from the inn's stable) of fine restaurants, shops, wineries and historic sites. The living room invites guests to sit by the fireplace, read a book or work on a jigsaw puzzle, and the six guest rooms manage to provide a feeling of seclusion and privacy in spite of the fact that the inn is on busy Sonoma street on the edge of downtown. Breakfast is served in the dining room looking out on Spain Street. All rooms have private baths, and some have whirlpool baths or ornamental fireplaces.

Victorian Garden Inn
$$$ • 316 E. Napa St., Sonoma • (707) 996-5339

It's a farmhouse built in 1870, but the growth of the city has left this inn within blocks of the downtown plaza. The wraparound porch with wicker chairs could make you believe the past is present. But it's the gardens that make this inn unique. Lawns and paths wind through the trees and along the creek, with occasional spots to sit and contemplate. The four guest rooms—one in the main house and the rest in a century-old water tower—have private baths and are elegantly decorated. Woodcutter's Cottage is a private retreat with a fireplace, claw-foot tub and garden view. Breakfast is served in the dining room, on the patio or in your room.

Trojan Horse Inn
$$$$ • 19455 Calif. Hwy. 12, Sonoma • (707) 996-2430, (800) 899-1925

Rebuilt after a tragic fire in 1990, this inn has turned into a charming B&B decorated with English and French antiques, a fact you'll especially appreciate if you join other guests for complimentary wine and hors d'oeuvres between 6 and 7 PM. Each of its six rooms has a different theme, decorated individually. Especially popular is the room called Grape Arbor, boasting a fireplace and double Jacuzzi, but all rooms are furnished with antiques of the 1880s era, when the original house was built. Children older than 12 are welcome with advance notice, but be advised: This inn is recommended in the book *Best Places to Kiss By in the Bay Area*. A full breakfast is served along the lines of French toast or banana pancakes, lemon chicken sausage, fresh fruit and Starbucks coffee.

Above the Clouds
$$$$$ • 3250 Trinity Rd., Glen Ellen • (707) 996-7371

The mountain road called Oakville Grade (up Trinity Road on the Sonoma side) straddles the Mayacamas Mountains that rise between the Sonoma and Napa valleys. Trinity Road sprouts from Calif. 12 about 8 miles north of the Sonoma Plaza, and winds through thickets of manzanita and scrub oaks for 3 miles before reaching Above the Clouds bed and breakfast inn. While the inn may not be exactly "above the clouds," it certainly is above everything else: It's a secluded mountain retreat that surveys forests and catches the sunset. Three guest rooms are furnished with antique iron or brass beds, and each has a private bath, queen bed, down comforters and lots of pillows. Robes are provided for those who want to take advantage of the swimming pool and Jacuzzi spa. A gourmet breakfast is served. You should book well in advance.

Beltane Ranch
**$$$$ • 11775 Calif. Hwy. 12, Glen Ellen
• (707) 996-6501**

The place has an exotic—even romantic—past. The land was first settled in 1882 by Mary Ann "Mammy" Pleasant, whose exploits as a madam to San Francisco's upper crust (plus suspicions of a possible homicide in her posh establishment) had led to alarming headlines. It was said she conducted black magic sessions too. But Mammy had another side: She became known as "the western terminus" of the Underground Railroad, making frequent trips to the South to secretly help thousands of blacks escape to Canada.

Beltane Ranch's architectural style suggests Deep South, with a stylish veranda set off with an elaborate gingerbread railing. But the Ranch's recent past is more mundane. In the 1920s it was the bunkhouse for a turkey ranch. Inside there are six guest rooms (including one cottage), each with an individual outdoor entrance. The rooms are rustic but cozy, furnished with antiques. The 1,600 acres include a working vineyard, and the owner is happy to tour the grounds with you and explain what viticulture is all about. The grapes are sold to Kenwood Vineyards (see our Wineries chapter).

A full breakfast is served, and it may include omelettes and homemade scones served on your own veranda or in the garden. This is a popular lodging place, and reservations are definitely recommended during the harvest season of August through October.

Gaige House Inn
**$$$$$ • 13540 Arnold Dr., Glen Ellen
• (707) 935-0237**

An elegant Italianate Victorian, restored from its original 1880s construction and recently refurbished, Gaige House Inn has a prime location at the edge of the village of Glen Ellen in the heart of Wine Country. It has six guest rooms and one suite in the main house, and eight garden rooms with outside entrances. The signature room is the Gaige Suite, a spacious sunny room with large windows on three sides and a wraparound deck overlooking the garden. You'll awake in your four-poster bed and step into a bathroom that's larger than most bedrooms. The creekside setting includes a large swimming pool and Jacuzzi. A formal breakfast is included, as are afternoon hor d'oeuvres and beverages.

Glenelly Inn
**$$$ • 5131 Warm Springs Rd., Glen Ellen
• (707) 996-6720**

This is one of the few Wine Country bed and breakfast inns that was actually built as an inn. Visitors of the 1920s and '30s came by railroad and basked in the sun on the inn's long verandas. The long verandas are still there, now with wicker chairs to provide a perch to watch the sun set over the Sonoma Mountains. Each of the eight rooms has a private entrance. They are furnished in a country motif, with antique furniture and Scandinavian down comforters. The Jack London Room has a sleigh bed and wood-burning stove, and all rooms have claw-foot tubs and antique sinks. An outdoor spa is set amid native landscaping. In the morning, a full breakfast is served in the common room by a large cobblestone fireplace. It's a great experience, with hot entrees, homemade bread and muffins, fresh fruit and fresh-squeezed orange juice.

Tanglewood House
**$$$$ • 250 Bonnie Way, Glen Ellen
• (707) 996-5021**

On a quiet country road a mile from Glen Ellen, Tanglewood House is a retreat occupying more than an acre of park-like, secluded gardens. Only one room is available—a large luxurious suite that occupies an entire wing of this lovely house. It has its own private entrance and patio and a spacious sitting room with fireplace, cathedral ceiling and color TV. A magnificent pool is available to guests, and there is a full breakfast in the morning.

Cavanagh Inn
**$$ • 10 Keller St., Petaluma
• (707) 765-4657**

There's a feeling of turn-of-the century elegance here that few modern houses achieve.

It was built for lumberman John Cavanagh in 1902, a time when his company was known for providing some of the finest rare heart-red-wood available. His house paneling shows he picked the best of what he had for his residence. The mansion's four bedrooms are furnished in Victorian style, though one of them has a special addition Cavanagh wouldn't believe—a tub with a whirlpool ready to froth with bubble bath.

There's a three-bedroom cottage beside the main house, built for two Cavanagh sisters. Bedrooms here are less formal, furnished with wicker, and two of the three rooms share a bath. Owners Ray and Jeanne Farris tell guests they can park their cars and forget them—the inn is within walking distance of most everything they'll want to visit, including Petaluma's historic district with its antique shops. Jeanne's love of cooking shows in her breakfast offerings. A typical morning might include pears in butterscotch sauce and fluffy scrambled eggs topped with crab and seafood sauce.

Goltermann Gardens & Country Inn
$$$$ • 1000 Skillman Ln., Petaluma
• (707) 762-1761

In northwest Petaluma's Leghorn Valley, Goltermann Gardens is a romantic country retreat. This rural farmhouse estate, set on more than 7 acres, was once home to 10,000 white Leghorn laying hens. The Goltermanns have turned the family farm into an elegant inn. Lush landscaping with mature trees, lawns and a lake allows you the freedom to enjoy fishing, horseshoes, croquet and hiking. Five spacious suites that include king or queen beds, fine linens and elegant bathroom fixtures offer an opportunity to enjoy a relaxing, pampered stay—for days or for weeks. This is also a popular site for romantic weddings and receptions, with a wisteria-covered pergola as a dance pavilion. A two-day minimum is required. This is one of those fabulous properties that's not so easy to categorize—the type mentioned in this chapter's introduction.

The Gables Inn
$$$$ • 4257 Petaluma Hill Rd., Santa Rosa
• (707) 585-7777

Built in 1877 at the height of Victorian Gothic Revival architecture, this home was built with 15 gables rising above some unique keyhole-shaped windows. There are seven rooms in the main house, five up a mahogany staircase, and two accessible to disabled guests, some of which include fireplaces, and all of which share central

air conditioning. Each room is furnished in unique decor that displays its history and character; each has a claw-foot tub in its private bath. An adjacent cottage is furnished with a kitchenette, TV with video library, stereo, woodstove, two-person whirlpool tub and private phone/data port. A lavish country breakfast is served. A large sundeck looks out across acres of country just outside Santa Rosa.

Melitta Station Inn
$$ • 5850 Melita Rd., Santa Rosa
• (707) 538-7712

Once this was a busy railroad station; before that it was a general store and post office. Today it's a warm inn with six guest rooms (five if the two-room suite is opened) furnished with antiques and folk art. The inn's former life is evident in its unique plank flooring and hand-sawed fir boards with the sawyer's strokes still well-marked. The style here is American antique, with lots of collectibles to admire. The setting is part of the charm: The inn is surrounded by state parks, hiking trails and biking opportunities. A full buffet breakfast is served by the wood-burning stove in the large sitting room on the balcony.

Pygmalion House
$$ • 331 Orange St., Santa Rosa
• (707) 526-3407

It was built in 1880 down near Railroad Square, where Santa Rosa had its beginnings. Now this Queen Anne home has been restored to a bed and breakfast inn of five rooms, all with private baths featuring showers and claw-foot tubs. It's furnished with pieces that include Gypsy Rose Lee antiques and memorabilia. Decorated in the European style, the parlor has a fireplace, TV and telephone. There's a private garden and parking behind the inn. A hearty breakfast and afternoon treats are served.

Country Meadow Inn
$$$$ • 11360 Old Redwood Hwy.,
Windsor • (707) 431-1276

This inn is a farmhouse from the 1890s in a setting of grape arbors, vegetable gardens, fruit trees and terraced flower beds. This is not your granddad's farmhouse—it's elegant and charming with private baths, whirlpool tubs and air conditioning. Outside there's a tennis court and swimming pool. Yet the farming influence is not forgotten: Breakfast abounds with farm-fresh eggs, preserves made from homegrown fruits and berries and fresh baked breads and pastries. Five romantic, country-style guest rooms are furnished in antiques or wicker; three have fireplaces and one has a whirlpool. The Garden Suite is a truly romantic hideaway with a separate sitting area.

Northern Sonoma

Belle de Jour Inn
$$$$$ • 16276 Healdsburg Ave., Healdsburg • (707) 431-9777

This inn's hilltop setting is on 6 acres and looks out on rolling hills. The farmhouse, a single-story Italianate built around 1873, is the residence of the innkeepers, and it is here guests enjoy a hearty breakfast. Guests are quartered in five white cottages, all with fireplaces and some with decks. Each cottage is its own country experience. The Caretaker Suite, for instance, has a king-size, canopy bed and a fireplace in the sitting room. There's a sunny studio atelier room with a high, vaulted ceiling, and the grand Carriage House that has everything, including views and tub for two.

Camellia Inn
$$ • 211 North St., Healdsburg • (707) 433-8182

The inn is overtaken by blooming camellias from November to May, hence the name. Built in 1869, the house served at one time as Healdsburg's first hospital, and in fact, the room you rent might have been the lab. There have been a few other incarnations since then, but the Lewants (Ray, Del and daughter Lucy) run a friendly and efficient operation with nine rooms. As a plus, the Camellia Inn is just two blocks from historic Healdsburg Plaza and its chic shops and boutiques. When you return to your room from your excursions you might recuperate from the rigors of shopping in your whirlpool tub for two, light up the gas fireplace if you're chilly and have a lovely night's sleep in your four-poster bed. The Camellia Inn includes a family suite—unusual in an industry largely geared toward couples.

Breakfast is served buffet style, with a selection of entrees and breads that will keep your energy up until noon (maybe later!). Sometimes it's quiche on breakfast custard, and it's always accompanied with fruit, cereal, sourdough toast and homemade jam. Bon appetit!

George Alexander House
$$$$ • 423 Matheson St., Healdsburg • (707) 433-1358

This historic house was built in 1905 by George Alexander, the 10th child of Cyrus Alexander. Cyrus was the first settler in the north county, and Alexander Valley is named for him (see our History chapter). There are four rooms in this lovely inn, which has "gone upscale" in the last couple of years under its energetic new owner, Don Krohn. The Alexander room has a fireplace and bay windows, while the Back Porch has a private entrance with a deck, wood-burning stove and whirlpool tub for two. If you're hungry for a hearty breakfast, you'll be happy to see such menu items as ricotta pancakes with sauteed apples. Two spacious parlors are available to guests, as is the sauna in the new garden. Stay two nights (a minimum on weekends) and get a bottle of wine.

Grape Leaf Inn
$$ • 539 Johnson St., Healdsburg • (707) 433-8140

The seven elegant guest rooms in this 1900 Queen Anne Victorian are a perfect backdrop for romance. Each room is named for a wine varietal, and all are lushly furnished with iron beds, armoires and warm oak accents. The four upstairs rooms will put you in a honeymoon mood with tubs for two. Most luxurious is the Chardonnay suite, with cedar wood walls and stained-glass windows. In the evening you can enjoy a glass of wine with a tray of cheese and bread. Grape Leaf Inn is near shopping, restaurants, wineries, golf, tennis, fishing, ballooning and canoe rentals. After a busy day about town and country, you can relax on the front porch. Breakfast is served in style in the dining room. The inn is known for its daily wine tasting presentation, offering seven varietals.

Haydon Street Inn
$$ • 321 Haydon St., Healdsburg • (707) 433-5228

In a quiet residential area within walking distance of Healdsburg's historic plaza, this Victorian inn has eight charming guest rooms. One of the most popular is the Turret Room, tucked into the slope of the roof, with a step-down entrance to the sleeping level. Each of the other rooms is distinctively different in decor, from iron bedsteads and handmade rugs to French antique furnishings. Six of the guest rooms are in the main house, a 1912 Queen Anne structure, and two are in the adjoining two-story Victorian cottage. The Garden Room has two walls of plantation-shuttered windows overlooking the garden. All rooms have private baths; those in the cottage also have double whirlpool tubs. If breakfast is your idea of the right start to the day, this is your place. You can get fired up for a full, energetic Wine Country adventure with scones slathered with orange butter, frittatas, croissants, French toast, quiches, fresh-baked breads, oven-roasted potatoes, meat side dishes—plus an aromatic house-blend coffee. When guests return from their ramblings, they'll be greeted with a snack treat to tide them over to dinner.

Healdsburg Inn on the Plaza
$$$$$ • 110 Matheson St., Healdsburg
• (707) 433-6991

The front entrance is unpretentious enough, but it opens onto a handsome art gallery. A staircase leads to the 10 antique-filled rooms—most with fireplaces, all with private baths, some with whirlpool tubs for two. Once a Wells Fargo building, the inn now rates high on the luxury scale. A solarium in the roof garden is the common area where guests meet for breakfast and afternoon refreshments, when wine and fresh buttered popcorn, coffee, tea and a bottomless cookie jar are available.

Honor Mansion
$$$$$ • 14891 Grove St., Healdsburg
• (707) 433-4277

The architecture, decor and surrounding gardens give this inn a feeling of turn-of-the-century grace. You can almost imagine women in ankle-length frocks carrying on polite conversation with gentlemen in tennis sweaters as they stroll along the garden path. Its eight guest rooms are furnished with antiques and feather beds, and each has a private bath. The place has a fascinating history, and the innkeeper will be glad to regale you with the life of the Squire Butcher family over a breakfast of home-baked pastries and gourmet entrees.

Madrona Manor
$$$$$ • 1001 Westside Rd., Healdsburg
• (707) 433-4231

Tucked away in the lush Dry Creek Valley, Madrona Manor is an estate for which adjectives like elegant and majestic were invented. Originally built in 1880 by business tycoon John Paxton, Madrona Knoll Rancho, as it was then called, became one of the grandest showplaces in all the valley. Today it stands as a wonderful exponent of a bygone era of grandeur and refined taste. The Manor's accommodations include 21 rooms in four buildings on 8 acres of wooded and manicured grounds. Seventeen of the rooms have fireplaces, and eight have a balcony or deck. A buffet-style breakfast is included. Need more elegance? World-class gourmet dining can be enjoyed each evening in a romantic candlelight setting.

Midnight Sun Inn
$$$ • 428 Haydon St., Healdsburg
• (707) 433-1718

Somewhat different from many bed and breakfast inns, Midnight Sun is decorated in a modern country style, with almost no antique decor. The linens are top-of-the-line, as are the beds and mattresses. There are three guest rooms in the main house: "Juliet's Balcony" invites a second-story stroll across the entire front of the house. Inside, there's a canopy bed to stretch out in. The other two rooms are the Enchanted Garden Room and the Safari Room. The latter has jungle-patterned sheets and mosquito net for atmosphere. There's also a cottage in the back yard; it has a Wine Country theme, and is said to be the most romantic room of all. Both the Garden Room and Juliet's Balcony have Jacuzzis for two.

Villa Messina
$$$$$ • 316 Burgundy Rd., Healdsburg
• (707) 433-6655

The setting is unbelievable, with a 360-degree view of three exquisite valleys—Alexander, Dry Creek and Russian River. The Italian villa-style inn was built in 1986 on top of the foundation of a former water tower. The inn's five guest rooms are furnished with antiques, and the floors are carpeted with Oriental rugs. All have private baths, plus TVs, VCRs and phones. Some have Jacuzzis or fireplaces. For breakfast the chef prepares such treats as fresh-squeezed orange juice and blueberry pancakes with bacon. He also bakes his own breads. There is a swimming pool and hot tub. Kids are discouraged, but babies are okay.

Hope-Bosworth House
$$$ • 21238 Geyserville Ave., Geyserville
• (707) 857-3356

Driving down Geyserville Avenue, you'll have no trouble instantly recognizing the Hope-Bosworth House—it's the Queen Anne with the picket fence covered with "roses of yesteryear"—varieties that were popular when the house was built in 1904. George Bosworth picked out the pattern for his home from a "pattern book" and had it constructed entirely of heart redwood.

All the rooms are a step into the past. The original oak-grained woodwork is evident everywhere, from the sliding doors in the hallway to the upstairs bedrooms. Polished fir floors and antique light fixtures enhance the period furnishing. At 9 AM a country breakfast is served in the formal dining room and includes fresh fruit, egg dishes, homemade breads and pastries and coffee or tea.

Hope-Merrill House
$$$ • 21253 Geyserville Ave., Geyserville • (707) 857-3356

In its former life, it was a stagecoach stop of the 1870s. Now it's an enchanting inn, listed on the Sonoma County Landmarks Register. Anyone interested in architecture will recognize the squared-off look of Eastlake Stick Style, popular between 1870 and 1885. J.P. Merrill, who was a land developer, saw to it he had the best of everything for his house, and he built it entirely of redwood. The Inn has eight rooms with charming names like Bachelor Button, Peacock and Carpenter Gothic, all with queen beds and private baths. Four rooms have fireplaces, two have whirlpool baths and one has a sitting room. Please take note of the restored Victorian hand-screened wallpaper—it's stunning! Breakfast is superb, served in the dining room. There's a swimming pool.

Abrams House Inn
$$ • 314 N. Main St., Cloverdale • (707) 894-2412

A restored 1870s Victorian, Abrams House Inn offers four guest rooms, one of them a special suite with a four-poster bed and private porch. There are also three parlors, two with TV and VCR, the other a library/game room. A wicker-decorated upper deck gives a lovely view of a rose garden, gazebo and a deck with a hot tub. And for those who simply must bring business with them, there's a fax machine and copier available. Breakfast is ample (to put it mildly), and in the evening you can enjoy a decadent dessert with Abrams House's own specially blended hot cocoa.

Mountain House Winery and Lodge
$$$$ • 33710 Hwy. 128, Cloverdale • (707) 894-5683

In its former life, Mountain House was a stagecoach stop and inn, flanked by a barn and some outbuildings. Now this 1890s-era homestead has been converted to a bed and breakfast inn, operating in conjunction with Mountain House's newly established winery. Accommodations at Mountain House include three suites (all with fireplaces) at the top of the winery building, three suites in the inn, and four cottages next to a lake, three of them one-bedroom and one two-bedroom—a great bonus for families. There is a spa too.

In the morning, you can look forward to quiche or other hot breakfast specialties and fruit in season. This is a great place to get married or to have a conference, if that's your inclination. The banquet room and tasting room (with full kitchen available to caterers) provides a grand background for either occasion.

Vintage Towers Inn
$$$ • 302 Main St., Cloverdale • (707) 894-4535

Mining executive Simon Pinchower had an unusual idea when he asked an architect to design him a Queen Anne house in 1913. He wanted three towers, all built in different shapes—one round, one square and one octagonal—so his house would be different than its neighbors.

Pinchower is long gone, but his legacy has given travelers a fine way to find their way to Vintage Towers Inn. Each of the three tower suites has its own sitting area, sleeping quarters and private bath. Three of the other five rooms also have private baths, and two share a conveniently located bath. The wide front veranda's porch swing is a pleasant place to relax after a day of touring the countryside. A hearty breakfast can be expected.

Sonoma Coast

Bay Hill Mansion
$$$$$ • 3919 Bay Hill Rd., Bodega Bay • (707) 875-3577

Recently built in the Queen Anne Victorian style, this new inn is perched on the coastal hills of Calif. Highway 1 and affords a full, sweeping, panoramic view encompassing everything from Marin County's Point Reyes to Jenner, on the Russian River to the north. Beyond that, there's the bay itself. For a unique experience, watch the harbor lights from the soothing warmth of the hot tub. Five elegant guest rooms are available, furnished with antiques, cozy down comforters and elegant pastel wallpaper with a 1900s motif. There is also a comfortable parlor perfect for fireside chats while guests enjoy an evening glass of wine and hors d'oeuvres. A gourmet breakfast makes the morning beautiful—nothing could go wrong on a day that starts with French toast made with homemade cinnamon bread.

Photo: The Blue Violet Mansion

The Blue Violet Mansion, built in 1886, sits on spacious grounds filled with trees, flowers and shrubs.

West County/Russian River

The Inn at Occidental
$$$$$ • 3657 Church St., Occidental
• (707) 874-1047

This inn is the type of romantic getaway where the main thing guests want is an opportunity just to be together. Jack Bullard, owner of The Inn, is a lifelong collector of fine art and antiques. The result for guests is that each of the 16 rooms is decorated with meticulous care in a theme related to a specific piece of art. The effect is that of a gallery with beds—a showplace in the rugged hills of western Sonoma County. Each of the rooms (including the eight-room expansion completed in 1999) has a private bath. One room is outfitted for wheelchair access, and all but one have fireplaces and decks. The new units have double spa tubs and views to the courtyard. A full breakfast is included.

The Farmhouse Inn
$$$$ • 7871 River Rd., Forestville
• (707) 887-3300

In 1878 it really was a working farm, with a row of cottages off to the side for the workers. Now it's a country inn by the side of the road,

and the workers' cottages have become charming private guest rooms with amenities the farm workers never dreamed could exist. All but one of the eight guest rooms has a sauna, and all but one boasts a fireplace. Some are furnished in natural wicker, some in brown wicker and many have brass beds. But above all, the place is designed for guest comfort and not filled with knick-knacks that occupy the space guests need to use.

This is only one of four country inns in the county that has a public restaurant, and it is here that breakfast is served each morning to the inn's guests. The Farmhouse also features "The Barn" events center, where business events and weddings can be held. The Barn can accommodate 100 guests.

Ridenhour Ranch House Inn
$$ • 12850 River Rd., Guerneville
• (707) 887-1033

Louis Ridenhour came to this land in 1850 and began farming 940 acres of land along the Russian River. This house, however, was not built until 1906. What guests find today is a large living room overlooking redwoods, and eight guest rooms, each with a private bath. One of them, Hawthorne Cottage, has a fireplace and cozy window seat. Korbel Champagne Cellars is within walking distance (see our Wineries chapter), and the Russian River is five minutes away by foot. Breakfast is ample.

Applewood Inn
$$$$ • 13555 Hwy. 116, Guerneville • (707) 869-9093

Sixteen stylish rooms and suites fill three multi-story Mediterranean-style villas set among apple orchards and redwood trees. Each is individually decorated, romantic and formal, yet familiar—like the home of a wealthy great-aunt you may have visited. This is no stuffy Victorian museum piece; it feels like a private home. The newer rooms have fireplaces, sitting areas, private verandas or decks, and either couples showers or Jacuzzi baths for two. The common area is centered around a huge stone fireplace. A new restaurant seats 50. The kitchen, once reserved for breakfast, now offers dinner Tuesday to Saturday.

Fern Grove Cottages
$$$ • 16650 Hwy. 116, Guerneville • (707) 869-8105

A small, quaint village of 22 romantic cottages, Fern Grove Inn provides a stylish country atmosphere and a base for exploring the back roads of the neighborhood. Cottages range from spacious one-bedroom suites to intimate guest rooms with sitting areas. All have a refrigerator; some have fireplaces or spas. Stroll the gardens, swim in the pool, feel romantic in general! The buffet breakfast features homemade pastries.

Mendocino County

U.S. Highway 101

Thatcher Inn
$$ • 13401 U.S. Hwy. 101 S., Hopland • (707) 744-1890, (800) 266-1891

It stands like a sentinel of the past—the hotel you've seen in a hundred Western movies, elegant as it was the day it was built in 1890. A carpeted stairway leads from the lobby to the 20 rooms on the two floors above, which are richly furnished and individually decorated with brass and iron beds and period furnishings. The handsome bar lounge is straight out of *Gunsmoke*. But if the decor is of yesteryear, the amenities are strictly modern (as in bathrooms and air conditioning). Thatcher Inn sits in the heart of Mendocino wine country, close

to redwood forests and hiking trails. An outdoor pool provides the background for patio dining, and it's here that breakfast is served, weather permitting.

Fetzer Valley Oaks Bed & Breakfast
$$$ • 13601 Eastside Rd., Hopland • (707) 744-1250

Located in the Fetzer Vineyards complex of tasting room and organic gardens is a charming 10-room bed and breakfast inn, housed in the ranch's original carriage house. Each room is beautifully appointed and features panoramic views of the surrounding vineyards (or organic gardens) from a private patio. The interiors are country casual, with overstuffed chairs pulled up to large coffee tables in the sitting rooms. All guests enjoy continental breakfast and access to a secluded pool. Two master suites have whirlpool tubs in their oversized bathrooms, separate bedrooms, large sitting rooms and small kitchens. (For more on the Fetzer complex, see our Wineries chapter.)

Calif. Highway 128

Anderson Creek Inn
$$$ • 12050 Anderson Valley Way, Boonville • (707) 895-3091

This inn is a rambling ranch house set on 16 acres at the junction of two creeks, with views of the hills beyond. Each of its spacious and spotless five rooms offers a different view and feeling, and each has a private bath, king bed and complimentary bottle of local wine. Two rooms have fireplaces, and one has a Franklin stove. The friendly family livestock includes llamas, sheep, horses and a goat. Come in March and see the newborn lambs! Breakfast is a special event and is served in the courtyard, weather permitting.

Pinoli Ranch Country Inn
$$ • 3280 Clark Rd., Philo • (707) 895-2550

This is the place to get away from it all—to experience total peace and tranquility. The inn is a mile off the main highway through Anderson Valley (Calif. 128) and is peacefully secluded, nestled on 100 acres with incomparable views of the entire valley. Guests can cycle around the quiet country roads, ride horses or visit some of the dozen or more wineries in the area. The inn has three guest rooms, two with private baths, but the draw here is the remote great outdoors. One recent entry in the guest book: "A real plus is that it is so far off the road." A country-style breakfast is served, and well-mannered children are welcome.

Mendocino Coast

Whale Watch Inn
$$$$$ • 35100 Calif. Hwy. 1, Gualala
• (707) 884-3667
It would be hard to imagine a more stylish setting for whale watching than the Whale Watch Inn. Perched on a cliff's edge 5 miles north of Gualala, this charming complex of five buildings is set on 2 acres of woods and gardens. There are 18 rooms and suites, most with whirlpool tubs and all with fireplaces, private decks and awesome views of the rocky, cypress-clad coast and the soul-soothing sea. The inn's decor slants toward contemporary rather than traditional, elegant instead of woodsy. Romance is the calling card here. Televisions and telephones have been banned from all rooms. Leave the laptop at home, and be prepared for some serious creature comforts. Breakfast is hearty: fresh seasonal fruits, freshly baked pastries and an entree that changes daily, all delivered to your private deck.

Wharf Master's Inn
$$$$ • 785 Port Rd., Point Arena
• (707) 882-3171
When Point Arena bustled with sailors hauling lumber and fish to supply California's Gold Rush, the wharf master had only to step onto his porch to make sure all was proceeding in an orderly fashion in the harbor below. The view is much more peaceful these days. The 120-year-old Victorian and several newer buildings together form the Wharf Master's Inn, an accommodation that is hard to pigeonhole. The tariffs vary dramatically here, from $95 for a standard room with a balcony and queen bed, to $175 for a more optimally placed (and wheelchair-accessible) unit, to $225 for the sublime Eastlake suite. All of the 23 rooms have feather beds, private baths and TVs, and most have fireplaces and spa tubs. Please note that the inn does not serve breakfast; we just couldn't bring ourselves to call it a motel.

Glendeven
$$$$ • 8205 N. Calif. Hwy. 1, Little River
• (707) 937-0083
Named for a Scottish grand estate, Glendeven consists of 10 rooms in three separate buildings, one containing an art gallery. The gallery is a showplace for 10 local artists and craftspeople. The central building was a farmhouse from 1867 until the late 1930s. Names of some of the rooms give an idea of their locale and decor—Carriage House Suite, Farmhouse Garret, Bayloft. The mood is of casual elegance. It's light and spacious. All rooms have private baths, and most have fireplaces. Wine is served by the fireplace in the sitting room, to the tinkling music of the baby grand. Breakfast is generous and will be delivered to your room should the fancy strike.

Rachel's Inn
$$$$ • 8200 N. Hwy. 1, Little River
• (707) 937-0088
Rachel's Inn—which borders 2,160-acre Van Damme State Park and its wooded hills sloping toward the sea (see our Parks and Recreation chapter)—opened in 1984 after a massive remodeling job. The results are striking. The inn is surrounded by informal gardens and century-old cypress trees. Cliffs overlooking the ocean are just a stroll away. A lane behind the inn leads to the beach. Each of the 10 rooms is tastefully appointed but also different from the rest. The morning meal is also different. Rachel is a gourmet cook whose breakfasts show why she is so highly regarded for her culinary skills.

Seafoam Lodge
$$$ • 6751 N. Hwy. 1, Little River
• (707) 937-1827, (800) 606-1827
The lodge has eight separate buildings offering a total of 24 guest accommodations and a conference center. A forested hillside provides the backdrop for the lodge, which is perched on 6 acres of coastal gardens and pines above the inlet of Buckhorn Cove. Guests can look forward to panoramic ocean views and breathtaking sunsets from every private room. You'll have a front-row seat to the unfolding drama of sea and sky. Some rooms have kitchens, some have fireplaces, and all have VCRs. Two spas let you en-

BED AND BREAKFAST INNS

INSIDERS' TIP
Husbands have been known to get dragged, kicking and grumbling, into B&Bs. If this is your man, he might settle for Cedar Gables Inn in Napa. "Cute" is definitely not the word for it. There are vintage motorcycles in the living room, and the evening wine and cheese even switches to popcorn and beer during ABC's *Monday Night Football*.

joy the outdoor space. The Crows Nest Conference Center, with its magnificent ocean view, will accommodate up to 50 guests—perfect for business meetings, seminars, family reunions and wedding receptions. A continental breakfast is delivered to your room each morning. Pets and children are welcome.

Stevenswood Lodge
$$$$ • 8211 N. Hwy. 1, Little River
• (707) 937-2810

There could scarcely be a more enchanting setting than this lodge enjoys, surrounded on three sides by 2,160 acres of Van Damme State Park forest and within a short walk of the ocean, Fern Canyon and the headlands. The mood here is decidedly upscale, with nine one-bedroom suites and one guest room (with handicapped access) that overlooks the gardens. All the room options have beckoning views, cozy wood-burning fireplaces, spacious private baths and stocked honor bars. Breakfast is a gourmet delight to remember, and there is now an on-site restaurant.

The Victorian Farmhouse
$$$ • 7001 N. Calif. Hwy. 1, Little River
• (707) 937-0697, (800) 264-4723

How charming is this bluff-top house south of Mendocino? Thomas Kincaid, the commercial master of "picturesque," chose it as the subject of his painting, *Home Is Where the Heart Is, #2*. Your heart could definitely end up here, on a two-acre parcel bordered by a creek on the south. The house was built in 1877 by John Dennen, whose grandson would later buy Pullen Farm and turn it into Heritage House (see our Spas and Resorts chapter). The Victorian Farmhouse has no ocean views, but Buckhorn Cove—a public beach that feels quite private—is a five-minute walk. There are four rooms in the old structure, and six more split between two separate buildings. Seven of the units have fireplaces; two have double spa tubs. A full breakfast is served in-room, and co-owner Jo Bradley will cater to your dietary needs, adding to an overall feeling of attentive comfort.

Elk Cove Inn
$$$$ • 6300 S. Calif. Hwy. 1, Elk
• (707) 877-3321

Tucked away beneath enveloping foliage, secluded high atop a bluff overlooking nearly a mile of coastline, is the Elk Cove Inn. Built in 1883 as an executive guest house for a lumber company, this beachfront retreat captures the essence of peace and tranquility. "Room with a

view" would be an understatement here. Massive windows bring dramatic, panoramic views and the unspoiled beauty of the outdoors to each of the 14 large accommodation options (six rooms, four cottages and four luxury suites). A trail leads down to the beach, and an outdoor hot tub leads to tranquility. A multi-course gourmet breakfast is served daily in the oceanfront dining room.

Harbor House
$$$$$ • 5600 S. Hwy. 1, Elk
• (707) 877-3203

The main building of this inn was built in 1916 by the Goodyear Redwood Lumber Company as an executive residence and for the lodging and entertainment of company guests. Situated on a bluff overlooking Greenwood Landing, Harbor House is a sanctuary for relaxation and privacy that is reminiscent of a leisurely, romantic era.

The 10 guest rooms reflect the decor of those bygone days. A path descends the bluff, with benches placed along the way to a private beach below. A sumptuous breakfast and four-course dinner are included in the price. Products are all from local sources. In addition to homegrown vegetables, the cuisine includes naturally raised meats and cheeses from nearby farms. Rooms in the main building and adjacent cottages are individually heated and have private baths.

Sandpiper House Inn
$$$$ • 5520 S. Hwy. 1, Elk
• (707) 877-3587

In 1916 when the house was built, Elk was a bustling harbor where schooners loaded redwood for the San Francisco market. This house was also built by Goodyear Redwood Lumber Company. The gray, shingled inn is decidedly unpretentious, though it was then one of the finest homes in town. It's when you step inside that you realize its classic elegance. Coffered ceilings and raised panel walls are examples of the craftsmanship of the era. Its five rooms are tastefully appointed in the style of a European country inn, decorated with antiques, comfy chairs, fresh flowers and down comforters. All have private baths. Look forward to a breakfast of crepes and sausages served in an elegant style on a lace tablecloth that's brightened with a bouquet of fresh flowers.

Fensalden Inn
$$$$ • 33810 Navarro Ridge Rd., Albion
• (707) 937-4042, (800) 959-3850

Once a Wells Fargo stagecoach way station,

Fensalden rests on 20 tree-lined, pastoral acres on a majestic ridge crest. At this 400-foot elevation, the ocean and meadow views are spectacular. The inn's eight rooms are divided between the main house, the water tower house and a separate bungalow, with three common rooms in the main building. One is a guest's office, one a parlor, and the third is the Tavern Room, a namesake common for way stations in the raucous Old West lifestyle. (If you can't sense the history, check out the bullet holes that pock the original ceiling.) In the evening, wine and hors d'oeuvres are served in this room, while guests chat and view the sunset over the Pacific. In the morning, a gourmet breakfast is also served there. There's a minimum two-night stay on weekends. Retreats, seminars, meetings, and weddings are invited.

Agate Cove Inn

$$$$ • 11201 N. Lansing St., Mendocino • (707) 937-0551

Agate Cove Inn was built as a farmhouse in 1860, and for the past few decades it was a comfortably funky inn with spectacular views. With breakfast cooked on an antique woodburning stove, its current incarnation still feels like a farmhouse. The views are still breathtaking too. But recent renovations have added some glamour to Agate Cove's farm-princess image. Many of the eight cottages and two farmhouse units feature oversize tubs and showers for two, fireplaces and huge beds with down comforters. Still down-home, however, are those breakfasts—hearty meals served with an unobstructed floor-to-ceiling view of the headlands and the waves crashing against the rocks.

Blair House

$$ • 45110 Little Lake St., Mendocino • (707) 937-1800, (800) 699-9296

This is perhaps the best-known home in Mendocino, because millions of people have seen it watching *Murder, She Wrote*. The show's producers used the exterior of Blair House as Jessica's Cabot Cove home. The house was built in 1888 for Elisha Blair, a railroad worker who graciously loaned money to his fellow workers, then turned his loan business into a career as a financier. The extensive use of virgin, clearheart redwood, now prohibitively expensive, is probably what has kept the house so wellpreserved. Four guest rooms are equipped with plush queen beds and handcrafted quilts. Angela's Suite is a two-room suite with 10-foot ceilings and bay windows that offer a view

of both the village and ocean. Three other guest rooms share a large bathroom in the hall. Breakfast is now served on-site.

Inn at Schoolhouse Creek

$$$$ • P.O. Box 1637, 7051 N. Hwy. 1, Mendocino • (707) 937-5525

The amenity guests appreciate most about this coastal inn is its eight surrounding acres of outdoor space, replete with tall cypress trees and an open meadow. The east end of the property leads to Schoolhouse Creek itself, and for beach-goers Buckhorn Cove is a short walk to the south. The staff here marvels at how the Inn has managed to preserve the feeling of what Mendocino and environs were like 25 years ago. The Inn was hoping to add two rooms by the summer of 2000, bringing the total to 15—nine freestanding cottages, two suites and four units in a small lodge. Some have ocean views. There's nothing new or high-tech here—an aspect that appeals to repeat visitors. Families are welcome, and dogs are allowed in some rooms. The Inn has a hot tub on the property, situated at the top of the meadow and with a sweeping ocean view.

John Dougherty House

$$$$ • 571 Ukiah St., Mendocino • (707) 937-5266, (800) 486-2104

Historic John Dougherty House, built in 1867, is one of the oldest houses in Mendocino. The main house is furnished with country antiques of the 1860s. Two guest rooms are in the main house, six more are in the adjoining cottages or historic water tower. All are individually decorated, accented with dried flower wreaths and fresh flowers from the garden. The Captain's Room has a private veranda. Upstairs, the First Mate's Room has hand-stenciled walls and antique pine furniture. Some rooms have four-poster beds and village views (the two newest units boast spectacular vistas); most have a small refrigerator and a wood-burning stove; four now feature jet tubs. Breakfast is served by a crackling fire in the New England-style keeping room.

Joshua Grindle Inn

$$$$ • 44800 Little Lake Rd., Mendocino • (707) 937-4143

Situated on 2 acres, this lovely home was built in 1879 by Joshua Grindle, who came from Maine to get into the booming lumber business and stayed on to become the town banker. The house features unmistakably New England-style architecture, and the decor of the inn is a reflection of the same early-American heritage. There are five rooms in the main house, two in the cottage and three in the water tower. Some have views of Mendocino and the ocean; others have wood-burning fireplaces. All have well-lighted, comfortably arranged sitting areas and private baths. Breakfast is a time to enjoy a delicious morning meal as well as conversation with other guests around the circa 1830 pine harvest table. Every morning offers a new treat, as the menu constantly changes. (The owners have produced a cookbook of breakfast menus.) The inn has received many honors, including *Focus* magazine's Inn of the Year award.

Mendocino Coast Reservations
$-$$$$$ • 1000 Main St., Mendocino
• (707) 937-5033, (800) 262-7801

Visitors who prefer a self-catered vacation will appreciate this home rental service offering a choice of residences—from stately Victorians to panoramic perches to cozy cottages tucked away in the woods—all fully furnished. You'll be expected to meet the two-night minimum (longer minimums may be in effect during peak season and holidays), and weekly rentals are available. Although availability may be limited, those without reservations are invited to drop in. As the price code indicates, a wide range of homes is available, from quaint and spartan to totally extravagant.

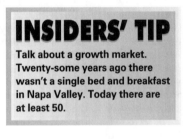

INSIDERS' TIP

Talk about a growth market. Twenty-some years ago there wasn't a single bed and breakfast in Napa Valley. Today there are at least 50.

Nicholson House
$$ • 951 Ukiah St., Mendocino
• (707) 937-0934, (800) 962-0934

Nicholson House, built in 1905 and located in the heart of Mendocino, was home to three generations of Nicholsons until 1976, when it was converted to an apartment and office building. Now it's a bed and breakfast, preserving much of the history and charm of the original house. There are seven plush rooms in all, and throughout the property guests can enjoy great views of the coast. For the more reflective, there's a pond.

Sea Gull Inn
$$ • 44960 Albion St., Mendocino
• (707) 937-5204, (888) 937-5204

Built in 1878, one of Mendocino's oldest standing houses is also one of its oldest continuous inns. The Sea Gull began welcoming tourists in the 1960s, and Marlene McIntyre has been the sole proprietor since 1986. (A resident with roots, she managed the Sea Gull Restaurant and Cellar Bar for 20 years before that.) The Sea Gull Inn is a cozy place with a profuse flower garden, a holly tree shading the front porch and a resident feline named Dottie. It has nine rooms, some of which offer hints of ocean blue from the windows. All have private bathrooms, though the unit known as The Shed does not have bathing facilities. (The Shed also happens to be a great bargain at $45 per night.) Two rooms accommodate children. One of those is The Barn, a funky, self-contained structure with a private deck and a secondary sleeping loft. This is the only unit with a television. Continental breakfast might include offerings from the Mendocino Cookie Company.

Sea Rock Inn
$$$$ • 11101 N. Lansing St., Mendocino
• (707) 937-0926

You might quibble with the Sea Rock's designation as a bed and breakfast inn. The inn's 14 units are spread among a complex of buildings, and the breakfast is a continental buffet. You will not, however, argue with the view. Every room has an ocean vista, ranging from "peek" to "spectacular." And the grounds include benches perched atop the bluffs, crashing waves and barking sea lions far below. The Sea Rock comprises six private cottages, four deluxe suites, and four rooms in the refurbished Stratton House. Each unit also is equipped with private bathroom, queen bed, cable TV, VCR, telephone, hardwood furniture, fine linens and down pillows. Many have featherbeds and/or Franklin fireplaces. Some have whirlpool tubs, and two rooms have an ocean view from the tub. Children are permitted under close supervision. The Sea Rock Inn is about a half-mile north of Mendocino.

Whitegate Inn
$$$$ • 499 Howard St., Mendocino
• (707) 937-4892

The framework for this bed and breakfast inn is an elegant house dating from 1883. A cobblestone path bordered with primroses leads to a terrace and gazebo. Restored in splendid style, the house is furnished with a collection of French, Italian and Victorian antiques.

Award-winning gourmet breakfasts are served on bone china and sterling silver and include such offerings as caramel-apple French toast or eggs Florentine. Seven lovely bedrooms with private baths provide comforts from fireplaces to cable television. Guests receive a welcome basket and are invited to a wine and cheese serving at 5 PM. Please note: Whitegate Inn has a 14-day cancellation policy and charges $25 for a cancellation, $30 per extra person.

Annie's Jughandle Beach Inn
$$$$ • Gibney Ln. and Hwy. 1, Fort Bragg
• (707) 964-1415, (800) 964-9957

This five-room Victorian-style inn built in 1883 sits midway between Mendocino and Fort Bragg and is the only lodging along that stretch of Highway 1. Guests enjoy private baths, spa tubs, fireplaces, and, in some rooms, ocean views. Jean LaTorre and his wife Shannon like to use the phrase "Louisiana hospitality and cuisine with the country charm of the Mendocino coast." Shannon, the chef, is the one from Louisiana, so meals at the Jughandle Inn tend to have a Cajun flair. The place overlooks the Jughandle State Preserve, and footpaths lead down to the ocean. There's access to plenty of hiking trails nearby, and in the springtime visitors can watch the whales right from the inn during breakfast—and all through the day.

Country Inn at Fort Bragg
$$ • 632 N. Main St., Fort Bragg
• (707) 964-3737

Inside this 1890s residence, innkeepers Bruce and Cynthia Knauss' intention is to transport you back to "the carefree turn-of-the-century." The sloping ceilings, decorative wallpaper and inviting fireplaces are part of the journey. Each of the eight rooms has its own theme, such as "Granny's Attic," with its clothing niche, walnut wainscoting framed by redwood molding, and old-fashioned bathtub. The Country Inn is just a short walk from the beach and features a full breakfast, free newspaper, afternoon wine and cheese.

The Grey Whale Inn
$$$ • 615 N. Main St., Fort Bragg
• (707) 964-0640, (800) 382-7244

It was the first bed and breakfast in Fort Bragg, and it has gathered a coterie of longtime admirers who come back time after time for the ambiance and cozy comforts of its spacious guest rooms. Twelve rooms on the first and second floors offer various amenities—some have gas log fireplaces, some have views of the

coastline, some are in French country style, and one has an antique sleigh bed. Two rooms in the penthouse have private sundecks; one has a double-size Jacuzzi. All rooms have private baths. The recreation room has a pool table and VCR. Breakfast is lavish.

Lodge at Noyo River
$$$ • 500 Casa Del Noyo, Fort Bragg
• (707) 964-8045

Ensconced in forest, the Lodge overlooks busy, small-boat Noyo Harbor. Suites are particularly spacious, with a solarium-style parlor and bedrooms with king or queen beds, window seats and plenty of fluffy pillows scattered about. Most have fireplaces. There are seven guest rooms and suites in the main lodge (one is said to be haunted!) and nine in an adjoining modern building. All rooms have private baths, down comforters and first-class bathroom amenities. In the evening you can watch pink sunsets over the handsome Noyo bridge, then wake up in the morning to the far-off barking of harbor seals. A sumptuous breakfast is served in the wood-paneled dining room.

Old Stewart House Inn
$$ • 511 Stewart St., Fort Bragg
• (707) 961-0775

Stewart House is Fort Bragg's oldest, a pre-Victorian erected in 1876. The proprietors bill it as the perfect spot for families or honeymooners. A third-story deck overlooks the ocean, affording visitors the best view in town not located in a lumber mill. All six of Stewart House's rooms have a European flair. The most formal, the Queen Anne room, has a gas fireplace and a bathroom with a big soaking tub. (There's a Jacuzzi tub room below the main house.) An outside cottage has a Greek theme. The Carriage House is more of a family unit, with bunk beds for the kids, a minikitchen and a separate room for mom and dad. Need another family amenity? Stewart House sits right across the street from the depot where the Willits-Fort Bragg Skunk Train arrives and departs.

Lake County

Forbestown Inn
$$ • 825 N. Forbes St., Lakeport
• (707) 263-7858

It's hard to miss this inn, which takes up the full half-block between Eighth and Ninth streets in downtown Lakeport. The two-story farmhouse and carriage house were built in 1863 for Lake County purveyor Henry McGee, whose son became the first Superior Court judge in San Francisco. The landscaping is immaculate; the four rooms welcoming, full of country antiques. Some have private bathrooms, some don't. You get refreshments in the afternoon and a full breakfast made to order anytime you want it (within reason). One major improvement to McGee's property: a swimming pool for guest use.

Arbor House Inn
$$ • 150 Clearlake Ave., Lakeport
• (707) 263-6444

Who says Lake County lacks refinement? The Arbor House Inn, a late-1800s Victorian about a block and a half from Clear Lake, has five tastefully appointed rooms, each with a unique set of antiques. Each unit has a private Jacuzzi tub (some are doubles), a king or queen bed, a TV and an outside entrance. Outdoors you'll find a spa and cottage gardens with a koi pond. The three-course breakfast is a winner, and guests receive complimentary wine and cheese in the afternoon. As of now, they have no problem with children.

Kristalberg Bed & Breakfast
$$ • 715 Pearl Ct., Lucerne
• (707) 274-8009

Clear Lake is the largest natural body of water within the boundaries of California, and you can see practically every drop of it from this hilltop inn between Lucerne and Glen Haven. Set in oak woodland, Kristalberg offers 200-degree views and a contemporary Cape Cod house. Two of the three guest rooms face the lake, and one of those is a master suite with early American furnishings, a whirlpool tub and a balcony. The full breakfast stresses organically grown foods, including herbs and vegetables straight from the garden. Ask about bringing children, and while you're at it ask about off-season discounts. Pearl Court is off of Bruner Drive, about a half-mile from Calif. Hwy. 20.

Featherbed Railroad Company
$$$ • 2870 Lakeshore Blvd., Nice
• (707) BR-GUEST, (800) 966-6322

Here's the perfect site for a training session: nine old Santa Fe or Southern Pacific cabooses converted into guest rooms. The oldest car, the Mint Julep, is about 70 years old. Each room has a feather bed and a TV/VCR, and six of them have two-person Jacuzzi tubs. There is a swimming pool on the grounds, and if that's too tame you can go jump in Clear Lake, which happens to be right next door. Full breakfast is served in one of three locations: in the dining room of the hosts' house, on the veranda or, upon request, in your cozy railcar.

Spas and Resorts

From that legendary day in the 1860s when Sam Brannan raised his wine glass and, with a probably unreasonable blood-alcohol level, proclaimed his new health resort "the Calistoga of Sarafornia," this area has been attracting the infirm, the consumptive and, much more likely, those who simply like to be pampered. The hot water that naturally percolates through various portions of the Wine Country is the active ingredient that started the spa craze, but it's really the scenery and generally hedonistic atmosphere that allow it to thrive today.

Some of the nation's finest full-service resorts are here—heavyweights like Meadowood and the Sonoma Mission Inn—and most of them revolve around mud, steam, massaging fingers and the like. You can find variety though. Silverado Country Club is the favorite of golf nuts, and the Little River Inn sings the siren's song of the Pacific coastline.

And don't feel priced out of this chapter. Many of the spas that greeted sore-kidneyed travelers in the middle of this century are alive today. Their glory is faded but not gone. Outpaced at their own game by the corporate entries, they have become a second tier of options for you. Places such as Dr. Wilkinson's offer a wide range of relaxation facilitators, but at a lower level of luxury—and price.

A word about what you will find here: To qualify for inclusion in this chapter, an inn has to offer amenities and services above and beyond a standard, pleasant lodging. If it isn't a full-service spa with mineral pools, massage and the like, it has to present a comprehensive package for visitors—that is, accommodations, a restaurant and multiple activities. In other words, it has to be a place where you can spend two or three days without ever leaving the boundaries of the property. The unspoken assumptions in the following listings are these: All rooms have private bathrooms; children are welcome, but pets are not; major credit cards are accepted; and you will leave happier and more forgiving of this world than when you arrived.

LOOK FOR:
- **Napa County**
- **Sonoma County**
- **Mendocino County**
- **Lake County**

Price Code

For room prices, refer to our dollar code printed below. Rates are for double occupancy on a weekend night in high season (generally, May through October). Most spas and resorts offer discounts for off-season or midweek visits. The tariff usually includes use of facilities such as tennis courts and gyms, if there are such things, but you will pay separately for spa services. The dollar code does not reflect taxes and tips.

$	**$80 or lower**
$$	**$81 to $120**
$$$	**$121 to $160**
$$$$	**$161 to $200**
$$$$$	**$201 and higher**

Napa County

Silverado Country Club & Resort
$$$$$ • 1600 Atlas Peak Rd., Napa • (707) 257-0200, (800) 532-0500

It is hard not to be impressed by this mega-resort at the base of Atlas Peak. For one thing, it's big. Silverado comprises 1,200 acres and 280 cottage suites—every one of them a deluxe accommodation with living room, wood-burning fireplace, full kitchen and a private patio or terrace. Most of the hubbub is centered around the two 18-hole, Robert Trent Jones Jr.-designed golf courses. But there is a slew of additional activity, including mountain-bike rentals, eight swimming pools, jogging trails, 17 plexi-paved tennis courts, and a brand-new, 16,000-square-foot spa and gym. Check-in and concierge service is in the circa-1870s Colonial Mansion, originally owned by Civil War Gen. John F. Miller. There you'll also find a conference center with 12,000 square feet of flexible meeting space (including a 5,200-square-foot grand ballroom) and a fully staffed catering and conventions department. Dining options include the Bar and Grill for breakfast and lunch and either Vintner's Court or the Mesquite-influenced Royal Oak for dinner (see our Restaurants chapter).

Auberge du Soleil
$$$$$ • 180 Rutherford Hill Rd., Rutherford
• (707) 963-1211, (800) 348-5406

What began as a restaurant in 1983 has blossomed into one of the Wine Country's most exclusive resorts, nestled among 33 acres of olive trees and chaparral. The whole operation exudes brightness and health, with terra cotta tile floors, fresh bouquets, natural wood and leather furnishings and Mediterranean color schemes. The 31 guest rooms and 19 suites all have private terraces, fireplaces, down comforters and stereo CD systems. The sizable bathrooms have double sinks and huge tubs under skylights.

The recreational opportunities include three tournament-surfaced tennis courts, a swimming pool, a whirlpool tub and an exercise room. There is a sculpture garden and three separate facilities for meetings, receptions or special occasions. The Auberge du Soleil restaurant is profiled in the Restaurants chapter. The spa services are an attraction in their own right. You can get a facial, a body wrap or a scalp treatment, and choose from a variety of massage styles. The spa also delves into Ayurvedic treatments (a holistic approach developed in India some 5,000 years ago), yoga and somatics, based on "neuromuscular retraining principles." Auberge du Soleil is not really geared for children younger than 16.

Meadowood Napa Valley
$$$$$ • 900 Meadowood Ln., St. Helena
• (707) 963-3646, (800) 458-8080

In the 1800s, Chinese laborers harvested rice in the small valley known as Meadowood. (The 800-foot tunnel they built still drains the valley during heavy rains.) The full-service, Relais & Chateaux estate that now graces the area would have been beyond the wildest dreams of those immigrants. There are 85 suites, lodges and cottages, spread among 250 acres and often tucked into the hillside scenery. All accommodations feature high-beamed ceilings, heated bathroom floors, private porches and down comforters. If you're feeling active, choose among two pools, a whirlpool, saunas, seven tennis courts, two championship croquet lawns, a nine-hole golf course and a 3-mile hiking trail. The Health Spa features a dizzying array of fitness classes, personal training, yoga, skin-care treatments, salt treatments and body wraps.

Meadowood's staff of resident experts includes a wine director who leads Friday night wine receptions and a croquet pro—one of only two in America. The resort also has five private conference and event rooms with a total reception capacity of 200. And if you happen to get hold of your delinquent ex-husband's Visa card, this might be the place to head: Meadowood's four-bedroom suites top out at $2,430. Yes, that's for one night. (See the Meadowood listing in our Restaurants chapter for even more decadence.)

White Sulphur Springs Resort & Spa
$$$ • 3100 White Sulphur Springs Rd., St. Helena • (707) 963-8588, (800) 593-8873 in Calif. and Nev.

California's oldest hot-springs resort (established in 1852) retains its 19th-century charm, thanks to a laid-back management style and an idyllic setting. Take Spring Street west from downtown St. Helena; soon the town ends, but the road keeps going until you're tucked into a forest of redwood, fir and madrone. White Sulphur Springs has gone by many names (the least impressive: Bob's Steak House) and survived under numerous owners, including, in succession, the Methodist Church Conference, the Northern California Zionist Youth Commission and the Sanatana Dharma Foundation.

The 330-acre resort now has 37 rooms—14 in the Carriage House (shared baths), 14 in The Inn (private baths) and nine creekside cottages. There is a warm (85 to 92 degrees) sulphur pool

INSIDERS' TIP
If you stay at Indian Springs on a weeknight (Sunday through Thursday) between November 1 and March 31, the Calistoga-based spa will give you complimentary mud baths for two.

SPAS AND RESORTS

fed by a natural spring, and you can smell it anywhere in the main residential area. Children are OK in the cottages. The spa treatments involve massage therapy and aroma/thermo therapy, including herbal facials, mineral mud wraps, seaweed wraps and herbal linen wraps.

Putah Creek Resort
$ • 7600 Knoxville Rd., Lake Berryessa
• (707) 966-0770

Don't expect any caviar or hot collagen wraps here. This is an old-fashioned sportsman's resort, right on Lake Berryessa between the Putah Creek and Pope Creek bridges. There are 27 rooms in the motel, some of which have kitchen facilities. Be advised that there are no nonsmoking units. Putah Creek has a 300-seat restaurant and bar, a playground area, a boat launching ramp and a 100-slip marina. They'll sell you gas and rent you a Jet Ski, a ski boat or a pontoon boat. Small dogs are accepted.

Silver Rose Inn & Spa
$$$$ • 351 Rosedale Rd., Calistoga
• (707) 942-9581, (800) 995-9381

The Silver Rose is building a reputation as the top-of-the-food-chain spa in the northern Napa Valley. The setting is quite pleasant—a quiet road just off the Silverado Trail, about a half-mile south of Calistoga. The inn has a total of 20 rooms divided between two buildings, Inn on the Knoll and Inn the Vineyard. Most units face onto vines and, beyond that, the rocky Palisades. (Some have young vines planted right outside the windows.) Each room is themed, e.g., the gold-accented Cleopatra Room and the saddle-and-boot-filled Western Room.

Guests are free to make use of the Jacuzzi, tennis courts, putting green and wine bottle-shaped swimming pool, and breakfast is served in the tiled dining hall. There is also a state-of-the-art conference room. The spa services include massage, body and facial treatments, various water treatments, hydrotherm massage and herbal body wraps (some available in-room). Prices range from $50 for a reflexology session to $249 for a 3-hour-plus, all-purpose body reclamation project. Most of the Silver Rose's king beds can be split into twins to accommodate corporate retreats. The spa has been working on a winery and restaurant, to open sometime in 2000. No children younger than 15, please.

Dr. Wilkinson's Hot Springs
$$$ • 1507 Lincoln Ave., Calistoga
• (707) 942-4102

This has been a Calistoga institution since John Wilkinson opened his spa in 1952. And "the works"—mud bath, facial mask, mineral whirlpool bath, steam room, blanket wrap and half-hour massage—is still the most popular package (though it now costs $99, rather than the original $4.50). Doc is a local legend who once served as the town's mayor. Often as not this fit octogenarian can be found prowling the town's streets, serving as a walking billboard for his health treatments. Dr. Wilkinson's has 43 rooms, some with kitchens, all with refrigerators and private bathrooms. Rooms in the adjacent five-unit Victorian are slightly more expensive. Individual spa services start at $45 for a half-hour massage. Children must be 14 or older to take a mud bath. Doc also offers an on-site salon where you can get facial and skin-care treatments or select from a wide range of related products.

Nance's Hot Springs
$$ • 1614 Lincoln Ave., Calistoga
• (707) 942-6211

Nance's is another of those venerable old spas on Calistoga's historic main drag. Established in 1923, the rambling, white-and-red, two-story complex is just earthy enough to lend an unassailable air of authenticity. The price is right too, with no room more than $90. All units have kitchenettes and HBO, and guests receive unlimited access to the hot mineral pool. Other sensuous offerings include mud baths, whirlpool baths, mineral steam, blanket wraps and massage. Nance's Works—a combination of all of the above—will run you $70 to $90. Sorry, no children. At the other end of the age spectrum, seniors receive a 10 percent discount for both lodging and spa activities between Sunday and Thursday.

Indian Springs
$$$$$ • 1712 Lincoln Ave., Calistoga
• (707) 942-4913

If this collection of teal-and-white buildings evokes the heyday of the recuperative spa, it's appropriate. Indian Springs is on land that was once part of Sam Brannan's inspired attempt to make this town the Saratoga of the West. The bathhouse and Olympic-size swimming pool date to 1913, and most of the bungalows were built in the 1930s. The spa's scattering of squat buildings (most units are duplexes), open vistas and billowing steam might make you think you're living under the Woodrow Wilson administration. In addition to the 17 studio and one-room units, Indian Springs offers the Merchant Bungalow, a three-

Photo: Lou Zauner

From this porch at Little River Inn on the Mendocino Coast, Silas Coombs watched for ships coming in to the lumber mills.

bedroom, two-bath suite that sleeps six and goes for $500 a night. The spa services include 100-percent volcanic ash mud baths, mineral baths, massage, facial or body polish treatments and combinations thereof.

Calistoga Spa Hot Springs
$$ • 1006 Washington St., Calistoga
• (707) 942-6269

Considering Calistoga Spa's services, excellent in both quality and quantity, this has to be considered something of a bargain. The spa is a block off Lincoln Avenue, set next to the old Gliderport runway and behind the Depot and other commercial buildings (on the site of the old Roman Olympic Pool). All 57 rooms come with kitchenettes (all the basics provided except an oven), air conditioning and cable TV; two suites have full kitchens. Guests are free to use the small but well-maintained gym (the only one in Calistoga) and four naturally heated mineral baths that range from 83 to 105 degrees. And then there is the typical lineup of spa services: mud baths, mineral baths, massage and steam-and-blanket combos. Prices start at $16 for a basic steam-and-blanket; a mud dunk, mineral bath, blanket wrap and one-hour massage go for $92. Calistoga Spa also has a

conference room that accommodates as many as 40 people.

Roman Spa
$$$ • 1300 Washington St., Calistoga
• (707) 942-4441

The Roman Spa is a straight-up motel, but you can get pampered next door at Calistoga Oasis Spa. The two establishments have the same owners, though they're run separately. Roman Spa, just a block from downtown Calistoga, has water everywhere you turn: lily ponds; a large, heated outdoor pool; an indoor, hydro-jet therapy pool; and outdoor hydro-jet and Finnish-style saunas. The 60 rooms include everything from a single with a queen bed to a family suite with two full rooms. About a third of the rooms have kitchen facilities, and there are five smoking rooms. They do not take credit card reservations over the phone here; you'll need to send a check or show up in person.

Golden Haven Hot Springs
$$ • 1713 Lake St., Calistoga
• (707) 942-6793

This is a comparatively affordable spa in a quiet section of Calistoga. The exterior is nothing special, but the rooms are clean and full of conveniences, including air conditioning, color TV and refrigerators. There is wide variation in price. For instance, a room with one queen goes for $59 on a Wednesday in April, while a king bed with a private Jacuzzi goes for $149 on a weekend. Children are allowed on weekdays only. All the soothing spa treatments are there if you want them. The lineup features mud baths (including private rooms for couples), herbal mineral baths, herbal facials and massage. Those fees range from $42 for a half-hour massage to $159 for a mud bath, hour massage, and herbal facial package. Golden Haven also promotes a "European body wrap" guaranteed to take off six inches of unsightly fat. Guests use the swimming pool and hot mineral pool free.

Calistoga Village Inn & Spa
$$$ • 1880 Lincoln Ave., Calistoga
• (707) 942-0991

Another of the town's older (post-World War II) spas, the Village Inn is a long row of whitewashed bungalows along the northern reaches of Lincoln Avenue, just before it hits the Silverado Trail. There are plenty of reasons to be semi-clothed here: a swimming pool, a wading pool (children are welcome), a Jacuzzi and a dry steam room. Among the numerous spa treatments are mud baths, massage, salt scrubs, facials, foot reflexology and body wraps. The inn also offers 16 different types of mineral bath, including the aromatic seaweed bath, Dr. Singha's mustard bath and the Moor mud baths. A package known as The Ultimate features a mud bath, salt scrub, mini-facial and one-hour massage for $155. Guests of the inn receive a 10 percent discount for all the above. The Village Inn has two conference rooms, 42 guest units and a restaurant, Speckmann's, that serves up robust German cuisine for dinner.

Sonoma County

Sonoma Mission Inn & Spa
$$$$$ • 18140 Sonoma Hwy.,
Boyes Hot Springs
• (707) 938-9000, (800) 862-4945

The style is Spanish-influenced early California, a sprawling pink building with red tile roof, arcade and bell tower. Lobby décor features heavy Spanish furnishings, grouped around a massive fireplace, where guests sip late-morning coffee on Sunday while reading the *San Francisco Chronicle* or the *Wall Street Journal*. It would be no surprise to see a Hollywood star or two, for they frequently escape Southern California to come for a spa treatment or a week of avoirdupois reduction. The health and fitness program reads like a Jane Fonda workout—aerobics, aromatherapy, body sculpting, yoga, herbal wrap, seaweed sauna, steam room—it goes on from there. To compensate for and recharge after all this activity, there are two great restaurants: the Grille, in the main building, and the nearby Mission Inn Cafe. Both offer low-calorie cuisine (see our Restaurants chapter).

The Inn itself has a colorful history. The first spa was built in 1860 by an eccentric doctor who burned it down after a tiff with his wife. The 1890s saw establishment of a popular resort that brought San Francisco society by rail and auto to "take the waters." The present Mission Inn dates to 1927, when it took shape in the style of a California mission. (The present "historic" section dates to those buildings.) In 1985, a total renovation brought 70 new rooms and a conference center. The hot springs, however, lay dormant, lost in the earth until 1993, when the legendary waters were brought back to the surface from 1,100 feet below the Inn. This is the water that today fills the two pools and whirlpools.

The Kenwood Inn
$$$$$ • 10400 Sonoma Hwy., Kenwood
• (707) 833-1293, (800) 3-KENWOO(D)

Intimate in scale with a peaceful, Old World charm, the Kenwood Inn offers the ambiance of an Italian country villa nestled in the heart of Sonoma Valley. The Inn, which has 12 private suites around a central courtyard and fountain, is situated on a secluded hillside facing more than 1,000 acres of sloping estate vineyards. The suites contains feather beds, down comforters, European antiques and lush fabrics, private baths and fireplaces. A complimentary bottle of wine greets guests on arrival. Breakfast is served either in the dining room or at outdoor tables in good weather. A full-service spa pampers guests and day visitors alike with

SPAS AND RESORTS

The Sonoma Mission Inn and Spa, located in Boyes Hot Springs, is a luxurious resort with its own natural hot springs.

six different therapeutic massages, 10 special skin-care treatments and spa body treatments such as clay and chamomile, seaweed body wrap and ancient Ayurvedic body purification rituals. Half-day spa experiences are available, including the popular couples "togetherness massage," as well as the Fango facial. Spa treatments are priced individually.

Mendocino County

Orr Hot Springs
$$ • 13201 Orr Springs Rd., Ukiah
• (707) 462-6277

The hot spring waters bubble up from the earth into a redwood tub and spill over into the swimming pool below. The spa has had a checkered history, and at present could only be described as rustic. The first bath house was built in the 1850s and is now used as a dormitory. A lodge and eight bungalows were put up in the 1930s and serve as the main buildings today. During the 1970s the 26-acre hot-springs facility was sold to some back-to-earth flower children who turned it into a commune. The present owner is one of those members (the rest have long since

dispersed). Besides the basic facilities (some of which have half-baths), camping is also an option. Day-use is another option. The situation here is informal; you can bring a picnic lunch and store it in the communal kitchen. Another informality: Clothing is optional.

Vichy Springs Resort
$$$$ • 2605 Vichy Springs Rd., Ukiah
• (707) 462-9515

Named after the world-famous springs first discovered by Julius Caesar in France, the waters of Vichy Springs surge forth from miles within the earth and are virtually identical in chemistry to those of the French namesake. Available in abundance for bathing and swimming, the waters are naturally warm and effervescent, filled with minerals and energy renowned for healing and restorative qualities. Also restorative and soothing is the idyllic park-like setting of the resort—the oldest continuously operating mineral springs spa in California. Opened in 1854 and now a California Historical Landmark, it was a favorite retreat of Mark Twain, Jack London and Presidents Ulysses S. Grant, Benjamin Harrison and Teddy Roosevelt. Today the resort is restored and renovated to tastefully combine its historic charm with modern comfort and conveniences.

Twelve individually decorated rooms with private baths have been created from the ancient, broken-down former facilities that date to the 1860s. (Five creekside rooms were added in 1997.) These are so attractive that the company that supplied the paint brings people to Vichy Springs to have a look. There are also four cottages with kitchens, bedrooms and living rooms. Two of them were built in 1854 and are the oldest standing structures in Mendocino County. The third was built in 1997, the fourth in 1999. Just steps away from the accommodations are the renovated indoor and outdoor bathing tubs, therapeutic massage building and mineral-water-filled, Olympic-size swimming pool. Offered at varying rates are therapeutic massage, Swedish massage and herbal facial. Day visitors are also welcome to use the pool, baths and the property.

Heritage House
$$$$ • 5200 N. Hwy. 1, Little River
• (707) 937-5885, (800) 235-5885

Sprawling across 37 private acres of pristine coastline, Heritage House is a classic country inn, opened in 1949 and still maintained by the same family. A total of 64 accommodations are mainly grouped in clusters of two, three or four private rooms under a common roof, which imparts a cottage-like feeling. One of the favorites is the sumptuous Carousel set of suites, housed in a secluded building offering unobstructed ocean views, huge decks and elegant furnishings. The Water Tower suite includes a spiral staircase leading to a sleeping loft. But the most requested rooms were built for the filming of the movie *Same Time Next Year*, which was written while author Bernard Slade stayed at the inn. Dining at Heritage House is a world-class experience (see our Restaurants chapter). The inn is open from Valentine's Day through Thanksgiving weekend, and for holiday celebrations from Christmas through New Year's Day.

Little River Inn
$$$$ • 7751 N. Hwy. 1, Little River,
• (707) 937-5942

Built in 1853 by Silas Coombs, a lumberman from Maine, this classic coastal resort once was the Coombs' family home. It is now run by the great-grandchildren, who keep the flavor of the past while expanding for the future. Eucalyptus trees, planted as a windbreak for the Coombs' orchard, now shelter a golf course.

The wisteria-covered front porch of the original home, where Silas once spotted ocean freighters, now beckons guests into the dining room. In the music room, the Emerson square grand piano, which survived its trip around Cape Horn in 1850, is still being played. The inn has a long tradition of hosting Hollywood celebrities—Joan Fontaine and a crew of 40; Jonathan Winters, who provided impromptu entertainment; Ronald Reagan, who sprawled on the floor to illustrate football plays.

Reservations for the 65 rooms here are required year-round. There is no charge for children younger than 18. Sunday brunch and dinner are served.

Stanford Inn by the Sea – Big River Lodge
$$$$$ • Calif. Hwy. 1 and Comptche-Ukiah Rd., Mendocino
• (707) 937-5615, (800) 331-8884

This elegantly rustic lodge has so many diversions that guests hardly need to ever leave. A firm believer in preserving the health of our environment, owner Jeff Stanford keeps a stable of bicycles for guests to use in exploring the countryside and a fleet of canoes and kayaks for exploring Big River. His terraced gardens are tended organically and are so prolific he donates produce to the local senior center. Besides that, he also keeps grazing llamas, horses and a few cats. Jeff serves vegetarian dishes in the Ravens restaurant, along with organic wines. Hors d'oeuvres are available in the evening, champagne with breakfast.

The site is stunning, sloping from a high meadow down to the sea. And the 33 accommodations have all the amenities expected of the finest hotels—wood-burning fireplaces, down comforters, ocean views, decks, refrigerators, VCRs. Some have kitchens. There's a heated indoor swimming pool and group Jacuzzi/sauna.

Sweetwater Spa & Inn
$$ • 955 Ukiah St. (spa), 44840 Main St. (inn), Mendocino • (707) 937-4140

The Sweetwater complex takes up most of the two blocks between Ukiah and Main streets in the village of Mendocino, and that's not all. Besides the 10 units downtown, the company has six more in Little River and two separate houses elsewhere. One of the homes, Redwood Cottage, is a popular lodging about five minutes east of Mendocino. The other is Sweetwater Cove, a three-bedroom, two-bath structure on a spectacular stretch of coastline between Caspar and Fort Bragg. (The Cove goes for upwards of $200 per night.)

The spa offers a variety of massage options, including the ever-popular Sweetheart Special—stay two nights in any room, book two massages and receive a $25 discount. Sweetwater also has hot tubs and sauna, with prices that vary according to privacy and tub size. Kids are welcome in all units except the Ocean Suite, which sits above the massage room and must be kept hush-hush.

Lake County

Konocti Harbor Resort & Spa
$$$ • 8727 Soda Bay Rd., Kelseyville
• (707) 279-4281, (800) 660-LAKE

Most people know Konocti Harbor as a premier concert venue for post-40 rockers (see our Nightlife chapter), but there's a lot going on here even after the last drum beat. The resort has 100 acres of lakefront property and 250 guest accommodations that range from basic rooms to apartment suites to beach cottages to fully equipped VIP suites. Many, but not all, of the rooms have views of Clear Lake. The price spectrum is wide, so call for more information. Basic rooms are $49 every night of the year; deluxe rooms with balconies vary in price according to season, but expect $99 on in-season weekends; Jacuzzi suites with fireplaces are $229.

Konocti Harbor bustles with activity. There is a tennis complex, a gym, two swimming pools, two wading pools, shuffleboard courts, horseshoe pits, sand volleyball courts and a softball field. And because the lake is primary among attractions, the resort has a 100-slip marina, a launch ramp and a certified boat repair shop. It also offers a rental fleet (ski boats, Waverunners, etc.) and, believe it or not, a bass fishing pro. Konocti's Dancing Springs Spa features massage, herbal wraps, loofa treatments, facials, manicures and more. If you must mix business and pleasure, the meeting facilities can handle groups from 10 to 700.

Harbin Hot Springs
$$ • P.O. Box 782, Middletown
• (707) 987-2477, (800) 622-2477

Legendary among latter-day hippies, New Age shamans and women who run with wolves (or swim with fishes), Harbin is a nonprofit retreat and workshop center set on 1,160 unencroached acres north of Middletown. Here you can let your hair, and practically everything else, hang down without inhibition. The guest accommodations range from camping ($25 per weekend night for one adult) to dormitory lodging ($45 per person) to rooms with shared baths ($105 for two) to rooms with full, private baths ($150) to cabins ($185). Harbin's health treatments include various forms of massage—from Swedish to acupressure—facials, aromatherapy and "watsu," a form of warm-water massage developed at the retreat. You don't have to leave the compound for meals, either.

The Stonefront Restaurant, open for breakfast and dinner, specializes in organic vegetarian ingredients, and there are two cafes and a health-food store. The group facilities handle conferences and events for parties of 14 to 300, including scheduled workshops on topics such as relationships and meditation. Alcohol and drugs are not permitted on the premises, and meat, fish and poultry are not allowed in guest kitchens. Children are allowed only to camp and are relegated to daytime pool use. From Big Canyon Road about a mile north of Middletown, go west on Harbin Springs Road. Follow the road 2 miles.

Camping

Most world-class vacation spots demand a basic decision: Are we going to disappear into the mountains with a tent and a camp stove and commune with nature? Or are we going to pack some slacks and dresses and live among the civilized? The Wine Country forces no such determination. One of the most attractive features of this area is that you can walk into practically any restaurant or winery, no matter how lofty the reputation or shiny the brass, in a clean T-shirt and a pair of Levi's and suffer not even a downward glance from the hostess.

As a result, many return guests have developed a satisfying routine: Pull into a campsite at a local state park or RV park, fry up some bacon and eggs in the morning and then drive off (or, better yet, bicycle off) for a day of winetasting and sightseeing. Once you're in the tasting room, no one can tell the campers from the four-star hotel guests (unless you blow your cover by offering the manager a s'more). Of course, some people actually want to rough it when they rough it. Have no fear, the upper reaches of Mendocino and Lake counties offer remote mountain campgrounds that a wine taster wouldn't stumble upon in a thousand years. Many of them afford opportunities for backpacking, hiking and fishing. And then there is the plethora of breezy lakeside sites in Lake County. You can consider them the compromise choice between the wild and the tame.

If we don't say otherwise, assume that each campground has piped, potable water, a desirable part of any outdoors experience. If it doesn't, arrange to bring or pump your own. And please note that some of the listed sites are part of the region's state parks. In those cases we have provided all the basic camping information here, but for a more thorough description of the park, you should turn to our Parks and Recreation chapter.

LOOK FOR:
• **Napa County**
• **Sonoma County**
• **Mendocino County**
• **Lake County**

Napa County

Napa Town & Country Fairgrounds
575 Third St., Napa
• (707) 253-4900

Your chances of spotting a deer or a black bear aren't good here. Then again, you won't be far from your morning cafe latte. The fairgrounds are just off Third Street in Napa, as it approaches the Silverado Trail. There are about 75 motorhome spaces though the group campground can accommodate anywhere from 15 to 500. On site are restrooms and showers, and close by are a laundry and a market. Pets are permitted on leashes.

The cost is $15 per night for a site. Note that Town & Country is closed to campers for the latter half of July and most of August.

Pleasure Cove Resort
Wragg Canyon Rd., off Calif. Hwy. 128, Lake Berryessa
• (707) 966-2172

This family-oriented campground is one of five around Lake Berryessa. Pleasure Cove has 105 sites for tents or motor homes, 20 of them with water and electrical hookups. The wheelchair-accessible sites have picnic tables and fire pits, and there are restrooms, showers, ice, a restaurant and bar, propane and groceries. Pleasure Cove also has a boat ramp if you're prowling for trout. The cost is $16 per night for a tent site, $18 with hookup. Pets are $2 extra.

Spanish Flat Resort
4290 Knoxville Rd., off Calif. Hwy. 128, Lake Berryessa • (707) 966-7700

Another possibility for a recreational jaunt to Berryessa is Spanish Flat, which has 120 campsites for tents or motor homes, a few of them with partial hook-ups. Picnic tables, fire pits, flush toilets and showers are provided. The hosts also have complete marina facilities, a boat launch and rentals. A laundry and a restaurant are a short drive away. The fee is $20 per night.

INSIDERS' TIP

To reserve a campsite in one of California's state parks, you must go through the DESTINET booking service at (800) 444-PARK. Don't forget that DESTINET will add a one-time $6.75 surcharge to any reservation.

Bothe-Napa Valley State Park
Calif. Hwy. 29, south of Calistoga • (707) 942-4575 (info), (800) 444-PARK (reservations)

While a million or so industrious tourists whiz by on Calif. Highway 29, you can lay next to your tent and look up at the boughs of oaks and pines, or at the stars of the Milky Way. The park has a first-rate campground along Redwood Creek, with nine tent-only sites and 50 for tents or RVs up to 31 feet long. You get picnic tables and fire pits, toilets and showers. Wheelchairs can be used here, and pets are allowed (campground only) for a $1 surcharge. There is a spring-fed swimming pool, where you can take the plunge for $3 ($2 for children); that's in addition to the $16 standard nightly rate. There are blackberries for the pickin' in summer. (For more on Bothe-Napa Valley State Park, see our Parks and Recreation chapter.)

Napa County Fairgrounds
1435 N. Oak St., Calistoga • (707) 942-5111

If you're going to pick a municipal campground, you could do a lot worse than Calistoga's. The scenery is nice, you can walk to restaurants and spas, and right next door is Mt. St. Helena Golf Course (see our Parks and Recreation chapter). There are about 60 drive-through campsites with electrical hookups, plus a small grassy area for tents; the cost is $18 a night for RVs, $10 for tents.

Restrooms, showers and propane are available, but campfires are not permitted. Pets are allowed on leashes. The campground is closed from mid-June through mid-July as the grounds are prepared for and cleaned up after the Napa County Fair (see our Festivals and Annual Events chapter).

Lower Hunting Creek
Knoxville-Devilshead Rd. • (707) 462-3873

This is one of the Wine Country's least-known campgrounds and, because of its isolation, that isn't likely to change anytime soon. Lower Hunting Creek has only five sites for tents or RVs, but it does have picnic tables, fireplaces, shade shelters and vault toilets. Pets are permitted on leashes. Be forewarned that the campground is popular with off-road enthusiasts and hunters. From Berryessa-Knoxville Road, turn south on Knoxville-Devilshead Road and drive for 2 miles. You can get a map of the area from the Bureau of Land Management, which administers the site. There is no charge for camping here.

Sonoma County

Southern Sonoma

Sugarloaf Ridge State Park
2605 Adobe Canyon Rd., Kenwood • (800) 444-7275

This locale in the Mayacamas Mountains has 50 campsites for tents or motor homes up to 27 feet long. There is piped-in water and restrooms. Hiking is the main recreation at this popular state park (see our Parks and Recreation chapter). Pets are OK. Campsites are $16.

Spring Lake Park
Newanga Ave., Santa Rosa • (707) 539-8092

A group camping area and 30 family campsites (four for tents only) at Spring Lake Park have centrally located restrooms and shower facilities. Also available are 200 picnic sites, barbecue pits, a bikeway, a hiking trail and equestrian trails. No electricity is available at this campground, which is open all week during the summer (the week before Memorial Day until the week after Labor Day) and weekends only during the winter. Please reserve at least 10 days in advance during high season. Tent and RV sites are $15. It's $5 for an extra vehicle and $1 for a dog, which must be vaccinated and leashed.

als and a launch ramp. The charge for either a tent site or an RV at Liberty Glen is $16 year-round.. Piped water, flush toilets, solar-heated showers and a sanitary disposal station are available in the developed area.

Northern Sonoma

Windsorland RV Trailer Park
9290 Old Redwood Hwy., Windsor
• (707) 838-4882

There are 56 full-hookup, pull-through sites available here, with laundry, playground, a small store, showers and restrooms. A pool is open seasonally. The park is open all year, and night registration is available. Tent sites cost $20, and RV sites are $25. There's a special senior RV rate of $15.

KOA Kampground
26460 River Rd., Cloverdale
• (707) 894-3337

This campground has 152 campsites (50 for tents), plus a swimming pool, recreation hall, store, minigolf course, stocked fishing pond, ball courts and horseshoe pits. Up 1 mile from the Russian River, it's open all year. Tent sites for two people cost $25; RV sites with full hook-ups are $29. There are also eight Kamping Kabins for two (with no water or electricity) at $45. Rates are lowered during the winter months.

Lake Sonoma—Liberty Glen
3333 Skaggs Springs Rd.,
Lake Sonoma
• (707) 433-9483

Eleven miles northwest of Healdsburg, off Dry Creek Road, this Lake Sonoma park offers more than 17,000 land and water acres. Lake Sonoma facilities include a visitors center and fish hatchery (see our Kidstuff chapter), with 118 campsites available for tents or RVs up to 50 feet. There are two group sites for up to 50 campers (advance reservations required). In addition, there are 15 boat-in/hike-in primitive campgrounds around the lake, and a privately operated marina that offers boat rent-

Sonoma Coast

Bodega Bay RV Park
2000 Calif. Hwy. 1, Bodega Bay
• (707) 875-3701

Full hookups and dry spaces are available, with hot showers, laundry room, volleyball court and horseshoe pits close at hand. This park has about 70 spots for RVs, is open all year and offers night registration. RV sites with full hookups are $25 for two people; those with no hookups are $17 for two people. It's $2 for each additional person.

Doran Park
Doran Beach, 1 mile south of Bodega Bay
• (707) 875-3540

Park facilities include 125 sites for RVs or tents, 10 tent-only sites and one group camping area for tents only. There are tables, fire rings and a trailer disposal site. What to do? Try fishing, beachcombing, clamming, boating and picnicking.

A boat ramp and fish-cleaning station are available. Tent and RV sites are $15 for two people. There's an extra charge of $5 per vehicle and $1 per dog.

Salt Point State Park
25050 Calif. Hwy. 1,
Jenner
• (707) 847-3221

This 31-site campground offers picnic areas, hiking trails, diving, horseback trails and the beautiful, adjacent Kruse Rhododendron State Reserve (see our Parks and Recreation chapter). It's open all year, but there are no RV hookups. Piped water and flush toilets are available. Cost of sites is $16 (senior rate is $12), plus $5 for an extra vehicle and $1 for a dog. In early winter this is headquarters for local abalone divers.

INSIDERS' TIP

Camping in one of the more remote spots of Mendocino National Forest, it's highly tempting to bend down to that crystal-clear stream for a drink. Don't do it. The fresh water of California is often populated by a protozoan called *Giardia lamblia*. You probably won't die if you take in *Giardia*, but you'll wish you could. It results in severe abdominal cramping and diarrhea that can last for weeks. So be safe and boil your water or pump it through a filter. (Water purification tablets do not kill *Giardia*.)

CAMPING

West County/Russian River

ity and water cost $24 for two people. Additional campers are $5 each.

Village Park Campground
6665 Calif. Hwy. 12, Sebastopol
• (707) 823-6348

Village Park is open from May 1 to October 31 for overnight or weekly stays. Laundry facilities, restrooms with showers and hot water are offered, and children and pets are welcome. Fees for the 13 tent sites are set at $10. RV sites (there are 22 of them) are $12 with electricity.

River Bend Campground
11820 River Bend, Forestville
• (707) 887-7662

Eleven miles from U.S. 101, off the River Road exit, this campground has 48 RV hookups and 44 tent sites and offers such amenities as canoe rentals, volleyball, barbecue pits, basketball courts, restrooms, hot showers, groceries, teepees for rent and the story of Paul Bunyan on a statue. It's open all year. Weekday rates are $15 for tent sites and $18 for RV sites. Weekend rates are slightly higher—$18 for tent sites, $25 for RV sites.

Faerie Ring Campground
16747 Armstrong Woods Rd., Guerneville
• (707) 869-2746

You can pick one of these 42 campsites—33 for tents, nine full hookups—in either a sunny or shady location. Hot showers and flush toilets are available. It's near the Russian River, 1.8 miles north of Calif. Highway 116, and it's open all year. Rates are $15 for two people in the winter, $20 for two in the summer (generally May through October). Faerie Ring also has a popular adults-only area that goes for $20/$25.

Schoolhouse Canyon Campground
12600 River Road, Guerneville
• (707) 869-2311

This camping option is amid a 200-acre wildlife sanctuary. Tent and RV sites are set in the redwoods and offer hot showers, beach life, fishing, hiking and nature trails. It's open April through October. Fees for tent sites are set at $20 for two people, and RV sites with electric-

INSIDERS' TIP

If you get on the road and decide you want the comfort of a motor home after all, call Adventure in Camping at (800) 417-7771. This company will haul a fully equipped trailer to your campsite, level it, light the appliances and explain its operation. They retrieve the trailer when your stay has ended. Adventure in Camping has 18- to 27-foot rigs that begin at $146 for two nights.

Gualala Point Regional Park
Calif. Hwy. 1, 0.5 mile south of Gualala
• (707) 785-2377

There are 26 sites at this dramatic location right on the ocean. The overnight camping area is across the highway from the park's day-use facilities, and it contains tables and stoves. Water and restroom facilities are nearby. Recreation options for day-use or overnight campers include fishing, bike trails, hiking (one trail beside the bluff is especially good for birdwatching) and picnic areas. It's open all year and offers 19 family campsites for tents and motor homes up to 28 feet, seven walk-in campsites and a trailer sanitary station. There's plenty of beachcombing to be done. The cost is $15 for all sites, $4 for an extra vehicle and $1 for dogs.

Mendocino County

U.S. Highway 101

Manor Oaks Overnighter Park
700 E. Gobbi St., Ukiah
• (707) 462-0529, (800) 357-8772

There are 53 motor-home spaces (15 of which are drive-through) with full hookups. Picnic tables, fire grills, restrooms, showers and a swimming pool are provided. A laundry and ice are available, and right next door are the tennis courts and barbecue facilities of Oak Manor Park. Leashed pets are allowed in the campground. The overnight fee is $20, and Manor Oaks is open year-round.

Quail Meadows Campground
23701 N. Calif. Hwy. 101, Willits
• (707) 459-6006

Most of the 49 motor-home spaces here have full or partial hookups, and there is a special section for tents only. Amenities include patios, picnic tables, restrooms, showers and a sanitary disposal station. A laundry, propane, ice and TV hookups are available. Pets are al-

Photo: Bill Hoban

Vista Point, north of Irish Beach, gives visitors a unique look at the Pacific Ocean.

lowed on leashes. Sites cost from $14 to $24, with a 10 percent discount for seniors or Good Sam Club members.

Willits KOA
1600 Calif. Hwy. 20, Willits
• (707) 459-6179

There are 21 sites for tents only and 50 RV spaces (27 of which are drive-through) with full or partial hookups. Piped water, flush toilets, showers, picnic tables, a playground, a swimming pool and a sanitary dump station are provided. And that's just the beginning. The Willits KOA has hiking trails, a fish pond, a petting zoo, minigolf, an arcade, weekend barbecues and even seasonal horseback riding. A grocery store, laundry and RV supplies are available, too. Pets are allowed on leashes. Tent sites cost $24, full RV hookups are $28, and the 12 recently added cabins go for $40 each.

Calif. Highway 128

Hendy Woods State Park
18599 Philo-Greenwood Rd., Philo
• (707) 937-5804

The park campground offers 92 sites for tents or RVs up to 35 feet long, including four wheelchair-accessible sites. Piped water, flush toilets, hot showers, a sanitary disposal sta-

tion, picnic tables and fire pits are provided. A grocery store and a propane gas station are available nearby. Pets are permitted. The fee for campsites is $16; each extra vehicle is $5. (For more on Hendy Woods State Park, see our Parks and Recreation chapter.)

Paul M. Dimmick Wayside State Camp
Calif. Hwy. 128, 8 miles east of
Calif. Hwy. 1 • (707) 937-5804

There are 25 campsites for tents or RVs up to 35 feet long. Restrooms, fireplaces and picnic tables are provided, and pets are permitted, but there is no potable water. The nearby Navarro River is the highlight here. In summer it's a spot for swimming or canoeing; in late winter, the river gets a fair steelhead run. The state camp is open year round. The camping fee is $12 a night, and an extra vehicle will run you $5.

Mendocino Coast

Manchester State Park
41500 Kinney Rd., Manchester
• (707) 937-5804

This popular state beach offers 46 campsites for tents and motor homes up to 30 feet long. It also includes a 40-person group site and 10 environmental camps. Most sites have piped water, chemical (non-flush) toilets, picnic tables and fireplaces. The campground has a sanitary dump station. No pets are allowed. The fee is $12 for tents or RVs. (For more on Manchester, see our Parks and Recreation chapter.)

Van Damme State Park
Calif. Hwy. 1, 3 miles south of Mendocino
• (707) 937-5804

At an elevation of 100 feet, Van Damme has great ocean views and 74 campsites for tents or motor homes up to 35 feet long. There are also 10 primitive campsites reached by a 1.7-mile hike, plus a group camp that accommodates 50 people. Piped water, flush toilets, a sanitary disposal station, hot showers, picnic tables and fireplaces are provided in the main campground. A grocery store, laundry and propane are available nearby. Pets are permitted. The fee is $16 per site ($10 for the environmental hike-in camp, $75 for the group site). An extra vehicle is $5. (See our Parks and Recreation chapter for more on Van Damme State Park.)

Russian Gulch State Park
Calif. Hwy. 1, 2 miles north of Mendocino
• (707) 937-5804

Set near some of California's most beautiful coastline, this park offers 24 campsites for tents or RVs up to 30 feet long. Some special sites are provided for hikers and bicyclists, so that they don't have to compete for space with RVs. There is also a wheelchair-accessible site and a 40-person group site. Piped water, hot showers, flush toilets, picnic tables and fireplaces with cooking grills are provided. Pets are permitted. The campground is open April through October. The fee per night is $16, or $60 for the group site. An extra vehicle costs $5. (For more on Russian Gulch, see our Parks and Recreation chapter.)

Jackson State Forest
State Department of Forestry, 802 N. Main St., Fort Bragg • (707) 964-5674

Pick up a camping permit and campground map at the Department of Forestry's Fort Bragg offices. There are 18 separate campgrounds scattered throughout this large state forest, with as few as two or as many as 24 campsites. Both tent-pitchers and RVers can find accommodations here. No piped water is available, but pit toilets, picnic tables and fireplaces are provided. Pets are permitted. Two equestrian campgrounds are available (check that campground

map). There is no fee at any of the campsites in this state forest. Although the camping is primitive, the redwood forest is an amazing attraction. (See our Parks and Recreation chapter for more on Jackson State Forest.)

Mackerricher State Park
24100 Mackerricher Park Rd., Fort Bragg
• (707) 937-5804

There are 11 walk-in campsites (for up to four people) and 139 sites for tents or motor homes up to 35 feet long—but no hookups—at this beautiful coastal park 3 miles north of Fort Bragg on Calif. 1. One site is wheelchair-accessible. Piped water, hot showers, flush toilets, a dump station, picnic tables and fireplaces are provided. Pets are permitted, and the overnight fee is $16, plus $5 for an extra vehicle. (Mackerricher State Park is further detailed in our Parks and Recreation chapter.)

Fort Bragg Leisure Time RV Park
30801 Calif. Hwy. 20, Fort Bragg
• (707) 964-5994

The wooded setting is a highlight here for RV campers. There are 82 sites for tents or RVs, many with full or partial hookups. Restrooms, picnic tables, cable TV, fire rings, coin-operated hot showers and a sanitary disposal station are provided. A laundry is available, and pets are allowed on leashes. The fee is $22.50 for full hookups, $20.50 for partial hookups and $16.50 for tents.

Lake County

Loch Lomond Park
Calif. Hwy. 175
• (707) 928-5044

Off Calif. Highway 175 on the northern slopes of Cobb Mountain is Loch Lomond, a peaceful campground with about 20 RV or tent spaces. They have picnic tables, fire grills, restrooms and showers, and a swimming pool and store are across the road. The overnight fee is $10 for a two-person tent site, $12 for full hookup.

Shaw's Shady Acres
7805 Cache Creek Way, Clearlake
• (707) 994-2236

Cache Creek is a small stream that pours out of Clear Lake, and at least three privately owned campgrounds are set along it. Shaw's has 13 sites for tents or RVs—six RV and two tent sites on the waterfront, five tent sites under the walnut trees. You'll find picnic tables, standing barbecues, restrooms, showers and a laundry. Need more? How about a swimming pool, a rec patio, a beer-and-wine bar and a market. Oh, and if you want your recreation right out on the creek, they have a pier, boat ramp, fishing supplies and boat rentals. The cost is $16 per night for two people, plus $2 for each additional person age 5 or older. North of Lower Lake on Calif. Highway 53, turn west at the Old Highway 53 turnoff; make a left on the frontage road and drive a quarter-mile to Shaw's.

Garners' Resort
6235 Old Calif. Hwy. 53
• (707) 994-6267

One of the southernmost campgrounds on Clear Lake, Garners' is just north of Lower Lake. The resort has 25 sites for tents and 40 for motor homes. It has flush toilets, showers, a recreation room, a swimming and wading pool, a laundry and a grocery store. Of course, it offers boat rentals and a pier for anglers. The fee is $16 per night.

M&M Campgrounds
13050 Island Dr., Clearlake Oaks
• (707) 998-9943

Have you promised your spouse a trip to some exotic island but just haven't been able to squirrel away any money? Your problems are solved! This park is actually on an island in the marshy area between Clear Lake and the town of Clearlake Oaks, just off Calif. 20. (Don't worry, the road is elevated.) M&M has 37 spaces, flush toilets, showers and a boat ramp. Boat rentals and a market are just down the street. The nightly fee is $13.

Edgewater Resort and RV Park
6420 Soda Bay Rd., Kelseyville
• (707) 279-0208

Edgewater is one of the higher-quality campgrounds around Clear Lake, in terms of both atmosphere and amenities. It boasts more than 150 trees of 19 varieties on the grounds. The resort has 61 spaces. Some of them work better as tent spaces, some are more appropriate for RVs, though the proprietors will mix and match as necessary. Here you'll find picnic tables, fire grills, restrooms, showers, a volleyball court, horseshoe pits, a clubhouse, a general store, a swimming pool and laundry facilities. There's also a long fishing pier, a boat ramp and a beach. You can even rent a boat here, and in the summer you might catch a musical event.

Pets are allowed on leashes. The cost is $25 per night, or $75-$250 for a cabin that sleeps from four to 12. Big groups are encouraged.

Clear Lake State Park
Soda Bay Rd., near Kelseyville
• (707) 279-4293 (info), (800) 444-PARK (reservations)

There are actually four separate campgrounds within the park: shady Cole Creek; Kelsey Creek, which is right on the water; and Upper and Lower Bay View, nice ridge-top spots. Not all of them are open through the winter. The park is popular with boaters, anglers and those wanting nothing more active than staring at the herons in the tules while sipping a cold drink. All together, Clear Lake has 147 campsites for tents or motor homes, plus a few primitive hike-in/bike-in sites. There are plenty of picnic tables, fire grills, restrooms and showers, plus a grocery store and a laundry. Some sites are wheelchair-accessible. The park charges $15 a night for tenters, $16 for RVers (up to eight people). (For more on Clear Lake, see our Parks and Recreation chapter.)

Kelly's Kamp
8220 Scotts Valley Rd., west of Upper Lake
• (707) 263-5754

Just far enough removed from Clear Lake that it avoids much of the traffic, this campground is on Scotts Creek, close to the Blue Lakes. Kelly's has 75 sites for tents or RVs, plus picnic tables, fire grills, flush toilets, showers, a laundry and a small camp store. The fee is $17 for up to four people, another $2.50 for electricity.

Holiday Harbor RV Park
3605 Lakeshore Blvd., Nice
• (707) 274-1136

Alongside Calif. 20 in the town of Nice, Holiday Harbor has a full-service marina, a boat ramp and reliable bass fishing. It also has 30 RV spaces with full or partial hookups. The park is equipped with picnic tables, restrooms, showers, a rec room and a laundromat. The overnight charge is $16 to $17.50.

Pine Acres Resort
5328 Blue Lakes Rd., north of Upper Lake
• (707) 275-2811

See our Hotels and Motels chapter for a full description of Pine Acres. Note here, however, that the resort also has 32 spaces for motor homes, most with full or partial hookups. The facilities include picnic tables, flush toilets, showers and a

CAMPING

grocery store. Some of the campsites are on the shore of Upper Blue Lake, and Pine Acres has the requisite moorings, boat ramp, fishing supplies and boat rentals.

The camping fee is $17 a night for tents, $19 to $20 for RVs. From Upper Lake, go 6 miles northwest on Calif. 20, turn left on Irvine Street and proceed two blocks. Turn right on Blue Lakes Road.

Bear Creek Campground
Bear Creek Rd., north of Upper Lake
• (707) 275-2361

This one is secluded, untrampled and picturesque, set at about 2,000 feet, at the confluence of Bear Creek and Blue Slide Creek (just past the Rice Fork of the Eel River). There are 16 sites for tents or motor homes, plus picnic tables, fire pits, vault toilets and access to hiking trails—but no piped water, so lug your own or bring a purifier.

Make no reservations, pay no fee. Pets are permitted on leashes. From Upper Lake, drive 17 miles north on Elk Mountain Road, then make a right onto Bear Creek Road and proceed another 8 miles. The grounds are closed to campers from mid-October through the end of April.

Middle Creek Campground
Elk Mountain Rd., north of Upper Lake
• (707) 275-2361

Among the campgrounds in the mountains of northern Lake County, this one is the closest to the towns of Clear Lake (about 8 miles north of Upper Lake). Middle Creek is at an elevation of about 2,000 feet, where the West and East forks of the Eel River come together. There are 12 sites for tents or small RVs, plus picnic tables, fire pits and vault toilets. Water is on the gravity system. You can bring a pet if it is leashed. Middle Creek, popular with dirt bikers, costs $4 per night for campers, and you can't make reservations. From Upper Lake, drive north on Elk Mountain Road (Forest Service Road 1N02).

Lower Nye
Rice Creek Rd., north of Upper Lake
• (707) 275-2361

This is a good starting point for a backpacking trip into the rugged Snow Mountain Wilderness. Lower Nye sits on the periphery of that protected area, at 3,300 feet on Skeleton Creek. The tiny campground has six sites for tents or motor homes, with picnic tables, fire pits and vault toilets. There is no piped water, and it is closed from mid-September through April. There is no charge for camping. From Upper Lake, go 17 miles north on Elk Mountain Road, veer right on Bear Creek Road and drive another 7 miles. Turn left on Rice Creek Road and proceed 14 miles to Lower Nye.

Sunset Campground
Potter Valley-Lake Pillsbury Rd., east of Potter Valley in Mendocino County
• (707) 275-2361

Largest of the five public and private campgrounds set around scenic Lake Pillsbury, Sunset has 54 sites for tents or RVs. It also has picnic tables, fire pits and vault toilets. You can angle for trout on the northeast rim of the lake or jump on the nature trail that begins near the campground. A boat ramp is close at hand. You pay $10 a night here, and reservations are not accepted. Lake Pillsbury is accessed via Potter Valley-Lake Pillsbury Road.

Fuller Grove
Simmons Rd., east of Potter Valley
• (707) 275-2361

Another option for Lake Pillsbury visitors, Fuller Grove has 30 spots for tents or motor homes. You get picnic tables, fireplaces, vault toilets and access to a nearby boat ramp if you want to get on the water. The cost is $10 per night. Pets are permitted but must be kept under control. From the Eel River Information Kiosk at Lake Pillsbury (follow the signs and you can't miss it approaching from the west), proceed 2.2 miles to the lake shore, make a right and drive another half-mile.

Restaurants

Here's the Wine Country's dirty little secret: Some return visitors don't come for the wine. In fact, rumors persist that some of them are actual teetotalers. They come for the food, and if you've ever wielded a knife and fork in these parts, you know why.

Let's say you will be spending the day in Napa Valley, lumbering up and down Calif. 29 with the rest of the wine seekers. Because of some rare pituitary condition, your doctor has told you to eat nothing but chicken dishes every night for three months. You're a week into the diet, and you are so sick of poultry you're thinking of vandalizing a KFC outlet. Take heart. You are about to be introduced to the wonders of Wine Country cuisine. Wine Spectator Greystone Restaurant will spit-roast that chicken with toasted orzo, olives, preserved lemon and sun-dried tomatoes; Celadon will roast it Indian-style, with ginger and red curry, and serve it with saffron-basmati risotto; Compadres will turn it into arroz con pollo; Catahoula will take that little sucker and roast it with tasso potatoes and garlic-lemon escarole; Soo Yuan will shred it and serve it in mu shu pancakes; All Seasons Cafe will roast it and deliver it with creamer potatoes, carrots and baby leeks (with a thyme-infused jus, of course); Pacifico Restaurante will add chayote and potato and bury it all with mole sauce; the Calistoga Inn will marinate the chicken in lime and crust it with Jamaican jerk sauce; Auberge du Soleil will redefine it as rosemary-roasted petite poulet with artichoke-eggplant ragout; Yoshi-Shige will offer traditional chicken teriyaki; Atlas Peak Grill will let the bird swim in achiote marinade, then grill it with roasted red peppers and potatoes. What's that, the same doctor demands you consume only salmon for lunch? Enough already! By now you should have an idea of the breadth of cuisine that awaits you here. It isn't your average meat and potatoes, though you can find that if you want it.

The Wine Country has become something of a magnet for chefs, more so since the opening of the Culinary Institute of America's "campus" north of St. Helena (see our Education and Child Care chapter). Of course, food and wine complement one another in business just as they do on the table. The same breed of traveler becomes preoccupied with both worlds.

You taste wine all day, get hungry and, seeking to preserve the happiness of your taste buds, opt for a first-rate restaurant. There on the menu are some of the wines you have been sampling. And if you attend a wedding the next day, it might be catered by the cafe at which you ate yesterday. Sometimes it's hard to separate the two industries (especially somewhere like Domaine Chandon, where winery and dining room sit side-by-side). So eat, drink and be married, and don't fret about the impossibility of visiting every restaurant in our four-county area.

As you read these entries remember that, unless we say otherwise, you can count on certain things: The restaurant serves beer and wine but does not have a full bar, it accepts major credit cards, it is wheelchair-accessible, and it takes reservations. Most of the upscale restaurants do not have children's menus, but the down-home places do. Lastly, most restaurants here define their dress code as "classy casual," "snappy casual" or, most often, "Wine Country casual." What that basically means is to look well-groomed. Tuck in your shirt, or change it if you just dumped half a glass of

LOOK FOR:
- **Napa County**
- **Sonoma County**
- **Mendocino County**
- **Lake County**

Price Guidelines

Refer to this price code as you peruse our Restaurants section. The dollar figure refers to the average price of two entrees only—no appetizers, no dessert, no drinks, no tax or gratuity. We don't actually expect you to eat that way—or to forego the tip!—we just wanted to keep the calculations simple.

$	$18 or less
$$	$18 to $25
$$$	$25 to $35
$$$$	$35 or more

Pinot Noir on it. Other than that, it is unlikely you'll be underdressed. Even the highest-rated establishments tend to allow Levi's, collarless shirts, even shorts and shoes with no socks in the summer. And that, some say, is one of the nicest things about eating here.

Napa County

Alexis Baking Company
$$, no credit cards • 1517 Third St., Napa • (707) 258-1827

What began as a wholesale bakery has become one of Napa's coolest hangouts, whether you're eating lunch or light dinner or just sipping oak-roasted coffee and contemplating the always-engaging art on the walls. ABC puts together a variety of salads, soups and specials, changing the lineup daily. The gorgonzola cheeseburgers and the focaccia sandwiches go over big, but it's the fresh baked goods that have inspired the most loyalty. Save room for a piece of chocolate-caramel cake or apricot pistachio cake, or just pig out on muffins and cookies. The Baking Company is open seven days for breakfast and lunch, carrying the lunch menu through dinner on Thursday and Friday.

INSIDERS' TIP

If you eat in a few high-end Napa Valley restaurants, you'll no doubt run across a reference to Forni-Brown greens under the Salads heading. Forni-Brown is a small organic producer in Calistoga, and, yes, their salad greens are uniformly delicious.

Atlas Peak Grill
$$$ • Monticello Rd. (Calif. Hwy. 121) and Vichy Ave., Napa • (707) 253-1455

On the east end of Napa, just a mile from Silverado Country Club, sits this Hansel and Gretel-esque, garden-ensconced stone and brick cottage, a not-so-old-fashioned steak house with global nuances. The corn-fed beef is the staple—New York cut, filet mignon or Chicago rib eye with your choice of sauce and accompaniments. Or try the Filet Christiana, tender filet mignon in puff pastry with mushroom and Cabernet sauce. Chef Roberto Estenzo also offers tempting Mediterranean specialties, which he adapts to the season. The bar has a substantial wine list, but is particularly renowned for its classic martinis (never infused) and generous selection of single malt scotches. Atlas Peak is open for dinner Wednesday through Sunday.

Bistro Don Giovanni
$$$ • 4110 St. Helena Hwy. S., Napa • (707) 224-3300

Damn it all, we just can't avoid the word. Giovanni Scala's restaurant is "romantic." The subdued earth tones, the unpolished wood and the tiles, the vineyard views, the fireplaces in and out—your date will be putty in your hands. Just make sure you can still concentrate on the food. Donna Scala does the cooking, favoring regional Italian dishes and tossing in a bit of Provence. The pan-seared salmon filet with buttermilk mashed potatoes is excellent, as is the grilled portobello mushroom appetizer. The restaurant is also noted for its risottos and pastas. Don Giovanni is open seven days a week for lunch and dinner. The menu changes daily, and there is a full bar.

Celadon
$$ • 1040 Main St., Ste. 104, Napa • (707) 254-9690

In Napa Valley, you'll be hard-pressed to find better quality for your dollar than you get at this bright creekside cafe in the rear of the Main Street Exchange (next to the Opera House). Celadon, painted in the pale greens and blues implied by the name, has a long slate counter and an open kitchen. They offer daily fish satays, nightly fish specials, and "the best burger in town" (we'll stay out of that brawl). Another favorite among the very local crowd is the jerked pork with spicy black beans and pineapple salsa. Celadon also has a well-conceived wine list, with 10 by-the-glass choices. It's open for lunch Monday through Friday and dinner Monday through Saturday. Seating is "upon arrival"—i.e., no reservations.

Chanterelle
$$$ • 804 First St., Napa • (707) 253-7300

A chanterelle might be a large, floppy fungus, but this dining room was voted Most Romantic Restaurant in Napa in 1994 and 1996. It must have something to do with the big, plush chairs and the widely spaced tables. Chanterelle does things in the Mediterranean style, favoring the French. Try the hazelnut-crusted rack of lamb with wild mushrooms and baby leeks, the angel hair pasta with saffron and grilled prawns or the poached salmon in a fine herb champagne sauce. And try to act amo-

Photo: Tina Luster-Hoban

Outdoor dining is a staple in the North Bay area. Here, people lunch near the waterfront in Petaluma.

rous. Chanterelle is open for lunch and dinner seven days a week and brunch on Sunday. The restaurant has a full bar.

Foothill Cafe
$$$ • 2766 Old Sonoma Rd., Napa
• (707) 252-6178

"People are scared to come in sometimes," chef/owner Jerry Shaffer says of his small, 40-seat restaurant in southwest Napa. That's because Foothill Cafe sits in a nondescript little strip mall, an unlikely venue for a locally adored restaurant. Enter the cafe and your faith will be rewarded with food that relies heavily on fresh local produce and a hickory smoker in the kitchen. Nightly specials accent favorites such as baby-back ribs and roasted free-range chicken breast with creamy polenta. The decor is frenetic, thanks to Shaffer's repeated excursions to Baja California. Foothill Cafe is open for dinner from Wednesday through Sunday.

La Boucane
$$$ • 1778 Second St., Napa
• (707) 253-1177

At 71, Jacques Mokrani must be starting to slow down, right? "My skills improve every day," retorts the indomitable, Algerian-born chef/restaurateur. By now his La Boucane, housed in a 120-year-old Victorian, is a Napa Valley landmark. There is a white tablecloth, a red rose and silver utensils on every table. Classical music strums in the background. And out comes the classic French cuisine: a Chilean sea bass Bretonne appetizer; onion soup Lyonnaise; crisp roast duckling with orange sauce for two; and, if you're smart, one of Mokrani's renowned souffles.

La Boucane's wine list sticks exclusively to Napa Valley. And remember what it says at the bottom of the menu: "We will prepare any dish upon request, providing we have the ingredients on hand." And if "on hand" means he has to run across the street to Safeway, the chef says, then so be it. The restaurant is open for dinner every night but Sunday.

Old Adobe Bar and Grille
$$ • 376 Soscol Ave., Napa
• (707) 255-4310

Old Adobe's name is more authentic than you might guess. The dining room is housed in the second-oldest intact adobe building in Northern California, constructed in 1840. The 3-foot-thick walls and exposed rafters in the dining room are original, and the murals depicting Mexican village life were painted in the 1920s. Old Adobe serves up variations of Mexican standards but really specializes in steaks and prime rib, adding daily fresh fish and pasta specials. The restaurant does dinner seven days a week and lunch Monday through Friday. It also offers Sunday brunch. There is a full bar.

RESTAURANTS

Piccolino's Italian Café
$$ • 1385 Napa Town Center
• (707) 251-0100

Food has always meant comfort to Joe Salerno, who grew up stirring pots and making sausage with his extended Italian family in upstate New York. Salerno now does his best to create fond memories at Piccolino's, his unpretentious, child-friendly restaurant in downtown Napa. The café offers fresh fish dishes, house-made sausage and four types of pizza. The pasta entrees are highlighted by the colorful fettuccine Calabrese, with its multitude of simple ingredients; and the lasagna, a family recipe that employs a light ricotta shipped in from the East Coast. Lasagna and spaghetti are available in immense family-style portions. The wine list is primarily Napan, though it does include a small line of Italians. Piccolino's is open daily for lunch and dinner, plus brunch on weekends. See our Nightlife chapter for information on live music.

The Royal Oak
Vintner's Court
$$$$ • Silverado Resort,
1600 Atlas Peak Rd., Napa
• (707) 257-0200, (707) 257-5428

Two separate restaurants are housed in The Mansion at Silverado. To the left of the main lounge is Vintner's Court, larger and more formal, with stolid, oak-sided walls and lots of glass. To the right is the more rustic Royal Oak, with its open beams and open kitchen. Vintner's Court serves fresh California cuisine with Mediterranean and Pacific Rim influences—for example, seared Chilean seabass with mango and jicama, or fresh Sonoma foie gras with figs. The Oak is more traditionally American, with big steaks and filet of salmon. Peter Pahk is executive chef for both restaurants. Both offer full bar service. The Royal Oak is open seven days a week for dinner. Vintner's Court is open Monday through Thursday for dinner off the menu, Friday night for seafood buffet and Sunday morning for brunch. The 2-inch-thick waffles have inspired all sorts of devotion.

Yoshi-Shige
$$$ • 3381 California Blvd., Napa
• (707) 257-3583

Good sushi restaurants are hard to find north of San Francisco. One of the best is Yoshi-Shige, a 10-year-old place with Japanese decor and a menu of more than 60 sushi items, not to mention entrees such as chicken teriyaki and shrimp-and-vegetable tempura. The sushi dishes range in price from $3.50 to $8.50, so how much you spend depends on how much you are willing to devour. Yoshi-Shige serves sake in addition to its beer and wine. It's open for lunch and dinner every day and night except Monday.

Bistro Jeanty
$$$ • 6510 Washington St., Yountville
• (707) 944-0103

Philippe Jeanty became head chef at Domaine Chandon a year after it opened, and over the next 20 years he turned it into a world-class restaurant. There was much local handwringing when Jeanty flew the coop in 1997. But his comfortable, two-room bistro opened in April of 1998 and quickly occupied a niche that, Philippe explains, is part Paris, part French countryside. You won't find a single pasta on this small menu, no Caesar salad or hamburgers. Instead, be on the lookout for lamb tongue and potato salad, rabbit and sweetbread ragout with white beans and truffle oil, and mussels steamed in red wine. The setting is just as authentic, with French furnishings and paintings by Guy Buffet. And the color of the walls? Dijon, of course. Bistro Jeanty is open for lunch and dinner seven days a week. It has a full bar.

Brix
$$$ • 7377 St. Helena Hwy., Yountville
• (707) 944-BRIX

Spicy, grilled rare Hawaiian Ahi tuna with sesame-ginger aioli and daikon ponzu? Smoked salmon pizza with sour cream, tobiko and Maui onions? Thai-pesto smoked rack of lamb with spicy peanut satay and Zinfandel glaze? What do you call this? "Asian fusion" if you're Brix, the restaurant just north of Yountville. Brix is surrounded by 10 acres of vineyard and a couple of acres of olive trees; one dining room wall is all glass, revealing the restaurant's herb garden. They have a full bar, including what the *San Francisco Chronicle* called an "Academy Award-winning wine list." Brix is open for lunch and dinner, seven days a week.

Compadres Mexican Bar & Grill
$$ • 6539 Washington St., Yountville
• (707) 944-2406

Mexican fare is more than appropriate here, on a portion of the land grant deeded to Salvador Vallejo by the Mexican government in 1838. Compadres is a sprawling, 165-seat restaurant with both indoor and outdoor seating. There is depth to the Margarita list, which includes what *San Francisco Focus* magazine once ordained the best Margarita it had sampled. The food is wide-ranging, too, with traditional Jaliscan carnitas, seafood tacos, daily fish specials and at least eight types of enchilada. Compadres is open seven days a week for breakfast, lunch and dinner.

The Diner
$$, no credit cards • 6476 Washington St., Yountville • (707) 944-2626

The Diner isn't a true '50s holdover but, established in 1976, it predates by far the bandwagon diners you now see in every city. Occupying a former Greyhound bus depot, this restaurant is nothing short of a landmark—a place where winery owners sit next to their vineyard workers, and no one feels out of place. The restaurant is progressive: It has its own gardens and on-site organic bakery. But the look is classic, with wooden booths, marble tabletops and Fiestaware.

The Diner is best known for its breakfasts but is open for lunch and dinner as well (though it's closed Mondays). If there is a house specialty—excluding the buttermilk shakes—it would have to be the German potato pancakes with homemade sausage and organic Gravenstein applesauce. Dinner includes a few Mexican dishes. The restaurant takes reservations only for parties of six or more.

Domaine Chandon
$$$$ • 1 California Dr., Yountville • (707) 944-2892

Domaine Chandon is Napa Valley's only restaurant and winery contained on the same grounds. Parked against the hills west of Yountville, it sits amid century-old oaks and the winery's own vineyards. The atmosphere is elegant, immaculate and *très français*. The menu changes weekly but returns to a few of chef Robert Curry's favorites, such as smoked trout or salmon, foie blond pate, caramelized scallops and local lamb. Domaine Chandon is open for dinner every night except Monday and Tuesday. It's open for lunch seven days a week. Note that reservations here should be booked well in advance.

The French Laundry
$$$$ • 6640 Washington St., Yountville • (707) 944-2380

What does Yountville have that Manhattan and Los Angeles don't? How about the best chef in America? That's what the prestigious James Beard Foundation called Thomas Keller

in May 1997. Keller's restaurant, The French Laundry, is so esteemed that it doesn't even bother hanging a sign out front—you have to search for the address plate at the corner of Washington and Creek streets. The restaurant, in a century-old fieldstone house that was, indeed, a French steam laundry for many years, has been compared to a three-star country establishment in France. The menu here is strictly prix fixe: $80 per person for a five-course vegetarian offering, $90 for a more robust five-course meal, or $105 for the nine-course Chef's Tasting Menu. Keller, though a devotee of traditional French principles, is also known for his whimsical takes on common meals, like "macaroni and cheese" that turns out to be butter-poached Maine lobster with creamy lobster broth and Mascarpone-enriched orzo, or "coffee and doughnuts" that are, in fact, fresh-baked cinnamon-sugared doughnuts with cappuccino semi-freddo. The French Laundry is open for dinner seven days a week and lunch from Friday through Sunday.

Mustards Grill
$$$ • 7399 St. Helena Hwy., Yountville • (707) 944-2424

Roadhouse meets fine dining at Mustards Grill. The restaurant is situated on Calif. 29, and the casual dining room looks onto a beautiful swath of the Napa countryside. But the real action here is in the kitchen. One of the most consistently popular restaurants in the valley, Mustards is also one of the oldest, established in 1983.

The menu changes seasonally, but classics like Mongolian pork chops (marinated, grilled chops with braised cabbage and garlic mashers) and hanger steak are available year round. Everything is made from scratch here—don't miss the house-made ketchup served with paper-thin onion rings. Chef/owner Cindy Pawlcyn has crafted a menu that tends toward creatively reinvented American classics, with daily fish specials providing the haute end of the cuisine. After dessert (most impressive is the lemon tart with 6-inch-high brown-sugar meringue), you can order a cigar and retire to the smoking patio. Mustards has a full bar with "way too many wines" and is open for lunch and dinner seven days a week. Look for the new Mustards Grill cookbook.

Piatti Restaurant
$$$ • 6480 Washington St., Yountville • (707) 944-2070

Dwelling on the Mediterranean end of Italy,

RESTAURANTS

the Piatti menu is filled with fresh herbs and seafood. Chef Peter Hall offers daily pizza, pasta and fish specials. Some things remain constant, though, like the pappardelle "fantasia": wide saffron ribbons with shrimp, arugula, fresh tomato and spicy lemon-wine sauce. The spice-rubbed rotisserie chicken is another favorite. Piatti has osso bucco and live music every Wednesday. The dining room is warm, with stucco walls, handpainted murals, white pine and fireplaces. The restaurant has a full bar (with many Italian wines) and is open for lunch and dinner seven days a week.

Auberge du Soleil
$$$$ • 180 Rutherford Hill Rd., Rutherford • (707) 963-1211

Before Auberge du Soleil the inn, there was Auberge du Soleil the restaurant. It's known as one of Napa Valley's premier eateries, not just for the food but for the remarkable vistas from the dining terrace. Chef Andy Sutton (his wife, Katie, is resident chef at The Hess Collection winery) stresses wine as an ingredient, along with low-fat recipe alternatives. The dining room is in theme with the entire resort—rustically classy, with thick cedar columns, rough-timbered ceilings, fireplaces and French doors. You can start with the famous Seven Sparkling Sins, a platter with treats ranging from sevruga caviar to truffled quail eggs. If still sitting upright, you can move on to oak-barrel-roasted sterling salmon or morels and veal medallions. Better yet, let Auberge surprise you with its ever-changing, five-course "Taste of the Wine Country" menu—it costs $75 per person (or $114 with wine pairings) and is available every night but Saturday. The restaurant is open for lunch and dinner seven days a week, and it has a full bar.

The Restaurant at Meadowood
$$$$ • 900 Meadowood Ln., St. Helena • (707) 963-3646

The bigshots in the Meadowood kitchen have been known to argue with one another from time to time, but you can forgive them. They're married. Together, executive chef Didier Lenders and his wife and chef de cuisine, California native Maria del Pilar Sanchez, consistently conjure dishes worthy of Meadowood's sterling reputation (see our Spas and Resorts chapter). Recent examples include seared sea scallops steamed in corn husks with vanilla bean butter, and tian of lamb loin with shiitake mushrooms. Of course, if the house-smoked sturgeon with warm potato fritters and

Osetra caviar is being offered as an appetizer, you'll have a hard time even thinking about a main course. As an alternative, you can select the chef's daily, four-course vintner menu. It runs $56, or $80 with four wine pairings.

And the wine list, by the way, is phenomenal. Sticking exclusively to Napa Valley, it represents nearly all 300 of the county's wineries. And if all of that isn't enough, there is the dining room itself—a comfortable pastel room overlooking the resort's manicured golf course. The Restaurant at Meadowood has a full bar, and is open for dinner seven nights a week, plus Sunday brunch.

Brava Terrace
$$$ • 3010 St. Helena Hwy. N., St. Helena • (707) 963-9300

If you wandered in from a winter downpour in the French countryside, this is just the type of food you would hope to find. Chef Fred Halpert offers 10 or so regular main courses, plus once-a-week specialties. For example, on Thursday it's braised short ribs, and on Saturday it's coq au vin. Thankfully, the osso bucco with garlic mashed potatoes never leaves the menu. Set in an A-frame building, the dining room has hardwood floors and a big stone fireplace. Brava Terrace is open for continuous lunch and dinner. From May through November the restaurant is open seven days a week; off-season, it's closed on Wednesday. It has a full bar.

Gillwoods Restaurant
$$ • 1313 Main St., St. Helena • (707) 963-1788
$$ • 1320 Napa Town Center, Napa • (707) 253-0409

You have to get up pretty early in the morning to beat the locals to Gillwoods, St. Helena's favorite breakfast spot. It's casual, intimate and filled with good cheer and caffeine. The big draw always has been the scrambles—eggs and cream cheese mixed with various ingredients. (Our personal favorite: the salmon scramble with capers.)

The restaurant is open for breakfast and lunch seven days a week and does not take reservations. Gillwoods now has a second location in Napa Town Center. The menu is the same there, except it includes dinner on Friday and Saturday nights. Reservations for six or more are accepted in Napa.

Green Valley Cafe
$$ • 1310 Main St., St. Helena • (707) 963-7088

Small, cozy and reasonably priced (i.e., exactly what you *don't* expect in St. Helena), Green Valley Cafe is the perfect place to sup before or after a film at Cameo Cinema. If you don't make reservations, you'll probably wind up at the counter. No matter where you sit, you will be treated to Delio Cuneo's Northern Italian cuisine. (Cuneo was born near Portofino.) Green Valley offers daily fresh-fish specials, but otherwise sticks to a simple, well-executed menu. Locals tend to gravitate toward the lasagna (with tomatoes, ham, mozzarella and basil), the braised lamb shank with polenta or the *melanzane*—eggplant topped with tomato and bechamel sauces and Parmesan cheese. The wine list is a mix of Napa Valley and Italy. Green Valley Cafe is open for lunch and dinner from Tuesday through Saturday.

Model Bakery
$ • 1357 Main St., St. Helena
• (707) 963-8192

You'd think it was a film set if those whiffs of fresh-baked bread didn't call you from the kitchen. The look is perfect for a small-town bakery, with a black-and-white checkerboard floor, ceiling fans, display windows and bench seats overlooking the sidewalk, and oversized wall mirrors at either end of the room making the place look twice as big as it is. The Model Bakery makes scones, croissants, danishes, bagels and at least a half-dozen types of muffins. The repertoire includes six or so daily breads, plus regular daily specials. They bust loose on Friday with five specials: whole wheat, seeded, oatmeal, sour rye and pumate-basil. The bakery also sells juices, soups and pre-wrapped sandwiches and, as you would guess, coffee and espresso drinks. It's open every day but Monday.

Pairs Parkside Cafe
$$ • 1420 Main St., St. Helena
• (707) 963-7566

The idea at Pairs is expressed in the restaurant's name: to pair food and wine to the advantage of both. Each dish on the menu, even appetizers, comes with a varietal recommendation. For instance, Chardonnay is suggested for the lemon-fried calamari, Sauvignon Blanc for the vegetarian spring rolls and Merlot for the grilled rosemary lamb chops. (Let us be so bold as to suggest black coffee with the warm cinnamon apple crisp; don't mention it.) Your wine choice is helped by the fact that all of Pairs' 25 or so wines are sold by the glass. In general, you can call the cuisine California Asian. The dining room walls are mottled with ochre and sienna, lending a casual, earthy feel

to the experience. The restaurant is open for lunch and dinner every day except Tuesday.

Pinot Blanc
$$$ • 641 Main St., St. Helena
• (707) 963-6191

German-born restaurateur Joaquim Splichal and his original Los Angeles restaurant, Patina, have garnered just about every food award imaginable. Over the last decade Splichal and his wife, Christine, have opened six other L.A.-area eateries and one notable Napa Valley relative: Pinot Blanc, a country bistro on the south side of St. Helena. Pinot Blanc attempts to create a weathered, Mediterranean-style oasis, with a roomy patio and a perimeter of olive trees and flowers. The always-creative pasta, fish and meat dishes are complemented by a *plat du jour*. Monday it might be Bellwether Farms spring lamb with potato, fava beans and truffle oil; Sunday it could be braised pig with herb-mustard spaetzle and red cabbage. Off the dining room are three private rooms for special events and wine tastings. Pinot Blanc is open seven days a week for lunch and dinner.

Showley's at Miramonte
$$$ • 1327 Railroad Ave., St. Helena
• (707) 963-1200

For more than 60 years the restaurant Miramonte stood as a grand landmark just behind Main Street in St. Helena. The famed eatery closed in 1989, but Grant Showley almost immediately moved into the vine-covered building (which was built as a cooperage in 1870) to fill the void. Showley is of the California cuisine school, but he adds some interesting spins, serving locally hunted wild boar in November and fig-based dishes whenever his 110-year-old fig tree (said to be the largest in the county) goes to harvest. The restaurant is open six days a week (closed Monday) for lunch and dinner. It has a patio and five separate rooms that are perfect for private parties from 14 to 75 diners.

Taylor's Refresher
$ • 933 Main St., St. Helena
• (707) 963-3486

If all fast food was this delightful then, well, the rainforest would be getting turned into cow pasture at an even faster clip. Retired traveling salesman and pharmacist Lloyd Taylor opened the Refresher for business in 1949. It's now owned by the Gott family, who spruced it up—but managed to retain the quaint atmosphere—in 1999. Taylor's cooks up lunch and early dinner seven days a week. The menu includes burgers, hot dogs and fountain treats. There are nice picnic grounds behind the eatery.

Terra
$$$$ • 1345 Railroad Ave., St. Helena
• (707) 963-8931

In St. Helena, "off the beaten track" means anything off Main Street, and Terra qualifies. It sits one block away in a historic landmark, a hardy fieldstone foundry constructed in 1884. The open redwood-beamed ceilings in the two dining rooms give you the feel of a Tuscan villa. Chef Hiro Sone's one-page menu aims for southern France and northern Italy, though he admittedly takes a few geographic liberties. Two appetizers should give you an example of what to expect: the fried rock shrimp with organic greens and chive-mustard sauce, and the terrine of foie gras with Belgian endive, walnuts and Fuji apple salad. The most popular main course might be the broiled, sake-marinated sea bass with shrimp dumplings in shiso broth. Terra is open for dinner every night except Tuesday.

Tomatina
$ • 1020 Main St., St. Helena
• (707) 967-9999

If tourists ever had a reason to complain about St. Helena, it was probably about the lack of inexpensive food. Tomatina, occupying the south half of the Inn at Southbridge (see our Hotels/Motels chapter), effectively bridged the gap when it opened in 1996. With Tra Vigne's Michael Chiarello serving as executive chef and Jim Humberd as on-site chef, the restaurant has become popular with local families. You order cafeteria-style, but servers bring you the food and drink. The Napoli-inspired thin-crust pizzas are recommended, as are the piadine—pizza crust removed from the big, wood-burning brick oven and topped by a selection of salad mixes and dressings. On hot days, the lemonade, simple syrup mixed with lemon juice and soda water, is irresistible. Tomatina is open for lunch and dinner seven days a week. The restaurant does not take reservations.

Tra Vigne
$$$ • 1050 Charter Oak Ave., St. Helena
• (707) 963-4444

Chef Michael Chiarello (see previous listing) has scrambled to the top of the Napa Valley food chain on the strength of this cozy trattoria in St. Helena. The stone building is an old landmark, and Tra Vigne has become a contemporary one. The regional Italian menu encourages grazing, with a host of interesting small plates, pastas and pizzas to complement the meats and fish. The restaurant is open for lunch and dinner seven days a week. There is a full bar and a wine cellar stocked with Italian reds and whites, plus a good selection of Californians.

Wine Spectator Greystone Restaurant
$$$ • 2555 Main St., St. Helena
• (707) 967-1010

Don't worry, eating at the Culinary Institute of America's restaurant doesn't make you a guinea pig for fresh-faced chefs-in-training. Remember, this branch of the CIA focuses on continuing education. Because most of the students are signed up for short study programs, it isn't practical to hire them for the kitchen. So the staff is quite professional, and executive chef Todd Humphries puts them to work preparing Mediterranean-inspired cuisine, including some dishes he brought from his former San Francisco restaurant, Campton Place.

Try the Greystone seafood paella (saffron rice, shrimp, mussels, monkfish and chorizo) or the popular grilled hanger steak with wild mushrooms. And try not to dribble while craning your head around the dining room, with its cement floor and stone walls lightened by blues and yellows. Greystone has a full bar. It is open seven days a week for lunch and dinner. Tuesdays and Wednesdays from mid-January through March are reserved for Winter Evenings in Wine Country, a series of special food and wine events.

All Seasons Cafe
$$$ • 1400 Lincoln Ave., Calistoga
• (707) 942-9111

If you read the food-and-wine magazines, you've probably been introduced to All Seasons. It has been profiled in *Gourmet*, *Wine Spectator* and *Appellation*, among others, and its high standards haven't faltered a bit over more than 15 years of operation. Mixing the quaint and the luxurious, the cafe has a wine bar that makes use of a truly exceptional wine list—it ranges far beyond the valley and is especially deep in Pinots and Zinfandels. The menu changes often here, but you can expect "seasonal California" dishes along the lines of grilled rib-eye steak with Cabernet glaze and creamy horseradish sauce, or English pea risotto with asparagus, spring garlic, tomato and mushrooms. The chef is John Coss. All Seasons is closed for lunch on Wednesday; otherwise, it's open for lunch and dinner daily.

A rustic fireplace waits to warm diners at Auberge du Soleil.

Brannan's Grill
$$$$ • 1374 Lincoln Ave., Calistoga
• (707) 942-2233

The Calistoga culinary scene got a major shakeup in March of 1998, when Brannan's Grill opened at the town's central intersection (Lincoln Avenue and Washington Street). It's physically arresting both inside and out, with refinished trusses and ironworks (all original to the 1911 building, long used as a motor garage) and storm windows that open onto Lincoln in warm weather. Most notable is the bar, a mahogany Brunswick design that was shipped around the cape in the late 1800s. The food is regional American, decidedly carnivore. Try the grilled hanger steak with hominy grit cakes or the voodoo shrimp, sauteed with oregano, rosemary, basil, dry-cured olives and cane sugar. Brannan's has a full bar. It's open seven days a week for lunch and dinner in high season, but lunch is Friday through Sunday in the winter. If you enjoy the experience, you might also consider eating at Checkers, Brannan's less formal sister restaurant just down the street at 1414 Lincoln.

Cafe Sarafornia
$$ • 1413 Lincoln Ave., Calistoga
• (707) 942-0555

Calistoga's most popular breakfast spot playfully incorporates the other half of Sam Brannan's legendary malapropism: "I'll make this the Calistoga of Sarafornia." The busy, sun-infused dining room has a central counter and sidewalk booths. Regulars swear by the cheese blintzes, the Brannan Benedict (two poached eggs with guacamole, bacon and Cajun cream on toast), the chicken-apple sausage and the Wildcat Scrambler (three eggs scrambled with mushrooms, Italian sausage, spinach and choice of cheese). The burgers are good at lunchtime. The cafe does not take reservations, which makes it easy to spot on Sunday morning—it's the place with the line out the door.

Calistoga Inn & Restaurant
$$$ • 1250 Lincoln Ave., Calistoga
• (707) 942-4101

The Inn is a popular place any time of year, but business really booms in the summer, when dining moves to the delightful creekside patio.

INSIDERS' TIP

The gardens at Cafe Beaujolais have become so attractive to passersby that the restaurant now provides Saturday tours twice monthly in spring and summer. Landscape designer Jaen Treesinger developed the gardens to allow drought-tolerant shrubs to thrive amidst edible flowers and herbs.

(The meat is even grilled outside, over hardwood.) Rosie Dunsford, that Jill of all trades—in addition to being innkeeper and executive chef, she was a recent Calistoga City Councilwoman—serves up regional American cuisine. The marinated Australian lamb sirloin, the Jamaican jerk half-chicken and the tri-tip sirloin finished with bleu cheese butter are all winners. There are fish specials too. The Inn is open for lunch and dinner every day of the year but Christmas. The restaurant has a full bar, including an extensive wine list and its own line of beers (look for Napa Valley Brewing Company in this chapter's Close-up on microbreweries).

Calistoga Roastery
$, no credit cards • 1631 Lincoln Ave., Calistoga • (707) 942-5757

This place must be doing something right: Half the inns and restaurants in the vicinity boast about serving Roastery coffee. Owners Clive Richardson and Terry Rich roast almost 20 varieties of beans—sometimes right on the spot in a preserved 1919 Probat roaster, the oldest of its kind in the nation. If the regular house coffee isn't exciting enough for you, there is a selection of espresso drinks, frappes and ice cream mochas, not to mention iced teas, Rocket Juices and Italian sodas. Yes, there are fresh-made baked goods too: bagels, croissants, scones of various stripes, banana bread, granola and more. And where else in Napa Valley can you get poached eggs on toast for $2.95? The Roastery opens at 6:30 AM every day and doesn't close its doors until 6 PM. It's an atmosphere designed for lounging, so bring a newspaper.

Catahoula Restaurant & Saloon
$$$ • 1457 Lincoln Ave., Calistoga
• (707) 942-2275

You can praise the food at Catahoula, just don't call it Cajun. Chef/owner Jan Birnbaum hails from Baton Rouge (the catahoula hound is the state dog of Louisiana), but he admits to taking creative liberties with his native cuisine. Birnbaum cooks up wonderful gumbos, but the menu also includes interesting combinations such as grilled quail with eggplant oyster stuffing and glazed cumin carrots, and whole oven-roasted fish in spicy tomato broth. Dessert is big here. How about a chewy molasses cookie and chicory-Kahlua ice cream sandwich with fresh peaches? The wood-fired oven dominates a dining room that manages to be elegant though decorated with industrial-looking "found art." Both restaurant and saloon are housed in the historic Mount View Hotel building (see our Hotels/Motels chapter). Catahoula serves dinner nightly, and breakfast, lunch and dinner on weekends.

Hydro Bar & Grill
$$ • 1403 Lincoln Ave., Calistoga
• (707) 942-9777

In a town where the sidewalks sometimes roll up at dusk, the Hydro is the restaurant that doesn't sleep. It offers dinner until 11 PM on weekdays and midnight on weekends, then greets you for breakfast the next morning. (It's closed only for lunch on Thursday.) Bright and roomy in an old brick building, this is an affordable complement to its sister restaurant across the street—All Season Cafe. Hydro does daily fish specials and top-notch hamburgers. Few can resist the lasagna with . . . deep breath . . . goat cheese, Fontina, spinach, roasted red peppers, mushrooms, caramelized onions, oven-dried tomatoes, roasted garlic and spicy tomato sauce. The full bar has 20 carefully selected microbrews. They don't take reservations here.

Napa Valley Ovens
$, no credit cards • 1353 Lincoln Ave., Calistoga • (707) 942-0777

If that bite of almond croissant tastes familiar, maybe you had its twin for breakfast yesterday. The Ovens supplies numerous Napa Valley restaurants, markets and bed and breakfast inns with bread products. The lineup is as formidable as it is divine. There is garlic rosemary bread, calamata olive bread and perhaps 10 more varieties on a given day. The owners make everything from scratch, putting almond flour in the marzipan and imported French butter in the flakier-than-thou croissants. Napa Valley Ovens serves espresso drinks and coffee, including an iced version in the summer. The sunny, colorful bakery is open daily from 7 AM until 3 PM in the heavy season; it's closed on Tuesdays in the winter.

Pacifico Restaurante Mexicano
$$ • 1237 Lincoln Ave., Calistoga
• (707) 942-4400

Calistoga isn't your typical small town, so why should Pacifico be your typical Mexican restaurant? Instead of mountain ranges of rice and beans, the kitchen cooks up traditional specialties from Jalisco, Veracruz and Oaxaca. The restaurant is especially noted for its fish dishes, such as grilled fish tacos with avocado tomatillo salsa, or *camarones a la diabla*—sautéed prawns with garlic, onion, arbol chilies and lime.

There is a full bar, and the Margaritas won't let you down. Pacifico is open seven days a week for lunch and dinner. It's also popular for Saturday and Sunday brunch. (The morning favorites are Huevos Benito and Huevos Pacifico, Mexican eggs Benedict with a mulato chili hollandaise.) The restaurant takes reservations for parties of seven or more.

Soo Yuan
$ • 1354 Lincoln Ave., Calistoga
• (707) 942-9404

On what do you base your dining experience? If friendly service and a cozy family atmosphere are paramount, you will have a hard time beating Soo Yuan.

The Fang family opened its first restaurant in Taipei in 1974, and they have operated in Calistoga since 1985. The tried-and-true favorites include the pepper-sauce spareribs, the asparagus with prawns and the grandly presented mu shu pancakes. If you can't reach a decision, go for the multi-course Soo Yuan Special Dinner ($10.50 per person). Soo Yuan is open daily for lunch and dinner.

Triple-S-Ranch
$$$ • 4600 Mountain Home Ranch Rd., Calistoga • (707) 942-6730

Step back in time, or at least up in elevation, to the huntsman's lodge-style restaurant at the Triple-S (see our Hotels and Motels chapter). Inside the rustic red building, a converted 1920s barn with corrugated tin roof, are wood-paneled walls, mounted elk and deer heads and a sign promoting Rocky Marciano's training session at the Napa Valley Fairgrounds. The portions are immense (we dare you to eat the 16-ounce New York steak!), the meat succulent.

The restaurant does serve chicken, seafood and vegetarian pasta dishes, but who drives up to a lodge to eat eggplant parmigiana? Oh, and the Triple-S goes through about 2,000 pounds of onions each year to make its famous onion rings—when you see the size of the serving, you'll think the whole ton is right there in front of you. Dinner is served seven days a week. There is a full bar.

RESTAURANTS

Infidels in the Kingdom:
A Guide to Wine Country Brewpubs

Do you prefer ambers and blacks to reds and whites? Do you put more stock in a drink's head than its legs? Is the born-on date more important than the vintage? Does your mouth water when you hear a bottle go *pssshhh* instead of *pop*? Would you rather get your bubbles from a stein than a champagne flute?

If the answers are yes, you're not as lost as you think you are. The microbrew craze has taken root, even here in Wine Country. About 20 microbreweries and brewpubs reside in our four-county area, and the number seems to grow every few months. The stereotype has the groomsmen heading to the brewpub while the bridesmaids gather at the winery, but the reality is that you're likely to see the same sort of people (maybe even the exact same people) at the two sorts of tasting rooms. Beer lovers and wine lovers both tend to be taste-bud-dominated devotees of the good life. And as you'll see below, beer critics can heave those heavy adjectives just like wine critics.

To help us get a handle on "California Beer Country," we turned to Thomas Dalldorf, editor and publisher of *Celebrator Beer News*, a tabloid-format journal of suds in America (and beyond). Dalldorf and his staff reviewed some of their favorite pubs for our guide — not every microbrewery in Wine Country, but a representative few. They stress that the brewers not reviewed would be likely to score just as highly.

Also, note that our space limits forced us to truncate these reviews; amazingly, the folks at *Celebrator* can and do go into even more exhaustive detail when talking about their favorite thing. If you like *Celebrator's* bent, you can call (800) 430-BEER for information on distribution and subscriptions. Now pass those pretzels, please.

Third Street AleWorks
610 Third St., Santa Rosa • (707) 523-3060

Experience can make all the difference, and at the Third Street AleWorks in Santa Rosa, it shows. Third Street AleWorks showcases both the experience of the owners, who were formerly associated with the Good Earth restaurants, and brewer Grant Johnston, formerly with Marin Brewing Company. The result is a comfortable and inviting pub atmosphere highlighted by a selection of innovative and fiercely traditional styles of ale.

"Here, I'm really mixing American flavors with British flavors," said Johnston, a disciple of English brewing methods. "I want to get away from that whole West Coast thing. You're not going to find any dry-hopped pale ales coming out of this brewery."

The AleWorks Rye Ale, a popular seller, is surprisingly light in color, with a distinctive rye malt character from less than 20 percent rye in the mash. The American Wheat Ale is an unfiltered example of the style, with a round flavor, dry finish and light hop character. Its companion, the American Dark Wheat, was one of the pub's first beers when it opened in March 1996, and is one of Johnston's old homebrew recipes.

The AleWorks Mild Ale is an outstanding example of the style, one not often found in America's microbreweries. This copper-colored ale is based on the milds of Northern England, a style that is often called a "session beer," due to the ability to have several pints over a late-night chin-wag without being completely anesthetized.

Seasonal beers include a blackberry ale, which is released during the summer, a smoked beer in the fall and a barley wine for the winter.

Photo: Buckhorn Saloon

Beer in Wine Country? You bet your hops. Brewpubs like Anderson Valley Brewing Company are scattered throughout this vinicultural holy land.

AleWorks occupies an almost ideal location in downtown Santa Rosa, across from a major parking garage and at the entrance to UA Cinema 6, one of the busiest movie theaters in the county. The decor combines bright corrugated metal and dark wood to create a relaxing and slightly funky interior. The two-story, open interior space is highlighted by a round silo-like area near the front door, a hanging bicycle and antique Olympic rowing scull, and historical pictures of the city. The second floor has billiards and long picnic-style tables overlooking the main dining area.

The reasonably priced menu includes a selection of interesting appetizers, salads, sandwiches, burgers and pub specialties such as pasta and barbecue beer shrimp.

Bear Republic Brewing Company
345 Healdsburg Ave., Healdsburg • (707) 433-BEER

In the late 1970s, Healdsburg boasted a handful of restaurants: a pizza parlor that served platter-sized pizzas with soggy centers, a couple of so-called greasy spoons and a colorful parade of Mexican taquerias. Two decades later, time and money have swept away the sleepy small-town aura — Healdsburg's charm now encompasses classy places to eat, drink and be merry. One of those places is Bear Republic Brewing Company.

Bear Republic is in the clock tower building across from Healdsburg's historic Plaza and is fronted by rose bushes, a bubbling fountain and an inviting expanse of green grass. The 5,000-square-foot brewpub unfolds beneath high ceilings. Amid brass trim and warm woods, its bright windows look out to the patio. The wall behind the bags of grain and the malt mill sparkles with a vibrant mural of scenic Healdsburg, while colorful cycling jerseys decorate another wall.

Bear Republic Brewing Company was conceived by Richard R. Norgrove and his son, Rich, in 1994. Rich, 27, was operations manager of Salsa Cycles in Petaluma (a small but revered supplier to the mountain bike industry) when his first

(Continued on next page)

beer of note, Red Rocket Ale, garnered a cult-like following in biking circles. Richard and Rich's ride since has been successful and meteoric.

The clientele at Bear Republic is a pleasant surprise, a vivid cross-section of folks. Sleekly attired businessmen — ties loosened, sunglasses perched by their beer mugs — mix with laborers in dusty blue jeans at the copper-topped Honduran mahogany bar. Families cluster around big round tables. A group of twenty-somethings, some with strategic body piercing and tattoos, quaff Bear Republic brews alongside a smattering of seniors and couples.

John Cammack, who heads up the fast-paced kitchen at Bear Republic, enlivens and expands on traditional pub offerings. The most popular beer continues to be the house IPA, but there are others worth noting. Red Rocket Ale is Richard's flagship brew, using a blend of Northwest hops for a full-bodied, caramel brew the color of terra-cotta gemstone. All Bear Republic's microbrews are aged three weeks before tapping and are available to go in 5-gallon kegs and 1-gallon reusable boxes. Rich also features one beer on tap from a local guest microbrewer, as well as homemade root beer and cream soda for the kids.

Mendocino Brewing Company
13351 S. U.S. Hwy. 101, Hopland • (707) 744-1015

Hopland, as the name implies, was a major area for hop cultivation until the 1950s, when changes in climate and a shaky local economy forced farmers to sow pear trees and grapevines (see our History chapter). So it's a fitting locale for Mendocino Brewing Company, the oldest microbrewery in California. Established in 1983, after the close of the New Albion Brewery, the beers originally were sold only on draft in the tavern or over-the-counter in 1.5-liter magnums. The world's first 42-pound six-pack soon became legendary but could not allow the company to meet its increasing demands.

Standard six-packs began rolling out of the facility in 1987. In 1994 the company was one of a select few small manufacturers to be accepted on the Pacific Stock Exchange. More recently, the company opened a new 80,000-barrel-a-year brewhouse 12 miles north of Hopland in Ukiah.

Red Tail Ale, the brewery's best-known label, is full, malty, complex and dry; Blue Heron Pale Ale is delightfully hoppy and crisp; Peregrine Pale Ale is soft, fruity and assertive; Black Hawk Stout is roasty, dry and rich with a full body. Seasonal offerings include the Yuletide Porter, a ruby, dry and slightly spicy brew, and Springtide Ale, golden, spiced and refreshing, with different spices used each year.

The pub is inside a 100-year-old brick building once known as the Hop Vine Saloon. An outdoor beer garden (featuring trellised hops), a dart room and a stage for musical acts complement the tasty bill of fare and cozy atmosphere.

Anderson Valley Brewing Company
14081 Calif. Hwy. 128, Boonville • (707) 895-2337

Imagine that it's 1873, and you're a sheep rancher working hard under the blazing sun. Nothing sounds better than a chilly brew or a few shots of whiskey to celebrate the end of another strenuous day. If you are lucky, you live in the heart of Anderson Valley, because the Buckhorn Saloon has just been opened for business!

A new Buckhorn Saloon exists today — on the same site the original saloon stood 125 years ago — along with the Anderson Valley Brewery, established in 1987 by Dr. Kenneth and Kimberly Allen. The 10-barrel brewhouse, located beneath the saloon, is now emerging from the back burner on the heels of the company's recent expansion operation. A 15,000-square-foot production facility has been erected a mile away and includes a 30-barrel stainless steel brewery. A new brewhouse opened in summer of 1998.

As for Anderson Valley Brewing's product, the Boont Amber Ale is smooth and copper-colored with a rich caramel malt flavor; Poleeko Gold is a crisp, golden pale ale with a flowery hop nose and dry finish; Barney Flats Oatmeal Stout is a silky smooth, rich potion with traits of chocolate and toffee; High Rollers is a sparkling, tangy wheat beer; Deep Enders Dark is a roasty, robust porter with complex roasted coffee notes and a good length.

The brewery started bottling six-packs in 1997. The Buckhorn Saloon offers a full menu of tasty dishes, an outdoor beer garden and a unique gift shop.

North Coast Brewing Company
444 N. Main St., Fort Bragg • (707) 964-2739

When an historic building — used as a church, mortuary, and college — became available in the heart of old Fort Bragg in 1988, Mark Ruedrich, Joe Rosenthal and Tom Allen grasped the opportunity and opened the North Coast Brewing Company Tap Room and Grill. The operation has recently expanded to produce 15,000 barrels a year in a 17,000-square-foot facility across the street from the restaurant, which houses the original 7-barrel brewery.

Red Seal Ale is a copper-red pale ale with a generous hop quality and perfect balance; an unfiltered golden summer quencher, Blue Star is a wheat beer especially tasty with a lemon slice; Acme Pale Ale is a golden rendition of an 1861 California classic; Acme Brown Ale is nutty, with a good malt character; Scrimshaw Pilsner is crisp, light and spicy; Old No. 38 Stout is dry with smooth, roasty chocolate and coffee flavors; Old Rasputin Russian Imperial Stout is a fruity, richly complex brew with toffee connotations and a warming effect on the finish.

North Coast also produces seasonal ales, all available in bottles. Visitors can savor the beers fresh at the restaurant, which also sports an eclectic menu with an emphasis on local ingredients.

The rundown of other Wine Country brewpubs and microbreweries includes Downtown Joe's, 902 Main Street, Napa, (707) 258-BEER; Napa Valley Brewing Company, 1250 Lincoln Avenue, Calistoga, (707) 942-4101; Dempsey's Ale House, 50 E. Washington Street, Petaluma, (707) 765-9694; Lagunitas Brewing Company, 1280 N. McDowell Street, Petaluma, (707) 769-4495; Moonlight Brewing Company, P.O. Box 316, Fulton 95439, (707) 528-2537; Powerhouse Brewing, 268 Petaluma Avenue, Sebastopol, (707) 829-9171; Russian River Brewing Company, 13250 River Road, Guerneville, (707) 887-2294 and Mount St. Helena Brewing Company, 21167 Calistoga Highway (Calif. Highway 29), Middletown, (707) 987-2106.

Wappo Bar & Bistro
$$$ • 1226 Washington St., Calistoga
• (707) 942-4712

One of the few Calistoga restaurants not found on Lincoln Avenue, the compact Wappo Bar is easy to miss—and that would be a big mistake. The scene is fairly informal and always gratifying, especially in the summer when the arbor-protected brick patio takes center stage. (They have live music there on Sunday evenings.) Signature dishes include the chili relleno with pomegranate sauce, the duck carnitas, and the Chilean sea bass with Indian spices. And ridiculous as it sounds, you have to try the table water here—"marinated" with cit-

rus, cucumber and mint, it is highly addictive. The Wappo Bar is open for lunch and dinner six days a week (closed Tuesdays).

Sonoma County

Southern Sonoma

The General's Daughter
$$$$ • 400 W. Spain St., Sonoma
• (707) 938-4004

It could win a contest for "prettiest little restaurant in the county" hands down. The

General's Daughter is in a house erected in 1864 for Gen. Vallejo's daughter (hence the name). It had been standing dilapidated and unappreciated for years when Suzanne Brangham undertook its renovation in 1994 and turned it into a first-class restaurant. The place is gorgeous, set in lush landscaping with an interior decor of antiques and lively murals (the Honduran mahogany bar is a standout). Lunch is served on the wide front porch in fair weather. The food is traditional Californian. For lunch, you might want to try the West Texas grilled skirt steak salad with black beans, corn, avocado, romaine hearts and whole grain mustard vinaigrette. Or consider the warm peach tart tatin with a ginger crème anglaise for dessert. Lunch and dinner are served daily, with brunch on Sunday.

The Swiss Hotel
$ • 18 W. Spain St., Sonoma
• (707) 938-2884

It's a wonderful old building—a remarkably preserved adobe that was once the home of Gen. Vallejo's brother, Salvador, who built it in 1850. He didn't live there long; a year later the sheriff put it up for sale to pay Salvador's debts. It became "The Swiss" when a stagecoach operator bought it and changed the name. Today it is easily recognizable by the Swiss flag flying over the door.

For decades the restaurant was patronized largely by local families who came for the generous family-style Italian dinners. The barroom was a hangout for locals as well, who came to meet and greet friends. It even drew a few celebrities: Herb Caen is said to have tippled there, as have Tommy Smothers, Jim Corbett and even the late Charles Kuralt.

The menu has moved a bit upscale from the days of the massive Italian feasts, but the pastas are still served al dente, and the pizzas are turned out of wood-burning brick ovens. It's open daily for lunch and dinner.

Marioni's
$ • 8 W. Spain St., Sonoma
• (707) 996-6866

It faces onto the Plaza and is an ever-popular favorite with locals. The outdoor tables in front are a big draw—they're a wonderful place to see and be seen while sipping coffee or wine or having a noontime sandwich. Marioni's adjoins the next-door Swiss Hotel and is actually operated by branches of the same Marioni family. Cioppino is a good bet for dinner here. But you can also enjoy a great vegetarian sandwich for lunch, per-haps served with an unusual minted soup that is a lovely shade of apple green and goes down very smoothly. A full bar is featured, and both bar and restaurant are open daily for lunch and dinner in summer, dinner nightly and lunch Friday through Sunday in winter.

Magliulo's Restaurant and Pensione
$$ • 691 Broadway, Sonoma
• (707) 996-1031

As you enter Sonoma along Calif. Highway 12, you'll see a number of formerly grand houses now turned into commercial establishments lining the wide thoroughfare. Among them is Magliulo's Restaurant. It's in a fine old 1884 Victorian, replete with fine-wood interior decor and an other-world atmosphere.

Chef Lou Magliulo is in charge of the kitchen here, and he excels with such specialties as veal scaloppini and chicken piccata. One of the real attractions here in summer is the opportunity to dine outdoors on Magliulo's backyard brick patio. A full bar is featured, and lunch and dinner are served daily.

Cafe at Sonoma Mission Inn
$$$ • 18141 Sonoma Hwy., Sonoma
• (707) 939-2410

This is a great place for breakfast—the eggs Benedict with rosemary potatoes will draw you back here time after time. Since this is connected to the Mission Inn Spa (see our Spas and Resorts chapter), the menu also includes dishes for the calorie-watcher that are equally good—especially apple oat cakes with walnuts and crème fraîche. Lunch and dinner are also served each day, with a fine wine list and full bar. Service is friendly but not intrusive.

Grille at Sonoma Mission Inn
$$$$ • 18141 Sonoma Hwy., Sonoma
• (707) 938-9000

If you're ready to go upscale, walk to the main building of the Inn for a Sunday brunch overlooking the pool, or have lunch or dinner in an ambiance that has country-club class—elegant but not stuffy. The Grille offers a seasonal Wine Country menu prepared with fresh, locally grown foods in an exuberant style. Entrees here range from pasta to lamb loin and include fresh seafood in a wide range of presentations. The award-winning wine list features 300 selections from Napa and Sonoma vineyards. This is one of Sonoma County's most expensive restaurants, but it's ideal for celebrations or special occasions. Reservations are recommended for dinner. The Grille is open daily.

RESTAURANTS

Della Santina's
$$$ • 133 E. Napa St., Sonoma
• (707) 935-0576

This is an intimate, no-frills Italian trattoria-pasticceria that faces onto the main street, but the food is authentic Italian prepared from recipes inspired by owner Dan Santina's grandmother. All food is prepared from scratch, using a rotisserie to contain the flavors of all the herbs and spices used in such dishes as locally raised chicken, rabbit and duck. The menu offers traditional Northern Italian dishes such as lasagna bolognese, pressed squab and all sorts of antipasti. One of the best entrees—maybe the best in all of Wine Country—is pollo allo spiedo, a traditional Italian roast chicken. Della Santina's serves lunch and dinner every day. Because the restaurant is small, reservations are advised.

Ristorante Piatti
$$$ • 405 W. First St., Sonoma
• (707) 996-2351

You enter Piatti from either the El Dorado Hotel lobby or the door on W. First Street. Either way, you'll soon be enveloped with the marvelous aromas from the open kitchen at the back of the dining room. Alfresco dining is also available amid the trees on the gorgeous patio courtyard off the dining room. While you're looking over the menu, you'll be served fresh breads with a saucer of olive oil, balsamic vinegar and garlic dipping sauce. As for the menu, it features the best of Tuscany pastas, pizzas and grilled meat and fish. Piatti is the winner of numerous Sonoma Valley restaurant awards. A full bar features select Sonoma Valley wines at lunch and dinner seven days a week.

La Casa Restaurant
$$ • 121 E. Spain St., Sonoma
• (707) 996-3406

In a town dedicated to Italian cuisine, La Casa's smashing Mexican food is as welcome as a breeze in the heat of summer. The ambiance is as close to authentic as you can get north of the border, with Mexican woven leather chairs and a tiled bar. The nachos are sensational here, the salsa and chips addictive. The food is so memorable that La Casa is often the first place former residents head for dinner when they return to the area for a visit. For a view of the Mission and Barracks (see our Attractions chapter), ask for a window seat. Or choose to eat outdoors on the patio facing onto El Paseo de Sonoma courtyard. La Casa's thin,

crisp tortilla chips and salsa are now available at the upscale Sonoma Market grocery. Fiesta hour (from 4 to 6 PM Monday through Friday) is extremely popular among the locals, thanks to the ambiance and the great Margaritas.

Depot Hotel Cucina Rustica
$$$ • 241 W. First St., Sonoma
• (707) 938-2980

Located in a historic stone building a block from the Plaza, this was once a hotel, but it is now a delightful restaurant serving Northern Italian cuisine. It's owned by Chef Ghilarducci, who does wonders with such dishes as ravioli al bosco (shiitake mushrooms and herbs sauteed with white wine and shallots) and hand-stuffed tortellini. One of the real delights of the restaurant is its garden, with Roman fountain and poolside dining. Vegetarian dishes and heart-healthy choices are also offered. The wine list is strictly Sonoma Valley and Carneros and has won *Wine Spectator* magazine's Award of Excellence several times. Lunch is available Wednesday through Friday from 11:30 AM to 5 PM, and dinner is served Wednesday through Sunday from 5 PM on.

Zino's Ristorante
$$ • 420 First St. E., Sonoma
• (707) 996-4466

The place has the look of an intimate Italian bistro, housed in a historic building made from stones quarried nearby. It's owned by Zino Mezoulin, a native of Algeria, whose Italian specialties have proved so popular with locals that for the summer months he has opened an outdoor dining room bordering on El Paseo de Sonoma courtyard. If you like seafood, try the linguine in Zino's special putanesca sauce or the linguine con vongole—it's made with lots of clams, broth and cream. Zino's is open for lunch seven days a week and dinner every night but Monday. A bar is available, and an extensive wine list offers wine by the glass or bottle.

Mary's Pizza Shack
$$ • 18636 Calif. Hwy. 12, Sonoma
• (707) 938-3600

The place does look a bit like an upscale shingled shack, but Mary's pizza is a Sonoma tradition, and people pour into the eatery to line up at the counter for pizza. Mary Fazio opened her first restaurant when she was 45 in 1959, using $700 in savings and pots and pans from her own home. There were no printed menus or prices, and people paid what they could afford. She was mobbed with customers.

She encouraged children to watch her make pizzas and gave them slices of salami as they watched. Though Fazio died in 1999, Mary's Pizza Shack is growing and branching out, with the first franchised copycats in Sonoma and Napa counties spreading to other California areas. It is estimated that more than 10 million families have dined at Mary's since she opened her doors. It's good pizza! Mary's is open daily for lunch and dinner.

Garden Court Cafe & Bakery
$$ • 13875 Sonoma Hwy., Glen Ellen
• (707) 935-1565

This is a small, 10-table cafe on the side of the road, but on any given weekend day, there are as many people outside waiting to get in as there are inside eating. Breakfast is the big draw here, with eggs Benedict in three varieties leading the popularity list and a variety of omelettes following close behind. The owner is chef, and he bakes some wonderful sticky buns, brownies and scones. The cafe is open for breakfast and lunch seven days a week.

Glen Ellen Inn Restaurant
$$$ • 13670 Arnold Dr., Glen Ellen
• (707) 996-6409

Set inside a Cape Cod-style cottage, this tiny restaurant delivers one delight after another. Stenciled grape leaves trim the ceiling, and white linens and candles grace the tables. You have three choices of where to eat—the indoor dining room, the sun porch or the patio. The chef learned his skills in New York and uses local ingredients to cook with a French accent. Particularly impressive is the California Jambalaya—prawns, bay shrimp, chicken, sausage and honey-smoked ham simmered with cayenne, vegetables and tomato sauce on a bed of couscous. Yes, this is a chef who can hold his own with the finest. The desserts are truly decadent. If you can manage two, go for the Bailey's Irish Cream Mousse scented with chocolate, and the French vanilla ice cream rolled in toasted coconut and drizzled with caramel sauce. The restaurant is open for dinner every night except winter Wednesdays.

Kenwood Restaurant
$$$$ • 9900 Sonoma Hwy., Kenwood
• (707) 833-6326

The parking lot is always full—a sure sign of the restaurant's well-deserved popularity. The chef does a great piece of work on bouillabaisse, using seafood from Bodega Bay in a flavorful broth. His roast duck, using local fowl,

is crispy on the outside, tender inside. And his prawns in succulent sauce with puff pastry are sheer inspiration. *Gourmet* magazine recently voted this one of the top 20 restaurants in the entire Bay Area. One of the real pleasures of dining here is the opportunity to drink in the exquisite view as the late-afternoon sun hits the peaks of Sugarloaf Ridge. The scene is particularly rewarding from the deck. The wine list is acclaimed for featuring the best wines produced in Kenwood (bar drinks are also available). Lunch and dinner are served Wednesday through Sunday.

J.M. Rosen's
$$$ • 54 E. Washington St., Petaluma
• (707) 773-3200

It's unfortunate that the first thing to greet your eye when you walk in the entrance here is the kitchen. Having said that, the dining area is charming, overlooking the Petaluma River and the Old Town beyond. If you choose to be served on the large deck, you'll have a first-class view of the yacht harbor as well. The cuisine is Californian, and the emphasis here is on garden-fresh products. Rosen's is open for lunch and dinner every day except Monday.

River House
$$ • 222 Weller St., Petaluma
• (707) 769-0123

River House, which opened in October 1997, offers the charming architectural setting of an 1888 Queen Anne Victorian.

The plan from the beginning was to have a full-service restaurant with banquet rooms featuring American cuisine and using most Sonoma fresh produce and local meats. Because "American cuisine" covers a lot of territory, a new segment of the country is to be featured each month—Lousiana Cajun cooking one month, New England seafood cuisine the next. Dinner is served daily, brunch on Sunday.

McNear's Restaurant
$$ • 23 N. Petaluma Blvd., Petaluma
• (707) 765-2121

It's friendly, funky and great fun. Every square inch of the walls is covered with historic memorabilia and old photographs, including old sleds, skis, street signs, flags and banners. The name McNear looms large in Petaluma history, stretching back to 1856 when John McNear came to town, created a business empire and became the first owner of the McNear Building. The goal of the present-day owners is to provide a meeting, eating and entertainment spot for locals and fun-loving visitors. Barbecue is the house specialty, with an extensive menu to back that up; the saloon is well-stocked. The dining room is large, but the sidewalk cafe in front is the popular place to sip espresso on Sunday morning. McNear's is open for lunch and dinner every day of the week, plus breakfast on Sunday.

Volpi's Ristorante
**$$ • 124 Washington St., Petaluma
• (707) 765-0695**

There's a lot of Old World charm in this place run by the Volpi family—it's been on the local scene since 1925 (in a building that was once a speakeasy). This is family-style dining in an unhurried atmosphere. The cuisine is Italian, created by chef Glen Petrucci, who specializes in homemade pastas, veal and seafood. If you're up to it, you can listen to live accordion music Friday and Saturday evenings. Lunch is served Wednesday, Thursday and Friday and dinner Wednesday through Sunday.

Twisted Vines
**$$$ • 16 Kentucky St., Petaluma
• (707) 766-8162**

This is something a little different—a combination wine shop and restaurant. The local restaurant reviewer gives it five stars, for both food and wine. Fresh fish is flown in from Hawaii every day, and mahi mahi is one of the most popular features on the menu. They take pride in using only the best ingredients, including the local poultry, which they transform into their special, half-roasted chicken. You can select a wine off the racks to enjoy with your food (paying only retail plus a $5 corkage fee), or you can buy it by the glass. It's a tiny place, so it's best to call ahead. The restaurant is open for lunch and dinner Tuesday through Saturday. Look for it in the Lanmart Building.

John Ash & Co.
**$$$$ • 4330 Barnes Rd., Santa Rosa
• (707) 527-7687**

John Ash is no longer there, but the cuisine he created carries on, with each entree made a masterpiece by tending to taste, texture, color and design. Nothing here is ordinary.

The fare is "wine country cuisine," i.e., California cuisine using only the freshest produce from local farmers and local goat cheeses. John Ash's signature dish is its Dungeness crab cakes. A recent redecoration has made this delightful Wine Country restaurant more alluring than ever. From the Spanish stucco exterior to the works of art that decorate the interior, the atmosphere is warm and inviting. Large, arched windows give an open airy feeling to the dining room. The wine list is one of the best in Wine Country, with a good selection sold by the glass. John Ash & Co. is adjacent to Vintners Inn, a Provençal-style hotel arranged around a central plaza and fountain, all set in a 45-acre vineyard (see our Bed and Breakfast Inns chapter). The restaurant and bar are open for dinner seven days a week, but John Ash & Co. does not serve lunch on Monday.

Equus
$$$$ • 101 Fountain Grove Pkwy., Santa Rosa • (707) 578-6101

Because this is the restaurant for Fountaingrove Inn (see our Hotels and Motels chapter), the decorating theme is horses and honors Equus, the legendary horse. The chef creates both classic favorites and imaginative dishes that surprise with their originality. The menu changes with each season, and in summer one lovely dish to try is African-spice roasted Petaluma duckling with basmati rice, served with summer vegetables and port essence. You may choose to sink into a spacious booth, or dine center stage under the coffered mahogany ceiling. In the lounge, you can sip cocktails and listen to romantic music played on the grand piano. Take time to examine the Gallery of Sonoma County Wines, a display of nearly 300 premium wines, chosen personally by each winery's own winemaker. Lunch is served from Monday through Friday and dinner is served daily.

Omelette Express
**$$ • 112 Fourth St., Santa Rosa
• (707) 525-1690**

If you happen to be walking around Railroad Square on a weekend morning, you'll see as many people on the sidewalk waiting to get into

INSIDERS' TIP
Mustards Grill, north of Yountville on Calif. 29, is an almost-guaranteed good time and great meal, as so many diners have learned over the years. The only problem is securing a reservation on short notice. Remember, then, that the restaurant stays open between lunch and dinner. You should consider a light lunch, a light late "supper" and a prodigious Mustards dinner at 3 PM.

RESTAURANTS

this restaurant as there are patrons inside. The menu lists 48 different varieties of the humble omelette—both plain and fancy, including vegetarian and seafood. None costs more than $9. The choices for lunch include two dozen "Pullman Car" sandwiches. You might want to bite into the Hot Express Special—mushrooms, grilled onions, melted jack and cheddar cheese, served open-face on dark rye. It's open seven days a week and most holidays.

Lisa Hemenway's Restaurant
$$$$ • 714 Village Ct., Santa Rosa
• (707) 526-5111

This lovely restaurant is nestled in a courtyard of Montgomery Village shopping center. The atmosphere is posh, comfortable and romantic, with archways, terra cotta tiles and paintings by local artists to complete the mood. Lisa Hemenway was a protegé of John Ash and has traveled six of the seven continents to add to her cuisine knowledge. You might want to try her version of grilled prawns with Thai peanut sauce. Meals are hearty here. All are made with fresh, locally grown ingredients. There's a daily fish entree, freshly caught, along with daily pasta and salad specialty. Don't miss the perfect orange-currant scones! There's a full bar and award-winning wines. Lisa's is open for lunch and dinner every day but Sunday.

Mistral
$$$ • 1229 N. Dutton Ave., Santa Rosa
• (707) 578-4511

French food—Provençal to be precise—is the focus here. Homemade pasta and hand-stuffed ravioli are prepared daily. Other specialties include fresh seafood, duck and lamb. Much of the game and produce used is grown by local farmers. Relax in the wine bar, and choose from an extensive list. The outdoor terrace is the perfect spot for summertime luncheon. Mistral is open for dinner nightly and lunch Monday through Friday.

Mixx
$$$ • 135 Fourth St., Santa Rosa
• (707) 573-1344

Billed as an American bistro, the atmosphere here is intimate and elegant without being stuffy. Chef Dan Berman takes an ethnic melting-pot approach to California cuisine, shaping it into Cajun, Indian, Italian and straight Californian. One house specialty is ravioli, but Berman also does wonderful things with fish. Berman's wife is responsible for the desserts. Dinner is served nightly except Sunday; lunch is offered Monday through Friday.

La Gare French Restaurant
$$$ • 208 Wilson St., Santa Rosa
• (707) 528-4355

La Gare has been voted "most romantic" and "best restaurant" by *The Press Democrat* newspaper. The *Sonoma County Independent* also has awarded La Gare its "best restaurant" award for the past five years. Tucked away in historic Railroad Square, it's a favorite of the locals, who come for hearty, country-style, traditional French cooking. Romantic it is, with the lace curtains, soft lighting and stained glass. It is one of the few places in Wine Country that you are offered French wines. La Gare ("railway station") is open for dinner Wednesday through Sunday.

Northern Sonoma

Lotus Thai Restaurant
$$ • 109-A Plaza St., Healdsburg
• (707) 433-5282

Here's where Bangkok meets Healdsburg. Open for lunch and dinner six days a week (excluding Monday), the chef has managed to strike a near-perfect balance between offering authentic dishes of Thailand and acknowledging the tastes and desires of Californians. This is arguably the most succulent chicken satay with the best peanut sauce in the county. It's a neat, clean and well-lit storefront restaurant. Service is unobtrusive and adequate. If you're looking for dessert, try the crispy and sweet fried banana.

Bistro Ralph
$$$ • 109 Plaza St., Healdsburg
• (707) 433-1380

The place is plain enough, with white-linen-covered tables lined up

INSIDERS' TIP
Does a picnic fit into your Napa Valley tour more sensibly than a restaurant stop? Some of the county's best take-out delicatessens include Vallerga's Market at 426 First Street in Napa; Oakville Grocery on the corner of Calif. 29 and the Oakville Cross Road; the V. Sattui Winery at the intersection of Calif. 29 and White Lane south of St. Helena; Dean & DeLuca, practically across the highway from V. Sattui; and Palisades Market at 1506 Lincoln Avenue in Calistoga.

RESTAURANTS

The General's Daughter restaurant is in a home built in 1864 for Gen. Vallejo's daughter.

along one wall in an arrangement reminiscent of earlier San Francisco Italian restaurants. It's narrow and noisy, but the food is prepared with an imaginative touch and fresh ingredients. Chef-owner Ralph Tingle can be seen at the farmer's market any Saturday morning, selecting from the seasonal bounty of vegetables that will be on his menu that night. He follows the Farm Trails map to find the best in meat vendors and duck farms as well (see our Close-up on Farm Trails in our Shopping chapter). The smoked salmon starter with an unusual focaccia pastry is a good choice. The Bistro is open for lunch and dinner on weekdays and for dinner only on weekends.

Madrona Manor
$$$$ • 1001 Westside Rd., Healdsburg
• (707) 433-4231

Nestled on a wooded knoll surrounded by lush vineyards, Madrona Manor is a majestic sight, its mansard roof rising three stories into the treetops (see our Bed and Breakfast Inns chapter). The dining room is opulent, the atmosphere romantic. Renowned chef Todd Muir specializes in California French cuisine, utilizing Sonoma County's abundance of fresh local products. An eclectic, changing menu features such dishes as Peking duck with almond coconut rice, stuffed mild chilies and salmon steak with mixed herbs. It's open daily for dinner, but prior to eating, you might want to stroll through the delightful 8-acre gardens. Long story short: Madrona Manor is everything you love about Wine Country.

Dry Creek General Store
$ • 3495 Dry Creek Rd., Healdsburg
• (707) 433-4171

It's an old-time grocery store that looks like it's been there forever, but if you've been cruising the Dry Creek vineyards for hours and your tummy says it's picnic time, you'll love the simple, delicious homemade sandwiches and salads, the wine selection and the gourmet food section. Take your purchases to any one of the many wineries in the area, buy yourself a bottle of their best, and settle in for a beautiful picnic. The store is open seven days a week, from 6 AM to 6 PM.

Chateau Souverain, The Cafe at the Winery
$$$$ • 400 Souverain Rd., Geyserville
• (707) 433-3141

For those who appreciate things French, the architecture of the majestic building is alone worthy of a visit. The chateau is a cross between a Sonoma hop kiln and a Loire chateau, overlooking the Alexander Valley out to the Mayacamas mountain range. The chef says his menu "has a French country theme with California influences." On that basis he turns out wondrous inventions like rosemary focaccia pocket with roasted vegetables and a delightful wild mushroom penne pasta with a portobello gorgonzola cheese sauce. This is a winery (see our Wineries chapter), and, as might be expected, the wine list is strictly Chateau Souverain, priced to encourage enjoyment (and future purchase) at a figure below market price. It's open daily for lunch and Friday, Saturday and Sunday for dinner. Reservations are recommended.

Hoffman House
$ • 21712 Geyserville Ave., Geyserville
• (707) 857-3264

Situated next door to the Geyserville Inn (see our Hotels and Motels chapter), this year-old deli is run by Elvie Nelson. The main features are sandwiches customized to the customers' wants. She bakes her own bread, and her French sourdough baguettes make the sandwiches a big area favorite. Bicyclists gather here on weekend mornings to pick up provisions and meet friends before heading down the trails that meander through the nearby vineyards. Elvie turns out reubens, meatball sandwiches and a special one made with portobello mushrooms. Hoffman House is open every day.

Sonoma Coast

Lucas Wharf & Bar
$$$ • 599 Calif. Hwy. 1, Bodega Bay
• (707) 875-3522

This is a cozy, romantic place, with a vaulted ceiling and a fireplace to warm you when the weather chills out (as it often does on this coast). Seafood will never be fresher than it is here, for this is a commercial fishery that supplies grocers and the public with fresh Pacific catch. The chef's special of the day is based on the best of the day's catch—salmon, halibut, crab, calamari, oysters—and while you enjoy it, you can bask in the glow of the setting sun or watch sea birds and the excitement of fishermen delivering their bounty at the pier. Lucas Wharf is a great place to pick up fresh cracked crab or custom smoked fish. The restaurant is open for lunch and dinner seven days a week. Fresh crab season is mid-November through

June, and fresh salmon season is mid-May through September.

Bay View Restaurant
$$$$ • 800 Calif. Hwy. 1, Bodega Bay • (707) 875-2751

Bay View is part of Inn at the Tides, one of the most relaxing hostelries at Bodega Bay (see our Hotels and Motels chapter). The restaurant features a menu that changes weekly and goes well beyond the local catch. Look for grilled Ahi tuna on the menu, bouillabaisse, scaloppine of veal, duck breast and rack of lamb. Cocktails are served in the lounge, a romantic setting as the sun goes down over the Pacific. The restaurant is open for dinner Wednesday through Sunday.

The Tides Wharf & Restaurant
$$$ • 835 Calif. Hwy. 1, Bodega Bay • (707) 875-3652

If it looks familiar, it's because you saw it in Alfred Hitchcock's film, *The Birds*. If you didn't see the movie, you can get a taste of the action through a poster on the wall. Aside from the renown that has come from Hitchcock and Tippi Hedren fending off birds, the restaurant has earned its own fame as the longstanding favorite of regulars who have been popping in since the place was a one-room affair. From a seat at the window, you can watch kids, grandparents and lovers dropping their lines to catch fish or snag a crab, and wait for the commercial fishing boats to come in and dump their loads. A very nice lunch can be made of the special seafood chowder, some sourdough bread and a glass of Chardonnay. The restaurant is open every day for breakfast, lunch and dinner, and it offers full bar service. You might want to pick up some cracked crab in the marketplace as you leave, if it's in season. If not, get a bag of saltwater taffy!

River's End Restaurant
$$$$ • 11048 Calif. Hwy. 1, Jenner • (707) 865-2484

From its position on a bluff where the Russian River flows into the Pacific, River's End has perhaps the most spectacular view on this part of the coast—at least that's what the locals claim. Menu offerings here have left local seafood far behind and moved on to upscale comfort foods. Here you can have beluga caviar for an appetizer, whiskey-marinated lobster for the fish course and roasted rack of lamb filled with oysters for the entree. For those without wallets fat enough for such a meal, the com-

plete-dinner house specialties sound almost as exciting—say, beef Wellington or medallions of venison. Either way, it's open for breakfast, lunch and dinner, Friday through Sunday.

West County/Russian River

Chez Peyo Country French Restaurant
$$$ • 2293 S. Gravenstein Hwy., Sebastopol • (707) 823-1262

A charming restaurant in a beautiful garden setting, Chez Peyo features the cuisine of the French Basque nation. Its name comes from the owner, Pierre Lagourgue – "Peyo" is Basque for "Pierre." While Peyo relies heavily on traditional French cooking with its grand sauces, he has also turned to what he terms California-French, using fresh herbs and lighter sauces. Produce is garden fresh, utilizing baby greens and baby spinach for salads. Fresh fish and seafood figures frequently on the menu, one of the most popular dishes being baked mussels. But for a real treat, one must try Peyo's paella, made in the Basque fashion with mussels, clams, shrimp, scallops, linguica (a Basque sausage), chicken and ham tossed with saffron rice. It's sensational. So is the appetizer of baked brie and garlic—the aroma pulls you into the restaurant even if you are only passing by. Peyo's is open for lunch and dinner Wednesday through Sunday, and serves a Sunday brunch.

Mom's Apple Pie
$$ • 4550 Gravenstein Hwy. N., Sebastopol • (707) 823-8330

It's a small cafe, but word has gotten out that Mom bakes a mean apple pie, and customers now come from around the globe—from as far away as Spain and Germany. Apples come from the owner's own Gravenstein orchard, and all varieties of pie are baked from scratch (the old-fashioned way, without so much sugar) in the six ovens in the back kitchen. The cafe is open for lunch and dinner, and locals rave about the breaded fried chicken and the six varieties of soup, all made right there in the kitchen.

Union Hotel Restaurant
$$ • 3731 Main St., Occidental • (707) 874-3555

It seems like the Union Hotel dining room has been there forever, housed in a building that goes back to 1879. It's not been around quite that long, but the same family has run it

RESTAURANTS

since 1925. The great fame of the place comes from the huge portions of pasta that are served family-style—it's known far and wide for the heaping helpings. It's a custom that was first established by Bill Howard, who settled in Occidental in the 1870s and opened a dining room to feed the wood cutters who came from Tuscany to work the forest (see our History chapter). The portions remain outsized, and the family really knows how to cook pasta. But there are other great items on the menu—chicken cacciatore for one. The establishment has its own bakery and makes great croissants and muffins to serve in its cafe. The restaurant is open for lunch and dinner every day, still serving family-style meals and drinks from the saloon.

INSIDERS' TIP

Most visitors assume Brix, the name of the restaurant just north of Yountville, is simply a cute misspelling. It's actually more appropriate to the setting than that. Winemakers note the sugar content of their fermenting liquid using the Brix scale of measurement.

Negri's
$$ • 3700 Bohemian Hwy., Occidental
• (707) 823-5301

It's a toss-up whether the hungry folks of Sonoma County head first for Union Hotel or Negri's—they're both terrific purveyors of great Italian meals. Negri's has been cooking pasta since 1940. Its fame is well-established, as is the expertise of the family that has been running the place since it opened. A family-style meal starts out with a tureen of minestrone that's so popular people come in to buy it by the bucket. The pasta list is long, including vegetarian spaghetti, penne pasta and homemade ravioli. After that, if you choose, you can order some of their other specials—among them deep fried calamari, grilled red snapper and prawns. Negri's is open for lunch and dinner every day and has a full bar.

The Farmhouse Inn
$$$ • 7871 River Rd., Forestville
• (707) 887-3300

The bed and breakfast service has now been expanded to include dinner, and the Farmhouse restaurant is open to visitors as well as guests. The dining room seats no more than two dozen, but the chef does a terrific job on a varied menu of fish, beef, pasta and poultry. Among the entrees is sea bass sauteed with sweet pepper, scallions and an orange sauce. Save room for dessert because the chocolate pecan pie is the best you'll ever taste! The restaurant is open for dinner Thursday through Sunday.

Topolos
$$$ • 5700 Gravenstein Hwy. N., Forestville • (707) 887-1562

You can dine indoors or outside on the patio here. Either way, the food is Greek, and it's very good. If you go for lunch, you can sample a little of several of their favorite items on a special combination plate—spanakopita, polenta, moussaka and dolmathakia. Outdoor dining is on a patio that seats 100. It's broken up into different areas by a wisteria arbor and a fountain, and is covered with a shade cloth so it can be used on sunny days. The restaurant is affiliated with Russian River Vineyards (see our Wineries chapter), so the wines served are made right on site. Topolos is open for lunch and dinner seven days a week, and for brunch on Sunday.

Applewood Inn & Restaurant
$$$$ • 13555 Calif. Hwy. 116, Guerneville
• (707) 869-9093

Snuggled among the redwoods of Pocket Canyon near Guerneville, Applewood Inn is famed for its sophisticated meals. It's one of those special places you want to keep to yourself, but you can't stop talking about it. The fire-lit dining room serves 30 at individual candlelit tables with windows facing the redwoods on three sides. The restaurant does wonderful things with a crisp duck breast in a blackberry-basil essence. But whatever you choose, save room for the caramelized apple cheesecake afterwards. Applewood is open for dinner Tuesday through Saturday.

Mendocino County

U.S. Highway 101

Valley Oaks Deli
$ • Fetzer Vineyards, Calif. Hwy. 175 and Eastside Rd., Hopland
• (707) 744-1737

This gourmet deli is in the visitors center of Fetzer Vineyards (see our Wineries chapter) and offers an extraordinary selection of fresh salads and sandwiches, all made daily with organic vegetables, fruits and herbs grown in Fetzer's adjacent Bonterra Garden. You might like to try a grilled vegetable sandwich on focaccia with Jambalaya pasta salad. For dessert, go for a cappuccino and the "devil's triangle," if you're a chocolate lover. If you are on your way to a picnic, Valley Oaks will supply you with a special gourmet bag lunch, created to fit your needs. The deli is open daily from 9 AM to 5 PM and adjoins the tasting room—you may want to pick up some of Fetzer's best and take it all out to a table on the patio.

Thatcher Inn
$$ • 13401 U.S. Hwy. 101 S., Hopland • (707) 744-1890

The Grand Dining Room offers a casual-yet-elegant ambiance that's immediately evident as you enter this Victorian-era room for dinner Wednesday through Saturday. The walls are decorated in dark green shades, and the dining room chairs are padded in rich rose hues to match the maroon carpeting. It's a scene from the 1890s for sure. In true Western style, the chef turns out a great steak, which goes well with the Fetzer wines that are featured. If you prefer, you can order a single-malt Scotch whiskey from the informal Lobby Bar, which is home of one of the largest collections of single-malts in the West. Dinner is served from 5 to 9:30 PM. (See our Hotels and Motels chapter for more on Thatcher Inn.)

North State Cafe
$ • 247 N. State St., Ukiah • (707) 462-3726

The logo contains a statement that says it all: "A Casual Experience in Fine Dining." The atmosphere here is that of a fine restaurant, without being too dressy—somewhere between tank tops and neckties. The special niche that's apparent on the menu is properly known as "California Italian," using fresh local ingredients for pasta sauces that are served with fresh fruits and vegetables.

The building was the Palace Hotel 100 years ago, but the Palace burned somewhere along the road of history and has been rebuilt across the street. Still, when the staff goes down to the wine cellar, some of the traces of the fire are visible among the concrete foundation partitions.

Ukiah is not a town with a heavy influx of tourists, and the Cafe's clientele is estimated to be about 95 percent local—much of the patronage coming from the staff at the nearby courthouse. The Cafe is open for lunch Monday through Friday from 11 AM to 2 PM, and for dinner Wednesday through Saturday from 5 to 9 PM.

Mendocino Coast

Pangaea Cafe
$$$, no credit cards • 250 Main St., Point Arena • (707) 882-3001

Walls are lined with paintings by local artists, giving the small restaurant a feeling of serenity. The food is distinctive, based on the chef's long experience living in other parts of the world (the Middle East, Portugal, Spain), and a changing menu reflects the global influence. Breads are baked in a brick oven and made fresh every day. Although the tendency is toward vegetarian and fish dishes, any poultry or meat served is from free-ranging fowl and animals. Mendocino County wines are featured, often from small, offbeat wineries that don't get much attention. When it comes to desserts, you've hit the culinary big time with the chocolate cake with brandied cherries. Pangaea is open for dinner Wednesday through Sunday.

Albion River Inn Restaurant
$$$$ • 3790 N. Calif. Hwy. 1, Albion • (707) 937-1919

A spectacular ocean view, California cuisine and an award-winning wine list combine to make this an especially romantic dining place. Piano music Friday through Tuesday nights adds to the allure of Albion River Inn. Seafood figures heavily in the menu, as might be expected at this oceanside restaurant. Sauteed local rock cod is pan-seared and finished with rock shrimp, capers and fresh dill. The oysters are imported from Washington, sauteed with mushrooms and finished with wilted spinach. Halibut from Alaska finds a home on a bed of shiitake mushrooms. Albion River Inn Restaurant serves dinner seven nights a week—from 5:30 to 9 PM Sunday through Thursday and from 5 to 9:30 PM on Friday and Saturday. Reservations are essential. (See our Hotels and Motels chapter for more on Albion River Inn.)

The Ledford House Restaurant
$$$$ • 3000 N. Calif. Hwy. 1, Albion • (707) 937-0282

If you've ever been to Provence, in southern France, you'll recognize the style and ambiance of this restaurant. Expansive windows make you a part of the Pacific vista. Add candlelight and music, and you've got the basis for a most romantic evening—a memorable occasion. The food is Mediterranean, and the menu changes monthly. Regulars are rack of lamb, steak and Pacific salmon. But you might want to be adventurous and try the tiger prawns flamed in vermouth for dipping in a smoky hot-and-sweet mustard sauce. Dinner is served Wednesday through Sunday from 5 PM, and reservations are advisable.

Heritage House
$$$$ • 5200 N. Calif. Hwy. 1, Little River
• (707) 937-5885

The dining room is opulent, the ambiance elegant. Quite simply, dining at Heritage House is a world-class experience. Chef Velasquez (named one of America's 10 best new chefs by *Food and Wine* magazine) uses only the freshest local ingredients and premier quality foods that are personally selected for his seasonal menus. His pan-seared, fresh Pacific Coast Ahi is a sureshot choice. The view from the dining room is of the spectacular Pacific. On sunny days, visitors may enjoy breakfast on the oceanview deck. Breakfast and dinner are served daily (reservations are advisable for dinner), but the Heritage House is closed from January 2 through mid-February. (See our Spas and Resorts chapter for more on Heritage House.) There is a full bar.

Little River Inn
$$$$ • 7750 N. Calif. Hwy. 1, Little River
• (707) 937-5942

In one of the prettiest garden settings anywhere, the inn's dining room offers scrumptious country meals for breakfast and dinner, as well as Sunday brunch. Unlike most coastal restaurants, the menu here is not partial to seafood, but leans to classics like leg of lamb filet, Cornish game hen and grilled pork chops. Salads are made from locally grown lettuces and greens. Desserts too may feature local items—don't fail to leave room for the ollalieberry cobbler! The restaurant at Little River Inn is open every day. (For more on the inn, see our Spas and Resorts chapter.)

Cafe Beaujolais
$$$$ • 961 Ukiah St., Mendocino
• (707) 937-5614

It was once a Victorian farmhouse, then at the edge of town. But the town has expanded and engulfed the farm. The ambiance inside is not overwhelming—two dozen well-spaced tables occupy a rather plain room. But the food! It's been praised by restaurant critics for more than two decades and remains something of a

legend in Mendocino. The cuisine has been influenced by France, Italy, Asia and Mexico and features local produce and free-range poultry as much as possible. Entrees run from sturgeon with truffle sauce, for example, to boneless veal roast. One of the most popular features is the posted Country Menu, with a fixed price of $25 for the entire dinner, including dessert. During good weather, there is the option of dining on the large deck in back, which faces onto a beautiful garden. Another option: Call and ask what the menu is for the evening, pick up the entire meal at the "call window" and dine in your hotel room. An array of breads baked on the premises in the wood-fired brick oven not only serves the restaurant, but also can be purchased by non-diners. Dinner is served nightly from 5:45 PM, but closing time (set at 9 PM) is blurred by the fact they'll keep serving as long as folks keep coming.

Mendocino Hotel Restaurant & Garden Room
$$$ • 45080 Main St., Mendocino
• (707) 937-0511

Perhaps it's the graciousness of the hostess, or maybe it's the welcoming decor of this Victorian dining room, but somehow just being here is a pleasant experience. California cuisine is the specialty, and it is influenced considerably by local seafood. Service is warm but not intrusive. The Victorian Room is open for dinner Sunday through Thursday from 6 to 9:30 PM, and Friday and Saturday from 6 to 10 PM. Breakfast and lunch are available in the Garden Room, a large, airy room with a skylight ceiling that really was a garden at one time. (See our Hotels and Motels chapter for more on the Mendocino Hotel.)

955 Ukiah Street Restaurant
$$$$ • 955 Ukiah St., Mendocino
• (707) 937-1955

Located in what was once an artist's studio down a garden path next door to Cafe Beaujolais, this may be one of the major reasons visitors from California and the rest of the country like to come to this coast. The enduring fame of the city of Mendocino is irrevocably connected to the palates of a few thousand visitors who know good restaurants when they find them. And the word is out that Ukiah Street is one of the best on the Mendocino Coast. Basing its fame less on elegance per se than on memorable meals, the restaurant offers a wide-ranging menu and uses local products whenever possible. Options include steaks, roast duck, lamb, and pasta. The restaurant is open Thursday through Sunday from 6 PM.

The Moosse Cafe
$, no credit cards • 390 Kasten St., Mendocino • (707) 937-4323

Take a seat on the deck, relax and let your eyes wander off to the Pacific, then order some delicious food—maybe an eggplant sandwich or smoked salmon pâté. If the weather is inclement, the cafe itself is warm and casual and the service agreeable, with beer and wine available. For the most part, the menu features fresh regional ingredients in its selections. The cafe is open seven days a week for lunch and dinner.

MacCallum House Restaurant
Grey Whale Bar & Cafe
$$$$ • 45020 Albion St., Mendocino • (707) 937-5763

Daisy MacCallum's 1882 Victorian house is one of the earliest of Mendocino's lumber era. If it looks familiar to you, it may be that you've seen it in a magazine. Its position always seems to fit into the "perfect picture" of the City of Mendocino. It's now a bed and breakfast inn, but the dining room is open to the public, as is the Grey Whale Bar & Cafe, where cafe fare is served at friendly prices on the sun porch or parlor. The dining room is more formal, warmed by a stone fireplace. The menu emphasizes fresh local seafoods and organic produce from neighboring farms. Among the choices, you might consider grilled portobello mushrooms or pan-seared duck breast. Dinner is served nightly, and a Sunday brunch is available after 11 AM. MacCallum House is closed from the first of January to mid-February.

Garden Grill
$$$ • Mendocino Coast Botanical Gardens, 18218 N. Calif. Hwy. 1, Fort Bragg • (707) 964-7474

The Grill's setting is unsurpassed: it's located in the spectacular Mendocino Coast Botanical Gardens—47 acres of blooming rhododendrons, azaleas, heather and 100 other native plants, with the bounding Pacific as a backdrop (see our Attractions chapter). You can dine indoors in the light-filled dining room or outside on the deck overlooking the lush coastal landscape. The specialty here is grilled steak, seafood and vegetarian selections. It's open for lunch Wednesday through Saturday from 11 AM to 2:30 PM and for dinner Thursday through Saturday. There's also a Sunday brunch from 10 AM to 2:30 PM.

Wharf Restaurant
$$$ • 32260 N. Harbor Dr., Fort Bragg • (707) 964-4283

The Wharf is a favorite spot for locals and travelers alike, as it has been for more than 40 years. It's right down at the working end of the Fort Bragg fishing industry, and as you relax and enjoy a cocktail or specialty of the house, you can watch the boats bringing in the catch of the day. Pride of the chef is the menu of fresh seafood, with steaks as an alternate. The Wharf is open for lunch and dinner seven days a week.

The Restaurant
$$$ • 418 Main St., Fort Bragg • (707) 964-9800

Like the meeting place of the friends on television's *Seinfeld*, this place is simply called The Restaurant, and it has been for the past two decades. A distinguishing feature is that the walls are covered with the paintings of local artist Olaf Palm. The owners-chefs are Jim and Barbara Larsen, who make everything on the menu except the bread. They offer light meals like grilled polenta with mozzarella and sauteed mushrooms, and they serve a delightful chicken piccata cooked in fresh lemon and white wine sauce. But whatever you eat, save room for the desserts because they're memorable—especially the tiramisu, an Italian concoction of sponge cake, cream cheese, espresso and bittersweet chocolate. The Restaurant presents live jazz on Friday and Saturday. It's open for dinner Thursday through Tuesday from 5 to 9 PM, for lunch on Thursday and Friday from 11:30 AM to 2 PM and for Sunday brunch from 10 AM to 1 PM. Reservations are recommended for Sunday brunch.

Egghead's Restaurant
$$ • 326 N. Main St., Fort Bragg • (707) 964-5005

It's known as the "local's favorite," and yes, the locals do brag that there are no better omelettes or eggs Benedict in the entire United States. Beyond that, Egghead's features some 40 varieties of crepes, specialty pancakes and waffles for breakfast. For lunch, there are creative salads, unusual sandwiches and many unique vegetarian treats. The restaurant is distinguished by another feature: a yellow brick road that runs from the front door to the kitchen (here it's known as Oz). A collection of photos and theater bills on the wall along the row of booths shows Dorothy, the Cowardly Lion, the Tin Man and the rest of the

Wizard cast. Eggheads is open seven days a week.

The Rendezvous
$$ • 647 N. Main St., Fort Bragg
• (707) 964-8142

California continental-style seafood, poultry, veal and steak are served in cozy, comfortable surroundings in one of Fort Bragg's classic early homes. Chef Kim Badenhop studied in Switzerland and France under master chefs, and much of the food served at The Rendezvous reflects the labor-intensive European style of cooking. Seasonality is important to him, and his menus reflect this—in winter, he works with wild game and Dungeness crab; in summer, fresh vegetables and king salmon figure strongly on his menu. Dinner is served Wednesday through Sunday, and reservations are advisable.

Lake County

Sunflower Chinese Restaurant
$ • 14521 Lakeshore Dr., Clearlake
• (707) 994-1268

Exotic it isn't, but it's hard to beat the Sunflower for dependable, Western-friendly Szechuan and Mandarin cuisine. All the favorites are here: beef with broccoli, sweet-and-sour pork, Mongolian beef, etc. They'll withhold the MSG upon request. It's a clean establishment within view of Clear Lake, and the restaurant has a full bar. It's open for lunch and dinner every day but Sunday.

Sicilian Country Steakhouse
$$$ • 5835 Main St., Kelseyville
• (707) 279-0704

There is so much of southern Italy at this downtown Kelseyville restaurant that you'll feel like driving up on a motor scooter, wearing no socks. The menu includes baked zitti, fresh ravioli and tortellini, and four kinds of gnocchi. You also will find a number of veal and chicken dishes, not to mention some of the best steaks around. Oh, and don't forget the robust cioppino alla Siciliano. Ask about the children's menu. Sicilian Country Steakhouse is open for dinner seven nights a week in the summer, closed Monday and Tuesday in the winter. There is a full bar.

Tee Room Restaurant
$$$ • Buckingham Golf & Country Club, 2855 Eastlake Dr., Kelseyville
• (707) 279-1140

You don't have to be a weary golfer, or even a guest of Konocti Harbor Resort (only five minutes away, see our Spas and Resorts chapter) to eat here. You just have to be a devotee of the Southwestern cuisine chef Lauretta Bonfiglio developed at her former restaurant, Lauretta's, in Aspen, Colorado. The Tee Room has a small menu with dishes such as herb-rubbed rack of lamb in a Zinfandel and garlic sauce, and grilled filet mignon in a brandied mushroom sauce. The dining room offers nice views of the golf course and looming Mount Konocti. It's open for dinner Wednesday through Sunday in the summer and Wednesday through Saturday in the winter.

Park Place Restaurant
$$ • 50 Third St., Lakeport
• (707) 263-0444

This pleasant bistro emphasizes fresh, local produce and casual taste. It's just a couple blocks from Clear Lake—from the deck you can see the water and, behind it to the southeast, Mount Konocti. Park Place makes its own pasta daily—one reason its tortellini and ravioli dishes are so popular. The gorgonzola bread and Mediterranean pasta salad, meanwhile, are more than a meal in combination. The restaurant is open for lunch and dinner seven days a week.

INSIDERS' TIP

Not sure about pairing food and wine, and too shy to ask? (Hey, it's a guy thing.) Here's some advice from Craig Schauffel, who specializes in such combinations as the chef de cuisine at Pairs Parkside Cafe: "You should echo the wine's body and flavors with the food: light-bodied wine with light food, high acid wine with high acid food, sweet wine with sweet food. As a simple rule of thumb, always drink white wines before red, dry before sweet and young before old. Your menu would follow by serving lighter foods first, progressing to a fuller food, then ending the meal on a sweet note."

Nightlife

Let's make one thing clear right off the bat: Gravenstein apples we have; the Big Apple we ain't.

The Wine Country has attractions, restaurants and scenery that, taken as a whole, might well stand up to any in the world. What we don't have is swinging, party-'til-dawn nightlife. Most towns around here start rolling up the sidewalks after sundown. (Oh, maybe they'll stay up until 11 PM on Saturday night.) It probably has something to do with all the activity our visitors tend to pack into their days and early evenings. After hours of driving, gawking, drinking wine, eating decadent meals and then drinking more wine, only the truly heroic have enough stamina left to search for evening action.

There are a few exceptions to this pattern. The downtown areas in Petaluma and Santa Rosa heat up pretty good on the weekend. In old Santa Rosa, in the area just east of U.S. Highway 101 between, say, Third and Fifth streets, you'll dig up a lot of live bands. Guerneville, too, can be lively in the summer, especially in the town's thriving gay bars. In those places that hop, last call might arrive at 2 AM. In general, you can expect your bartender to turn into a pumpkin at midnight.

Here are a few Wine Country clubs, bars and pubs that can be relied upon for entertainment, or at least for a cool beer in a warm atmosphere. Figure on paying no cover charge unless we state otherwise. The listings are followed by movie theaters in the four counties. Check a local newspaper for more up-to-date information. And please observe the same common sense about drinking and driving that applies anywhere. California's legal blood-alcohol threshold is a stringent .08, so taking to the road after more than one drink can be expensive and inconvenient, as well as dangerous. If you need a taxi, consult our Getting Around chapter.

LOOK FOR:
- Bars and Clubs
- Movie Theaters

Bars and Clubs

Napa County

Downtown Joe's
902 Main St., Napa
• (707) 258-2337

This riverside microbrewery offers a variety of rock, pop and blues bands every Wednesday—8:30 PM to midnight—and Friday, Saturday, and Sunday evenings—9:30 PM to 1:30 AM. There is no cover.

Marlowe's
1637 W. Imola Ave., Napa
• (707) 224-2700

Napa's most popular Latino hangout features outrageous banda groups—with blinding outfits and 10-piece horn sections—every Saturday night. Those shows generally run from 9 PM to 1:30 AM, cost $15 and reel in dozens of immigrants from the Mexican states of Michoacan, Jalisco and Guerrero. Marlowe's puts on different faces other nights. Friday is house/hip-hop, Wednesday is Country Night (including dance lessons from 7:30 to 9:30 PM) and Sunday afternoon features Dixieland jazz. The cover for these peripheral shows ranges from free to $7.

Silverado Country Club & Resort
1600 Atlas Peak Rd., Napa
• (707) 257-0200

A classy joint indeed, Silverado features jazz piano from 5 to 9 PM on the patio terrace, Wednesday through Saturday. On Friday and Saturday nights the soloist is followed by a band that plays from 9 PM to 1 AM. The regular act of late has been the five-piece Paul Martin Band. There is never a cover.

The Carriage House Restaurant
1775 Clay St., Napa • (707) 255-4744

This is a veritable House of Karaoke. The Carriage House gives you an opportunity to warble every Tuesday, Thursday, Friday and Saturday from 9 PM to 2 AM. There is a $5 cover on weekend nights.

Hemphill's Lounge
3385 California Blvd., Napa
• (707) 255-9744

Your chances of spotting Drew Barrymore are practically nil at this little hideaway, but you can try karaoke on Thursday night (9 PM to 1:30 AM) or listen to pop music on Friday (9 PM to 2 AM). There is no cover.

Piccolino's Italian Cafe
1385 Napa Town Center, Napa
• (707) 251-0100

On Friday and Saturday evenings, this centrally located restaurant provides jazz accompaniment, perhaps spiced with a little R&B or salsa. Hours are generally 5 to 9 PM, and there is no cover.

Violette's at the Mansion
443 Brown St., Napa • (707) 253-2583, (800) 959-2583

At the rear of one of Napa Valley's finest inns (see our Bed and Breakfast chapter) is a charming French restaurant, and its Friday- and Saturday-night performances—classical guitar, jazz, blues or even harp—have become quite popular. Reservations definitely are required. Dinner seating is at 7 PM, and the price of $85 per person includes a seven-course prix fixe meal. Dessert seating—$40 per couple for a sampler—is at 8:30.

Piatti Restaurant
6480 Washington St., Yountville
• (707) 944-2070

See our Restaurants chapter for a sample of Piatti's fare. See our Festivals and Events chapter (December, Napa County) for a description of David Auerbach's music. But if you want to combine the two, you should come here on a Wednesday night. The dinner shows begin at 7 PM.

Ana's Cantina
1205 Main St., St. Helena • (707) 963-4921

This tropical-themed Mexican restaurant heats up from 9:30 PM to 1:30 AM most Friday and Saturday nights, with a stream of bands that run from Latin-Mediterranean to jazz to rock to reggae. Forget about a cover. Wednesday and Sunday are karaoke night. Thursday is open-mike night.

Calistoga Inn & Restaurant
1250 Lincoln Ave., Calistoga
• (707) 942-4101

The bartender slings Napa Valley Brewing Company beers here, and every Saturday from 8:30 to 11 PM (and often on Tuesdays and Fridays), live music fills the small oblong bar. The material varies but tends toward intimate, singer-songwriter stuff. Wednesday is open-mike night.

Hydro Bar & Grill
1403 Lincoln Ave., Calistoga
• (707) 942-9777

Calistoga's late-night eatery is a perfect spot for sultry jazz, low-down blues piano or luny rock 'n' roll, and that's just what you get most nights of the week. Show times vary, but the music usually doesn't die until 1:30 AM on Saturdays. There is no cover.

Surfwood
1410 Lincoln Ave., Calistoga
• (707) 942-4700

The Surfwood, popular among the locals, has always offered occasional blues or rock performances. Show time is generally 9:30 PM to 1:30 AM. There is no cover.

Sonoma County

Murphy's Irish Pub
464 First St. E., Sonoma • (707) 935-0660

This pub keeps sleepy Sonoma awake, usually every Thursday through Sunday night. The genre is hard to predict. It could be blues one night, traditional Celtic the next. Or it could be folk ballads followed by a melodious string ensemble. There is no cover, but expect a two-pint minimum.

Copperfield's Cafe
140 Kentucky St., Petaluma
• (707) 762-8798

Sonoma County's hippest bookstore chain goes one step further at this Petaluma branch, laying down poetry on Thursdays and storytelling on Fridays.

Kodiak Jack's
256 Petaluma Blvd. N., Petaluma
• (707) 765-5760

With so many cowboy boots stomping at one time here, we hope Jack's foundation is structurally reinforced. There is West Coast swing dancing on Mondays, intermediate dancing on Tuesdays, line dancing on Wednesdays, "beginner couples" on Thursdays and power country on Fridays and three out of four Saturdays each month. There's a restaurant with cuisine to match the country theme. Call for cover information.

Mystic Theatre & Dance Hall
23 Petaluma Blvd. N., Petaluma
• (707) 765-6665

Not as big as Konocti Harbor, not as polite as the Luther Burbank Center, the Mystic Theatre might be the Wine Country's coolest venue. Built in 1911, it's a vaulted, double-decker palace that wouldn't be out of place on the Sunset strip. Much of the music—Friday and Saturday nights, plus the occasional Thursday or Sunday—is local, but the managers will occasionally hit you with a passing-through bigshot such as legendary jazz pianist and vocalist Mose Allison, jittery rockers The Reverend Horton Heat or side-saddle angel Emmylou Harris. The cover charge can range from $3 to $20.

Inn of the Beginning
8201 Old Redwood Hwy., Cotati
• (707) 664-1100

Monday through Saturday, this tripped-out club gets Cotati jumping. You could hear shoulder-dipping funk one night, cow punk the next, psychedelia the night after that. The Inn keeps its hipness in order with regular appearances by California-based The Mother Hips, country rock's genius band ready to explode. In some ways, little has changed since the Inn played host to Janis Joplin and Neil Young so many years ago. Call for cover information.

Tradewinds
8210 Old Redwood Hwy., Cotati
• (707) 795-7878

If the musical fare at Inn of the Beginning doesn't grab you, wander across the street to Tradewinds. This small club has music most weekend nights. Expect a lot of blues and R&B, and watch for Derek and the Aces, the roots-rock band that used to be regulars here.

A'Roma Roasters and Coffeehouse
95 Fifth St., Santa Rosa • (707) 576-7765

Come down to Railroad Square on a Friday or Saturday night and get groovy while sipping on a hot cup of chai. A'Roma does a lot of folk music, plus some world beat, jazz and blues.

The Cantina
500 Fourth St., Santa Rosa
• (707) 523-3663

Generation Next moves to its own beat at the Cantina, in the heart of downtown. Thursday is college night during the spring and summer, when the downtown farmers market fills the Fourth Street area. Fridays and Saturdays (when they charge $2 and up), you get a mix of top 40, R&B, disco, house and Latin beats.

Clo's Ice Creamery
557 Summerfield Rd., Santa Rosa
• (707) 539-6100

Name another place in America that offers both amped-up rock 'n roll AND drive-thru dairy-product sales, and we'll buy you a frozen yogurt with your choice of topping. The back room of Clo's has become one of Sonorma County's hottest venues. Call for a concert schedule and cover charges.

Club Rumors
120 Fifth St., Santa Rosa
• (707) 545-5483

Five nights a week this is the place to get your dance on in downtown Santa Rosa. DJs spin the discs Friday and Saturday nights (for those 18 and older on Friday, 21 and older on Saturday). Sunday is Club Diva, Monday is swing night and Tuesday is country dance night. Cover is usually about $5.

The Moonlight Bar & Grill
515 Fourth St., Santa Rosa
• (707) 526-2662

This downtown club rocks with straight-up screaming guitars, or something weird like surf or ska, most nights of most weeks. The cover is usually $2 to $3.

Sweetriver Saloon
248 Coddingtown Center, Santa Rosa
• (707) 526-0400

Seating a comedy club in the middle of a mall should provide a lot of grist for the comics. Sweetriver makes you laugh every Friday and Saturday night, starting at 9 PM. The cover is $7 (no joke).

Bear Republic Brewing Company
345 Healdsburg Ave., Healdsburg
• (707) 433-2337

Another microbrewery that also offers music (again, see our Restaurants chapter Close-up), Bear Republic often has entertainment on Friday night. It might be blues; it might be reggae; it might sound like heaven after a couple of pints.

Tamale Malone's Irish Cantina & Grille
245 Healdsburg Ave., Healdsburg
• (707) 431-1856

Drawing on the under-exploited bond between the cultures of Ireland and Mexico, Malone's (on Healdsburg's central plaza) is open seven days a week with a full-service bar, Mexican cuisine and live entertainment on Friday and Saturday nights.

Jasper O'Farrell's
6957 Sebastopol Ave., Sebastopol
• (707) 823-1389

O'Farrell's keeps Sebastopol busy just about every night of the week. Tuesday is open-mike night. Friday through Monday you get music, music, music—mostly blues, some rock, some soul, some original songwriting, and even the occasional Celtic group. On Thursdays groove to the Sonny Lowe Blues Band. It's very eclectic and very local.

Marty's Top o' the Hill
8050 Bodega Ave., Sebastopol
• (707) 823-5987

Marty's schedules musical acts—don't be surprised to encounter hard-core metal—every Friday and Saturday night. Thursday and Sunday are karaoke nights.

The Powerhouse Brewing Company
268 Petaluma Ave., Sebastopol
• (707) 829-9171

This brewpub-cum-night spot (see the Close-up in our Restaurants chapter) offers a mix of local and national talent, heavy on the blues. Sometimes there is no cover, but it can be as much as $12 for acts like the Nervis Brothers, those New Orleans boogiers.

INSIDERS' TIP
For unparalleled coverage of the Wine Country social scene, pick up a free copy of the weekly *Sonoma County Independent*, available in bookstores, coffee houses, etc., throughout the county. It will tell you all you need to know about current music, film and drama. Unfortunately, our other three counties have no equivalent.

Main Street Station
16280 Main St., Guerneville
• (707) 869-0501

When the sizzle of Guerneville gets a little too hot, duck into the Station for some cool, breezy jazz. Two house bands have been ruling lately—the Benny Barth Jazz Tri on Tuesdays and the Vickie Anne Jazz Trio on Wednesdays. Other hipsters blow in and out on Thursdays, Fridays and Saturdays. There is no cover charge.

Rainbow Cattle Company
16220 Main St., Guerneville
• (707) 869-0206

It celebrated its 20th anniversary in October 1999, but the Cattle Company hasn't slowed down a bit. It's still where the Russian River's gay clientele congregates for loud, uninhibited fun. The club has a DJ on Friday and Saturday nights and holidays.

Molly Brown's Saloon
14120 Old Cazadero Rd., Guerneville
• (707) 869-0511

It's a mixed crowd at Molly's, and that is a lot of the appeal. Whatever your age, racial mix or gender flavoring, you're welcome here (though some wouldn't hesitate to call it a gay bar). It was the Red Barn until 1983.

Mendocino County

Greenwood Pier Cafe
5926 S. Calif. Hwy. 1, Elk • (707) 877-9997

If you find yourself in the village of Elk, south of Albion on the rugged Mendocino coast, you might be surprised to hear the cadence of a jazz piano on the breeze. It will lead you to Greenwood Pier Cafe, which has music every Friday and Saturday from 5:30 to 9 PM.

Patterson's Pub
10485 Lansing St., Mendocino
• (707) 937-4782

Beer and tall tales are paramount at Patterson's, but the pub also keeps you occupied with four sports-occupied TV sets. The pub also has live music on occasion, though it

NIGHTLIFE

is rare. Look for the old London cab in the driveway. Patterson's is open daily.

The Caspar Inn
14957 Caspar Rd., Caspar
• (707) 964-5565

About halfway between Mendocino and Fort Bragg (8 miles or so) is Caspar, home to this old-style roadhouse. The inn hosts bands —rock or blues or funk or reggae—most nights from Thursday through Sunday. Expect a $5 to $10 cover and a lot of dancing bodies. Sunday is open-mike night, and Caspar's presents swing dance lessons on Thursdays at 7 PM.

Headlands Coffee House
120 E. Laurel St.,
Ft. Bragg • (707) 964-1987

This is the epicenter of local culture in Fort Bragg, a hipster java joint where there's almost always something interesting to listen to as you stay wired. Sunday is classical music night: maybe a string trio, maybe a guitar-and-flute combination. On Friday there is usually a jazz piano trio. Beyond that you're most likely to encounter jazz or acoustic singer-songwriter stuff.

Rendezvous Restaurant
647 N. Main St., Ft. Bragg • (707) 964-8142

This restaurant in the heart of Fort Bragg accompanies its food with the sounds of local musicians, every Saturday evening. Lately the tendency has been toward vocals with electric piano.

Lake County

Konocti Harbor Resort & Spa
8727 Soda Bay Rd., Kelseyville
• (707) 279-4281

In a few short years, Konocti Harbor has managed to place itself among the top music venues in Northern California. The resort actually has several different sites for performance. The Konocti Field Amphitheater, which operates between May and October, puts you under the stars for major concerts. This lakeside amphitheater seats 5,000, all within 200 feet of

the stage. It pulls big acts, some contemporary, some revived. The lineup has included the likes of Wynonna, Vince Gill, Styx, the Doobie Brothers and Tim McGraw. Tickets usually range from $29 to $49.

Predating the amphitheater was the Joe Mazzola Classic Concert Showroom, a 1,000-occupancy dinner theater with two VIP balconies and tiered seating. The showroom tends to show stars of yesterday or acts more appropriate to an intimate setting. Like who? Like Ray Charles, Eddie Money, Tanya Tucker and Bill Cosby. These tickets are in the $35 to $60 range, more if you include buffet dinner. But wait, there's more. The Full Moon Saloon, right next to Clear Lake, has live entertainment Fridays and Saturdays year round, and seven days a week from June through Labor Day. The saloon has indoor and outdoor seating and a sizable dance floor.

> ## INSIDERS' TIP
> Curb Records artist Philip Claypool is a Calistoga resident. He's a familiar face at local bars, filling up the small rooms with his downtown Memphis sound. You can sing along when he gets to these lines: "She kicked my dog. She slammed the door. She stole my heart and my brand-new Ford."

Movie Theaters

Napa County

Napa CineDome 8, 825 Pearl Street, Napa •(707) 257-7700

Uptown Cinema, 1350 3rd Street, Napa • (707) 256-0150

The Magnum Cinema (70 mm films), 6525 Washington Street, Yountville • (707) 944-0470

Cameo Cinema (occasional art movies), 1340 Main Street, St. Helena • (707) 963-9779

Sonoma County

Sebastiani Theatre (historic building; occasional art movies), 476 First Street E., Sonoma • (707) 996-2020

Sonoma Cinemas, 200 Siesta Way, Sonoma • (707) 935-1234

Washington Square Cinema 5, 219 S. McDowell Boulevard, Petaluma • (707) 762-0006

UA Empire Cinemas, 6470 Redwood Drive, Rohnert Park • (707) 584-0123

Pacific Theatres 16, 555 Rohnert Park Expressway W., Rohnert Pack • (707) 586-0555

Airport Cinema 8, 409 Aviation Way, Santa Rosa • (707) 522-0330

Lakeside Cinema 5, 551 Summerfield Road, Santa Rosa • (707) 522-0330

UA Cinema 6, 620 Third Street, Santa Rosa • (707) 528-8770

UA Coddingtown Cinemas, 1630 Range Avenue, Santa Rosa • (707) 544-1970

UA Movies 5, 547 Mendocino Avenue, Santa Rosa • (707) 528-7200

The Raven Film Center, 115 North Street, Healdsburg • (707) 433-5448

Clover Cinemas, 121 E. First Street, Cloverdale • (707) 894-7920

Sebastopol Cinemas, 6868 McKinley Street, Sebastopol • (707) 829-3456

Rio Theater, 20396 Bohemian Highway (Calif. Hwy. 116), Monte Rio • (707) 865-0913

Mendocino County

Forks Theater, 40 Pallini Lane, Ukiah • (707) 468-4336

Ukiah 6 Theatre, 612 S. State Street, Ukiah • (707) 462-6788

Arena Theatre, 214 Main Street, Point Arena • (707) 882-3020

Coast Cinemas, 167 S. Franklin Street, Fort Bragg • (707) 964-2019

Lake County

Clearlake Cinema, 3380 Washington Street, Clearlake • (707) 994-7469

Lakeport Auto Movies (drive-in), 52 Soda Bay Road, Lakeport • (707) 263-5011

Lakeport Cinema 5, 52 Soda Bay Rd., Lakeport • (707) 263-4215

NIGHTLIFE

Wineries

A state of mind as much as a place, Wine Country demands that you slow down and savor its pleasures: handsome wineries that house aging vintages, historic towns, and scenery that rivals any on earth. Ideal grape-growing conditions have made Napa, Sonoma, Mendocino and Lake counties famous for producing some of the best wines in the world. When you visit, you are in the midst of some of the most valuable cropland on the continent.

More than 400 million gallons of juice are squeezed from grapes each year, bottled and set aside to age as wine. But it takes marketing to turn the product into cash, so most wineries want visitors to stop in, look around, taste the product, buy it and keep on buying it. It's difficult to imagine a trip to Wine Country without at least a day or two set aside for a sampling of the region's wineries. If you take time to drop by more than a few, you'll discover each winery has its own special story to tell. Genial guides and tasting room hosts gladly explain the mysteries of the craft, reminisce about vintage years and share hopes for this year's crop.

Don't rush through Wine Country. There's nothing to be gained from sprinting between tasting rooms. Take the time to learn about the winery, the winemaking process and especially its people. Usually they are as mellow and unhurried as the wines themselves.

LOOK FOR:
- **A Taste of Each Region**
- **Getting Your Bearings**
- **A Winetasting Primer**
- **Wineries to Visit**

A Taste of Each Region

So . . . with more than 600 wineries within the four counties, where does one begin? First, we'll give you a taste of what separates our four-county coverage area from the rest of the winemaking areas of this state and the world—qualities that have given our region the undisputed title of California's Wine Country. Next, we'll provide a brief overview of the wine and wineries of each of the counties in our coverage area. Then comes the part where you get to pick and choose: detailed listings for more than 120 individual producers throughout Wine Country.

Quality, Not Quantity

Despite the number of wineries here and the number of acres under viticulture, it's interesting to note that Wine Country's grape harvest represents only a relatively small contribution to California's total wine production. The annual grape harvest of Sonoma County adds up to a minuscule 4 percent of the state's total volume, about the same as neighboring Napa County. This deceptively small percentage stands in stark contrast with the lofty reputation Wine Country's vintages have deservedly attained.

There are dozens of wineries here, but they are not the oil-refinery-scale tank farms of the jug wine, bulk business. Nearly all our wineries are small- to medium-sized operations, often family-owned. This is as good a reason as any to visit—you will nearly always find a tasty vintage to call your own personal discovery. One of Napa Valley's winemakers

WINERIES

captured Wine Country philosophy: "The people I deal with are all happy people; wine is a happy product." Perhaps the region's most memorable quality, at any time of year, is its warm and welcoming spirit.

But there's more to the great wines produced in this region, and it doesn't all have to do with the smaller operations and intense attention to detail—these are things you might find in some other locations. What we have that cannot be reproduced are the unique marriages of land and climate. Pour yourself another glass of your newly discovered favorite red, and read about the climatology of fine wines.

The Information on Appellations

It's this simple: The quality of the grapes is the key to the quality of the wine. Where grapes are grown makes up almost 80 percent of the characteristics of a specific wine. The mellow in your Merlot? The zest in that Zinfandel? The panache of a particular Pinot Noir? It all can be traced back to the grapes, the climate that fostered their growth and the ground they came from.

Areas with hot days, warm nights and deep, peat-rich soils might be good for growing corn and other vegetables (and even table grapes), but they produce wine grapes that are too high in sugar content and, therefore, not good for creating fine wines. A cooler, dryer climate and the volcanic soils so common in Napa, Sonoma, Mendocino and Lake counties lead to the production of world-class wines.

Within this four-county area, there are also many microclimates. Each of these areas has specific characteristics that affect the wine grapes grown there. In the wine industry, these special growing regions are referred to as "American viticultural areas" (AVAs) or "appellations," a word you will run into frequently in this guide. How important is this term? Some grapes grow better in one appellation than in another. Also, the same grape grown in one appellation may produce a wine that is distinctly different than one made with the same grade of grapes grown in another appellation. A Merlot grown in Carneros, for example, produces a wine that is complex, with some light and soft fruit flavors; the same grape grown in the Dry Creek appellation may bring about a wine with a full, robust character that is bursting with flavor.

There are 11 AVAs in Sonoma County alone, and another 13 in Napa County. Additionally the two counties share one—the aforementioned Carneros, a cool region bordering San Pablo Bay at the southern reaches of both the Napa and Sonoma valleys. At first, it may sound to the novice as if the wine snobs are splitting hairs. But the differences in the wines from different appellations (and different winemakers within the same appellation), when tasted side by side, are distinct and remarkable.

Appellations also are important economically. A wine labeled with a certain appellation name must be produced using a minimum of 75 to 85 percent of grapes from that region. For example, a "Sonoma Valley" Zinfandel must take at least 85 percent of its Zinfandel grapes from the Sonoma Valley AVA. Such distinctions add value to the wine and raise the shelf price. By comparison, a Zinfandel with the appellation "California" on the label means that the grapes could have come from anywhere in California. These wines often are produced with grapes from less-prestigious growing areas such as the San Joaquin Valley, where the long, hot summers allow production of massive quantities of grapes that are used primarily for jug wines and the so-called "fighting varietals" (wine industry jargon for lower-priced varietals).

The generally dryer and cooler microclimates of Napa, Sonoma, Mendocino and Lake counties produce fewer grapes, but they are of a much higher quality for making fine wine. Grapes from these regions are more expensive (often as much as four to five times higher per ton), and they are in high demand.

Of course, grapes are not the only element that goes into making a fine wine. The object of the winemaker's craft—a blend of skill, experience, science, art, taste and inspiration—

INSIDERS' TIP

In addition to their highly regarded tours, the folks at Robert Mondavi Winery also offer wine-and-food seminars from 10 AM to 2 PM every Friday, May through October. Detailed information on wine growing and tasting is supplemented by a lunch prepared by winery chefs—along with Robert Mondavi wines, of course.

is to take the special qualities of certain grapes and maximize their potential. Without getting too high-falutin' about it, a tour of Wine Country can include the dimension of a search for the perfect blend of the region's finest grapes and the winemaker's skill.

Where'd That Come From?

Wines labeled with a certain appellation name must be produced using a minimum of 75 to 85 percent of grapes (depending on the varietal) from that specific region. Below are the recognized appellations of the four counties in Wine Country. Note that the North Coast appellation is a broad one, applying to wines from several different counties including Napa, Sonoma, Mendocino and Lake.

Napa County
Atlas Peak, Chiles Valley, Howell Mountain, Los Carneros, Mount Veeder, Napa Valley, North Coast, Oakville, Rutherford, Spring Mountain District, St. Helena, Stags Leap District, Wild Horse Valley, Yountville

Sonoma County
Alexander Valley, Chalk Hill, Dry Creek Valley, Knights Valley, Los Carneros, North Coast, Northern Sonoma, Russian River Valley, Sonoma Coast, Sonoma County Green Valley, Sonoma Mountain, Sonoma Valley

Mendocino County
Anderson Valley, Cole Ranch, McDowell Valley, Mendocino, Mendocino Ridge, North Coast, Potter Valley, Redwood Valley, Yorkville Highlands

Lake County
Benmore Valley, Clear Lake, Guenoc Valley, North Coast

Sources: *Appellation* magazine; Mendocino Wine Growers Alliance; Lake County Visitor Information; Bureau of Alcohol, Tobacco and Firearms; The Wine Institute

Napa County

Most people think first of Napa County, where the wines have been established as the yardstick by which other American vintages are measured. Even the French have taken notice of this world-famous source. Compared to Europe, however, where vineyards have flourished for centuries, Napa Valley still is in its infancy. Yet it has grown quickly, with such an intense concentration of wineries that there is some concern traffic and crowds will destroy the bucolic landscape, particularly in summer when tourist count is high.

Those who know the region well are inclined at such busy times to abandon the main highway through the valley, Calif. Highway 29, and turn onto the Silverado Trail, which runs parallel to the east. From there, they can cross over, using any of several connecting lanes that bind the two north-south roads. Silverado Trail is a delight in itself, winding between meadows and wooded slopes to the east and vineyards to the west. Its slight elevation produces some striking vineyard panoramas, eminently suited to photography. (For more on negotiating the byways of Wine Country, see our Getting Around chapter.)

Napa boasts so many tasting rooms it is almost impossible to classify them as a group. They range in style from rustic to elegant, sparse to cluttered, disarmingly casual to alarmingly commercial. But beyond atmosphere and physical trappings, the valley's tasting rooms provide the makings of a truly unique wine experience. In these pockets of hospitality you will find an abundance of wines rivaling any in the world.

Photo: Viansa Winery

The inside tasting room at the Viansa Winery not only offers wine but a selection of gourmet foods.

At its widest, Napa Valley is no more than 3 miles across. It is 27 miles from north end to south end, framed on both sides by hulking mountains. Most of the valley's 2 million annual visitors come to see its groomed vineyards—some just planted, some ancient, with gnarled vines that stand like regiments of old soldiers. Visitors come to sip the nectar of the gods; to luxuriate in handsome, turn-of-the-century bed and breakfast inns; and to further excite their palates with gourmet dining that rivals that of most major cities. Visitors also learn something more: Wineries are great places to find some unexpected entertainment. Musical events are a feature at several wineries—Sunday jazz at Domaine Chandon, for instance (see our Arts and Culture chapter). St. Supery's guided tour includes a look at a Victorian home restored as a living museum of the late 1800s. At Sterling Vineyards, an aerial tram lifts passengers high over the valley floor to a wine tasting deck affording an unequaled view of Napa Valley's upper reaches.

Food-and-wine pairings are staged in several wineries, and many have picnic grounds that give new meaning to the great outdoors. Artesa has a charming museum with some 17th-century winemaking casks and paraphernalia from its home country of Spain.

Sonoma County

The Napa and Sonoma valleys are separated by the Mayacamas Mountains. Close up, the two counties are as different as they are alike. If Napa is a smooth James Bond, or perhaps Maurice Chevalier, Sonoma is a rangy, quietly self-assured John Wayne—the country cousin with surprising qualities.

But when people say they are going to visit "Sonoma," just which Sonoma do they mean? Are they talking about Sonoma County—a sprawling giant one-and-a-half times the size of Rhode Island? Or are they referring to the Sonoma Valley, Jack London's famed "Valley of the Moon," where Count Agoston Haraszthy fathered the California wine industry? Maybe they simply mean the town of Sonoma, the historic little pueblo nestled in the southeast corner of the county, and site of the state's last mission (see our History and Area Overview chapters for more on all these incarnations of Sonoma).

Each of these Sonomas is distinctly different, and when you begin discussing grape-growing and winemaking, it gets even more complicated.

Sonoma County, as mentioned previously, is home to at least 11 distinct wine-growing appellations and shares an 12th, Carneros, with Napa County. Saying that a wine comes from Sonoma doesn't really say enough to those who know their wines. There are differences—sometimes subtle, sometimes dramatic—among the same types of wine produced by different Sonoma County vintners in different appellations.

Grapes are planted in every corner of Sonoma County except right along the Pacific. Major grape-growing areas include the Russian River, where ocean fog makes the climate ideal for Pinot Noir and Chardonnay, and for an exceptional Sauvignon Blanc; Los Carneros (which, again, Sonoma shares with Napa County), where wind and fog from San Pablo Bay create conditions that produce intensely flavored Pinot Noir and Chardonnay; Sonoma Valley, which has so many microclimates virtually any grape grows well; Alexander Valley, known for its Cabernet Sauvignon and Sauvignon Blanc; and Dry Creek Valley, where the wines have been earning much publicity and numerous gold medals of late. Sauvignon Blancs from virtually any area of Sonoma County would be considered excellent and superior to the same wine produced in less-prestigious wine grape regions of California.

The handsome, green countryside of the Russian River valley, which extends south of Healdsburg to Sebastopol, east to Mark West Springs and west to Guerneville, is a quiet corner of Sonoma County that has remained relatively unknown to tourists. It is one of the county's large viticultural areas, subject to heavy rainfall and considerable fog. White grapes predominate, and some wineries produce popular sparkling wines.

Thousands of acres of vines bask in the north county's rumpled hills and river bottomlands. Wineries range from small, family-operated enterprises where bottle labels still are applied by hand, to huge corporations where ageless winemaking skills are blended with computerized technology. Several years ago, seven small wineries got together to create the Russian River Wine Road, an informational program to tell the public about their scenic and uncrowded wine region. This pamphlet is available at many locations in the area, including the visitors bureau in Healdsburg.

Wine experts have been calling Sonoma County "a work in progress." While Napa seems increasingly pigeonholed as a source for Cabernet and Chardonnay, Sonoma's image is still evolving. There's plenty of room for discovery because of its diverse soil types and weather.

INSIDERS' TIP

"Tours by appointment. No picnic facilities." You'll see those words a lot during your Wine Country stay—in this book, for instance. But as Dick Steltzner of Steltzner Vineyards points out, many newer wineries have to say that. It's standard verbiage in the use permits now issued by the County of Napa. (Older wineries retain the rights stated on their original permits.) What does it all mean? Only that it never hurts to ask. "By appointment" can mean inquiring five minutes before taking a tour. And wineries without official picnic grounds have been known to turn a blind eye to small groups bearing baskets of cheese.

One current development in the winemaking fraternity of Sonoma County has been the relatively quiet genesis of E. & J. Gallo's Sonoma Series. Convinced that Sonoma is the place to grow the world's finest wines, the Gallos have been quietly accumulating hundreds of acres in the county for 20 years. They are now one of the county's biggest landowners with 6,000 acres—about 2,500 of them covered with grape vines and more being planted. Gallo is headquartered near Healdsburg, but don't look for winetasting experiences here (hence, no subsequent listing). They're not laying out a welcome mat for the public. The driveway entrance has a simple sign that reads "Private Property," in English and Spanish.

The bottom line is this: Sonoma County is huge. How does a prospective wine tasting explorer know where to begin?

If you have only one day to tour the Sonoma County area of Wine Country, you can't go wrong if you start in the Sonoma Valley. It is the closest of the premium wine-growing regions to San Francisco, only 45 minutes from the Golden Gate.

Your tour might well begin with a stop at the Sonoma Valley Visitors Bureau (which is also the office of the Sonoma Valley Vintners and Growers Association) on Spain Street. It's next to the Sonoma State Historic Park headquarters, across the street from the lovely, green central Plaza in the center of the town of Sonoma (see our Attractions and History chapters). For an easy mix of shopping and browsing and winetasting, walk around the town square before taking a free trolley three blocks east for a winery tour and tasting at Sebastiani Vineyards.

If you are eager for some serious winetasting, there are more than a half-dozen small- to medium-sized wineries within a 15-minute drive of Sonoma Plaza. These include Ravenswood, known for its excellent Zinfandels; Buena Vista, which also has a tasting room on the Plaza; Gundlach Bundschu; and Bartholomew Park Winery (all are listed in this chapter). If you are headed back to San Francisco, as you enter the region nearest San Pablo Bay you will be traveling through the Carneros region with its many wineries. Stop in at Viansa (which also has an outstanding deli) and Cline Cellars. If you are able to visit and taste the wines of even half the places mentioned, you will have had a full and enjoyable day. The big-name producers in the county include Sebastiani, Glen Ellen, Clos du Bois and Korbel, but don't neglect the smaller wineries: Benziger, Kenwood, Foppiano, Hop Kiln, Ferrari-Carano, Chateau Souverain, Simi and so on. Another possibility would be to visit places

Area wineries often offer tours in which visitors can see how wines are aged to perfection

like the Family Wineries of Sonoma Valley or the Wine Room, where you can taste the wines of multiple wineries in a single spot.

Besides the wine itself, touring Sonoma County offers the sheer pleasure of driving along winding roads with views of vineyards and farms that alternate between the dramatic and the sweetly rural. From some mountaintops and parts of the Carneros district at the southern border, the skyline of San Francisco is visible on clear days (and nights).

Mendocino County

While not as well known as Sonoma or Napa, Mendocino County is gradually getting the word out that some fantastic wines are being made around Ukiah and closer to the coast in the Anderson Valley, originally an area of orchards and sheep and cattle ranches. Discovered during the 1970s as a fine growing area for wine grapes, this rolling valley, split by the Navarro River, is now marked by uniform lines—vines of Pinot Noir, Chardonnay, Gewurtztraminer and Zinfandel.

To prove to the world that Anderson Valley is the finest but least recognized Pinot Noir-producing region in the country, vintners there held the first annual "Pinot Noir Weekend" in May 1997 and promised annual renewals. Participating wineries offer vineyard and winery tours, a look at the history of growing Pinot Noir and lots of tastings from both barrels and bottles to prove they know their business.

If anyone deserved to be called the grandfather of Mendocino wine success, it would be Adolph Parducci. From the end of Prohibition until the end of the 1960s, Parducci Wine Cellars

Variety Show

Don't know your Gamay from your Pinot Grigio? Who can blame you? The French have had thousands of years to learn the characteristics of various grapes. In typical American fashion, we have tried to catch up in a few decades, and we expect ourselves to incorporate Italian and German varietals as well. It can rapidly become perplexing.

On the other hand, too many wine drinkers, even some experienced ones, seem intent on limiting themselves to Chardonnay and Cabernet Sauvignon, with an occasional Merlot to lend a feeling of anarchy. They don't know what they're missing. There are a lot of delicious grapes out there, and some of them are obscure even in Wine Country. Don't be afraid to try any of them. And be fair to blends, which can make for some of the finest (and most coveted) bottles around. Remember, this is about personal taste — if you like it, it's a good wine.

The following list of varietals is neither complete nor guaranteed to apply to every wine you taste. It will, however, give you a general idea of what to expect when you sip a certain type. With a little practice (and practice was never this fun) you might even develop a pet grape or two.

Barbera: The grape variety has its origins in Italy, and Italian families in Sonoma and Napa make most of this varietal. It's a dry, full-flavored wine, often served with pasta or seafood stews in spicy tomato sauces.

Blanc de Blancs: The phrase means white wine made from white grapes, usually describing sparkling wines made to be light in style.

Blanc de Noirs: The phrase means white wine (usually sparkling wine) made from black grapes (usually Pinot Noir).

Cabernet Sauvignon: Currently this is the bedrock of California's dry red wines.

Photo: Tina Luster-Hoban

Chardonnay grapes ripen on the vine at a Napa Valley vineyard. The wine they will yield is one of many Wine Country specialties.

Young wines tend to be more tannic (the quality that makes your cheeks pucker); the good ones become more velvety when aged.

Chardonnay: A dry white wine, it's enjoying the same prestige as red Cabernet Sauvignon. It's frequently called upon to complement the rich, buttery flavors of creamy sauces or lobster.

Fume Blanc: A white table wine, it is almost always dry. Some say it has a smoky flavor; you might consider that when you taste it. It's a great companion to well-seasoned poultry dishes.

Chenin Blanc: A white table wine, it is sweet enough to be considered a before-dinner wine, while still suitable for dinner. It's great with lunch or picnics.

Gamay Beaujolais: Light and fresh, it is the fruitiest of the red wines. It's usually served slightly chilled.

Gewurztraminer: Its spicy characteristic is so pronounced that many people prefer to drink it with appetizers rather than as a dinner wine.

Grey Riesling: This is a white that should be consumed when the wine is still young. It is spicy and sweet.

Johannisburg Riesling: A grape variety originated in the Mosel region of Germany, this white table wine is marked by a faint hint of sweetness. It is declared by many to be the perfect accompaniment to seafood.

Merlot: A currently trendy red table wine, Merlot is one of the traditional grapes of Bordeaux (along with Cabernet Sauvignon and Cabernet Franc).

Petite Sirah: Always dry, this red table wine is well suited to heavy meals centered around well-seasoned meats or pasta.

Pinot Noir: An infamously delicate grape, it is the principal representative of France's Burgundy reds. Pinot Noir thrives in relatively cool, moist areas with coastal breezes.

Sauvignon Blanc: This is a favored dry wine for table use, particularly with fish. Though it has acquired somewhat of a bad rap because of the many herbaceous $3.99 brands, Sauvignon Blanc can be happily complex.

Semillon: Often combined with Sauvignon Blanc, this is a fruity white wine.

Zinfandel: This red table wine comes from the most widely planted grape in the state (though the majority of it is picked for white Zinfandel). The grape, often grown in hot microclimates, produces a hardy, chewy red wine.

in Ukiah carried the Mendocino flag almost unaided. In 1918, when fear of the oncoming Prohibition was driving everyone else out of the business, Parducci bought some casks, a crusher and some elementary equipment and began making wine in an old barn in Cloverdale. He survived the Prohibition years in part because the law allowed home winemakers to have 200 gallons of "juice" for their own use.

By 1927 Parducci had pulled together enough money to buy some land in Ukiah Valley (now fondly called the Home Ranch) and planted 100 acres of grapes. From that time on, he and his four sons learned the meaning of hard work—tending the vineyards, harvesting the grapes, building a winery. With the repeal of Prohibition in 1933, they opened a small tasting cellar in the basement of their home. Soon the charming family winery became a favorite stopping place for tourists. They'd sample from the spigot, have their jugs filled and watch the Parducci label being pasted on the bottles. Today Parducci is one of the great names in wine.

Another major player in Mendocino County wine is Fetzer, just off U.S. Highway 101 in Hopland. In the 1950s Bernard Fetzer bought the vineyards that had originally been established in the Redwood Valley by gold miner Anson Seward a century earlier. Some of the vines actually dated back to Seward's earlier planting. During the next 10 years, Fetzer experimented with some Bordeaux-type varietals with considerable success, selling his Cabernet Sauvignon and Semillon wines by air freight to home consumers all over the country. The Valley Oaks Ranch, purchased by the Fetzer family in 1984, is now their headquarters.

If Parducci and Fetzer are the most easily recognized names, by no means do they stand alone. There are more than 35 other wineries in the Mendocino County area, producing an abundance of award-winning vintages. The business of winemaking is the largest non-manufacturing industry in the county. Mendocino's wine regions are divided into six valley areas, each noted for the different varieties of grapes produced under slightly different climatic conditions. In the southeast areas of Sanel and McDowell valleys look for the wines of Fetzer, Milano, McDowell, Jepson and Duncan Peak. Ukiah Valley lies farther north along U.S. Highway 101, and it's here that some of Mendocino's largest and oldest vintners make their home. Look for Hidden Cellars, Dunnewood, Parducci, Alambic, Fremont Creek, Mendocino, Whaler, Domaine St. Gregory and Zellerbach.

The Redwood and Potter valleys, on the northern frontier of California's commercial grape-growing territory, are home to Redwood Valley Cellars, Lolonis, Frey, Gabrielli, Konrad and Elizabeth. Anderson Valley, home to some of the most beautiful countryside in the state, is the region for wines by Navarro, Husch, Greenwood Ridge, Christine Woods, Lazy Creek, Brutocao, Yorkville, Handley, Roederer, Claudia Springs, Pepperwood Springs and Scharffenberger.

Lake County

Although agriculture has been the mainstay of Lake County's economy for decades, only some 3,500 acres are devoted today to wine grapes. Still, for the relatively small number of acres, Lake County wines are winning more awards per acre than any other area in the world. You find some of the most respected names in the wine industry here including Wildhurst, Guenoc, Steel and Roumiguiere Vineyards.

Certainly wineries are not new to the region. The first vineyard in Lake County was planted in 1872 near Lower Lake. By the end of the 1880s, grape acreage had increased to 5,000, and famed actress Lillie Langtry started her own winery, Guenoc, bringing in an expert winemaker from Bordeaux. The home she built is still on the property and plans to make a television series on her life are on the Hollywood agenda (see our History chapter).

Getting Your Bearings

One of the best places to get a handle on everything you've ever wanted to know about the state in general and, more specifically, Wine Country is the California Welcome Center, a handsome, 43,000-square-foot building overlooking lovely Roberts Lake just off U.S. 101 in Rohnert Park in Sonoma County. It is adjacent to the Doubletree Hotel, and "walking bear" directional signs on U.S. 101 point the way to the center. It was established by the California Division of Tourism in 1995 to help visitors navigate this enormous state, realizing that much confusion exists on the length of time it requires to move from one locale to another. Aside from maps and brochures, there's an interactive kiosk at the center with audiovisual information and a knowledgeable staff to answer questions and make suggestions.

This is also the information center for the Sonoma County Winemakers Association, and visitors may be surprised to find a selection of some 200 different wines to sample. A demonstration vineyard outside the building tells the story of how grapes become wine, and visitors can walk through a small vineyard featuring several different varieties of wine grapes—mostly red—and even taste the grapes if the season is right. Extending from the building and overlooking the lake is a large deck, complete with tables and chairs. During good weather, umbrellas come out on the tables, and guests enjoy their picnic lunches, receptions or brunches in a relaxed setting.

A Winetasting Primer

During your enological experience, remember that the pleasure of wine comes from several senses—sight, smell, taste and touch. Here are a couple of suggestions to keep you from feeling completely lost during your first winery adventures. Rest assured that you will learn much more as you travel from tasting room to tasting room.

INSIDERS' TIP

If you have the time, try to visit local wine shops (listed in this chapter) before making major purchases at winery tasting rooms. Counter-intuitive as it may be, you can often find better deals and a wider selection at the shops.

Photo: Tina Luster-Hoban

Goosecross Winery, a small winery in Napa County, was using the services of this mobile bottling truck for a couple of days. The mobile unit can bottle 1,500 to 2,000 cases of wine a day.

Sight: Hold the glass to the light and enjoy its colors. If you really want to put the wine to the test, hold a white napkin or sheet of thick white paper behind the glass in ordinary sunlight.

Smell: Swirl the wine gently in the glass to release its fragrances. Sniff sharply to carry them to the nerve ends high in the nose.

Taste: Take a drink and roll it in your mouth to reach all the taste bud areas. Connoisseurs learn to draw in air over the wine still in their mouth. It looks silly, but it carries fumes to the nasal cavity, where most of the subtle olfactory differences emerge. Try to pick out tastes that are familiar to you, such as berry or pepper.

Touch: Chew the wine, just as if you were munching on some mashed potatoes. Note the amount of astringency present and get the "feel" of the wine.

Aftertaste: Swallow the wine and note the taste sensations remaining, also known as "the length." The aftertaste should always be pleasant, though it's often quite different from your first impression upon sipping.

Wineries to Visit

With some 600 wineries in the four counties of Wine Country, it is not possible to list all of them here, and it would, in fact, be overwhelming for the visitor to digest. To make your decision easier, we have not listed those wineries that limit their hospitality to "appointment only." All the wineries we include are open to the general public, although some do require appointments for tours. Complete, exhaustive lists of all wineries are available at the California Welcome Center or the Napa Valley Wine Library at 1492 Library Lane in St. Helena.

Outside Napa Valley, winemakers often provide samples of their wines without charge. However, should you request to sample their more expensive Reserve wines or their Library (non-circulating) wines, a small fee may be involved—say, $2 to $5. Wineries that produce sparkling wine (champagne) serve by the glass, and there is always a charge, with a couple of exceptions: Korbel Winery in Sonoma County has stated they will never charge to taste their product, and Kornell Cellars south of Calistoga also pours gratis.

The list of wineries that follows only scratches the surface of the possibilities. You will no doubt find new favorites of your own as you tour the area. As we have done throughout the book, we arrange the winery listings in the geographical sequence explained in our How to Use This Book chapter. The general breakdown is Napa County wineries, followed by those in Sonoma, Mendocino and Lake counties.

Napa County

Domaine Carneros
1240 Duhig Rd., Carneros
• (707) 257-0101

This imposing winery was inspired by the Louis XV-style Chateau de la Marquetterie in Champagne, country estate of the Taittinger family, which founded Domaine Carneros in 1987. The atmosphere is elegant and *tres française*, with a looming portrait of Madame de Pompadour in the main lobby. You can have your beverage ($6 to $10 per glass, with complimentary hors d'oeuvres) in the salon or on the patio, which is swept by breezes off San Pablo Bay. Domaine Carneros offers three types of sparkling wine (Brut Cuvee, Blanc de Blancs and Brut Rose) and its Famous Gate Pinot Noir. Free winery tours are at 11 AM, 1 and 3 PM during the week, and hourly from 11 AM to 4 PM on weekends. On dry Friday mornings at 11:15, the winery offers vineyard tours that explain layout, planting techniques and vine care. Cost of the vineyard tour is $10 and includes a tasting. Domaine Carneros is open daily from 10:30 AM to 6 PM.

Carneros Creek
1285 Dealy Ln., Carneros
• (707) 253-WINE

San Franciscan Francis Mahoney started a trend in 1972 when he established the first winery in Carneros after the repeal of Prohibition. Carneros was little more than lonely cattle land then, but its Bay-cooled hills are now coveted by grape growers. Carneros Creek is a modest, homey facility, with arbor-covered picnic tables in back that offer a view to magnificent Artesa. The winery's reputation is steeped in Pinot Noir, which still makes up 85 percent of its production. (It also produces Chardonnay.) The winery is open from 10 AM to 5 PM daily, and tours are by appointment. The tasting fee of $2.50 applies to purchase.

Artesa Winery
1345 Henry Rd., Carneros
• (707) 224-1668

For a moment, if you can, forget Artesa's rich history and its world-class champagnes. Forget the 270-degree views of the Carneros hills and the small on-site museum with its 500-year-old wine casks. Those factors are more than enough to recommend Artesa, but the physical presence of the winery takes precedence. The building was designed by Barcelona architect Domingo Triay. Dug into the top of a hill, with native grasses planted over its sloping walls, it looks like a half-unearthed Mayan ruin—until you get inside, where the breezy central atrium and reflecting pools are nothing but modern elegance. Artesa is owned by Codorniu, one of the world's biggest producers of champagne, or cava. The Raventos family has been making wine since the 16th century (a Codorniu married a Raventos in 1659) and making *methode champenoise* sparkling wine since 1872. The Napa outpost bottles three varieties, including the limited Reserve Cuvee, and you can try them for $4 to $6 per glass. It also offers Chardonnay, Cabernet Sauvignon and Pinot Noir ($8 for six tastes). There are two free tours daily, and reservations are recommended. Artesa is open from 10 AM to 5 PM daily.

Monticello Vineyards
4242 Big Ranch Rd., Napa
• (707) 253-2802, (800) 743-6668

Proprietor Jay Corley is a big fan of Thomas Jefferson. So big, he named his winery Monticello and built a small-scale "Jefferson House," patterned after the founding father's Virginia mansion, to serve as the company's offices and culinary center. It's a pretty setting on Big Ranch Road, which heads north out of Napa city about halfway between Calif. Highway 29 and the Silverado Trail. There is a vivid rose garden and a shady picnic area called The Grove. Monticello makes Cabernet, Chardonnay, Merlot, Pinot Noir, Champagne and, weather permitting, a late-harvest Semillon. Monticello is open from 10 AM to 4:30 PM daily. Tours are at 10:30, 12:30 and 2:30 during the summer, by appointment otherwise. You can taste for $4.

Trefethen Vineyards
1160 Oak Knoll Ave., Napa
• (707) 255-7700

When Capt. Hamden McIntyre built the Eshcol winery in 1886, the three-story, wooden, gravity-flow architectural design was standard. Grapes were crushed on the third floor, fer-

mented on the second and stored at ground level. Today the old Eshcol building is the centerpiece of Trefethen Vineyards, and it's the last gravity-flow winery building in Napa Valley. Trefethen is a throwback in another way too: All of its grapes come from the surrounding vines, making it the valley's largest contiguous vineyard under single ownership. There are 600 acres of Chardonnay, Cabernet Sauvignon, Riesling and Merlot plus gardens, walnut trees and oaks. It was Eugene Trefethen, an executive for Kaiser (the massive construction firm responsible for, among other projects, Hoover Dam and the San Francisco-Oakland Bay Bridge), who bought the estate in 1968. His son, John, and John's wife, Janet, started the winery five years later. Trefethen is open from 10 AM to 4:30 PM daily. Tasting is complimentary, unless you opt for the Reserve package—four wines for $5.

The Hess Collection
4411 Redwood Rd., Napa
• (707) 255-1144

The "collection" is a stunning assemblage of modern art (see our Arts and Culture chapter). The Hess is Donald Hess, the Swiss millionaire whose holdings include Valser St. Petersquelle, one of Switzerland's most popular mineral waters. Hess doesn't do anything halfway. In 1986 he leased Mt. LaSalle Winery, the Christian Brothers' original Napa Valley home, and set about renovating the 1903 bastion halfway up craggy Mount Veeder (the southernmost peak in the Mayacamas Mountains). The result is magnificent. Hess keeps it simple as far as the wines go, with Chardonnay and Cabernet Sauvignon, bottling both under The Hess Collection label and a second, lower-priced label called Hess Select. Hours are 10 AM to 4 PM. There is a $3 tasting charge, and you can also ask to sample Valser, the aforementioned mineral water. Hess now owns some 900 acres on Mount Veeder and, since 1996, half of Glen Carlou, one of South Africa's best-known wineries.

Clos Du Val
5330 Silverado Trail, Napa
• (707) 259-2200

Clos Du Val is French in more than name only. Founder John Goelet is descended from a distinguished Bordeaux wine merchant family, the Guestiers, and president/winemaker Bernard Portet is a sixth-generation vintner from the same French region. They crushed their first Napa Valley harvest together in 1972, and their ivy-covered, stone tasting room opened in 1983. It is open from 10 AM to 5 PM daily, and the tasting charge is $5 per person (refunded with purchase). Clos Du Val now produces seven wines, including its signature Reserve Cabernet Sauvignon. Almost as much as for its vintages, the winery is known for the series of whimsical, wine-related illustrations it commissioned from famed graphic satirist Ronald Searle in 1977. Tours are given by appointment, and you can picnic on the grounds.

Chimney Rock Winery
5350 Silverado Trail, Napa
• **(707) 257-2641**

At the foot of the hills east of the Silverado Trail—including the outcrop from which it draws its name—is Chimney Rock, a stately white structure of Cape Dutch style, cloaked (in the summer) or picketed (in the winter) by a row of poplars. Ask if you can see the wine cellar, where resides a faithful reproduction of the Ganymede frieze depicting the Gods' cup bearer atop a fierce eagle. The winery makes Fume Blanc, Chardonnay and Cabernet Sauvignon. The tasting fee is $3, and the hours are 10 AM to 5 PM daily. Tours are by appointment.

Stag's Leap Wine Cellars
5766 Silverado Trail, Napa
• **(707) 944-2020**

Stag's Leap founder Warren Winiarski was a liberal arts lecturer at the University of Chicago, but his destiny should have been clear: In Polish, "winiarski" means "from wine" or "winemaker's son." Founded in 1972, Stag's Leap was a little-known family winery until 1976, when it outshone the best of French Bordeaux in the famous Bicentennial tasting in Paris (see Close-up, "The Discovery of California," in this chapter). Since then it has been a Napa Valley landmark. The winery produces several types of wine, red and white, under both its own label and Hawk Crest, a line of accessible, reasonably priced wines crushed at other facilities. Its reputation, however, is staked upon Cabernet Sauvignon, especially the versions made from the Stag's Leap and Fay vineyards, including the world-renowned Cask 23. The winery is open from 10 AM to 4:30 PM daily. There is a $5 charge for tasting and free beverages for the designated driver. You can picnic in the shade of oaks. (Note: Stag's Leap Wine Cellars is not to be confused with Stags' Leap Winery or the Stags Leap District, all of which get their name from the rock outcropping that overlooks the scene.)

Pine Ridge Winery
5901 Silverado Trail, Napa
• **(707) 252-9777, (800) 575-9777**

The pines aren't only high on the ridge. There is a grove of them surrounding the picnic area, making for a cool experience on a hot Napa day. Owner-winemaker Gary Andrus has been growing grapes since 1978. Pine Ridge currently produces Chardonnay, Chenin Blanc-Viognier, Cabernet Sauvignon and Merlot. You can taste current releases for $5, sample five limited releases for $12 or enjoy two reserve reds for $10. Tours begin at 10:15 AM, 1 and 3 PM and should be booked in advance. If you can't fit one of those into your schedule, investigate the Pine Ridge Demonstration Vineyard adjacent to the winery. It displays various combinations of rootstock, clone and trellising apparatus—all you need to distinguish your Geneva double curtain from your traditional French double guyot. The winery is open 11 AM to 5 PM daily.

Steltzner Vineyards
5998 Silverado Trail, Napa
• **(707) 252-7272**

Dick and Christine Steltzner started making wines for bulk sale in 1977, and they opened their Silverado Trail winery in 1983. (The current structure was built in 1992.) Steltzner is noted for its reds, as are all labels within the Stags Leap appellation. Its wines include Cabernet Sauvignon, Claret and a South African varietal called Pinotage. Steltzner is open 10 AM to 4:30 PM Monday through Saturday and noon to 4:30 PM on Sunday. Tasting is $3, and tours are by appointment.

Silverado Vineyards
6121 Silverado Trail, Napa
• **(707) 257-1770**

This is no Mickey Mouse winery, despite ownership by Walt Disney's daughter, Diane Disney Miller, and Diane's husband, Ron Miller. (Walt's widow, Lillian, died in 1997.) It isn't a '90s-style corporate takeover, either, as the Millers are longtime Napa Valley denizens. Silverado offers great views above the Trail and a winery crafted of native stone and redwood. It made its reputation with Chardonnay but probably is best known these days for its estate-grown Cabernet Sauvignon. The winery has begun construction on a new production facility and hopes to have a new barrel cellar sometime in 2000. There is no charge for tasting. Silverado is open 11 AM to 4:30 PM daily, but tours are by appointment and take place at 11 AM and 2 PM on weekends.

Robert Sinskey Vineyards
6320 Silverado Trail, Napa
• (707) 944-9090, (800) 869-2030

This is another multi-generational operation, with founder Robert Sinskey, M.D., having passed the reins to his son, Rob. Sinskey Vineyards, which has been crushing grapes since 1986, is known for tackling Merlot and the tricky Pinot Noir, grown in the winery's Carneros vineyards. ("Heathens in the land of Cabernet," as they describe themselves.) Winemaker Jeff Virnig also creates small quantities of a half-dozen other varieties, including a Stags Leap District Claret and a Pinot Blanc. The cathedral-like winery combines Napa Valley stone and California redwood. There is a $5 fee for tasting (keep the glass), and you just might get a nibble from the Vineyard Kitchen. Tours are by appointment. Robert Sinskey is open from 10 AM to 4:30 PM daily.

Domaine Chandon
1 California Dr., Yountville
• (707) 944-2280

Domaine Chandon, child of world-renowned Moet-Hennessy, is a trendsetter. It was California's first French-owned winery (established in 1973), and the first to use the Champagne varietal Pinot Eunier in sparkling wine. It welcomes visitors to Le Salon, an open, terraced, cafe-style tasting room where you get samples ($8 for three cuvées, $12 for five) and complimentary hors d'oeuvres. Chandon's renowned tours run every hour (on the hour, except for opening and closing times), and they pretty much tell you everything you need to know about fermentation, aging, riddling and disgorging. The scenic winery produces several types of sparkling wine plus brandy and pear liqueur. Summer hours are 10 AM to 6 PM Monday and Tuesday, 10 AM to 8 PM Wednesday through Sunday; winter hours are 10 AM to 6 PM daily. See our Restaurants chapter for information on Chandon's exclusive eatery, and keep your eyes peeled for musical events at the winery.

Goosecross Cellars
1119 State Ln., Yountville
• (707) 944-1986,
(800) 276-9210

Goosecross likes to refer to itself as a microwinery, and the feeling is unquestionably intimate on this lonely lane off the Yountville Cross Road. The winery was established in 1985 by college buddies David Topper, the CEO, and Geoff Gorsuch, the winemaker. ("Goosecross"

is an Old English derivation of Gorsuch.) The Cellars are open 10 AM to 5 PM daily. They produce Chardonnay and Cabernet Sauvignon, in quantities that barely surpass 7,500 cases a year. If you have some free time Saturday from 11 AM until about 12:30 PM, sign up for the acclaimed Goosecross Wine Basics class, a hands-on crash course designed to remove the "snobbery and mysticism" from grape appreciation. The free, hands-on class includes a full tour of the vineyard and winery.

Cosentino Winery
7415 St. Helena Hwy. S., Yountville
• (707) 944-1220

Mitch Cosentino crafts a variety of wines and sells them in an affable, low-key setting right next door to Mustards Grill (see our Restaurants chapter). Cosentino's Meritage reds stand out, as do his Merlots and Zinfandels. He also is no stranger to dessert wines. The winemaker prides himself on his "punched cap fermentation" process, a traditional, labor-intensive technique that involves continually dunking the floating grape skins (the cap) into the juice during fermentation. The $4 tasting charge applies to purchase, and you get a souvenir glass too. Cosentino is open 10 AM to 5 PM daily.

La Famiglia di Robert Mondavi
1595 Oakville Grade, Oakville
• (707) 944-2811

You can call this one "The Winery Formerly Known as Vichon." Robert Mondavi purchased the facility in 1985, when it was 5 years old, and changed the name in 1997. It is now dedicated to the "First Family's" lineup of Italian varietals, including Sangiovese, Barbera and Nebbiolo. The owners (Mondavi has partners) also have been busy renovating the winery. It already has wonderful valley views from the steep Oakville Grade and exemplary picnic grounds. The winery is open from 10 AM to 4:30 PM daily. Tasting is free; tours are by appointment.

Silver Oak Cellars
915 Oakville Cross Road, Oakville
• (707) 944-8808

Wine & Spirits' 1996 poll of restaurants determined that Silver Oak produced the most popular Cabernet Sauvignon in America. Their secret? Do one thing and do it well. Silver Oak is all Cabernet, all the time. The winery even follows a specific routine for all its vintages: For example, they use 100 percent Cabernet Sauvignon grapes and they ferment the wine

Photo: Korbel Russian River Brewing Company

Besides champagne, wine and brandy, Korbel makes beer too. These fermenting vats belong to the Russian River Brewing Company, which is on-site.

for at least 30 months in American oak barrels. Silver Oak was founded in 1972 by Ray Duncan and Justin Meyer, who had recently abandoned his post as the Christian Brothers' Napa Valley winemaker. His company has two winery sites: one in Napa Valley at the site of the Oakville Dairy, and another in Alexander Valley in the old Lyeth Winery. The Oakville facility has a tasting room in an impressive masonry structure. It is open 9 AM to 4 PM Monday through Saturday. There is a $5 tasting charge, but the Shott souvenir glass is far superior to the usual handout. Tours are by appointment only, and because the tasting room can get swamped on summer Saturdays, the winery suggests arriving early or calling ahead on those days.

Robert Mondavi Winery
7801 St. Helena Hwy. S., Oakville
• **(707) 226-1395**

Here it is, the Yankee Stadium of American wineries, with Bob himself playing the part of Babe Ruth. More than any other individual, Robert Mondavi is credited with educating the world about the virtues of California wine. His innovations are prolific. He took a disregarded varietal known as White Pinot, changed the fermentation and released it as Chenin Blanc; sales quintupled the next year. He almost single-handedly popularized Sauvignon Blanc

by producing a drier version that he renamed Fume Blanc. Mondavi still actively promotes the industry, but sons Michael (president and CEO) and Timothy (winegrower) run the winery.

Robert Mondavi Winery is known for its wine-and-food programs, art exhibits (displayed in the Vineyard Room) and jazz and classical concerts. But most of all, it is known for its tasting tours: a complimentary one-hour tour offered throughout the day; a $15 essence tasting (which matches a particular varietal with some two-dozen steeped or crushed aromatic essences) every Tuesday at 10 AM and again at 2 PM during the dry season; and an in-depth, Advanced Winemaking tour that costs $20 per person and takes three to four hours (conducted at 10 AM every Sunday and Wednesday). Oh, and they make wines too. Outside the tours, you can purchase by the glass. Mondavi is open from 9 AM to 5 PM May through October, and 9:30 AM to 4:30 PM from November through April.

Turnbull Wine Cellars
8210 St. Helena Hwy. S., Oakville
• **(707) 963-5839, (800) TURNBUL**

Publisher Patrick O'Dell bought Turnbull Wine Cellars in the spring of 1993. The winery is just north of the Oakville Cross Road, and its vineyards are primarily contained within

Photo: Tina Luster-Hoban

The reservoir tower at Silver Oak Winery in Napa Valley overlooks the vineyards.

the Oakville Viticultural Area. Turnbull's production is about 10,000 cases per year, with most of it in Cabernet Sauvignon, Merlot and Sangiovese. The facility, which features a collection of Ansel Adams prints, is open daily from 10 AM to 4:30 PM; tours are by appointment. The $3 tasting charge is refunded toward the purchase of wine.

Oakville Ranch Winery
7850 Silverado Trail, Oakville
• (707) 944-9500

This group has been making wines since 1989 but has been in the hospitality business only since August 1996, when it purchased a 100,000-case facility on the Silverado Trail. (Oakville Ranch produces only about 4,500 cases per year; the site is also rented for custom crush.) The winery bottles under two labels: Oakville Ranch Vineyards, made 100 percent from estate fruit, is the premium line ($5 for tasting), while Oakville Ranch Cellars ($3) is a group of less expensive wines made from purchased grapes and sold only from the tasting room. The estate vineyards are at 1,000 feet, the highest in the Oakville appellation. Oakville Ranch produces many types, including award-winning Cabernets, fine Chardonnays and Robert's Blend, a Cabernet Franc and Sauvignon composition named for Robert Miner, the winery's late founder and also a founder of Oracle Corporation. Oakville Ranch is open daily from 11 AM to 6 PM from April through October and 11 AM to 5 PM November to March. Tours are by appointment.

St. Supéry Vineyards & Winery
8440 St. Helena Hwy. S., Rutherford
• (707) 963-4507, (800) 942-0809

More than its intriguing historical setting and its rich lineup of wines, St. Supéry is known for its Wine Discovery Center. You can wander through the display vineyard and the exhibit gallery (don't miss the SmellaVision display) alone, or sign up for a free guided tour. French businessman Robert Skalli's establishment is the only major winery to grow most of its grapes in isolated Pope Valley, beyond the hills to the east of Napa. St. Supéry (named for a previous owner of the property) has a lengthy list of wines, with all the standards plus sur-

prises such as a dessert Moscato and a Zinfandel Rosé sold only at the winery. Skalli also produces kosher Chardonnay and Cabernet under the Mt. Maroma label. (Former Israeli Prime Minister Benjamin Netanyahu reportedly gushed over the stuff at a White House visit.) There is a $3 charge for sampling, but the glass is equivalent to a lifetime pass to the tasting room. The facility is open daily from 9:30 AM to 6 PM April through October and 9:30 AM to 5 PM November to March.

Peju Province Winery
8466 St. Helena Hwy. S., Rutherford
• (707) 963-3600

If everything looks familiar as you head into Peju Province, it isn't necessarily a case of déjà vu. Herta Peju's prolific flower beds have been photographed for numerous garden magazines. Husband Tony sticks to winemaking, and his Cabernet Sauvignon has been winning awards. (He also makes Chardonnay, Cabernet Franc, Colombard, Merlot, a dry rosé and, occasionally, a late-harvest Chardonnay.) The Pejus opened their French Provincial-style facility in 1991. They produce only about 15,000 cases a year. You can taste for $3, which applies to any purchase, and tours are self-guided. Peju Province is open daily from 10 AM to 6 PM.

Niebaum-Coppola Estate Winery
1991 St. Helena Hwy. S., Rutherford
• (707) 968-1100

Yes, it's that Coppola, a winemaker almost as long as he has been a director. Francis and his wife, Eleanor, purchased a lavish Victorian and prime acreage in 1975, then discovered the story behind the locale. The house was built in 1881 by Gustave Niebaum, a Finnish sea captain who founded Inglenook, perhaps the most respected winery in California before corporate raiders used the name to sell jug wine. Enchanted by the history, Coppola used the substantial profits from *Bram Stoker's Dracula* to reunify Niebaum's original estate in 1995. The purchase included the original chateau, which the director renovated (check out the staircase made from exotic Belizean hardwoods). It now houses the tasting room and a museum of wine and film. The director's five Oscars stand at attention on the second floor.

INSIDERS' TIP

Where did all that mustard planted in vineyard rows come from? Some say the Spanish missionaries, as they explored the intimidating valleys and hills, scattered mustard seeds behind them to mark a golden route home to their missions. (There is no historical basis for this, but it is not a difficult story to believe.)

Niebaum-Coppola releases several wines under the Francis Coppola Family Wines label, but is best known for Rubicon, its Cabernet Sauvignon-Merlot-Cabernet Franc meritage that is made to last 100 years. Niebaum-Coppola is open daily from 10 AM to 5 PM. There is a $7.50 charge for tasting, and you get to keep the glass.

ZD Wines
8383 Silverado Trail, Rutherford
• (707) 963-5188

ZD might be last on the alphabetical list, but it has been first elsewhere, such as the Los Angeles County Fair, where the 1996 Chardonnay recently was named Best of Class. And the label is clearly bipartisan—it has been served at the White House during each of the last three presidential administrations. This is a true family affair. Norman and Rosa Lee deLeuze co-founded the winery, and their three children have taken up the cause—Robert as winemaker, Brett as marketing director and Julie as administrative director. ZD got its start in Sonoma County in 1969, then moved to Napa a decade later. Today it primarily makes Chardonnay, Pinot Noir and Cabernet Sauvignon. Tasting is $5, which is refundable toward purchase. ZD is open from 10 AM to 4:30 PM daily, and tours (maximum 15 people) are by appointment.

INSIDERS' TIP

The Wine Library of Sonoma County is in Healdsburg's Public Library at Piper and Center streets. A separate room with a wine librarian on duty houses a collection of books, magazines and pamphlets. Library hours are 9:30 AM to 6 PM Tuesday, Thursday, Friday and Saturday. Doors are open until 9 PM Monday and Wednesday.

Mumm Napa Valley
8445 Silverado Trail, Rutherford
• (707) 942-3434, (800) 686-6272

The setting in Mumm's tasting salon is one of the most soothing in the valley, with a long wall of glass that faces uncluttered vineyard. (It's definitely the place to bring a date.) You can buy a glass of champagne for $3 to $6 or a "taster" of three samples for $7.50. They offer tours of the winery on the hour; the last stop is the photo gallery, which is reason enough to make a pilgrimage (see our Arts and Culture chapter). Mumm Napa Valley was launched in 1979, a co-venture between G.H. Mumm of France and Joseph E. Seagram and Sons of New York. The winery currently bottles three Bruts—Blanc de Blancs, Blanc de Noir, and Brut

Prestige—and a vintage sparkler, DVX, its tête de cuvée. It is open 10:30 AM to 6 PM daily from April to October and 10 AM to 5 PM daily from November through March.

Beaulieu Vineyard
1960 St. Helena Hwy. S., Rutherfod
• (707) 967-5200

The oldest continuously producing winery in Napa Valley? It isn't Charles Krug or Beringer. It's Beaulieu, which was founded by Georges de Latour in 1900 and survived Prohibition by turning out sacramental wines. By 1940 Beaulieu might have been the nation's most famous winery, a status no doubt aided by de Latour's recruitment of young, Russian-born enologist Andre Tchelistcheff, who was more or less the Luther Burbank of the wine industry. The current director of winemaking, Joel Aiken, has pioneered new cellaring and vine management programs, and he oversees a lengthy list of varieties. The Napa Series is made up of Cabernet Sauvignon, Chardonnay, Pinot Noir, Sauvignon Blanc, Zinfandel and Merlot; the Signet Collection includes everything from Viognier to Pinot Gris. (The Georges de Latour Private Reserve Cabernet, hunted by collectors, remains BV's benchmark product.) Tasting is $5, or for $18 you can sample five of Beaulieu's top-tier wines. Beaulieu is open from 10 AM to 5 PM daily, with tours every hour between 11 AM and 4 PM.

Grgich Hills Cellar
1829 St. Helena Hwy. S., Rutherford
• (707) 963-2784

The Grgich is Miljenko Grgich. The Hills, you might be surprised to learn, is a reference not to the rugged terrain around Rutherford, but rather to Austin Hills of the Hills Bros. coffee family. Hills added his business acumen to Grgich's winemaking skills back in 1977, and they have been making tasty wines ever since. Grgich Hills is known for its buttery, creamy Chardonnay, though it also produces Sauvignon Blanc, Zinfandel, Cabernet Sauvignon and a late-harvest dessert wine. The winery offers two by-appointment tours daily: 11 AM and 2 PM on weekdays, 11 AM and 1:30 PM

The Discovery of California

In 1976, as Sparky Anderson's Big Red Machine moved toward its second World Series title and the nation buzzed over Patty Hearst's bank robbery conviction, California wines were about as trendy as straight-legged jeans and short hair. A handful of wineries were producing vintages to domestic acclaim, but few Europeans knew the difference between Schramsberg and Scharffenberger. And even in America sales were anything but spectacular.

It was a rare vintner who hung up a sign and opened a tasting room. Who would stop, except to use the restroom? Still, *le vin de Californie* had its fans, and one of them was Steven Spurrier, a 34-year-old transplanted Englishman who had become one of Paris' most influential wine merchants. His Cave de Madeleine wine shop was highly regarded, and the six-week courses offered at his Academie du Vin were standard curriculum for the French Restaurant Association's chefs and sommeliers.

Spurrier's American associate, Patricia Gallagher, visited dozens of Napa, Sonoma and Santa Clara Valley wineries in the summer of 1975, and Spurrier made the rounds the next spring. Together they tasted more than 100 labels. They identified those they liked best, and Spurrier proceeded to step out onto a limb. He proposed a crucible — a blind taste test matching the best of France against the best of the United States.

It was the perfect time for patriotic fervor. The U.S. was immersed in its bicentennial celebration of nationhood, with the clock ticking down on the biggest, most commercial Independence Day bash ever. The French, meanwhile, were placing credit where they felt credit was due — squarely on their own heads. One headline in the popular weekly *Paris-Match* read "How France Won the American Revolution." And the head curator of the Chateau de Versailles stated succinctly, "If it hadn't been for Louis XVI, you would not be free."

It was in this charged atmosphere that Joanne Dickenson of Tchelistcheff Wine Tours International hand-carried Spurrier's top picks across the Atlantic, holding her breath and checking them through customs in their less-than-impenetrable cardboard cases. "I don't think some of these wines have even been tasted on the East Coast," Gallagher said at the time.

Indeed, some were barely known outside the San Francisco Bay Area. And yet on May 24, 1976, on a patio of the Hotel Intercontinental in Paris, six California Pinot Chardonnays (as they were called at the time) stood ready to butt bottles with four white Burgundies, and six California Cabernet Sauvignons stared down four Bordeaux reds. To ensure fairness, the organizers did their best to compare wines "of similar quality." What that meant was that the French wines, though borrowed from the most esteemed producers, were a bit younger than ideal, because their California counterparts had not fully aged.

The nine assembled judges were nothing less than the royal courtesans of Gallic wine. Here was Pierre Tari, secretary-general of the Association des Grands Crus Classes; Aubert de Villaine, co-manager of Romanee-Conti, makers of what might be the world's finest Burgundy; Odette Kaan, editor of the *Revue du Vin de France*; and Pierre Brejoux, inspector-general of the Institut National des Appellations d'Origine. The press drank French champagne and waited for the challenger to be knocked to the floor.

(Continued on next page)

Each jurist held before him or her a score card and, like some character from *Les Miserables*, a hard roll with which to clear the palate between entries. The judges were immediately able to distinguish between wines from either side of the Atlantic — or so they thought. "Ah, back to France?" mused Raymond Oliver, owner of Le Grand Vefour restaurant and recognized doyen of French culinary writers, after sipping a 1972 Napa Chardonnay.

"That is definitely California. It has no nose," another proclaimed after downing a Batard Montrachet '73. Yet another judge, upon learning that the wine he had just given a mere 14 (out of 20) points was the revered Mouton Rothschild, quickly re-evaluated the wine's "finish" and changed his score to 18.

When all of the whites had been evaluated, the top-rated Chardonnay was a 1973 made by Chateau Montelena. Montelena's champion was everything the French deplore in a wine. Not only were the grapes picked from young vines, it was a blend of fruit from two different districts — blatant disregard for France's strict appellation code. Some Francophiles would grumble about the blend. (Though just as many Americans would claim that the choice of France's vintage, its best in nearly a decade, gave the Europeans an edge, and rumors danced that the wines were not uniformly chilled.)

Still, the mood actually remained jovial when the white results were announced, for it is red wine that courses through the heart of French culture. Then came the shocking news: the number-one Cabernet was a 1972 from Stag's Leap Wine Cellars. When the upset victory was announced, the reaction was uproar. One Gallic wine editor, pinning her notes to her bosom, asked, "You aren't going to let these notes circulate, are you?"

"Yes, indeed," Spurrier replied. "They are going straight to California."

For the moment, Napa Valley occupied the highest point on the gobal landsape of wine. And the news couldn't have been more timely for the California wine industry, which was in the early stages of the region's most severe drought of the 20th century.

Jim Barrett, general manager and part-owner of Chateau Montelena, was touring France with legendary winemaker Andre Tchelistcheff, but he wasn't at the tasting. He was sitting down to lunch at Chateau Lascomb in the Haut-Medoc region when he got the phone call. Barrett was thrilled, but not to the point of chest-pounding. When asked for a comment, he kept it to, "Not bad for kids from the sticks."

He quickly wired Miljenko Grgich, then the winemaker at Montelena and now co-owner of Grgich Hills Cellar: STUNNING SUCCESS IN PARIS TASTING ON MAY 24 STOP TOOK FIRST PLACE OVER 9 OTHERS WITH LE PREMIER CRU WINE STOP TOP NAMES IN FRANCE WERE THE BLIND TASTERS STOP. You could forgive Grgich's initial confusion, as he didn't even know his wines were entered in a contest. And yet he was not surprised. "We had the

Photo: Stag's Leap Wine Cellars

And the winner is . . . This Stag's Leap Cabernet topped its established French competitors and helped put California on the winemaking map in 1976.

grapes, the cooperage, the art of winemaking, and the money" to stay apace with France's best, he explained.

Warren Winiarski, proprietor of Stag's Leap, wasn't in France at all. He didn't hear the news until Tchelistcheff returned to California the next day. A few days later, Spurrier sent a congratulatory letter to Stag's Leap to confirm the report.

Meanwhile, one prominent French grape grower characterized the event as a direct attack on his nation's wine industry. And no less than Baron Philippe de Rothschild phoned one unfortunate judge to ask, "What are you doing to my wines? It took me forty years to become classified as a premier grand cru!"

In the New World, the immediate fanfare was as deafening as a single cork being extracted from a bottle. Two weeks later, however, *Time* magazine ran a short recap entitled "Judgment of Paris," a playful reference to the Greek legend in which Aphrodite was rewarded for her beauty. Brief as the article was, it touched off a frenzy. Wine stores and individual collectors swarmed Montelena and Stag's Leap in search of the victors. At the Wine and Cheese Center in San Francisco, a man lunged through the door of the sedate tasting room and pleaded, "Have you got any Montelena?!" A shop in New York got 400 calls in one day.

Nobody got rich right away, though. Stag's Leap had bottled only 2,000 cases of the '73 Cabernet and was running low before the tasting. One-third of the '74 vintage had been released, but the bulk needed more bottle aging and would not hit the market until October. Montelena not only was out of the '73 Chardonnay — it didn't have a single bottle of wine to sell. Prices did not go up.

And yet a small snowball had begun to roll down the slope of popular consciousness. California wines were about to enter a new age. In the mid-1970s producers made about $150 million a year from non-jug wines; today it's more like $2.5 billion. Wine economist Jon Fredrikson calls the Paris tasting "a major turning point in consumers' attitudes" and a factor in the subsequent "staggering revolution in vineyard technology."

California vintners looked back fondly as they celebrated the 20th anniversary of the Judgment in 1996. Bottles of the winning wines were sent to Washington, D.C., to claim their place as part of the Smithsonian Institution's permanent collection. And at that year's Napa Valley Wine Auction (see our Festivals and Annual Events chapter), one of the most coveted lots was a re-creation of the Paris event that featured appearances by Barrett, Winiarski and Spurrier, plus dinners at the key wineries with guest chefs Julia Child, Wolfgang Puck and Thomas Keller.

One lingering irony of the 1976 tasting is that, if you use the same point system to rate the countries as was applied to the wines, the whites show a statistical dead heat. Chalone Vineyards' '74 Chardonnay showed third and Spring Mountain's '73 fourth; a '72 Freemark Abbey ranked sixth but two other California wines — a '72 Veedercrest and a '73 David Bruce, brought up the rear. And the French reds, in aggregate, actually outperformed the Americans. There was a big fall-off after Stag's Leap. Ridge's 1971 "Mountain Range" occupied the fifth spot, and the rest clustered at the bottom — in order, a '71 Mayacamas, a '72 Clos du Val, a '70 Heitz Cellar and a '69 Freemark Abbey.

Perhaps that is one reason why, even now, Winiarski is loath to say he "beat" the French. "We felt as though we were joining in a group," he says. "It gave us confidence that the soil, climate and skills we possessed were adequate — more than adequate — to produce wines that could compete with the great wines of the world."

Don't look for any similar contests in the near future. California wines have moved far beyond the point of having to prove themselves to anyone — even to the likes of Baron Rothschild.

on weekends. Tasting costs $3 on weekends, and that includes the glass; it's free during the week. Grgich Hills is open 9:30 AM to 4:30 PM daily.

Villa Mt. Eden Winery
Conn Creek Winery
8711 Silverado Trail, St. Helena
• (707) 963-9100

You can break two bottles of wine with one stone here. The Silverado Trail tasting room houses Villa Mt. Eden and Conn Creek, sister wineries owned by Stimson Lane Vineyards of Woodinville, Washington. Villa Mt. Eden is descended, however tenuously, from Mt. Eden Vineyards, established in 1881 as the 11th bonded winery in Napa Valley. It now produces seven basic varietals, including Cabernet Sauvignon, Chardonnay, Zinfandel and Pinot Noir. Volume should increase after the recent purchase of more than 400 vineyard acres, 237 in the Stags Leap area and another 192 in Monterey County. There is no tasting fee, hours are 10 AM to 4 PM daily, and tours are by appointment. Conn Creek bottles a tiny amount of reserve wines, primarily Cabernet and a Meritage.

Beaucanon Winery
1695 St. Helena Hwy. S., St. Helena
• (707) 967-3520

If this built-in-1987 winery looks like it was transported from Bordeaux, with its vaulted ceilings and unpartitioned interior, it's no accident. Beaucanon is owned by the de Coninck family, which owns some 15 chateaux in France. Siblings Louis and Chantal de Coninck run the California operations, bottling Chardonnay, Cabernet Sauvignon and Merlot under two lines, Beaucanon Napa Valley and La Crosse Napa Valley. There is no tasting charge. Beaucanon is open daily from 10 AM to 5 PM.

Franciscan Oakville Estates
1178 Galleron Rd., Rutherford
• (707) 963-7111

This is part of the spreading Franciscan Estates empire, which also includes Mount Veeder Winery and Quintessa in Napa County, Estancia in Sonoma and Monterey, and Veramonte in the Casablanca Valley in Chile (the homeland of owner Augustin Huneeus). Outside the winery, which is right off Calif. 29, you'll encounter an ornate fountain and the Rutherford Bench, a tongue-in-cheek reference to a local geologic feature. Inside you can taste wine from Franciscan and Mount Veeder.

It's $4 for a basic tasting, $7 for reserve wines, and either applies to any purchase. Operating hours are 10 AM to 5 PM daily. Franciscan specializes in Cabernet Sauvignon, Merlot and Cabernet Franc, with all the grapes for Magnificat (a meritage blend) coming from its 240-acre estate in the heart of the Oakville appellation. It also sets itself apart through its experiments in "wild" yeast fermentation—using the native yeast of each vineyard to help ferment those particular grapes. The winery's Cuvée Sauvage Chardonnay is 100 percent wild yeast, barrel fermented.

Rutherford Hill Winery
200 Rutherford Hill Rd., Rutherford
• (707) 963-7194

Rutherford Hill produces numerous varietals (including a Zinfandel port), but the name has become nearly synonymous with Merlot. It's also known as one of the most pleasant places to visit, with picnic grounds amid shady oaks and olive trees, and stunning views of Napa Valley. (Because of its popularity, you might think about calling ahead to reserve a table.) Beyond all that, Rutherford Hill's wine caves are said to be some of the most extensive in America, with nearly a mile of tunnels, galleries and passageways. The caves are the main feature of the tours given three times daily during the week (11:30 AM, 1:30 and 3:30 PM), and five times on weekends (add 12:30 and 2:30 PM). Normal tasting is $4, and you leave with the glass; or you can pay $8 for the reserve tasting. Regular hours are 10 AM to 5 PM daily.

Raymond Vineyard & Cellar
849 Zinfandel Ln., St. Helena
• (707) 963-3141, (800) 525-2659

Proprietors Roy Jr. and Walter Raymond get their last name from their father (Roy Sr.) and their winemaking skills from both sides of the family tree. Their mother was the former Martha Jane Beringer, granddaughter of the famed Jacob Beringer. The family played an active part at Beringer until 1971, when they established this winery. Now Roy Jr.'s son Craig and Walter's daughter Krisi have joined the team. Raymond has a strong reputation for Chardonnay and Cabernet Sauvignon, though it also bottles Sauvignon Blanc, Merlot and Pinot Noir. It produces under four distinct brands: Amberhill, Raymond Estates, Raymond Napa Valley Reserve and Raymond Generations. The winery's Napa Valley vineyards are supplemented by a large Chardonnay plot in

Photo: V. Sattui Winery

The V. Sattui Winery welcomes picnickers, who enjoy its ample shaded areas and extensive choice of wines.

Monterey County, on the Central Coast. All told, Raymond owns more than 500 acres. Tasting is free though you can request a library wine for $2.50. The facility is open from 10 AM to 4 PM daily, but tours are by appointment.

Milat Vineyards
1091 St. Helena Hwy. S., St. Helena
• (707) 963-0758, (800) 54-MILAT

This is another intimate, family-run winery, 2 miles south of St. Helena. The Milats have been growing and selling grapes to Napa Valley wineries since 1949, and in 1986 they finally decided to affix their own label. Brothers Bob and Mike Milat (with wives, Joyce and Carolyn) wear all the hats. Milat bottles Chardonnay, Chenin Blanc, Zinfandel, Cabernet Sauvignon and a blush table wine called Zivio, selling the bulk of their production from the tasting room. Milat is open 10 AM to 6 PM daily. The $2 tasting fee includes a souvenir glass or wine credit.

V. Sattui Winery
1111 White Ln., St. Helena
• (707) 963-7774

If you have made a few trips to Napa Valley, you probably know V. Sattui as the place

with all the picnickers. It's a favorite for itinerant eaters, primarily because of an ample, shady picnic area and well-stocked deli featuring homemade items. Daryl Sattui is a fourth-generation winemaker, the great-grandson of Vittorio Sattui, who founded the business in 1885. Daryl's current wine list is immense, with two Chardonnays, two Johannisburg Rieslings, two Zinfandels, four Cabernet Sauvignons and many others, all of them sold exclusively at the winery. V. Sattui offers self-guided tours and does not charge for tasting. The winery is open daily from 9 AM to 6 PM in summer and 9 AM to 5 PM in the winter.

Heitz Wine Cellar
436 St. Helena Hwy. S., St. Helena
• (707) 963-3542

The winery you visit is not the current Heitz facility, but rather the original facility opened by Joe and Alice Heitz in 1961. They now do their winemaking at a 160-acre holding on Taplin Road, just east of St. Helena, aided by two of their children: David is the vice president and winemaker, Kathleen is chief operating officer. The winery built its reputation on Chardonnay, though now it is known more for its Cabernet Sauvignon. Three special cabs are vineyard-designated: Martha's Vineyard (near Oakville), Bella Oaks Vineyard and Trailside Vineyard (both near Rutherford). Heitz also makes Zinfandel and Napa Valley's only Grignolino, a light red. There is no charge for tasting. Heitz is open 11 AM to 4:30 PM daily.

Prager Winery & Port Works
1281 Lewelling Ln., St. Helena
• **(707) 963-PORT, (800) 969-PORT**

Prager makes Chardonnay and Cabernet but is really known for its Port, which accounts for about 85 percent of production. One of the top sellers is the Royal Escort Port, produced from Petite Sirah grapes. Jim and Imogene Prager ditched a commercial insurance business in Orange County and founded the winery in 1980, and they have been joined by children John, Jeff, Peter and Katie. Prager's facilities are inside an old carriage house, part of the John Thomann Winery and Distillery, constructed in 1865. The intimate tasting room is plastered with money donated by visitors—everything from Indonesian rupiah to Toys R Us Geoffrey dollars. There is a picnic table in front of the winery, and the $5 tasting fee can be applied to purchase. Prager is open daily from 10:30 AM to 4:30 PM.

Sutter Home Winery
277 St. Helena Hwy. S., St. Helena
• **(707) 963-3104**

What was once a small, family-run winery is now a gigantic family-run winery, the nation's fourth-largest (actually, the number-one table-wine brand name), thanks to unqualified marketing genius. The facilities date back to 1874, the name to 1906, when the new Swiss-American co-owner named it after her father, John A. Sutter (not to be confused with the California pioneer of the same name). Sutter Home has been owned by the Trincheros since 1947, and the family gets credit (or blame, depending on your outlook) for inventing white Zinfandel—which it originally called Oeil de Pedrix, "Eye of the Partridge"—in the 1970s. More recently, the winery introduced innovations such as 187-milliliter, "single-service" bottles and VinLoc seals, an aluminum alternative to traditional cork. Sutter Home has numerous vineyards in Napa and Lake counties

but grows the bulk of its grapes in the Sacramento Valley, Sacramento Delta and Sierra foothill regions. The company produces nine varieties of wine beyond the Zinfandel plus Fre, the best-selling nonalcoholic wines in America. They even make seven types of pasta sauce! There is no charge for tasting (the wine, that is). The facility is open daily, from 10 AM to 5:30 PM in the summer and 10 AM to 4:30 in the winter.

Louis M. Martini Winery
254 St. Helena Hwy. S., St. Helena
• **(707) 963-2736, (800) 321-WINE**

Louis M. was an Italian immigrant, born near Genoa, who founded the L.M. Martini Grape Products Co. in Kingsburg, California, in 1922. The "Grand Old Man" built his Napa Valley winery 11 years later, and it's still in the family, now headed by his grandchildren, Carolyn and Michael Martini. The company's vineyards are far-flung, stretching from Sonoma Valley to the Russian River Valley to Lake County to Chiles Valley to Pope Valley (two areas in eastern Napa County). The winery makes a wide range of wines, from Cabernet Sauvignon to Barbera to Merlot. It also produces cream sherry and dry sherry. There are picnic grounds at the facility, which is open from 10 AM to 4:30 PM daily, and production tours are offered (call for the schedule). You can taste current releases for free, or pay $6 for library wines and get a souvenir glass.

Merryvale Vineyards
1000 Main St., St. Helena
• **(707) 963-2225, (800) 326-6069**

Merryvale is hard to miss, as it sits in Sunny St. Helena. That's not a reference to the town, but to the old winery that dates back to the 1930s. The stolid stone structure took new life when it was founded as Merryvale by four partners (the same four who started San Francisco's Pacific Union Realty) in 1983. And then Merryvale was purchased by the Swiss family Schlatter in 1996. The facility produces several varietals, including Chardonnay, Cabernet Sauvignon, Merlot and a dessert wine called Antigua. The tasting charge is $3 for the stan-

INSIDERS' TIP
A champagne cork can exit the bottle at 62 mph. To avoid the misery of spilling all the sparkling wine and sending the cork through your antique grandfather clock, note this technique: Don't twist the cork. Place a cloth towel over the cork, hold it firmly and gently rotate the bottle clockwise.

Photo: Beringer Winery

The Beringer Winery in St. Helena is a historical landmark.

dard choices, $5 for reserve wines and $10 for a special "connoisseur" selection. There are no tours, but Merryvale does offer wine component tasting seminars every Saturday and Sunday at 10:30 AM. Cost is $10, and reservations are recommended. The facility is open from 10 AM to 6:30 PM daily.

Beringer Vineyards
2000 Main St., St. Helena
• (707) 963-7115

Just as you pass through the "Row of Elms" that forms a canopy over Calif. 29 just north of St. Helena, what you'll see to the west is Beringer Wine Estates, arguably the most majestic of all Napa Valley wineries. Beringer produces a half-dozen wines that vary from high-quality to high-volume. The tours, which run every half-hour, are extremely popular. They include the wine caves tunneled into the hillside, and a finale in the tasting room, where for $3 you receive mouthfuls of three or four different wines. You can also choose to pay for a tasting of reserves ($2 to $7) in the Founders Room. The winery is a preserved historical landmark built by Jacob and Frederick Beringer in 1876. The tasting room, with its pine floors and slate roof, was Frederick's mansion. Beringer is open from 9:30 AM to 5 PM daily.

Charles Krug Winery
2800 Main St., St. Helena
• (707) 967-2200

There is a lot of history working at this 19th-century structure. It was Napa Valley's first winery, founded in 1861 by the eponymous Prussian immigrant, political theorist and editor of *Staats Zeitung*, the Pacific Coast's first German-language newspaper. Charles Krug, the winery, also shares the history of the Mondavi family, that dynasty of California winemaking. Cesare Mondavi bought Krug in 1943; his wife, Rosa, took over upon Cesare's death in 1959 and their son, Peter, became general manager in 1966. Now Peter's sons, Marc and Peter Jr., oversee most of the winery's operations, including the winemaking, marketing and sales. Charles Krug bottles at least 10 varieties of wine, including the full-bodied Vintage Selection Cabernet Sauvignon and Generations, a traditional Bordeaux blend. The facility is open daily from 10:30 AM to 5:30 PM, and tours are at 11:30 AM, 1:30 and 3:30 PM. There is a $3 charge for tasting ($5 for reserves.)

Markham Vineyards
2812 St. Helena Hwy. N., St. Helena
• (707) 963-5292

The fortress north of St. Helena, with its

fountains and eucalyptus trees, has seen a lot of change in its 120-plus years. It was built of stone quarried from nearby Glass Mountain by Bordeaux immigrant and failed prospector Jean Laurent in 1874, but it was used for bulk wines until 1977, when the winery was purchased by Bruce Markham. He sold the business 11 years later to Mercian, Japan's largest wine company. And in 1993, the winery officially reopened after a multimillion-dollar renovation that included restoration of Markham's 6,000-square-foot stone cellar. The tasting is not in the old structure, but rather in a new addition on its north side. There is a $3 fee for four white wines, $5 for four reds. Markham's Merlot, Sauvignon Blanc and Chardonnay all, at various times, have been rated No. 1 in the state by *Wine Spectator*. Markham is open daily from 10 AM to 5 PM.

St. Clement Vineyards
2867 St. Helena Hwy. N., St. Helena
• (707) 967-3033

The St. Clement winery is eye-catching anytime, but especially at night, when the pristine yellow Victorian is bathed by floodlights. The house dates to 1878, when it became Johannaburg winery, the eighth in Napa Valley. It was a private residence for most of the 20th century, until Dr. Bill Casey started St. Clement in 1975. Beer giant Sapporo USA has owned the label since 1987. The winery bottles five varietals and is best known for its Carneros Chardonnay and Cabernet Sauvignon. The $2 tasting charge applies to any purchase. St. Clement is open from 10 AM to 4 PM daily. They give daily tours at 10 AM and 2 PM, but you must make reservations. If you are feeling flushed as you leave, use it as an excuse to sit on the porch swing on the veranda—you'll want to stay there all month.

Freemark Abbey Winery
3022 St. Helena Hwy. N., St. Helena
• (707) 963-9694

No, Freemark Abbey was never home to a group of wine-mad monks. The name comes from a triumvirate that purchased the winery in 1939: Charles Freeman, Markquand Foster and Albert (Abbey) Ahern. Long before that (starting in 1886, to be exact), the winery was known as Tychson Hill, named for California's first female vintner, Josephine Tychson. The current winemaker (and managing partner), Ted Edwards, concentrates on four varietals: Cabernet Sauvignon, Chardonnay, Merlot and Johannisberg Riesling. Among those are three

esteemed single-vineyard wines—Cabernet Bosche, Sycamore Vineyards Cabernet Sauvignon and Carpy Ranch Chardonnay. You also should keep an eye out for the Edelwein Gold, a Sauterne-like dessert wine made only when conditions are right (10 times since 1973). The facility is open daily from 10 AM to 5 PM during the summer, 10 AM to 4:30 PM during winter. There are regular tours at 2 PM every day, and the $4 tasting fee includes the souvenir glass.

Folie á Deux Winery
3070 St. Helena Hwy. N., St. Helena
• (707) 963-1160

Give this one extra credit for a sense of humor. "Folie á deux" is a French term that means "shared madness of two." It's a psychiatric diagnosis that the original owners, two mental health professionals, found appropriate. They even requisitioned a logo that resembles a Rorschach inkblot. You don't have to be not-all-there to enjoy Folie á Deux's wines, however. Wine-maker Scott Harvey is one of the best in the business, and his broad selection includes Sangio-vese, Cabernet Sauvignon and Muscat. He also makes a special Amador Zinfandel from the oldest Zin vines in California, those of the 1870s Grandpere Vineyard. There is no charge for a sampling of five basic wines, nor for a cave tour (Friday, Saturday and Sunday, at 11 AM and 1 PM). You can sample reserve wines for $5. The tasting room is a century-old farmhouse, and there are picnic grounds overlooking the vineyards. Folie á Deux is open from 10 AM to 5 PM daily.

Rombauer Vineyards
3522 Silverado Trail, St. Helena
• (707) 963-5170

If the name rings a bell, think of food, not wine. Vintner Koerner Rombauer's great aunt, Irma Rombauer, has been in practically every kitchen in America. She's the author of *The Joy of Cooking*. Koerner makes six types of wine, including two—a Cabernet Franc and a Zinfandel—sold only from the tasting room. There is no charge for tasting. Rombauer is at the end of a long, steep driveway, and its views of the Napa Valley floor are hard to match—you should think about taking advantage of the picnic tables. It is open from 10 AM to 5 PM daily.

Wermuth Winery
3942 Silverado Trail, Calistoga
• (707) 942-5924

When you consider great winemakers, you naturally think of, uh, Newfoundland. That's where Ralph Wermuth is from anyway, and his small Upvalley winery has been making drinkable vintages since 1981. The wines are all dry, all crushed from Napa Valley grapes such as Colombard and Gamay, and all sold only on the premises. The $1 tasting fee is refundable with purchase, and you can get a quick tour of the facilities if you arrange it in advance. Wermuth is open daily from 11 AM to 5 PM, though Ralph is forced to close shop for errand runs on occasion.

Kornell Rombauer Cellars
1059 Larkmead Ln., Calistoga
• **(707) 942-0859**

This one isn't as gargantuan as some of Napa's other champagneries, but it's a treat for visitors: a sublime spot on one of the valley's less-traveled crossroads, a charming picnic area behind the 1906 stone building and sparkling wines sold only on the premises. The winery was known as Larkmead Cellars back in the old days, when it produced still wines. Now it is owned by Koerner Rombauer (of Rombauer Vineyards) and grape-grower Richard Frank. Kornell's champagne line includes Blanc de Blancs, Blanc de Noirs, Brut and Rouge. There is no charge for tasting, and they claim the longest you'll ever have to wait for a tour is 10 minutes. Kornell is open daily from 10 AM to 5 PM.

Schramsberg Vineyards and Cellars
1400 Schramsberg Rd., Calistoga
• **(707) 942-4558**

When Richard Nixon and Chinese Premier Chou En-Lai raised a glass of bubbly for their "Toast to Peace" in 1972, it was a 1969 Schramsberg Blanc de Blancs they sipped. That was only one of the historic milestones marked by a one-of-a-kind winery. German immigrant Jacob Schram founded the business on Diamond Mountain in 1862, planting the first hillside vineyards in Napa Valley. Schram developed a good reputation, but the operation had crumbled by the time Jack and Jamie Davies (and their investors) purchased the property in 1965.

Jack and Jamie set about restoring Schram's old house and gardens and, most importantly, devoting the winery to champagne production. They were the first Californians to use Chardonnay and Pinot Noir grapes, the traditional Champagne varietals, in their sparkling wines, and their place in Wine Country history is now cemented. (The valley still mourns Jack, who died in 1998.) Schramsberg makes six types of champagne, including the world-

renowned J. Schram tête de cuvée. You must book a tour to taste—three releases for $7.50 or a vertical selection of one varietal for $10. To find Schramsberg, which is open daily from 9:30 AM to 4:30 PM, turn onto Peterson Drive from Calif. 29, about 3 miles south of Calistoga.

Dutch Henry
4310 Silverado Trail, Calistoga
• **(707) 942-5771**

The two families that own Dutch Henry, Chafen and Phelps, run it like a mom-and-pop winery. (There is no relation to famous vintner Joseph Phelps—"unfortunately," says Scott Chafen.) They pour in the cellar, and a tour consists of looking in different directions while you get the lowdown. The winery produces only about 3,000 cases a year, and its line includes Chardonnay, Zinfandel, Sirah and Pinot Noir. Some of their 70-year-old zin vines are being pulled up because of a malady called "leaf curl," but don't worry, another vineyard is lined up as a replacement. Dutch Henry does no distribution away from the winery. There has never been a tasting charge, but the owners have been thinking of implementing one during the summer, so call first if it's an issue. The winery is open from 10 AM to 4:30 PM daily.

Stonegate Winery
1183 Dunaweal Ln., Calistoga
• **(707) 942-6500**

Stonegate is less heralded and less imposing than its Dunaweal neighbors, Sterling and Clos Pegase (see next listings). Founded in 1973, it is now owned by California Wine Company, which also runs Bandiera Winery, near Cloverdale. Stonegate gets many of its grapes from the Calistoga area. It plucks Sauvignon Blanc from the vineyard around the winery, and Merlot and Cabernet Sauvignon from its plantings in Chiles Valley. Tasting is free. Stonegate provides tours and picnic tables and is open daily from 10:30 AM to 4:30 PM.

Sterling Vineyards
1111 Dunaweal Ln., Calistoga
• **(707) 942-3300**

The Napa uninitiated can be forgiven for unfailingly asking, "Is that a monastery up on the hill between St. Helena and Calistoga?" Not exactly. It's Sterling Vineyards, with its white stucco, Ionian-style architecture and knoll-top regality. Winetasting here literally has been elevated to an event. A gondola takes you to the top of the hill, where you are free to sip samples, wander on a self-guided tour, art-gaze in the Three Palms Gallery or eat at a table on the terrace, with its wide-angle views of the valley below. It's $6 for the whole experience ($3 for children ages 4 to 18, free for tots). Most of Sterling's production falls among four wines—Cabernet Sauvignon, Chardonnay, Sauvignon Blanc and Merlot, including several vineyard-designated versions. It also bottles small lots of lesser-known wines that it sells only at the winery, such as Malvasia Bianca and Charbono. Sterling was founded by English paper broker Peter Newton in 1964, sold to Coca-Cola in 1977, then to Joseph E. Seagram and Sons in 1983. Newton left behind a Brit legacy—the old bells of St. Dunstan's Church, which chime on the half-hour. Sterling is open every day from 10:30 AM to 4:30 PM.

Clos Pegase
1060 Dunaweal Ln., Calistoga
• (707) 942-4981

Jan Shrem's winery is named for the winged horse Pegasus, whose hooves are said to have unleashed the Spring of the Muses, bringing both wine and art to the masses. Shrem, who built his fortune publishing reference and technical books in Japan, is preoccupied with both wine and art. His collection of sculpture and painting is profiled in our Arts and Culture chapter, and his wines—Cabernet Sauvignon, Chardonnay, Merlot and Petite Sirah Port—are some of the best in the valley. The winery itself, designed by renowned Princeton architect Michael Graves, is a stark, modern landmark of earth tones, angles and curves. Public tours depart at 11 AM and 2 PM daily and include the 20,000-square-foot aging caves. The tasting fee is $2.50 for two Chardonnays and a Merlot, or $5 for three different Cabernets. Clos Pegase is open from 10:30 AM to 5 PM daily.

Cuvaison Winery
4550 Silverado Trail, Calistoga
• (707) 942-6266

When Silicon Valley engineers Thomas Cottrell and Thomas Parkhill started a small Upvalley winery in 1969, they called it Cuvaison, a French term for the fermentation of wine on the grape skins. The name remains, though the winery is now owned by Thomas Schmidheiny, CEO of the world's largest cement company (Holderbank) and one of the richest men in Switzerland. John Thacher is the winemaker (and president), and he is particularly known for his Chardonnay. Cuvaison gets more than 90 percent of its grapes from its 400-acre vineyard in Carneros. Tours are at 10:30 AM, and tasting is $4 (or $5 for reserve wines), which includes a souvenir glass. The winery has a pleasant, oak-shaded picnic area and is open from 10 AM to 5 PM daily.

Vincent Arroyo Winery
2361 Greenwood Ave., Calistoga
• (707) 942-6995

Cozy? Not only is Vincent Arroyo a family operation, but Vincent is the only member of the family. He pretty much runs the show, with help from a few employees and a gregarious black lab named Joy. There is nothing special about the tasting room—it's in a modern barn of a barrel house—but Arroyo has found a serenely perfect spot just north of Calistoga, tasting is free of charge, and the wines themselves are first-rate. (The standbys are Chardonnay, Cabernet Sauvignon and Petite Sirah, and all are sold only at the winery.) Bring a picnic and watch the hawks circling overhead. The winery is open daily from 10 AM to 4:30 PM.

Graeser Winery
255 Petrified Forest Rd., Calistoga
• (707) 942-4437

Want to get a feeling for the Napa Valley wine industry circa 1890? Take a drive to Graeser, about 2 miles northwest of Calistoga. The tasting room is in an 1886 home. If no one answers, ring the doorbell, a rope attached to the bell tower over the house. It's a bucolic setting once known as La Perlita del Monte ("The Pearl of the Mountain"), and Richard Graeser can genuinely claim a unique microclimate for his grapes, which are the traditional Burgundian varietals: Cabernet Sauvignon, Cabernet Franc and Merlot. The winery is open daily from 10 AM to 5 PM. There is no charge for tasting, and picnics should be mandatory. Ask about Graeser's Adopt-a-Vine program.

Chateau Montelena
1429 Tubbs Ln., Calistoga
• (707) 942-5105

Montelena was one of the two Napa Valley wineries—Stag's Leap being the other—that rocked the French establishment at a famous blind tasting in Paris in 1976 (see this chapter's Close-up). It was a Chardonnay that prevailed that day, and the winery still makes one of the valley's best, along with top-notch Cabernet Sauvignon and Johannisberg Riesling (the latter grown in northward Potter Valley and sold only in the retail room).

Chateau Montelena's name and origins go back much further than 1976. The winery was started by Alfred L. Tubbs in the late 1800s, but no wine had been produced for 50 years when new owner Jim Barrett filled the barrels again in 1972. The building, nothing short of a hilltop castle with walls 3 to 10 feet thick, dates back to Tubbs' day, and a subsequent owner, Yort Frank, added Jade Lake and its Chinese gardens. Montelena is open daily from 10 AM to 4 PM and gives daily tours at 11 AM and 2 PM; call to reserve. The $5 tasting charge applies to any purchase.

Hans Fahden Vineyards
5300 Mountain Home Ranch Rd., Calistoga • (707) 942-6760

This winery has no intention of serving your one-stop wine-shopping needs. It produces one varietal: an estate-grown Cabernet Sauvignon that can cozy up to barbecued lamb or chocolate truffles. Hans Fahden was the name of the founder, an immigrant from Hamburg who sold more prunes and walnuts than grapes. His grandsons, Lyall and Antone, reclaimed the overgrown land and re-established the winery in 1982. It's a breathtaking location between Calistoga and Santa Rosa, in the hills of eastern Sonoma County. There is no tasting charge, and you are encouraged to use the flowering picnic grounds. The facility is open 10 AM to 4 PM daily.

Sonoma County

Southern Sonoma

Bartholomew Park Winery
1000 Vineyard Ln., Sonoma • (707) 935-9511

The winery and adjacent park are named for Frank Bartholomew, former foreign correspondent with United Press International (later its president). The winery's picnic sites, set among native oaks, are unequalled, with picnic tables overlooking vistas of vineyards. Frank's wife, Antonia, who lived to age 90, is responsible for building the reproduction of Agoston Haraszthy's Pompeian-style villa (see our History chapter), which stands sentinel over the vineyards he once cultivated. Within the winery there is a small museum celebrating the life of Haraszthy and the achievements of Frank Bartholomew in his days with United Press. An innovative feature has been added to amuse and educate winery visitors during the crush season—the Punch Down Club. One component of winemaking and a fermenting "must" is a relatively thick cap of skin that

floats to the top and must be pushed back down four or five times a day. Members of the club can participate in this somewhat messy operation, then receive a bottle of "their" wine when it has aged. The winery offers complimentary tastings (except for large groups) and tours and is open 10:30 AM to 4:30 PM daily. The nearby villa may be toured Wednesday through Sunday at varying hours. During the summer, the winery presents a jazz concert once a month.

Buena Vista Winery
18000 Old Winery Rd., Sonoma • (707) 938-1266

Huge shade trees surround Buena Vista, the oldest premium winery in California, established in 1857 by Count Agoston Haraszthy (see the Close-up on Haraszthy, "The Father of California Viticulture," in our History chapter). The fountain courtyard, a lovely picnic spot, is home to a self-guided historic tour, but there's also a guided historic presentation daily at 2 PM (plus one at 11 AM in summer). Two of the winery's stone buildings are registered as state historic landmarks. Chinese laborers dug long tunnels into the hillside for wine aging, and Buena Vista's buildings are made from the salvaged rock. The Press House, built in 1862, houses a gift shop, displays a fine collection of art and offers complimentary tastings. The Heritage Bar, on the second floor, features rare, intensely flavored vintage wines from the Carneros region. The 1997 season marked 140 years since the globe-trotting Count Haraszthy turned a shovel of sun-baked earth and proclaimed the birth of Buena Vista Winery. Today Buena Vista supplies wine to all 50 states and 30 countries around the world, an accomplishment that would not surprise the enterprising count. The winery is open 10:30 AM to 5 PM; tours are complimentary.

Buena Vista has a second tasting room in downtown Sonoma, at the southeast corner of the plaza (494 First Street East) in Pinelli's Corner Store (once the historic Pinelli Mission Hardware Store). There is no charge for any tasting. Daily tasting hours are 11 AM to 5:30 PM, and the phone number is (707) 939-0579. Both the winery and the downtown Sonoma tasting room feature wines by Buena Vista, Robert Stemmler and Haywood.

Cline Cellars
24737 Calif. Hwy. 121, Sonoma • (707) 935-4310

After spending his childhood learning farming and winemaking from his grandfather

Avaleriano Jacuzzi (of spa fame), Fred Cline founded Cline Cellars in 1982 in the sandy soils of Oakley, California in Contra Costa County. His brother Matt joined him in 1991 as winemaker, and they relocated to the Sonoma Valley. The tasting room is in an 1850s farmhouse with a large, old-fashioned porch. Picnic grounds surrounded by 1,100 rose bushes make for a very pleasant lunch stop, with sweeping views of the Sonoma Valley on a site that was once a Miwok village. Tastings, which are complimentary, feature Rhone-style red wines—Syrah, and Mouvedre—as well as several white wines. Facilities are available for special events and weddings. The winery is open 10 AM to 6 PM daily.

Gloria Ferrer Champagne Caves
23555 Calif. Hwy. 121, Sonoma
• (707) 996-7256

The vineyards stretch across the hills, and from the hillock above, the Spanish-style winery overlooks the estate vineyards and the rolling Carneros hills. This is one of seven wineries owned and operated by the Ferrer family of Barcelona, which has produced *methode champenoise* sparkling wine for 100 years. You can tour the facility with its state-of-the-art caves and learn the secrets of the class *methode champenoise* process. Others may choose to linger on the vista terrace, noshing gourmet appetizers and sipping sparkling wine. Picnic tables are available for those who buy a bottle of wine to go with the comestibles. There is often musical entertainment on weekends, and there's plenty of banquet and meeting space. Tastings are by appointment.

Gundlach Bundschu Winery
2000 Denmark St., Sonoma
• (707) 938-5277

Jacob Gundlach and his brother-in-law, Charles Bundschu, established this winery in 1858 on land east of Sonoma that they called Rhinefarm. The enterprise gained international fame in the late 1800s and survived the 1906 earthquake, but fell to Prohibition, when its owners were reduced to selling grapes to other vintners. The resurrection of the winery began on Halloween 1970, when Jim Bundschu, great-great-grandson of the founder, decided to turn his winemaking hobby into a viable business. Operating on a shoestring budget, he and his brothers-in-law converted a dairy's milk tanks into fermentation vats and squeezed grapes with a muscle-wrenching, hand-operated basket press. Today Gundlach Bundschu produces

50,000 cases of premium, award-winning wines a year, specializing in Merlot, Pinot Noir, Chardonnay, Cabernet and Zinfandel. Picnic tables are in a grove of oak trees overlooking a lake. The winery also offers cave tours every half-hour throughout the summer. Another attraction at Gundlach Bundschu is a 6-foot by 140-foot mural dedicated to the winery's farmworkers, completed in spring 1998.

Jim Bundschu's lighthearted humor is legendary, and local residents like to drive out to the tasting rooms occasionally just to see the wacky posters he creates as part of his marketing plan. In one, Bundschu's mother, behind the wheel of a 1947 Kaiser on the edge of the family vineyards, is exchanging words with a motorcycle cop who says, "If you can't say Gundlach Bundschu Gewurztraminer you shouldn't be driving." The room for complimentary tastings is open daily from 11 AM to 4:30 PM, and self-guided tours are offered.

Ravenswood Winery
18701 Gehricke Rd., Sonoma
• (707) 938-1960, (888) 669-4679

The advertising copy says it all: "Serious wines, handcrafted by people who think wine should also be fun." Beneath a photo of the winery staff, sitting partially clad and hunkered down in wine barrels, their philosophy is announced: "It's what's in the barrel that counts!" What's in the barrel is often some of the best Zinfandel in the world. This winery also features picnic facilities and a barbecue in the vineyard every weekend from May through September. The winery is open daily from 10 AM to 4:30 PM, with tours (10:30 AM, by reservation) and complimentary tastings of Zinfandel, Merlot and Cabernet Sauvignon.

Roche Winery
28700 Arnold Dr., Sonoma
• (707) 935-7115

This small, family-operated winery is the first you see as you enter the Sonoma Valley from the south, just north of Sears Point raceway. Owners Joseph and Genevieve Roche started with 10 acres in 1982, expanded to 25 acres in 1987 and plan to remain a small winery with carefully crafted estate wines. Housed in a modified barn at the top of a small hill, the setting commands a sweeping view of the valley, the bay and the lights of the communities beyond. The tasting room features free sips of Chardonnay, Pinot Noir, Muscat and Merlot, or $3 glasses of reserve wines. (Roche's Merlot is sold by lottery.) Lovely picnic facilities are

Photo: Lou Zauner

Korbel, near Guerneville, was one of Wine Country's first makers of sparkling wines.

available, and the winery is open daily from 10 AM to 6 PM in the summer and 10 AM to 5 PM in the winter.

Schug-Carneros Estate Winery
602 Bonneau Rd., Sonoma
• (707) 939-9363

This lifelong dream of owner-winemaster Walter Schug spans four decades and two continents. A native of Germany's Rhein River valley and a graduate of a prestigious German wine institute, Walter left for California determined to find success with his Pinot Noir, which has since been proclaimed no less than world-class by critics in both the United States and Europe. The winery, built in 1990 of post-and-beam architecture, reflects the Schug family's German heritage. Schug still maintains close ties to Europe (one-third of Schug wines are sold there), and it's a likely possibility you'll meet European neighbors while you're in the tasting room to enjoy complimentary sips (or reserve wines at $2 per taste). The winery is open daily from 10 AM to 5 PM.

Sebastiani Vineyards
389 Fourth St. E., Sonoma
• (707) 938-5532

One of the few original family wineries still remaining, Sebastiani is extremely proud of its wines and its Italian heritage. Founder Samuele Sebastiani learned winemaking from the monks in Franetta, Italy before he came to America in 1894 at the age of 19 and went to work hauling cobblestones. In 1904 he bought the old Sonoma Mission vineyard, where the padres had been making altar wines for 80 years. He sold his first vino to local Italian stonecutters in demijohns the size of beach balls.

The winery is three blocks east of Sonoma Plaza, set amid the vineyards from which Sebastiani produces its special Sonoma Cask and Cherry Block Cabernet wines. A great convenience for visitors is the winery's trolley, which allows people to park at the winery and catch a shuttle back to the plaza. The winery has a picnic area and also gives daily tours, the first at 10:30 AM and the last at 4 PM. Be sure to spend some time in the wine-aging cellars marveling at the largest collection of hand-carved casks in America. Some date back to the mid-1880s. The tasting room is open from 10 AM to 5 PM, and tastings are complimentary.

Viansa Winery and Italian Marketplace
25200 Arnold Dr., Sonoma
• (707) 935-4700

When Sam Sebastiani visited the homeland

of his grandfather in Italy, he was astounded to see that Franetta, Italy, looked exactly like the Sonoma Valley. "It looked so much like Sonoma I damn near fell over," he said. The winery that Sam and his wife, Vicki (Viansa combines Sam and Vicki) established is about as Italian in aura as you will find this side of the Atlantic. Specimen olive trees were imported from Italy, the architecture is Italian, and the garden paths that wind between levels of the winery are in Tuscan style.

The winetasting room (sips are complimentary) is also a tasting room for some stunning gourmet foods—a manifestation of Vicki's longstanding interest in hospitality. (Her cookbook is on sale at the gift shop.) Visitors can wander about, picking up samples of olive-anchovy pesto, hot sweet mustards, blood-orange vinegar and other aromatic foods. Vicki and her kitchen staff have also developed some unusual specialties such as focaccia, sandwiches and fine salads that are available at the food counter —all splendid foods for a picnic. Plenty of picnic tables are available at various patio levels overlooking Sonoma Valley and Sam's award-winning wildlife preserve with a few thousand birds. Sam Sebastiani adheres to his loyalty to Italian-style wines; his winery features Piccolo Toscano (a Chianti type of grape), Sothena (a Dolcetto grape) and Nebbiolo (the name of the grape and the wine) plus 40 other varieties. Wine and food tasting is offered from 10 AM to 5 PM daily.

Arrowood Vineyards & Winery
14347 Sonoma Hwy., Glen Ellen
• **(707) 938-5170**

It had been the philosophy of Richard Arrowood to make only reserve-quality Chardonnay and Cabernet Sauvignon. But he has been unable to resist experimenting with unusual varietals, so his portfolio has now expanded to include limited quantities of Merlot, Viognier and Pinot Blanc. Hospitality and personal service are a top priority at Arrowood, whose new tasting room is open daily from 10 AM to 4:30 PM. Tastings are $3 per person. When visitors finish savoring the wines, they can savor the spectacular view from the vineyard veranda.

Benziger Family Winery
1883 London Ranch Rd., Glen Ellen
• **(707) 935-3000**

You could easily spend an entire, pleasant day here at the Benziger Family Winery, perched on the side of Sonoma Mountain high above the Sonoma Valley floor and the town of Glen Ellen. Guests can browse world-renowned art in the Imagery Art Gallery (which spotlights the award-winning art created for Benziger labels), picnic in the redwood grove, visit an experimental vineyard, enjoy complimentary winetasting (or five reserve wines for $5) and take in a one-of-a-kind educational vineyard tour aboard a motorized tram. The Benzigers emigrated from White Plains, New York, to their mountain ranch next to Jack London State Park (see our Parks and Recreation chapter). They have since built a reputation for grape-growing innovation that produces award-winning wines in the Imagery series—Merlot, Chardonnay and an unusual Cabernet Franc, a Bordeaux varietal—year after year. They also founded the Glen Ellen Winery (see subsequent listing) and later sold it. Winetasting is available from 10 AM to 5 PM. The winery also conducts six tram tours daily, with additional tours on weekends.

Chandelle of Sonoma
15499 Arnold Dr., Glen Ellen
• **(707) 938-5862**

Flying is the theme of Chandelle Winery's colorful labels. They feature paintings of vintage aircraft—a salute, no doubt, to five-star Gen. "Hap" Arnold, who happens to be the grandfather of owner Robert Arnold. (Arnold Drive is also named for the general.) Robert and his wife, Mary Evelyn, opened a sales room for Chandelle wines in Jack London Village in Glen Ellen, the only place the wines are sold. Chardonnay and Cabernet wines are Chandelle's specialties. The winery is open daily for sales only (no tasting) from 10 AM to 4 PM Monday through Saturday and 11 AM to 4 PM on Sunday. Note that Chandelle is closed Sunday in winter.

Glen Ellen Tasting Room
14301 Arnold Dr., Glen Ellen
• **(707) 939-6277**

A new tasting room and history center has been opened by Glen Ellen Winery, housed in the historic Chauvet Winery building in Jack London Village (next to Gen. Vallejo's 1850 grist mill). A fascinating display of historical photographs and other memorabilia delineates the colorful history of Glen Ellen and its world-famous figures, including writer Jack London and his wife, Charmian (see our History and Attractions chapters for more on London). A special Train Room displays photos of trains that actually came through Sonoma Valley in bygone times. Once a month, the winery presents special events, which run the gamut from a ghost story contest to a program of readings, food and dance inspired by the work of novelist and food writer M.F.K. Fisher. No wines are made here, but you can taste Glen Ellen and M.G. Vallejo wines as well as the winery's new line of premium varietals: Expressions. The tasting room is open daily from 10 AM to 5 PM.

Many wineries have lovely common areas to help you enjoy your visit.

Wellington Vineyards
11600 Dunbar Rd., Glen Ellen
• **(707) 939-0708**

Operating a small, family vineyard and winery producing just 6,000 cases a year, John and Peter Wellington nevertheless produce a wide range of wines, concentrating on reds like Zinfandel, Merlot and Cabernet. They also produce a couple of unusual wines, unique to the area, including a Rhone-style blend, Côtes de Sonoma. The winery and tasting room are surrounded by vines, some as old as 100 years. The tasting room is open daily for complimentary sips from 11 AM to 5 PM.

Chateau St. Jean
8555 Sonoma Hwy., Kenwood
• **(707) 833-4134**

Nestled against the tranquil slopes of Sugarloaf Ridge, Chateau St. Jean (named for owner Ken Sheffield's sister and pronounced "gene") was founded in 1973. An elegant château on the grounds of this 250-acre estate was built in 1920 and is now a showplace surrounded by beautiful gardens. It's a lovely spot for picnicking. Chateau St. Jean's Cabernet Sauvignon has been served at the White House, and Queen Elizabeth has been served their Chardonnay. The tasting room is open daily from 10 AM to 4:30 PM.

Mayo Family Wineries
9200 Sonoma Hwy., Kenwood
• **(707) 833-5504**

It has been the lifetime dream of real estate broker Henry Mayo (see our Real Estate chapter) to own a home in the vineyards of Sonoma County and to raise his own grapes. Now he has achieved both goals. His first grapes were planted in 1989, harvested in 1993. At first he planned to simply raise and sell his grapes, since his location in Santa Rosa was not conducive to offering a tasting room. However, his son, Jeffrey, has now joined him, and they have developed an interesting plan to publicize their wines. Using the Mayo real estate offices on the main highway through Kenwood (now on the upper floor), they have turned the main floor into a tasting room and have rented tasting-room space to six other winery owners who join them in pouring their wines. Each winery owner takes one day to pour the wines of all, so there is always a knowledgeable owner on duty. The wineries represented, along with the Mayo family's, are Sable Ridge Vineyards, Nelson Estate Winery, Sunce Winery, Noel Winery, Tantalus Cellars and Deerfield Ranch Winery. Tastings are complimentary, and the room is open daily from 11 AM to 6 PM.

Kenwood Vineyards
9592 Sonoma Hwy., Kenwood
• **(707) 833-5891**

When the Pagani brothers founded this winery in 1906, Jack London lived on the estate next door. Both estate owners are gone now, and the winery was bought by three college chums, all wine lovers, in 1970. The grapes they use are still grown on the London ranch, and

Visitors enjoy a look at the Beringer Wine caves, which tunnel into the hillside.

the label on a special bottling shows a picture of a wolf and Jack London's signature. The tasting room is rustic, the sips are complimentary, and the atmosphere is charmingly informal. Kenwood is known for its Sauvignon Blanc, Zinfandels and Cabernets. One of the charming features of this winery is the free food-and-wine pairings on weekends. The tasting room is open daily 10 AM to 4:30 PM.

Kunde Estate Winery
10155 Sonoma Hwy., Kenwood
• (707) 833-5501

The ranch that has seen four generations of Kundes since 1904 stretches for 1.5 miles along Sonoma Highway and extends from the valley up into the mountains above. Founder of this winery (and of the family) was Louis Kunde, who arrived in California from Germany in 1884. He bought a vineyard that had been planted in 1879 and used an old barn as the winery. Today's tasting room is a replica of that old barn, built on the site of the original. The Kunde family ages its wine in 30,000 square feet of caves dug into the hillside, providing an ideal environment for natural aging. Timbers from the old barn were used to handcraft tables and benches. Picnic grounds are surrounded by scenic vineyards. There's a nice gift shop inside, and tours are available Friday through Sun-

day. Chardonnay vineyards surround the tasting rooms, where samples are complimentary. Kunde Estate is open daily from 11 AM to 5 PM.

Landmark Vineyards
101 Adobe Canyon Rd., Kenwood
• (707) 833-0053

Perhaps the most spectacular aspect of this Spanish Mission-style winery is its expansive interior courtyard, facing onto dramatic, hulking Sugarloaf Mountain—a perfect setting for the weddings that often take place there. Ample room for guests outside can be augmented by adequate seating in the dining room (with kitchen available) to make the wedding a memorable day for everyone. The hospitality center at Landmark is a magnificent facility featuring a granite tasting bar, a warm fireplace for chilly days and a full-wall mural by noted Sonoma County artist Claudia Wagar. The pond-side picnic area is a picturesque location for lunch or for just lounging and watching the clouds drift by. A tower conference room offers a 360-degree view that must be distracting to those attending the meetings held there. Landmark's production focuses on Chardonnay, and three labels have won awards: Overlook, from Sonoma County vineyards; Damaris Reserve, from Alexander Valley appellation; and Two Williams Vineyard, from southern Sonoma Valley. Tastings are complimentary, and the room is open daily from 10 AM to 4:30 PM.

St. Francis Winery and Vineyards
8450 Sonoma Hwy., Kenwood
- **(707) 833-4666**

Joseph Martin, who left the corporate world in 1971 to become a vintner, named his winery after St. Francis of Assisi and San Francisco de Solano Mission in Sonoma. His first harvest came in 1979 with production of 4,000 cases. Today his benchmark varietals are Chardonnay and Merlot, rich with character and complexity, but the portfolio also includes Cabernet Sauvignon and Zinfandel. A pleasant Wine Garden patio is furnished with picnic tables and umbrellas and faces panoramic views of vineyards and mountains. Complimentary tastings are available daily from 10 AM to 4:30 PM.

Smothers Winery and Remick Ridge Vineyards
9575 Sonoma Hwy., Kenwood
- **(707) 833-6131**

The tasting room may be small, but it's filled with Smothers Brothers memorabilia, including gold records adorning the walls. If you ask if the television stars might be in, someone will point to a corner where a full-size, cardboard cutout replicates the brothers standing together. Tommy Smothers (the goofy one in the act) bought 110 acres of vineyard land in 1972, and his brother, Dick (the straight man), bought a home and 30 acres of vineyard in the Santa Cruz mountains two years later. When Dick added Vine Hill Vineyard next to Tom's acreage, the Smothers Winery was born. The famous brothers had their first crush in 1977 and opened the tasting room in 1985. Dick has since sold out to his brother. Now Tommy grows the grapes, but the wine is made in Glen Ellen by Richard Arrowood. They produce Chardonnay, Cabernet and a small amount of Merlot. There is a small picnic area, and the tasting room, fronting Sonoma Highway, is open daily from 11 AM to 4 PM.

Matanzas Creek Winery
6097 Bennett Valley Rd., Santa Rosa
- **(707) 528-6464**

On the face of it, Bill and Sandra MacIver were unlikely candidates to suc-ceed in the wine business. He had a 20-year military career behind him; she had no experience but a vision of creating a perfect wine. In 1978 they came together as partners in marriage and business, and today, Matanzas Creek Winery is recognized as one of the country's best.

Ensconced at the base of Bennett Mountain, the new, environmentally conscious winemaking facility boasts one of the most sophisticated research laboratories in California. There, Matanzas Creek's winemakers have conducted more than 100 experiments in progressive winemaking. In the early 1990s, Matanzas released a new wine made in a radically progressive winemaking program named Journey. Although its $70 price raised some controversy, the first 1990 Chardonnay sold out on release and was hailed by critics as the finest Chardonnay ever produced in America. The tasting room is open from 10 AM to 4:30 PM every day. Tastings are $3 to $9, depending on what is poured. Picnic facilities are available as well as a self-guided garden tour that includes the largest planting of high-quality lavender in Northern California. Look for handmade lavender products in the gift shop.

Paradise Ridge Winery
4545 Thomas Lake Harris Dr., Santa Rosa
- **(707) 528-9463**

Welcome to Paradise! For Walter and Marijki Byck, Paradise came to be on the day in 1994 when they opened the doors to their new winery, a California-style structure with breathtaking views from the decks. In fact, the view is so exciting the winery stays open late on Wednesday evenings just so visitors can catch the sunset. After purchasing a 156-acre ranch adjoining the old Fountain Grove Winery, the Bycks planted 18 acres of Sauvignon Blanc and Chardonnay grapes, determined to produce the finest wines possible. In addition to their award-winning wines, they also feature a historical exhibit and world-class sculpture garden. Tastings are complimentary. The tasting room is open daily from 11 AM to 6 PM and until sunset on Wednesday.

De Loach Vineyards
1791 Olivet Rd., Santa Rosa
- **(707) 526-9111**

Cecil and Christine De Loach have established a

INSIDERS' TIP
Phylloxera, the voracious little plant louse that brought devastation to vineyards in the late 19th century, works at a grapevine's roots. Tiny insects suck the life out of the vine, usually taking three to five years to fully destroy it.

reputation as leading producers of premium wines and professional leaders in the industry ranks. He has served on the board of directors of the Wine Institute, and she is past president of the Sonoma County Wineries Association, both positions of prestige. Together, they cultivate 500 acres of vineyards in the Russian River Valley, producing Pinot Noir, Chardonnay and Gewurztraminer as well as some remarkable Zinfandel, from vines that were planted between the turn of the century and 1934. The winery also makes Sauvignon Blanc, Merlot and Cabernet Sauvignon plus a distinctive White Zinfandel. Picnic facilities are on the lawn in front of the winery, which is situated among the vines. Tours and tastings are complimentary. The tasting room is open daily from 10 AM to 4:30 PM, and tours are conducted at 11 AM and 2 PM, by appointment only.

Martini & Prati Wines
2191 Laguna Rd., Santa Rosa
• (707) 823-2404

This is what wineries used to be! It's a unique experience—the only place in Sonoma County where you can sometimes fill a jug straight from the tank. It is said to be the oldest winery in continuous operation in the county, and it's still owned by the Martini family who opened it. If you have a picnic in mind, visit Elmo's Groceria and Italian Country Store, which is on-site. The Italian family tradition is reflected in the handcrafted style of wines produced—exceptional Sangiovese, Barbera, Vino Grigio, Muscato and Port. To add to a lovely day, take a stroll through the landscaped grounds, which include an acre of lavender. The tasting room is open daily from 11 AM to 4 PM, with tours offered at 11 AM.

Northern Sonoma

Armida Winery
2201 Westside Rd., Healdsburg
• (707) 433-2222

Tastings here are charmingly casual (and complimentary), and the setting is spectacular. Built on the side of a hill, the winery looks out on the Dry Creek and Russian River valleys, with Alexander Valley, Geyser Peak and Mount St. Helena to the east and south. High on the hillside, three geodesic domes represent the winery, lab and administrative offices. If you've been looking forward to a game of bocce ball (or if you'd like to learn what it is!), there's a court near the picnic grounds, overlooking a pond. Vineyards are south of the winery, producing Amida's four varietals: Merlot, Chardonnay, Pinot Noir and the recently added Zinfandel. Tasting-room hours are 11 AM to 5 PM daily.

Belvedere Winery
4035 Westside Rd., Healdsburg
• (707) 433-8236

This winery, in the coastal foothills of the Russian River Valley, takes its name from the Italian word for "beautiful view." A trip to the winery reveals just that. Taste world-class wines while you enjoy a picnic on the sunny deck or under an oak tree in a beautiful garden setting. The picturesque vineyards of the Russian River Valley will spread out before you. Belvedere specialties are Zinfandel, Chardonnay, Merlot and Cabernet Sauvignon from their premium vineyards in the Alexander, Dry Creek and Russian River valleys. Tastings are complimentary from 10 AM to 4:30 PM daily. Belvedere has a second tasting room on the southeast corner of the Healdsburg Plaza.

Davis Bynum Winery
807 Westside Rd., Healdsburg
• (707) 433-5852

Davis Bynum made wine at home in Berkeley for many years, then started a winery there in 1965. In 1972 he purchased an 82-acre ranch in the Russian River Valley and moved his operation. Most of the wines are made from grapes produced in the cool, coastal Russian River Valley, which gives them intense varietal character. Davis-Bynum has become more vineyard-specific over the last two years, concentrating on smaller batches for higher quality. Wines produced include Fume Blanc, Zinfandel, vari-

INSIDERS' TIP

Some of Wine Country's back roads beckon bicycle enthusiasts, particularly the two-lane country roads of the Dry Creek and Alexander valleys in Sonoma County. Quail scurry across the paths, and swallowtail butterflies enjoy roadside tastings of their own. Caution is required, though, for the roads are narrow and curves frequent. In Napa County, Silverado Trail is ideal for bikes—the road is level, and a multitude of small side roads invite exploration. (See our Parks and Recreation chapter for more on bicycling in Wine Country.)

ous Chardonnays, three levels of Pinot Noir, estate grown Merlot and Cabernet Sauvignon. With the winery perched on a hillside, the picnic grounds offer a most pleasant view. The tasting room, where samples are complimentary, is open daily from 10 AM to 5 PM.

Foppiano Vineyards
12707 Old Redwood Hwy., Healdsburg
• (707) 433-7272

This is the oldest family-owned winery in Sonoma County. It was founded by John Foppiano, a disenchanted gold miner, who decided to get back to his farming roots. He supported his wife and 10 children by selling vegetables to San Francisco customers before deciding to get into grape growing in 1896. Foppiano survived Prohibition by shipping fresh grapes to the East Coast. The winery is now being run by fourth-generation Foppianos, producing 200,000 cases a year of Cabernet Sauvignon, Petite Sirah, Zinfandel, Merlot, Pinot Noir, Chardonnay and Sauvignon Blanc. Some of the producing vines are 100 years old. Tastings are complimentary, and a self-guided vineyard tour is available. Winery hours are 10 AM to 4:30 PM daily.

Hop Kiln Winery
6050 Westside Rd, Healdsburg
• (707) 433-6491

Housed in an old stone building that was once a hops barn, the tasting room at Hop Kiln displays a fine collection of winemaking tools and a gallery of old photos showing the history of the hop industry, which bustled in the early 1900s when that crop was extensively grown in Sonoma County for beer manufacturing. The Hop Kiln was declared a state historic landmark in 1977 and has been the setting for several motion pictures, including *The Magic of Lassie*, and the TV show *Homeward Bound*. The tasting room is cool, rustic and pleasant and serves complimentary samplings of Zinfandel, Chardonnay and two blends, Marty Griffin's Big Red and Thousand Flowers. You can enjoy a picnic beside a picturesque pond inhabited by local wildfowl while sipping wine and enjoying crackers, cheese and salami in the picnic area. Winery hours are 10 AM to 5 PM daily.

Kendall-Jackson Winery
Wine Country Store
337 Healdsburg Ave., Healdsburg
• (707) 433-7102

The hugely successful Kendall-Jackson operation encompasses 14 wineries owned by proprietor Jess Jackson and his family. The largest of these is Kendall-Jackson itself. The company lists the 13 others under the heading "Artisans and Estates": Cambria, Edmeades, Camelot, Cardinale, Stonestreet, Vina Calina (Chile), Calina (Chile), Mariposa (Argentina), La Crema, Robert Pepi, Lakewood, Hartford Court and Kristone.

To learn more about each winery and the wide span of varietals Kendall-Jackson produces, the Healdsburg store is a virtual command central. Once you've arrived in Healdsburg, the friendly folks at the K-J store will be happy to direct you to one or both of their other locations: Kendall-Jackson Wine Center, 5007 Fulton Road, Fulton, (707) 571-8100; and Cardinale Winery, 7600 St. Helena Highway, Oakville, (707) 945-1391.

The K-J Wine Country Store is open daily for complimentary tastings from 10 AM to 4:30 PM. The Wine Center, where tastings also are free, is open daily from 10 AM to 5 PM.

Mill Creek Vineyards
1401 Westside Rd., Healdsburg
• (707) 431-2121

Beautifully landscaped, the winery is on a knoll above the vineyard, which has been operated since 1975 by the Kreck family. The tasting room, complete with working waterwheel and a mill pond, is in an air-conditioned two-story redwood building. The bar top, trusses and beams are all made from one redwood tree from the Kreck ranch on Mill Creek Road. A 3,000-square-foot picnic deck overlooks the Dry Creek Valley, Fitch Mountain and Mt. St. Helena. It is occasionally used for company picnics or seminars. Winery hours are 10 AM to 5 PM daily, and tastings are complimentary.

Rabbit Ridge Vineyards
3291 Westside Rd., Healdsburg
• (707) 431-7128

The vineyards occupy 45 acres of hillside, with the winery buildings at the top of Rabbit Ridge. The operation was literally built from the ground up by Erich Russel, a teacher who spent a summer working at Chateau St. Jean and decided that wine was the life for him. The tasting room is open and serving from a selection of 20 different wines (including Chardonnay, Sauvignon Blanc and Cabernet) each day from 11 AM to 4:30 PM.

Rodney Strong Vineyards
11455 Old Redwood Hwy., Healdsburg
• (707) 431-1533

In 1959, long before Sonoma County was

"discovered" as a premium grape-growing region, Rodney Strong began an exhaustive search for the very best vineyards. Ultimately, he selected several vineyards in the Chalk Hill, Alexander Valley and Russian River Valley appellations. The winery, a low-lying building with a roof spreading across it like the wings of a giant eagle, is situated among acres of prime vineyards. The winery's estate wines are named after the individual vineyards where the grapes grow—for example, the Charlotte Home, a Sauvignon Blanc, and Alexander's Crown, a Cabernet. Picnic areas are available. For special occasions there's a garden area adjacent to the vineyards (contact the vineyard for availability). Tours are conducted daily at 11 AM and 3 PM. Free tastings are offered from 10 AM to 5 PM daily.

Windsor Vineyards Tasting Room
308-B Center St., Healdsburg
• (707) 433-2822

The wines of Windsor Vineyards are sold direct to the consumer only. A tasting room has been established in Healdsburg. In 1959, Windsor was one of the first wineries to stake a claim to Sonoma County. Vineyards were set out in three valleys—Alexander, Dry Creek and Russian River.

Windsor offers a wide variety of wines that have brought home several awards. A novel promotional idea is to label bottles with a special personalized message or logo. The tasting room, where samples are complimentary, is open Monday through Friday from 10 AM to 5 PM and 10 AM to 6 PM Saturday and Sunday.

Dry Creek Vineyard
3770 Lambert Bridge Rd., Healdsburg
• (707) 433-1000

Dry Creek Winery started in 1972 when ex-Bostonian David Stare began turning an old prune orchard into an award-winning winery. A trip he took to France in 1970 apparently inspired him to leave Boston and head for the University of California at Davis, where he studied viticulture and enology. Stare's was the first new winery in Sonoma County's Dry Creek Valley since the days of Prohibition, and it led to a dramatic wave of change in this long-neglected grape-growing region.

Stare now owns 135 acres of vineyards and also buys grapes from local growers to produce Fume Blanc, Chenin Blanc, Cabernet Sauvignon and other wines, including his estate-bottled Meritage (a Bordeaux blend). The gray stone winery he built resembles a French country wine chateau. The tasting room, voted among the top 10 in Sonoma County by *Sonoma Business*, is casual and informal. When the weather turns cool in October, there's a warm fireplace. When the sun spreads warm yellow patches on the lawn, a picnic lunch in the gardens is a perfect idea.

The tasting room, where samples are complimentary, is open daily from 10:30 AM to 4:30 PM. The first weekend of June marks Dry Creek's annual open house.

Ferrari-Carrano Vineyard & Winery
8761 Dry Creek Rd., Healdsburg
• (707) 433-6700

The Wine Shop at Villa Fiore (the name of the chateau of sorts that houses the Ferrari-Carrano operation) is one of California's friendliest and most enchanting wine country destinations. Visitors will discover magnificent gardens, critically acclaimed wines and unique gifts. They will also be impressed by the spectacular underground barrel cellar where the wines of Don and Rhonda Carrano age. Among the wines poured at the Wine Shop are Fume Blanc, Chardonnay, Merlot and a late harvest dessert wine called Eldorado Gold. Wine tastings cost $2.50 (refundable with the purchase of wine) and are offered daily from 10 AM to 5 PM.

Lake Sonoma Winery
9990 Dry Creek Rd., Geyserville
• (707) 431-1550

The newest member of the Korbel family (obtained in 1996), Lake Sonoma Winery is notable for its breathtaking view of Dry Creek Valley and Warm Springs Dam. Gourmet picnic fare is available in the deli and can be enjoyed on the wooded picnic grounds with a bottle of Chardonnay, Cabernet, Zinfandel or Cinsault. The winery is adjacent to Lake Sonoma Recreation Area and is open daily from 10 AM to 5 PM. Tastings are complimentary.

Lambert Bridge Winery
4085 W. Dry Creek Rd., Healdsburg
• (707) 431-9600

Established in 1975, the winery takes its name from a neighboring landmark that spans Dry Creek. Beyond connecting the east and west side roads of the valley, this one-lane trestle bridge serves as a connection to Dry Creek Valley's pastoral past. Many of the wines of this small, high-quality winery are available only in the charming tasting room, where the wine-stained tasting bar was made from oak casks. Is the weather chilly? A crackling fireplace cheers frosty days. Sunny? Lambert Bridge's picnic grounds may be the most elegant in Dry Valley. Gourmet mustards are available to go with the winery's wines, which include Fume Blanc, Pinot Noir and Zinfandel. The winery, with complimentary samplings, is open daily from 10:30 AM to 4:30 PM.

Pezzi King Vineyards
3805 Lambert Bridge Rd., Healdsburg
• (707) 431-9388

This recent entry is committed to the natural farming of premium hillside vineyards in the scenic Dry Creek Valley across from Dry Creek Vineyard (see previous listing). Six picnic pavilions with redwood trees for shade offer panoramic views of Dry Creek Valley. The James Rowe family released its first Zinfandel and Cabernet Sauvignon in March 1996, and they also produce a fine Chardonnay. The tasting room, where samples are complimentary (except for a $2 reserve taste), is open daily from 10 AM to 4:30 PM.

Preston Vineyards
9282 W. Dry Creek Rd., Healdsburg
• (707) 433-3372

According to the folks at family-owned Preston Winery, "Having fun is no scandal." They take pride in being known as the alternative winery: the place to go when you want something different—and delicious. You can not only taste some unusual wines, but also enjoy some fresh bread baked in the forno and picnic among flowers, herbs, vegetable gardens and olive trees. If that's not enough fun, you can play a game of bocce ball on the house courts.

Preston is slightly off the beaten path, but with so much going for it, the adventure is worth it. The 115 acres of grapes are grown without insecticides and produce quirky wines such as Beaujolais, Viognier, Moscato Curioso and Marsanne. You can sample them free in the tasting room, which is open (along with the bocce courts) from 11 AM to 4:30 PM daily.

Quivira Vineyards
4900 W. Dry Creek Rd., Healdsburg
• (707) 431-8333

For centuries, European explorers searched for the legendary New World land called Quivira. It was thought to be on the Pacific Coast in the region now known as Sonoma County. Three centuries ago European mapmakers placed it just about where the Quivira Winery is located now. Whatever else you find out here about the legends of Quivira, you will also encounter some excellent Sauvignon Blanc, Zinfandel and a Rhone-style

blend. The tasting room (samples are complimentary) is open daily from 11 AM to 5 PM. Picnic grounds offer a splendid view of Dry Creek Valley.

Clos du Bois
19410 Geyserville Ave., Geyserville
• (707) 857-3100

This is one of Sonoma County's most honored wineries. They have access to some 1,000 prime acres in Alexander and Dry Creek valleys, from which they produce Sauvignon Blanc, Chardonnay, Gewurztraminer, Pinot Noir, Merlot, Zinfandel and Cabernet Sauvignon. With such a roster, it's remarkable that they seem to do all of them well, some superbly. In addition, they produce an exceptional Winemaker's Reserve Cabernet Sauvignon, and their reserve Chardonnay from the Flintwood vineyard is impressive.

One aspect of the Clos du Bois tasting room that is appreciated by all is the extremely knowledgeable and friendly staff, who pour a wide variety of wines daily. If you're a neophyte and it shows, they will never blink an eye but patiently offer you their expertise. Tastings are offered from 10 AM to 4:30 PM daily.

Canyon Road Winery
19550 Geyserville Ave., Geyserville
• (707) 857-3417

A warm and friendly tasting room serves Canyon Road's Cabernet Sauvignon, Sauvignon Blanc and Chardonnay, as well as wines of the Venezia and Nervo labels. A country deli and gift shop encourages the idea of a picnic shared with a bottle of Canyon Road wine.

A novel idea that could prove interesting is the Roadies Club, which uses a newsletter to advise of opportunities to join in the autumn crush and do a little grape stomping. Other benefits of Roadie membership include a seminar on wines in the spring, a chance to visit with the winemaker and an opportunity to receive shipments of select wines at discount prices. Samples are complimentary, and the tasting room is open daily from 10 AM to 5 PM.

Chateau Souverain
Independence Ln. at U.S. Hwy. 101,
Geyserville • (707) 433-8281

This architecturally striking winery is one of the few with a restaurant—The Cafe, which is open daily for lunch and Friday, Saturday and Sunday for dinner. (Call 707-433-3141 for reservations.) See listing for "Chateau Souverain, The Cafe at the Winery" in the Sonoma

Roederer Estate ages its best wines in 1,100-gallon casks that are hand-carved and made from fine-grained Center-of-France oak.

County section of our Restaurants chapter for more information.) Award-winning wines are offered for sampling in Chateau Souverain's "room with a view." Cabernet Sauvignon, Merlot, Zinfandel, Pinot Noir and Sauvignon Blanc are produced from selected vineyards within the Alexander Valley, Dry Creek and Carneros appellations. The tasting room is open daily from 10 AM to 5 PM.

Fieldstone Winery
10075 Calif. Hwy. 128, east of Healdsburg
• (707) 433-7266

Eleven miles east of Healdsburg in the Alexander Valley, a unique winery structure built underground (using native stone from the surrounding fields) is surrounded by the family's 40-acre estate. Beautiful picnic grounds under spreading oaks are the setting for sum-

mer events, including concerts, Shakespearean plays and dinners. The estate-bottled wines include Cabernet Sauvignon, Merlot and Petite Sirah plus three stylish whites—Sauvignon Blanc, Chardonnay and Gewurztraminer. Picnic facilities are available, and complimentary tasting hours are 10 AM to 5 PM daily.

Geyser Peak Winery
22281 Chianti Rd., Geyserville
• (707) 857-9400, (800) 255-WINE

One of the fastest-growing wineries in Sonoma County, Geyser Peak dates back to 1880 but is presently owned by the Trione family of Santa Rosa. With sales of its wines zooming in the United States, the company also distributes in Switzerland, Germany and Hong Kong. Food and a lovely picnic area overlooking Alexander Valley are available, and hikers will find two hiking trails—the Panoramic Trail, winding up behind the winery; and the Margot Patterson Doss Trail, named for a well-known San Francisco walker and writer. Geyser Peak is known particularly for its Chardonnay.

Geyser Peak publishes an outstanding newsletter, available by writing the folks at P.O. Box 25, Geyserville 95441. You might also want to join The Cellar Door Club for discount opportunities on Geyser Peak wines and a chance to attend special events. Samples are complimentary (unless you want to pop $5 for the reserve wines), and tasting room hours are 10 AM to 5 PM daily.

Hanna Winery
9280 Calif. Hwy. 128, Healdsburg
• (707) 431-4310

Founded in 1985 by Dr. Elias S. Hanna, a Marin County surgeon, Hanna Winery now has two hospitality centers—one at 5353 Occidental Road in Santa Rosa and this newer one in Alexander Valley. This winery annually produces about 34,000 cases of Sauvignon Blanc, Chardonnay, Cabernet Sauvignon, Merlot and Pinot Noir. The patio of the new visitor center in Healdsburg is a lovely place for a picnic, with sweeping views of the Alexander Valley and Hanna's magnificent hillside vineyard. It's also a grand setting for weddings or corporate events. The tasting room (samples are complimentary) is open daily from 10 AM to 4 PM.

Johnson's Alexander Valley Wines
8333 Calif. Hwy. 128, Healdsburg
• (707) 433-2319

From time to time, the tasting room roars with the mighty sound of a 1924 theater pipe organ. Tom Johnson makes the wine; Jay Johnson repairs old organs. This is a small, family winery producing seven varietals (Zinfandel and Cabernet are two) from family vineyards, all sold only at the winery. Picnic tables are available, and you may enjoy an informal tour hosted by a member of the Johnson family. Special events are scheduled periodically; if you wish to know about them, contact the winery and ask to be placed on the mailing list for winery news. The tasting room is open daily from 10 AM to 5 PM.

Pedroncelli Winery
1220 Canyon Rd., Geyserville
• (707) 857-3531

The charmingly rustic J. Pedroncelli Winery, tucked 2 miles up Canyon Road from U.S. 101, was born in 1927, when John Pedroncelli, a native of Lombardy, Italy, bought the vineyard property, which was planted in 1904. During Prohibition, the winery sold grapes to home winemakers; after the repeal, it sold wine in bulk to other wineries. Today, Pedroncelli is run by John's sons, John and James, using grapes harvested from the Dry Creek Valley to produce excellent Cabernet, Zinfandel and Pinot Noir wines. Picnic tables invite a pleasant lunch. Ask about getting on the winery's mailing list for its newsletter. The tasting room, where samples are free, is open daily from 10 AM to 4:30 PM.

Simi Winery
16275 Healdsburg Ave., Healdsburg
• (707) 433-6981

In 1881 two Italian immigrant brothers, Guiseppe and Pietro Simi, bought a winery near the grain depot in Healdsburg for $2,250 in gold coins. With more business than they could handle, they built a magnificent, hand-hewn stone winery. Business doubled. Then, in the midst of success, both brothers died, and Guiseppe's teenage daughter Isabelle took over. Prohibition was a blow for her, but when it ended, she had one of the winery's enormous redwood tanks rolled outside and created a retail tasting room. Until she was in her late 80s, Isabelle could be found there, still selling Simi wines.

Simi is now owned by the French company Moet-Hennessy, which has turned Simi's distinctive wines into part of a winemaking estate of worldwide recognition. There's a picnic area, and samples of the winery's complex, intensely flavored wines are available in the tasting room from 10 AM to 4:30 PM daily. Tours, recognized as being among the industry's best, are conducted daily at 11 AM, 1 and 3 PM.

Trentadue Winery
19170 Geyersville Ave., Geyersville
• (707) 433-3104

Founded in 1969, family-owned and operated, Trentadue has achieved an outstanding reputation not only for rare and unusual wines, but also for highly regarded, better-known varieties. Visitors are offered complimentary tastings of the many varieties (including Petite Sirah, Cabernet and Sangiovese) and can spend time browsing through a fine collection of wine-related gifts, fine crystal and china personally selected by Evelyn Trentadue. A gourmet food shop can supply items to take to the picnic area. The tasting room is open daily from 11 AM to 4:30 PM. Trentadue has a second retail outlet at 320 Center Street in Healdsburg.

West County/Russian River

Mark West Vineyards & Winery
7010 Trenton-Healdsburg Rd., Forestville
• **(707) 836-9647**

Named after British mariner and adventurer Marcus West, Mark West Vineyards encompasses 120 acres on a portion of the former San Miguel Rancho Spanish Land Grant in the Russian River Valley appellation. Cradled between the Mayacamas Mountains and the Pacific Ocean in a valley of rolling hills, the area is well-suited to growing Chardonnay, Gewurztraminer, Pinot Noir and Merlot grapes. Aside from the tasting room, where sips are complimentary, you will find tree-shaded picnic grounds, an espresso bar, a gift shop and the largest private collection of insect-eating plants in the United States. The tasting room is open Thursday through Sunday from 11 AM to 4:30 PM.

Topolos at Russian River Vineyards, Winery & Restaurant
5700 Gravenstein Hwy., Forestville
• **(707) 887-1575 (winery),**
• **(707) 887-1562 (restaurant)**

This small, family-owned winery, established in 1963, is immediately recognizable amid the Forestville landscape because of its unique architecture. Its unusual design was inspired by the historical presence of hop kilns in the area and by the Russian stockade at Fort Ross. Visitors can sample complimentary sips of Zinfandel, Chardonnay, Petite Sirah and Alicante Bouschet, and browse the gift shop. Greek cuisine is served at the adjoining restaurant, open for lunch and dinner. The tasting room is open daily from 11 AM to 5:30 PM.

Korbel Champagne Cellars
13250 River Rd., Guerneville
• **(707) 824-7000**

When the three Korbel brothers emigrated from Bohemia, they settled in a redwood forest along the Russian River, tried several different enterprises and finally settled on winemaking. The handsome, brick winery was built in 1886, and the story behind the quaint turreted tower at the south end is a romantic one. Before leaving Prague, the youngest Korbel inadvertently fired his pistola in the midst of the townfolk who had gathered to hear the news called out by the town crier. He was jailed briefly, and upon his release the three brothers fled the country. The tower of the winery is a sentimental duplicate of the jail where young Joseph spent his last days in his home country.

Korbel has an excellent program that includes a complete tour of both the champagne cellars and the antique rose garden that surrounds the old summer house. Visitors see how champagne is made and peruse a fascinating collection of old winemaking tools. Korbel California Champagne is produced in the *methode champenoise*, the traditional French method in which the second fermentation takes place in the same bottle. Complimentary tastings are offered daily from 9 AM to 4:30 PM, tours on the hour from 10 AM to 3 PM.

Mendocino County

The wineries of Anderson Valley are clustered along a 6-mile stretch of Calif. 128 near Philo. Morning fog off the Pacific, afternoon breezes and hillside vineyards make Anderson Valley a special place to grow cool-climate wine grapes, notably Pinot Noir, Chardonnay and Gewurztraminer.

Farther north along U.S. 101, the Ukiah Valley is where the county's grape-growing began. Today it's where some of Mendocino's oldest and largest vintners make their home.

U.S. Highway 101

Fetzer Vineyards
Calif. Hwy. 175 and East Side Rd., Hopland
• **(707) 744-1737**

Bernard Fetzer, a lumber executive, purchased the winery's Redwood Valley Home Ranch in 1958 as a place to raise his large family and grow fine grapes for home winemakers. The family began making wine commercially in 1968. In 1981, Fetzer's 11 children took over and helped the winery grow into one of the leading varietal wine producers in the world. Fetzer wines are well-made and almost always reasonably priced; the family has worked hard to keep that image while earning critical praise and tons of gold medals, especially for their Chardonnay.

The tasting room and visitors center features intimate vineyard and garden tours and offers tastings of new releases as well as older wines. A full-service deli with a spacious picnic area is also open to the public. The 50-acre Valley Oaks Ranch is home to vineyards, dozens of old barns, a dining pavilion overlooking Lake Fume and the 5-acre Bantera Garden. All grapes and plants are grown organically, without use of pesticides or synthetic fertilizers. Also on the property is a charming seven-room bed and breakfast inn (see our Bed and Breakfast Inns chapter). In 1982 Brown-Forman purchased the Fetzer label as well as the Hopland winery. The Fetzer family continues to grow grapes for Fetzer Vineyards under an exclusive contract. The tasting room is open from 10 AM to 6 PM daily. There is a $4 tasting fee, which includes four tastes and your choice of a commemorative Fetzer wine glass or a purchase discount.

Jepson Vineyards
10400 S. U.S. Hwy. 101, Ukiah
• (707) 468-8936

In addition to producing Chardonnay and Sauvignon Blanc, Bob and Alice Jepson, along with winemaker Kurt Lorenzi, have created a special niche by producing alambic pot still brandy, estate-grown and bottled. In fall 1996, Jepson also released its first red wine, a Pinot Noir produced from select Sonoma County vineyards. The winery's tasting room, where sips of a generous 8 to 10 wines are complimentary, is open every day from 10 AM to 5 PM.

Milano Winery
14594 S. U.S. Hwy. 101, Hopland
• (707) 744-1396

In the early 1900s, Vincenzo Milone came to Mendocino County with his father, discovered some agriculturally rich land near Hopland and planted grapes. They also built a hop kiln at the foot of Duncan's Peak, near their home. Today that hop kiln is the tasting room for Milano Winery—a name coined from the two current owners, MIL-one and Grazi-ANO. The kiln is one of the few left over from the days when the nearby village of Hopland was earning its name growing and curing hops. The tasting room is open from 10 AM to 5 PM daily.

Dunnewood Vineyards and Winery
2399 N. State St., Ukiah
• (707) 462-2987

The affirmed goal at Dunnewood is to make premium California wines and sell them at very reasonable prices. Winemaker George Phelan calls on a depth of resources (Dunnewood is owned by Canandaigiua Wine Company) to make wines using techniques usually reserved for vintages costing two to four times as much as the $6 to $8 range where consumers find Dunnewood. The winery is noted for its Merlot, Cabernet Sauvignon and Chardonnay.

Committed to educating consumers about food and wine pairings, Dunnewood has instituted a couple of unique aids. One you can take to the restaurant with you is a clever pocket sommelier that will advise you instantly what wine you should order to complement your poultry, fish, pasta or beef dinner. Another of their educational aids is for home use. Peel back the Dunnewood label to reveal a recipe for use with that particular wine. The tasting room staff is super-friendly, offering complimentary samples from 10 AM to 5 PM daily. Stop by the gift shop or have a picnic.

Parducci Wine Cellars
501 Parducci Rd., Ukiah
• (707) 462-9463

Since 1932, Parducci Wine Cellars has made wine according to a simple philosophy: Wine is an honest, natural product that should never be over-processed, never be masked by too much oak and never have its essential flavor and aroma filtered away. Parducci is Mendocino's oldest operating winery, but is dedicated to contemporary consumers, using modern winemaking techniques and evolving wine styles. Parducci's conviction is that whites should be fermented cold and bottled cold to retain the liveliness, crispness and freshness of the varietals that make up the wine. Served cold, Parducci white wines show a slight spritz from carbon dioxide, a natural retainer of the varietal flavors for which Parducci wines are famous. The tasting room is open Monday through Saturday (except major holidays) between 10 AM and 5 PM, and Sunday 10 AM and 4 PM.

Redwood Valley Cellars
7051 N. State St., off U.S. Hwy. 101, Redwood Valley • (707) 485-0322

This is actually a tasting room for Barren-Pauli Winery in Petaluma. Redwood Valley Cellars also produces wine from grapes grown in Potter Valley. Located between Ukiah and Willits, at the West Road exit off U.S. 101, Redwood Valley Cellars offers tastings and picnicking daily from 9 AM to 5 PM.

Calif. Highway 128

Greenwood Ridge Vineyards
5501 Calif. Hwy. 128, Philo
• (707) 895-2002

Allan Green, a graphic artist turned winemaker, has crafted in the cool climate of Anderson Valley a lovely winery and tasting room with a wraparound deck and a view of the hilltop ridge where his vines grow. On one wall of the tasting room are the ribbons he has been awarded for the excellence of his wines—White Riesling, Late Harvest Riesling, Sauvignon Blanc, Chardonnay, Zinfandel, Pinot Noir, Merlot and

Cabernet Sauvignon. Three Greenwood wines have been included in the *Wine Spectator's* annual list of the "Top 100 Wines of the World." In another corner of the tasting room (samples are complimentary, by the way), you'll see Green's collection of 5,000 wine corks, arranged innovatively into a sculpture. On a sunny day, it's pleasant to sit on the deck of the tasting room, which is open daily from 9 AM to 6 PM in summer and 9 AM to 5 PM in winter.

Handley Cellars
3151 Calif. Hwy. 128, Philo
• (707) 895-3876

Fermentation science is a natural interest for Milla Handley, the winemaker and owner who is the great-great-granddaughter of brewing giant Henry Weinhard. After receiving her degree in enology and working six years in the wine industry, she and her husband, Rex, founded Handley Cellars in the basement of their home near Philo. Today's tasting room is a far cry from that basement winery. As visitors sip wine they are surrounded by the Handley family's collection of folk art from around the world. In fact, Milla's interest in the folk art of North Africa, Thailand and India has led her to instigate a monthly culinary adventure, asking visitors to taste the featured ethnic food of the month with different wines. Lucky participants get to decide which is best, then take home recipes such as cilantro pesto.

Located 6 miles northwest of Philo, the tasting room offers complimentary samples of their unusual Pinot Menieur, as well as an excellent Pinot Noir. It is open daily from 11 AM to 6 PM in summer and 11 AM to 5 PM in winter. There is an inviting garden courtyard for picnics.

Husch Vineyards
4400 Calif. Hwy. 128,
Philo • (707) 895-3216

Farming has been the occupation for three generations of the Oswald family, owners of Husch Vineyards. Theirs is the oldest winery in Anderson Valley and still contains some of its first varietal plantings. Originally planted in 1969 and bonded in 1971 by the Husches, it was purchased by the Oswalds in 1979. Currently, three members of the Oswald family are involved in the winery: Hugo, Miles and Ken. All Husch wines are made from grapes grown only on the family-owned vineyards, including the original 21-acre block of Pinot Noir, Gewurztraminer and Chardonnay. The tasting room is rustic, friendly and open daily for complimentary samples from 10 AM to 6 PM in summer and 10 AM to 5 PM in winter.

Navarro Vineyards
5601 Calif. Hwy. 128, Philo
• (707) 895-3686

Ted Bennett has been making Anderson Valley Gewurztraminer since 1973, and over the years he has developed a successful formula for this grape, which requires a long growing season. His wife, Deborah, serves guests in the tasting rooms. "We're not a big corporate winery," she says. "We're the '70s homesteaders who happened to like wine." Navarro Vineyards seeks to make a fine wine but doesn't forget about "the guy in a camper van with three kids who just wants to enjoy a bottle," says winemaker Jim Klein, whose efforts produce 30,000 cases a year. The tasting room offers complimentary sips daily from 10 AM to 6 PM in summer, 10 AM to 5 PM in winter.

Scharffenberger Cellars
8501 Calif. Hwy. 128, Philo
• (707) 895-2065

In the scenic setting of Anderson Valley—dotted with rural hamlets, blessed with an abundance of organic produce, refuge to talented artists—Scharffenberger seems right at home. They were pioneers in the production of premium sparkling wine in this valley and have established a reputation for excellence. Scharffenberger wines were served by President Reagan when he was in the White House. Scharffenberger Cremant was selected for the 1988 Moscow Summit because the Soviets preferred a slightly sweeter sparkling wine. The winery stages a monthly art show—if you get in touch with them, they'll keep you posted. The tasting room is open daily from 11 AM to 5 PM. There's a $3 fee for sampling Scharffen-berger, but one fee is waived with each bottle purchased.

Roederer Estate
4501 Calif. Hwy. 128, Philo
• (707) 895-2288

The wines created by the European firm

INSIDERS' TIP

On the walls of Sam Sebastiani's office at Viansa Winery hangs his philosophy: "I was not delivered into this world in defeat, nor does failure course in my veins. I am not a sheep . . . I am an eagle and I refuse to walk with the sheep. The slaughterhouse of failure is not my destiny. I will persist until I succeed."

headed by Madame Orly-Roederer have been world-famous for 200 years. Now they are being produced in Mendocino's Anderson Valley under the direction of her grandson, Jean-Claude Rouzard, who came to Anderson Valley in 1981 in search of the perfect vineyard land. To create the perfect wine, Roederer uses only the first juice, pressed from the pulp with minimal skin contact. Subsequent pressings are not used, and even the first pressing is further critiqued, with 30 percent later discarded to be faithful to the Roederer style.

Roederer Estate winery is open every day from 11 AM to 5 PM. A $3 sampling fee is charged but is deducted from each bottle of wine purchased.

Yorkville Vineyards & Cellars
Calif. Hwy. 128 at Mile Marker 40.4, Yorkville • (707) 894-9177

The 30-acre vineyard owned by the Wallo family lies at 1,000 feet above sea level, where sun-filled days and cool nights combine to create premium-quality grapes. Since its establishment in 1982, the Yorkville Vineyards estate has been farmed organically. Instead of pesticides and herbicides, they count on seasonal cover to serve as an alternative for insects to attack instead of the vine. The cover also provides a host environment for beneficial insects that prey on unwelcome ones. Yorkville Vineyards has been certified organic by the state of California every year since 1986. Yorkville grows seven Bordeaux varietals and makes at least one unusual wine—Eleanor of Aquitaine, a half-and-half blend of Sauvignon Blanc and Semillon, aged in French oak barrels only. Picnics are encouraged, and complimentary tastings are offered from 11 AM to 6 PM daily in summer, 11 AM to 5 PM daily in winter (call in advance in winter).

Lake County

Guenoc and Langtry Estate
21000 Butts Canyon Rd., Middletown • (707) 987-9127

Whose charming countenance is that you see gracing bottles of Guenoc wine? It's Lillie Langtry—the "Jersey Lily," beloved stage actress of the late 19th century (see our History chapter). Langtry ran the business from 1888 to 1906, and her palatial home is still the centerpiece of the property. The 400 acres of vineyard sit on the border of Napa and Lake counties in Guenoc Valley, the only federally approved appellation un-

der single proprietorship. Grower Orville Magoon helps produce a wide range of wines, from Chardonnay and Cabernet Sauvignon to Petite Sirah and even the occasional Port. There is no charge for tasting, though you can opt to pay $4 for a selection of reserve wines. Tours are by appointment, though you can take a self-guided tour of the grounds anytime. Hours are 11:30 AM to 5 PM daily.

Ployez Winery
11171 S. Calif. 29, Lower Lake • (707) 994-2106

You probably thought the only thing French in Lake County was the fries at Burger King, but along comes Gerald Ployez, a fourth generation winemaker from Champagne whose east-of-the-Atlantic family still bottles under the Ployez-Jacquemari label. Gerald and his wife, Shirley, opened this winery in September, 1997. Gerald concentrates mostly on Chardonnay and Sauvignon Blanc, though he produces three types of red, too. He also makes Lake County's only sparkling wine, a Brut. Over the next two to four years, the couple plans to plant about 23 acres around the winery in Chardonnay and Cabernet Sauvignon. Ployez is open daily from Memorial Day weekend through October, and Thursday through Sunday in the low season; the hours are always 11 AM to 5 PM, though they are experimenting with a 9 PM closing time on Fridays. Tours are by appointment, and there is no charge for tasting.

Wildhurst Vineyards
3855 Main St., Kelseyville • (707) 279-4302, (800) 595-9463

When Myron and Marilyn Holdenried started this winery in 1991, it was really just a case of diversification: Myron is a fifth-generation Kelseyville farmer. In fact, he had already been growing grapes for 25 years. Wildhurst started at the site of the old Steurmer Winery in Lower Lake, then moved to Kelseyville in 1996; a year later it unveiled its tasting room in a refurbished I.O.O.F. Hall. (The winery is two miles away, and not open to the public.) Wildhurst is primarily noted for its Merlot, but makes three other reds and a couple of whites, all under the Clear Lake appellation. Myron still sells grapes to Beringer, Kendall-Jackson and Fetzer, but the top 25 percent of his crop is crushed for Wildhurst. The facility is open from 10 AM to 5 PM daily in the summer (May 1 through January 1), and Wednesday through Sunday from noon to 5 PM in the winter. Tours are by appointment, and there is no tasting fee.

Steele Wines
4350 Thomas Dr., Kelseyville
• **(707) 279-9475**

Kendall-Jackson was the pride of Lake County until it "went Sonoma" a couple of years ago. But Lake still can brag of its hold upon one of the men who nurtured that winery to prominence: Jed Steele. The former winemaker at K-J produced his first self-named vintage in 1991 and is going strong in the building formerly occupied by Konocti Winery. Jed dabbles in a number of varietals, but generally sticks to Chardonnay, Pinot Noir and Zinfandel, with grapes from as far south as Santa Barbara County and as far north as Mendocino. Steele is open Monday through Saturday from 11 AM to 5 PM, May through October; it's closed during the winter. There is a $1 charge for tasting, and you are encouraged to enjoy a picnic lunch among the lush gardens. You also might stumble upon a farmer's market if you arrive Saturday morning, or the Harvest Festival (see our Festivals and Annual Events chapter) if you get there on the second weekend of October.

Wine Shops

As you would expect, they don't just make 'em, pour 'em and sell 'em in the Wine Country, there are also a variety of stores dedicated to the display, presentation, storage and properly outfitted enjoyment of wines. In addition, some shops offer amazing selections of wines from our four-county coverage area and beyond, along with all the decadent accouterments. So light up that fat, pricey cigar and take a look at a few of our favorite wine shops.

Napa County

The Vintage 1870 Wine Cellar
6525 Washington St., Yountville
• **(707) 944-9070, (800) WINE-4-US**

Ironic that the stables of the old Groezinger Winery would end up as the one piece of the property expressly devoted to wine. Unlike most wine shops, this one is licensed for tastings—they pour about a dozen selections, all day long. On the shelves you'll find everything from $5 bottles to an imperial of Mondavi 1978 Reserve Cabernet Sauvignon that goes for $1,000. The Cellar also sells a few cigars.

St. Helena Wine Merchants
699 St. Helena Hwy. S., St. Helena
• **(707) 963-7888, (800) 729-9463**

Across the road from V. Sattui Winery is this unpretentious purveyor of wines. The Merchants aim to carry the sort of small-availability labels that out-of-state visitors read about, but can't find at home—Harlan, Dominus and Maya come to mind as examples. Don't be surprised if you bump into a local winemaker or two during your visit.

Dean & DeLuca
607 St. Helena Hwy. S., St. Helena
• **(877) DEAN-WIN(E)**

When those classy New Yorkers set up shop in Wine Country (see our Shopping chapter), it changed the face of retail wine sales in Napa Valley. D&D has the most extensive collection of California wines you could ever hope to see: 1,200 labels, and that's just 750-milliliter bottles. The wines are arranged alphabetically within varietal categories. Forget about trying to note every wine; by the time you make it to the last Zinfandel, they probably will have added a few more bottles. "We try for the newest, the latest, the hottest, the best," says John Hardisty, who manages the wine section. Rarely does Dean & DeLuca fall short of its goals.

Calistoga Wine Stop
1458 Lincoln Ave., No. 2, Calistoga
• **(707) 942-5556, (800) 648-4521**

Before you even get to the wine, there's a lot of history worth noting here. The Wine Stop is in The Depot, that big yellow wood building that was what it claims to be. Built in 1868, it's the second-oldest train station left in California (though no trains have stopped here since 1963). The wine shop itself is jammed inside a 19th-century boxcar, which limits the elbow room but somehow doesn't impair the Napa-Sonoma-concentrated selection. (Owner Tom Pelter estimates that 75 percent of his stock is made in those two counties.) Pelter is a bundle of help, whether you're selecting or trying to get it home. He's also something of a Port aficionado, which explains the high density of Portugal's fortified wine in his store.

Enoteca Wine Shop
1345 Lincoln Ave., Calistoga
• **(707) 942-1117**

Discreetly cached on the second floor of Calistoga's 111-year-old I.O.O.F. building is this classy wine shop. ("Enoteca" is an Italian word meaning "wine cellar" or "wine library.") Proprietor Margaux Singleton learned the trade while purchasing wine for such respected establishments as La Casa Sena Wine Shop in Santa Fe and All Seasons Cafe in Calistoga, and she has been accepted to enter the arduous Master of Wine program, headquartered in England. She and co-owner Frederick Schrader taste every wine before stocking it (no, they're not looking for assistants). They tend toward artisanal vintners who produce hundreds of cases rather than tens of thousands. And they draw from all over the world, as evidenced by their affection for the likes of Chateau Musar in Lebanon.

Sonoma County

The Wine Exchange of Sonoma
452 First St. East, Sonoma
• **(707) 938-1794, (800) 938-1794**

Looking for a more efficient way to sample local wines than driving from one place to another? Interested in a place that carries hard-to-find wines and will even ship them anywhere allowed by law? The Wine Exchange is the place for you, with some 800 premium wines and 280 beers in stock. It's opposite the Sonoma Plaza, with a tasting bar that features 18 wines and six draft beers. The store is open from 10 AM to 6 PM Monday through Saturday, and 11 AM to 6 PM on Sunday.

The Wine Rack Shop
536 Broadway, Sonoma
• **(707) 996-3497**

For wine enthusiasts who believe in giving their bottled treasures the very best care—or those who simply like to own wine accessories—this is a place to spend some happy time browsing and buying. You'll find every form of wine rack imaginable plus such niceties as cork pullers, chilling cabinets, glasses and stemware in every shape and size, stacks and bins, and wine accessories you never dreamed existed but will be glad to find out about. If you're uncertain how to best care for your wines, owner Dan Whetstone will give plenty of helpful advice; he has served as cellarmaster for Gallo, Beringer and Sebastiani. So it's not surprising to learn that in recent years, Dan has specialized in custom wine cellars. The shop is open 10 AM to 6 PM every day.

Taylor & Norton Wine Merchants
19210 Sonoma Hwy., Sonoma
• **(707) 939-6611**

You'll have no trouble finding every local and regional wine you've been looking for in this wine shop. More than that, Taylor & Norton carries wines from other U.S. areas (some not so easy to locate in this heavily promoted wine region), as well as wines from Europe and other foreign wine-producing regions. Ask owner Gregory Taylor anything—he's a knowledgeable expert. While shopping for wine, you might want to browse through a handsome selection of antique wine decanters and glasses, some from the Victorian era. They're pricey, but so beautiful you may not be able to resist taking home a souvenir. The store is open 10 AM to 6 PM Monday through Saturday.

Attractions

LOOK FOR:
• Napa County
• Sonoma County
• Mendocino County
• Lake County

Attractions? We don't need attractions. We're the California Wine Country, for crying out loud. Pardon the attitude, but people here figure we'll do just fine without any roadside dinosaurs. Anyway, what are winery tours, tasting rooms, glorious state parks, volcanic mud baths and world-class restaurants if not attractions?

All those selling points are detailed in other chapters. In this chapter, you'll find everything worth visiting that defies categorical lumping. That might be a culturally rich historical site (such as Fort Ross), a museum (such as the Napa Firefighters Museum), a scenic jaunt (such as the Skunk Train) or even a good old-fashioned bit of hokum (such as the Old Faithful Geyser). We also have included separate sections on spas, balloon and glider rides, and guided tours that range from quirky to luxurious.

Lastly, let us point out the complete absence of anything approaching a major amusement park in the four-county area. We suppose there are those who would consider such a dearth a major shortcoming, but most residents and our regular visitors would fight a Rollercoaster World tooth and nail if it reared its ugly head.

Napa County

Seguin Moreau Napa Cooperage
151 Camino Dorado, Napa
• (707) 252-3408

Ever wonder how they make the oak barrels used to age wine? Stop by this working cooperage south of Napa (across the span of the Butler Bridge) and see for yourself. Seguin Moreau allows self-guided tours. You will see the staves being arranged by hand, the barrels molded by fire and the metal bands hammered—just as they have been for centuries. Admission is free.

Hakusan Sake Gardens
1 Executive Way, Napa
• (707) 258-6160

We begin with kernels of high-grade Sacramento Valley rice, milled at the company's private mill in Williams, California. Hakusan is one of only seven sake makers in the United States, and the only one in Wine Country. Sake, while comparable to wine in body and complexity, actually is brewed, like beer. It therefore is made to be refrigerated and consumed within a year, not aged. Hakusan, at the intersection of California highways 29 and 12, is open from 10 AM to 5 PM every day. There are self-guided tours, and for $1 you can sample about five varieties, both hot and cold. The brewery's offerings include cooking sake and sweet plum sake.

RMS Distillery
1250 Cuttings Wharf Rd., Napa
• (707) 253-9055

Step inside the Barrel House of the former Alambic Distillery, where hundreds of casks of brandy lie aging. But don't linger unless you're looking for a good buzz; the scent is enough to curl your nose hairs. The distillery, the largest one of its kind in North America, was started as a joint venture of Remy Martin and Schramsberg Vineyards in 1982 (Schramsberg is no longer involved). They offer 40-minute tours from 10:30 AM to 4:15 PM, taking you into the Barrel House, the video and aroma room, and the Still House, where eight huge alambic stills, much like those used for centuries in Cognac, do their business. A variety of spirits may be purchased in the expanded retail room. Cuttings Wharf Road leaves Calif. Highway 12/121 about 1.3 miles west of Calif. 29.

Rivership Grand Romance
500 Main St., Napa
• (707) 256-3100, (800) 750-7501

Formerly known as the *Petaluma Queen*, the rivership *Grand Romance* now plies the Napa River between the Main Street Landing and the marshes south of town. The Mississippi-style sternwheeler is 122 feet long "and every inch a lady," the brochure says. *Grand Romance* has an observation deck at bow, a bar aft and two restaurants in between. You can sign up for a linen-and-china dinner, lunch or weekend champagne-brunch cruise (ranging from $34 to $49 per person), a sightseeing trip ($17 for adults, $10 for children) or late-night dance cruise on Friday or Saturday ($15). Most of the excursions last about two hours; reservations are required for all of them. *Grand Romance* can also be rented for charter cruises.

Napa Firefighters Museum
1201 Main St., Napa
• (707) 259-0609

We're not saying you should make an entire day of it, but the Firefighters Museum will give you a deeper appreciation of the folks that fight the flames. Inside you'll see a hand pumper and a steamer, hose carts, engines, ladder trucks, old fire equipment and uniforms and photos from many eras of puttin' out fires. There is no admission fee, and the museum is open 11 AM to 4 PM Wednesday through Sunday.

California Veterans Home
California Dr., Yountville
• (707) 944-4918

There is a museum in the old chapel of the Veterans Home. It features rotating displays of documents, photographs, models, uniforms and weapons from various eras of U.S. military history. Unfortunately, the museum is open only on Friday and Saturday, noon to 2 PM. However, just strolling around the manicured grounds of this Spanish Revival complex, much of which dates back to 1918, is a pleasure. The landscaping comprises a working horticultural exhibit, with dozens of trees and plants labeled. Look for the signs on Calif. 29 just south of Domaine Chandon.

Napa Valley Museum
55 Presidents Circle, Yountville
• (707) 944-0500

Looking like a Lexus in a parking lot full of Packards, the Napa Valley Museum opened to the public in 1998, on the site of the California Veterans Home in Yountville. A major capital project that was years in the planning, the non-profit museum celebrates the artistic, historical and cultural heritage of the valley. Its central, permanent exhibition is "California Wine: The Science of an Art." Using music, the spoken word and the power of technology (including 26 videodisc players and nine microcomputers), it effectively presents the winemaking process in near entirety.

Temporary exhibitions have included Gold Rush photography and a collection of 19th-Century prints by Andrew Jackson Grayson, a local bird artist of renown. The Napa Valley Museum is open Wednesday through Monday from 10 AM to 5 PM (until 8 PM on the first Thursday of the month). Admission is $4.50 for adults, $3.50 for students and seniors age 60 or older, and $2.50 for youth ages 7 to 17.

Silverado Museum
1490 Library Ln., St. Helena
• (707) 963-3757

A California museum devoted to a Scottish novelist might seem a bit weird, but, hey, Robert Louis Stevenson did help immortalize the area with his *The Silverado Squatters*. He also penned classics such as *Treasure Island, Dr. Jekyll and Mr. Hyde* and others you'll read all about at the museum. It has first editions, artifacts from the Stevenson home, personal letters and photographs, and a few original manuscripts (though most of those reside at Yale University). Silverado Musuem is closed Monday but open every other day from noon to 4 PM.

Bale Grist Mill State Historic Park
3369 Calif. Hwy. 29, St. Helena
• (707) 963-2236

This is a working reminder of the days when "milling" involved more than driving to Safeway for a bag of all-purpose flour. Dr. Edward Bale built the wood-framed mill in 1846, and it has been painstakingly refurbished. The park is open 10 AM to 5 PM daily, but the best times to visit are weekend days at 11:30 AM, 1, 2:30 and 3:30 PM. That's when the park cranks up the wooden, 36-foot water wheel and gets those original quartz stones to grinding wheat or corn. (The wheel has been undergoing extensive repairs and will not be operational until sometime in 2000.) Also displayed are artifacts such as 50-pound sacks of grist, worn millstones and the whisks used to clean them. Admission is $2 for adults, $1 for kids. From here you can hike to adjacent Bothe-Napa Valley State Park (see our Parks and Recreation chapter).

The Sharpsteen Museum
1311 Washington St., Calistoga
• (707) 942-5911

Photo: Lou Zauner

Christopher Prevost will take you on a high-flying ride at Aeroschellville.

If every small town in America had a museum as lively and authentic as the Sharpsteen, maybe we wouldn't be so ignorant of history. The museum was founded in the 1970s by Ben Sharpsteen, who produced such films as *Fantasia* and *Snow White* for Walt Disney. The crowning piece of his legacy is a 32-foot, scale-model diorama that lays out the grounds of Sam Brannan's Calistoga spa, circa 1860 (see our History chapter for more on Brannan). One of the original cottages from that spa serves as a museum annex.

The Sharpsteen also has a restored Bill (Finest Kind) Spiers stagecoach that once ran from Calistoga to Middletown, an exhibit on the local Wappo tribe, an interactive display on geothermal activity and a bunch more. The museum is open 10 AM to 4 PM daily from April through September and noon to 4 PM daily from October through March. There is no admission charge, thanks to the eager volunteer staff. They do, of course, accept donations.

Old Faithful Geyser of California
1299 Tubbs Ln., Calistoga
• (707) 942-6463

About every 40 minutes on the yearly average (depending on how much water is in the aquifer), the earth gurgles, puffs and blows a stream of boiling hot water 60 feet into the air off Tubbs Lane. Welcome to Calistoga's geyser, one of only three in world that can call themselves "Old Faithful" without shame. Both the visitors building and the private home on the property are heated entirely by thermal means. There is a working seismograph in the entryway (the geyser is said to predict earthquakes), and outside near the erupting pond,

for some reason, is a pen of Tennessee Fainting goats, a rare breed suffering from myatonia, which causes them to lock up and topple when startled. The Old Faithful complex is open from 9 AM to 6 PM daily in the warm months, 9 to 5 PM in the winter. Admission is $6 for adults, $5 for seniors and $2 for kids ages 6 through 12.

Sonoma County

Southern Sonoma

Depot Park Museum
270 First St. W., Sonoma
• (707) 938-1762

This is more than a museum; it's an authentic piece of Sonoma city's history. Originally the depot was on the downtown plaza, much to the chagrin of Sonomans, who felt the plaza had been turned into a railroad yard, turntable and all. After some pressure, the depot was moved in 1890 to its present site, where Northwest Pacific operated until it went out of business, and the city bought the property. It was gradually sinking into oblivion when the Sonoma County Historical Society took over the depot in 1976. But while the society was setting about restoring it, the depot burned. By 1978 it had been rebuilt, and the museum now houses a terrific collection of historic memorabilia focusing on the 19th century. Several rooms are furnished in Victorian style, and a good deal of emphasis is placed on the life of General Mariano Vallejo (see our History chapter). Pioneer artifacts and exhibits of Native American culture are nicely displayed. Temporary exhibits shed light on specific historical periods, crafts and events. The museum is open Wednesday through Sunday from 1 to 4:30 PM. There's no admission, but donations are welcome.

Train Town
20264 Broadway, Sonoma
• **(707) 938-3912**

Train Town is the most well-developed scale railroad in America—a joy for anyone of any age. It is just plain, clean fun for old and young. You climb into a miniature train, one-fourth the normal size, and chug your way through 10 acres of planned landscaped park filled with thousands of native trees, animals, bridges over lakes, tunnels, waterfalls and replicas of historic buildings. Two miniature steam engines (on weekends; during the week it's likely to be diesel) and handcrafted railroad cars take passengers on the 20-minute ride to Lakeville, a pint-sized, Western-flavored hamlet populated with geese and ducks. Along the way there's a stop to pet some llamas and goats. Trains operate daily in summer from 10 AM to 5 PM. In winter they are on a shorter, weekend schedule. Train cars are protected overhead, but if showers start, passengers get to go around twice. The fare is $3.75 for adults and $2.75 for children 12 and younger and seniors. The expanded sidelights include a carousel, a ferris wheel, and a petting zoo.

Vintage Aircraft Co.
23982 Arnold Dr., Sonoma
• **(707) 938-2444**

You step back into the 1940s when you step onto the tarmac and check out Christopher Prevost's fleet of authentic, 1940 Boeing-built Stearman biplanes. One of the planes is a North American-built, World War II Navy SNJ-4, designed and built to train pilot candidates for the Air Force and Navy. Meticulously restored and maintained, the planes will tempt thrill-seekers to take one of several rides offered by Prevost. A leisurely 20-minute ride over Sonoma Valley is $89 for one passenger, $139 for two. Want to go for aerobatic maneuvers? That would be $99 for one passenger, $159 for two. Add loops and rolls, and you're looking at $149, $199 for two. The Kamikaze, said to be "intensely aerobatic and not for the faint of heart," is priced at $129, $179 for two. It's the experience of a lifetime! Weekday flights are by appointment. On weekends, Prevost does accept drop-ins, but appointments are recommended.

Sears Point Raceway
Calif. Hwys. 37 and 121, Sonoma
• **(707) 938-8448**

You'll see some of the top names in the racing world compete here each year on the grueling road course, the rugged motocross dirt track and the drag strip. Legends such as Mario Andretti, Al Unser (Sr. and Jr.) and Bobby Allison have all toured the track as well as Hollywood celebrities such as Paul Newman, Clint Eastwood and James Garner. Annual events include NASCAR road races and sports car racing by the Sports Car Club of America with TRANS-AM, Formula Atlantic and Pro Formula Ford entrants. Bike events include AMA motorcycle road races and several motocross races. Prices for events vary. (See our Spectator Sports chapter for more details.)

Historic Sonoma
Various sites

Few spots in Sonoma County evoke such a definite sense of place as the town of Sonoma, and the best spot to drink in this feeling is the 8-acre **Sonoma Plaza**, a state and national landmark and the largest plaza in California. It is an ideal picnic spot, with numerous tables under nearly 200 trees, a playground and a duck pond. A monument honors the raising of the Bear Flag here in 1846 (see our History chapter).

Surrounding the plaza are some of the buildings that marked the start of the village, then owned by Mexico and ruled by Gen. Mariano Vallejo. It makes a lovely walking tour, and one $2 ticket, available at any of the following sites, will give you access to the Mission, the Barracks, Vallejo's home and the Petaluma Adobe.

Mission San Francisco Solano, founded in 1823 as the last of California's Franciscan missions, is diagonally opposite the plaza's northeast corner. Today's mission is a faithful recreation of the original. Only the priests' quarters date from the founding. It's open daily from 10 AM to 5 PM.

Sonoma Barracks, across from the mission, housed Vallejo's Mexican troops, sheltered

ATTRACTIONS

Vintage Railroad: All Aboard the Napa Valley Wine Train

As soon as you set foot in Napa County, the ads are everywhere. Tourist brochures, billboards, and bus benches urge you to ride it with someone you love. Napa motels promote themselves as "Minutes From" it. Leaflets lie in the living rooms of practically every bed and breakfast inn in the land.

And if you spend any significant time driving the length of the valley, you will eventually see it: a chain of exquisite railroad cars, painted "burgundy, champagne gold and grapeleaf green," rumbling along at a luxuriously unhurried gait. It's the Napa Valley Wine Train, the uncontested champion of Napa tourist attractions.

To get the full story of the Wine Train, you have to jump back to 1864, when ground was broken for a railway terminus at Soscol Landing, a port-of-call south of Napa. Sam Brannan needed a reliable method of transporting the upper crust of San Francisco to his new resort in Calistoga (see our History chapter), and now he had a train to meet the ferry. The first 5 miles of track, extending to Main Street in Napa, became operative in 1865, just 10 years after California's first railroad line connected Sacramento and Folsom.

The Napa tracks would thrive for decades. The Southern Pacific Railroad Company assumed control in 1885 and ran the train for more than 100 years. But Southern Pacific discontinued passenger service in 1929, and by 1984 the company sought government approval to abandon the line altogether. It looked like the old Napa Valley Railroad was dead. In stepped Vincent DeDomenico, son of Sicilian immigrants who rose to prominence as president of Golden Grain Macaroni Company and later purchased the famed Ghirardelli Chocolate company. DeDomenico, who had built an empire out of Rice-A-Roni, bought the track and right-of-way from Southern Pacific for $2.25 million.

DeDomenico's namesake son then took the lead. Vincent Jr. had once refurbished yachts in Scotland; he knew what would be involved in piecing together a vintage train. So the company mounted a nationwide search, and before long had found what it desired. They purchased five Pullman coach cars, all built in 1915. Four of them, made for the Northern Pacific Railroad Company, had most recently been used to transport vacationing skiers for the Denver & Rio Grande Western Railroad. They were converted into parlor cars. The fifth coach, built for the Southern Railway Company, became the kitchen car. Two more units, 1917 Pullman sleepers, were converted into dining cars.

Meanwhile, the company bought four 1,800-horsepower, diesel/electric passenger locomotives from the Canadian National Railroad in Montreal. The locomotives were manufactured in the 1950s. (In the summer of 1997 the Wine Train added a double-decked dome car, built for the Milwaukee Road Railroad Line in 1947.)

All of the cars were in a dilapidated state. Beyond spiffing them up, the DeDomenicos had to bring the amenities up to modern standards. They installed new, 4-inch concrete floors and built new roofs. They upgraded the lighting, plumbing, heating and air conditioning, and they made the six-wheel trucks (the wheelbases) road-worthy.

And then there were the tracks. Before the first Napa Valley Wine Train ever rolled down the line, crews laid some 16,000 tons of ballast rocks along the bed. They laid 6 miles of new track at stations and terminals and replaced about 16,000 old railroad ties, many of which dated to the '40s. All in all, the track renovation cost $1.7 million. Limited passenger service finally began September 16, 1989.

The Wine Train Depot is at 1275 McKinstry Street in Napa, near the corner of Soscol Avenue and First Street. Unlike the train itself, the depot is not a restored

Photo: Ketchum Public Relations

The Napa Valley Wine Train returns you to a time when railroad travel was the height of luxury.

piece of grandeur. It's more like a small convention center, with patrons drifting along carpeted floor to the sound of jingling cash registers.

Before you board, a Wine Train representative conducts a quickie seminar, explaining how the senses of taste, smell and touch combine to help you enjoy that complimentary glass of wine you're holding. The crowd is casual and enthusiastic, a diverse demography of ages, genders and races.

As you board, an employee is there to snap your photo in front of the train. When you return to the depot, you can purchase the souvenir in a variety of packages.

The train cars are exquisite, with Honduran mahogany paneling, brass bathroom fixtures, etched glass partitions, crystal chandeliers and wool carpeting. Norman Roth, the San Francisco-based designer who oversaw the interior design, patterned the cars after early-20th-century classics such as the Venice-Simplon Orient Express and the Andalusian Express, and they aren't far off the mark.

The dining tables are predictably tasteful, with white damask linens and bone china, silver flatware and lead crystal. Fresh flowers adorn the tables, classical music wafts overhead.

Patrick Finney, who grew up not far away in Woodland and is known for Southwestern cuisine, is the chef. One of the most popular aspects of the ride is the glass-walled kitchen car, where you can watch Finney and his staff of six sear your tuna or grill your filet mignon on propane-fired ranges. (You can, in fact, walk freely about the length of the train, including the Wine Bar car.)

The food is complemented by some 40 still wines and a small selection of sparkling wines; some are big names, some small, but all are from Napa Valley. Finney prints a wine recommendation for each dish on the menu, perhaps a 1994 Scheutz-Oles Zinfandel with the pork tenderloin or a 1995 Atlas Peak Sangiovese with the free-range chicken. (The Wine Train has liquor, too.)

All in all, you'll travel 36 miles from Napa to St. Helena, past 26 wineries and countless acres of vines. As with most trains, there is a "wrong side of the tracks"

(Continued on next page)

to be passed through as you make your way out of town, with barbed wire, junked cars and the like. But once you're free of the town, the view opens into a panorama of vineyards and farmhouses. The best sections are when the train breaks away from Calif. 29, giving you the impression that you're chugging through remote countryside.

Though the Wine Train owns the right-of-way clear to Calistoga, it would have to rip through profitable vineyard land to connect the tracks, and that's a battle for which the company isn't ready. So St. Helena is the midpoint, and there is no turnaround loop there. The two engines, connected back-to-back, are moved along parallel tracks to the back of the train, which then becomes the front. And then it's time for you to move, too.

Unless you are in the dome car, you will either start with an hors d'oeuvres course in the parlor and move to a dining car for lunch, or eat the first two courses in a dining car, then retire to the parlor for dessert.

And despite the finery of the dining cars, the parlors are the pinnacle of the trip. With plush seats that swivel 360 degrees, you can point yourself at the window and watch the Wine Country pass by at a leisurely 15 to 20 miles per hour. It's a hypnotic sensation.

Make no mistake, you'll be the center of attention. Motorists and pedestrians can't help but swing their heads to take in the sight of your elegant mode of transportation. No doubt you'll also see a few "NO WINE TRAIN" signs planted next to the tracks. The reasons behind this antagonism are complicated and not always unified. As one winery tasting room manager told us, "I'm in favor of the Wine Train now. The problem was that when they first bought the right-of-way, they sort of arrogantly pushed their way in, without trying to sway the public over to their side." Others simply object to idling behind a gate in a long line of cars while the train slips across Calif. 29.

Claiming it gets a bum rap, the Napa Valley Wine Train ownership now seems to go out of its way to be a good corporate neighbor. For example, because of the age of the train cars, the Wine Train isn't required to be accessible to the disabled. It is. And as DeDomenico Jr. points out, his company is much more cooperative than Cal Trans when it comes to giving access to city and county agencies who want to lay pipes or cables along the highway. You could also make an argument that most of the passengers would be clogging the roads with their rental cars if they weren't on board the train.

In any case, the Wine Train is immensely popular and clearly here to stay. One thing even most locals don't realize about the Wine Train is that it leads a double life as an after-hours freight service, hauling everything from giant aluminum wine vats to living room recliners for Napa Valley customers. Under an interchange agreement, the Napa Valley Railroad transports goods to Roctram, a Southern Pacific hub south of Napa. From there, shipments headed east are moved to Cordelia Junction near Sacramento; shipments destined for overseas are taken to the Port of Oakland. The system allows Napa businesses an efficient, cost-effective shipping alternative. The DeDomenicos would also like to see their trains used as regular transportation to the ferry terminal in Vallejo, a throwback to the 19th century.

For now, the luncheon train takes three hours and boards at 11 AM Monday through Friday, 12:10 on Saturday and Sunday. The dinner train is a three-hour cruise that boards at 6 PM Monday through Friday, 5:30 PM on Saturday and Sunday. The Champagne brunch train runs for two and a half hours and boards at 8:30 AM on Saturday and Sunday. All-inclusive tariffs (for train fare and food) are $59.50 for brunch, $68.50 for lunch and $75 for dinner. You can also pay $29.50 to ride in the deli car, then purchase your lunch a la carte. The Wine Train accepts most credit cards, but smoking is not permitted anywhere on board.

Look for special events. Most Fridays there is a Vintner's Luncheon, wherein you get to taste the creations of a designated Napa Valley winemaker. These lunch excursions are $95 per person. And once a month, on a Thursday or Friday, you can sign up for "Murder on the Wine Train Express," a full dinner and "real life theatre," with characters in 1915 period dress. The cost for that is $99 per person.

In July 1996, the Wine Train began offering an optional winery stop at Grgich Hills Cellars. Grgich Hills was the logical geographic choice: Its location gives passengers just enough time to hop off, take a private tour and jump back on, and it doesn't force them to brave a crossing of Calif. 29. The train eventually wants to offer several such disembarkations, but is currently locked in battle with the St. Helena City Council. Whenever you ride the Napa Valley Wine Train, and whichever package you choose, reservations are a must. You can call (707) 253-2111 or (800) 427-4124.

the Bear Flag soldiers and served as a U.S. military headquarters in the 1840s and 1850s. Today the Barracks are restored to their Mexican-era appearance, with exhibits inside and an attractive gift shop with California items. Grizzly bears once battled bulls in the enclosed courtyard behind the Barracks, while spectators gambled on the outcome. It's open 10 AM to 5 PM daily.

Toscano Hotel, a few doors down First Street from the Barracks, served as an unpretentious hotel for Italian immigrants (hence the name Toscano, which means "man from Tuscany"). The two-story frame structure with kitchen has free docent tours on Friday, Saturday and Sunday from 1 to 4 PM.

Salvador Vallejo Adobe (Swiss Hotel) has a bar and restaurant that have long been favorites of residents and visitors alike. The locally famous drink, "Bear's Hair" sherry, is served in the saloon. Originally the adobe was built for Gen. Vallejo's brother, Salvador, in the 1840s. It has been known as the Swiss Hotel since the 1880s.

Salvador Vallejo Adobe (El Dorado Hotel), a Monterey Colonial adobe, has had a checkered history as a government office, college, winery and hotel. Salvador Vallejo built it between 1836 and 1846. Subsequently it was occupied by the Bear Flag party members and U.S. Gen. John C. Fremont during the opening days of the Mexican-American War. Presbyterian settlers operated Cumberland College at the adobe from 1858 until 1864.

El Paseo de Sonoma (Pinelli Building) is one of several plaza structures built of native stone. The building survived a 1911 fire when Augustino Pinelli let firefighters douse flames with his barrels of wine. Today several shops and restaurants can be found on the passageway behind First Street East and Spain Street. **Blue Wing Inn**, on E. Spain Street across from the mission, was once a rowdy gold rush-era saloon visited by future President U.S. Grant, legendary then-Lt. William Tecumseh Sherman, Kit Carson and notorious bandit Joaquin Murietta. This wisteria-covered, two-story adobe now contains shops and residences.

Vasquez House, in the courtyard of El Paseo de Sonoma off Spain Street, was built by "Fighting Joe" Hooker, a U.S. Army officer and later a Civil War general, while he was stationed in Sonoma. The restored, frame dwelling houses a museum and serves as headquarters for the Sonoma League for Historic Preservation. It's open Wednesday through Sunday from 1:30 to 4:30 PM. There is no charge, and refreshments are available for purchase in the tea room.

General Vallejo's Home (Lachryma Montis) is not on the plaza but three blocks down W. Spain Street. Gen. Vallejo built this Gothic Revival home at a cost of $50,000 in 1851 and named it Lachryma Montis ("tears of the mountain") because of a spring on the property. Abandoning Spanish-style architecture, he built a grand Victorian and furnished it with European imports. He had redwood lumber hauled in from the port at Vallejo, while bricks and marble mantels were shipped from Hawaii. Landscaping, a glass pavilion (now gone) and every convenience of the time were included. The Vallejos' 15th and 16th children were born at Lachryma Montis.

Vallejo's once-great holdings eventually were reduced to only the acreage around this home. Many of the original furnishings are still in place. The kitchen is set aside in a separate building, to keep the heat of cooking away from the rest of the house. A charming little guesthouse remains on the property, and a short walk up the hill leads to the room of one of the Vallejo children. Picnic tables are set around a stream that runs through the property. Now a state historic park, Lachryma Montis is open 10 AM to 5 PM daily.

Jack London State Historic Park
2400 London Ranch Rd. off Arnold Dr.,
Glen Ellen • (707) 938-5216

Jack London called it his "Beauty Ranch," but he wanted to achieve more than aesthetic satisfaction here. His goal was to achieve a scientifically operated ranch where new techniques could be developed. Many buildings remain from his experiment in ranching: stone stables where he kept his prize horses, remnants of the winery and distillery, the last vestiges of his famous scientific piggery and the farmhouse where he lived for five years and wrote most of his stories. In the center of the 800 acres is the rubble of Wolf House, the lava-stone mansion he had hoped to live in, burned to the ground in 1913. The half-mile trail to the Wolf House ruins passes through a forest of oak, madrone and buckeye trees. Nearby is London's grave, marked only by a stone from the ruins of the house.

At the top of the hill, as you enter the state park, is the House of Happy Walls, built by London's wife, Charmian, after his death. This fascinating museum provides a look at the life of a man who was first and foremost an adventurer. It contains memorabilia of his life as a war correspondent, his trip around the world with Charmian in a ship he built himself and a load of information about his writing life. Displayed are some of the 600 rejection slips he received, the first from *Saturday Evening Post*. Seven miles of hiking, mountain biking and equestrian trails are available. The museum is open daily from 10 AM to 5 PM, and admission is $6 per car ($4 when seniors are riding). There are ample picnic sites.

INSIDERS' TIP

If you are staying in San Francisco and seeking a one-day Wine Country tour, consider the working relationship shared by Blue-and-Gold Fleet and Napa Valley Holidays. You can take the Blue-and-Gold ferry to Vallejo, where Holidays' bus will pick you up to begin its usual Napa Valley tour (see listing in this chapter). The whole package costs $45 per person.

Petaluma Historical Museum
20 Fourth St., Petaluma
• (707) 778-4398

A large, freestanding, stained-glass dome accents the beauty of this 1906 Carnegie Free Library—one of the hundreds that philanthropist Andrew Carnegie built and donated early this century. You'll find a 19th-century, horse-drawn fire wagon here, along with Native American artifacts, pioneer relics and displays describing Petaluma's dairy and poultry beginnings. An exhibit about the Petaluma River illustrates how the town became an important manufacturing and trading hub when Petaluma was one of California's largest cities.

By the way, this Victorian riverfront town has one of California's best-preserved downtowns. (It's on the National Register of Historic Places.) Petaluma's all-American appearance has not escaped the notice of Hollywood filmmakers, and movie sites can be found all over town. Some of the films shot here include *Peggy Sue Got Married, Basic Instinct* and *Phenomenon*, starring John Travolta.

The museum offers brochures for self-guided walking tours of the city, featuring the famous Iron Front buildings and beautiful Victorian homes. In addition, guided tours of historic downtown are led by docents costumed in Victorian attire on Saturday and Sunday at 10:30 AM May through October. It's free, but donations are accepted. Admission to the museum is also free, and hours are 10 AM to 4 PM Thursday, Friday, Saturday and Monday, and Sunday 12 to 3 PM.

Petaluma Adobe State Historic Park
3325 Adobe Rd. at Casa Grande Rd.,
Petaluma • (707) 762-4871

Once the headquarters of Gen. Mariano Vallejo's 100-square-mile Rancho Petaluma, this enormous two-story adobe overlooking Petaluma stands as a monument to California's early history. A self-guided tour of the structure offers views of the period-furnished kitchen, the living quarters where the Vallejo family stayed when they spent their summer holiday at the rancho and the rooms where guests were assigned. The rustic chairs and candle sconces are of Spanish motif. The rancho workshops, where once 2,000 Indians wove blankets and clothes, are empty. Outside you will find replicas of the beehive ovens where bread was baked for the rancho inhabitants. Occasionally the ranger in charge may put in a loaf or two, using the same recipe the Vallejo servants used. The ranch is open daily (except Thanksgiving, Christmas and New Year's Day) from 10 AM to 5 PM. The $3 admission fee, $2 for children ages 6 to 12, entitles you to visit any of the sites on historic Sonoma Plaza (see previous listing).

Passengers explore the historic area of Willits by horse-drawn carriage.

Luther Burbank Home and Gardens
Santa Rosa and Sonoma Aves.,
Santa Rosa • (707) 524-5445

Horticulturist Luther Burbank settled in Santa Rosa as a young man in 1875, drawn to the area for its climate and soil conditions. He had barely stepped down from the train when he declared it to be the most salubrious climate in the country. During his 53 years in Santa Rosa, Burbank changed the horticultural world, improving and hybridizing more than 800 plant varieties, including the well-known Burbank russet potato. In daily life he was just a gardener at heart and often found time to trade seeds with his neighbors. At age 69, Burbank married his 27-year-old secretary, who took up his work after he died in 1926. He is buried beneath the cedar of Lebanon tree in front of his home.

This national historical landmark features Burbank's home, a carriage house and the greenhouse where he performed his experiments. Outside you'll find a lovely garden filled with the plants Burbank introduced to the world. Docent-led house tours are offered on the half-hour Tuesday through Sunday from April through October. Tours, which are $3 for adults and free for children 12 and younger, run from 10 AM to 3:30 PM. The gardens are open daily at no charge.

Jesse Peter Native American Art Museum
Santa Rosa Junior College,
1501 Mendocino Ave., Santa Rosa
• (707) 527-4479

This museum is dedicated to arts and crafts created by Native Americans from the 19th century up to the present day. The collection contains an extensive assortment of baskets, including the extraordinarily beautiful baskets of the Pomo tribe. Most items displayed represent the work of California tribes, although beadwork of the Plains and Plateau tribes is on hand as well as some Eskimo art. There are replicas of a Southwestern pueblo, a Pomo roundhouse and a Klamath River xonta (a family shelter). The museum is on the campus of Santa Rosa Junior College and is open noon to 4 PM Monday through Friday (except for school holidays) from mid-August through May.

Sonoma County Museum
425 Seventh St., Santa Rosa
• (707) 579-1500

This museum is housed in the old post office built after the 1906 earthquake, a structure moved and restored as a part of local grassroots activities. The lower floor is devoted to an extensive collection of art exhibits, exhibits on the history and heritage of the county and photographs of the local landscape and people. Included in the collection are Sonoma County landscapes by early California painters William Keith and Thomas Hill. The second floor is given over to exciting temporary exhibits. Past ones have included a displays of cartoon art and a woodworking exhibit of bowls, boxes and furniture. The Wild Oat Gift Shop has a particularly intriguing assortment of books and items with Sonoma County themes. The museum and gift shop are open Wednesday through Sunday year round, from 11 AM to 4 PM. A $1 donation is requested.

Redwood Empire Ice Arena
1667 W. Steele Ln., Santa Rosa
• **(707) 546-7147**

Outside of Charlie Brown, who will always be universally loved, the Redwood Empire Ice Arena may be the most public gift Charles Schulz has given Sonoma County. His career started in Minnesota and ballooned to fame, with his work appearing in more than 1,800 newspapers in 65 countries worldwide. Schulz, a resident of Sebastopol and later Santa Rosa, rolled out the adventures of Snoopy, Lucy, Linus and Charlie Brown.

The arena offers a full range of skating, and many world champions have glided across the ice here. The arena is open daily, but hours vary, with mornings reserved for special programs and classes. The cost is $7.50 (including skate rental) for adults and teens and $6.50 for children younger than 12. Aside from the arena, visitors will delight in the gift shop with hundreds of items from the lives of the Peanuts gang.

Safari West
3115 Porter Creek Rd., Santa Rosa
• **(707) 579-2551**

This is a little different than those drive-through safari parks where tourists outnumber perplexed animals by about 100-to-1. Safari West is a private preserve and working ranch dedicated to conservation and propagation of endangered species. You can experience the thrill of a dusty African safari—gaze at herds of zebra or watch a giraffe crane its mammoth neck to eat out of your hand. The 240 acres of Safari West are home to 400 exotic mammals and birds.

Guests spend an unparalleled two-and-a-half hours on a unique educational trek through the rolling hills of the preserve. Accompanied by a naturalist, groups get the rarest of opportunities to photograph herds of antelope, eland, gazelle, zebra and many more types of animals. Because the critters live in vast acreage, they are comfortable with vehicles and can be seen up close. (One group was even treated to the birth of an antelope.) Wear comfortable clothing and bring sunscreen and a hat. Oh, and the proprietors can customize tours if you have a particular interest in, say, springboks. Cost of a basic tour is $48 for adults and $24 for children 16 and younger. Safari West now includes overnight accommodations. The south African-made "tents" include hardwood foors, bathrooms and king-sized beds. They go for $350 per night for two adults ($225 on weeknights). Overnight guests also receive a 20 percent discount on the tours. Visits are by appointment only. It is suggested you do not bring pets.

The Petrified Forest
4100 Petrified Forest Rd., Calistoga
• **(707) 942-6667**

It's not as spooky as it sounds, unless you think too hard about the advancing wall of muddy volcanic ash that leveled these trees about 3 million years ago, following massive eruptions to the northeast. The trees lay unmolested until 1870, when a gent later known as "Petrified Charlie" Evans happened upon a rock-hard stump while tending his cows. The rest is tourist-industry history. A short loop takes you past all the highlights, including The Monarch, a petrified, 105-foot redwood with a diameter of 6 feet. The museum and store—open 10 AM to 4:30 PM—are housed in the big red Ollie Bockee House. You'll want to sit on the porch. Admission is $4 for adults, $3 for youngsters ages 12 through 17 and $2 for kids ages 6 to 11. Seniors 60 and over pay $3.

Northern Sonoma

Windsor Waterworks and Slides
8225 Conde Ln., Windsor
• **(707) 838-7760**

This recreational park offers welcome relief from hot summer days. Among the attractions are an inner-tube slide, a speed slide and a body slide, a splash fountain with squirt guns, a swimming pool and wading pool, a large picnic area with barbecue pits and an arcade. Kids can also play table tennis, horseshoes and volleyball. The park's newest attraction is an inflatable ship on which children can bounce. A snack bar is available. The park is open every day from May through September from 11 AM to 7 PM. The entrance fee is $13.25 for those 13 and older and $12.25 for kids ages 4 to 12. There's a special rate of $9.75 after 4 PM for the "afternoon splash." (See our Kidstuff chapter for more on this attraction.)

Healdsburg Museum
221 Matheson St., Healdsburg
• (707) 431-3325

This museum is in a refurbished Carnegie library building and features both permanent and changing exhibits. The county's history is depicted from prehistoric times to the present, and displays include antique firearms, 19th-century clothing, tools and an outstanding collection of Pomo basketry and crafts. The archives contain more than 5,000 historical photographs and newspapers dating back to 1865. Healdsburg Museum is open Tuesday through Sunday from 11 AM to 4 PM. Admission is free.

Northwestern Pacific Railroad Passenger Excursion Service
Healdsburg to Willits
• (800) 550-2122

This is train travel that gets passengers thinking of the days when railroad was the way to go. The round trip from Healdsburg to Willits is a relaxing nine hours, departing at 8:30 AM and arriving at 6:30 PM, with stops at historic Hopland and Ukiah. The trip begins with a continental breakfast. If you're traveling coach, you'll enjoy a delicious deli lunch, and you may purchase beer or wine. First-class travel includes a three-course gourmet lunch, fine Sonoma and Mendocino wines and the fabulous dome car. You may elect to get off at Hopland or Ukiah and reboard on the return trip. Price of first-class fare is $150; coach fare is $89. Coach-only, one-way fare from Healdsburg to Ukiah is $39, to Willits $50.

West County/Russian River

Luther Burbank Gold Ridge Experiment Farm
7781 Bodega Ave., Sebastopol
• (707) 829-6711

On his 18-acre experimental farm, Burbank built a cottage and worked to perfect Gravenstein apples, plums, cherries, grapes and lilies. Although he lived and worked in Santa Rosa, this is where he conducted his horticultural research between 1895 and 1926. Free guided tours, available by appointment from April through mid-October, explore Burbank's gardens and visit his restored cottage. The gardens are open for free self-guided tours year round.

West County Museum
261 S. Main St., Sebastopol
• (707) 829-6711

The Western Sonoma County Historical Society's collections are presented in this restored railroad depot. The Triggs Reference Room contains books, photographs, magazines, newspapers, audiotapes and videotapes on local history. West County Museum is open Thursday through Sunday from 1 to 4 PM. There is no admission fee, but donations are welcomed. If you'd like to learn more, visit www.seb.org on the World Wide Web and click on "community orgs."

Greenwood State Park Visitors Center
Calif. Hwy. 1, Elk
• (707) 877-3458

This small history center tells the story of the tiny town of Elk, from its founding by the Greenwood brothers in the late 1800s through its history as a logging and lumber town. Displays include a large mural depicting the journey lumber took—by cable, down cliffs, into mule wagons and across the rocks to waiting ships. The center also contains historic photographs, artifacts, a story rail tracing the history of the local lumber industry and archives. The visitors center is open on Saturdays and Sundays, March through October, from 11 AM to 1 PM.

Fort Ross State Historic Park
Calif. Hwy. 1 and Fort Ross Rd., Jenner
• (707) 847-3286

On a grassy, windswept bluff north of Bodega Bay stands a ruddy, wooden stockade, its main gate facing out over the Pacific Ocean toward the coast of what was once Russia, more than 5,000 miles away. The 14-foot walls are

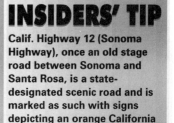

INSIDERS' TIP

Calif. Highway 12 (Sonoma Highway), once an old stage road between Sonoma and Santa Rosa, is a state-designated scenic road and is marked as such with signs depicting an orange California poppy on a blue background.

ATTRACTIONS

Photo: Bill Hoban

Disembarking from the Skunk Train, passengers head for the depot at Willits.

made of weather-beaten redwood. Inside is a small chapel, dedicated to St. Nicholas and topped with an orthodox cross. In another building, seal and otter pelts hang on the walls above casks marked in Cyrillic characters.

Now part of a state historic park, Fort Ross provides a fascinating glimpse into the history of the settlement founded with the aim of providing food for the fledgling Russian colony in Alaska, where Russia's eastward push ended in the early 1800s. The settlement survived for 29 years as a trading post and agricultural center. Restored structures include the chapel, the commandant's house, blockhouse and stockade. The museum in the visitors center exhibits Russian and Native American artifacts. The gift shop offers crafts made by the local Pomo tribe as well as goods imported from Russia. There are hiking trails, and a campground is 2 miles south of the park (see our Camping chapter). The park is open daily from 10 AM to 4:30 PM. There is no entrance fee, but there is a $6 charge for parking, $5 for seniors.

Berry's Saw Mill
Calif. Hwy. 116 and Cazadero Hwy.,
Cazadero • (707) 865-2365

This authentic sawmill offers visitors an opportunity to see trees sawed, split and planed into usable lumber. Guided tours are not of-fered, but visitors may explore the mill on an informal basis. It's open at no charge Monday through Friday from 7:45 AM to 4:30 PM.

Mendocino County

Real Goods Solar Living Center
13771 U.S. Hwy. 101, Hopland
• (707) 744-2100

At the Solar Living Center, you'll learn about creating electricity from renewable resources and the beauty of passive and active solar architecture and earth-friendly building materials. It's 100 percent solar- and wind-powered. You can shop from a wide selection of environmentally conscious products such as solar panels, hemp goods and water filtration systems and enjoy a tour of the 12 acres of beautiful, permaculture organic gardens and ponds. For the kids there's a special area for playing and learning, including a unique solar calendar; they call it a 21st-century Stonehenge. The Solar Living Center is open daily from 10 AM to 6 PM.

Grace Hudson Museum and Sun House
431 S. Main St., Ukiah • (707) 467-2836

Grace Hudson Museum is an art, history and anthropology museum focusing on the life works of Grace Hudson, who painted more than 650 oils, primarily of the local Pomo people. She was already a talented painter when she married ethnologist Dr. John Hudson and focused her art on Native American subjects. The museum displays Hudson's portraits of Pomos, exhibits of Native American arts and crafts and changing shows by local artists. Sun House, which shares the site, is a charming Craftsman bungalow that served as the Hudson residence. The museum is open Wednesday through Saturday from 10 AM to 4:30 PM and noon to 4:30 PM on Sunday. Tours of the Sun House are offered on the hour, noon to 3 PM.

Held-Poage Memorial Home and Library
Mendocino County Historical Society, 603 W. Perkins St., Ukiah
• (707) 462-6969

A treasure trove of historical information, the library holds 4,500 books on county, state and national history, 13,500 historical photographic negatives and microfilms pertaining to Northern California history. There are also documents, maps, scrapbooks, genealogies and more. Researchers from all over the United States contact the society for assistance. All this information is housed in the historical Queen Anne-style Victorian home built in 1903 for William D. Held and Ethel Poage Held, who were dedicated to the collection of archival materials about California. The home is open every day but Sunday from 1:30 to 4 PM. It is closed holidays, and donations are accepted.

Pomo Visitor Center
Marina Dr., Lake Mendocino, Ukiah
• (707) 485-8285

This small museum was built by the Army Corps of Engineers and is operated by the local Coyote Tribal Council. The round shape of the center is modeled on the Pomo ceremonial dance house, where cultural knowledge was passed down through the generations. On display are examples of Pomo basketry, a demonstration of clam-shell money-making and some Pomo games and a hands-on exhibit of different animal skins. The Army Corps has staged its own exhibit—a large aquarium of various fish found in Lake Mendocino. A gift shop operated by the Tribal Council contains items made by local Native Americans. Admission is free, and the museum is open from 9 AM to 5 PM daily from June through October.

Mendocino County Museum
400 E. Commercial St., Willits
• (707) 459-2736

This large, modern museum displays artifacts and interpretations of the cultural history of the county, with a particular focus on local Pomo and Yuki tribes. A fascinating aspect is the collection of oral history interviews from Mendocino citizens. It's open Wednesday through Sunday from 10 AM to 4:30 PM. Admission is free, but donations are gladly accepted.

Anderson Valley Historical Museum
Calif. Hwy. 128, 1 mile north of Boonville
• (707) 895-3207

In a century-old schoolhouse on the side of the road, this museum showcases Anderson Valley pioneer life. Displays include a sheepshearing shed, a blacksmith shop, Pomo Indian basketry and tools, and antique agricultural and lumber industry equipment. There is also an exhibit devoted to "Boontling," the valley's unique folk dialect. From September through May, it's open Friday, Saturday and Sunday from 1 to 4 PM; in summer, from 11:30 AM to 4 PM. To simplify: When the flag is flying, the museum is open.

Point Arena Lighthouse and Museum
Lighthouse Rd., Point Arena
• (707) 882-2777

The lighthouse, built after the San Francisco earthquake of 1906, still shines a warning to keep ships off the dangerous rocks and shoals. The light is now automated, and the old Coast Guard facilities have been turned into a maritime museum, with several guest cottages run by a local nonprofit organization. Visitors may climb the light tower and view the broad agricultural terraces that run down to the sea or admire the ancient Fresnel lens that remains in place in the light room at the top. Offshore, scuba divers enjoy the Arena Rock Underwater Preserve, an area of abundant marine flora and fauna, as well as the sunken wreck of a freighter. The lighthouse museum is open daily

> **INSIDERS' TIP**
> Movie buffs may recognize some of Mendocino's streets as settings for movies such as *East of Eden; Same Time Next Year; The Russians Are Coming, The Russians Are Coming;* and, recently, *Dying Young*.

from 11 AM to 3:30 PM on weekdays and 10 AM to 3:30 PM on weekends. Admission is $3 for adults and teens and $1 for kids younger than 12. For more information, try negotiating the rocks and shoals of the World Wide Web to www.mcn.org.

Ford House Museum
735 Main St., Mendocino
• (707) 937-5397

The Ford House, built in 1854 as the second home in Mendocino, was originally the residence of a Mendocino lumber mill owner. Today it serves as a museum and visitors center for Mendocino Headlands State Park. This is where to find out everything you need to know for your visit to the charming village of Mendocino and the wild shores off the Headlands. During the whale migrations from January through March, there are docent-led whale-watching walks that leave from Ford House on Saturday. At the height of the wildflower season in late spring, knowledgeable docents lead walks through a riot of color and tell about the flowers. The museum also posts displays on topics such as tide pools, whales and sea vegetation. Ford House is open daily from 11 AM to 4 PM. Admission is free, as are the docent walks, though small donations are encouraged.

Kelley House Museum
45007 Albion St., Mendocino
• (707) 937-5791

The house looks like a home transplanted from a Maine coastal town, a reflection of the fact that many New Englanders did come to Mendocino in earlier times. Its walls display a collection of historic photographs of days when redwood logs were loaded onto waiting ships via chutes and long piers. Displays tell the story of the logging and shipping industries that turned a wild, lonely coast into a thriving, driving city. The house is open from Friday through Monday from 1 to 4 PM. There is a $2 (suggested) admission fee.

Anchor Charters
Noyo Harbor, North Harbor Dr., Fort Bragg
• (707) 964-3854

Once on the endangered species list, the gray whale has made a comeback and can be seen traveling between the Bering Sea and Baja California from late November through late April. Although whales can be seen from shore, it is exciting to board a charter boat and see them directly in the waters they inhabit. The really lucky watchers get so close they can reach out

This heavily tattooed hunter is part of the Maori collection on exhibit at the Triangle Tattoo Museum.

and pet one. Dress for any weather because it can change quickly from sunny and warm to cloudy and cool. Bring along a camera with a telephoto lens, a telescope (just like the old mariners) or a pair of binoculars. Other whale-watching excursions leave from Noyo Harbor as well. Anchor Charters cruises last approximately two hours and are $25 per person.

Mendocino Coast Botanical Gardens
18220 N. Calif. Hwy. 1, Fort Bragg
• (707) 964-4352

This 47-acre delight is one of only three botanical gardens in the United States actually situated oceanside. Founded in 1961, the Mendocino Coast Botanical Gardens were purchased by grants from the California Coastal Conservancy and have been operated as a non-profit public trust since 1992. The collections here are divided into garden "rooms" of perennials, rhododendrons (which grow wild in great abundance in this county), heathers, succulents, ivies, fuchsias, dwarf conifers and other native species. Two creeks flow through the gardens, and more than 3 miles of trails provide easy access to the coast and opportunities for visitors to enjoy and learn about plants and nature.

A cliff house overlooks the ocean, where you can enjoy the drama of the sea, and the coastal bluffs are a vantage point for the gray whale migration. A favorite haunt of local painters who visit with easels in tow, the grounds include picnic tables tucked in quiet spaces for those who have had the foresight to bring lunch. Two miles south of Fort Bragg and 7 miles north of Mendocino, the gardens are open daily from 9 AM to 5 PM from March to October and 9 AM to 4 PM from November to February. Admission is $6 for adults, $5 for seniors, $3 for children 13-17, and $1 for kids 6-12.

Footlighters Little Theater
245 E. Laurel St., Fort Bragg
• (707) 964-3806

It's a lot of fun: a Gay Nineties night of family theater that's been going on since 1943. Plays are written by the cast and performed by most of the same people year after year—the oldest cast member is 85 and the youngest is 6. There's a little light can-can, a chance to hiss the villain and plenty of laughs. The audience sits around tables drinking coffee, beer or soft drinks and munching on pretzels. The theater itself is a leftover from silent film days and has a white-painted fireplace decorated with a painting of a can-can dancer. The cast makes its own costumes, and nobody is paid. In fact, they pay dues to belong! Performances are every Wednesday and Saturday at 8 PM, Memorial Day to Labor Day. The $7 ticket price may be going up.

Triangle Tattoo Museum
356B N. Main St., Fort Bragg
• (707) 964-8814

It's one of only a dozen places in the world dedicated to the documentation and preservation of tattoo history. The museum displays thousands of images of skin art, including those from several different countries and different periods in history. Several color prints of New Zealand's Maori people are displayed, showing both men and women with the cultural markings called Moko. Other tattoo portraits highlight designs from Borneo, Samoa, Japan, India, Burma, Zaire and Native American tribes. The tribal roots section includes an exhibit on the oldest documented finding of tattoos—on a 5,300-year-old Bronze Age iceman discovered in a glacier in 1983. The museum is open noon to 6 PM from Sunday through Thursday, noon to 8 PM on Friday and Saturday. Admission is free, and tours given upon request. Five tattoo artists are on hand, ready to make their point, and international guests have been known to stop by.

Guest House Museum
343 N. Main St., Fort Bragg
• (707) 961-2840

Much of Fort Bragg's history is displayed here. Built for the Fort Bragg Redwood Company in the 19th century, the building later became the guesthouse for friends and customers of C.R. Johnson, founder of Union Lumber Company. It is built entirely of redwood. Looking at the collection of photographs and artifacts telling the history of Fort Bragg, it becomes overwhelmingly apparent how rooted in the lumber business this community is. Historic equipment such as steam donkeys, rigging blocks, locomotives and high wheels once used in log harvesting are on display across the street at the Fort Bragg Depot Mall. The museum is open Tuesday through Sunday from 10:30 AM to 2:30 PM. Admission is $1.

Skunk Train
Laurel Street Depot, Fort Bragg
• (707) 964-6371

The pioneering logging railroad called California Western connects Fort Bragg on the coast with inland Willits by a tortuous 40 miles of steel—a distance that could be covered in 23 miles by an efficient crow. The terrain was scarcely conducive to easy track laying. The longest straight section is less than a mile long. In 1885 it was established to haul logs to the mill, and it still is a working line. But today, its greatest fame is as a railroad buff's excursion. The Skunk, a name that derives from the odor of earlier gas engines, passes through the scenic, dense redwood forests, crossing more than 30 bridges and trestles and negotiating two deep mountain tunnels. At Northspur, the halfway point, you find food treats, cold beer, juices and soft drinks. Those who wish may spend some time here, catching the next train back from Willits at a half-day fare. The fare for the full-day round trip is $35 for adults and $18 for children 3 to 17. The half-day trip is $27 for adults, $14 for children, though check on family packages. Reservations are recommended.

Lake County

Lower Lake Schoolhouse and Museum
16435 Main St., Lower Lake
• (707) 995-3565

The 1,000 or so residents of Lower Lake went all out when they decided to build a community schoolhouse in 1877. The two-story brick building, with its Mansard roof and Cobb

Mountain lumber, stands today to remind us how plain and unimaginative most of our new educational facilities are. The Lower Lake Schoolhouse was more than that too. They held dances, traveling minstrel shows, films, even circus acts, and the building's preservation committee seeks to capture that atmosphere with art exhibits and performances in the second-floor auditorium. The museum features a period classroom plus exhibits on pioneer families and local mining history. It's all open Wednesday through Saturday from 11 AM to 3 PM. There is no admission fee, but you might want to make a donation.

Anderson Marsh State Historic Park
Calif. Hwy. 53 at Anderson Ranch Pkwy., Lower Lake
• (707) 994-0688, (707) 279-2267

Eighty-four percent of the original marshland around Clear Lake has been destroyed, which makes Anderson Marsh that much more important to the wildlife that breeds in the ecosystem. There are 540 acres of wetlands or tule marsh plus oak and riparian woodland within the 1,000-acre park. The visitors center is in a farmhouse erected in the 1860s by farming brothers Achilles and John Melchisadeck Grigsby, with a prominent addition by John Still Anderson, a Scottish rancher whose family lived on the property for about 85 years. There are five short nature trails in the park, including the Cache Creek Trail, a 1.1-mile route with interpretive displays. Dogs and bicycles are not permitted on trails. The park is open from 10 AM to 5 PM Wednesday through Sunday, and parking is $3 per vehicle.

The Clear Lake Queen
Library Park, Lakeport
• (707) 994-5432

This recent attraction is made to feel old. It's an 84-foot, triple-deck, paddlewheel boat that would look more at home in the Mississippi Delta. (Sorry, the wheel is just for show—the *Queen* is powered by two massive diesel engines.) You can watch the shoreline activity—we don't know if the animals or the humans will be more intriguing—while you eat lunch or dinner. The boat used to pick up at Ferndale Resort in Kelseyville, and might sometime add a stop in Clearlake. High-season prices run from $16 to $18 for sightseeing only to $28 for a two-hour lunch or brunch cruise to $35 for a three-hour dinner. (The dining floors are warm and enclosed.) The *Queen* runs Wednesday through Sunday during the summer, Fri-

day and Saturday during the winter, and features music and dancing once a month. The price goes up those nights.

Lake County Museum
255 N. Main St., Lakeport
• (707) 263-4555

It has been said that the Pomo Indians who lived in the vicinity of Clear Lake were the most skillful basket weavers on the planet. Judge for yourself at this museum, where dozens of twined and coiled baskets are on display. Other Pomo artifacts include dance costumes and a small boat and hut. Lake County Museum also houses a research library and remnants of the early white settlers, including a firearm display. It's all inside a magnificent 1871 brick building that used to be the county courthouse. It is open Wednesday through Sunday from 11 AM to 4 PM (closed Sundays in the winter). A suggested donation is $2 for adults and $1 for children.

Balloons and Gliders

It's hard to find a Wine Country brochure that doesn't include a photo of a multicolored hot-air balloon drifting over vine-scored hills. Somewhere along the way, ballooning became part of the everyday lexicon here. It is a natural fit. Hot-air balloons are splashy, even extravagant, but in a way that celebrates the physical environment rather than tramples it. They connote old-fashioned gentility in the same way a horse-drawn carriage does, and that sort of wistful pleasure is what the Wine Country is all about. Of course, the awe-evoking vistas have something to do with the popularity of our balloons and gliders too. You don't realize just how underpopulated the region is until you get some altitude and take in all the green space between towns.

As for the frequently asked questions: Yes, the flying machines are quite safe. Most pilots are FAA-certified; feel free to ask about their qualifications when you phone. It is true that balloon pilots have limited control over the direction of their rigs, except on a vertical scale. This means there is always a chance you'll make an unscheduled stop in an open field, but it will likely be a gentle one, and the company's chase team will be right on your heels. (Gliders are much easier to steer.)

As for capacity, the balloon gondolas accommodate anywhere from four to 16 passengers. Those of average size hold six to eight

The Sharpsteen Museum in Calistoga gives visitors a great overview of the history of the area.

people. You should dress in layers when riding in a balloon. The shifts in altitude, the breezes and the heat from the fire make it hard to predict what level of clothing will be comfortable. And if you are a tall person, be sure to bring a cap—radiant heat from the burner can be unpleasant after an hour or so.

Napa County

Balloons Above the Valley
5091 Solano Ave., Napa
• (707) 253-2222, (800) GO-HOT-AI(R)

These guys launch from Domaine Chandon in Yountville. They will take you on a drifting, one-hour flight and give you a champagne brunch for $175 per person.

Adventures Aloft
Vintage 1870, Yountville
• (707) 944-4408, (800) 944-4408

This group of experienced balloon pilots charges $185 for adults, $150 for youth ages 6 to 16. They will shuttle you to the launch site from anywhere in Napa Valley for no extra charge, with coffee and pastries served upon arrival and a sparkling wine breakfast afterward. You have the option of helping to blow up the balloons (no, your cheeks won't get

tired) before your one-hour flight. Reservations are required.

Napa Valley Balloons, Inc.
P.O. Box 2860, Yountville 94599
• (707) 944-0228, (800) 253-2224

This is a scenic ride before you ever leave the ground. The company launches from Domaine Chandon at dawn, after a continental breakfast. Postflight, you get a champagne brunch at Napa Valley Grille and a color photo of the occasion. In between you'll spend an hour in the air (three to five hours for the entire experience), gawking at the scenery. Meet the van at the southwest corner of Washington Square. It costs $175 per person, and reservations are required.

Bonaventura Balloon Company
Rancho Caymus Inn, 1145 Rutherford
Cross Road, Rutherford
• (707) 944-2822, (800) FLY-NAPA

Not long ago, *The Napa Valley Register* ran a breathtaking photo of a hot air balloon gliding over Mt. Pinatubo in the Philippines. Piloting the balloon was Joyce Bowen, and though she isn't likely to make your Napa Valley flight such an adventure, she will certainly show you a good time. Bonaventura works "the heart of the valley," from Oakville to St. Helena. The balloons take off at sunrise and stay aloft for 60 to 90 minutes. The company never rushes a flight (only one per balloon each day) and never puts more than six people in the basket. The price, $165 to $195 per person, includes breakfast at either Rancho Caymus or Meadowood Resort.

Sonoma County

Aerostat Adventures
P.O. Box 2082, Healdsburg 95448
• (707) 579-0183, (800) 579-0183

Aerostat enjoys an exclusive launch site out of the Rodney Strong vineyards near Healdsburg. The location affords spectacular views of the Dry Creek Valley, Alexander Valley and Russian River wine regions as you fly over famous and secluded vineyards. Upon touchdown passengers can look forward to a big champagne brunch. Cost of the flight and brunch is $180.

Air Flambuoyant
250 Pleasant Ave., Santa Rosa
• (707) 838-8500, (800) 456-4711

This is the largest and most experienced family-owned balloon company in North America, flying since 1974. Their specialty is small groups, though they also take large groups.

The flight lasts one hour, followed by a grand breakfast. Flights depart early to take advantage of favorable early-morning weather conditions. They leave from the Healdsburg area and fly over the wine valleys of Dry Creek and Russian River. Two or three times a year the captain, who has flown balloons all over the world, performs a wedding while aloft. (Yes, that's legal!) Flights are individually planned but usually cost about $180 per person. Ask about group packages and special offers.

Lake County

Crazy Creek Soaring
18896 Grange Rd., Middletown
• (707) 987-9112 for gliders,
(707) 987-9393 for skydiving

See the rolling range and forested hills of Lake County from 3,000 feet. Or better yet, put a parachute on your back and watch those shrubs get bigger and bigger. Glider rides range from $90 per person for 20 minutes to $115 for 30 minutes to $145 for 40 minutes. True daredevils can sign up with an aerobatic pilot who will take you through a series of rolls and loop-the-loops for $150. The jumps start at $135 for a beginner tandem leap.

Spas

Our Spas and Resorts chapter is filled with full-accommodation spas—places that will rub you, wrap you, soak you and give you a bed to rest your delirious body. The Calistoga area also has several walk-in facilities that offer equally rejuvenating services. The only difference is that after the treatment, you'll have to get yourself together long enough to make it to your hotel—or maybe just to the restaurant next door. Here are a few walk-in possibilities.

Mount View Spa
1457 Lincoln Ave., Calistoga
• (707) 942-5789, (800) 772-8838

In the Mount View Hotel building (see our Hotels and Motels chapter), but run separately, is the ultimate in luxury. The tasteful furnishings, the personalized service, the waffle-weave cotton robes in the dressing rooms—they all combine to set a mood of elegant decadence. Mount View offers five types of massage, from Swedish to reflexology; customized whirlpool baths with additives such as fango mud, mineral salts, powdered milk whey and herbal bath oils; and body wraps. The latter include the herbal linen wrap, the stress-relief hydro wrap (a warm, aloe vera-based gel) and the Dead Sea mud wrap, which is painted over your entire body like a dusky leotard. All of it is performed in private rooms. The massages cost $35 (for 25 minutes) to $90 (for 85 minutes). A bath treatment followed by a 55-minute massage runs $85; add an herbal wrap and a 25-minute basic cleansing facial and pay $170.

Lincoln Avenue Spa
1339 Lincoln Ave., Calistoga
• (707) 942-5296

Set in an old stone building in the heart of town, this spa is an upscale companion to Golden Haven Hot Springs (see our Spas and Resorts chapter). Lincoln Avenue specializes in the easygoing Swedish/Esalen style of massage, with rates ranging from $40 for back, neck and shoulder work to $80 for a full body massage and a foot reflexology treatment. The mud treatments ($49) are longtime favorites too. Lie for an hour on a steam table while wearing a suit of herbal mineral body mud (with 34 herbs), sea mud (with kelp) or mint mud. If you're not allowed to play in the mud, try on the herbal wrap. The spa also does facials and acupressure "facelifts." Packages are available, of course, such as the Ultimate Pamper Package, a four-and-a-half-hour slice of heaven that costs $239.

Lavender Hill Spa
1015 Foothill Blvd., Calistoga
• **(707) 942-4495, (800) 528-4772**

This intimate retreat bills itself as "A Garden Spa for Couples," and, indeed, the verdant grounds in back of the bathhouses are a suitably romantic spot for post-massage reverie and sweet talk. Inside, Lavender Hill offers elegant trappings and a warm staff. Choose from four basic bath treatments: volcanic mud bath, seaweed bath, herbal bath wrap or aromatherapy mineral salt bath, all of which come with a facial mask, blanket wrap and light foot massage. Other options include aromatherapy facials, therapeutic massage and foot reflexology. Prices range from $45 for a basic half-hour massage to $145 for a bath treatment with one-hour massage and mini-facial. The spa's owner produces his own line of ultra-pure products, Quan Yin Essentials, which can be purchased on the premises.

The Calistoga Massage Center
1219 Washington St., Calistoga
• **(707) 942-6193**

The Massage Center is for connoisseurs of massage. They offer deep tissue and sports massage, shiatsu, Thai and esoteric methods called cranio-sacral and Jin Shin. Select a mode and a duration—it's $40 for 30 minutes, $70 for an hour or $105 for 90 minutes. (Swedish/Esalen-based massage is a little less expensive, running $38, $60 and $90.) The center also offers massage for two ($115 for an hour each), massage instruction for couples ($210 for three hours), foot reflexology ($70 for an hour), herbal facials ($65 an hour) and various combinations of the above. Ask about discounts for students, seniors, Upvalley residents and anyone visiting Tuesday through Thursday.

INSIDERS' TIP
Sonoma's bike path runs west-east from Calif. Highway 12 to Sebastiani Winery on the eastern edge of the city. Although it's a bike path, it's more likely to be used by walkers. Along the way you pass Vallejo's Lachryma Montis home, the Depot Museum and the Vella Cheese Company and meet a lot of friendly people.

Tours

Napa County

Napa Valley Holidays
• **(707) 255-1050**

Eli and Laura Glick's company customizes tours for parties of any size. Napa Valley Holidays' basic fee is $250 for two people, and that's an all-day commitment—perhaps four to six wineries, lunch and an on-board docent brimming with behind-the-scenes information and anecdotes. The Glicks also are happy to help visitors with recommendations and reservations for dinner, spas and the like. Soon they might resume the regularly scheduled bus pickups they used to offer.

Napa Valley Bike Tours
4080 Byway E., Napa
• **(707) 255-3377, (800) 707-BIKE**

You feel the breeze, you burn the calories, but someone else wrestles with the logistics. Sound all right? These winery tours begin at 9:30 AM, end about 3 PM and cost $85 per person. Along with a bicycle and helmet, you'll get a fully catered picnic, a friendly guide and a support van to lug bottles of wine (and bodies of worn-out riders). Group size is limited to 10 to ensure safety and individual attention. You can also arrange half-day group tours of 10 to 40 cyclists for $55 per person. Napa Valley Bike Tours also rents cycles by the hour ($7) and day ($22).

Wine & Dine Tours
345 La Fata St., Ste. D, St. Helena
• **(707) 963-8930, (800) WINE-TOU(R)**

A full-service company? Wine & Dine does everything but brush your teeth for you. In addition to guided tours, they handle restaurant reservations, accommodations, ground and air transportation, corporate meetings and event planning, balloon flights, spa treatments and golf. A typical day tour might include transportation, tours and tastings at three wineries and a nice lunch at one of the wineries. Rates vary, but figure on $400 total for a car (1-6 people) plus $45 per person for lunch.

Napa Valley Tours and Trail Hikes
315 Clark Way, Angwin
• **(707) 965-2000, (800) 964-4142**

These guys give you no shortage of options for getting outdoors and getting informed in Napa. They not only do winery tours but also

ATTRACTIONS

offer an overlook hike with a gourmet picnic lunch, and a Mount St. Helena hike. They now offer van service to the peak too. Small backpacks are provided, but it's up to you to wear sensible shoes. Tours range from $79 for a half-day winery circuit to $198 for an all-day, one-on-one trek.

Destination: Napa Valley Tours
295 West Ln., Angwin
• (707) 965-1808

If your tastes are more highbrow than hedonistic, this might be the package for you. Destination: Napa Valley Tours offers chauffer-driven private tours of wineries, but goes far beyond that to incorporate local lore and wine industry history. Prices for a full-day experience range from $65 to $100 per person, depending upon location of pickup and return. (They'll go all the way to San Francisco to get you.)

Getaway Adventures & Bike Shop
1117 Lincoln Ave., Calistoga
• (707) 942-0332, (800) 499-BIKE

Getaway will rent you a bicycle anytime you drop in, but they can do a lot more than that upon request. They do winery tours: six varied wineries, a champagne cellar visit and a shady picnic lunch for $89 (which includes basic tasting fees). They do an all-day Mount St. Helena extreme: a 4,000-foot, off-road descent for $89. And they even do kayak trips: Lake Berryessa, Lake Hennessy or the Russian River for $109.

Sonoma County

Carriage Occasions
530 Irwin Ln., Santa Rosa
• (707) 546-2568

Limousines and antique cars simply not ostentatious enough for you? OK, how about a horse-drawn carriage? This company will meet you in Napa, Sonoma or Alexander Valley and customize a two to three-hour winery tour. Prices vary from city to city. You must book in advance, and they primarily work Saturdays and Sundays.

Festivals and Annual Events

LOOK FOR:
• Event Schedules
January through
December

There's a spirit of *joie de vivre* in this laid-back business of growing grapes and turning them into wine. Whereas life in, say, the banking business seems structured, here in the pastoral setting of Wine Country, a relaxed peacefulness sets in, and the inhabitants turn their attention to having fun and making life more entertaining. Some of this ebullience and joy spills over into a multitude of annual festivals and events. In this locality, we celebrate everything!

Autumn is the time of the "crush," when grapes have ripened and are mashed into juice. Harvest fairs abound, sometimes accompanied by a participatory grape stomp. In village plazas, we all celebrate the glory of another harvest with a sipping, food-noshing salute to wine and the visual arts. Don't forget this is also the land of the Gravenstein apple. We make it a point to remember, shaking up life with an Apple Fair. And while we're at it, let's throw in a little music. How about an Old Time Fiddle Contest? Fiddlers aren't your thing? No problem: We've got jazz festivals and other events that feature different musical styles.

Along the Pacific coast, fishermen bring in the best Dungeness crab in the world (we earnestly believe). To help you prove us right, we've listed a couple of events where you can sample seafood of all kinds and also watch some crazy amateur sailors heading out into the bay in home-made boats built with Styrofoam or milk cartons. We have an exciting, colorful history, and we keep it alive in events throughout the area. We even pay special homage to the rose, for it was plant wizard Luther Burbank who came to this countryside and developed the simple rose into an art form not yet dreamed of.

The wineries themselves are a big part of this celebratory milieu. They have such big, impressive buildings and lovely grounds that they're really ripe for special events. Almost any summer week, there's something great going on in one winery or another. Wine caves have wonderful acoustics, for instance, and if you haven't heard Shakespeare's words in that kind of auditorium, you've got something new to look forward to. And picture this: Imagine sitting on green, rolling estate lawns, sipping wine and listening to a symphony concert while squirrels scamper up the trees around you. These particular events are not free, but the experiences are to be savored for a lifetime.

Perhaps no festival presented in Wine Country surpasses our joyous celebration of mustard. In some areas of the country, mustard is considered an undesirable weed. In Wine Country, it is venerated for the cheer-inspiring swaths of yellow it spreads across the vineyards and open fields. Napa Valley's annual Mustard Festival is launched the first weekend in February with a multitude of separate events.

We couldn't possibly list all the fun-filled and educational events that go on throughout a given year, but we've picked out several we think you will love as much as we do. Many cost nothing; most very little.

January

Sonoma County

Old-Time Fiddle Contest
Citrus Fairgrounds, 1 Citrus Fair Dr., Cloverdale • (707) 894-9550

Sixty or more contestants, novice to pro, gather at the fairgrounds on Citrus Fair Drive for an old-fashioned fiddling contest. But some of the best action is not on the stage, it's in a side room where curious visitors can look in on some wild, free-form jamming. This free event is sponsored by the Cloverdale Historic Society on the fourth Saturday of January. An area has been blocked off for a cafe, where the World Famous Hamburger Ranch & Pasta Farm serves its award-winning burgers. The indoor event usually draws a festive crowd of about 1,200. The year-2000 contest was the 25th annual. You can click on www.cloverdale.net for details.

February

Napa County

Mustard Magic
The Culinary Institute of America at Greystone, 2555 Main St., St. Helena • (707) 259-9020

This grand fête officially launches the annual Napa Valley Mustard Festival on a Saturday in late January or early February (in it fell on January 29). The focus is on the arts, including an exhibition and silent auction of entries in the Mustard Festival Fine Art Contest. Other pleasantries include hors d'oeuvres and desserts created by prominent local chefs, ultra-premium winetastings and music (live opera in 2000). Admission to Mustard Magic is $75 to $95, $125 at the door.

Blessing of the Balloons
Domaine Chandon, 1 California Dr., Yountville • (707) 944-8793

Only seven or eight balloons usually ascend to mark the first weekend of the Mustard Festival, but the Blessing draws anywhere from 200 to 400 people. Picture the blue light of dawn, a field of erupting mustard and drifting planes of mist as Native American spokesman Rolando Solis offers traditional encouragement. There is no charge—except maybe a case of frostbite if you forget to dress warmly.

Chocolate Cabernet Fantasy
Sterling Vineyards, 1111 Dunaweal Ln., Calistoga • (707) 942-0680

Looking for a little decadence? Nero might have been attracted to this three-hour get-together off Dunaweal Lane, about 2 miles south of Calistoga. The Soroptimists fix the desserts (mostly chocolate), Sterling donates its renowned Cabs, and you take care of the rest. There is dance music too. The Fantasy is held on a Friday or Saturday night around Valentine's Day. Tickets are $20, with all proceeds going to charity.

Sonoma County

Japanese Cultural Festival
Rohnert Park Community Center, Snider Ln. and Rohnert Park Expy., Rohnert Park • (707) 795-7863

Spend the first Saturday in February immersing yourself in the culture of the Japanese courtesy of the City of Rohnert Park. Practice the art of paper-folding known as origami, listen to taiko drummers and observe the formal, elaborate, ancient art of the tea ceremony. It happens at the city community center, and it's all free except for food booths and trinket vendors, where you can spend some money.

Citrus Fair
Cloverdale Fairgrounds, 1 Citrus Dr., Cloverdale • (707) 894-3992

Here's how to brighten up winter. On the weekend nearest President's Day, the citizens of Cloverdale come together in a jolly event organized by the Citrus Fair Association. It starts off with a downtown parade then moves out to the Fairgrounds, where everyone livens up with square dancing, country-western dancing, line dancing and regular dancing. There is a carnival for young people, and beer tast-

INSIDERS' TIP

The Clear Lake Team Bass Tournament in March is good family fun, but it is not without its restrictions. Contestants must be 18 years of age or accompanied by a legal guardian, and all standard State of California fishing regulations apply.

ing and winetasting for grownups. Fifteen dollars will get you a glass that 60 to 70 participating wineries will fill. On Sunday you can attend a concert by a popular Western music group such as Smokin' Armadillo. Admission each day is $6 for adults, $3 for seniors and kids ages 6 to 12.

Mendocino County

St. Mary's Mardi Gras
Redwood Empire Fairgrounds,
1055 State St., Ukiah
• (707) 462-3884

For Ukiah, it's the biggest money-raising event of the year, a two-day celebration on a weekend in mid-February that raises money for St. Mary's Elementary School. On Saturday night, there's a dinner and dance held at Carl Purdy Hall at the fairgrounds, with live music by one of the local bands. But Sunday is given over to family fun, with carnival rides and game booths for children. For adults, a wine auction gives bidders a chance to vie for bottles of the vintners' best or for weekend getaways contributed by hotels or resorts. Entrance to the event is free; carnival tickets cost varying amounts.

March

Napa County

Mustard on the Silverado Trail
Various locations • (800) 686-6272

The wine producers that line Napa Valley's "other" north-south artery, the Silverado Trail, demand overdue attention on a weekend in early March. About 15 wineries—including Mumm Napa Valley, Round Hill, Rutherford Hill, Sterling and ZD (see our Wineries chapter)—go above and beyond the call of duty, offering special tours, wine-and-food pairings, entertainment, barrel tastings and so forth. It's a great way to familiarize yourself with the "quiet side" of the valley, and it's free of charge. The two-day open house series is part of the Mustard Festival.

Napa Valley Classic Irish Festival
Kolbe Academy, 1600 F St., Napa
• (707) 255-6412

Nobody dyes the Napa River green for St. Patrick's Day, but the folks at Kolbe Academy (see our Education chapter) do a fine job of celebrating from 2 to 5 PM on an afternoon near the holiday. Food, including wine and ales, is inside the school. The entertainment is in the yard (weather permitting), and includes bagpipes, singing and traditional Irish dancing. Figure on $25 for adults, $15 for children ages 4-12. This is the academy's one major fundraiser each year.

The Awards
Various locations • (707) 259-9020

Lest your springtime excursions begin to convince you that mustard is merely a treat for the eyes, here is an evening that pits Napa Valley's best chefs in a spread-off. Guests get to taste the entries, along with food and wine. There is live music as well. The event, which moves each year and costs $75 in advance ($100 at the door), is held the night before The Marketplace (see next listing). It is coordinated by Barry Levenson of the Mount Horeb Mustard Museum in Wisconsin. The organizers of the competition remind you: When engaging in casual gastronomical activity, always use a condiment.

The Marketplace
Napa Valley Exposition, 575 Third St.,
Napa • (707) 259-9020

This is the Mustard Festival's signature event. The Exposition's halls and open spaces come alive with cooking demonstrations by celebrity chefs, wine and mustard tastings, gourmet food products, micro-brews, fine art, local crafts, horse-drawn carriage rides, eclectic musical offerings on three stages, historical displays and barrel-making demonstrations. It's a two-day event (11 AM to 5 PM both days) on a weekend in mid-March. Admission is $7 for adults, $2 for children 12 or younger. Net proceeds benefit a wide range of nonprofit groups.

A Taste of Yountville
Washington St., Yountville
• (707) 944-0904

Come on down! Yountville likes to boast that it has "more gourmet restaurants and premium wineries than any other town of comparable size," and on the third weekend in March, the hamlet sets up a solid-mile gauntlet of food, olive oil, vinegar, mustard, wine and beer for the sampling public. Local merchants get into the act with fashion shows, tours, furniture restoration displays and even tips on table setting. Most demonstrations are free, and tasting tickets are reasonable (around $1). Even if you are beyond temptation, it might be worth your time to stroll the six blocks through downtown just to hear the live music and watch the entertainment. This is a Mustard Festival event.

The Photo Finish
Mumm Napa Valley, 8445 Silverado Trail, Rutherford • (707) 259-9020

With this grand finale, the Mustard Festival usually leaves 'em longing for more as it heads into hibernation for a year. Mumm's hallways and visitors center are filled with lovers of photography, food, wine and music (doesn't leave many of us out, does it?) on the last Saturday in March or the first in April. The food is by Napa Valley chefs, the wine is primarily from Silverado Trail labels, and the camera work is by the contestants in the annual Napa Valley Mustard Festival Photography Contest. Awards are presented in the tasting room at about 9 PM. Tickets to the Photo Finish cost $65 in advance or $75 at the door.

Sonoma County

Spring Craft Fair
Petaluma Community Center, 320 N. McDowell Blvd., Petaluma • (707) 778-4380

It happens the second weekend in March, and you'll see everything from wood crafts to jewelry to pottery in this show. A comprehensive array of talent is always displayed—everything is handcrafted and lots of things are one-of-a-kind. There's music and refreshments at this free event along with stuff for the kids to do.

Mendocino County

Whale Festivals
Mendocino and Fort Bragg • (707) 961-6300

One of the best reasons to visit the Mendocino Coast in winter is to watch the gray whales cut through the choppy seas during their annual migration, a 12,000-mile round trip from the Arctic Circle to Baja California. It's a cause for celebration, and there are festivals in two cities—in Mendocino the first weekend in March and in Fort Bragg on the third weekend—to welcome the migrating mammals. Whale-watching cruises set out from Noyo Harbor (various prices). There's music, marine art exhibits, discussions about whales at state parks, samplings of wine, beer and chowder all over the towns (pay as you taste) and more.

Lake County

Clear Lake Team Bass Tournament
Library Park, Lakeport • (707) 263-5092

This two-day tournament used to draw 200 to 225 boats. Lately, in the face of competing tourneys and a gradual decline in take at the lake, it has been more like 100. Still, that's enough to give ulcers to the resident largemouth, smallmouth and spotted bass. There is a $100 entry fee per boat, and this is the only tournament in the area to offer a 100 percent payback (not to mention a Saturday night dinner). Boats enter the water at Library Park on a weekend in March, and weigh-ins are held at 3 PM. Winners are determined by total combined weight for the two days.

April

Napa County

April in Carneros
Various locations • (800) 825-9475

The Carneros area, in the bay-cooled hills between Sonoma and Napa, is emerging as the Wine Country's next great appellation. You can judge for yourself over one weekend in mid-April, when 20 or more wineries open their doors and stage special events. About a quarter of the participating producers are normally open by appointment only, and others don't even have proper wineries there—guests are welcomed instead to production facilities. New vintages are released, accompanied by barrel tastings, food pairings, music and even cigar-smoking demonstrations (inhaling optional). Maps are distributed at the open houses, and there is no charge for attending. The circuit tends to be less crowded on Sunday.

MaiFest
Napa County Fairgrounds, 1435 N. Oak St., Calistoga • (707) 942-5356

Upvalley's wurst festival is one of its best. Watch traditional German folk dancing. Sway to the soothing oom-pah-pah of Ottmar Stubler and His Pretzel Benders. More to the point, eat and drink in the robust style of Bavaria. Spaten is the most-requested brew at this all-day Saturday event in late April or early May, though

Napa Valley Brewing Company offers its competent lineup of microbrews along with three or four wineries. Tickets are $10 in advance, $12 at the gate. Food and beverages are extra (though reasonable), as are raffle tickets. First prize is two roundtrip airline tickets from San Francisco to Munich. MaiFest bankrolls a scholarship fund for Calistoga High School.

Sonoma County

Sheepshearing at the Adobe
Petaluma Adobe State Park,
3325 Adobe Rd., Petaluma
• **(707) 762-4871**

On a Saturday in mid-April, 4-H'ers and docents gather at the adobe building that was once the ranch home of General Vallejo (see our History chapter) to demonstrate the arts of wool cleaning, weaving and sheep-shearing. It's all done to pay homage to the way of life Vallejo and the people of his time knew. Looms are available for those who want to try their hand at the craft. Bring along a picnic and make a day of it. There's no charge for the event, but park admission is $3 per adult ($2 for ages 6 to 12).

Butter and Egg Days
Various locations, Petaluma
• **(707) 762-2785**

Petaluma celebrates its storied past through this popular event. Once known as the world's egg basket, Petaluma is now largely dairy country, thus the hometown Butter & Egg Day parade. This includes an egg toss in downtown and a parade of marching bands and (best of all) residents dressed as chickens and pats of butter. Viewers might also see giant papier mâché cows resembling Chinese dragons and floats designed to look like Victorian villages. The "Cutest Little Chick In Town" contest adds to the fun. It all happens the last complete weekend in April, and there are also food booths, other entertainment and an antique fair.

Apple Blossom Festival
Various locations, Sebastopol
• **(877) 828-4748**

It's a weekend in April, and it's a salute to the apple—an annual revival of fairs held at the turn of the century. They'll crown the Apple Blossom Queen, watch a mile-long parade march down Main Street and spend two days having a good time with plenty of music—blues, country and gospel. There's an art show,

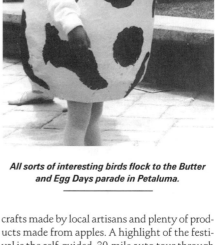
All sorts of interesting birds flock to the Butter and Egg Days parade in Petaluma.

crafts made by local artisans and plenty of products made from apples. A highlight of the festival is the self-guided, 30-mile auto tour through the West County's scenic apple orchards (maps and road signage provided). The festival is sponsored by the local chamber of commerce, and events are held in Ives Park (282 High Street) and at the Veterans Memorial Building next door. Admission is $5 for adults, $2 for seniors and children ages 11 to 17.

Bodega Bay Fishermen's Festival
Westside Park, Bodega Bay
• **(707) 875-3422**

This annual event takes place at Westside Park during a weekend in April. Features include foot races, the Blessing of the Fleet, a boat parade and a bathtub race that includes tubs crafted out of anything that floats—from Styrofoam, milk cartons, wine boxes, you name it. Directions to the park are well-posted. A $3 donation is requested.

Lake County

Pear Blossom Festival
Lake County Fairgrounds, 401 Martin St.,
Lakeport • **(707) 263-6181**

This popular event has little to do with pears

or flowers and everything to do with square dancing. As many as 600 people—enough to fill three pavilions—join hands and promenade their partners at the fairgrounds. Prominent "callers" usually show up to fire off instructions to the dancers, while vendors outside sell down-home food and Western outfits. You can join in, or you can just watch the choreography. There is no admission fee.

May

Napa County

Villa Ca'Toga Tour
**Buses serve Sharpsteen Museum,
1311 Washington St., Calistoga
• (707) 963-4171**

Carlo Marchiori is one of the eminent *tromp l'oeil* artists in the world, and Villa Ca'Toga—a mansion and work-in-progress on the outskirts of Calistoga—is his vision come to life. Faux pillars, staircases and hanging plants are painted in three-dimensional realism on two-dimensional walls. Alcoves end abruptly at painted backdrops, and surprises lie around every corner (even for the initiated—Marchiori is constantly adding new sculptures). For two or three days in May, the house is open to the public. Because there is no parking at Villa Ca'Toga, buses run every half-hour from the Sharpsteen Museum at 1311 Washington Street. You can join a docent trained by Marchiori himself, or you can wander at your own discretion. Tickets are $25, a donation to the city-owned Sharpsteen.

Hidden Gardens Tour
Various locations • (707) 255-1836

The people at Napa County Landmarks were confronted with 106-degree temperatures for the first Gardens Tour in 1996, and El Niño washed out the 1997 edition. They were undaunted, and subsequent tours have been a big success. This is an organized, go-at-your-own-pace walking tour of pocket gardens and historic homes on a weekend in May or June. Explorers hit six to eight pleasances, and then enjoy

an outdoor reception. It costs $18 on tour day. If you buy tickets in advance, it's $10 for members of Napa County Landmarks and $12.50 for non-members. Landmarks also offers self-guided walking tours on 10 Saturdays between May and September. Call for details.

Picnic Day
Fuller Park, Napa • (707) 253-0376

On the Friday before Memorial Day, normally serene Fuller Park becomes a squirming, squealing square full of toddlers and preschoolers. Community Resources for Children sponsors this free event. There is ice cream and oodles of activities and games, from face-painting to bubble-blowing to lamb-petting. About 300 kids usually show up, at least 250 of whom wind up fighting over the same toy. To get to Fuller Park from Calif. Highway 29, take the Downtown Napa exit (Second Street), turn right at Jefferson Street and proceed two blocks.

Sonoma County

Luther Burbank Rose Festival
**Various locations, Santa Rosa
• (707) 545-1414**

Find a spot along Santa Rosa's streets on a mid-May weekend to watch a parade that dates back to 1894 and now draws more than 20,000 people. Floats created with thousands of roses are the highlight of the parade, which begins in front of Burbank's home and winds its way through Santa Rosa to the Veterans Memorial building. The event honors the world-famous horticulturist who improved 800 plant varieties, including the Santa Rosa rose, while living in Santa Rosa (see our Attractions chapter). Other festival events take place at various sites in the downtown area and include street fair exhibits, food booths, performances by singing groups, carnival rides, folk dancing, an antiques fair, a firefighter's competition and displays of firefighting equipment. There's an awards ceremony to honor the best of the parade floats.

Sheepdog Trials
**City Park, end of
Second St., Cloverdale
• (707) 894-5541**

Anyone who has watched these clever little

INSIDERS' TIP

It may complicate your suitcase packing, but the layered look is *de rigeur* in the Wine Country— and not just so you can show off your brightly hued Patagonia windbreaker. The temperature is apt to drop 30 degrees in a single 24-hour period, turning a perfectly warm day into a chilly evening. You need to be prepared for both.

Photo: Tina Luster-Hoban

Vintage 1870 in Yountville houses a variety of shops and eateries and is a popular venue for special events.

herding dogs at work can't help but be amazed at their skill and determination. They love their work and it shows. On the third Saturday in May, sheepdog trials are held at City Park (at the end of Second Street) starting at 9:30 AM. At 11:30 AM, there's a lamb barbecue followed by a ram auction. It's all free except the food. The event is sponsored by the Wool Growers' Association and largely attended by farmers.

Black Bart Festival
124 S. Cloverdale Blvd., Cloverdale
• (707) 894-4470

Honoring the memory of Black Bart, an 1849 bandit who robbed stages without firing a shot in the wild days of the Gold Rush, the citizens of Cloverdale close off the main boulevard of town and turn the day over to celebration. Events include a pet parade and cow-chip tossing (the local Boys & Girls Club collects the cow chips). A foot race starts at 9 AM, and everything else happens after 10 AM—judging of homemade wines, a barbecue from 5 to 7 PM and country music and dancing outdoors on the plaza. It's on a weekend in May or June, and it's all free except the food.

Sonoma Country Fair and Twilight Parade
Various locations, Healdsburg
• (707) 431-7644

Scheduled for the last weekend in May, this is the longest-running event in Healdsburg and the only fair in California that's nonprofit. The Future Farmers of America sponsor this event, in which everything's free except the food. There's a parade on Thursday, a livestock show and auction on Friday, and kids' activities on Saturday. Food and game booths are run by local youth organizations.

Mendocino County

Willits Celtic Renaissance
1119 Madrone Cir., Willits
• (707) 459-1450

The Celtic Renaissance is a throwback to 16th-century Scotland. For two days on the third weekend in May, Recreation Grove is filled with guild booths, where vendors dressed in period costume sell jewelry, swords and weaponry of a bygone era. Some booths represent the English (their brothers) as well as Germans, who are said to have fought as mercenaries for the Scots. The event draws some 1,500 people a day to live Scottish life as it was 400 years ago and to enjoy events where javelins are hurled and water balloons catapulted. Jugglers juggle, and wenches walk about selling tidbits of food. The money collected goes for scholarships for local high school students on their way to college. Admission is $7 for adults, $5 for seniors and free for kids younger than 11.

Great Rubber Ducky Race
Wages Creek, Westport
• (707) 964-2872

Westport is the northernmost town on the Mendocino Coast. It's isolated, and the residents like it that way. But the locals have a sense of humor, proven by their annual Great Rubber Ducky Race. It takes place on Mother's Day and is held on the wide, white sand beaches of Wages Creek just north of the town. Anyone who wants to enter can simply bring a rubber ducky from home (some people fancy them up a bit), launch it in the creek and wait to see how long it takes to float downstream to meet the ocean. Meanwhile, the barbecue coals are lighted (the menu is beef, not duck). Everyone is cool and laid back, watching the clouds float across the blue sky and keeping an eye on the fleet of ducks bobbing downstream.

The event is organized by the Westport Village Society to preserve the headlands as open space. Westport is a small town, but the ranks of rubber-ducky race entrants may reach 300, drawing heavily from nearby Mendocino 9 miles south. Those who go there faithfully each year call it "a real hoot" and "a barrel of fun." The sunshine is free; race entry combined with the beef dinner is $10. It's a great day!

Lake County

Red Hot 'n' Roll
Lake County Fairgrounds, 401 Martin St., Lakeport
• (707) 263-5092

For those of you on the classic vehicle tour, this is your first Wine Country stop. It's a new event on a weekend in May or June, featuring restored cars and motorcycles, beer tasting, a chili cookoff, a bluegrass fiddlers' jam and—that staple of hot-rod events—a doll show. The admission fee is about $3.

Lake County Outdoor Passion Play
Calif. Hwy. 29, Lakeport
• (707) 279-0349

We guarantee you will not find anything else like this in Wine Country. The extravagant dramatization of Jesus Christ's resurrection, staged the third weekend in May, features colorful costumes and an ecumenical cast of 150, not counting sheep, goats or pigeons. Father Philip Ryan of St. Mary's Parish says you can hear a pin drop when Pontius Pilate enters in a horse-drawn chariot. The play used to be one afternoon only, but with some 3,000 people attending, they had to carry it over for two days. (The show runs from 4 to 6 PM.) Bring food and lawn chairs and settle next to Clear Lake. There is no charge, not even for parking, though donations are gladly accepted.

Memorial Day Parade
Main St., Lakeport
• (707) 263-5092

Lakeport chooses the Saturday before Memorial Day for its biggest annual parade. The procession of civic floats and marching bands heads down Main Street as 500 to 600 people crowd the sidewalks. There are additional activities at Library Park before and after, including a pancake breakfast, music, a crafts fair and a barbecue. The only charge is for food.

June

Napa County

Napa Valley Wine Auction
Meadowood Napa Valley, 900 Meadowood Ln., St. Helena
• (707) 942-9775

You can't say you've reached the upper echelon of Wine Country society until you have lifted your bidder's paddle at the Auction. This is Napa Valley's glitziest annual event, not to mention one of the nation's eminent charity auctions. (It has raised nearly $17 million for local healthcare since it was started in 1981.) The Wine Auction takes place the first Thursday-through-Sunday block in June. Thursday features barrel tasting—that's tasting from a barrel. Local vintners then stage a series of simultaneous gatherings: intimate Thursday-night dinners or Friday luncheons. These gatherings display a wide range of formality and whimsy. Saturday offers hot-and-heavy auctioning (both silent and live), followed by a sumptuous feast prepared by a team of renowned chefs at the Meadowood resort. On Sunday most Napa Valley wineries have open houses. All this, and you wouldn't believe how much more, for just $2,000 per couple.

Berryessa Lions Annual Lizard Races
Pleasure Cove, Lake Berryessa
• (707) 966-2172

People can get pretty hot-blooded watching these cold-blooded creatures scamper across indoor-outdoor carpet on the first Saturday in June. Show up with a blue-bellied lizard and a feather and you, too, can enter the fray. (The feather is to be used only if your racer stalls.) There is no entrance fee, and the champions leave with nothing more than blue ribbons. Lizard "owners" are divided by age group, giving the adults a chance to win too. You reach Pleasure Cove via Calif. Highway 128—about 5 miles east of Calif. 121, turn left on Wragg Canyon Road.

Vintage 1870 Father's Day Invitational Auto Show
Vintage 1870, 6525 Washington St., Yountville • (707) 944-2451

When Dad begins to rebel against wide ties and cheap cologne, take him to a car show for Father's Day. The north parking lot of Vintage 1870 will be double-parked with 85 to 90 cars—from Vipers to DeSoto Coupes and from a 1939 Packard limousine to a boss old Woody. While you examine the cars, you can eat, drink (everything from Calistoga water to margaritas) and listen to music. The show runs from 11 AM to 4 PM and is free to the public, excluding food.

Wine Country Kennel Club
Napa Valley Exposition, 575 Third St., Napa • (707) 253-4900

The dog days of summer start a little early in Napa—on a weekend in late June, to be exact. That's when some 2,000 well-groomed pooches strut around the halls and grounds of the Exposition. There are separate shows on Saturday and Sunday, each from 8 AM until about 6 PM. Saturday features an obedience competition; Sunday, a canine good-citizenship test. There are eight age-and-experience classes (including two puppy classes) and seven dog groups: sporting, hound-working, terrier, toy, non-sporting, herding and miscellaneous breeds. The entry fee is generally $22 per dog, and no cash prizes are awarded. The animals vie for points, ribbons, trophies and the ever-popular pat on the head. There is no charge to spectators. The Lions Club provides food, including a pancake breakfast.

Beringer Celebrity Golf Classic
Chardonnay Golf Club
2555 Jamieson Canyon Rd., Napa
• (707) 255-0950

Tired of being ignored as you scream at televised sporting events? The last Wednesday in June is your chance to bend the ear of a famous athlete or coach. Bay Area luminaries like Jim Plunkett, Bill Walsh and Vida Blue have been spotted at recent Beringer Classics. The tournament had been staged at Silverado Country Club for years, but it moved to Chardonnay's Shakespeare course in 1997. Corporate groups pay a $1,500 entry fee; individuals pay $375 (just $300 if they don't feel the need to be paired with a big shot). It's expensive, yes, but the price includes a pre-golf dinner at Beringer. More important, the event funds about half the annual athletic program at Justin-Siena High School, the only Catholic high school in Napa County.

Sonoma County

Ox Roast
Sonoma Plaza, Sonoma • (707) 938-4626

For more than 30 years, the first Sunday in June has been marked by aromatic smoke rising from the town's central plaza. The annual Ox Roast is one giant picnic with barbecued beef, corn on the cob, and plenty of beer and wine. You'll pay $3 to $9 for the meal (beer and wine are extra, and there's also a vegetarian plate), and it all goes to benefit the local community center. The plaza is smack-dab in the center of town. You can't miss it. Just follow the smoke signals.

Stumptown Daze
Main St. and Rodeo Grounds, Guerneville
• (707) 869-1959, (800) 253-8800

This is a great treat for Dad on Father's Day

weekend. A parade, with school bands and pre-school kids on bikes, starts at 11 AM Saturday and follows a route that's subject to local politics, so you might want to call in advance to find out where to park your folding chair. Those who arrive before the parade starts can enjoy a $5 cowboy breakfast ($3.50 for kids) served from 7 AM to noon by the Guerneville Rotary Club. When the parade reaches the rodeo grounds, there is a barbecue ($7 for adults, $4 for those younger than 16). At 2 PM the rodeo starts, with all those events you expect—calf roping, bull riding and barrel racing. On Sunday there's another cowboy breakfast from 7 to 11 AM, more free rodeo and some horseback games. Where'd the name originate? Guerneville gained the moniker "Stumptown" in its early days when redwood trees were mercilessly chopped down, leaving only a forest of stumps.

Mendocino County

Spring Carnival
**Redwood Empire Fairgrounds,
1055 N. State St., Ukiah
• (707) 462-3884**

It's free to enter the gates to the spring fair, held the first weekend in June each year. Entrance to the carnival field is also free, with varying prices for individual thrill rides. Grandstand shows are held Friday and Saturday afternoons from 2 PM on and feature motor sports events such as stock car races. Admission to the grandstand is $10, but kids younger than 3 get in free. The fair is sponsored by the Redwood Empire Fair Association.

Lake County

Middletown Days
**Various locations, Middletown
• (707) 987-3678**

For more than 35 years, the southernmost burg in Lake County has taken the opportunity to say, "Welcome to Middletown," on the third weekend of June. The three days of activity include an old-fashioned hoedown at the arena in Central Park (noon to midnight on Friday); a parade that courses down Main Street on Saturday at 11 AM; lots of music, including

a live band that performs at 9 PM on Saturday; and a gymkhana (Sunday, noon to dusk) that offers various tests of equine skill, concluded by the outrageous "hide ride," wherein competitors sit on a cowhide and get dragged around by a horse. The only costs are for entering events and for food, and those are quite reasonable.

July

Napa County

Napa County Fair
**Napa County Fairgrounds, 1435 N. Oak St.,
Calistoga • (707) 942-5111**

You could be forgiven for expecting to find 9-pound Chardonnay grapes or prize-winning Pinot pies at the eminent wine region's annual fair. But the five-day brouhaha (during the Fourth of July weekend) is more down-to-earth than that. Yes, there is plenty of wine to taste, but there are also the usual assortment of carnival rides, livestock exhibits, arts and crafts and cavity-creating snacks. The fair also includes one or two nights of sprint car racing (see our Spectator Sports chapter) and two nights of concerts, with recent headliners such as country heavyweights LeAnn Rimes, Toby Keith and Faith Hill. Admission is $5 for adults; $2.50 for kids ages 6 to 12. Two separate events—the Miss Napa County Fair Pageant and the Champagne Art Preview—are held on the eve of the fair. Expect about 35,000 people over the five days.

> **INSIDERS' TIP**
> If you plan to watch Calistoga's Fourth of July Silverado Parade on Fair Way, near the end of the route, you had better dress for showers. The fire trucks have been known to hose down the crowd—strictly in retaliation, of course.

Fourth of July Celebrations
**Napa • (707) 257-9529
Calistoga • (707) 942-6333**

Veterans Park is the gathering place for a slew of activity in Napa, including food, carnival games and winetasting. Since 1995 the patriotism has expanded to include eight hours of music at the park by a lineup of five or six bands. When your ears are properly ringing, you can treat your eyes to a fireworks display. There was some uncertainty about this event at press time, so please call for details.

Serving as interlude to the Napa County

Fair is a sublime slice of Americana. People come from miles around for Calistoga's annual Silverado Parade, placing lawn chairs along the route hours in advance. Past parades have featured the sparkling rigs of the volunteer fire department, horsemen, bikers, clowns, a kazoo corps, floats ranging from sweet to absurd and, for some reason, a large group of high-school martial-arts students from Kyoto, Japan. The procession starts at 11 AM, and you do not want to miss it.

Bastille Day
Domaine Chandon, 1 California Dr., Yountville • (707) 944-8844

More than 200 years after the fact, what does the revolutionary capture of Paris' most infamous prison mean to Napa Valley tourists? Party! French bands play folk songs or classic Parisian cafe music from 11 AM to 6 PM, and the visitors center staff dresses up "French style." That phrase is interpreted liberally, so you have an equal chance of being greeted by a slinky French maid, Louis XIV or a two-legged poodle. There is no admission fee, and you can "liberate" sparkling wine by the glass or bottle for the going rate. The 1998 edition was Chandon's 20th.

Napa Valley Shakespeare Festival
**Rutherford Grove Winery,
1673 St. Helena Hwy, St. Helena
• (707) 253-3208**

Talk about a midsummer night's dream. Bring a picnic basket, blanket and a couple of low-backed chairs to Rutherford Grove and see the Bard's most popular works acted under the stars. The Festival starts the weekend after the Fourth of July, and performances are usually held at 7 PM on Friday through Sunday nights for the next four weeks. You can rent a lawn chair for $3. All beverages must be purchased on site, but parking is free. The admission fee is $15, $10 for seniors, students and children younger than 12. In 1999 the scheduled plays are *Comedy of Errors* and *The Merchant of Venice*.

Meadowood Croquet Classic
**Meadowood Napa Valley,
900 Meadowood Ln. • (707) 963-3646**

This is no carefree backyard play day. Members of the U.S. Croquet Association flock to Meadowood in late July for a week of serious mallet-wielding. Guests at the resort may watch the preliminary competition for no charge during the week. On Saturday comes the finale: the championship round plus an auction (for charity) and an early-evening gourmet dinner. It's an elegant affair, with some 200 diners attired in natty whites and seated adjacent to the croquet courts. The finale package costs upwards of $100 per person.

Sonoma County

Old-Fashioned Fourth of July Celebration
Sonoma Plaza • (707) 938-4626

You'd think someone rolled back the clock a few decades to see how Sonoma celebrates Independence Day. In fact, some Insiders say the Fourth of July is their favorite holiday here. Arrive early for a good place to watch the 10 AM parade that circles the Sonoma Plaza, and be sure to wear red, white and blue like everyone else! Among the favorite annual entries is the Hometown Band, with its stirring Sousa marches. After the parade, townsfolk assemble in the Plaza for more band music, the singing of the national anthem, a patriotic speech and the presentation of awards for parade entrants. Locals laze around the rest of the day, then reassemble at nightfall for the big finale—a fireworks display put on by the city fire department (partially funded by an appreciative public) in a large field next to the Vallejo Home.

Salute to the Arts
Sonoma Plaza • (707) 938-1133

On the third or fourth weekend in July, the entire Sonoma Plaza in the heart of town is transformed into an elegant, lively outdoor setting featuring five stages filled with theater troupe performances and a variety of music and dance. Fine art by Sonoma Valley artists, children's activities and the best in local cuisine, wine and handcrafted beers are available. Admission to the festival is free. Tickets for food and wine may be purchased for $1 per taste, or you can employ various package prices that include a souvenir wine glass and plate.

Fort Ross Living History Days
**Fort Ross State Park, Fort Ross
• (707) 847-3286**

On the last Saturday in July, some 100 volunteers and staff participants don period attire and re-enact a typical day at Fort Ross in the mid-1800s, during the days of Russian settlement when the commandant and his wife lived elegantly in the wilderness surroundings (see our History chapter). Bring a picnic! Weather here is unpredictable, so bring a sun hat and warm clothes. Admission is $10 per vehicle, $9 if there are seniors in the car.

Mendocino County

Willits Frontier Days
Various locations, Willits
• (707) 459-6330

A three-day event during the Fourth of July weekend, it's claimed to be "the longest, continuous rodeo in California." Besides roping and steer riding, there is a Fourth of July parade, horseshoe pitching, dances, a carnival, cowboy breakfast, talent show, barbecue and crafts show. Most of it happens in midtown or on the rodeo grounds.

Lake County

Clearlake International Worm Races
Redbud Park, Clearlake
• (707) 994-3600, (800) 525-3743

Gentlemen and ladies, start your invertebrates. The Clearlake International Worm Races take place at Redbud Park on Independence Day, at the end of a parade route that begins at Austin Park. You'll also encounter food and craft vendors and after-dark fireworks. But let's face it, most people show up to see the slimy thoroughbreds. The 1999 races marked the 31st running of an event started by C.C. Schoenberger, a direct descendant of Mark Twain. You can train your own nightcrawler or red worm, or you can rent one for 50 cents immediately prior to the starting gun. There is a $2 entry fee. Racers start in the bull's eye of a 2-foot-diameter circle; the first to inch its way across the perimeter is the winner.

Lake County Roundup
Main St., Lakeport
• (707) 279-4517

They ride into town from as far away as Los Angeles and Oregon on a weekend after the Fourth, resting their steeds in the middle of Main Street. Palominos? No, but maybe Mustangs. The Roundup is an annual classic car show featuring food, music (highlighted by the Konocti Clickers, a group of cloggers) and close to 300 cherry street machines. There is no charge for viewing, but please don't kick the tires. The day before the show, there is a picnic and poker tournament at the county park plus a parade. All proceeds from food sales go to Hospice of Lake County.

Lake County Rodeo
**Lake County Fairgrounds, 401 Martin St.,
Lakeport • (707) 263-6181**

The Rodeo is staged at the same time as the Roundup (see previous listing). For two days in early July, the unsullied Lake County air is filled with dust, the thunderous beat of hooves and, yes, possibly even the smell of manure. This is a full-menu rodeo with calf roping, steer wrestling, bronc riding, bull riding, etc. After the second day's competition, you can set the woods afire at the rodeo dance. The dance is included in the admission fee of $8 to $10.

August

Napa County

Napa Town and Country Fair
**Napa Valley Exposition, 575 Third St.,
Napa • (707) 253-4900**

You can join the 65,000-odd people who come to the Exposition over five days in early to mid-August—just don't call it a county fair. Napa's one and only official county fair is in Calistoga in July (see previous listing), but this is a more-than-reasonable facsimile. There are homemade jams and oversized zucchini, 4-H livestock, crowd pleasers such as a lumberjack competition, a high-diving exhibition, wine-tasting and a kiddie carnival. Headliners at this event have spanned the range from Chubby Checker to Chinese acrobats.

Admission is $7 for adults and teens and $4 for seniors and children ages 6 to 12. There is an additional charge for events in the grandstand, specifically a rodeo and a demolition derby.

Mostly Mozart
Various locations
• (707) 252-8671

On a Sunday afternoon in August, the Napa Valley Music Associates occupy a local winery or landmark to offer tribute to that impish Austrian composer. This musical event usually begins with a "legacy," a series of dramatic vignettes and musical samplers from the life of Wolfgang Amadeus M., and possibly Schubert or some other classical giant. Then featured visiting artists usually play chamber music. Tickets are about $30, and they include the legacy, the concert, a reception and often a tour of the venue. All proceeds benefit NVMA's ongoing music programs.

Photo: Sonoma Index-Tribune

The annual Blessing of the Grapes takes place at the Mission San Francisco de Solano.

historic downtown district by the river. A $3 donation gets you in to the festival, with kids younger than 15 admitted free. Kids can also enjoy a rare experience listening to park rangers sing old sea chanteys, and then everyone can join in on a sing-along. It's an all-day event, from 9 AM to 7 PM.

Sonoma County Folk Festival
**Cinnabar Performing Arts Theater,
3333 Petaluma Blvd. N., Petaluma**
• **(707)838-4857**

Renowned throughout the United States since 1986, this is a wonderful indoor music festival. It's a one-day event held in August, with a varied lineup of musicians. You'll hear everything from traditional and original acoustic music to blues, Caribbean grooves, country and '40s music. Instrumental workshops offer a chance to learn to play a variety of folk instruments from dulcimer to banjo, and there is a kids-for-kids concert.

Dixie Jazz Festival
Doubletree Hotel, 1 Doubletree Dr., Rohnert Park
• **(707) 539-3494**

A late August weekend of solid jazz brings traditional purveyors of the genre from across the country. They play Dixieland and ragtime from 2 PM to midnight on Friday, 10 AM to midnight Saturday and 9 AM to 6 PM Sunday. Don't miss the gospel services Sunday morning. There are five venues at the Doubletree Hotel (formerly Red Lion Inn) at 1 Doubletree Drive in Rohnert Park. For admission prices, which come in a variety of packages, call the above number.

Cotati Accordion Festival
La Plaza Park, W. Silva Ave. and Redwood Hwy., Cotati
• **(707) 664-0444**

On the weekend before Labor Day, accordion players from around the world descend on La Plaza Park. For them, this is a world classic—a two-day extravaganza with professionals playing tangos, clogging music from Ire-

Day of the Queen at Silverado
Silverado Country Club & Resort, 1600 Atlas Peak Rd., Napa
• **(707) 257-4044**

For one day in August, Silverado Country Club becomes a large, lush hat passed for Queen of the Valley Hospital (see our Healthcare chapter). The full bill includes a fashion show, tennis tournament and golf tournament, lunch, an evening barbecue, dancing and a silent auction. The cost depends on how many events you mix and match. The fashion show and lunch are $45; golf and lunch are $130; golf, tennis and the barbecue are $255; you get the idea. The 1999 event raised $90,000 toward a new CT scanner.

Sonoma County

Petaluma River Festival
Petaluma River Turning Basin, Petaluma
• **(707) 769-0429**

On a pleasant summer day, the turning basin (the area where boats and yachts turn around) is a picture to remember, filled with yachts and sailboats, and an ancient schooner (official vessel of the City of Petaluma). In mid-August the whole waterfront area comes alive with boat races, food vendors, arts and crafts booths filled with quality items and an opportunity to stroll around the

land and everything in between. Two stages are set up side by side for nonstop entertainment, while a jam tent gives visitors a chance to bring their own instruments and squeeze with the pros. The event's appeal is largely to a mature crowd, but on the morning of the second day, kid players show what they can do. Admission is $8 for one day, $15 for both. Kids 12 and under are admitted free.

Old Adobe Fiesta
Petaluma Adobe State Park,
3325 Adobe Rd., Petaluma
• (707) 762-4871

General Vallejo's heyday, the 1840s, is recreated here on his rancho, with costumed volunteers displaying craft demonstrations, food preparation, blacksmithing and other period activities from 10 AM to 4 PM (see our History chapter). There is also Hispanic music, Native American dancing and a whisker contest. Enjoy food, kid games, farm animals and more. Park admission is $3 for adults, $2 for kids 6 to 12.

Gravenstein Apple Fair
Ragle Rd., 1 mile north of Bodega Hwy.,
Sebastopol • (707) 571-8288

Traditionally scheduled for a mid-August weekend at Ragle Park in Sebastopol, the Apple Fair features local cuisine and food demonstrations, an animal petting zoo, arts and crafts, and of course, lots of Gravenstein apples and plenty of pie. Music and kids' activities fill the day. Admission is $5 for adults, $4 for seniors and kids ages 6 to 18 and $1 for kids younger than 5.

Mendocino County

Redwood Empire District Fair
Mendocino County Fairgrounds,
1055 N. State St., Ukiah
• (707) 462-3884

Held the second weekend in August at the fairgrounds on N. State Street, it's a bang-up event (literally, if you consider the Destruction Derby) with a big carnival, country-western concerts, lots of livestock events and plenty of family fun. Admission is $6 for adults and teens, $3 for kids 12 or younger. There is some free seating in a grandstand.

Art in the Redwoods
Various locations, Gualala
• (707) 884-1138

Art in the Redwoods, held the third weekend in August. includes fine art, crafts, food and beverage booths, games for children and day-long musical and theatrical entertainment. The event is sponsored by Gualala Art Center, and the fun takes place at the center and Bower Park. There is a $5 admission charge and plenty of stuff to buy.

Lake County

Blackberry Festival
Anderson Marsh State Historic Park,
Calif. Hwy. 53, Lower Lake
• (707) 994-0688

Anderson Marsh is worth a visit any time of year (see our Attractions chapter), but it's especially alluring the second Saturday in August, when the rangers (with help from the Rotary Club and the park's Interpretive Association) set back the clock to the turn of the 20th century. The circular white picket fence serves as a time machine. Outside the fence, there is thoroughly modern live music, food and crafts; inside it, you'll see throwbacks such as butter churning, flint napping and Victorian melodramas—all of which is mere pretense for eating blackberry pie and ice cream on a long summer day. That combination is likely to draw 4,000 to 6,000 people. Cost is $3 for adults, $2 for kids.

Summerfest
Konocti Harbor Resort & Spa, 8727 Soda
Bay Rd., Kelseyville
• (707) 279-4281, (800) 660-LAKE

Konocti Harbor has no qualms about long goodbyes. Lake County's premier resort takes 10 days to say "so long" to summer, ending with a fireworks show the night before Labor Day. Summerfest is actually a bundle of smaller outdoor events, each of which charges a separate admission fee of $30 to $50. The 1999 event also included a Celebrity Quarterback Shootout that drew a number of retired NFL slingers; that one cost $500 a head, though it included tickets to the other events. Meanwhile, standing for all 10 days is Festival Row, a carnival that includes laser tag, water slides, a karaoke bar and lots of

> **INSIDERS' TIP**
> The first day of the Napa County Fair in July is usually designated as Kids Day. All children 12 and under enter free.

evening entertainment. Summer is so impressed it returns to Lake County every year.

September

Napa County

Symphony on the River
Third St. Bridge, Napa • (707) 254-8520

The Napa Valley Symphony brings its music to the masses for one night a year—the Sunday before Labor Day. The action centers around the Third Street Bridge in downtown Napa, where the symphony performs between 7 and about 9:15 PM. Main Street is blocked off between Second and Third streets, and many people also watch from China Point near the First Street Bridge. The show is followed by fireworks and preceded by a mixer at Veterans Park, where vendors sell food, wine and crafts starting at about 3 PM. It's all organized by Friends of the Napa River. (Note: There is a looming possibility that the 2000 event might be canceled due to bridge construction; please call.)

Music Festival for Mental Health
Staglin Family Vineyard,
1570 Bella Oaks Ln., Rutherford,
• (707) 963-1749

Granted, it's not a very sexy title, but the event itself, staged in a big, open-sided tent overlooking the winery and Napa Valley, is rather divine. On a Saturday or Sunday in late September, four hundred guests arrive for a reception with wine and hors d'oeuvres. At 3:30, there is a classical concert directed by a celebrity guest conductor. Half the attendees (those smiling broadly) then stay for a lavish dinner prepared by a renowned chef such as Charlie Trotter or Traci des Jardins. Some 40 to 50 small, ultrapremium Napa Valley wineries pour their goods throughout. The base price is $250 per person for the reception, $1,000 if you stay for dinner, and the best tables are reserved for $10,000 to $50,000. Every penny funds much-needed research into mental illness, primarily through the National Alliance for Research on Schizophrenia and Depression.

Sonoma County

Sonoma Valley Harvest Wine Auction
Various locations, Sonoma
• (707) 935-0803

Events during the Labor Day weekend occur at various wineries and vineyards and include a wine auction and dinner dance, celebrity-chef dinners, barbecue picnics, entertainment and winetasting panels. It's three days of irreverent fun and frivolity to raise money for various charities while avoiding the pretentiousness of other wine auctions. (Tuxes may be worn, but only when accompanied by a "Kick me" sign.) Sunday's auctions culminate with an extravagant dinner buffet and live dance band.

Prices and package deals vary widely year to year as do the charities that benefit. Get information on tickets from Sonoma Vintners and Growers Alliance at the listed number.

Russian River Jazz Festival
Johnson's Beach, Guerneville
• (707) 869-3940

At least eight internationally recognized jazz artists get together the first week in September for two all-day concerts at Johnson's Beach on the Russian River. Food and drinks are available. Prices for jazz under the redwoods range from $26 to $65 for two days.

Valley of the Moon Vintage Festival
Sonoma Plaza • (707) 996-2109

The 100-year-old Valley of the Moon Vintage Festival, held annually on the last weekend in September on the Plaza in Sonoma, is among the oldest wine harvest celebrations in the country. It features a traditional Friday evening winetasting party and a full weekend of historical pageants, the blessing of the grapes, parades, concerts, wine and food tastings. The festival is easy to find—just drive to Sonoma, and it'll be smack in the center of town. If you want to attend the Friday night winetasting event, however, you'll need to order tickets at least a month in advance—it's a sellout every year.

Mendocino County

Roots of Motive Power Festival
Mendocino County Museum, 400 E.
Commercial St., Willits
• (707) 459-2736

This is a way to relive the excitement and dangers of everyday lumberjack work in the redwoods. In mid-September the Mendocino County Museum brings out some of the tools of the trade—antique locomotives and yarders and old steam donkeys (a steam-powered machine that replaced the donkey for pulling large logs). What really draws a crowd is the two-day lumberjack handcar race event, held in front of the Skunk railroad depot (see our Attractions chapter). Two handcars, with four people aboard each, engage in a drag race, pumping for 100 feet or so. Want to see how well you'd do as a lumberjack? It costs $5 to enter the races. It's a popular contest, and during the two days some 40 teams head down the track, pumping away. Other than the race entry fee, the entire event is free.

Fiesta Patrias
**Redwood Empire Fairgrounds,
1055 N. State St., Ukiah
• (707) 463-8181**

To celebrate Mexican Independence Day on September 16, the Latino Club of Ukiah stages a Fiesta Patrias event to select a Latina queen. Actually the object is not so much a beauty contest as a way to raise money for a scholarship fund. The contenders spend a lot of time and energy before the event in soliciting money from merchants, selling tamales and tickets and other fund-raising endeavors. One queen is selected for her beauty, but the real winner is the girl who collects the most money. Each year some $10,000 is made available to help local students of Latin descent go to college. The festivities include fireworks and folk dancing.

Mendocino County Fair and Apple Show
**14400 Calif. Hwy. 128, Boonville
• (707) 895-3011**

This is a traditional three-day family event held on a mid-September weekend and highlighted by a rodeo, sheepdog trials, rides for kids of all ages and country-western dancing in the unique town of Boonville, famous for its self-created language "Boontling." (see the Area Overview chapter and the Insiders' Tip in this section). Admission is $6 for adults and $3 for children younger than 12.

Paul Bunyan Days
**Various locations, Fort Bragg
• (707) 964-8687**

Held each year on Labor Day weekend, this community celebration is a tribute to Paul Bunyan, the legendary giant lumberjack and folk hero who seems to show up everywhere there's lumber, from the north woods of Minnesota to the forests around Seattle. Numerous events keep things hopping for four days. A Sunday logging show gives visitors a look at what professional loggers do in the way of very

strenuous activity. Watching the loggers costs $6, but other events like the parade, the 19th-century dress revue, the fiddlers' contest and the fire department water fight are free. The location changes, so call for the current site.

Winesong
**Botanical Gardens of Mendocino County,
18220 Calif. Hwy. 1, Mendocino
• (707)961-4688**

More than 60 wineries and 50 restaurants participate in this winetasting and auction, held at the unique Botanical Gardens in mid-September. This delightful 47-acre botanical garden is the site of many public functions, including art shows, weddings and civic affairs. Winesong benefits the Mendocino Coast Hospital Foundation. The site is filled with native plants—rhododendrons, heather, fuchsia and dwarf conifers. Two creeks flow through the gardens, and more than 3 miles of trails allow visitors to find their way to the cliff house overlooking the dramatic seascape. It's a perfect site to sample Mendocino's famous wines. There's no entrance fee, but there is a charge for the wine.

Lake County

Lake County Fair
**Lake County Fairgrounds, 401 Martin St.,
Lakeport • (707) 263-6181**

The winetasting tables are the only reminders that this isn't Missouri or Iowa. Lake County throws an old-fashioned fair every Labor Day weekend, with a carnival, livestock exhibits, draft-horse wagon rides and four days of goings-on. There are musical acts, a horse show and a mini-rodeo (bull riding only). The sun can still get a bit aggressive here in early September, but there is plenty of shade at the fairgrounds. The cost is $6 for adults, $3 for children.

West Coast Seaplane Splash-In
**Clear Lake, Lakeport
• (209) 736-4554**

Lake County's annual D-Day comes on the Friday before the last weekend in September, when 35 to 40 seaplanes descend upon tranquil Clear Lake. They range from straight float planes to amphibians, from pre-war to contemporary. It's a loosely organized event that includes a safety seminar and a Friday or Saturday night dinner at the Skylark Motel in Lakeport. There is no fee for watching the invasion, and you can bet on good weather: The event's had only two bad years in nearly 20.

Photo: Bill Hoban

*This sign welcomes visitors to Willits, a north-coast town kick-started
by the 19th-century lumber boom.*

Kelseyville Pear Festival
Various locations, Kelseyville
• **(707) 279-2550**

The citizens of Kelseyville have figured out a constructive use for those late-season Bartletts. On the last Saturday of September, they stuff the succulent fruits into pie crusts, cookie batter, jam jars, ice cream and anything else they can think of, and they build a whole weekend around them. There's even a pear-packing competition among the local packing houses. You'll also enjoy a parade down Main Street (led by antique tractors), followed by a petting zoo, craft vendors and a dance perfor-

mance, and it's all free. In conjunction with the Pear Festival is the Kelseyville Quilt Show, a two-day event featuring at least 100 fine bedspreads—some old, some new, some for sale, some just to admire. The Quilt Show is at the Kelseyville Presbyterian Church at Third and Church streets, and admission is $3. Also part of the festival is a fine art show at the Bank of Lake County, 4280 Main Street.

Pedal 'Round the Puddle
Library Park, Lakeport
• **(707) 263-1845**

A major cyclist alert goes out to Clear Lake

residents on a Sunday in late September or early October. About 250 pedalers start at Library Park (which hugs the lake between First and Third streets in Lakeport) and embark on one of three rides: a 30-miler, a 60-miler or a 100-miler, the last of which pretty much circumnavigates the elongated "puddle." Any type of bike is welcome as long as you have the entry fee ($25 to $35). The Pedal is organized by the Lakeport Rotary Club.

October

Napa County

Southwest Art in the Wine Country
Lee Youngman Galleries,1316 Lincoln Ave., Calistoga • (707) 942-0585

If Native American spirit guides, dusty cowboys, fiery desert sunsets and howling coyotes are your idea of art, you shouldn't miss this annual show at an Upvalley winery. About 35 artists usually display varied works in late September or early October. Saturday is by RSVP only; Sunday is open to the general public, at no charge. A silent auction benefits the Boy Scouts of America.

Calistoga Beer and Sausage Festival
Napa County Fairgrounds, 1435 N. Oak St., Calistoga • (707) 942-6333

You might think you have to speak in hushed tones when you discuss beer in the Wine Country, but this festival is well-regarded. (The 2000 edition is the 17th annual.) The sudsfest features a chili cookoff, music and samples from about 30 microbreweries (see the Close-Up in our Wineries chapter), not to mention sausage companies, mustard makers and, quite possibly, pretzels from Snyders of Hanover. Twenty dollars gets you in the door and entitles you to a bottomless souvenir cup and borderless plate. It's a one-day affair in late September or early October.

Old Mill Days
Bale Grist Mill State Historic Park, 3369 N. St. Helena Hwy., St. Helena • (707) 942-4575

The folks at the Grist Mill celebrate the end of harvest by partying like it's 1869. Coopers, weavers, storytellers and old-time fiddlers don period costumes to lend a touch of authenticity to the 19th-century goings-on. The kids can make cornhusk dolls or dye wheat. And the park rangers offer nonstop tours of the mill, which (if it's restored in time) will be busy grinding whole-wheat flour and cornmeal. It's a two-day event in mid-October. The cost is $4 for adults and $2 for children.

Napa Valley Open Studios Tour
Various locations
• (707) 257-2117

Come see real, live artists in their natural habitats! On successive weekends in mid- to late October, Napa Valley creative types throw open the doors to their studios and welcome the self-guided with refreshments. The format tends to be Upvalley one weekend and Downvalley the next. The Napa Valley Arts Council distributes maps prior to the free event; all you do is drive and gawk. At least 80 artists usually participate, including big names such as Earl Thollander, Catherine Anderson, Davis DeSelle and Ann Hunter Hamilton. The settings run from valley tip to valley bottom, and the media run from photography to metal sculpture to oil painting. If nothing else, the tour shows that all artists do not live in cramped, unkempt studio apartments. You must be thinking of writers.

Hometown Harvest Festival
Adams St., St. Helena
• (707) 963-5706

For decades, St. Helena marked the end of the grape harvest with a municipal celebration. Sometime in the 1960s, the city fathers decided to adopt a more refined image, and the harvest bash was abolished. It made a welcome comeback in 1987. The festival, a one-day event on a Saturday in October, includes arts and crafts, a fun run, a carnival, winetasting and a canine Frisbee-catching contest. The highlight is the pet parade, an advancing column of dogs, cats, horses, llamas, roosters and lizards. (One recent costume award went to a hamster.) Most of the action swirls around St. Helena Elementary School, on Adams Street between Oak and Stockton streets. There is no admission fee, and most of the proceeds from vendor sales go toward building St. Helena a new community center.

Sonoma County

Fall Colors Festival & Car Show
Various locations, Geyserville
• (707) 857-3745

On the last Sunday in October, Geyserville's streets are lined with autos, old and new, for the Kiwanis Car Show. The day starts with a pancake breakfast at 7 AM; the rest of the day is filled with music and arts and crafts shows. After breakfast, admission to the events is free.

Sonoma County Harvest Fair
1350 Bennett Valley Rd., Santa Rosa
• (707) 545-4203

This harvest festival on the first full weekend in October features a world-championship grape stomp, winetasting, produce exhibits, food, arts, crafts, amateur beer and wine booths, music and kids' exhibits. General admission is $5, but it's $2 for seniors on Friday and $2 for kids ages 7 to 12.

Mendocino County

Country Pumpkin Fest
Various sites, Ukiah
• (707) 462-4706

The Pumpkin Fest is a two-day event at the end of October that draws more than 12,000 visitors to celebrate Ukiah's rich agricultural tradition. The event starts with a parade on Saturday morning then goes on to a vast assortment of entertainment. Home-cooking contestants vie for the best pumpkin recipe. (There is a small fee to enter.) Most of downtown Ukiah participates in the event, and it's all free except for what you eat or purchase from vendors.

Lake County

Harvest Festival
Steele Winery, 4350 Thomas Dr.,
Kelseyville • (707) 279-1420

The only thing better than watching people peel off their shoes and stomp the juice out of ripe grapes is hopping into the tub yourself. Well, here's your chance. When Steele bought Konocti in 1995, it continued the old winery's traditional harvest bash, with crafts, barbecue, music, winetasting and the oldest form of crushing. It's

a two-day event on the second weekend of October, with a Lakeport Chamber of Commerce-sponsored vineyard run on one of the days.

November

Napa County

Napa Valley Wine Festival
Napa Valley Exposition, 575 3rd St., Napa
• (707) 253-3563

Encouraging kids to drink is not good, but encouraging kids through a drinking festival is another matter altogether. This gig on the first Saturday in November raises about $50,000 a year for the Napa Valley Unified School District. The fun includes a live auction, with about 50 valley wineries pouring and 1,000 guests sipping, student-provided music as a backdrop and a pasta dinner for sustenance. Tickets are $30 in advance, $35 at the door. There are also golf and tennis tournaments at Napa Valley Country Club, though they may precede the festival by a week.

Festival of Lights
Vintage 1870, 6525 Washington St.,
Yountville • (707) 944-2451

This isn't so much the lighting of a tree as the lighting of a town. At about 6 PM the day after Thanksgiving, all of Yountville flicks its switches and is bathed in fairy lights. Christmas is beckoned with singers, street performers, hayrides and roasted chestnuts from 2 to 9 PM. There is no admission fee, though you must buy tickets for food and wine. The extravaganza sets off a month of special dinners, musical performances and the like around Yountville. The festival celebrated its 10th anniversary in 1998.

Christmas Parade
Napa • (707) 257-0322

Napa's Yuletide parade, a tradition since the early 1960s, gets moving at 11 AM the Saturday after Thanksgiving. It starts at the Cinedome Theater at Pearl Street and Soscol Avenue and moves west on Pearl. The parade turns left on Main, right on Second, right on School, right down First, left on West and back to Pearl. Making all those right-angle turns are high school bands, dance groups, scout troops, church floats, horses, clowns and a waving, hirsute man in a red suit. When Santa retires to the rotunda at Napa Town Center after the parade, the holiday season has officially come to Napa.

Sonoma County

Santa's Arrival
Petaluma Riverfront,
Petaluma
• (707) 769-0429

On the last Saturday in November, Santa makes his way into Petaluma by boat. While awaiting his arrival, the children stay busy with a variety of entertainment options. As might be expected, Santa's first move is to start handing out candy canes. Then he steps into an antique wagon chosen from the collection at the county museum (considered the largest collection in North America) and leads a parade of beautiful wagons in a circular route around town. It ends in historic Petaluma, where merchants hold a "Share the Spirit" event with an array of treats for all.

Mendocino County

Thanksgiving Festival
Mendocino Art Center,
45200 Little Lake Rd., Mendocino
• (707) 937-5818

A jolly festival at the Mendocino Art Center to survey the newest in professional arts and crafts occurs the weekend after Thanksgiving. Every inch of the center (and outside it, if the weather is cooperative) is filled with booths displaying crafters' works, from tie-dye to watercolors. A separate room has been reserved for kids to play, and there is always a visit from Santa. Stick around for the blackberry sundae—it's scrumptious.

December

Napa County

Carols in the Caves
Various Napa and Sonoma wineries
<Listing info>• (707) 224-4222

David Auerbach is a local multi-instrumentalist. That term is defined at his performances, where he is likely to play two dozen musical devices including dulcimers, pan pipes and psalteries. As you might guess, he specializes in

unusual folk instruments, and he brings out the best of each in the flawless acoustic environment of wine caves. The Carols series consists of a minimum of eight simple, informal concerts, two or three per weekend between Thanksgiving and Christmas—and sometimes running into January for a Twelfth Night celebration. Locations vary from year to year and week to week. The first half of Auerbach's show tends toward the unfamiliar and esoteric; the second half encourages audience participation with well-known carols. Cost for each show is about $30 per person, unless it includes dinner, in which case you'll pay at least $125. It is customary for the host to pour complimentary wine during the intermission (or dinner).

Holiday Candlelight Tour
Various locations • (707) 255-1836

On the second Saturday in December, Napa County Landmarks (a local preservation society) organizes a 3 to 8 PM walking tour in a selected historic neighborhood. The stroll and open houses are usually in Napa but can turn up anywhere in the county. Many of the hosts put out cookies or cider, and there is a sweets-and-wine reception from 4 to 10 PM at a particularly fabulous building. One recent tour was in the district surrounding St. John's Catholic Church in Napa, with a reception at the Jarvis Conservatory. Expect eight or nine stops, with strolling carolers and glowing luminaries along the way. The cost is $15 for Napa County Landmarks members, $18 for everyone else signing up in advance. It's $25 if you pay at the door.

Pioneer Christmas
Bale Grist Mill State Historic Park,
3369 N. St. Helena Hwy., St. Helena
• (707) 942-4575

Ever wonder how Americans celebrated Christmas in the 1850s? Well, don't expect any Tickle Me Elmos or Muzak renditions of "Silver Bells" if you visit the Bale Grist Mill on a weekend day in mid-December. What you can expect are Christmas carols sung to the accompaniment of mandolin and fiddle. You can string popcorn and cranberries, drink apple cider and, for a nominal charge, decorate gingerbread cookies. Longtime miller George Stratton probably will be there giving tours and, if the State Parks Service can repair the wheel in time, he may be grinding out fresh flour and corn-meal too. Adults pay $4; it's $2 for the kids.

Sonoma County

Russian River Heritage Christmas
Various locations, Guerneville
• (707) 869-9000

In the early 1800s, Russians from Fort Ross made their way up the river and settled for a time. Guerneville folks have not forgotten their heritage. Costumed carolers sing Russian folk songs, Russian sweets are sold by vendors and shop windows are decorated with Russian dolls and toys. Kids can ride in a Russian carriage, and Father Christmas hands out small candies.

Dickens Street Faire
Various locations, Cloverdale
• (707) 894-4470

For two days during the first weekend in December, Cloverdale shop owners and street vendors dress in period costumes, ply their arts and crafts and sell their wares. There is enter-tainment, horse-drawn carriage rides, storytelling and St. Nicholas holiday music from 10 AM to 4 PM each day.

Mendocino County

A Smalltown Christmas
Various locations, Ukiah
• (707) 462-4705

Santa flies into the local airport, and from there he rides a fire truck around town to visit all the shopping centers. A music program is held in the downtown area and is followed by the "Truckers Light Parade." Kick off the Christ-mas spirit with this event, the first weekend in December.

Lake County

Christmas Open House
Anderson Marsh State Historic Park,
Calif. Hwy. 53, Lower Lake
• (707) 994-0688

This is sort of a wintry version of the Black-berry Festival (see August), held on a Saturday (usually) in early December. The historic house is spruced up with handmade 19th-century holi-day decorations. Come inside for Christmas car-ols, cider and cookies. There is no admission charge.

Shopping

LOOK FOR:
• Malls
• Unique Shops
• Antiques
• Bookstores

Wine Country is not the land of the mega-mall, nor of endless discount outlet store complexes. Although we have both malls and outlets here, they have not yet taken total control.

Instead, what you're likely to encounter are one-of-a-kind shops selling one-of-a-kind items in towns that are tucked amid sprawling vineyards or washed by the wild Pacific. But don't be fooled—these are not the quaint country villages of TV's Cabot Cove or Mayberry USA. These are cosmopolitan communities—meccas for lovers of fine wines, fine foods and all things unique and excellent.

Wine Country shopkeepers are savvy and world-wise in their selection of merchandise. Informed shoppers will recognize the possibilities immediately and plunge in right away. For them, shopping is a game, a challenge to find all that's new and special and "just right," at prices that will turn friends green with envy. For these advanced "shopaholics," Wine Country is just the place, and now is the time.

On the other hand, if your idea of shopping is going out to buy socks when you finally run out, even you may fall under the spell cast by the picturesque streets of St. Helena and Calistoga. You may find yourself popping in and out of the shops and galleries clinging to the four sides of Sonoma's historic Plaza. And in the end, you may find yourself hooked. A stroll among Mendocino's dozens of specialty shops is certain to bring the credit cards out of your jeans pocket.

Wineries add to the galaxy of possibilities here. Drop in at one of the winery gift shops, and you'll see lots of things to bring home to friends—if you haven't already loaded them down with bottles of Zinfandel. And if you're into antiques, you're a goner for sure. Napa alone has enough antique items to fill 24,000 square feet in just one building. Santa Rosa has devoted most of a city block to the sale of antiques. Tiny Sebastopol (population 7,575) has about 15 antique shops, including one collective with more than 100 dealers. And those are just the big ones.

Oh, yes, and about those malls and outlets. If you've had enough of boutique shopping and yearn for something more mainstream, head for Napa Factory Stores (a maze of classic-label clothing emporiums) or to the Petaluma Village Factory Outlet, where the dazzling possibilities may keep you rooted to the place for days. Almost every town in Wine Country has some sort of mall or shopping strip—generally anchored by a food market and a drug store, with various other shops between. We have listed those that are larger, especially those with nationally recognized stores or with particularly intriguing specialty shops. You'll find these in our first section of listings.

Next, we detail the various specialty shops scattered throughout Wine Country, and we follow that up with a breakdown of antique stores and bookstores throughout the four-county region. Remember, listings within the different subject headings are arranged in the geographic order outlined in How to Use This Book: We start with Napa County, then move on to Sonoma, Mendocino and Lake counties. Expect these stores to keep reasonably regular hours—if operating times are particularly unusual, we'll let you know in the listings. It's always a good idea to make a call if you're not sure when a place is open.

Malls

Napa County

Napa Premium Outlets
Calif. Hwy. 29 at First St. exit, Napa
• (707) 226-9876

The factory stores have done the improbable in Napa Valley—in the middle of Wine Country, they've become a big tourist draw in and of themselves. The immense Napa facility features more than 45 premium designers and brand-name outlets, including heavy hitters such as **Calvin Klein**, **Nautica**, **Ellen Tracy**, **Ann Taylor Loft**, **BCBG**, **Max Studio**, **J. Crew**, **Timberland**, **Tommy Hilfiger**, **Jones New York** and **Dansk**. You can expect savings of 25 percent to 65 percent off normal retail price tags. Napa Premium Outlets also has the Courtyard Cafes with a choice of quickie cuisines, plus the table-service Fujiya Restaurant. The stores are open Monday through Thursday from 10 AM to 8 PM, FRIDAY AND SATURDAY FROM 10 AM TO 9 PM, and Sunday from 10 AM to 6 PM.

Napa Town Center
First St., between Coombs and
Franklin Sts. • (707) 253-9282

Roughly bordered by First, Franklin, Pearl and Coombs streets, Napa Town Center is the pulsing heart of the city's downtown shopping. The courtyard mall has winding pathways through cobblestone paseos, and at least 20 shops, including **McCaulou's Department Store**, **Waldenbooks**, and **Miller's Outpost**. It also houses the **Napa Valley Conference and Visitors Bureau**, the stationary welcome wagon for a high percentage of Wine Country tourists. Napa Town Center is bordered by a half-dozen or more restaurants and snack shops. The Center presents two Bridal Fairs each year and holiday events at Christmas, plus regular **Popcorn Pete's** Kid Club Shows. And every Friday from May through September it hosts the **Chefs Market**, which gathers together purveyors of produce, baked goods, crafts and more.

Vintage 1870
6525 Washington St., Yountville
• (707) 944-2451

You can't miss Vintage 1870 any more than you could have missed the building when it dominated the landscape as the Groezinger Winery. Built (as you might guess) in 1870 by Gottlieb Groezinger, the massive red-brick winery now contains a warren of specialty shops

featuring fine art, foodstuffs, T-shirts, antiques, home and garden accessories, clothing, linens—more than 40 shops on two levels. Vintage 1870 has several cafes, snack shops and restaurants for the hungry purchaser, as well as a trellis-shaded picnic garden. It also has an excellent wine cellar—see our Wineries chapter for more details. Get there early enough and you can watch the hot-air balloon departures.

St. Helena Premium Outlets
Calif. Hwy. 29, 2 miles north of St. Helena
• (707) 963-7282

The St. Helena collection of factory stores is much smaller than its relatives in Napa and Petaluma, but a poor cousin it isn't. The tucked-away line of shops on the west side of the highway includes **Brooks Brothers**, **Donna Karan**, **Joan & David**, **Movado**, **Coach** and **London Fog**. Traditional retail establishments would have a hard time matching the prices here (25 to 65 percent less at the outlets), and even more trouble matching the parklike setting, which includes picnic tables. The outlets are open daily from 10 AM to 6 PM.

Sonoma County

The Plaza areas in the cities of Sonoma and Healdsburg could easily be considered shopping centers. But with so many wonderful stores meriting individual listings, we have placed the write-ups for those shops under the subsequent "Unique Shops" heading. What follows is information on the more traditional mall-type alternatives in Sonoma County.

Petaluma Village Premium Outlets
2200 N. Petaluma Blvd., Petaluma
• (707) 778-9300

It's outside the mainstream shopping area of Petaluma, but it's an irresistible magnet for shoppers looking for bargains on the finest designer fashions and name-brand merchandise. The maze of stores includes **Brooks Brothers**, **Levi's**, **Jones New York**, **Mikasa**, **Reebok**, **Saks Fifth Avenue** . . . and that's just a start. If you're tired of boutique shopping, this is your place. You'll find about 50 shops to get lost in, every day of the week. Hours are 10 AM to 8 PM Monday through Saturday and 10 AM to 6 PM on Sunday.

Raley's Towne Center
6547 State Farm Dr., Rohnert Park
• (707) 545-3844

It's new, and it's a cool, wonderful place to

spend a summer day or escape a rainy, wintry one. Find dress bargains at **Ross Dress for Less**, or sink into a slice of pizza at **Little Caesars**. There is also a **RadioShack**, **Kragen Auto Parts**, **Beauty Store & More** and **Precision Hairstyling** represented in this center. Hours of individual stores will vary.

Coddingtown Regional Mall
U.S. Hwy. 101 and Steele Ln., Santa Rosa • (707) 527-5377

This is the old standby shopping mall for locals. Some Wine Country patrons come just to spend a few Sunday hours sitting on the comfy benches and sipping Orange Julius drinks while people-watching—or are they just waiting to get up their steam for another charge at the 100 shops along the runways? Anchor stores are **Macy's Department Store**, **Gottschalks** and **JCPenney**, with lots of likely favorites filling the spaces between such as **Miller's Outpost**, **Cobbie Shoe Shop** and **Clothes Time**. One of the most charming shops here or anywhere is **The Classic Duck**, crammed with exquisite gift and home accessories that will keep you spellbound while time passes and spouses wait.

Montgomery Village
Montgomery Dr. and Farmers Ln., Santa Rosa • (707) (707) 545-3844

This is an architecturally appealing shopping center, dripping with ivy and landscaped with exotic shrubs and plants. Montgomery Village was built using the ranch-style Town and Country architecture so popular in the 1950s. The shops are tidy and specialized. You can find kid stuff at **Gingerbread Storybooks and Whimsy**, perk up your home decor with finds from **Home Sweet Home**, be dazzled by gorgeous tabletop settings at **Company's Comin'**, pick up some stylish leisure clothes at **Barbara Friday Weekend Wear** or indulge in awe-inspiring baked goods at **Michelle Marie's Patisserie**. (A co-author of this guide served a Michelle Marie creation at his daughter's 30th birthday party, inadvertently rendering every guest speechless for a full 15 minutes following "Happy Birthday to You.") In all, Montgomery Village includes 50 shops and a few restau-

rants. Shops are open seven days a week from 10 AM to 9 PM.

Santa Rosa Plaza
Downtown exit off U.S. Hwy. 101, Santa Rosa • (707) 544-SHOP

This shopping mall is downtown, poised at the end of Fourth Street, which itself is a cozy five-block shopping street that's recently been revitalized by the arrival of a humongous **Barnes & Noble** bookstore. The anchor stores of Santa Rosa Plaza are **Macy's**, **Mervyn's** and **Sears**. More than 110 additional specialty shops, eateries and special services are lined up on two levels, with lots of apparel shops (**Eddie Bauer**, **Gap**, **Victoria's Secret**) and places to buy cards, music, jewelry, sporting goods and more. Shops are open seven days a week.

Mendocino County

Depot Marketplace & Museum
401 N. Main St., Fort Bragg • (707) 964-6261

For most of this century, the California Western "Skunk" depot has been the busiest place in town—at least when the train heads out for Willits on its run (see our Attractions chapter for more on the train). Now the depot at the end of Laurel Avenue attracts crowds for another reason. Four years ago an old Ford garage was turned into a shopping mall and railroad museum. Some unusual little shops are clustered around immense hunks of equipment and a steam engine that occupies center stage as you enter.

Boutique Mystique displays gorgeous quilts that are nothing like the ones your great-grandmother turned out to use up old scraps of material. They're a little pricier (around $900), and they're real works of art.

Fuchsiarama has more gorgeous quilts glorifying its walls. (The name comes from Fuchsiarama, a lovely spot 2 miles north of Fort Bragg that is smothered in fuchsia blossoms. It's a great place for a picnic.)

Tylart Shop is for you if you've got any Scandinavian blood. You'll recognize the trolls there when you see them—those ugly elves whose very name has terrified schoolchildren for

SHOPPING

centuries. This shop has them by the hundreds, and they're hardly scary at all. Depot Marketplace shops are open from 10 AM to 6 PM in summer, and until 5 PM in winter.

Unique Shops

Napa County

Shackford's
1350 Main St., Napa • (707) 226-2132

World-class restaurants necessitate a lot of chefs, and most Napa Valley kitchen whizzes do their shopping at Shackford's. So do the common cooks, and one step into the store will show you why. This is the Nirvana of pots and pans. You'll find whole aisles of knives (Wusthof Trident, Sebatier, Forschner and many more), pans (Calphalon, All-Clad, Look, etc. etc.) and cutting boards (wood, acrylic, poly, yada-yada-yada). The Kitchen Aid mixers are lined up like a Panzer division, and the pot racks hang like chandeliers. What else? Dozens of cookie cutters and candy forms, canning supplies, every possible component of cake decoration and gadgets too numerous to look at, let alone mention. It's all priced competitively.

The Beaded Nomad
1238 First St., Napa
• (707) 258-8004

There aren't many stores where prices start at 3 cents. The Nomad stocks more types of beads than you thought existed on the seven continents of this world—beads of metal, thread, plastic, glass, wood, fimo (a polymer clay), ceramic and even hemp. The bins in which they nest become a three-dimensional quilt of colors, shapes and designs. You can assemble your beads right there in the store (mixing is encouraged), and they'll provide design assistance and repair. The shop even offers classes in basic and advanced stringing. It also carries masks and jewelry from various exotic locales.

JHM Stamps & Collectibles
The Book Merchant and Sirius Bindery
1330 Second St., Napa
• (707) 226-7511 (JHM), (707) 259-1326 (Book Merchant)

Double your high-brow pleasure at one address housing two business. JHM, the only stamp shop within a 40-mile radius, has been on Second Street for more than 20 years. They have stamps from all over the world and a wide range of philatelic supplies—albums, refill pages, catalogs and more. JHM also has boxes of blank postcards, from every state in the union. The Book Merchant deals in antique and collectible books, especially those concerning local history. You might find a five-part library of Freemasonry, old pulp paperbacks, a 24-volume Dumas collection, signed first editions or the complete work of Dickens in 20 volumes. The prices range from $5 to $1,000. The bindery is especially popular with people trying to preserve family relics.

Inti
1139 First St., Napa
• (707) 258-8034

That this store was named for the Incan sun god tells you all you need to know about the business. It's a hodgepodge of imported multi-ethnic crafts popular with hippie kids— and anyone else looking for interesting decorations that won't devastate their checkbooks. Inti has jewelry, wood carvings, furniture, musical instruments, purses, candles, incense, batiks from Bali and rugs from Peru. Oversized tapestries hang on the walls, and clothing from India and Indonesia hangs on racks. Look for the *arpilleras*—long Peruvian quilts that tell stories through applique.

Napa Valley Keyboards
1141 First St., Napa
• (707) 224-5397

When a local winery or resort needs a grand piano for a one-night fete, it goes to Napa Valley Keyboards. That's partly because this is the only piano store in Napa County, but also because of the shop's sterling reputation. They have both new and old pianos of varying sizes and new electronic keyboards too. All pianos are tuned twice—once in the store and again after delivery. One drawback: Few of them fit in the trunk of a rental car.

Paint Your World
1349 Napa Town Center, Napa
• (707) 226-7484

Looking for a completely original gift? Hire yourself as the artisan. At Paint Your World, you buy a plain ceramic piece (anything from a plate or cup and saucer to a serving bowl or switch plate) for the going rate and decorate it yourself. The materials charge is $6 for the first hour or $9 for the live-long day, and most customers finish in about an hour. The store provides a spectrum of paints, a work station and an apron. They glaze and fire your pieces, and you return to pick up the finished product. All the materials are non-toxic and dishwasher-safe. Paint Your World also hosts kids' parties at $16 to $20 per child, and they toss in cake, juice, balloons and the ceramic article of choice.

Overland Sheepskin Company
6505 Washington St., Yountville
• (707) 944-0778

If it once bleated, you'll find it here. Overland's Jim Leahy began making sheepskin coats by hand in Taos, New Mexico, in 1973. Now the family-owned company sells its woolly wear at 11 locations around the country, including this locale in Yountville. Try on the sheepskin slippers, or sit on a stack of amazingly plush rugs. Almost everything is 100 percent sheepskin, from the car seat covers to the coats (even the lining). Overland sells leather goods made by other manufacturers, including Australian outback dusters, hats, footwear and water-buffalo bags from India.

INSIDERS' TIP

Not every state will allow interstate wine shipments into their territory, so ask your wine merchant in advance.

Mosswood
6550 Washington St., Yountville
• (707) 944-8151

When you have fully decorated your house and it's time to turn to the garden, Mosswood is here for you. This place has fountains, bird feeders, statuary, weather vanes, wind chimes and more. The line of birdhouses is particularly impressive, with copper-domed, thatched-roof and pebbled models. Mosswood also carries decorative interior accessories, including the Gracey Knight collection of bright, handpainted furniture, featuring dozens of different knobs and pulls.

Napa Valley Grapevine Wreath Company
8901 Conn Creek Rd. (Rutherford Cross Road), Rutherford
• (707) 963-8893

While most grape growers are pruning, stacking and burning vines in the winter, this company is building its inventory. The Wood family (a partner in the original Freemark Abbey investment group) trims its 80 acres of Cabernet Sauvignon plants, strips the leaves and fashions the vines into decorative wreaths—and a whole lot more. They make dozens of styles of baskets, plus cornucopias, hearts, crosses, stars, wine carriers, even rein-

deer and magic wands. All of it is handmade, distinct and highly durable.

Dean & DeLuca
607 St. Helena Hwy. S., St. Helena
• (707) 967-9980

Twenty years after the first Dean & DeLuca opened in SoHo in 1977, the ultrapremium food purveyors brought their act to Napa Valley. And while the massive wine section (see our Wineries chapter) is what sets this one apart from the other four branches, there is plenty more to woo your senses. Such as? Such as jam and marmalade jars by the dozen, and an ocean of olive oil compartmentalized into 16-ounce bottles. You can find dried beans and rice, dried fruit, tins of dried herbs, teas and coffees, cigars, chocolates and sweetly packaged edibles you never knew existed. And you can complete the experience with a high-quality cooking utensil, a cookbook or a basket. Dean & DeLuca has a sandwich-and-salad bar called Market Cafe, an espresso bar and bakery, fresh produce and a central deli with no end of meats, cheeses and olives. But most of all it has its reputation for service, a commodity delivered by a squadron of friendly attendants in white chef's coats.

St. Helena Olive Oil Co.
345 La Fata St., Suite C, St. Helena
• (707) 967-1003

Olive oil is as ancient a pursuit as wine, and it gets the same reverent treatment at the St. Helena Olive Oil Co. You can sample a few varieties in the tasting room, then tour the aging and bottling operations. Most of the fruit comes from the Central Valley, but the company recently contracted with a Napa Valley olive grower. That product will go into the high-end Cask 85 line. St. Helena Olive Oil also imports balsamic vinegar from Italy and makes a few types of its own, including five flavored balsamics (with fresh berries) and a Cabernet vinegar. Everything is natural—no sugars or preservatives—and available in 60-ml., and 250-ml., or 375-ml. vessels. Access La Fata Street via Dowdell Lane, which exits Calif. 29.

Napa Valley Olive Oil Co.
835 Charter Oak Ave., St. Helena
• (707) 963-4173

For more than 50 years, this white clap-

SHOPPING

Photo: Bill Hoban

The Grace Hudson Museum and Sun House contains a fine collection of gifts, books, crafts and jewelry.

board barn has been distributing premier olive oil to Napa Valley and the world. The old mill and hydraulic presses are still here, but the olives are actually pressed in the Sacramento Valley now. Still, the Particelli family bottles and packages all of its oils in St. Helena (except for the extra virgin). That's a lot of bottling—about 100,000 cases per year. The oil is available in sizes ranging from pints to gallons.

Flying Carpets
1152 Main St., St. Helena
• (707) 967-9192

If you don't have the cash for a six-month trip to the Middle East and Asia, you might settle for a half-hour in this store. Flying Carpets has rugs from 14 countries. Some are old (more than a century in a few cases), some are new, all are handmade. There are about 1,000 in the store at any given time (give or take a couple hundred)—rugs on the floor, on the walls and rolled up and posted like dandy soldiers. Ray Tokareff, who co-owns the business with his wife, Marsha, teaches "rug appreciation" at Napa Valley College. The shop also does washing, repair and appraisals.

Vanderbilt and Company
1429 Main St., St. Helena
• (707) 963-1010

"Barn" would be too pedestrian a word for this up-market emporium of home furnishings. But the effect created by the room's high open beams and skylights is not far removed. Inside are semi-enclosed alcoves devoted to, say, boldly painted Vietri tableware or the ornately muraled Wright Collection of furniture. Vanderbilt has glassware from Salas and Schott, a brimming Crabtree & Evelyn cupboard, linens and tablecloths, pillows and pillowcases, candles, baskets and woven or twisted wine racks.

Tivoli
1432 Main St., St. Helena
• (707) 967-9399

Look for the eye-catching checkerboard of grass and cement with oversized stone globes. It's basically the front lawn of Tivoli, a furniture shop that is co-owned with Bale Mill (see subsequent listing). About two-thirds of what's stocked here is designed and built by the company. Tivoli has a European bent, and it tends toward the huge and the grand—mirrors and pots and beds that Shaquille O'Neal might appreciate. You'll notice a lot of iron and aluminum and pine that's left rough or given a "distressed" finish.

Calla Lily Fine Linens
1222 Main St., St. Helena
• (707) 963-8188

None of this "we sell a little bit of everything" here. Calla Lily inhabits a well-defined realm of linens, towels, rugs and bathrobes, and only the best of each. The colors tend to be soft and muted, the prices steep, but the owners explain that some of the linens will last decades. Calla Lily also handles custom orders, and offers select personal care products for the discriminating visitor.

R.S. Basso Home
1219 Main St., St. Helena
• (707) 963-0391
186 N. Main St., Sebastopol
• (707) 829-1426
115 Plaza St., Healdsburg
• (707) 431-1925

Ron and Mary Basso began making custom sofas and chairs in the early 1980s in Sebastopol, and their presence has spread to two additional Wine Country locations, plus others in Palo Alto and Danville. They also opened a fabric store last fall. The Bassos still manufacture the frames to specification in Sebastopol, and you can choose from thousands of fabrics to cover yours. They ship all over the country, or farther—Ecuador on at least one occasion. The St. Helena store is packed with a lot more than couches. R.S. Basso has fine art, floor and table lamps, figurines, wrought-iron chandeliers and framed sketches and photos from eras past. And check out the magnificent mirrors, framed by embossed tin, inlaid stone tiger stripes or handpainted Devonshire roses.

Tantau
1220 Adams St., St. Helena
• (707) 963-3115

Owner Sally Tantau has been an interior designer in Napa Valley for more than 25 years, which helps to explain the inviting layout of this store. Tantau features the functional artwork of many valley locals, including drapery rods shaped like olive branches, colorful tissue boxes and hand-painted tables. You'll also find jewelry, festive bowls, cups and plates, upholstered furniture by Lee and Shabby Chic, wall art and candles, plus enough picture frames to surround every head in Wine Country.

Tapioca Tiger
1234 Adams St., St. Helena
• (707) 967-0608

Not all kid stores are alike, as this one adeptly proves. Tapioca Tiger finds some items made just down the road, and others manufactured overseas. The shop specializes in clothing (boys and girls, newborn to size 7) and toys. The clothes are highly original designs, everything from sweetly sophisticated European items to funky domestic lines. Many of the toys are handmade by small producers—items like wooden dinosaurs and dressable plush cats. Tapioca Tiger also features children's bedding and furniture.

Fideaux
1312 Main St., St. Helena
• (707) 967-9935

Greeting customers on a recent visit to this shop was a shirt that read, "I Kiss My Dog on the Lips." If that sentiment warms your heart rather than turns your stomach, this is the store for you. Dogs and cats are shaggy royalty here. Fideaux offers numerous squeeze-and-squeak toys, a wide selection of pet collars, collapsible dog dishes for hiking, even pet futon beds (made for the Fideaux label) and wine-barrel doghouses. They also stock the basics: shampoo, food, kitty litter, etc. Feel free to bring Ranger or Lucky with you, if he or she is on a leash.

WilkesSport
1219 Main St., St. Helena
• (707) 963-4323
10466 Lansing St., Mendocino
• (707) 937-1357

The well-heeled crowd that buys its tailored suits from the Wilkes Bashford Company of San Francisco probably looks here for its weekend activewear. The shop has a small but flawless selection of pants, sport coats, shirts, shoes and accessories, featuring fine Italian fabrics. Examples of the manufacturers are Zegna for men and Piazza and Sempione for women.

Amelia Claire
1230 Main St., St. Helena
• (707) 963-8502

Lady, if you really want to go local, drop into Amelia Claire and emerge with a new ensemble. Rene Sculatti's boutique specializes in sun hats, shoes and accessories for those see-and-be-seen summer months. Name a color and a decorative twist for your head, and you'll probably find both here—and you may even find it at impulse-buying prices.

Bale Mill Classic Country Furniture
3431 St. Helena Hwy. N., St. Helena
• (707) 963-4595

The old sign out front says "Pine Furniture," but Bale Mill has gone way beyond that. The company now stocks both the in-demand and the unexpected: huge iron canopy beds and pillars, wicker chairs, marble tables, stone fountains, copper lamps and even a few antiques like typewriters and clocks. Some of the wood is painted or varnished, but some of it is left rough. It's all contained in an old white house perched on Calif. Highway 29 north of St. Helena. Don't forget to investigate the rooms upstairs.

Calistoga Pottery
1001 Foothill Blvd., Calistoga
• (707) 942-0216

Sally and Jeff Manfredi run this pottery studio from the back of their home, and, while popularity has surged, in some ways it's all very similar to how it was in 1980. Everything is fired on-site. And they have remained loyal to a handful of rugged-looking glazes because their customers, in turn, have remained loyal to Calistoga Pottery. The company aims for utilitarian stoneware—platters, plates, pitchers, bowls, mugs, kettles, etc.—that complements food. (Sally used to be a painter, Jeff a chef.) Much of the work is made to order, but you can always find some pots for sale on the shelves. The Manfredis will hand-letter messages at no charge.

Wexford & Woods
1347 Lincoln Ave., Calistoga
• (707) 942-9729, (800) 919-9729

If your mud bath is over, but you just can't stand the thought of ending your spa experience, rinse off and stroll into Wexford & Woods. Close your eyes, breathe in the mingled scents of innumerable skin- and hair-care products, then start exploring. You'll find triple-milled soaps from France, organic cleansers from Australia and Dead Sea bath salts from Israel, not to mention soap bars of every possible size, color, fragrance and ingredient—but all of one lofty quality. Nearly every line can be sampled, and most of it is 100 percent natural. Wexford & Woods also has a wide selection of baskets they will custom pack and gift wrap for you.

The Artful Eye
1333-A Lincoln Ave., Calistoga
• (707) 942-4743

Several media are represented at this shop—ceramics, oil painting, iron—but what stands out immediately is the collection of colored glass, most of it mouth-blown (often referred to as handblown). The vases, oversized wine-glasses and decorative flowers seem to writhe in the light as you look around the room. The Artful Eye also offers wearable art like jewelry (from paper to gold) and clothing. Note that there is a sister store in Healdsburg.

The Candy Cellar
1367 Lincoln Ave., Calistoga
• (707) 942-6990

If you have not just one sweet tooth but a whole gumful of them, abandon all hope when you enter this place. You'll see barrels filled with saltwater taffy, jawbreakers, swirls, crunches, bubble gum, lollipops and all the Jelly Bellies of the rainbow. Most of it is sold by weight, so you can mix and match. Anyway, you'll probably head straight for the award-winning fudge—10 to 15 flavors mixed right on the spot, including the likes of chewy praline, maple nut, rocky road and caffe latte. And remember: Pretend you're shopping for your nephew, and no one will shoot you any reprimanding glances. The Candy Cellar also sells stuffed animals and puzzles.

INSIDERS' TIP

If your timing is on, you can let the Farm Trails come to you. Wine Country features some two dozen farmers' markets, with growers setting up stalls to offer fresh produce. The markets are usually held once a week during summer and fall, but the day varies, so inquire locally.

Sonoma County

Southern Sonoma

Along the dozens of buildings from yesteryear that rim the Plaza, visitors come to search out galleries, specialty shops and fine boutiques—to find the unusual, the elegant, the unexpected. Beyond the main streets are more shops tucked into El Paseo de Sonoma, a charming enclave behind the corner of East Spain and First streets. The path down the Mercato leads to more wonderful shopping. The Plaza is Sonoma's main shopping scene. Here are just some of the shops you can explore. Unless otherwise noted, they are all open seven days a week.

Spirits in Stone
452 First St. E., Sonoma
• (707) 938-2200

Laura and Tony Ponter are on a mission: to import the best in elegant, simple sculpture from the Shona ("people of the mist") tribe in Zimbabwe, and to demonstrate that "the spirit in stone" has much to teach us all about dignity, compassion and peace. There is something almost magnetic about these profound sculptures—a feeling that you must reach out and touch them, and you are encouraged to do so. Large pieces are pricey, but the smaller sculptures are affordable and tempting for any lover of fine things. (See the gallery listings in our Arts and Culture chapter for more information.)

Viva Sonoma
180 E. Napa St., Sonoma
• (707) 939-1904

How about a nice courtyard where you can sit among fruit trees or admire garden art while your companion shops? Viva Sonoma has taken up residence in Sonoma's second-oldest wood house (built in 1865 and located just a block east of the Plaza) and beautifully filled it with imported folk art, ceramics, linens and more. If you've wondered how the local women put together that "Sonoma look," this is a great place to shop for some of its essentials, including dresses and skirts of natural fibers.

Sign of the Bear
435 First St. W., Sonoma
• (707) 996-3722

Here's a great place to pick up handmade kitchen utensils, paella pans, cookie molds, madeleine pans, wooden bowls, immense Italian platters, spaghetti drainers—all those things you need to feel like a professional chef or to make a friend who actually is one very happy.

The Flag Store
20089 Broadway, Sonoma
• (707) 996-8140

How often do you run into a store totally devoted to flags of the world? You'll find every flag here, including some in the category of "discontinued country." Owner Dallas Dutson is a leading authority on flags and serves as a consultant to the White House on the subject. The flags come in every size and every price. Maybe you'll find one for your alma mater or favorite historic event.

Bear Moon Clothing
117 E. Napa St..,, Sonoma
• (707) 935-3392

This is the place to go to find products that keep the environment in mind. Brand names include S.F. City Lights, Royal Robbins, Mishi and Woolrich Outdoor Wear. You'll find clothing and soft linens, cottons, tencel and down-to-earth blends for life's simple pleasures. It's all natural. The store's motto, "quality clothing in natural fabrics with fashion and the environment in mind," pretty much sums up what Bear Moon is all about.

Sonoma Cheese Factory
2 W. Spain St., Sonoma
• (707) 996-1931

This may be the most popular shop on the Plaza. People come to watch the cheese-making process at the back of the store, or to buy one of the dozens of varieties of Sonoma Jack or Cheddar cheese. There's an array of gourmet items to go with the cheese—take it all home or turn it into a picnic on the green Plaza lawn. If you like, they'll make you a sandwich to eat at the sidewalk tables.

Vella Cheese Company
315 Second St. E., Sonoma
• (707) 938-3232

Some of the best cheese in the world is made on E. Second Street, around the corner from the main drag, by Thomas Vella and his son, Ig. They've been in the same 1905 rough-cut stone brewery building since 1931. The shop doesn't have the same exposure as the main street shops, but Vella Dry Jack has won international prizes, and the Cheddar is so sharp it makes your mouth pucker.

Milagros
414 First St. E., Sonoma
• (707) 939-0834

Following the covered passageway called El Paseo, which winds between East Spain and E. First streets, you'll suddenly believe you've wandered into another country and another time. There before you is Milagros, a fabulous store of affordable fine Mexican folk art—whimsical Oaxacan wood carvings, Spanish Colonial sconces, hand-crafted jewelry from all over Latin America, Talavera bowls and wonderful masks. This shop also features a rare collection of religious Mexican folk art. Milagros, which means "miracles" in Spanish, is named after the figures sold in front of churches in Mexico.

Sonoma Rock & Mineral
414 First St. E., Sonoma
• (707) 996-7200

El Paseo courtyard has another shop worthy of a visit, particularly if you're interested in things lapidary. It's hard to believe the earth holds such wondrous rocks and stones. The display is professionally arranged in a spacious setting, with beautiful polished stones to buy.

The Legacy Gift Shop
452 First St. E., Sonoma
• **(707) 935-9447**

If you love decorating your home, you'll go crazy here. Big things, small pieces—tableware and vases, chairs and umbrella stands, candle holders in 100 shapes—they're all exquisite additions to a home that's cherished. The Legacy also is a great spot to find a memorable gift for a new bride. The shop is along the Mercato, the shop-filled promenade off First Street E.

La Villeta de Sonoma
27 Fremont Dr., Sonoma
• **(707) 939-9392**

Take out your Visa or MasterCard because you're going to melt when you see the beautiful hand-crafted terra cotta designer accessories in this unusual shop. It opened in mid-1997, and is a branch of a larger store in Guadalajara, where artisans respected in their fields turn out urns and plates, paintings and furniture that are styled from the beautiful museum pieces of the Mediterranean. What you see here won't remind you of Mexico—it will remind you of Portugal or Italy, Greece or Spain, even North Africa. It is all created by some of Mexico's best creative sculptors and ceramic artists. There's always something new because the owner, Mardo, travels back to Guadalajara and other Mexican cities about every six weeks. Prices? Anywhere from $4 to about $10,000. The shop is at the junction of Calif. Highway 116 and Calif. 121.

Other Southern Sonoma Shops

The Olive Press
14301 Arnold Dr., Glen Ellen
• **(707) 939-8900**

Inspired by the cooperatives of northern Italy, the Olive Press was created by a group of olive aficionados. Its purpose? To press olives for commercial producers, small-harvest growers and hobbyists eager to make olive oil from homegrown olives. Visitors can sample a premium selection of olive oils, and during harvest season (October through March) they can view the pressing process. A bounty of olive-related specialty foods and gifts is available for purchase.

SNOOPY'S Gallery and Gift Shop
1667 W. Steele Ln., Santa Rosa
• **(707) 546-3385**

SNOOPY'S Gallery features a museum containing awards, drawings and personal memo-rabilia from Peanuts creator Charles M. Schultz. The gift shop has the largest selection of Snoopy products in the world. The Redwood Empire Ice Arena is one block away on the right (see our Attractions chapter).

Sonoma Outfitters
145 Third St., Santa Rosa
• **(707) 528-1920**

For sports enthusiasts, this is the place to go. It's immense (more than 11,000 square feet), and the inventory is sure to cover everything you need for just about any sport. There's an enormous amount of boating and camping equipment—Mountain Hard Wear tents and sleeping bags, Vasque and Rockport shoes, Old Town canoes, rubber and plastic kayaks, tents of every size, Marmot ski clothing, in-line skates, you name it. It's all sports equipment from wall to wall. The knowledgeable staff can help outfit you and your family for almost any outdoor recreation.

Northern Sonoma

Healdsburg

The pretty Plaza that makes Healdsburg so charming was built in 1852 by Harmon Heald, who sold lots for $15. Today, $15 wouldn't pay for a day's rent, and the stores that sold harnesses and hardware in Heald's day are now occupied by charming shops filled with jewelry, books, fine art, clothing and home furnishings. These shops are open every day.

The Artful Eye
706 Center St., Healdsburg
• **(707) 433-9190**

The one-of-a-kind jewelry, sculpture, paintings and drawings on display in these elegant surroundings are created by artists from across the country, although the shop also features local artists. Perhaps you'll find yourself drawn to some exquisitely wrought bijou by the same impulse that inspires all buyers here—these pieces speak to your soul; they call out to you.

The Irish Cottage
112 Matheson St., Healdsburg
• **(707) 433-4850**

If your passion is country decor, you'll want to dawdle here. The owner returns to her homeland in Ireland from time to time to find genteel Old Country pieces to add to her collection of distinctive pine tables, antique furniture, primitives, collectibles and

Wine Country's Fabulous Farm Trails

Wandering from one winery to another, Wine Country visitors are likely to come across green and white signs posted in some farm yards announcing "Farm Trails." Wine isn't the only thing this countryside turns out. Produce is our other forte.

Agriculture is as important to Wine Country as movie-making is to Hollywood. And just leave it to California farmers to turn our agricultural Eden into an attraction for the family.

Farm Trails was organized in 1973 by a group of farmers dedicated to the

promotion and preservation of the agricultural heritage of the region. During the ensuing 25 years it has guided consumers through the spectacular countryside to "experience a farm," sample local fresh foods and wines or select a rare plant from a specialty nursery. Maps and a guide have been printed to lead you to 100 farms open to the public, all eager to sell their goods directly to drop-in consumers. You can pick one up at the California Welcome Center in Rohnert Park or at a number of Wine Country visitors bureaus, hotels, fruit stands and grocery stores.

The maps outline in fine detail the tranquil backroads and old-time farms that lie slumbering off the main thoroughfares. You'll never forget your first tangy bite of a Gravenstein apple picked right off the tree, or the juicy you-pick-it strawberry you pop in your mouth. This is where tomatoes come in multiple hues — yellow, orange and red. Fresh salad greens are sprinkled with pansy, nasturtium and rose petals. Take home jams, jellies and chutneys made from local berries and apples, and don't forget to sample speckled butter lettuce, red orach spinach, dragon

Photo: Lou Zauner

You never know what you'll run into on the Farm Trails.

tongue beans, melons, raspberries, cherries, walnuts and, for the home winemaker, grapes for crushing. The product index includes other intriguing headings — hayrides, goats (pygmy), llamas and emus and pigs (Vietnamese), quails (and quail eggs), bees, wax and pollen.

While Sonoma County may seem rural, Napa County produces specialty foods that have become world-famous — olive oils in various degrees of virginity, flavored vinegars, microbrewed beers, award-winning mustards, salsas, cider, candies, baked goods and wines that have won awards but won't appear on your grocer's shelves. There's even a farm where weavers can buy angora wool and mohair for home spinning.

Does all this remind you of Provence in France, or Tuscany in Italy? Perhaps we have grown so accustomed to this fresh food and produce we are only now discovering that such comparisons are valid on many levels. Like those cherished European regions, we have rural landscapes with flowing hillsides grazed by sheep and cows, vineyards thick with choice grapes and a striking seashore where fishermen daily pull in catches of crab and shrimp. The area offers a chance to find out what goes on behind the scenes beyond the level of supermarket shopping.

The produce of the Farm Trails group is as diverse as California's terrain and climate. From the fog-chilled valleys near the coast to the sunbaked fields inland, you'll find everything from smoked salmon to cacti and, best of all, have a chance to chat with the people who make their living from agriculture. Here you can learn the pleasures and pitfalls of an industry that's seldom showcased.

One of the first farms to join the Farm Trails organization was Kozlowski Farms, which also was one of the first Sonoma County farms to go organic. The farm started as a raspberry ranch in 1947 and turned into a roadside sales stand when Carmen Kozlowski decided to cook up some raspberry jam and sell it to passersby. Now that same kitchen is turning out 65 different products, all from the fields of organic fruits where it all started. Besides raspberry jam, you can buy fresh berries and organic apples in season, mustards, salad dressings, cider, fresh pies, tarts and cookies. And Carmen, who has retired, no longer has to worry every time a big car drives up that it might be the county authorities asking for a kitchen permit.

There's really no limit to what you might run into as you toodle along the Farm Trails. In Napa County, along with the olive oils mentioned, pick up some dried fruit, lively vinegar or, if you can manage it, some naturally raised lambs, goats or suckling pigs. Wreaths made of grapevines might be easier to pack out — they are charming and lasting. You also might find yourself in a wooden drying shed where the walls, ceiling and floor are dense, bright cushions of dried flowers — calendulas, Johnny jump-ups, bachelor buttons and sunflowers — it's summer's bounty preserved for winter's enjoyment.

Admittedly, this is not supermarket shopping. Sometimes you'll be drawn down narrow farm roads and into rough-hewn barns to buy your goods. That's the adventure part of the journey. What makes it worthwhile is the intimacy of these visits to farmers' homesteads. Some trails meander through countryside so beautiful it's hard to leave it at day's end. That in itself is a reward! The trail guides and maps issued by each county are your passport.

You'll discover products you didn't know existed, and you'll find new ways to use the ones you're used to seeing. Lace a spinach salad with strips of smoked duck, sun-dried tomatoes and goat cheese. Bake a persimmon pie. Liven up potato salad with some zippy new mustard. Use quail eggs next time you make deviled eggs and garnish them with fresh herbs. You also might want to plan your trip to coincide with a number of fairs, festivals and other agricultural events taking place. Your Farm Trails map and guide will reveal what's happening and where.

SHOPPING

decorative accessories. But it's not all Irish, and it's not all antique. The cottage is cozy and cluttered, with plenty of linens, pillows, rugs and textiles to warm up your home with country coziness.

Robinson & Co.
108 Matheson St., Healdsburg
• **(707) 433-7116**

Billed as "purveyors of fine coffees and cookwares," the store lives up to the claim. You encounter the aroma of coffee beans when you walk in, and there is a varied inventory of everything dear to the heart of a cook. The shop is contemporary and glossy, filled with all the accouterments you need to become a world-class chef, including the cookbooks that tell you how to go about it. David Robinson, the store's personable and welcoming owner, will be happy to acquaint you with a wide range of other products, including Italian porcelain, European and Australian pottery, French hand soaps, spices and Williamsburg candles.

Oakville Grocery Co.
124 Matheson St., Healdsburg
• **(707) 433-3200**

This is a branch of the same wonderful gourmet grocery store whose jam-packed shelves in the Napa Valley have attracted passersby for decades. At this location it has metamorphosed into a gentrified, glossy emporium of most everything gourmet and delicious. Here you can stock your kitchen pantry with exotic mustards, duck pate, caviar, Greek olives and everything imaginable beyond that. The vegetable section has a display of onions, carrots and other good things that are so fresh and perfectly formed you may think they're made of porcelain. You can eat lunch here too, selecting salads, sandwiches and yummy desserts to be eaten under umbrellas on the patio.

Art and All That Jazz
119 Plaza St., Healdsburg
• **(707) 433-7900**

Jessica Felix, whose works have been shown at the Smithsonian Museum as well as prominent galleries across the country, has been designing spirited jewelry since 1970. Her shop serves as a gallery that includes the work of others in art glass, ceramics, photography, collage and an eclectic selection of jazz and Brazilian music. But her works take center stage in this shop. Jessica demonstrates an uncanny ability to take simple ideas and transform them into powerful images that incorporate the spirit

worlds of Alaska, the Canadian northwest and Africa. She's also proud of the store's new wine design jewelry.

West County/Russian River

Traditions
145 N. Main St., Sebastopol
• **(707) 829-3667**

This is a sort of outdoor-indoor gardening shop, with all those tools you need to rearrange your petunias or prune the wisteria. But it's a lot more than that—a sort of one-stop center for all sorts of neat things. Buy a birdhouse for the patio or a colorful pot to fill with growing plants. Get some stuffed animals or Beanie Babies for the kids, or a box of popular Yankee candles. There are flowered throw rugs for indoors or out and a charming line of greeting cards from England.

Hearth Song
156 N. Main St., Sebastopol
• **(707) 829-0944**

Lucky is the kid who gets toys from this shop. The emphasis here is on toys that stimulate the imagination—bug catchers, for instance, to capture bugs and hold them for live study. You can buy magic wands and gardening tools made for kids so they can grow their own plants. You can buy games and puzzles, hippity-hop balls, tether balls, teepees. Some of the products are made in Europe. In addition to the retail sales, a mail-order catalog is available. Call (800) 525-2502 for more information.

California Carnivores
7020 Trenton-Healdsburg Rd., Forestville
• **(707) 838-1630**

It's been called "Little Shop of Horrors," but it's one of the most fascinating shops you'll see in a month of Sundays. About 550 carnivorous plants grow here, with about 120 varieties for sale. These are the meat-eaters of the plant world and are endless fun to watch. An unsuspecting fly circles above the Venus's-flytrap and makes what will be its final landing. In two seconds it triggers a hair-like finger, the plant snaps tight with a crushing device more terrifying than anything in a James Bond movie, and it sucks the life out of the fly. Other plants, like the pitcher plant or the bladderwort, are even more unkind to insects. The plants are easy to care for and inexpensive—you could get a dandy one for between $4 and $10 and perhaps be fly-free forever. If you'd like to send one to a friend, a mail-order service is provided.

Mendocino County

U.S. Highway 101

Real Goods Store
13771 S. U.S. Hwy. 101, Hopland
• (707) 744-2100

Built as part of the Solar Living Center (see our Attractions chapter), Real Goods is both a retail store and educational center. A thousand items are available, and hemp is one of the prime products promoted. The hope is that such items will free the planet from the use of petroleum products and end the destruction of forests. Stop in (or order a catalog), buy some hemp socks or a solar-powered fountain and learn to spurn bugs without noxious repellents. The array of products you can buy is mind-boggling.

Hoyman Browe Studio
323 N. Main St., Ukiah
• (707) 468-8835

Trained in the European school of pottery making, Douglas Browe and his wife, Jan Hoyman, have established a studio in the traditional, old-time format—training apprentices and displaying their work. Much of the output from the studio is sold to restaurants across the country, but the showroom at the studio doesn't just have pots. There are tea sets, huge presentation platters, jardinieres and 10-gallon flower pots, as well as tableware with bright designs of fruits, flowers and vegetables. More good news: These pieces are available as seconds with tiny, undetectable flaws.

Mendocino Bounty
200 S. School St., Ukiah
• (707) 463-6711

This small shop is filled with food and wine made in Mendocino County, and stuff for the kitchen. You'll find colorful bowls, linens and gift baskets filled with products. If you wish, the basket can be custom-designed—let's say a pasta basket filled with grape-seed oil, organic herbs and unusual pastas that are hard to find anywhere else. There's a breakfast basket with honey, local syrup, breakfast cakes and a special waffle mix prepared by Mendocino's famous Cafe Beaujolais (see our Restaurants chapter). If you'd like a snack while you shop, there's

a small copper bar with stools where you can sample lasagna made at Boonville Farms and various other treats.

Grace Hudson Museum
431 S. Main St., Ukiah
• (707) 467-2856

Grace Hudson's portraiture of Native Americans—particularly the Pomo tribe—brought her national recognition. The museum's gift shop collection of Native American crafts, books and jewelry reflects that same fascination. A fine sampling of books explores all facets of Native American culture, and there's a nice selection of items for children. The gift shop is open Wednesday through Sunday. A jaunt through the museum is free, but donations are appreciated (see our Attractions chapter).

Moore's Flour Mill
1550 S. State St., Ukiah
• (707) 462-6550

Just before you leave Ukiah heading south, you'll spot a brown, shingled building on the right with an immense water mill wheel. It's the home of some of the best home-style bread you'll ever eat, but more than that, it's the place to stock up on spices at wholesale prices. The mill wheel grinds the flour for the bread, which is also available for sale.

Marlana River Designs
30 E. San Francisco Ave., Willits
• (707) 459-0910

A family of designers, sculptors, potters and painters has combined its talents to establish a large factory producing tableware with bright colors and happy designs. The products are shipped all over the world and supply several restaurants in this country. Each piece is hand-thrown and hand-painted. Visitors are invited to tour the factory and visit the showroom, where they can buy from a wide selection of dishes, bowls, pots, candle holders and sundry other items.

Mendocino Coast

Velvet Rabbit
38140 S. Calif. Hwy. 1, Gualala
• (707) 884-1501

Shop to operatic music while you browse

> **INSIDERS' TIP**
>
> Do the plates and bowls for sale in Calistoga Pottery look familiar? They might, because the company's goods have been used in prominent local establishments like Tra Vigne, Brava Terrace, Robert Mondavi Winery and Foothill House.

Grinding flour the old-fashioned way, Moore's Flour Mill in Ukiah is a fascinating stop.

through the works of selected artisans in a variety of fields. You'll find everything here that goes by the name of art—stained glass, bronze sculptures, carved stone, wooden boxes from England, china, crystal, hand-blown glass and shells from all over the world.

The Melting Pot
Main and Lansing Sts., Mendocino
• (707) 937-0173

This store is huge—a two-story emporium of candles, pots, sparkling glass, fine art, outside garden stuff and carved birds so real you wait for them to take off in flight. According to *Niche* magazine, this is one of the Top 100 retailers of American crafts in the nation. The owner started the business as a candle shop in the early 1970s and was overwhelmed when, on the first day, someone came in and bought 25 black candles. He thought he had found a pot of gold and immediately started expanding. Now he operates with 6,000 square feet of floor space and still specializes in candles.

The Courtyard
Kasten and Main Sts., Mendocino
• (707) 937-0917

Here you'll find all those kitchen gadgets you didn't think you'd ever need but suddenly are convinced that maybe you do. How about a new garlic press? Or a potato peeler made in Switzerland? The display of imported English

teapots is large enough to convince you you're back in Sussex. Maybe you'll go home with a matching set of table linens and crockery. If you don't know how to cook, the shop will take care of that too—there is a large library of cookbooks.

Lark in the Morning Musique
10460 Kasten St., Mendocino
• (707) 937-5275

If you have a passion for musical instruments, you shouldn't pass this one up. From alpenhorns to zithers, they fill every corner and hang from the ceiling—dulcimers, mandolins, banjos (with four or five strings), hurdy-gurdies, ukuleles, concertinas and accordions, harps, bagpipes and drums of every size. You can spend from $1 to $4,000. If you want something small for the kids, you'll find that there too—bongo drums, harmonicas or Irish tin whistles. Ask to get on the catalog list.

The Golden Goose
45094 Main St., Mendocino
• (707) 937-4655

Don't even think of saving this shop for the end of your shopping tour. They've got beds covered with down quilts and down pillows so fluffy you'll be overcome by the need to plop into bed and forget the rest of your stops. If you'd like to take home a bed full of luxurious sheets and down, it will probably run up a bill of about $1,500. To go with it, you can pick up a flannel nightshirt made in England that looks like sheep's wool. There goes another hundred bucks! This is sheer luxury.

Panache
Kasten and Albion Sts., Mendocino
• (707) 937-1234

You'll find art galleries all over town because Mendocino is artists' heaven. But it's worth stopping in here to see the metal sculpture of Don Quixote that's on exhibit front and center. It's like none other. Panache is also the place to buy the fruit and vegetable paintings of Gerald Stinski, who moved to Mendocino in 1991 to pursue his art dreams. Now his paintings sell as fast as he turns them out, all with four-figure price tags.

The Irish Shop
45050 Main St., Mendocino
• (707) 937-3133

Did you forget to pick up that fisherman's sweater last time you were in Killarney? You'll find it here, along with anything you might need from Scotland or Wales. The shop also carries high-quality food products such as the award-winning Christine and Rob's Old Fashioned Oatmeal, as well as Norwegian sweaters, Geiger jackets from Austria, men's caps, dolls, mohair afghans and hand-made Teddy bears.

Deja-Vu Hat Co.
10470 Lansing St., Mendocino
• (707)937-4120

Who wouldn't want to see the largest selection of hats in Northern California? There's something for everyone who owns a head—felts, fine fur, straws, Stetsons, Akubras, Borsalinos, Panamas and Deja-Vu's own dress hats.

Mendocino Coast Botanical Gardens
18218 N. Calif. Hwy. 1, Fort Bragg
• (707) 964-4352

This 47-acre showcase garden displays wondrous collections of rhododendrons, azaleas, heathers and succulents. Some of these species have also been made available in a retail nursery that helps support the nonprofit effort. Travelers might consider one of the sempervivum ("live forever") succulents, to take a piece of Northern California back home. They're inexpensive (about $4), and they travel well. There's also a gift shop with cards, vases and so forth, as well as a shop for outdoor garden supplies (including some irresistible ceramic frogs). Admission prices are $6 general, $5 for

seniors, $3 for juniors 13 to 17 and $1 for kids 6 to 12. (For more on the Mendocino Coast Botanical Gardens, see our Attractions chapter.)

Harvest Market
171 Boatyard Dr., Fort Bragg
• (707) 964-7000

Well, yes, it's a grocery store. But this is the one you wish was just around the corner from your kitchen. Homegrown produce, fresh local seafood and fresh-baked bread are imaginatively displayed. The folks at Harvest Market will make you a picnic basket to go or fill your ice chest with the best foods in town.

Hot Pepper Jelly Company
330 N. Main St., Fort Bragg
• (707) 961-1422

Come on in! These people have 30 varieties of jelly they want you to sample. Don't neglect the old-time favorites, ginger pepper, Chardonnay conserve or very cherry marmalade. For kicks, try the jalapeño pepper jam—give your taste buds a shock! All Carol Hall jellies are made by hand in small batches. They're sold nationwide, and the lineup also includes chutneys, dessert toppings, fruit syrups, mustards, vinegars and salsa. The peach cobbler jam won an Oscar at the New York Fancy Foods Show. Ask for a free catalog.

For the Shell of It
344 N. Main St., Fort Bragg
• (707) 961-0461

Here you'll find pieces of the ocean, without the water. Long aisles hold everything from scallop shells for serving seafood to tiny shells made into earrings. They are not local shells, however—remember that the state parks system says not to carry any part of the beach away.

Fiddles & Cameras
400 N. Main St., Fort Bragg
• (707) 964-7370

You won't find any fiddles here, but this is one huge camera shop. The main question is this: Did you remember to bring along your binoculars for whale watching? If not, this is the place to buy a pair.

Lake County

Bright Lights Candle Company
16275-A Main St., Lower Lake
• (707) 994-3267

When this company was launched in 1993,

SHOPPING

it was a small operation that exclusively made candles designed by German maker Volker Wagner. Since then it has grown into a business that supplies about 3,000 gift shops in the United States, plus a few hundred more in Canada. The designs now include tapers, pyramids, balls, pillars, teardrops, flames and persimmons, plus a small number of wax statuettes created by local artists, all available in a variety of color combinations.

Peek through the glass of the retail room, and you'll see hot candles being hung on the taper rack.

J's Garden
9885 Lee Barr Rd., Lower Lake
• (707) 995-3608

They call Jeanette Grainger "The Herb Lady of Lake County," and no, she's not a Rastafarian. She grows pesticide-free culinary and medicinal herbs, stocking about 25 varieties (fresh and dried) at any particular time. Unlike the supermarkets, J's Garden guarantees freshness, discarding unsold dried herbs at the end of each season. The shop also sells herbal ancillaries like moth repellent, potpourri, cat toys and dream pillows.

Holdenried Farms
3930 Main St., Kelseyville
• (707) 279-9022

Before the Holdenrieds started Wildhurst Vineyards (see our Wineries chapter), they had this gift shop in the heart of old Kelseyville. The colors and aromas hit you as soon as you walk in the door. When your senses have stopped wobbling, you'll find teddy bears, baskets, soaps, linens, pottery, gourmet coffee, jams and jellies, enamelware, birdhouses and one or two (or a million) other temptations.

Lehman's Lollipop Farm
1446 Pitney Ln., Upper Lake
• (707) 275-3103

Lollipops don't really grow on trees. (Just think how easy it would be to get the kids to help with chores.) But if they did, Judy Lehman would harvest 'em. She has a little bit of everything in this gigantic country home north of Upper Lake: Christmas or-

naments, rock and lapidary products, artwork, dolls, stuffed animals, herbal concoctions, beaded and ceramic crafts, handmade stationery, pine-needle baskets and plenty more. The teapot is always on, and the price range is 50¢ to $5,000, so don't try to make out like there's nothing there for you. Pitney Lane is off of Elk Mountain Road.

Antiques

Napa County

Riverfront Antique Center
705 Soscol Ave., Napa
• (707) 253-1966

This is Antiquasaurus Rex, the most monstrous of all Wine Country antique shops: 24,000 square feet in a warehouse once used by the Roughrider men's clothing company. High ceilings and big banks of windows look down on more than 140 exhibitors offering everything from new pine furniture to real Victorian treasures. There are plenty of collectibles too.

Irish Pedlar Antiques
1988 Wise Dr., Napa
• (707) 253-9091

In the 1800s the Irish used pine exclusively in their furniture construction. Much of it was done in the home, in a primitive style. (No two pieces seem to be exactly the same dimension.) The Irish Pedlar specializes in the sale of such items, the bulk of it made between 1880 and 1890. They do sell some American pine, as well as ceramics and old American linens. All of it is authentically old, and nothing is broken or ripped. The shop is on the north side of the John Muir Inn.

The Neighborhood
1400 First St., Napa
• (707) 259-1900

Yes, it is almost big enough to be its own neighborhood. This showroom takes up half a block in downtown Napa, and inside it displays on two levels. Poke around and find everything from mission benches to barber chairs, framed photos of American Indians to ice

SHOPPING

sleds, and rough willow chairs to green bottles from the old Vichy Hot Springs in Sonoma.

Red Hen Antiques
5091 St. Helena Hwy., Napa
• (707) 257-0822

This is something of a local landmark about halfway between Napa and Yountville. It has been Red Hen since 1983, and it was the Napa Valley Garden Shop for many years before that. Look for the big chicken facing the highway. Inside you'll find a collective of 80 dealers peddling a wide range of goods.

Antique Fair
6512 Washington St., Yountville
• (707) 944-8440

This shop has been around for a long time (since 1971), but not as long as its merchandise. Antique Fair specializes in high-quality French antiquities from about 1890, *la créme* of Lyon and Paris estates. They have jewelry, statuettes, silverware, armoires and bookcases. And if they're known for one thing, it's probably old beds they have converted to queen size.

Erika Hills
115 Main St., St. Helena
• (707) 963-0919

Just south of St. Helena you will spy a line of statuary along Calif. Highwy 29, and behind it, a former church that has been painted ocher and converted into an antique store. This is Erika Hills, the namesake house of ancient delights. Inside you will find Limoges plates, Venetian glass, brightly accented Mexican chairs, Baroque angels from Austria and sturdy oak chairs salvaged right off the farm. Most, but not all, of the furniture is painted, and everything leans toward the high end.

St. Helena St. Helena Antiques
1231 Main St., St. Helena
• (707) 963-5878

This ultra-high-end locale feels like a turn-of-the-century shop in London or New England. Customers are met at the door by two life-size, cartoonish "greeters"—a chef and a winemaker—carved from single trunks. (They're menu boards from the 1860s.) Inside is everything from Provençal ceramics to 19th-century baskets to vintage pond boats.

If there is a specialty, it's wine-related items: corkscrews, bottles, racks and practically anything that might have been salvaged from an old winery.

Lone Dog Fine Art & Antiques
1345 Lincoln Ave., Ste. A, Calistoga
• (707) 942-1115

The shop is a relative newcomer, but proprietor Frederick Schrader has a wealth of experience in gathering artifacts. Lone Dog shares space with Enoteca Wine Shop (see our Wineries chapter) in the wonderfully restored I.O.O.F. building (also known as the Oddfellows building). It's the perfect setting for Schrader's collection, which includes framed lithographs of 19th Century local scenes, and wine-related tools and paraphernalia.

Sonoma County

Southern Sonoma

Country Pine Antiques
23999 Arnold Dr., Sonoma
• (707) 938-8315

Looking for English and Victorian or Georgian pine designs and furnishings from the period 1820 to 1900? Country Pine Sonoma either has it or can obtain it for you. This is a one-of-a-kind showplace of unique pine antiques that would fit perfectly in the modern home.

Margaret's Antiques
472 W. Second St., Sonoma
• (707) 938-8036

Tucked away cozily in a white cottage that dates to the 1870s and is now a historic landmark, Margaret's Antiques replaced the family that lived in the house for 100 years. The shop's specialties are art glass, china, furniture, dolls, pottery and linens from the 1800s, although they do have a few collectibles that are more recent.

Cat & The Fiddle
153 W. Napa St., Sonoma
• (707) 996-5651

With a storefront shop in the main Plaza shopping area, this place gets a lot of exposure. The specialty here is French tables, armoires and buffets, with some English and American antique pieces and gifts. The old is mixed in with some new things that go well with antique furnishings.

Chelsea Antiques
148 Petaluma Blvd. N., Petaluma
• (707) 763-7686

This is a collective that features a wonder-

SHOPPING

ful selection of decorative antiques, collectibles and architectural and garden items in three buildings. Chelsea represents just about every field of antique collecting.

Vintage Bank Antiques
101 Petaluma Blvd. N., Petaluma
• **(707) 769-3097**

It's one of those wonderful old banks that has ceilings two stories high and a small window on the second level overlooking the bank floor so the manager could monitor his tellers and cashiers. Today it's a collective for 48 dealers, giving you three floors to explore. Even the bank vault is within the dealers' domain. What you'll find here is lots of jewelry, furniture, vintage clothing, porcelain, gentlemen's collectibles, dinnerware and lots more.

Antique Marketplace & Annex
248 Petaluma Blvd. N., Petaluma
• **(707) 765-1155**

It claims to have the finest and largest selection of antique furniture in Petaluma. Included is a large selection of pine and country furniture.

Chanticleer Antiques
145 Petaluma Blvd. N., Petaluma
• **(707) 763-9177**

You'll find 7,000 square feet of collective shopping at Chanticlear, which specializes in unique furniture, pottery, clocks, Orientalia—everything from formal to primitive.

Kentucky Street Antiques
127 Kentucky St., Petaluma
• **(707) 765-1698**

Nine dealers display their collections here, showing everything from country to classic—furniture, china, glassware, toys, tools, old advertising, paper and jewelry.

Marianne's Antiques
111 Third St., Santa Rosa
• **(707) 579-5749**

Specializing in European furnishings, Marianne's has a wide variety of special items for your home or office. You'll find romantic beds, armoires, dressers, elegant furnishings and decorator items. Shipping service is available.

Whistle Stop Antiques
130 Fourth St., Santa Rosa
• **(707) 542-9474**

This is where it all began—Sonoma County's original collective, now 25 years old. With 10,000 square feet of space and more than

35 dealers, it's a collector's paradise with thousands of items from dishes to doorknobs. You'll also find clock repair, refinishing supplies, antique books and a wonderful assortment of glassware, jewelry, furniture and collectibles.

Sixth Street Antiques
52 W. Sixth St., Santa Rosa
• **(707) 570-1292**

This is the newest collective in Santa Rosa's Railroad Square, a stone's throw from the newly restored, historic Railroad Depot. There are 30 dealers, so you can browse the many showcases and dealer spaces stocked with merchandise at enticing prices. Choose from Depression glass, California pottery, tin advertising, silver, art and furniture. There's an auction here every month or two. Plenty of parking space is available on a huge paved lot. An added attraction at Sixth Street Warehouse is the addition of a fine arts gallery—Greg Bard Gallery—where you'll find works by award-winning artists.

The Blue Abbey
129 Fourth St., Santa Rosa
• **(707) 523-7540**

American oak furniture is featured here, along with fine china, sterling silver, vintage linens, quilts, crystal and jewelry, and a special collection of original Maxfield Parrish prints.

Railroad Square Basement Antiques
100 Fourth St., Santa Rosa
• **(707) 569-9646**

You enter this shop on Wilson Street. It features a fine collection of vintage furniture, glassware, pottery, kitchenware, china and cookbooks.

Northern Sonoma

Vintage Plaza Antiques
44 Mill St., Healdsburg
• **(707) 433-8409**

Look for the Big Blue Building, where more than 40 dealers showcase their wares in 20,000 square feet of space. You'll find furniture—classic to country—glass, china, silver, fine oil paintings by listed artists, plus some crazy things you never thought you'd need—gas station collectibles, metal signs and 1950s memorabilia.

Healdsburg Classics
226 Healdsburg Ave., Healdsburg
• **(707) 433-4315**

This is an enormous warehouse with a roster of some 20 dealers. It would be difficult to name something that isn't here, rather than what is. However, anyone looking for indoor-outdoor furniture or yard pieces will certainly not be disappointed.

Antique Harvest & Robert's Relics
225 Healdsburg Ave., Healdsburg
• **(707) 433-0223**
Items range from country pine to Victorian, with lamps, brass and art deco furnishings to boot. Meander through and check out the wares of more than 10 dealers.

Jimtown Store
6706 Calif. Hwy. 128, Healdsburg
• **(707) 433-1212**
Not only can you find American antiques, folk art and primitives here, you can also have some "real food" (as they advertise) and a truly good cup of coffee.

The Irish Cottage
112 Matheson St., Healdsburg
• **(707) 433-4850**
Located in the heart of the Plaza, the Irish Cottage has been specializing in antiques, collectibles and gifts since 1994.

Oldie's And Things
118 North St., Healdsburg
• **(707) 433-2885**
This very eclectic shop is full of antiques, collectibles, gifts and some newer things too.

Sonoma Coast

Wooden Duck Antique Shop
132 Bodega Ln., Bodega
• **(707)876-3176**
You'll spot the big yellow house (once a Druids hall) from the highway as you head toward the ocean. The store is open only Saturday and Sunday, but you'll find some fine 18th- and 19th-century furniture, plus a lot of Americana—pewter, glass, silver, whale oil lamps, plus some English Staffordshire china. There's also a fine collection of antique guns.

West County/Russian River

Llano House Antiques
4353 Gravenstein Hwy. S., Sebastopol
• **(707) 829-9322**
Housed in the oldest wooden building in Sonoma County, Llano House Antiques deals mainly in American oak furniture, Depression glass and kitchen collectibles.

Antique Society
2661 Gravenstein Hwy. S., Sebastopol
• **(707) 829-1733**
Along the 8-mile stretch of antique shops on Gravenstein Highway there are 15 antique stores. Antique Society is right when they claim "there's no place quite like" their collective. With more than 100 dealers, it is simply immense. You'll find just about anything you're looking for here, and they claim to have "country prices."

School Bell Antiques
3555 Gravenstein Hwy. S., Sebastopol
• **(707) 823-2878**
Housed in a charming old schoolhouse is a 24-dealer collective. The schoolhouse alone is worth the visit.

Sebastopol Antique Mall
755 Petaluma Ave., Sebastopol
• **(707) 823-1936**
Want to take home a star? You'll find fabulous studio portraits and scene stills of yesterday's film stars—say, John Wayne or Elvis—with autographs guaranteed authentic, all from the private collection of Laurel Proeme. A signed photo might be had for $75, with Elvis going for a little more. If you'd like to take Marilyn Monroe home with you, dig deep—you'll need at least $1,000. You'll find a lot more, and since this is a mall you can also stop for coffee, wine or lunch at a gourmet cafe.

Mendocino County

U.S. Highway 101

Hopland Antiques
13456 U.S. Hwy. 101, Hopland
• **(707) 744-1023**
Almost everything in this large building came from buying complete estates, so you'll find a lot of furniture, home accessories and some excellent estate jewelry.

Li'l Stinker Antiques
20029 N. U.S. Hwy. 101, Willits
• **(707) 459-2486**
It's all furniture here—no small stuff. Some of it dates back to the 1830s. The store has been in business under the same owner since 1967.

Whistlestop Antiques
350 N. Franklin St., Fort Bragg
• **(707) 961-0902**
Here they call about half the stock "tempo-

rary collectibles" and the other half antiques, on the assumption half the collecting community are "only temporary custodians." The extensive selection of elegant glassware includes Fostoria, Heisey, Cambridge and many others, as well as Depression glass and Carnival glass. They also carry a fine line of American furniture. To give a nice touch of nostalgia, a model train runs through the store from time to time.

Lake County

Decker's
14915 Olympic Dr., Bldg. G, Clearlake
• (707) 994-0952

Joyce Decker buys 90 percent of her wares locally, so the shop will give you a glimpse into the Lake County of the past. It's a small building, so they don't do much trade in large furniture. What they do have is a lot of cast-iron and kitchen gadgets, plus jewelry, toys, pottery and more.

One Man's Junk, Another Man's Gold
3780-B Main St., Kelseyville
• (707) 279-9744

At First and Main streets, One Man's Junk is truly in the heart of old Kelseyville. The shop offers neon signs, glassware and lots of kitchenware, plus an interesting concentration of petroleum memorabilia—restored gas pumps, oil cans, road maps and the like. If nothing else, you'll hear some good, lowdown blues on the speakers.

Bookstores

Napa County

Bookends Book Store
1014 Coombs St., Napa
• (707) 254-7323

Bookends counts a couple of big-chain book stores as neighbors in downtown Napa but manages to hold its own. How? With substantial sections on computers, business, biography, self-help, crafts, children's books and family (things like birth, child rearing and weddings).

Bookends has plenty of magazines and fiction and a large collection of travel guides and maps, including a comprehensive set of Wine Country maps.

Copperfield's Books
1303 First St., Napa
• (707) 252-8002

Wine Country literati have been relying on Copperfield's for years. The Napa edition, like its brethren in Sonoma County, is both well-stocked and well-staffed. This one sells new, used and rare books.

Open Door Book Store
1030 Clinton St., Napa
• (707) 252-4848

Has your third eye been a little bloodshot lately? The Open Door specializes in that arching umbrella known as the metaphysical: spiritual quests, Zen meditation, Buddhism, plus more down-to-earth fare such as *The Arthritis Cure Book*. They stock no fiction and no occult. They do have lots of cards and jewelry.

The bookstore is affiliated with the Napa Valley Center for Spiritual Living, a religious science community. The Center organizes ongoing classes, poetry readings and book review groups.

Waldenbooks
1370 Napa Town Center, Napa
• (707) 252-7326

If you are familiar with the printed word, you know about Waldenbooks. It's a national chain renowned for its hard-to-beat prices, whether you're hunting for fiction, coffee-table art books or travel guides like this one. Waldenbooks has a brimming periodicals rack too.

Main Street Books
1315 Main St., St. Helena
• (707) 963-1338

This business has been around since 1983, but recently re-invented itself. Main Street Books is now an extremely small shop that emphasizes used items. (It's the only Upvalley used-book store.) The cramped quarters and carefully selected titles are bound to remind you of a classic London book stall.

INSIDERS' TIP

If you're really on the hunt for bargains, you can bypass the up-market antique stores and head to the Salvation Army's distribution center for North Bay counties. It's at 200 Lytton Springs Road, just north of Healdsburg. The bargains galore are housed in a big complex of 1870s mission-style buildings. Originally built as a plush resort hotel, the property became a military academy for boys before the Salvation Army bought it in 1905.

SHOPPING

The Calistoga Bookstore
1343 Lincoln Ave., Calistoga
• **(707) 942-4123**

This bookstore, nicely set in the 19th-Century Oddfellows Building, knows its audience. Catering largely to tourists, it has a large collection of oversized coffee-table books and Northern California travel guides. And because this is a spa town, Calistoga Bookstore gets into the act with material on massage, reiki, reflexology, nutrition, yoga and other healthful pursuits. It even goes one step further—into Celtic and Arthurian, New Age and Eastern religion, feng shui and sexuality.

Please pet the feline "owner"; her name is Sara.

Sonoma County

Southern Sonoma

Sonoma Bookends Bookstore
201 W. Napa St., No. 15, Sonoma
• **(707) 938-5926**

It's a general interest bookstore with an eye toward tourists in the wide selection of Wine Country books. The store's travel section focuses on California, but there's also a fine selection of U.S. Geological Survey maps.

Readers' Books
127 E. Napa St., Sonoma
• **(707) 939-1779**

Described by *Travel & Leisure* as a "honey pot" ("You can't help but get stuck there"), Readers' is a bookstore with many rooms, one of which is strictly for children's books and serves as a gathering room for youngsters. The store has gained some fame for its authors' readings.

Adobe Drug
303 W. Napa St., Sonoma
• **(707) 938-1144**

It's a lot more than a pharmacy, with a fine gift section, a great collection of books by local authors and plenty of good, old-fashioned friendliness.

A couple strolls along Main Street in the historic, oceanside town of Mendocino.

Jack London Bookstore
14300 Arnold Dr., Glen Ellen
• **(707) 996-2888**

Used and new books are sold here, with a special concentration of books dealing with the life of author Jack London.

Book Warehouse
2200 Petaluma Blvd. N., Petaluma
• **(707) 778-6981**

This is a clearance bookstore tucked in the southwest corner of the Petaluma Village Premium Outlet. It sells the same range of books as any general bookstore, but all have been purchased from stock that has not been sold in other stores.

Wordsworth Books
281 McDowell Blvd. N., Petaluma
• **(707) 762-5665**

Wordsworth offers a complete selection of new hardcover and paperback books and wel-

SHOPPING

Photo: Bill Hoban

comes special orders. There's also a special section of bargain and used books.

Copperfield's Books
140 Kentucky St., Petaluma
• **(707) 762-0563**
210 Coddingtown Mall, Santa Rosa
• **(707) 575-0550**
2316 Montgomery Dr., Santa Rosa
• **(707) 578-8938**
650 Fourth St., Santa Rosa
• **(707) 545-5326**
138 N. Main St., Sebastopol
• **(707) 823-2618**
176 N. Main St., Sebastopol
• **(707) 829-0429**

Copperfield's has built its business on customer service and is highly respected by its customers. The shelves are filled with general interest publications, and there's a great children's section with occasional special events for children (see our Kidstuff chapter). The Fourth Street store in Santa Rosa and the Petaluma store both deal in new and used books.

Barnes & Noble
700 Fourth St., Santa Rosa
• **(707) 576-7494**

Having established the largest bookstore in all of Wine Country, Barnes & Noble has become a place for customers to relax in comfortable cushioned chairs (with a cup of coffee from the adjoining Starbucks) while deciding on book purchases. The business was established when Barnes & Noble purchased a defunct furniture store and helped revitalize the Fourth Street shopping district. This is a very large bookstore.

Crown Books
2080 Santa Rosa Ave., Santa Rosa
• **(707) 578-2044**

This store with discounted prices has certainly given the local independent booksellers a run for their money. The selection is decent here, and readers will find good prices.

Lakeside Village Bookstore
4275 Montgomery Dr., Santa Rosa
• **(707) 538-0579**

Both new and used books are sold here. A special incentive to stop in is a standing 20 percent discount on all kids' books.

Waldenbooks
583 Coddingtown Mall, Santa Rosa
• **(707) 542-7065**

Its location in a busy shopping mall makes this a very popular stop. It's a particularly tidy store with easy to locate sections, and there are large, enticing bargain bins at the front entrance filled with best sellers. The staff here is pleasant and helpful with special orders.

Northern Sonoma

Toyon Books
104 Matheson St., Healdsburg
• **(707) 433-9270**

Travelers looking for more information about Sonoma County's wineries will find a fine selection of wine-related books at the front of the store. The selection at Toyon Books is geared toward general reading, but a group of books specializes in spiritual and self-awareness subjects.

Levin & Company
306 Center St., Healdsburg
• **(707) 433-1118**

It would be hard to find a more appealing bookstore—a large, airy room displays books on three large islands in the center of the store. Beyond that there's a cozy room with a comfortable couch in the mystery novel section, and then another cozy room with books on women's studies. A WPA-style mural spans one wall.

There's also a children's room. Levin & Company offers primarily new books—quality fiction, interior design and garden titles. Upstairs in the loft, you'll find an art gallery displaying the works of some 15 local artists.

Sonoma Coast

Fort Ross Book & Gift Shop
19005 Calif. Hwy. 1, Jenner
• **(707) 847-3437**

Located 11 miles north of the town of Jenner, the state park has a unique selection of books highlighting the Russian settlers and Native Americans, plus the natural history of the Fort Ross area (see our History chapter).

Mendocino County

U.S. Highway 101

The Bookworm
202 S. State St., Ukiah
• **(707) 463-1901**

With some 60,000 titles, The Bookworm sells both new and used books.

The Mendocino Book Company
102 S. School St., Ukiah
• (707) 468-5940

It's billed as the largest bookstore between Santa Rosa and Portland, with special orders and mail orders welcome. It's a true family bookstore, featuring a special young readers room. In addition to books, there's an excellent selection of magazines and newspapers.

Leaves of Grass Bookstore
630 S. Main St., Willits
• (707) 459-3744

Besides the books, this store has an excellent selection of U.S. Geological Survey topographical maps. Also available are educational games and toys for kids, plus books on tape for travelers.

Mendocino Coast

Gallery Bookshop & Bookwinkle's Children's Books
Main and Kasten Sts., Mendocino
• (707) 937-2665

Here's a world-class bookstore stocking more than 25,000 titles, plus cards, magazines and newspapers. The section on local history is comprehensive, and Bookwinkle's is a perfect place to shop for children's books.

Book Loft
45050 Main St., Mendocino
• (707) 937-0890

The shelves are well-organized, the ambiance pleasant and the selection of books comprehensive yet discriminating. Categories are well-marked—best sellers, travel, psychology, metaphysical. In short, it's a delightful place to browse or shop. Tapes, CDs, magazines and newspapers also are available.

Ford House Visitor Center
735 Main St., Mendocino
• (707) 937-5397

This is one of Mendocino's earliest residences as well as the headquarters of the State Historic Park. Here you can find out about beach walks and whale watches. The selection of books covers everything that ever happened to Mendocino and the people who have lived here. There are even books about the movies that have been filmed in Mendocino.

Cheshire Bookshop
363 N. Franklin St., Fort Bragg
• (707) 964-5918

This full-service bookstore has been run by the same owner in Fort Bragg since 1973. The shop is spacious, uncrowded and well-organized.

Lake County

The Book Nook
3928 Main St., Kelseyville
• (707) 279-9752

The Book Nook specializes in children's books. There are many in the store, and "if it isn't here, we'll order it." They stock a lot of gift items—bookends, wind chimes and handmade bookmarks, for example.

The Book Stop
305 N. Main St., Lakeport
• (707) 263-5787

Hiding in Lakeport is the type of bookstore you'd expect to find in San Francisco (which explains why it has become a regular stop for city vacationers). The Book Stop is divided into five rooms: the main room, with more than 80,000 new and used tomes; the antiquarian book room, with both paperback and hardcover editions; the mystery room; the literature and nonfiction room; and the Nature and Discovery Shop, as profiled in our Kidstuff chapter. The store also has a religious section, a large supply of easy listening CDs, gardening tools and even a collection of minerals and fossils.

Catfish Books
1013 11th St., Lakeport
• (707) 263-4454

No, it doesn't deal primarily in fishing manuals. The name is simply a playful nod to nearby Clear Lake. Catfish has new and used material for all ages. Special orders are the house specialty.

Agape Christian Book Store
1859 N. High St., Lakeport
• (707) 263-3120

This Christian book store (pronounced uh-GAH-pay) has been in Lakeport for more than 20 years. It stocks Christian books, gifts, jewelry and Bibles—primarily geared to Protestant readers—by the dozen.

SHOPPING

Arts and Culture

LOOK FOR:
- Theater Companies and Venues
- Music and Dance Organizations and Venues
- Visual Arts Organizations, Venues and Galleries

There seems to be something about the landscape—the rolling hills, the valleys of neatly arranged vineyards, the crashing Pacific—that draws creative souls to seek inspiration in Wine Country. Writer Jack London may have been the first to feel the pull of the area's beauty when he arrived on the scene in the early 1900s. In love with what he called his "Valley of the Moon," he settled in on a ranch above Glen Ellen, wrote a thousand words a day and achieved fame as America's most prolific writer.

If he was the first to be so inspired, he was by no means the last. Today's Wine Country hosts an astonishing number of talented artistic types, many of them living in small villages they are transforming into pockets of culture. Says Doug Hundley, director of Ukiah Playhouse in Mendocino County, "I AM daily amazed at the level of talent in this small town."

Artists set up their easels along Mendocino's rocky shores or take their palettes and empty canvases to vine-covered inland valleys to express themselves, each in his or her unique style. The paintings they produce may sell for four-figure amounts to city folk who come specifically to search out the work of talented painters living in an artistic environment. Authors who populate best-seller lists have taken refuge here, comfortable in the anonymity of small-town life. Sam Keen, author of *Fire in the Belly*, has made his home in the Sonoma Valley, as did the late food guru M.F.K. Fisher, author of a dozen popular books.

On the music scene, singers who once were part of the metropolitan operatic world have left promising big-city careers behind them for the freedom to conduct productions in a less formal style and atmosphere. As for drama, the works of William Shakespeare have been performed by theatrical companies here so frequently he is being considered something of a local author. It all has the ring of a cultural heaven.

But while a pristine setting offers inspiration to the artist, the actor and the producer, it also often deprives them of venues to display their talents. In spite of an abundance of gifted locals, most small towns find it hard to raise money to build theaters, auditoriums and museums.

Nevertheless, the situation has left plenty of room for innovation. If a town has not been able to support any cathedrals of culture, adjustments of attitude are made, and some really great plays and musical productions wind up being performed in rather out-of-the-ordinary settings. Theater-in-the-round works in a church, for example, as do musical events—if the house of worship is blessed with a good piano. Orchestras and choral groups set up seating in veterans' halls or high school auditoriums. Surprisingly, it all works. If the production is good, audiences will overlook the spartan surroundings.

For their part, artists can be grateful for California's rainless summers. They band together in associations and spend weekends displaying paintings outdoors on town plazas. Wine Country hotels and restaurants invite artists to use their wall space, and everyone wins—talent is put on display, the decor is improved, sales are made.

But the greatest of innovations may be in the use of the wineries themselves, both as theatrical venues and art galleries. The spacious lawns are ideal for chamber music—Mozart among the oaks, with a glass of Merlot, never sounded better. At some wineries, stages are anchored to a hillside, and Shakespeare's immortal words and plots unfold as dramatically as in the outdoor settings where the originals were played out. Because of their acoustic properties, winery caves have also proven to be excellent performance spaces. Public rooms at wineries often become art galleries in themselves, places for local artists to be seen and admired. One winery, Buena Vista, even has installed an "artist in residence" program that allows a selected artist each month to not only display paintings, but also work on a canvas amid the winery visitors.

Meanwhile, in the last few years some small communities have made progress in building proper theaters for themselves. In Ukiah (population 17,000), a magnificent ongoing effort began in the mid-1980s to build a theater—with "love, blood, sweat and tears," according to the director. The novel approach was to issue a catalog of needs (10 pounds of nails, 40 feet of electrical cord, etc.), and the community responded in a splendid manner. Not infrequently the theatrical company itself does the subsequent work, taking over buildings that haven't been occupied for years and performing the labor required to turn warehouse into theater. No one likes to waste a good building, so abandoned grammar schools are becoming performing arts centers, churches have become theaters, a former library is now a museum.

Vineyards and wineries may be the mainstay of the Wine Country economy, and the wonder of the natural setting may be the glue that holds its people fast to their surroundings. But the area's arts and culture feed the soul. Who could ignore the thrill of a curtain going up or the excitement sparked when the conductor raises his baton and the drums roll? And when we see a painter dabbing at his canvas while facing a vineyard tinted russet and gold by autumn's palette —don't we all envy the artist just a little? In this chapter, we break our arts and culture offerings into three categories—theater organizations and venues, music and dance options and visual-arts venues and galleries—using our regular geographical sequence: Napa County, then Sonoma, Mendocino and Lake.

Theater Companies and Venues

Napa County

Dreamweavers Theater
101P S. Coombs St., Napa
• **(707) 255-LIVE**

This is Napa's only nonprofit live theater, supported by memberships, donations and ticket sales and completely staffed by volunteers. The troupe incorporated in 1987 and found a permanent home in 1990—a vacant warehouse in the Tannery Row complex that it converted into a cozy, black-box theater (it's been recently renovated) with 85 seats. Dreamweavers does four shows a year for four weekends each, with smaller projects filling the gaps. The 2000 lineup includes *Nuts, I Hard Hamlet, Dracula* and *Three Viewings*. Tickets normally cost $10 to $12. Dreamweavers also sponsors a young actors' theater, with performances by the kids.

Napa Valley College Theater
2277 Napa-Vallejo Hwy., Napa
• **(707) 253-3200**

The drama students of Napa Valley College stage several events at their campus theater during the academic year, August through May. Some examples of recent undertakings are *Amadeus, The Snow Queen, Oklahoma* and *De Donde*.

Prices range from $5 to $12; ask about student and senior discounts. See the Music and Dance section for more NVC productions.

Tucker Farm Center
1201 Tucker Rd., Calistoga
• **(707) 942-0967**

Nobody is trying to be ironic here. It really is a theater, but for most of its existence it has served as a working support center for local farmers. The stage company, mostly Calistogans, performs original works in the summer, fun musicals and comedies in the spring and fall. The theater building, which doubles as a meeting hall or whatever else the growers need it for, holds about 120 patrons for most performances. Admission is $10 to $20. The center is off Calif. Highway 29, just north of Bothe-Napa Valley State Park.

Sonoma County

Andrews Hall
276 E. Napa St., Sonoma
• (707) 938-4626

A classic brick structure, Andrews Hall is a leftover from 1916, when it was the Sonoma Grammar School. More recently it achieved modest national exposure when it was selected as one of the settings for the hit movie *Scream*. It's a small theater that's now part of the Sonoma Community Center and will seat up to 299—it takes on no airs for being grand. There's a friendly hometown atmosphere about it, and it offers a surprisingly diverse assortment of talent, with five major performances staged each winter season using mainly local actors.

The stage is small, so plays generally run to those requiring few actors and uncomplicated sets such as *Mame*, *A Child's Christmas in Wales* and murder mysteries. December usually brings a Christmas-themed production; in 1999 Andrews Hall staged *A Christmas Carol*. Occasional musical evenings bring the internationally recognized Brass Works of San Francisco or a performance by the Baguette Quartet. The intimate, 50-seat Black Box Theater behind Andrews Hall stages one-act plays, sometimes written by local authors. Admission is set at $10 to 12 per event at Andrews Hall, or a season of five performances is $60.

The venue also puts on regular guest artist lectures, in conjunction with the ceramics and art department. Workshops in disciplines such as writing and painting also enrich Andrews Hall's calendar.

Avalon Players
Buena Vista Winery,
18000 Old Winery Rd., Sonoma
• (707) 938-1266, (800) 926-1266

This group has been performing Shakespeare's plays at Buena Vista Winery since 1980 and has become something of a tradition among theater lovers. A lighthearted spirit of fun prevails, and people come from Los Angeles and San Francisco—there are even some regulars from as far away as Texas—to watch the Avalon group perform. One group of 30 friends has come every season for the past several years. Whole families attend, kids and grandparents included. This is "Shakespeare

with a twist"—the audience can expect an occasional actor to leave the stage and carry on his performance amidst the viewers. In 1998, the theater put on the French farce *La Bete*. Children are a part of the cast because the director, Kate Kennedy, also teaches acting to kids. The kids play demanding roles and often put in star performances.

Seating is at picnic tables and is on a first-come, first-served basis. It has become the custom among those who come often to bring some fanciful picnic fare and elaborate table settings. Buena Vista wine is available, of course. Tickets are priced at $18 for adults, $10 for kids. Buena Vista Winery is at the eastern edge of Sonoma. Once on E. Spain Street, follow the directional signs.

Sonoma Valley Shakespeare Festival
Gundlach Bundschu Winery,
4000 Denmark St., Sonoma
• (707) 588-3400

A group of Shakespearean actors using the name Odyssey Theatre has performed since 1982 on a stage at the base of a grassy hill above the Gundlach Bundschu Winery. The venue for the Sonoma Valley Shakespeare Festival is on the eastern edge of Sonoma, and audiences of some 150 to 200 people settle in on a grassy area below to watch. Most bring blankets and picnic fare, and wine is available. Limited bench seating is available for those who find blanket seating difficult. The cast consists of about 30 performers, semiprofessional to highly polished. The plays last more than two hours. A repertory of three each season (*Hamlet* and *A Midsummer Night's Dream*, to name a couple of recent productions) are performed in the original form, with slight adaptations to conform to the limits of the stage. Tickets are $10 to $18 per show, with season tickets available at $45. Performances are at 7 PM Friday, Saturday and Sunday from June to September.

Valley of the Moon Shakespeare Company
Sonoma Developmental Center,
15000 Arnold Dr., Eldridge
• (707) 996-4802

In late 1994, a group of professional Shakespearean actors decided to set up a company of their own and stage outdoor "Shakespeare Under the Stars" performances in the Sonoma area. From late August to late September they perform Saturday and Sunday nights at 7 PM. Past plays have included *The Comedy of Errors* and *The Tempest*, but selections

The wine-aging caves of Clos Pegase are laden with an extensive collection of glass, stone, ceramic, wood and terra cotta representations of Bacchus and his attendants, many of which are 18th- and 19th-century Italian and French originals.

change each year. With a core group and a few additional volunteer actors, some 25 to 30 people are involved in performances. Plays are staged on the extensive grounds of Sonoma Developmental Center in Sonoma's Valley of the Moon. Advance tickets are $12 for adults and $10 for students and seniors. Tack on $2 if they are purchased at the door.

Sonoma State University
1801 E. Cotati, Rohnert Park
• (707) 644-2353

This university is one of 20 campuses in the California state university and college system (see our Education and Child Care chapter). Performing arts get top billing at Sonoma State, with works from the pens of local playwrights and international favorites performed year round, along with dance recitals and musical concerts. The school's Everett B. Person Theatre, seating 475, gives students an opportunity to perform in such two-weekend productions as the Broadway play *Scapino* and the lesser-known *Another Part of the House*. Productions often include guest artists, who occasionally conduct workshops afterwards for students. A smaller theater seating 175 presents plays in the round, mostly student productions suitable for the more intimate stage. *Waiting for Godot* is a good example. There is also Warren Auditorium, which is devoted to music events throughout the year, from jazz to chamber music. Prices of tickets vary but generally run in the range of $5 to $20.

Spreckels Performing Arts Center
5409 Snyder Ln., Rohnert Park
• (707) 588-3400

This is one Sonoma County building designed specifically for the arts. When the City of Rohnert Park was developed in the late 1970s, an $8-million performing arts complex of 35,000 square feet was included in the master plan. It is the home of the Pacific Alliance Stage Company, founded by Spreckels director Michael Grice; Smuin Ballet/SF; and Orchestra Sonoma. The Spreckels Center also serves as a home away from home for top touring performers.

The center houses two theaters designed and built exclusively for dance, music and theatrical performances. The Nellie W. Codding Theatre seats 511 patrons and offers a variety of performances from nationally known arts groups. The innovative Bette Condiotti Experimental Theatre seats 175 and presents more unusual and creative programming as well as special productions by local arts groups, schools

and civic organizations. Both theaters are attractive, but the Codding Theatre is stunning with its red carpeting, luxurious fabric theater seats, and midnight blue catwalks and ceiling. Codding productions include Broadway hits, an extraordinary ballet program featuring 12 of the Bay Area's most charismatic soloists, a performance of *The Nutcracker* at Christmas and symphony performances. Main Stage ticket prices usually run $22 to $25.

Santa Rosa Players
Lincoln Arts Center, 709 Davis St., Santa Rosa
• (707) 579-8618, (707) 544-7827

A few blocks north of Old Railroad Square, in an old elementary school at Davis and Eighth streets, is the Lincoln Arts Center. Home of the Sonoma County Arts Council, the center houses a ballet school, radio station and fine-art printer. It is also the stage home of the Santa Rosa Players, performers of musicals, tragedies and comedies. The 1999 season included *Lend Me a Tenor, Kiss of the Spider Woman, I Hate Hamlet* and *Kiss Me Kate*.

Luther Burbank Center for the Arts
50 Mark West Springs Rd., Santa Rosa
• (707) 546-3600

The arts center became a reality in 1981 when the Christian Life Center, a religious organization, was forced to sell its holdings—this facility included—as part of bankruptcy proceedings. That left the door open for the Luther Burbank Foundation to move in and reopen it as a regional arts hub. It's still going strong, with big-name concerts and cultural events of all kinds. It serves as host to many groups, including the Actors' Theatre, the Redwood Empire Lyric Theatre, the Redwood Empire Ballet, Ballet California, the California Museum of the Arts and the Santa Rosa Symphony (see the symphony's listing in "Music and Dance" later in this chapter).

The center's cathedral beginnings are clearly visible in the 6,000-square-foot lobby, which twinkles with lights from multi-layered chandeliers that span the interior of the room. This provides an entrance to the theater that maintains the elegance of the sanctuary it once was. It's certain the Christian Life Center also spared no expense in making its pews and balconies the best its parishioners could buy. The seating capacity of 1,563 provides ample space to attend national and international quality performances across the spectrum of the arts world. Ballets, choral performances, symphonies, films, operas, concerts and fund-raisers of all kinds are held in this inviting setting.

There are other auditoriums at the Burbank Center. The East, seating 425, is ideal for school plays and recitals, giving them a professional touch with theatrical lighting, a sound booth and audiovisual equipment. The Chamber Chapel seats 325 and has a spectacular, high-vaulted ceiling and stained-glass windows. The Exhibit Hall, a 9,000-square-foot venue, lends itself to trade shows, art exhibits or wine-tastings. Half the entertainment world seems to have found its way to Luther Burbank Center at one time or another—take Engelbert Humperdinck, Ballet Folklorico de Mexico, Yo Yo Ma, Nanci Griffith, and the New Pickle Circus as samples of the diversity. Tickets run from $15 to $50, depending on the event.

Santa Rosa Junior College Summer Repertory Theater
11501 Mendocino Ave., Santa Rosa
• (707) 527-4343

Summer repertory productions by this group are approaching 30 seasons. Running from mid-June into early August, plays rotate throughout the season and include musicals, dramas and comedies. The 2000 lineup includes *The Wizard of Oz*, H.R. Gurney's *Tale of Sylvia, Romeo and Juliet*, and *Victor/Victoria*. Performances are held variously at the college, Luther Burbank Center for the Arts (see previous listing) or local high schools. This is a professional training program geared to actors in graduate school, all of whom come on scholarships for summer work. Paid directors are well-known and usually work on a rotating basis—six work each season. For students, it represents an excellent opportunity to find out if this is what they want to do, not only as performers but also as backstage people. One thing they discover is that it's hard work—14 hours a day, six days a week in season. Tickets range from $7 to $14, or $40–$60 for season passes. Musicals are in the high end of that range.

Sonoma County Repertory Theatre
415 Humboldt St., Santa Rosa and
104 N. Main St., Sebastopol
• (707) 544-7278, (707) 823-0177

Voted Sonoma County's "Best Theatre

Troupe for 1996," Main Street Theatre was formed in 1991 and in 1996 added a sister company in downtown Santa Rosa, the Sonoma County Repertory Theatre. Now working together as the Sonoma County Repertory Theatre, they offer an intriguing selection of fare. The 1999 season included *The Birthday Party, Let's Play Two* and, back by popular demand, *Sylvia*, a modern romantic comedy about a marriage and a dog.

In addition, the two theaters will continue to offer year-round, multi-disciplinary training for both children and adults, plus children's theater and a summer Shakespeare festival. Admission prices at both theaters are generally $15, or $10 for students and seniors.

Mendocino County

Ukiah Playhouse
1041 Low Gap Road, Ukiah
• (707) 462-9226

Offering an eclectic mix, Ukiah Playhouse stages five plays each season (October to June) including such recent fare as *Oklahoma!* and an adaptation of Studs Terkel's *The Good War*. In addition, the Playhouse offers readings fo original, unproduced scripts, one of them eventually selected for production. These can be tricky presentations, as the audience must become accustomed to the fact that there is no action on stage.

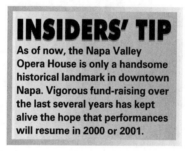

INSIDERS' TIP
As of now, the Napa Valley Opera House is only a handsome historical landmark in downtown Napa. Vigorous fund-raising over the last several years has kept alive the hope that performances will resume in 2000 or 2001.

Ukiah Playhouse has been producing plays since 1977, sometimes performing in rented spaces such as an abandoned 7-eleven. It was reborn and revitalized in the mid-1980s when members of the company set out to build their own theater. The whole community came together, with everyone donating materials to the cause—landscaping included. Over the years, improvements have been made, with a box office and dressing rooms added. It's a work in progress. The present structure seats 138 but will be enlarged to seat 198. Tickets for play productions are priced at $10 to $12. The staged readings are $4 or $5.

Willits Community Theatre
37 W. Van Ln., Willits
• (707) 459-2281

This company now performs works in a

small, intimate theater seating 74 playgoers. Until 1993 plays had been staged in different venues in Willits, mainly the Methodist Church and the Grange. The breakthrough in getting its own theater came when the company put on a phenomenally successful run of *The Music Man* at the local high school. Most of Mendo-cino County rushed to see the performance, thereby securing a bankroll big enough to start planning a theater. The community rose to the occasion, with donations that eventually transformed a former Volkswagen repair shop into a community theater. During more than 20 years of production, the company has staged dozens of plays, including *Blues in the Night,* a history of the blues that ran in February 1999. In recent years, the company has presented *Waiting for Godot,* a cabaret production of *Oh, Coward!* and the British mystery *What the Butler Saw.* Plays run Fridays and Saturdays from October to late June, with admission set at $5 to $12.

Photo: Tina Luster-Hoban

Napa was the birthplace of the loudspeaker and the Magnavox Corporation. The first speaker was invented by Peter Jensen and Edwin Pridham at 1601 First Street in 1915. This statue, by Franco Vianello, was dedicated in 1985.

Mendocino Theater Company
Little Lake and Caster Sts., Mendocino
• (707) 937-4477

It's a small, cozy theater—just 80 seats in nine rows—but the bill of fare is enticing, with a mix of comedies (*Picasso at the Lapin Agile*), drama (Eugene O'Neill's *A Moon for the Misbegotten*) and mainstream presentations. The theater adjoins Mendocino Art Center (see listing under "Visual Art Venues and Organizations" in this chapter), where the revival of the City

of Mendocino began in the 1940s with an influx of hungry artists looking for an inexpensive way of life (see our History chapter). The company produces six plays a year with shows Thursday through Sunday nights. Tickets are priced at $10 to $15.

Gloriana Theater
721 W. Franklin St., Fort Bragg
• (707) 964-7469

Here's musical theater in grand style, featuring a full cast with lavish costumes, sets and choreography. Past productions have included *Nunsense* and *Annie. Grease* and the West Coast premiere of *Quark*, a science-fiction drama, were included on the program for the summer of 1999. Looking at theater from a different angle, Gloriana also has experimented with a series called Showcase Performances, designed to combine the highest values of musical theater with an elegant simplicity of production style, minimal sets and simple costuming. Children's programs and workshops offer kids opportunities to express themselves in a creative environment through the skills and techniques of musical theater. For kids 4th grade and up, there are workshops in acting, singing, dancing and makeup.

Another offbeat sideline is the Rent-A-Singer and Rent-A-Costume program. For weddings, parties or other special events, Gloriana will send out a fully equipped theater company, a group of carolers, an a capella ensemble or their children's chorus. This group has been creating melodious magic since 1977, performing musical theater from *The Mikado* to *Fiddler On the Roof*, but until 1996 the company had makeshift arrangements. The building of a new theater has begun. It's small—just 150 seats with a full stage and backstage area—but it's a work in progress, and construction proceeds amid great excitement. The season is year-round, with performances Thursday through Sunday at 8 PM. Tickets are priced at $10 and $8, with discounts available for series of shows.

Warehouse Repertory Theatre
319 N. Main St., Fort Bragg
• (707) 961-2940

Artistic director Meg Patterson calls it "industrial strength theater," and her intention is to introduce audiences to people, emotions and situations that challenge experiences and stretch the mind. Patterson pulls out some heavy drama—plays such as Sam Shepard's Pulitzer Prize-winning *Buried Child,* Arthur Miller's *The Crucible* and Steven Dietz's original *Private Eyes.*

Patterson has high expectations for the Warehouse. She's hoping to make Fort Bragg as famous as Ashland, Oregon, as a center for summer Shakespeare and envisions an annual pilgrimage to a world-renowned shrine of serious theater in Mendocino County. From July through September she presents the Mendocino Coast Shakespeare Festival. Until last season, the repertory company was crammed into the upstairs of the Lions Hall. Bolstered by tremen-

dous community response, the group has a new, permanent home in an old lumber company that was miraculously transformed by means of sweat equity. The season runs April to December, with tickets priced at $10 and $15, or $5 for kids.

Lake County

Lake County Repertory Theater
P.O. Box 1753, Lower Lake 95457
• (707) 995-3565

The theater group was formed in 1981 but was inactive for several years as it searched for a home. They found it in 1994, at the Lake County Museum in Lower Lake (seating capacity 120). The theater stages two plays a year—one in spring and one in fall. Recent productions have included *Steel Magnolias* and *Dracula.* They prefer to keep things light. Admission is $6 to $7.

Lakeport Community Players
P.O. Box 220, Lakeport 95453
• (707) 263-4187

When the Lakeport campus of Mendocino College dropped its drama department for budgetary reasons in 1991, those staff members eventually reorganized as the Lakeport Community Players, an auxiliary of the Lake County Arts Council. They do splashy musicals, Woody Allen farces, mysteries and dramas. Recent examples: *Guys and Dolls* and *Harvey.* They are in the process of raising funds to renovate the Soper-Reese Theater (at Main and Martin streets), which they hope to make their permanent home. They also do melodramas at the Blackberry Festival and the Lake County Fair (see our Festivals and Annual Events chapter).

Music and Dance Organizations and Venues

Napa County

Jarvis Conservatory
1711 Main St., Napa • (707) 255-5445

The Jarvis Conservatory was founded in 1973 as a nonprofit generator of scholarships for students of the performing arts. The corporation took a great leap in 1994 when it acquired its own educational facilities. And what facilities they are, centered around the Lisbon

Winery, a registered historic landmark built in 1882. Performances are in a 221-seat theater in the acoustically superb, expensively equipped, stone winery building. The Conservatory's offerings feature a mix of students and visiting professionals. Recent artists have included the Jose Limon West Dance Troupe and pianist/conductor Donald Runnicles. The first Saturday of the month is opera night, and the specialty of the house is zarzuela, a splendidly costumed, melodramatic form of Spanish opera. Admission for all shows can range from $10 and $30.

Napa Valley Symphony
2407 California Blvd., Napa
• (707) 22-MUSIC

The symphony, conducted by Asher Raboy, plays with an assurance and aptitude you might not expect to find in a city of 65,000. Its primary venue is the Lincoln Theater at the California Veterans Home (see our Attractions chapter) in Yountville. The Napa Valley Sympony has tackled Beethoven, Tchaikovsky and Mahler, Baroque chamber music and jazzy compositions by Artie Shaw. It has welcomed guests such as pianist Ursula Oppens, clarinetist Todd Palmer and violinist Amy Oshiro. And on occasion it leaves the Lincoln for special performances at Robert Mondavi Winery or St. John's Catholic Church in Napa. Single tickets in section A are $32 for adults, $16 for students and children younger than 16; in section B, prices are $26 and $13. You also can subscribe to a series of five Tuesday evening or Sunday matinee concerts. Adult series prices range from $85 to $150.

Napa Valley College Theater
2277 Napa-Vallejo Hwy., Napa
• (707) 253-3200

The college's esteemed music program puts on a variety of performances, such as orchestra and vocal recitals, even cabaret nights, during the August-through-May academic year. The theater also has lured independent groups like the North Bay Philharmonic Orchestra, the North Bay Wind Ensemble and the Billy Browning Jazz Orchestra. Occasionally events are staged off campus, usually at wineries. Prices range from $5 to $10. Ask about senior and student discounts.

Chamber Music in Napa Valley
• (707) 252-7122

This group brings the soothing sounds of chamber music to the Wine Country. Recent guests include Isaac Stern, the Prazak Quartet (a renowned group from Prague) and tenor James Morris. Most performances are at the First United Methodist Church in Napa, though the chamber music sometimes drifts to the wine caves of S. Anderson or Clos Pegase. The church performances are generally $15, while winery shows are $25 and include winetasting.

Robert Mondavi Winery
7801 St. Helena Hwy., Oakville
• (707) 226-1395 ext. 4392

While Robert serves as unofficial wine ambassador to the world, his wife, Margrit Biever, does her part to make the winery a center of culture in the Wine Country. It seems as though there is always a note of music in the air here, whether it's the Preservation Hall Jazz Band kicking off the outdoor Summer Concert Series or Italian opera to benefit renovation of the Napa Valley Opera House. Call the winery for a schedule and admission fees.

Paulin Hall Auditorium
Pacific Union College, Angwin
• (707) 965-7362

The forested heights of Howell Mountain might be an unlikely spot for the sweet melodies of classical music, but Pacific Union College (PUC) is able to attract frontline talent to Paulin Hall. Recent performers have included soprano Marnie Breckenridge, Romanian-born pianist Eduard Stan and Troika Balalaikas, an American trio that dresses in traditional costume and plays the folk songs of Czarist Russia. The Fine Arts series usually runs from October to April. The cost per is $5 for adults and $3 for children per show, or pay $20 and $9, respectively, for five programs. There are numerous other events at Paulin that are not part of the Fine Arts series. Any shows requiring an organ take place in PUC's church sanctuary, which has the state's largest tracker pipe organ.

Sonoma County

Sonoma Valley Chorale
Veterans Memorial Building, 126 1st St. W., Sonoma • (707) 935-1576

This professional-level, 150-member chorus, under the direction of Jim Griewe, has been singing together since the early '70s. Performing a three-concert series annually, they bring audiences to their feet with music that might be classical, sacred, from Broadway, from the '40s or from Gershwin. The chorale has sung with

*Cesar Baldachini, who designed the "Cesar," the French equivalent of the Oscar, also designed this
giant bronze thumb which rises from the ground at the Clos Pegase Winery.*

the Napa Valley and Santa Rosa symphonies (see listings in this section) and even for the opening ceremony at a Giants baseball game. They've made two European tours, singing their way through France and Italy. Their regular venue is the Veterans Memorial building auditorium, which has tiered, theater seating for 400. Tickets are $12 for adults and $10 for seniors and students. Reservations can be made over the phone with ticket pickup at the door.

Cinnabar Theater
3333 Petaluma Blvd. N., Petaluma
• (707) 763-8920

In the summer of 1970, Marvin Klebe abandoned his career singing baritone with the San Francisco Opera Company, bought a 60-year-old, two-room schoolhouse on the outskirts of Petaluma surrounded by dairy cows and chickens, and began transforming the structure into a theater. Disenchanted with the usual regimentation of grand opera, Marvin's goal was to provide a stage for experimental works that would involve the local community.

Today Cinnabar Theater is a venue for an outstanding array of entertainers performing everything from Bach to rock. Candlelight concerts give a rare and romantic opportunity to hear chamber music the way some of our ancestors did. Concerts are held not only at Cinnabar Theater, but also in some of Petaluma's loveliest gardens and mansions, intimate art galleries and in the downtown Polly Klaas Theater (a school for young acting hopefuls). The Summer Music Festival presents the best in classical music, ethnic music, musical comedy, opera and children's music.

In 1983 Marvin and his wife, Jan, created Cinnabar Children's Theater workshop. In the first year the children mounted a musical production of *The Hobbit* that they wrote and publicized themselves. Children's programming and training play a role of growing importance at Cinnabar. Classes are packed. A free brochure outlining Klebe's many ventures is available. Performance tickets are priced at $8 to $18.

Santa Rosa Symphony
50 Mark West Springs Rd., No. 305,
Santa Rosa • (707) 546-8742

The Santa Rosa Symphony was founded by George Trombley in 1927. Thirty-two eager (and some talented) amateur musicians played for the first time at the local Elks Club. It is said that Mr. T (as his players called him) was fond of spirited selections. Under his direction the orchestra played Dvorak's *Slavonic Dance* at most concerts. These perfomances were enlivened by the gusto of Mr. T, who stomped his foot on the podium until the dust flew. Trombley's tenure lasted 30 years, when Maestro Corrick Brown took over the baton and held it for another 37 years.

The orchestra has long since left the Elks Club and now makes its home at the Luther Burbank Center for the Arts (see listing under "Theater Companies and Venues" in this chapter). It also has a new conductor, Jeffrey Kahane, the world-renowned pianist, who assumed the podium in 1995. It is the only orchestra of its size and quality (there are 80-plus musicians) between the southern border of Sonoma County and Eugene, Oregon. The concert season consists of seven three-day events plus a pops concert and picnic in June (table seating and lawn seating are available), a Redwoods Music Festival in August and other special events in August and September. Kahane is particularly eager to work with young people and has established a Symphony Youth Orchestra, providing two free concerts for children (particularly popular with kindergarten through 3rd-grade students).

Lake County

Lake County Community Chorus
P.O. Box 1216, Lakeport
• (707) 263-5526

The chorus, an auxiliary of the Lake County Arts Council, gets together a few times a year to belt out everything from Mozart to Christmas carols to Broadway standards. Admission is along the lines of $5. The chorus' venues include the Lower Lake Schoolhouse and Museum, and the Soper-Reese Theater.

Visual Arts Organizations, Venues and Galleries

To make it easier for you to skip from one gallery to the next one you will encounter, listings in this section are presented in the intra-county geographical sequence outlined in How to Use This Book.

Napa County

di Rosa Preserve
5200 Calif. Hwy. 121/12, Napa
• (707) 226-5991

The subtitle of this collection is Art & Nature, and, indeed, many of the pieces are blended into the scenery of Carneros, that cool-climate grape growing region on the north side of San Pablo Bay (see our Wineries chapter). Rene and Veronica di Rosa have been gathering artwork for 30 years, and their current display tends to the whimsical, even outrageous. All of it was produced in the Bay Area in the latter part of the 20th century. The indoor space includes a circa-1886 winery the di Rosas have converted into their home, plus some contemporary galleries full of works of various media. Rene originally moved to Carneros to grow grapes, which he did as Winery Lake Vineyards until he sold the planted land to Seagram, the corporate beverage giant, in 1986. Admission is $10 and by guided tour only. The Preserve offers two tours a day—9:25 AM and 12:55 PM—Tuesday through Friday from October through May, and Monday through Thursday from June through September, except for summer Tuesdays when the later tour gets bumped to 9:25 PM. Got that? Good, because there are also Saturday morning tours at 9:25 AM and 10:25 AM.

Jessel Miller Gallery
1019 Atlas Peak Rd., Napa
• (707) 257-2350

On the road to Silverado Country Club, in a stately, vine-covered, white-brick building, is the studio of esteemed watercolorist Jessel Miller. The gallery shows the work of both emerging and established artists, in media from oil to collage to jewelry. It also offers public tours, lectures and demonstrations. The gallery is open 10 AM to 5 PM daily.

Henry Joseph Gallery
2475 Solano Ave., Napa
• (707) 224-4356

This gallery is devoted to the California style—that spontaneous, impressionistic form spawned by a group of Californians in the 1930s. Painters such as Charles Surrendorf, Jade Fon and Justin Faivre made the California style easily distinguishable from traditional English watercolor. The gallery also represents prominent Napa Valley artists like Roger Blum, Bill King and Jay Golik. If you pop for an original, you can have it framed at the affiliated Napa Frame Studio. Hours of operation are 10 AM to 5:30 PM Tuesday through Friday and 10 AM to 3 PM Saturday.

Napa Valley Art Association
1520 Behrens St., Napa
• (707) 255-9616

The Napa Valley Art Association was formed as a nonprofit corporation in 1953, to provide local artists with satisfactory facilities. At the association's once-a-month meetings (usually on the fourth Monday), guest artists demonstrate their skills and ideas. Those demonstrations are often videotaped for future observation. You can pay a $24 annual fee for membership, or surrender a nominal $2 charge to attend a single meeting. The association hosts occasional shows of its members' work, —everything from still lifes to portraits and landscapes to abstracts, in all sorts of media. Call the association for further information.

The Hess Collection Winery
4411 Redwood Rd., Napa
• (707) 255-1144

Donald Hess, the Swiss businessman who made his millions bottling water before he turned to wine, is a passionate art collector, and some of the best of his collection is here in Napa Valley. His three-story, 13,000-square-foot gallery is part of the winery and just as much of a draw to visitors. Hess collects only works by living artists, and the list is impressive: Francis Bacon, Frank Stella, Henri Machaux and Theodoros Stamos, just to name a few. Some of the outstanding conceptual pieces include a group of oversized, headless figures fashioned by Polish artist Magdalena Abakanowicz, and a vintage Underwood typewriter going up in flames, a work by Argentinian Leopoldo Maler. There is no charge to enter the museum, which is open 10 AM to 4 PM daily.

Images Fine Art
North: 6540 Washington St., Yountville
• (707) 944-0404
South: 6505 Washington St., Yountville
• (707) 944-0606

North and south have never been closer than at these twin galleries in downtown Yountville. The northern room came first; the southern was added in 1996. Neither has a specialty, just best-selling artists represented in a dramatic, two-story space with vaulted ceilings. Con-

This jungle mural greets shoppers and walkers in downtown Santa Rosa.

tributors include David Dodsworth, Guy Buffet, Roy Fairchild and Pradzynski. Both galleries are open daily from 10 AM to 5 PM.

RAKU Ceramics Collection
Beard Plaza, 6540 Washington St., Yountville • (707) 944-9424

Raku, the process originally used to make bowls for tea ceremony in medieval Japan, involves using tongs to remove red-hot pots from the kiln, then cooling the ceramics quickly in the air or in water. Most of what you see here gets an additional copper-flashing technique. The pots, sprayed with copper, are covered with a pail after firing. When the pot is removed, the copper oxidizes and flashes in a rainbow of colors. RAKU has work by more than 75 ceramists, including Greg Milne, Ed Risak and Tom and Nancy Giusti, and is open daily from 10 AM to 5 PM.

Mumm Napa Valley
8445 Silverado Trail, Rutherford • (707) 942-3434

Mumm's corporate owners, Joseph E. Seagram & Sons, have been appreciative of photographers, making the winery perhaps Napa Valley's premier venue for that industrial art. Luminaries such as Imogen Cunningham, Galen Rowell, Sebastio Salgado and William Neill have been represented on the walls. But the rotating exhibitions have a hard time diverting attention from the winery's one permanent collection: "The Story of a Winery" by Ansel Adams. The legendary Californian was hired in 1959 to document construction of new wine cellars, care of the vineyards and the process of winemaking from vine to bottle. The Smithsonian Institution circulated the best of the photos for three years, and now Mumm has dozens of gelatin silver prints. There is no admission charge to the galleries, which are open from 10 AM to 5 PM daily.

I. Wolk Gallery
1235 Main St., St. Helena • (707) 963-8800

Ira Wolk's second-floor gallery is a definitive St. Helena establishment—tasteful art in a lovely, immaculate space. The gallery features everything from paintings and works on paper to photography and sculpture. It is open Wednesday through Monday from 10 AM to 5:30 PM.

The Gallery on Main Street
1359 Main St., St. Helena • (707) 963-3350

One of St. Helena's most prominent and centrally located spaces, the Gallery on Main focuses on, but is not limited to, images of vineyards and wine. It's primarily a venue for Northern California artists and traditional styles. An example is Gail Packer's extensive series of multiplate etchings, with frames designed by artist Hildy Henry. Other contributors include Garberville's Josh Adam and Hopland's Ray Voisard. The Gallery on Main is open daily from 10 AM to 5 PM.

Rasmussen Art Gallery
Pacific Union College, Angwin
• **(707) 965-7362**

Pacific Union College's stylish art gallery is largely a showplace for its own students, faculty and alumni. It isn't limited to these groups, though. Other recent exhibitions have included the drawings of Samuel Fleming Lewis and the experimental photography of Cliff Rusch. Admission is free, and the gallery is open from 1 to 5 PM on Tuesday, Thursday, Saturday and Sunday.

Clos Pegase Winery
1060 Dunaweal Ln., Calistoga
• **(707) 942-4981**

Art is everywhere at Clos Pegase, from the winery itself—something of a huge modern sculpture—to French and Italian carvings of Bacchus tucked into the wine caves. The variety is impressive too, from granite sculptures to watercolors to collages. Clos Pegase offers a self-guided walking tour of the premises, as well as guided tours of the facility and wine caves that take place at 11 AM and 2 PM (no reservation required). Among the pieces it holds are a giant bronze thumb by Cesar Baldachini (designer of the "Cesar," the French equivalent of the Oscar); Michael Scranton's *Wrecking Ball*, an enervating installation in the Reserve Room; and a Henry Moore sculpture (*Mother Earth*) in the portico. In addition to all that, a wine-in-art slide presentation, created by proprietor Jan Shrem, is given inside the caves at 2 PM on the third Saturday of each month (December and January excluded). The show is free.

Lee Youngman Galleries
1316 Lincoln Ave., Calistoga
• **(707) 942-0585, (800) 551-0585**

Owner Lee Love Youngman has long been surrounded by creative men. Her father, Ralph Love, was a painter from the Early California school who has work hung in major museums. And her husband, Paul Youngman, is noted for his contemporary landscapes, architectural renderings and marines. Lee's gallery has a decidedly Southwest bent. It represents more than 60 full-time artists, including big shots such as

Neil Boyle and Mark Geller. The gallery is open 10 AM to 5 PM Monday through Saturday and 11 AM to 4 PM Sunday.

Sonoma County

Spirits In Stone
452 First St. E., Sonoma
• **(707) 938-2200**

"Must touch to appreciate" is the byword when visiting this collection of Zimbabwe Shona sculpture. The form's sleek surface is beyond description. *Newsweek* has called Shona sculpture "the most important new art form to emerge from Africa this century." You can also find African photographs, paintings and music at this museum-quality gallery, which is open daily from 10 AM to 6 PM. (See our Shopping chapter for more on Spirits In Stone.)

Sonoma State University Art Gallery
1801 E. Cotati Ave., Rohnert Park
• **(707) 664-2295**

Changing exhibits of contemporary art are combined with works by artists known regionally, nationally and internationally. The gallery is open Tuesday through Friday from 11 AM to 4 PM and noon to 4 PM on weekends.

Valley of the Moon Art Association
Box 2097, Boyes Hot Springs 95416
• **(707) 996-2115**

This active art group of 100 or so members has been promoting and enjoying art since 1958. Open to painters in two-dimensional media and sculpture, the association puts on seven shows a year, mostly on the Sonoma Plaza in the center of town and often in connection with other events such as the town's Fourth of July celebration or Salute to the Arts (see our Festivals and Annual Events chapter). Members' talent levels range from beginner to the highly professional (some paintings fetch prices in the thousands). There are two types of membership, active ($30) and associate ($50), and members are expected to attend at least five meetings and either participate in the shows or help work at them.

Cultural Arts Council of Sonoma County
602 Wilson St., Santa Rosa
• **(707) 579-ARTS**

Curating new exhibits every eight weeks, the council serves as a resource center for artists and provides a gallery for their work. A

ARTS AND CULTURE

Photo: Sonoma Museum of Visual Art

The Sonoma Museum of Visual Art showcases contemporary work, like the sculpture by Carol Setterlund pictured above.

typical art competition commissioned by the Sonoma Land Trust challenged artists to portray imagery inspired by Sonoma County's agricultural environment. It's not just two-dimensional art. For five years the council has sponsored a gospel music concert, sharing a unique American art form in performances at Santa Rosa High School. The council also sponsors events such as First Night Santa Rosa, a New Year's Eve celebration of the arts in downtown Santa Rosa featuring jazz, rock, Big Band, mime, comedy, theater and dance.

Sonoma Museum of Visual Art
Luther Burbank Center for the Arts,
50 Mark West Springs Rd., Santa Rosa
• (707) 527-0297

The only fine arts museum serving the Northern California coast and northern San Francisco Bay Area, the Sonoma Museum of Visual Art (MOVA) is dedicated to exhibiting exciting and thought-provoking shows that challenge the mind and the eye while examining unique visions of beauty and form. Drawing from a wide variety of sources, Sonoma MOVA showcases original works by living artists who push beyond the traditional limits of painting, sculpture, photography and architecture. An interactive salon is held at Sonoma

MOVA on occasional Friday evenings throughout the year. These feature guest speakers from all walks of the artistic community. In the summer months, visitors can enjoy the outdoor Film Cafe, which pairs short experimental films with excellent local food and wine. Museum hours are 1 to 4 PM Wednesdays and Fridays, 1-8 Thursdays and 11 AM to 4 PM on weekends. Admission is $2, and a listing of current exhibitions is yours on the Web at www.lbc.net

The Ren Brown Collection
1781 Calif. Hwy. 1, Bodega Bay
• (707) 875-2922

Housed in a newly refurbished building with shoji screens and a small Japanese garden, this gallery is dedicated to showing contemporary art from both sides of the Pacific. The major focus is on modern Japanese prints by artists such as Shigeki Kuroda, Toko Shinoda and Ryohei Tanaka, whose works often appear in prominent museums. The items shown at Ren Brown represent the largest selection of contemporary Japanese prints in California. Also featured are the works of several regional California artists. You'll see watercolor, sculpture in stone and bronze, and acrylic paintings as well as woodcut, silkscreen, mezzotint and lithograph art. All in all, some 75 artists are represented on two floors of the gallery, which is open every day except Tuesday from 10 AM to 5 PM.

Christopher Queen Galleries
John Orr's Garden, No. 4, Duncans Mills
• (707) 865-1318

On Calif. 116 in historic Duncans Mills, this gallery features nationally known wildlife artists, including Thomas Brenders, John Bateman and Thomas Quinn. Serigraphs by John Powell and Don Hatfield also are on display. The Upstairs Salon features an extensive display of important early California artists. The galleries are open every day but Tuesday from 11 AM to 5 PM, and by appointment.

Sea Ranch Lodge
Calif. Hwy. 1 N., Sea Ranch
• (707) 785-2371

Various artists and photographers display their work in the Sea Ranch Lodge's Fireside Room overlooking the ocean (for more on Sea Ranch, see our Real Estate chapter). New exhibits are posted each month, introduced with a reception of wine and hors d'oeuvres.

Mendocino County

Gualala Arts Center
46501 Old State Hwy., Gualala
• (707) 884-1138

The small town of Gualala is an artist's heaven and an art lover's paradise. And the wonder of it is that such a small town (population 1,100) could support so many artists.

This is the classic story with Mendocino coastal towns. In the early 1900s, Gualala was a lumber mill center, abandoned when sawmills closed down (see our History chapter). But in the 1960s, the beauty of the area attracted artists and other creative people. They painted, photographed, wrote, acted and watched whales. They attracted other talented people, and during the last three decades Gualala has become recognized as a center for the arts, drawing people from miles around to soak up the cultural atmosphere.

The focal point of all this art activity is a new 15,000-square-foot arts center, established in 1997 and set in the forest. The scope of the center's activities is somewhat overwhelming. You'll find popular and classical music concerts, lectures, exhibits, youth and adult art classes, theater productions and meeting space for artists, photographers, quilters, poets, weavers and book groups. They do all this with one salaried

secretary, a professional executive director and a lot of volunteers.

The first Sunday of every month is given over to chamber music concerts (tickets are $15), but it's likely you will run into some kind of music event any time you happen to be in town. Admission fees in the same range are set for a wide variety of events from theater presentations to lecture series held in the multipurpose room (seating capacity, 350). The big event—the one in 2000 will be the 39th—is the mid-August Art In the Redwoods extravaganza (see our Festivals and Annual Events chapter), where more than 350 artistic entries attract the attention of some 5,000 people who attend. Another event occurs in December—a two-day tour of the private studios of local artists. There is no fee. You can send e-mail to the center at garts@mcn.org.

Alinder Gallery
39165 S. Hwy. 1, Gualala • (707) 884-4884

Internationally respected authorities Mary and Jim Alinder personally manage their gallery. While specializing in original Ansel Adams images, the gallery maintains an excellent inventory of work by many other great photographers. Alinder Gallery is open Tuesday through Sunday from 10 AM to 6 PM.

Mendocino Art Center
45200 Little Lake St., Mendocino
• (707) 937-5818

This is an educational organization that features classes in everything from furniture making to bead artistry. Year-round classes in fine arts, ceramics and children's art, conducted by paid artists-in-residence, draw students from around the country. A spacious gallery at the center features the work of established and emerging artists of local, regional and national reputation. An additional showcase gallery is at 560 Main Street, open every day from 10 AM to 4 PM. (For more on the Mendocino Art Center, see our Shopping chapter.)

Northcoast Artists Gallery
362 N. Main St., Fort Bragg
• (707) 964-8266

This is a cooperative gallery with 22 artists showing their work. Started in 1986 with nine artists, it's now like a family, with four members of the original group still involved. Others come and go. Artists in oil paintings, ceramics, woodwork and producers of silk-screens and fine paper products are featured. The gallery is open daily from 10 AM to 6 PM.

Lake County

Rolf Nord Kriken
3566 Big Valley Rd., Kelseyville
• (707) 279-9116

Kriken is a sculptor famed for his oversized bronze renderings. His works include the California Vietnam Veterans Memorial in Sacramento; the All Veterans Memorial in Cleveland; and the Danville Memorial in Danville, California. He does fine-art castings, too. Call between 9 AM and 4:30 PM for an appointment.

Lake County ARTS Council
325 N. Main St., Lakeport
• (707) 263-6658

What would the Lake County arts scene be without this umbrella organization? Let's hope we never find out. The ARTS council has its fingers in a lot of pots. It owns and operates Main Street Gallery at the above address, giving local artists a place to show and sell their work; it hosts open-mike nights for musicians, poets and storytellers on the first and third Thursdays of each month; it administers the Art in Public Places program, beautifying the county while giving artists a year-round forum; it showcases student artwork in vacant buildings (called Phantom Galleries) around the lake; and it compiles a Cultural Events Calendar published by the *Lake County Record-Bee* on the first Wednesday of each month. It does a lot more, too, but that should give you the basic idea.

American Photo Impressions
375 Brush St., Lakeport
• (707) 263-1231

Artist Tommy Gilliam III has an interesting, thoroughly modern medium: Polaroid photography. Gilliam takes Polaroids and physically alters the images, then enlarges them through normal photographic reproduction. His subjects include landscapes, nostalgia, florals and Southwest imagery. Call for an appointment.

D. Gutierrez Gallery
9445 Main St., Upper Lake
• (707) 275-2005

Dick Gutierrez is an award-winning artist known for realistic renderings of pastoral scenes and still lifes. Both framed and unframed prints of his work are available here. The venue is open 10 AM to 4 PM Friday through Monday.

Parks and Recreation

Think you can spend your entire vacation inside your hotel room watching Nickelodeon, ordering bottles of wine by delivery service and venturing out only to gorge yourself at the local restaurants? Read this chapter, and if you still don't feel so much as a muscle twitch, you have truly reached a higher state of vegetation.

First we present the primary parks and recreation areas in the four-county region, followed by separate sections on golf, bicycling, horseback riding, tennis, swimming, hunting and bowling. There is no individual section on hiking, as almost all of the parks offer trails. While campgrounds and primitive camping sites are mentioned in these listings, more specific information may be found in our Camping chapter. Likewise, we will mention many water-related activities in this chapter, but for more comprehensive information, you will want to dive into our On The Water chapter.

LOOK FOR:
- Parks
- Recreation
- Golf
- Bicycling
- Bowling
- Horseback Riding
- Hunting
- Swimming
- Tennis

Parks

Like the statewide system as a whole, the California state parks within the Wine Country offer an almost inconceivable diversity of ecosystems. While visitors to Mackerricher State Park are turning up their collars and waiting for the dense coastal fog to lift on a summer morning, folks are already in the water at Clear Lake State Park. See the grasslands of Austin Creek one day and the redwood canopy of Admiral William Standley the next, and try to convince yourself you're on the same planet. And that doesn't even address the historical parks, which are listed in the Attractions chapter.

Included in this section, along with the state lands, are major regional parks and recreation areas that offer more than a lawn and a playground. You're never far from one of them. (You're probably even closer to a municipal park—consult a local map or ask around.) Deciding where to go might depend on when you'll be there. Only the inland, northern entries, such as Mendocino National Forest, are likely to be affected by winter snow. Of course, all the parks have a chance of being wet and dreary between November and February. Spring and autumn are always safe bets. Summer takes more thought. The coastal parks and state beaches are wonderful retreats from the heat, but some of the valley parks will put you right into the oven.

Unless otherwise stated, parks are open year-round and 24 hours a day. Expect to pay an entrance fee to state parks, usually in the neighborhood of $5 for a carload. Most regional parks have no admission charge. Pets are welcome in campgrounds and picnic areas but usually not on trails or beaches. With millions of jittery city folks visiting California's parks each year, the campgrounds are often filled to the brim, especially between Memorial Day and Labor Day. You can make reservations up to seven months in advance by phoning PARKNET (see the number subsequently listed). All major credit cards and traveler's checks are accepted.

When It's Time to Park It

Here are some helpful numbers to keep in mind when considering a visit to one of the state parks.

California State Park Information • (916) 653-6995
PARKNET Camping Reservations • (800) 444-7275
PARKNET Customer Service/Cancellations • (800) 695-2269
Special Services for the Handicapped • (916) 653-8148
Caltrans Road/Weather Information • (800) 427-7623

Napa County

Bothe-Napa Valley State Park
Calif. Hwy. 29, 4 miles south of Calistoga
• (707) 942-4575

A trail of cars crawls along Calif. Highway 29, but you can leave it behind by exploring this 1,900-acre retreat. Follow shady Ritchey Creek with its redwoods and maples, then venture deeper into terrain covered by oak, hazel, laurel and madrone. From Coyote Peak you can gaze east into a rugged canyon—not a vineyard in sight. And in summer you can enjoy the cool, spring-fed swimming pool in the picnic area. There is a campground (see our Camping chapter) and a horse concession with guided rides. Bothe is just off Calif. 29, between Calistoga and St. Helena. Parallel to the highway runs a 1.02-mile trail that connects Bothe with the Bale Grist Mill Historic Park (see our Attractions chapter).

Robert Louis Stevenson State Park
Calif. Hwy. 29 between Calistoga and Middletown • (707) 942-4575

Between Calistoga and Middletown, at the crest of Calif. 29, is Stevenson State Park. Less than a mile from the trailhead rests a memorial to the noted author, who in 1880 spent his honeymoon squatting here and weathering a long illness. (His experience wound up as the basis for *The Silverado Squatters*; see our History chapter.) A steep 100 yards from the memorial, you will encounter a fire road/trail that winds 5 miles to the top of Mount St. Helena, offering brilliant views throughout. If you spin in a circle at the 4,343-foot summit, you'll probably be able to see the snow-capped Sierra Nevada Mountains to the east, the shining Pacific to the west, Mount Diablo to the south and, on good days, Mt. Shasta, 192 miles to the north. The trail is highly exposed, so bring

plenty of water. The picnic area near the highway is lovely, if a bit noisy.

Sonoma County

Southern Sonoma

Sonoma Valley Regional Park
13630 Calif. Hwy. 12, Glen Ellen
• (707) 527-2041

A 162-acre spread just outside Glen Ellen, Sonoma Valley has a paved, 2-mile bicycle trail and about 5 miles of hiking trails through meadows and oak-dense terrain, plus a picnic area. It's just off Arnold Drive, which intersects Calif. Highway 12 and runs through the heart of Glen Ellen, and is open daily from sunup to sundown. Just across the highway is Bouverie Wildflower Preserve.

Sugarloaf Ridge State Park
Adobe Canyon Rd., 11 miles north of Sonoma on Calif. Hwy. 12
• (707) 833-5712

Standing at the summit of Bald Mountain, you don't have to choose between Sonoma and Napa valleys—you can see them both at the same time. It's a startling view that is aided by identifying signs. And speaking of distant vistas, Sugarloaf recently added an observatory with the most powerful publicly accessible telescope in the state. The park as a whole is rugged and steep, an adventurous contrast to the gentle valleys below. Look for deer, gray fox, even bobcat and mountain lion. The chaparral can get hot in the summer, but you'll be shaded (sometimes by redwoods) if you stay next to Sonoma Creek.

Because day parking is limited, the road entering Sugarloaf Ridge tends to congest with spillover traffic, so try to arrive early on weekends. The 7-mile Bald Mountain loop is the highlight of the park's numerous and well-marked trails. The park is on Adobe Canyon Road, 9 miles east of Santa Rosa or 11 miles north of Sonoma on Calif. 12. (See our Camping chapter for more information.)

Helen Putnam Regional Park
411 Chileno Valley Rd., 1 mile southwest of Petaluma • (707) 527-2041

Just outside downtown Petaluma, 216-acre Helen Putnam Park has hiking, biking and horse trails that lead to exceptional views of town and farmland. There is a playground and a picnic area with a gazebo. The park is open sunrise to sunset. From Petaluma Boulevard, go west on Western Avenue and turn left on Chileno Valley Road.

Fairfield Osborn Preserve
6543 Lichau Rd., east of Cotati • (707) 795-5069

Formerly operated by The Nature Conservancy and now owned and managed by Sonoma State University, Fairfield Osborn is a jewel of a preserve that butts up against the western slope of 2,465-foot Sonoma Mountain, east of Cotati. The 210-acre holding has 6 miles of trails through oak woodlands, meadows and riparian forest. The preserve is not open to the public on a daily basis. However, on Saturdays and Sundays in the fall and spring, naturalists lead hikes at 10 AM and 1 PM. No reservations are required.

The cost is $3 for adults; children 12 and under are free. Please call for directions and exact dates.

Crane Creek Regional Park
6107 Pressley Rd., east of Rohnert Park • (707) 527-2041

No, Rohnert Park isn't made up entirely of Home Depots and Targets. This pleasant, 128-acre park is just east of Sonoma State University, in the foothills of the Sonoma Mountains. It has a picnic area and 3 miles of trails open to people on foot, bicycles and horses. Follow the creek past buckeye, oak and maple. Crane Creek is on Pressley Road; take Roberts Road east from Petaluma Hill Road. The park is open sunrise to sunset.

INSIDERS' TIP
This is not one of those areas where you spot white-chalk handprints on every vertical rock surface, but there are rock-climbing possibilities. Here are some sources for both equipment rental and knowledge: Sonoma Outfitters, 145 Third Street, Santa Rosa, (707) 528-1920; Marin Outdoors, 2770 Santa Rosa Avenue, Santa Rosa, (707) 544-4400; The Outdoor Store, 247 N. Main Street, Fort Bragg, (707) 964-1407.

Annadel State Park
Channel Rd., southeast of Santa Rosa • (707) 539-3911

One minute you're in Santa Rosa, largest city in Wine Country, and the next you're hiking in the solitude of in a 5,000-acre parcel of undulating meadow and oak woodland. Within Annadel, you'll find one large natural marsh and one man-made lake, Ilsanjo, stocked with black bass and bluegill. One of the best hikes is the Warren Richardson-Ledson Marsh Loop, a 7.5-mile outing that takes you to Ledson with its bulrushes, cattails and bird life. Primary trail junctions are marked, but you should think about carrying a park map to help you sort out the details. There are several picnic sites in the park, which is open 9 AM to sunset daily. Get there by taking Montgomery Drive to Channel Road on the east side of Santa Rosa.

Spring Lake Regional Park
Summerfield Rd., Santa Rosa • (707) 539-8092

Most of this 320-acre park is consumed by the central lake, popular with boaters and swimmers in the summer. Around the lake are a 2-mile bike path and a parcourse plus about 15 miles of hiking and equestrian trails. Spring Lake also has a developed campground, scads of picnic tables and a visitors center that's open on weekends. The park is attached to the north end of Annadel State Park. The west entrance is on Newanga Avenue, off Summerfield Road in Santa Rosa; the east entrance is on Violetti Drive, off Montgomery Road.

Northern Sonoma

Lake Sonoma
Stewarts Point-Skaggs Spring Rd., off Dry Creek Rd. • (707) 433-9483

Lake Sonoma's primary recreational offerings are detailed in the On the Water chapter. However, the 18,000-acre park that surrounds the lake is filled with possibilities of its own, including more than 40 miles of trails with periodic views of the lake. The visitors center has Pomo Indian artifacts, and the California Department of Fish & Game operates a nearby fish hatchery. A self-guided nature trail begins at the center. Lake Sonoma also has a large developed campground and 15 primitive campgrounds around the lake (see our Camping chapter). From Geyserville, go west on Canyon Road, turn right on Dry Creek Road and, after about 3 miles, bend left onto Stewarts Point-Skaggs Spring Road.

Sonoma Coast

Doran Regional Park
Westside Regional Park
Off Calif. Hwy. 1
• (707) 875-3540

These two recreation areas are on the south and northwest sides, respectively, of ultra-protected Bodega Bay. The bay's water-based attractions are profiled in our On the Water chapter. But the parks also feature wavy sand dunes and, at Doran, a 2-mile stretch of beach. Each park has a campground, with 47 sites at Westside and 128 at Doran, which is handled in our Camping chapter. Each is reached from Calif. Highway 1. For the southern park, turn west at Doran Park Road; for Westside, turn west at Bay Flat Road.

Sonoma Coast State Beach
Off Calif. Hwy. 1
• (707) 875-3483

Are you sure this isn't Big Sur? The 100-foot bluffs, the ruinous offshore rocks and arches, the coastal scrub plateaus, the black-sand coves—it all adds up to make you wonder if perhaps you should have made that left in Chinatown. The park stretches 16.6 miles along the jagged coastline and offers three trails. The main attraction is Goat Rock, a massive, wave-battered block that is connected to the land. In spring, the bluffs are decorated with lupine, sea pinks and Indian paintbrush. There is whale watching from Bodega Head and a seal colony at the mouth of the Russian River. Numerous marked and unmarked roads provide access to the beaches, some of them ending in parking lots, some not. All are found off Calif. 1 between Bodega Bay and the bluffs 4.8 miles north of Jenner, the town with the visitors center. There are two campgrounds, at Bodega Dunes and Wrights Beach. There also are two environmental camps; ask for a map at the visitors center. A final word: To get in this water, you'd have to be a lunatic, a harbor seal or a surfer—there are breaks off Miwok and North Salmon Creek beaches.

Stillwater Cove Regional Park
Calif. Hwy. 1, between Fort Ross and Salt Point • (707) 847-3245

Even if you're not an abalone diver or a surf fisher, Stillwater Cove is a worthwhile stop. It has a picnic area and 5 miles of hiking trails, amid the redwoods. It also has one developed campground with showers and flush toilets. In the park is a preserved, one-room schoolhouse from the 19th century.

Salt Point State Park
Off Calif. Hwy. 1
• (707) 847-3221

Salt Point and neighboring Kruse Rhododendron State Reserve (see subsequent listing) have a little bit of something for everyone. Salt Point has about 10 miles of battered coastline featuring sea stacks, arches and tafoni—those eerily sculpted knobs, ribs and honeycombs that look like they were crafted for horror movies. The inland portion of the 6,000-acre park has hiking trails through coastal brush, Bishop pine and Douglas fir, not to mention a ridge-top pygmy forest with half-pint cypress, pine and redwood. Salt Point also boasts one of California's first underwater parks, Gerstle Cove Marine Reserve, a favorite for scuba divers (and for fish, which are fully protected there). The park has two campgrounds plus walk-in campsites; see our Camping chapter for more on that. It straddles Calif. 1, about 16 miles north of Jenner or 18 miles south of Gualala.

Kruse Rhododendron State Reserve
Off Calif. Hwy. 1 on Kruse Ranch Rd.
• (707) 847-3221

Set like a hunch on the back of Salt Point State Park, this 317-acre reserve was donated in 1933 by Edward P.E. Kruse, whose family raised sheep, logged and harvested tanbark there. From April through June, the subdued forest of firs and second-growth redwoods is brightened by the pink of rhododendrons. The flowers are the result of a great fire that once occurred here—as the forest regenerates, it gradually pushes out the rhododendrons. Nature moves slowly, though, so you have plenty of time to view the blooms on 5 miles of hiking trails. The Kruse Reserve is off Calif. 1, toward the north end of Salt Point, and is open sunup to sunset daily.

Gualala Point Regional Park
Off Calif. Hwy. 1, 1 mile south of Gualala
• (707) 785-2377

It's not run by the state of California, but

Cyclists take a break among vineyards in the Dry Creek Valley of Sonoma County.

Gualala Point is impressive enough to be a state park. Anglers show up for both saltwater and freshwater fishing. Hikers enjoy 6 miles of trails. Picnickers have several site options, some with barbecue pits. And campers are greeted by a developed area in the redwoods. The visitors center is open 10:30 AM to 3 PM Friday through Monday.

West County/Russian River

Ragle Ranch Regional Park
500 Ragle Rd., 1 mile north of Bodega Hwy. • (707) 527-2041

This 157-acre park offers the usual family-oriented facilities—baseball diamonds, playgrounds, a soccer field, a volleyball court and picnic sites—but also claims hiking and equestrian trails through rugged oak woodlands and marshes. There is a parcourse too. The park is off Ragle Road, 1 mile north of Bodega Highway on the western perimeter of Sebastopol, and is open sunup to sunset.

Armstrong Redwoods State Reserve
Armstrong Woods Rd., near Guerneville • (707) 869-2015

In the 1870s, lumberman Col. James Armstrong saw the errors of his clear-cutting ways and preserved a large chunk of old-growth redwood forest. Today it forms the core of 805-acre Armstrong Redwoods Reserve, with its nature trails and dwarfed picnic area. Don't forget to say hello to the most impressive individuals in the park: the 1,400-year-old Colonel Armstrong Tree and the tallest tree in the area, the 310-foot Parson Jones Tree, (named for the Colonel's son-in-law). Next to the Jones Tree is a gigantic log cut that shows you how mature this now-defunct tree was when, say, Crusaders sacked Constantinople in 1204. To get to Armstrong from Guerneville, turn north off River Road onto Armstrong Woods Road and proceed 2.2 miles. The reserve is open daily from 8 AM to one hour after sunset.

Austin Creek State Recreation Area
Armstrong Woods Rd. • (707) 869-2015

Directly adjacent to Armstrong Redwoods Reserve is 5,683-acre Austin Creek State Recreation Area, a wild and rugged contrast. Austin Creek has miles of trails that hikers have to share with horses. (Mountain bikes are allowed only on paved roads, and on a five-mile dirt road called the East Austin Creek Trail.) Keep an eye open for deer, wild turkeys, raccoons and possibly even world-famous ceramic artists. One of the latter, Marguerite Wildenhain, lived here, and her home and workshop—Pond

Farm—are within the park, though off-limits since Wildenhain's death. There is a drive-in campground and four backcountry campsites within the recreation area. To get to Austin Creek, follow the directions for Armstrong Woods and, after reaching the entrance, continue another 3.6 miles to Bullfrog Pond Campground.

Mendocino County

U.S. Highway 101

Lake Mendocino Recreation Area
Lake Mendocino Dr., off U.S. Hwy. 101
• **(707) 462-7581**

About as pretty as man-made lakes come, Lake Mendocino is surrounded by 1,800 acres of hills, vineyards and pear orchards. There are 18 miles of riding trails and nearly as many of hiking trails. You can also take advantage of five day-use picnic areas and three developed campgrounds. (You can reach another 20 primitive campsites with a boat.) To get there, head east on Lake Mendocino Drive from U.S. Highway 101, just north of Ukiah, or go south on Marina Drive from Calif. Highway 20 near Calpella. (See our On The Water chapter for more details.)

Montgomery Woods State Reserve
Orr Springs Rd., north of Ukiah
• **(707) 937-5804**

Here you can find all your major appliances, from microwaves to washers and dryers. Oh, wait, that's Montgomery Ward. Montgomery Woods is an isolated sanctuary northwest of Ukiah. The 2-mile nature trail not only guides you alongside giant trees, but also takes you right through them, with steps and passageways carved into toppled specimens. You'll visit five redwood groves along Montgomery Creek, including the splendid Grubbs' Memorial Grove. You can pick up a printed guide at the beginning of the trail. Montgomery Woods has one creekside picnic site and no water. It is open sunrise to sunset. From downtown Ukiah, take Orr Springs Road northwest for about 12 miles.

Admiral William Standley State Recreation Area
Branscomb Rd., off U.S. Hwy. 101
• **(707) 445-6547**

Admiral Standley's namesake is small (45 acres), hard to get to, and rarely crowded. It's a beautiful piece of forest, with virgin redwoods coexisting with Douglas firs, madrone, rhododendron and mushrooms. However, there are no trails so don't wander far from the parking area. From U.S. 101 in Laytonville, turn left on Branscomb Road and drive 12 miles. The recreation area is set on either side of the road, and signs can be difficult to spot. It is open sunup to sundown.

Standish-Hickey State Recreation Area
U.S. Hwy. 101, 1 mile north of Leggett
• **(707) 925-6482**

This sizable park presents your basic gigantic redwoods plus access to the South Fork of the Eel River. The Big Tree Loop starts at Redwood Campground and ends near Miles Standish Tree, a 225-foot, 1,200-year-old giant that towers over its second-growth neighbors. Still visible on its side are the ax marks delivered, as the legend goes, by a 1930s evangelist who vowed to chop down the biggest tree he could find. Miles Standish lives on, while the evangelist has gone to that great lumber mill in the sky. In summer it's swimming that lures most visitors. The Eel is punctuated with deep pools formed by rock outcrops. The best is at the tail end of a wide bend, where the Big Tree Loop crosses the river. The pool is nearly 20 feet deep, with a sandy floor. There is no shade, so bring sunscreen and a hat. Standish-Hickey has three campgrounds and a picnic area.

Smith Redwoods State Reserve
U.S. Hwy. 101, 4 miles north of Leggett
• **(707) 925-6482**

Little more than a roadside attraction, Smith has no trails or picnic facilities. It does, however, give you an up-close encounter with some of the largest trees in the world. Don't be shy, big fella, give that tree a hug. You can walk through two stumps. And if you're in need of a dunk, both a 60-foot waterfall (across the highway) and the South Fork of the Eel River are close at hand. It is open sunup to sundown.

Calif. Highway 128

Mailliard Redwoods State Reserve
Fish Rock Rd., off Calif. Hwy. 128
• **(707) 937-5804**

There isn't much here for hikers or bikers, but if you're in the area, your eyes will appreciate the detour. Mailliard has 242 acres of virgin and second-growth redwoods along the headwaters of Garcia River. You can reach the park from Calif. 128, 7.3 miles east of Boonville. Turn south on Fish Rock Road and proceed about 3 miles. There is one picnic area nearly a mile into the park. Mailliard is open sunrise to sunset.

Hendy Woods State Park
Philo-Greenwood Rd., off Calif. Hwy. 128
• **(707) 937-5804**

This is one of the best places within the Wine Country boundaries to surrender to the majesty of the redwoods. There are campsites (see our Camping chapter), a picnic area and trails for hikers, mountain bikers and equestrians. The Gentle Giants All-Access Trail is a surfaced path that accesses Big Hendy, Anderson Valley's last extensive grove of old-growth coastal redwoods. Another short trail leads to the hermit hut, a partially collapsed, thatched-roof lean-to that the Boonville Hermit used as his abode from the end of World War II (when he jumped his Russian ship) until he died in 1981. To get to Hendy Woods, take Calif. 128 2.8 miles west of Philo and turn south on Philo-Greenwood Road.

Navarro River Redwoods
Calif. Hwy. 128 between Navarro and Calif. Hwy. 1
• **(707) 937-5804**

Because this is America, you get to enjoy the beauty of Navarro River without ever leaving your rental car. The park straddles Calif. 128 between Navarro and the coast, and the highway basically shadows the river. It's a shady corridor of second-growth redwoods, alders and tan oak. There are plenty of turnouts if you want a breath of fresh air or a short stroll. In the fall, you'll likely see people fishing for steelhead. Navarro River also has one overnight possibility featured in our Camping chapter—the Paul M. Dimmick Campground, about 6 miles west of Navarro. Bring water!

Mendocino Coast

Schooner Gulch
Off Calif. Hwy. 1, 3.5 miles south of Point Arena
• **(707) 937-5804**

This park contains two beaches, separated by a bulging headland. The north lobe is Bowling Ball Beach, named for the perfectly spherical boulders revealed at low tide. (It might be worth it to consult a tide chart before visiting.) The cliffs abutting this mile-long strand of hard-packed sand are misshapen and interesting. The south lobe is Schooner Gulch, which is rockier and preferred by fishermen. The actual gulch feeds into the sea amidst a jumble of logs. There

is no water in the park, so bring your own. It's open sunrise to sunset.

Manchester State Beach
Kinney Rd., off Calif. Hwy. 1
• **(707) 937-5804**

Manchester's diverse topography encompasses rocky shore, dunes (both grassy and bald), marshes, a lagoon and a coastal plane. It's a place where anglers, bird watchers and rowdy kids can find common ground. The avian wealth includes northern harriers, tundra swans, ducks, herons and pelicans. The drift-log shelters along the 5 miles of beach attest to the relentless winds that buffet the area. There is a primitive campground (noted in our Camping chapter) and hiking trails, including the 5-mile Beach-Inland Loop. To reach Manchester from Calif. 1, turn west onto Kinney Road and drive just more than a half-mile.

Greenwood Creek State Beach
Calif. Hwy. 1, near Elk
• **(707) 937-5804**

This park is quite small on the horizontal scale, but impressive on the vertical—it encompasses both the gravelly beach and the overlooking bluff, some 150 feet above. Most of the picnic sites are up top. From the shore you can see the three rock islands that punctuate the cove and watch for the bobbing heads of harbor seals. Greenwood Creek is west of Calif. 1, adjacent to the town of Elk. The visitors center is Elk's original mill office. Greenwood Creek State Beach is open sunrise to sunset.

Van Damme State Park
Calif. Hwy. 1, 2.5 miles south of Mendocino
• **(707) 937-5804**

Don't worry, you aren't likely to be bothered by overly aggressive action-adventure heroes in this fascinating park. What you will get is a smorgasbord of redwoods, beach, underwater bounty, swamp and pygmy trees. The Fern Canyon Trail is a 4.9-mile meander through a dark, cool fern forest. Separate mini-trails take you to the pygmy forest, with its 4-foot pines and cypresses, and a bog. Hikers and bikers share some trails but on others get the segregation they both seek.

Van Damme has both developed campgrounds and hike-in tent sites, as discussed in our Camping chapter. It has a picnic area on the beach and an undersea preserve. And don't miss the re-created surge channel at the visitors center. The park is 2.5 miles south of

Mendocino on Calif. 1—turn east for the main park, west for the beach.

Mendocino Headlands State Park
Main St., Mendocino
• (707) 937-5804

This is Mendocino's guarantee of seaside access for all—a wraparound park that frames the village on three sides. Spring brings wildflowers, winter ushers migrating gray whales, and summer draws sunbathers and hardy swimmers to Big River Beach, just south of the headlands. The miles of blowholes, arches and craggy stacks are there year round. There is a picnic area along Heeser Drive at the north end of town; in town is the Ford House Visitor Center with its fine historical displays. The Headlands Trail, 6 miles round trip, allows dizzying views of the shoreline. You can get to the park—open sunrise to sunset—from Heeser Drive and Main Street in Mendocino.

Russian Gulch State Park
Off Calif. Hwy. 1, 2 miles north of Mendocino
• (707) 937-5804

Here you have the option of walking along the coast, where waves crash like giant cymbals, or wandering through the serenity of the forest. The Headland Trail offers two sideshow oddities: a blowhole fed by a sea cave, and an inland punchbowl, connected to the sea by another, hidden cave. The Fern Canyon Trail, meanwhile, takes you alongside Russian Gulch to a delicate, 36-foot waterfall. It's a 6-mile round-trip stroll through alder, California laurel, redwoods and, of course, ferns. The park has campsites (see our Camping chapter) and a picnic area.

Caspar Headlands State Beach and Reserve
Point Cabrillo Dr., off Calif. Hwy. 1, Caspar
• (707) 937-5804

These twin holdings are small (less than 5 acres between them) and highly regulated. You can visit the bluff-top reserve, with its far-reaching views, only with a permit, obtainable at the Mendocino District Office, 2 miles north of Mendocino. Get a map there, too, as the reserve interlocks with a private housing development, and it's easy to trespass. The beach, about a quarter-mile long, opens onto a square bay. It's popular with swimmers, divers and anglers. This is no place for the meek. Caspar Headlands has no toilets, no picnic tables and no water. Undeterred? From Calif. 1 in Caspar, turn west on Point Cabrillo Drive. The park is open sunrise to sunset.

Jug Handle State Reserve
Off Calif. Hwy. 1, just north of Caspar
• (707) 937-5804

This is another coastal park that gives you surf-and-turf options. One trail roams the soaring headlands, with views of Jug Handle Bay to the north and a similar inlet to the south. Look for sea stacks and an arch. The Ecological Staircase Trail is a 5-mile, round-trip tour of three marine terraces—a geologic showcase that displays about 250,000 years of elemental activity. The first terrace is meadow-transition habitat, the second is a mixed conifer forest, and the third is redwood-Douglas fir complex. At the end of the line, for no extra charge, is a pygmy forest. The trails are for hikers only, and visitors should bring their own water. Jug Handle is open sunup to sundown.

Jackson State Forest
• (707) 964-5674

Sprawling between Willits and the coast in the vicinity of Calif. Highway 20, this state holding has 50,000 acres of oak, pine and redwoods, not to mention a pygmy forest. There are 25 miles of fire road and two other trails suitable as footpaths. It's a mixed bag—as state forests often are—with some pristine areas and others that have been logged or mined. Jackson has campgrounds in two areas. One is near the hamlet of Dunlap, about halfway between Willits and the coast. The other, highlighted in our Camping chapter, is about 6 miles east of Calif. 1. The Jackson forest headquarters are at 802 North Main Street in Fort Bragg; they have campground brochures.

Mackerricher State Park
West of Calif. Hwy. 1, 3 miles north of Fort Bragg • (707) 937-5804

Mackerricher is a prime slice of Northern

> ## INSIDERS' TIP
> Stocking up on firewood for a camping trip? See if you can track down some Pacific madrone (a tree named by Father Crespi of the Portola expedition in 1769). The madrone makes a delightfully smoke-free fire.

California coast, with 8 miles of beach, large dunes, grassy headlands and even freshwater Lake Cleone. Gray whales migrate offshore between December and March, and humans migrate to the headlands to watch them. If you're into cetacean anatomy, a 30-foot gray whale skeleton lies near the ranger station, just beyond the main entrance. The footpaths are varied. The Laguna Trail circles the lake and its marshy border. The Seal Point Trail leads to a (harbor) Seal Watching Station. And the Haul Road Bicycle Route is a one-time logging road that runs the length of the park, about 7 miles. It's closed to motorized vehicles and so is popular with cyclists and runners. Of course, you can simply walk down the beach for miles if you prefer. Mackerricher has two campgrounds (see our Camping chapter) and several picnic areas. The main entrance is 3 miles north of Fort Bragg, just west of Calif. 1. The Pudding Creek Day Area is only a half-mile north of Fort Bragg.

Westport-Union Landing State Beach
Off Calif. Hwy. 1,
just north of Westport
• (707) 937-5804

North of the town of Westport is a series of four oceanside bluffs, separated by creek canyons and interspersed with beaches. Together they form this skinny park, with its 50-foot cliffs and craggy shoreline. It's a favorite haunt for storm-watchers, who can practically feel the spray from the swollen waves. Anglers come for spawning surf smelt in spring and summer. Pete's Beach and the sand below Abalone Point are fun to explore, but they don't offer much room to operate, so watch out for sleeper waves—large, forceful waves that hit with little warning. Westport-Union Landing has several access points off Calif. 1, between a quarter-mile and 4 miles north of Westport. It offers open, grassy campsites but no water.

Sinkyone Wilderness State Park
County Rd. 431, west of Leggett
• (707) 986-7711

Wonder what the Mendocino Coast looked like before a certain bipedal mammal clogged

up the scenery? Here's your answer. The Sinkyone Wilderness is part of the Lost Coast, a once-busy stretch of shoreline that has been isolated by its lack of contact with major roads. There are two entrances to the park, one at the south end and another at the north. Between them lies a long expanse of unadulterated nature: forested ridges, rugged coast, black-sand beaches and riparian ecosystem. The Needle Rock Visitor Center is in a restored, turn-of-the-century ranch house; nearby is a short trail to Needle Rock Beach. There is a drive-in campground at Usal Creek (the south entrance) and walk-in sites near Bear Harbor in the north. To get to Usal Creek, follow Calif. 1 west from Leggett and, 14 miles later, turn right on County Road 431 and proceed 5.5 miles. To get to Needle Rock, make your way to Redway, 2.5 miles west of Garberville and U.S. 101. Turn south on Briceland Road and continue past Whitethorn; the road turns to gravel after 17 miles. It's another 7.2 miles to the visitors center.

INSIDERS' TIP
Not all the major hiking trails are on government land. One of the best in Napa County is the Oat Hill Mine Trail, a public right of way that ascends through private property in the hills east of Calistoga. The trailhead is near the three-way junction of Calif. 29, the Silverado Trail and Lake Street. Oat Hill Mine, an abandoned mercury source, is about 5 miles up the path. And the trail, thanks to a 1999 enhancement, now is connected to the parking area in Robert Louis Stevenson State Park, via the Palisades Crest Trail.

Lake County

Boggs Mountain Demonstration State Forest
Off Calif. Hwy. 175,
1 mile north of Cobb
• (707) 928-4378

Here's what pine trees do: They sway gently in the breeze and drop needles on your head. There, now you don't need a demonstration. You might want to visit anyway, to get a sample of the forest's 3,493 acres of oak, Douglas fir and ponderosa pine. There are 14 miles of trails for two legs, four legs or two wheels, and one developed campground. The main entrance is at the California Forest Service heliport.

Clear Lake State Park
Soda Bay Rd., near Kelseyville
• (707) 279-4293

It seems that the entire 100 miles of Clear Lake shoreline are devoted to leisure and recreation, and this 565-acre park is no exception. The visitors center, alongside Kelsey Creek Diversion, is a good place to start, with its broad porches and aquarium full of Clear Lake citizens. There is a boat launch and four campgrounds; some of the sites are shaded and/or next to the water (see our Camping chapter). There is a pleasant, gravel-beach swimming area facing Dorn Cove. When you've had enough splashing, take the Indian Nature Trail, featuring 20 interpretive stations, or the Dorn Trail, a 1.5-mile loop that offers some nice views of the water. Clear Lake State Park is on the southwest shore of the lake. Turn north off Calif. 29 in Kelseyville and follow the signs for the park. Three miles thereafter, you'll turn right on Soda Bay Road.

Cow Mountain Recreation Area
Scott Creek Rd., off Calif. Hwy. 29 in Lakeport • (707) 468-4000

This sprawling domain, administered by the federal Bureau of Land Management (BLM), has one leg in Mendocino County and another in Lake County, with the bulk of its 50,000 acres in Lake. It features about 40 miles of hiking, biking and equestrian trails that weave in and out of chaparral, oak scrubland and pine forest. It also has five small, primitive campgrounds. As in most BLM holdings, seasonal hunting is permitted, so don't wear that cap with the foam antlers. There is even a shooting range in the area, near Willow Creek Recreation Site. Nearly half of Cow Mountain's southern portion is accessible to off-highway vehicles. There are two main entryways into the park: From U.S. 101 in Ukiah, take Mill Creek Road east; or from Calif. 29 in Lakeport, take Scott Creek Road west.

Mendocino National Forest
• (707) 983-6118

If we tried to present a detailed account of the options here, the book would be called *Insiders' Guide to Mendocino National Forest*. This is an immense, million-acre tract of terrain in the North Coast Mountain Range that encompasses almost all of the upper half of Lake County and the northeast tip of Mendocino

Photo: Ahuva Simon-Sa'ar

Calistoga's Pioneer Park got new playground equipment in 1999, making it popular with both locals and visitors.

County, not to mention parts of Glenn, Tehama and Trinity counties. The forest boasts two wilderness areas (closed to motorized vehicles), 2,000-acre Lake Pillsbury, several smaller lakes and various tributaries of the Eel River. Trails? Yes, more than 160 miles, including off-highway vehicle paths near Upper Lake and Stoneyford. Campgrounds? Ten developed sites (see our Camping chapter) and numerous primitive camps. There are many routes into the forest. Perhaps the most prominent is Elk Mountain Road, which heads north from the town of Upper Lake. About a mile north of Upper Lake is a ranger station dispensing maps and advice. Another station is on Calif. 162, where the route name changes from Covelo Road to Mendocino Pass Road (about 2 miles north of Covelo in Mendocino County). There is no charge for day use of the forest.

Recreation

Let's say you break out in a rash at the sight of Winnebagos, or that you're wanted by the California Park Service for absconding with a Chumash arrowhead in 1973. Don't fret, there is plenty of recreational activity that goes beyond hiking and camping in the parks. Here we offer basic information on golf, bicycling, horseback riding, tennis, swimming, hunting and, yes, even bowling. That should keep you busy for a while. If you still run out of things to do, maybe you should consider picking up a pamphlet on Attention Deficit Disorder. Or better yet, turn to our On The Water chapter and read about a whole different order of activities.

Golf

The Wine Country isn't a hacker's mecca in the way of a Scottsdale or a Myrtle Beach. On the other hand, the mild climate and the stunning terrain do lend themselves to the links, especially for those who consider walking from fairway to green a form of exercise.

The facilities in our coverage area range from nine-hole pitch-and-putts to manicured, PGA-caliber courses. All of them have some sort of refreshment option—either a snack bar or a full-service restaurant. And practically all of them have pro shops where you can stock anything you forgot to pack. Following are some basic descriptions of the public courses; private clubs (with one major exception that does facilitate play by non-members) are not included.

Napa County

Silverado Country Club & Resort
1600 Atlas Peak Rd., Napa
• (707) 257-0200, (800) 532-0500

Although part of a private club, the two 18-hole championship courses at beautiful Silverado—designed by Robert Trent Jones Jr. and opened in 1965—can be accessed by Wine Country visitors. Guests at the Silverado re-

sort (see our Spas and Resorts chapter) are extended golfing privileges, and reciprocal arrangements with selected clubs around the country are also honored. Some allowances are made for non-guests who make arrangements two days in advance. Call to find out more. The club hosts the annual Transamerica Senior Golf Tournament, and you might find a celebrity or two asking if they can play through—former PGA Player of the Year and current NBC golf analyst Johnny Miller used to be the touring pro at Silverado and still plays the courses often.

Silverado offers a year-round golf package that includes a standard room for two with 18 holes of golf for $260. A less-expensive package is available mid-December through mid-January, when the weather is less predictable. Regular greens fees are $120 including cart, and clubs may be rented for $22.

Napa Golf Club
2295 Streblow Dr., Napa
• (707) 255-4333

With John F. Kennedy Memorial Regional Park and the Napa River to the west and the open spaces of Napa Valley College to the north, this is a nicely placed 18-hole, par 72 course that runs about 6500 yards. The cost is $23.50 during the week, $27.75 on weekends for non-residents; $16.25 on weekdays and $21.50 on weekends for locals. A cart is an additional $23. Ask about the reduced senior rates. Napa Golf Club is easy to walk but quite difficult to shoot. This is a challenging course.

Chardonnay Golf Club
2555 Jamieson Canyon Rd., Napa
• (707) 257-1900, (800) 788-0136

Southeast of Napa, where the cool breezes of San Pablo Bay keep the terrain lush and green, Chardonnay offers a public 18-hole, par 72, 6816-yard course called The Vineyards. The club also has a private course called The Club Shakespeare, a qualifying site for the 1998 U.S. Open. Rates for The Vineyards range from $40 to $80, depending on the season, and that includes a cart. There is a grass driving range, a bar and grill (Sandtrap), and tournament and

A sunbather lies out on a stretch of coast north of Portuguese Beach—part of the Sonoma State Beach area.

banquet facilities. And only in Napa Valley would you have to abide by the rule, "Vineyards are Out of Bounds." Jamieson Canyon Road is another name for Calif. Highway 12 between Calif. 29 and Interstate 80. Proper golf attire is required.

Chimney Rock Golf Course
5320 Silverado Tr., Napa
• (707) 255-3363

You'd be hard-pressed to find a nine-holer more delightful than this. The course takes its name from Chimney Rock, one of the picturesque outcroppings on the west-facing bluffs that loom over the Silverado Trail. The hills and the vineyards of the Stags Leap District are visible from practically anywhere on the 3400-yard links, which opened in 1965. Right next door is Chimney Rock Winery. Greens fees are $15 for nine holes and $20 for 18 during the week, $18 for nine holes and $24 for 18 on weekends. (After 3 PM you pay $14/$17.) Carts are $16 for nine holes, $22 for 18.

Yountville Golf Course
7901 Solano Ave., Yountville
• (707) 944-1992

Napa County's newest golfing attraction is a nine-hole course with true, fast greens and a backdrop of the historic Veterans Home buildings. Total yardage is 2700; par is 34. Yountville Golf Course is full of amenities, including a clubhouse that serves breakfast, lunch and appetizers (including alcohol), and a full pro shop. By the time you read this, the lighted, covered, 36-stall driving range may have been joined by a smaller grass range. Here are your greens fees: $18 for nine holes and $24 for 18 holes during the week; $24 for nine holes and $30 for 18 holes on Saturday and Sunday. Rent and electric cart for nine holes ($16) or 18 ($24).

Mount St. Helena Golf Course
Napa County Fairgrounds,
1435 N. Oak St., Calistoga
• (707) 942-9966

The course itself is modest—nothing special, one might go so far as to say—but Calistoga's scenic situation, within a horseshoe toss of rugged hills, makes this a fine place to spend a few hours. Play all day for $12 during the week, $18 on weekends. After 4 PM the price dips to $7 during the week and $10 on weekends. The nine-hole course is 2748 yards and par 34 for men, 2647 yards and par 35 for "ladies," as they say in the golf world.

Aetna Springs Golf Course
1600 Aetna Springs Rd., Pope Valley
• **(707) 965-2115, (800) 675-2115**

Depending on your definition of a golf course, this might be the oldest west of the Mississippi. Evidence indicates they were aiming for four holes at Aetna Springs as early as 1891. Today, it's a modest nine-hole course (par 35, 2690 yards) far off the beaten track, but it's worth every minute of drive time. Ancient oak trees and rocky streams add not only to the scenery, but also to the challenges of the course. And then there is all that history. Aetna Springs Resort was once a retreat for the mighty, and it later was purchased by the Unification Church. Debate now swirls around whether Napa County will allow the current owners to give the 672-acre property an elegance-restoring facelift. In the meantime, it's only $15 for 18 holes during the week ($9 for students and seniors) and $20 on weekends. Carts are $9 for nine holes, $16 for 18. From Angwin, go north on Howell Mountain Road, then turn left on Pope Valley Road. Proceed about 4 miles to the Aetna Springs sign.

Sonoma County

Sonoma Golf Club
17700 Arnold Dr., Sonoma
• **(707) 996-0300**

The clubhouse is strictly '90s, but Sonoma Golf Club dates back to 1926. It was designed by Sam Whiting and Willie Watson, the same duo that laid out the lake course at the Olympic Club in San Francisco, and it is beautiful. The facility has 83 sand bunkers, three lakes and surrounding views of the Mayacamas Mountains. The course plays 6583 yards from the regular tees. Soft spikes are mandatory, as are collared shirts and slacks. The tab is $70 during the week, $85 on Friday and $100 on weekends. That price includes cart and use of the driving range.

Los Arroyos Golf Course
5000 Stage Gulch Rd., Sonoma
• **(707) 938-8835**

This course is just southwest of Sonoma, adjacent to Calif. 116. It expanded to 18 holes in July 1997, becoming a par 58, but it's still on the easy side, with two par 4s and some long par 3s. Weekend greens fees are $12 for nine holes and $17 for 18. Play during the week for $10 or $15. Pull-carts are $2 and Los Arroyos has a snack bar.

Adobe Creek Golf & Country Club
1901 Frates Rd., Petaluma
• **(707) 765-3000**

Adobe Creek, designed by Robert Trent Jones Jr., is an 18-hole, par 72, 6986-yard course on the northeast edge of Petaluma (just south of Petaluma Adobe State Historic Park). It has a grass driving range, and greens fees range from $27 to $60 depending on time of the week and day. Weekends are $60, including cart. Collared shirts and soft spikes are mandatory.

Rooster Run Golf Club
2301 E. Washington St., Petaluma
• **(707) 778-1211**

Rooster Run opened in the spring of 1998, and by the turn of the century the young track looks to be Wine Country's supreme public-golf bargain. Situated across the street from Petaluma Airport, the course is subject to the same afternoon winds that bedevil its neighbor, Adobe Creek Golf Course. The front nine includes an island green on the par-3 number 6. You'll need an oasis after number 5, rated the course's most difficult. Rooster Run management likes to boast that the course includes "the toughest four finishing holes in Northern California golf." Believe it. Regular rates are $26 Monday through Thursday, $32 Friday and $42 on weekends; the corresponding rates for certified Petaluma residents are $20, $23 and $34. Seniors play for $15 Monday through Wednesday. Juniors pay $10 after 2:30 PM Monday through Thursday.

Mountain Shadows Golf Resort
100 Golf Course Dr., Rohnert Park
• **(707) 584-7766**

Mountain Shadows, just off U.S. 101 in Rohnert Park, has two championship courses and a spacious practice range. The 6675-yard North Course is scenic and friendly; the 6720-yard South Course is more challenging, with plenty of trees to foil your plans. Both are par

INSIDERS' TIP
Robert Louis Stevenson State Park is a potentially dangerous place. Mountain lions and rockslides? They're nothing compared to crossing Calif. 29 from the parking lot. The lot is just north of the road's crest, and vehicles tend to barrel down obliviously. Sorry, we have no secret passageways to divulge, just a piece of advice: Look both ways before crossing.

PARKS AND RECREATION

72. The fee is $20 Monday through Thursday, $24 on Friday. On Saturday or Sunday it's $32 for the south course and $35 for the north. Add $13 per person for a golf cart.

Sonoma Fairgrounds Golf Center
1350 Bennett Valley Rd., Santa Rosa
• (707) 577-0755

This user-friendly facility sits inside the racetrack at the Sonoma County Fairgrounds. It's right off Calif. 12, just east of U.S. 101, and it offers practice greens and a night-lighted driving range in case you feel like swinging after sundown. The nine-hole, par 30 executive course costs $9, another $3 for a replay on weekdays, or $12/$4 on weekends. After 3 PM you can pay $9 Monday through Friday, or $10 on Saturday and Sunday, and hack away to your heart's content.

Bennett Valley Golf Course
3330 Yulupa Ave., Santa Rosa
• (707) 528-3673

The tidy streets of Bennett Valley are a perfect place for a golf course, with the peaks of Annadel State Park forming a backdrop to the east. It's an 18-hole, par 72 course that runs 6600 yards. You'll pay $25 on weekends, $18 during the week if you're an out-of-towner; residents pay $18 and $14. A cart costs an additional $20. Bennett Valley has a snack bar/restaurant.

The Oakmont Golf Club
7025 Oakmont Dr., Santa Rosa
• (707) 539-0415 (West Course), 539-2454 (East Course)

This is one of the Santa Rosa area's premier facilities, with two 18-hole courses: the championship, par 72 West Course and the executive, par 63 East Course. Oakmont is just southeast of town, off Calif. 12 where it starts to bend down toward the Valley of the Moon. Prices range from $22 (after 2 PM on weekdays) to $39 (weekend mornings) for the West Course, and from $18 to $32 for the East Course. Carts are $24 each. You can choose between a snack bar and a sit-down restaurant. PGA director of golf Dean F. James is the resident expert.

Wikiup Golf Course
5001 Carriage Ln., Wikiup
• (707) 546-8787

Wikiup is a cul-de-sac neighborhood just north of Santa Rosa, and the com-munity pretty much revolves around the nine-hole, par 29 executive golf course. Weekday green fees are $10 for nine holes, $13 for 18; on Saturday and Sunday it's $12 for nine and $18 for 18.

Windsor Golf Club
6555 Skylane Blvd., Windsor
• (707) 838-7888

This is a challenging and well-maintained facility—a par 72, 6169-yard championship course—that has hosted the Nike Tour on several occasions. Greens fees are $24 Monday through Thursday, $29 on Friday and $42 on weekends. Twilight (after 2 PM) rates, meanwhile, are $18, $20 and $26 respectively. A full cart will cost you $22 or $16 after 2 PM. Windsor has a new restaurant and a snack bar, and golf lessons are available.

Healdsburg Municipal Golf Course
927 S. Fitch Mtn. Rd., Healdsburg
• (707) 433-4275

At the east edge of central Healdsburg, about a quarter-mile from one stretch of the Russian River and a half-mile from another, this course is a par 35 nine-holer. It costs $10 for nine holes, $16 for 18 holes on weekdays, and $12 and $18, respectively, on weekends. Carts are $5 each per person, per nine holes. It's also known as Tayman Park Golf Course.

Bodega Harbour Golf Links
1400 Calif. Hwy. 1, Bodega Bay
• (707) 875-3538

This seaside course offers wonderful salty breezes and ocean sparkle. Designed by Robert Trent Jones Jr., Bodega Harbour has rolling fairways, cavernous pot bunkers, native coastal rough and marshlands. (Remember, players are prohibited from entering the marsh on holes 16, 17 and 18.) The 18th has been voted the best finishing hole in Northern California. The par is 70, and the yardage measures 5630 from the white tees. Greens fees are $55 Monday through Thursday, $65 on Friday and $85 on Saturday and Sunday (all rates include cart rental). The clubhouse restaurant serves lunch daily, dinner on Friday and Saturday nights and breakfast on weekend mornings. Bodega Harbour Golf Links has golf-and-lodging packages in conjunction with several hotels in Bodega Bay, and with vacation rental agencies that offer private homes bordering the course. Contact Bodega Harbour for more information.

Sebastopol Golf Course
2881 Scott's Right-of-Way, Sebastopol
• (707) 823-9852

This is your one and only option in Sebastopol. It's a nine-hole, par 31 course. Weekdays you'll pay $10 for nine holes, $5 for an additional round; weekends it's $12 for one round and another $5 for two.

Northwood Golf Course
19400 Calif. Hwy. 116, Monte Rio
• (707) 865-1116

Most people don't think of something as sedate as golf when they plan a trip to the Russian River, but this is a course that could change their aspirations. Set in an elbow of the river, it's surrounded by water on three sides (though deprived of water views). Redwoods frame the links, and across the river to the south is haughty Bohemian Grove. Northwood is a par 36, nine-hole course. During the week it is $25 for 18 holes, $15 for nine; on weekends it's $35 for 18 holes, $20 for nine. Twilight rates ($15 on Saturday and Sunday, $13 on weekdays) are in effect after 3 PM.

Mendocino County

Ukiah Municipal Golf Course
599 Park Blvd., Ukiah
• (707) 467-2832

Mendocino County's biggest city has its only 18-hole golf course, par 70 Ukiah Municipal. The 5850-yard course is known to be fairly forgiving. Greens fees vary, but generally work out to $16 on weekdays, $18 on weekends. Add $20 if you want a cart. Ukiah Municipal has a snack bar.

Brooktrails Golf Course
24860 Birch St., Willits
• (707) 459-6761

Here's your chance to bounce a little white ball off the flank of a majestic coast redwood—in fact, that's just what you'll do unless you send it right down the middle. Brooktrails has 18 tees and nine greens. The course is a 5300-yard par 56 for 18 holes. It's $8.50 for nine holes and $10.50 for 18 holes weekdays, $9.50 and $13 on weekends. You can play all day for $15 during the week. Pull-carts are $3 for 18 holes. The Brooktrails snack shop sells hot dogs, sandwiches, beer and other refreshments.

Little River Inn
7751 Calif. Hwy. 1, Little River
• (707) 937-5667

The Inn, a popular vacation retreat (see our Bed and Breakfast Inns chapter), also has a nine-hole, par 35 golf course. Actually, it has an 11-hole course, so if you play 18 holes (par 71, 5458 yards) you can experience two new greens. There is a driving range (off mats, not grass) and a putting green. The rates for nine holes are $15 on weekdays, $20 on weekends and $9.50 in twilight hours—after 5 PM during Daylight Savings Time, after 3 PM during Standard Time. For 18 holes you pay $25 during the week, $30 on weekends. Carts are $16 for nine holes, $24 for 18

Lake County

Hobergs-Forest Lake Golf Course
16451 Golf Rd., Cobb
• (707) 928-5276

In the heart of the Boggs Mountain State Forest is this rarefied nine-hole, 2250-yard course with all par 3 and 4 holes. The layout is relatively level, despite the surrounding peaks. The fees are $12 for nine holes, $17 for 18 during the week, and $14 and $20, respectively, on weekends. Renting a cart for nine holes will cost you $12, while the fee for 18 holes is $20. The restaurant generally is open for dinner Thursday through Sunday.

Adams Springs Golf Course
14347 Snead Ct., Loch Lomond
• (707) 928-9992

Adams Springs is just north of Boggs Mountain State Forest. It's a challenging par 34, nine-hole course set among whispering pines (as if there were any other kind of pine), but the wide fairways are forgiving. You'll pay $10 for nine holes, $16 for 18 during the week, and $14 and $20, respectively, on weekends. Total yardage for Adams Springs is 2640. There is a snack bar, and carts rent for $20 for 18 holes.

Clear Lake Riviera Golf Course
10200 Fairway Dr., Clear Lake Riviera
• (707) 277-7129

Not even whizzing golf balls can foul the view at Clear Lake Riviera. To the west is 4,200-foot Mount Konocti, to the north a broad vista of the lake. It's a hilly, par 36, nine-hole course with two sets of tees and fine views, complemented by a putting green and an above-average dining room. The cost: $19 for nine holes, $25 for 18 during the week, and $24 and $33, respectively, on weekends. Those prices included cart rental.

Buckingham Golf and Country Club
2855 E. Lake Dr., Kelseyville
• (707) 279-4863

On a thumb that pokes into Clear Lake, with four fairways encircling the much smaller body of Little Borax Lake, is Buckingham Golf Course, a nine-hole, par 36 facility with tight fairways and plenty of shade. The weekday fees for the 3159-yard course are $15 for nine holes or $22 for 18; it's $18 or $26 on weekends. Cart rental is $9 per person for nine holes, $14 for 18. There is a snack bar on the course and a restaurant in the clubhouse (look for the Tee Room in our Restaurants chapter).

Hidden Valley Lake Country Club
19210 Hartman Rd., Hidden Valley Lake
• (707) 987-3035

This is Lake County's only 18-hole golf course, a par 72 with a relatively flat and open front nine and a back nine that winds through the hills and nuzzles the hefty homes of the Hidden Valley subdivision. There is a driving range and a putting green. Greens fees are $35 during the week and $45 on weekends including the a cart. Knock off $9 after 2 PM. The scene includes a sit-down restaurant and golf lessons.

Bicycling

If you drive for more than an hour without spotting a cyclist, pull over and consult a map. You may have inadvertently left the bounds of the Wine Country. Mad cyclist disease is rampant here. It overcomes tourists and locals in equal proportion, causing an army of sore-calved pedalers to choke the shoulders of winery lanes, isolated country roads and dirt tracks meant for nothing more aerodynamic than a goat.

Rentals are easy to find, and many of the establishments offer maps and sound advice. Not surprisingly, spring and fall are the ideal times to hop aboard. If you make a summer excursion, start early and take plenty of water. We have included a few popular cycling areas

and routes—this is but a scratch on the surface, meant to get you interested enough to dig deeper. After that we list shops that rent bikes. (Companies that offer special bicycle tours are listed in our Attractions chapter.) Call first to make sure the shop has what you want, i.e. a mountain bike or a road bike (some have tandems too). Expect to pay $8 to $12 per hour or $25 to $35 per day. Most shops throw in a helmet, plastic water bottle and saddle bag, and some will even deliver.

Promise us you won't be stupid enough to leave the driveway or parking area without a helmet.

INSIDERS' TIP
Depending on when you read this, Napa County may have an additional golf course in operation. The Yountville Golf Course, adjacent to the Veterans Home of California (see our Attractions chapter), was set to open June 1, 1999. It will be a par 34, 2750-yard, nine-hole course, and should include a pro shop, a restaurant, and a lighted, covered driving range. Call (707) 944-1992 to investigate.

Las Posadas State Forest

This is one of Napa County's most popular mountain-biking areas, located in the hills near Angwin. Miles of trails—from single-track to fire road—crisscross the dusty, pine-covered landscape. You can stumble upon some nice views of Chiles Valley to the east. From Howell Mountain Road just south of Pacific Union College, turn east on Las Posadas Road and go nearly to the end of the road. (Look for the "Beware of Mountain Lions" sign, an ominous entry point.)

Highland Springs Loop

Here is an intermediate, 34-mile ride for hybrid bikes. It starts near Kelseyville, on the south shore of Clear Lake, and follows the Old Toll Road, long ago replaced by Calif. 175 as a major motor vehicle route. The ride takes you through rustic Donovan Valley and over the mountains to Hopland. You can either return on Calif. 175 or retrace your tracks.

Annadel State Park

Annadel's miles of dirt and gravel roads let you customize your own combination of trails. A good one to start with is a double loop around Lake Ilsanjo and Ledson Marsh. Start from the parking area at the end of Channel Drive and take the Warren Richardson Trail up to the lake.

Skirt the lake counter-clockwise and turn left on the Rough Go Trail. Cross the dam and aim right at the next intersection, riding onto the Canyon Trail. Make a left at the Marsh Trail for a climb to Buick Meadows, then a descent to the marsh. Stay on the trail as it loops around the marsh, then make a right onto the Burma Trail, which will return you to the Warren Richardson Trail. It sounds complicated, but all intersections are well posted. The whole ride is about 12 miles. To get to Annadel from Calif. 12 east of Santa Rosa, turn south on Los Alamos Road, make a right onto Melita Road and merge onto Montgomery Drive. After 0.7 mile, turn left on Channel Road and proceed into the park.

Van Damme State Park

If you're visiting Mendocino, you can ride south about 3 miles on Calif. 1, an exhilarating romp with views of the spectacular coastline. After a nice downhill stretch to the park, turn left and follow signs to the Pygmy Forest. You'll be in Fern Canyon, on an old skid road used by ox teams to haul logs down to the mouth of Little River, site of a former lumber mill. After your only steep climb, on the Logging Road Trail, you'll reach the entrance to the Pygmy Forest. Dismount and do the nature trail on foot.

From here you can continue on to the Little River-Airport Road. Make a right and head back to the coast highway.

Bicycle Rentals

Napa County
Bicycle Trax, 796 Soscol Ave., Napa • (707) 258-TRAX
Napa Valley Bike Tours & Rentals, 4080 Byway E., Napa • (707) 255-3377
St. Helena Cyclery, 1156 Main St., St. Helena • (707) 963-7736
Palisades Mountain Sport, 1330B Gerard St., Calistoga • (707) 942-9687
Getaway Bike Shop, 1117 Lincoln Ave., Calistoga • (707) 942-0332, (800) 499-BIKE

Sonoma County
Sonoma Valley Cyclery, 20093 Broadway, Sonoma • (707) 935-3377
The Goodtime Bicycle Company, 18503 Calif. Hwy. 12, Sonoma • (707) 938-0453
The Bicycle Factory, 110 Kentucky St., Petaluma • (707) 763-7515; 1007 W. College Ave., Santa Rosa • (707) 566-8421; 195 N. Main St., Sebastopol, • (707) 829-1880

Sports Ltd., 587 Rohnert Park Expressway W., Rohnert Park • (707) 585-0505
Rincon Cyclery, 4927 Sonoma Hwy., Ste, H, Santa Rosa • (707) 538-0868, (800) 965-BIKE
Spoke Folk Cyclery, 249 Center St., Healdsburg • (707) 433-7171

Mendocino County
Catch a Canoe & Bicycles Too, Calif. Hwy. 1 and Comptche-Ukiah Rd., Mendocino • (707) 937-0273, (800) 320-BIKE
Fetzer Cycles, 290 Seminary Ave., Ukiah • (707) 462-4419
Fort Bragg Cyclery, 579 S. Franklin St., Fort Bragg • (707) 964-3509

Lake County
The Bicycle Rack, 302 N. Main St., Lakeport • (707) 263-1200

Bowling

Lest we be accused of catering to elitist ideals of recreation, herein is a quick look at bowling, a game even Ralph Kramden could appreciate. Most of the following lanes include cocktail lounges, video games and other stalwarts of the genre. Call to make sure you won't get edged out by league play. And here's hoping your memories of the Wine Country won't include any 7-10 splits.

Napa County
Napa Bowl, 494 Soscol Ave., Napa • (707) 224-8331

Sonoma County
Boulevard Bowl, 1100 Petaluma Blvd. S., Petaluma • (707) 762-4581
Double Decker Lanes, 300 Golf Course Dr., Rohnert Park • (707) 585-0226
Continental Lanes, 765 Sebastopol Rd., Santa Rosa • (707) 523-2695
Windsor Bowl, 8801 Conde Ln., Windsor • (707) 837-9889

Mendocino County
Yokayo Bowl, 1401 N. State St., Ukiah • (707) 462-8686
Noyo Bowl, 900 N. Main St., Ft. Bragg • (707) 964-4051

Lake County
Clearlake Bowl, 14060 Lakeshore Dr., Clearlake • (707) 994-6627

PARKS AND RECREATION

Lakeshore Bowl, 2773 Lakeshore Blvd., Lakeport • (707) 263-5223

Sports Bowl, 872 Lakeport Blvd., Lakeport • (707) 263-4828

Horseback Riding

Many of the trails in the state parks, state forests and recreation areas of the Wine Country are open to horses. You did bring yours, didn't you? If it wouldn't fit in your overnight bag, there are a few outfits that will rent you a steed. You provide the cowboy hat and the harmonica.

Sonoma Cattle Co. & Napa Valley Trail Rides
P.O. Box 877, Glen Ellen 95442
• (707) 996-8566

This is a private concessionaire that for 15 years has been leading groups into three Wine Country State Parks: Bothe-Napa Valley, Jack London and Sugarloaf Ridge (see previous listings in this chapter). The Jack London rides, April through November, skirt vineyards owned by the author's descendants. The Bothe ride also is available for reservation April through November, offering the shade of Ritchey Creek and the peace of the Mayacamas Mountains. The company operates year round in Sugarloaf Ridge, weather and trails permitting, and the views from atop a saddle are fabulous.

You can choose from a variety of forays, from a two-hour Sonoma Valley ride ($45 per person) to a 1 1/2-hour Napa Valley gallop followed by gourmet winery lunch ($75) to a half-day ride in Annadel State Park ($200). The prices rise if you are booking for seven or more people. Reservations are a must. Riders must be at least 8 years old. Open-toed shoes are not permitted, and the weight limit is 230 pounds.

Chanslor Guest Ranch and Stables
2660 Calif. Hwy. 1, Bodega Bay
• (707) 875-3333

You can lead a horse to the water, but you can't make him surf. Chanslor offers $50 beach rides from their inland property—over the dunes to Bodega Bay and back. There are other options,

too: the one-and-a-half-hour Salmon Creek Trail ($40), which winds into a canyon and around much of the company's 730 acres; the one-hour Eagle View ride ($30), with its impressive vistas; and a half-hour, $25 trek through the Wetlands Preservation Habitat, where you are likely to spot a couple of resident bald eagles. They don't do the inland rides in the winter.

Armstrong Woods Pack Station
P.O. Box 287, Guerneville 95446
• (707) 887-2939

If you have a sudden urge to get away from it all but can't muster the energy to disappear into the hills with a backpack, why not let some willing quarter horse do the work? Laura and Jonathan Ayers have been leading treks into Armstrong Woods State Reserve and adjacent Austin Creek State Recreation Area since 1983. Laura is a trained naturalist who can add some education to your ride. They take up to 10 people, and beginners are welcome. The options include a half-day trip to Horse Heaven, not a sugar cube forest but a meadow of volcanic soil ($50); a full-day lunch ride through redwoods and mixed conifer forest ($100); and a full-frills, overnight trip (about $180). Laura reports that the shorter excursions are most popular these days. The stables are 1 mile into the state reserve; follow the "Horses for Hire" signs. No shorts or sandals, and no offensive tackles— maximum weight is 210 pounds. Reservations are required.

Hunting

While some are out hunting for the perfect Zinfandel to complement that evening's lamb shoulders, others are combing the hills, rifle in hand, looking to bag something a little more mobile. The huge tracts of forested land within the Wine Country present numerous options for hunters. Below we offer an introduction to those options, highlighting the most popular areas and targets.

We stick primarily to public lands administered by the U.S. Forest Service, the Bureau of Land Management, the California Department

---

INSIDERS' TIP

A few rules to remember when encountering the California State Park system: (1) Do not disturb flowers, rocks, plants, animals or artifacts—and, yes, putting something in your pocket is considered a disturbance; (2) Do not gather firewood; and (3) Hunting or possession of firearms (loaded or unloaded) is probably prohibited, so check with the individual park beforehand.

Photo: Tina Luster-Hoban

This gazebo at the park at Lakeport, on Clear Lake, offers shade and a break from the beach.

of Fish & Game (DFG), and similar organizations. If you want to hunt on private land, be sure to obtain written permission from the landowner. And whether you're on public or private property, please don't leave any litter behind. It's the kind of behavior that gives hunters bad names.

California's hunting license year runs from July 1 through June 30. You can pick up resident licenses and regulation booklets at most sporting goods stores or at the Region 3 DFG Headquarters at 7329 Silverado Trail, near Yountville in Napa County. Each license costs $26.75 if purchased directly from the DFG, $28 from an agent. If you're visiting the area and just happen to have brought your rifle along, you can request a two-day, nonresident hunting license ($26.25) from the DFG. Call (916) 227-2271 for details.

When's Wabbit Season?

Here are the parameters of the hunting seasons for the most common game animals in the Wine Country:

Deer: opens the second Saturday in August, closes 44 days later.

Bear (northeast of Calif. 128 only): opens the second Saturday in August, closes the last Sunday in December.

Wild pig: open all year.

Cottontail rabbit, snowshoe hare: opens July 1, closes the last Sunday in January.

Jack rabbit, black-tailed and white-tailed rabbit: open all year.

Raccoon: opens November 16, closes March 31.

Badger and gray fox: opens November 16, closes the last day in February.

Wine Country Hunting Areas

Napa-Sonoma Marshes Wildlife Area
Department of Fish and Game
• (707) 944-5500

On the west bank of the lower Napa River, where it widens out before dumping into Carquinez Strait, are 2,000 acres of public lands divided into six units. The hunting areas are accessible by boat via Mud Slough, Hudeman Slough and Tolay Creek. Besides the abundance of waterfowl, you might scare up a pheasant or dove.

Cedar Roughs
Bureau of Land Management
• (707) 468-4000

This little-known, 7,000-acre pocket west of Lake Berryessa is run by the BLM. The only public access to Cedar Roughs is a 1-mile foot trail that begins on Pope Canyon Road, 3 miles north of the Pope Creek Bridge, which is at the lake. The trail rises steeply to a broad plateau of glades and forests that harbor deer, bobcat, bear, coyote, gray squirrel, rabbit, quail, dove and pigeon.

Petaluma Marsh Wildlife Area
Department of Fish and Game
• (707) 944-5500

This 1,900-acre tidal salt marsh is along the Petaluma River, north of its confluence with San Antonio Creek. The only access is by boat. (There are several public ramps along the river.) The marsh is a mecca for ducks, geese and other waterfowl.

Lake Sonoma Wildlife Area
Department of Fish and Game
• (707) 944-5500

The area around Lake Sonoma is leased by the California Department of Fish and Game from the U.S. Army Corps of Engineers. It is managed with the idea of providing special hunts for deer, wild pig and turkey, especially for junior hunters. The hunts are by permit only. Call the DFG for specific information and dates.

Jackson State Forest
State Forest Headquarters
• (707) 964-5674

Sizable Jackson State Forest, east of Fort Bragg in Mendocino County, is home to game animals such as deer, black bear, gray squirrel, rabbit, mountain and valley quail and band-tailed pigeon. Check for possible road closures and firearms bans within the forest.

Knoxville
Bureau of Land Management
• (707) 468-4000

Along the Napa-Lake county line, southeast of the town of Lower Lake, are 17,700 acres of public land in the Knoxville area. The rugged, isolated landscape tends to be hot in the summer and wet in the winter, but when did that ever discourage hunters? From Knoxville Berryessa Road south of the Homestake Mining Company, you'll see a signed access point. Follow the road and gun for deer, bobcat, gray squirrel, rabbit, quail, dove or pigeon.

Boggs Mountain
State Forest Headquarters
• (707) 928-4378

The State of California bought 3,460 acres on Boggs Mountain from the Calso Company in 1949 and turned them over to the state's

Forest Service. If you hunt here, use extreme caution, as the area is popular with hikers and bikers in addition to deer, mountain quail and gray squirrel.

Cache Creek
Bureau of Land Management
• (707) 468-4000

The Cache Creek drainage flows from Clear Lake south to Capay Valley in western Yolo County. Public access to the 45,000 acres of public land—divided among several state and federal entities—is via the Cache Creek Wildlife Area parking lot, 8 miles east of Clearlake Oaks on Calif. 20. With no public roads, the area is limited to walkers and horses, and certain areas are closed in the spring to let the elks calve. Resident game includes deer, rabbit, dove, quail and wild turkey.

Cow Mountain
Bureau of Land Management
• (707) 468-4000

The Cow Mountain Recreation Area (see the Parks section of this chapter) consists of about 54,000 acres of mountainous terrain. You're likely to find deer, rabbit, gray squirrel, bobcat, coyote, dove and quail. Public access is from Ukiah on Mill Creek Road, from Lakeport on Scotts Creek Road or from Kelseyville on Highland Springs Road/Old Toll Road.

Mendocino National Forest
National Forest Headquarters
• (916) 934-3316

As profiled earlier in the chapter, this sprawling territory covers about 1,700 square miles of the Coast Range mountains. With the exception of a state game refuge that lies outside the Wine Country, practically all public land in the forest is open to hunting. In addition to the forest headquarters in Willows, you can obtain district maps from the Forest Service office in Upper Lake (707-275-2361) or Covelo (707-983-6118). Common game includes deer, valley and mountain quail, band-tailed pigeon, turkey, rabbit, gray squirrel, black bear, blue grouse, dove, bobcat and coyote.

Swimming

If you are not fortunate enough to be staying (or living) next to the Pacific Ocean or one of the Wine Country's many lakes during those summer hot spells, you might feel the need to jump into a different body of water—specifically, the rectangular, chlorinated variety. Here is a partial list of public swimming facilities. All of them are open from Memorial Day weekend through Labor Day weekend; some are accessible for longer periods of time. Call for more information, including the lowdown on lessons, admission fees and no-kids or kids-only periods.

Public Swimming Pools

Napa County
St. Helena Community Pool, 1401 Grayson Ave., St. Helena • (707) 963-7946

Sonoma County
Petaluma Swim Center, 900 E. Washington St., Petaluma • (707) 778-4410

Alicia Pool, 300 Arlen Dr., Rohnert Park • (707) 795-7265

Benicia Pool, 7469 Bernice Ave., Rohnert Park • (707) 795-7582

Ladybug Pool, 8517 Liman Way, Rohnert Park • (707) 664-1070

Honeybee Pool, 1170 Golf Course Dr., Rohnert Park • (707) 586-1413

Finley Aquatic Complex, 2060 W. College Ave., Santa Rosa • (707) 543-3760

Ridgeway Swim Center, 455 Ridgeway Ave., Santa Rosa • (707) 543-3421

Healdsburg Municipal Swimming Pool, 360 Monte Vista Ave., Healdsburg • (707) 433-1109

Cloverdale Memorial Pool, 105 W. First St., Cloverdale • (707) 894-3236

Ives Pool, 7400 Willow St., Sebastopol • (707) 823-8693

Mendocino County
Ukiah Municipal Swimming Pool, 511 Park Blvd., Ukiah • (707) 467-2831

Willits Municipal Swimming Pool, 429 N. Main St., Willits • (707) 459-5778

Lake County
Middletown County Park Community Pool, 20962 Big Canyon Rd., Middletown • (707) 263-2295

Westshore County Park Swimming Pool, 250 Lange St., Lakeport • (707) 263-3077

In addition, many high schools open their pools to the public during summer vacation. To find out if such options exist in your area, call the municipal recreation numbers listed below in the Tennis section.

Lastly, some spas permit walk-in (dive-in?) swimmers who pay for day use of their mineral pools. Search our Resorts chapter for relevant information.

Tennis

If you think tennis is just the sort of vigorous-yet-natty sport that would flourish in the Wine Country, you're right on target. Because of the geographic enormity of the area, however, a complete list of available courts would be harder to handle than an Anna Kournikova first serve. Instead we provide a list of city recreation departments throughout the four-county region. The folks on the other end of the line will tell you where the courts are—many of them are after-hours high school facilities—whether you need reservations, what it costs to play there and whether the courts are lighted.

Rec Departments

Napa County
City of American Canyon Recreation, • (707) 647-4360
City of Napa Parks and Recreation, • (707) 257-9529
Town of Yountville Recreation, • (707) 944-8712
City of St. Helena Recreation Department, • (707) 963-5706
City of Calistoga Parks and Recreation, • (707) 942-2838

Sonoma County
Sonoma City Hall, (707) 938-3681
City of Petaluma Parks & Recreation, •(707) 778-4380
City of Cotati • (707) 792-4600
City of Rohnert Park Recreation Department, • (707) 588-3456
City of Santa Rosa Recreation & Parks Offices • (707) 543-3282
Town of Windsor Parks and Recreation, • (707) 838-1260
City of Healdsburg • (707) 431-3300
City of Cloverdale • (707) 894-2521
City of Sebastopol Recreation Information, • (707) 823-1511

Mendocino County
City of Ukiah Recreation • (707) 463-6237
City of Willits • (707) 459-4601
City of Point Arena • (707) 882-2122
Fort Bragg Recreation Center • (707) 964-2231

Lake County
City of Clearlake • 707) 994-8201
City of Lakeport Parks and Recreation, • (707) 263-5615

PARKS AND RECREATION

On the Water

LOOK FOR:
- **The Ocean**
- **The Rivers**
- **The Lakes**
- **Provisioners:**
  Charters,
  Watercraft,
  Lessons

If your idea of happiness is being near water—if you love to swim in it, surf on it, fish in it, canoe or kayak in it, windsurf on it, cut through its waves in a sailboat or lie on the beaches and look at it—we've got good news for you. It's all available in Wine Country.

We've got an ocean like none other; on our coasts, the Pacific is untamed, unpredictable, unusually beautiful. You'll find this northern coast bears little resemblance to its southern relative, that mild stretch of beach lined with sunbathers from Santa Barbara to San Diego. North of San Francisco the fog-swept sand dunes are spotted with wild grasses, and the weather can be chilly and blustery. The ocean thrashes wildly, flinging itself in frothy rage against the rocks. Then, just as you begin to think of this rugged shoreline as cold and brooding, the fury abates, the sun burns through the fog and the ocean turns a vivid shade of deep blue.

Compared to the ocean, our rivers are tame. They ramble along through countryside that is forested or laced with meadows, almost never working up to whitewater status. You won't have to cling to the edges of your kayak with white knuckles. These are laid-back rivers—places to relax, watch white clouds scud through the sky and pop open another soft drink.

The dry summer climate that is so good for growing grapes hasn't exactly made this a water wonderland for lakes. In fact, we've had to build dams to create our own lakes, flooding farmlands and, in one case, an entire city, houses and all. Only in Lake County will you find natural lakes in Wine Country. There are a handful there, including Clear Lake and the Blue Lakes. All are teeming with fish and great for swimming and watersports.

So here's a rundown on things you can do to take advantage of our waters. Just one caution—if you plan to fish, please remember that the most important piece of equipment you'll need is your fishing license. You can get one through the Department of Fish and Game, 7329 Silverado Trail, Napa, (707) 944-5500, or through most sporting goods stores.

The Ocean

To be specific, the Pacific.

Sonoma Coast

Along the wild and rugged shores of Sonoma Coast, the sea seems to be constantly battling the land, chiseling the earth into small coves, creating pocket-size beaches, building up sea stacks—those rocky islands that rise like tall sentinels offshore. This is one of the most beautiful and accessible stretches of shoreline in California, but it's important for visitors to keep in mind that the ocean here is treacherous. It's vital to be alert for rogue waves (appropriately named "sleeper waves") that can sweep people off coastal rocks into the sea. Every year there are deaths caused by unpredictable waves and strong undertows. Caution is the watchword.

The southernmost town on the Sonoma Coast is the New England-style village of Bodega Bay, home to approximately 300 commercial fishing boats. Bodega Bay Harbor offers some protection from the rough Pacific surf and is the base for a variety of sporting activities. The gentle beaches on the west side of the harbor afford a perfect spot for windsurfing or kayaking. There's hardly a day when you don't see the fluorescent sails of a windsurfer skimming across the waters here. Wide-open spaces protected from boat traffic offer the perfect place to practice your skills and meet the challenges of shifting winds and tides.

Surfers and boogie-boarders looking for the perfect wave will find that as far as the northern shores go, surfing here is as good as it gets. Some spots offer long, low waves crashing onto sandy beaches; others present the challenge of surfing into rocky coves. Two of the best spots along the coast are Salmon Creek, just north of Bodega Bay, and Goat Rock State Beach, farther up the coast near Jenner. But it's always a good idea to contact a local surf shop for knowledge—it's a long coastline, and you can spend a lot of time looking.

Sportfishing is big at Bodega Bay as well. Boats go out every day, and come back to Tides Wharf with rock cod, lingcod, halibut, salmon, albacore tuna and crab. Many, though, choose to cast a line from the surf, and lots of families find fun dropping a line right off the wharf behind the recently refurbished Inn at the Tides Restaurant.

North from Bodega Bay, 10 miles of secluded, sandy beaches lie hidden from the road by steep bluffs. Most of these Sonoma Coast state beaches have parking areas and paths leading to the surf. Once you've reached the sheltered beach coves, you'll enjoy walking barefoot (most people wear full clothing) along the headlands, water-carved arches and sea stacks. These beaches are ideal for fishing, beachcombing, picnicking, beach parties and wading, but the chilly waters are unsafe for swimming due to a strong undertow, rip currents and sleeper waves.

There are no lifeguards on the state beaches, but some of them have restrooms. Beach headquarters are just north of Bodega Bay at Salmon Creek, where you can get maps and information. Park rangers also offer whale-watching walks.

There are other, gentler activities along the coast—shell-searching for one. Discover a wide variety of shells on the beach. Admire them, play with them, photograph them, but don't take them home. Another pastime that's lots of fun and perfect for these beaches is kite flying. You can buy some wild ones at a couple of Bodega Bay shops—Candy & Kites and Bodega Bay Gifts 'N' Goodies. And bird watching, of course, is a never-ending fascination, with or without binoculars.

See our Parks and Recreation chapter for more information on the Sonoma Coast State Beach and other coastal-area recreation sites including Doran and Westside regional parks, Stillwater Cove Regional Park, Salt Point State Park, Kruse Rhododendron State Reserve and Gualala Point Regional Park.

Mendocino Coast

For sheer drama, nothing compares with the splendor of the view from the town of Mendocino, perched atop a high bluff, surrounded on three sides by the wild Pacific Ocean. Here the shoreline is punctuated by rugged offshore rocks, tiny coves and abundant sea tunnels. Add to that an ever-changing climate of swirling foggy mists, crystalline blue skies and raging winter storms that coax both natural flora and cultivated gardens into a wondrous profusion of colors. This is one of the most soul-stirring landscapes on earth. It's not uncommon to see people hunkered along a grassy bluff, contemplating nature for hours.

Perhaps the most popular attraction along this scenic seashore is at Russian Gulch State Park, where a unique "Punch Bowl" was formed when a large sea cave collapsed. Waves enter through a tunnel in one side and crash around the interior of the Punch Bowl, sending up a distinctive array of throaty echoes. Russian Gulch State Park is just 2 miles north of Mendocino (see our Parks and Recreation chapter).

Fishing is a popular sport along the Mendocino Coast. Greenwood Creek State Beach, a new day-use state beach near the town of Elk (at the intersection of Calif. Highway. 1 and Calif. Highway. 128), is popular with picnickers and ocean anglers who want easy access to the beaches. Surf fishers will find plenty of good spots to cast a line in hopes of snagging rock cod and other bottom fish. Additional angling spots along the Mendocino Coast include Manchester State Beach, on Kinney Road off Calif. 1, where there's a bonus of two creeks that have salmon and steelhead in abundance during winter. Surf fishing is good at Schooner Gulch State Park,

Photo: Tina Luster-Hoban

Children enjoy the swimming area on the shoreline of Clear Lake.

which has a different sort of bonus—a stunning perch for watching sunsets (see our Parks and Recreation chapter for more on Manchester State Beach and Schooner Gulch).

Abalone diving is a popular sport around these parts for the adventuresome, experienced diver. The abalone is a giant marine snail (as long as 6 to 8 inches) with a powerful foot that can lock a strong grip on rock surfaces. One of these mollusks can yield more than a pound of pure white meat. Because its meat is popular not only among humans, but also with other mollusks and fish, abalone is becoming an endangered species. Rules for abalone diving (including size limits) are strict. Abalone can be harvested from April to December, excluding July, but check with the state Department of Parks and Recreation at any state beach for regulations. And above all, consult with park rangers and local citizens about the dangers of abalone diving. Every year brings its share of drownings, even among veteran divers, along this shoreline.

For more information on other popular recreational spots on or near the Mendocino Coast— including Van Damme State Park, Mendocino Headlands State Park, Jug Handle State Reserve, Jackson State Forest, Mackerricher State Park, Westport-Union Landing State Beach and Sinkyone Wilderness State Park—see our Parks and Recreation chapter.

The Rivers

Napa County

Napa River

Though most of the Napa River's length snakes from Mount St. Helena to the town of Napa, the big-time angling is mostly confined to extreme points south, especially as the river broadens between the Butler Bridge (the airborne stretch of Calif. Highway 12/29) and Carquinez Strait. Summer fishing isn't great in these tidal waters, but autumn brings hungry striped bass and sturgeon. Try live bait such as mudsuckers or bullheads for the stripers, live bass shrimp or mud shrimp for the sturgeon.

The many sloughs that feed into Napa River in this marshy area are also good bets for striped bass. If you're looking for a full-service resort, try the Napa Valley Marina, (707) 252-8011, or Napa Sea Ranch, (707) 252-2799, both on or near Cuttings Wharf Road.

Sonoma County

Russian River

There's nothing glamorous about the Russian River—it's one of those summer places where everyone knows that going barefoot and keeping wet is the only way to spend the summer.

The Russian River actually runs south through a large section of Mendocino County to the north. At its upper reaches in Sonoma County, the river rolls past small wineries, many campgrounds and some of the best waters for canoeing in the area. There are 70 miles of canoeing waters between Cloverdale and Jenner at the Sea. Anyone who wants to cruise the entire length can count on a trip of three or four days. Most visitors opt for a one-day canoe trip of about 10 miles, which allows some time for swimming and picnicking. Besides canoes, river-trippers use kayaks, rubber rafts and inner tubes. The best canoeing is between March and October. It's a beautiful run through quiet waters among redwoods, past summer resorts, old homes and the occasional nude beach. (See our Provisioners listings in this chapter for information on area river outfitters.)

For more on Russian River area wineries, see our Wineries chapter. To find out about camping options, see our Camping chapter.

Mendocino County

Gualala River

Although the portion of the Gualala River most people see is the wide swath of sand that spreads out where the river joins the Pacific (and where kayakers set out to sea), the Gualala does wind far into the interior of the county, through forests of redwoods and groves of ferns. In a good wet year, when winter rains have drenched the land and the river is full, it is possible to kayak almost 10 miles inland. That would be a rare year, but even paddling only a mile or so upriver is rewarding, giving a different view of the natural splendors of Northern California. With some luck, you'll witness soaring ospreys, great blue herons and brown pelicans, catch a glimpse of the playful river otters and watch the variety of birds that call the forest home.

Motorboats are not permitted on the river, but anglers in rowboats sometimes make their way upstream to cast a line in search of trout. During winter rainy season, the river swells and roars out to sea, washing beach sands of summer and obliterating them.

Navarro River

Motoring along the rolling hills of Calif. 128 and into Anderson Valley, drivers suddenly encounter "a redwood tunnel to the sea" and their first look at the Navarro River.

For first-time visitors and longtime residents alike, the redwoods along the Navarro River are a magnificent sight to behold. Second-growth redwood groves stretch along the river bank, making a home for riverbed-dwelling birds such as the belted kingfisher, along with families of raccoons and black-tailed deer. This is a great river for kayaking, and some of the kayak companies operating out of Sonoma County bring groups here (see Provisioners, listed subsequently, for more information).

The Lakes
Napa County

Lake Hennessey

About 5 miles east of St. Helena is an 850-acre reservoir owned by the city of Napa and surrounded by rolling hills covered with grass and dappled with oak trees. Lake Hennessey was formed by the construction of Conn Dam. The Department of Fish and Game stocks Lake Hennessey with trout in the fall, winter and spring, and you'll find a few bass, bluegill and catfish as well. Motorized boats are allowed on the water if they don't exceed 14 feet and 10 horsepower; sailboats are permitted if they are 16 feet or shorter. Swimming and kayaking are prohibited. There is a $4 access fee for visiting the lake, and an additional $1 special fishing permit is also required. There is no particular place to pay for the fishing permit, so just be ready to fork over the buck if you see the Lake Hennessey caretaker.

Lake Berryessa

It was 40 years ago that Putah Creek was dammed, creating Lake Berryessa between two legs of California's Coast Ranges (and drowning the town of Monticello). The ragged perimeter formed by the obstruction gives Berryessa 165 miles of shoreline, more than surrounds massive Lake Tahoe. The north end of the lake is shallow, with gentle, grassy hills sloping down to the water. Contrast that with the south end and its steep, rocky terrain dotted with manzanita and oak. The eastern shore of the lake, meanwhile, is off-limits to the public.

The Bureau of Reclamation maintains three day-use facilities and a launch ramp at Capell Cove, plus picnic sites at Smittle Creek and Oak Shores. The trout and salmon fishing are great here in the spring. Cast between the dam and The Narrows, or troll in Markley Cove or Skiers Cove. Look for largemouth bass in the coves, smallmouth and spotted bass on the big island in the middle of the lake or at steep, jagged points in up to 40 feet of water. Bluegill usually hang out in the backs of shallow coves all around the lake, and catfish are plentiful at Capell Cove, Pope Creek and Putah Creek.

There are several marinas along Knoxville Road and Calif. 128. Keep in mind that this lake is heavily trafficked, especially in the summer. Berryessa welcomes more than 1.5 million visitors each year.

Sonoma County

Lake Sonoma

Designed to control Russian River flooding, the Warm Springs Dam has created some 3,600 surface acres of scenic recreational waters. Located 11 miles north of Healdsburg on Dry Creek Road, this is primarily a boating lake, although water-skiers and Jet Skiers are allowed in designated areas. Skiing is not always considered desirable because of the many full-growth trees that are partially submerged. Kayakers, however, have no trouble paddling their way through the treetops.

Fishing is the main recreational sport. Generally speaking, boat fishing is more successful than shore fishing, and the upper reaches of the river usually produce the best angling luck. Among the fish population are smallmouth bass, red ear sunfish, green sunfish and rainbow trout. A public boat ramp is available, as well as the full-service Lake Sonoma Marina. The fish hatchery is always great fun (see our Attractions chapter), and there's an interesting visitors center. Swimming is a possibility, but much of the shoreline is rocky.

Mendocino County

Lake Mendocino

Ten miles north of Ukiah off Calif. 20, Lake Mendocino offers a variety of activities, including waterskiing, pleasure boating, sailing, windsurfing and swimming. It's an aesthetically pleasing body of water and is popular in the Ukiah Valley, where temperatures tend to climb into the stratosphere in summer (see Provisioners, below, for some rental outlet options).

Everything you could want for fun in the water can be rented here—Sea-Doos, Jet Skis, fishing boats and pontoon boats. All you need to provide is a swimsuit. The visitor center offers a variety of information about the lake, Pomo Indian culture and the Coyote Valley. The Interpretive Cultural Center has exhibits of Pomo Indian crafts, pottery, jewelry and decorative arts. This area is a great place for a summer picnic.

Lake County

Clear Lake

They don't call this Lake County for nothing. It has several significant wet spots, but really it has Clear Lake. Three things about Clear Lake are, uh, clear: It is big, it is shallow, and it is old. With 43,785 acres of surface area, this is the largest natural freshwater lake within California. And yet the volume of water contained herein is not staggering. That's because the average depth of the lake is less than 30 feet.

Scientists are convinced that lakes of some sort have existed at this site for some 2.5 million years, possibly making Clear Lake the oldest lake in North America. They figure the upper arm, between Lakeport and Lucerne, has been under water continuously for 450,000 years.

In terms of its importance to the identity of the county, Clear Lake is the undeniable hub. Almost all the towns in Lake County are clustered around the shoreline, and access for all is faithfully preserved. There are 11 public ramps around the lake, providing an array of launch points. Remember that permission is required for use of beaches and ramps not posted "public." (While you're at it, remember to reduce your boat speed to 5 mph within 500 feet of shore.)

Clear Lake is known as the Bass Capital of the West. Two-thirds of the fish caught here are largemouth bass. Spring is the time to get them, especially from docks or in pockets formed in the beds of tule reeds. Two specific hot spots are the north end of the lake from Lakeport to Rocky Point, and the shoreline from Clear Lake State Park to Corinthian Bay. Bass might be the most plentiful, but they aren't the biggest fish to fry here. The Clear Lake record for a large-mouth bass is 17.5 pounds; the record for a catfish is nearly twice that. Channel catfish are nearly everywhere on the lake, but seem to be particularly active at Rattlesnake Island, Rodman Slough and Horseshoe Bend. The bluegill and crappie fishing is considered fair at Clear Lake.

Indian Valley Reservoir

Northeast of Clear Lake, in isolated terrain near the Colusa County line, is this 3,800-acre reservoir created by construction of the Indian Valley Dam. The lake is open to all boating, though a 10 mph speed limit is imposed. Two public launch ramps are available. If you're not swimming in the reservoir or hunting around it, you can fish for rainbow trout, largemouth and smallmouth bass, catfish or red ear perch.

Blue Lakes

Upper Blue Lake and Lower Blue Lake are two small, slender fingers alongside Calif. 20, just northwest of Clear Lake. Their scale is almost insignificant from a countywide perspective, but they are consistently popular because of their natural beauty, with pine trees creeping practically to the water's edge. The lakes attract canoers (because motor boats are relegated to 5 mph) and windsurfers (because of the steady breezes that flow from the canyons). It's a fairly hot spot for anglers, too, with varying supplies of trout, catfish, bluegill and largemouth bass.

Lake Pillsbury

Two-thousand-acre Lake Pillsbury is tucked away in the mountains of Mendocino National Forest—you must negotiate 15 miles of dirt road to get there—but it, too, is man-made. It's scenic nonetheless, as evidenced by the number of campsites constructed along its edge (see our Camping chapter for a sampling). It's warm, too—more than 70 degrees in the summer despite resting at 1,800 feet. The lake is open to all boating, with most of the rod-and-reel action devoted to black bass, rainbow and brown trout and bluegill. Lake Pillsbury's environs are laced with U.S. Forest Service hiking and biking trails.

Provisioners: Charters, Watercraft, Lessons

A sampling of Wine Country companies in the business of getting you in the water follows. You'll find information on renting everything from a Jet Ski to a kayak, and lots of these folks will teach you how to use them as well.

If you're planning an inland fishing trip, there are many top-notch places to pick up bait and tackle (also see King's Sport and Tackle listing, below). In Napa County, these include A&M Market, 2877 Solano Avenue, Napa, (707) 255-0400; and Sweeney's Sports, 1537 Imola Avenue, Napa, (707) 255-5544.

In Lake County, stop in at Don's Bait & Tackle, 14531 Lakeshore Drive, Clearlake, (707) 995-9668; Ed's Market, 3657 E. Calif. 20, Nice, (707) 274-8029; Garner's Resort, 6035 Old Highway 53, Clearlake, (707) 994-6267; Kits Corner Store & Gas, 7990 Calif. 29, Kelseyville, (707) 279-8954; or Lakeport Tackle, 1050 N. Main Street, Lakeport, (707) 263-8862.

Napa County

A Wet Pleasure Jet Ski & Watercraft Rentals
5800 Knoxville Rd., Lake Berryessa
• (707) 966-4204

A Wet Pleasure has a full lineup of aluminum fishing boats (14- or 16-footers), ski boats, pedal boats, 24-foot patio boats and Yamaha Jet Skis. Boat rentals cost $60 for eight hours.

Sonoma County

W.C. "Bob" Trowbridge Canoe Trips
13840 Old Redwood Hwy., Healdsburg
• (707) 433-7247, (800) 640-1386 (information and reservation line)

The company, named for the man who started it in 1953 (and whose granddaughter still helps run the shop), offers a wide range of outings on the Russian River from April to October on canoes accommodating two or three people. You can choose from a variety of trips: afternoon, half-day paddles for 2-3 hours; full days from 4-6 hours, or even a 5-day canoe excursion.

Bodega Bay Sport Fishing Association
1500 Bay Flat Rd., Bodega Bay
• (707) 875-3344

These folks operate three charter boats out of Bodega Bay for either full-day or half-day fishing trips for bay or ocean fishing. You'll be going after rock cod, lingcod, salmon (April through December), halibut and dungeness crab. Fishing tackle is available. Whale-watching trips run from November to February. The Association also specializes in evening cruises.

The cost of excursions ranges from $50 to $60 if you're going for the fish listed above, and you can fish for them in combinations. Going out 60 to 80 miles for salmon or halibut would require a negotiated cost. At the high end of the scale there's albacore tuna, and those trips will run you from $125 to $150.

The Association also operates from another location, a boathouse called Fish and Chips and Fishing Trips, at 1445 Calif. Hwy. 1. The phone number is (707) 875-3495. It's the culinary extension of the charter boat service, serving fish and chips, calamari, scallops, prawns, oysters, barbecued oysters, hot dogs, burgers, beer and wine.

Bodega Bay Surf Shack
1400 Calif. Hwy. 1, Pelican Plaza, Bodega Bay • (707) 875-3944

This shop is a hub of activity and a must-stop for any visitor eager to glean the optimum amount of local knowledge—particularly when it comes to Salmon Creek Beach (north of Bodega Bay) and Goat Rock State Beach (near Jenner, where the Russian River flows into the ocean and provides good wave conditions). Bob Miller, the shop's friendly and welcoming owner, has been here since 1984. His shop offers surfboards, wetsuit rentals and surfing lessons. Bike and kayak rentals also are available, along with a great selection of men's and women's beachwear and casual clothing.

High Tide Surf Shop
9 Fourth St., Petaluma
• (707) 763-3860

Located in the McNear Building, part of Petaluma's historic downtown, High Tide is a relative newcomer, having arrived in 1992. If you should pass through "the crossroads to the beach," as proprietor Len Crain likes to call the neighborhood, don't expect his shop to be open before noon. Then again, you might want to avail yourself of a High Tide public service, a continuous broadcast of the coastal weather report and surf conditions emanating from a not-so-loudspeaker above the recessed doorway.

High Tide stocks a complete line of custom

Photo: Bill Hoban

Boats line the docks situated between the Noyo River and the Fort Bragg harbor.

surfboards, body boards, skim boards and accessories, plus a large selection of wetsuits for men, women and children of all sizes and shapes. Even if the surf isn't calling your name, there's a rack full of Hawaiian shirts and a good selection of swim wear.

Windwalker Board Sports and School of Windsurfing
4347 Harrison Grade Rd., Occidental
• (707) 874-2331

Windwalker gives windsurfing lessons in Bodega Bay, where conditions are particularly favorable for learning the sport—a mile of 3-foot-deep water with consistent winds. The shop also rents wetsuits, boards and sails.

Windwalker is unique in another respect—it offers Bed and Breakfast packages in a variety of accommodations and a wide price range.

King's Sport and Tackle Shop
16258 Main St., Guerneville
• (707) 869-2156

You can buy just about anything you need for the outdoor life here. Whether you're a camping, fishing or archery enthusiast, or you don't know a striped bass from a catfish, Steve Jackson, King's friendly and knowledgeable owner, can provide you with sportswear, footwear, camping gear and accessories, fresh and saltwater bait and tackle, guns and ammo. He's also got custom, hand-tied flies, dry bags for river activities and equipment for abalone diving.

King's also provides guide service for fishing on the Russian River during steelhead, salmon and bass season. A local hunting guide is available to help you stalk wild boar, deer and turkey. King's rents kayaks ($22 a day for one-person kayaks, $33 for two) and gives guided river tours from May 1 to mid-October.

Mendocino County

Tally Ho II Old Fish House
Noyo Harbor, Fort Bragg • (707) 964-2079

Tally Ho II provides ocean charters fishing for salmon, rock cod and ling cod—rod and bait included. Two trips are made daily, at 7 AM and 1 PM. Whale-watching trips are provided January through March. Deep-sea fishing trips are $50; a two-hour whale-watching excursion is $20.

Lake County

Disney's Water Sports
401 S. Main St., Lakeport
• (707) 263-0969

No magic kingdom or amusement park rides here, just Jet Skis, aluminum fishing boats, patio boats, kayaks, ski boats, parasail rides, pedal boats, Ski Doos and water ski lessons.

On the Waterfront
60 Third St., Lakeport
• (707) 263-6789

Here you can rent 18-foot Bowrider ski boats, fishing boats, patio boats (with AM/FM stereo cassette!), pedal boats, a variety of personal watercraft (including stand-up and three-seat Jet Skis) and accessories such as skis and kneeboards.

Spectator Sports

The Wine Country approach to spectator sports isn't a whole lot different than the overall philosophy of living here.

For one thing, you will notice a well-balanced dichotomy between the sophisticated (such as PGA Golf) and the populist (welcome to sprint-car racing). Another example of sports imitating life in grapeland: Local events tend to be modest and folksy, but everyone appreciates having access to professional-scale happenings in the Bay Area and Sacramento. No fewer than eight pro sports franchises take the field (or diamond, or court, or rink, or pitch) within two hours of the Wine Country. Each is included in this chapter. And plenty of other Bay Area sporting events—from boxing matches to major golf and tennis tournaments—are not included. We had to draw the line somewhere.

Also note that some sports outings seemed more appropriately included in our Festivals and Annual Events chapter—the annual rodeo at the Sonoma County Fair is an example. And if the activity is more participatory than vicarious in nature, look for it in the Parks and Recreation or our On The Water chapters.

The radio stations listed below every franchise name are the teams' English-language flagship stations, and the phone numbers are ticket sources. For major events you also can try TicketMaster at (800) 523-1515. Now go buy a bucket of popcorn and an official program, and root, root, root for the home team.

LOOK FOR:
- **Baseball**
- **Football**
- **Basketball**
- **Hockey**
- **Soccer**
- **Golf**
- **Motorsports**
- **Running**
- **Bicycle Road Races**
- **Arm Wrestling**
- **Horse Jumping**
- **Horse Racing**
- **College Sports**

Baseball

San Francisco Giants
Pacific Bell Park, China Basin
• **(415) 468-3700**
• **KNBR 680 AM**

One of two franchises—the Los Angeles Dodgers being the other—to open Major League Baseball to westward expansion in 1958, the Giants have been a team of individual standouts but little collective success (notwithstanding a division title in '97 and a near-miss for the National League wild card berth in '98). The team has won four National League West championships and two pennants in its 40-or-so years in San Francisco, losing the World Series to the Yankees in 1962 and to the cross-bay Oakland A's in 1989.

Yet in the city that refers to itself as The City, style points are almost as valuable as titles, and the Giants have had plenty of style. The 1960s squads had big clout from legendary center fielder Willie Mays, first basemen Willie McCovey and Orlando Cepeda, and the brilliant pitcher Juan Marichal. The Giants didn't have a losing season in San Francisco until 1972, but they suffered several close eliminations. In each season from 1964 to 1966, for example, the team was in contention up to the final few games of the year.

The Giants of the 1970s and early '80s were perennial also-rans, but a slugging lineup that included

Will Clark, Kevin Mitchell and Matt Williams took the team to division titles in 1987 and 1989. Those three players are gone now, but Barry Bonds continues to be a one-man draw. When the moody Bonds is focused on business, he arguably is one of the five best all-around players in major-league history.

Candlestick Park, at the south end of San Francisco off U.S. Highway 101, was considered a jewel when it opened in 1960. But after years of frigid ninth innings and wind-tormented pop flies, Giants president Peter Magowan announced that the team would be moving to a new, privately financed stadium in the China Basin area of San Francisco. That stadium, Pacific Bell Park, is scheduled to host the home opener in the year 2000. Designed by the renowned architectural group of HOK Sports Facilities, it promises to be a nostalgic wonder along the lines of Baltimore's Oriole Park at Camden Yards and Cleveland's Jacobs Field. Pac Bell Park will hug San Francisco Bay—so close, in fact, that prodigious drives to right field will end up in salt water, to be retrieved by a canine employee. The stadium will include a brew pub, a bayside promenade that will allow people to peek through the fence for no charge, and, unlike 3Com Park, ample public transportation options. Current Giants ticket prices range from $10 to $24.

Oakland Athletics
Network Associates Coliseum,
off I-880, about 5 miles south of I-980
• (510) 568-5600 • KFRC 610 AM

The Athletics' history in Oakland has been the steepest of roller-coaster rides. The A's had been unqualifiedly dreadful in Kansas City, but they immediately posted their first winning record in 16 years after moving to the Bay Area in 1968. The A's improved steadily and soon captured three consecutive World Series (1972-74), a feat that no team has duplicated since. Those Athletics were the rollicking Mustache Gang put together by maverick owner Charles O. Finley. Reggie Jackson hit the home runs and made the headlines, but the strength of the team was pitching, led by starters Jim "Catfish" Hunter and Vida Blue and handlebar-mustachioed reliever Rollie Fingers. But Finley soon sold off his stars, and the Athletics sank into ineptitude. They played games in the late 1970s that drew fewer than 1,000 fans.

The team had no more sustained success until it was bought by the family of Walter Haas, the Levi's executive who became a model for professional sports owners. Under the Haas

family's benevolence, the shrewd personnel moves of general manager Sandy Alderson and the cool machinations of manager Tony LaRussa, the A's became Major League Baseball's best team from 1988 to 1990. Dave Stewart won 20 or more games four straight years, Dennis Eckersley was reborn as baseball's eminent closer, Rickey Henderson returned to his hometown to steal bases and runs, and hitting giants such as Jose Canseco and Mark McGwire drove opposing pitchers into deep depression. Oakland was upset by the Dodgers in '88 and the Reds in '90 but flattened the Giants in 1989's "Bay Bridge Series," which was interrupted by the 7.1-magnitude Loma Prieta earthquake.

Alas, the A's didn't have enough money to retain the superstars, and the team hit the rocks again in the 1990s as ownership passed to local businessmen Steve Schott and Ken Hofmann. Before long Oakland had traded McGwire to St. Louis, given up (once again) on Rickey Henderson, and watched Sandy Alderson leave to take a post with Major League Baseball. As 1999 rang to a close, MLB still had not approved a new ownership group, restarting the perpetual talk of the club's moving. Even in the best of times, the A's have had trouble drawing fans consistently, though a crop of talented youngsters—led by outfielder Ben Grieve, third baseman Eric Chavez and pitcher Tim Hudson—might change that.

Until the new regime settles in, and no doubt afterward, the recently renovated Oakland Coliseum will remain a delightful place to watch a ball game. The music is way ahead of the standard play list, there is a play room for bored kids, and rainouts are nearly as rare as no-hitters. (There were only 11 rain checks issued between 1978 and 1996.) The stadium lies south of downtown Oakland, right off Interstate 880. The cheapest A's ticket is $6; the most expensive is $24, and all of them are half-price if you are younger than 15 or older than 60.

Sonoma County Crushers
Rohnert Park Stadium, 5900 Labath Ave.,
Rohnert Park
• (707) 588-8300 • KBBF 89.1 FM

There may not be anyone named Bonds or Grieve on the field, but fans in Sonoma County have discovered what their ilk around the country already knew: Minor-league baseball is a heck of a lot of fun. The unaffiliated Crushers, 1998 champions of the independent Western Baseball League, play on a one-time cow pasture developed into a cozy, 4,150-seat stadium. (From U.S. 101, go west on the Rohnert Park

Expressway.) Both the team and the league got going in 1995.

On 45 home dates between late May and early September, the Crushers host teams from places like Chico, Salinas and Bend, Oregon. They promise good baseball. If they don't deliver? Who cares! A Crushers ticket can be had for $5 to $13—quite a bargain for an experience that includes a field-adjacent barbecue deck, a giant Korbel champagne bottle that "explodes" upon every Crushers home run and quite possibly the greatest name in the history of sports mascots: the Abominable Sonoman.

Football

San Francisco 49ers
3Com Park at Candlestick Point,
off U.S. Hwy. 101, about
1½ miles south of I-280
• (415) 656-4900 • KGO 810 AM

Despite their recent implosion, the 49ers retain a firm grip on the hearts and minds of greater Northern California. The caps, the T-shirts, the bumper stickers and the bar decorations are there to make sure you don't forget, not even for a minute, that the Wine Country is Niners country. It wasn't always this way, of course. The team had its core following for decades, but it wasn't until the harmonic convergence of Bill Walsh and Joe Montana that things went crazy.

The 49ers got their start in the All-America Football Conference in 1946, then became one of three AAFC teams (the Browns and Colts were the others) to join the NFL in 1950. Since then, no shortage of Hall of Famers and perennial all-pros have graced the gridirons of Kezar Stadium and Candlestick/3Com Park. There was quarterback Y.A. Tittle, with his balding head and golden arm. There was Hugh McElhenny, one of the finest open-field runners in history. There was halfback Joe Perry, an unlikely blend of power and speed. Throw in Leo Nomellini, Bob St. Clair (who actually ate, and eats, raw meat) and John Brodie, and San Francisco was blessed with plenty of attractions, but no championships. From 1946 through 1980, the 49ers had zero NFL title banners to fly.

That changed when Walsh, the academic head coach, and Montana, the uncanny quarterback, arrived in 1979. The 49ers were in the Super Bowl by January 1982, and they'd be back four times in the next 13 seasons. During this era, even a down year usually amounted

to an 11-5 record, an NFC West title and a loss in the conference championship game. Along the way, Montana was replaced by scrambling Steve Young. Wide receiver Dwight Clark was replaced by Jerry Rice, maybe the best player ever to wear an NFL uniform. Battering-ram safety Ronnie Lott was replaced by Tim McDonald. Even Walsh was replaced with protege George Seifert, who was in turn supplanted by Steve Mariucci in 1997. Through it all, the team hardly missed a beat—until 1999, when it sank to the bottom of the NFL.

The 49ers want a new, state-of-the-art stadium, not to mention an integrated commercial mega-complex, at the existing site of 3Com Park. And they want taxpayers to shoulder about $100 million of the project through bonds. Proposition D made that money available in 1997, and Proposition F changed the local zoning code. Both passed by the slimmest of margins in a highly charged election.

The aftermath has not been pretty, as a front-office feud among long-time owner Eddie DeBartolo, his sister Denise DeBartolo York, and general manager Carmen Policy resulted in Policy's departure for the NFL's new Cleveland Browns franchise. Dwight Clark soon left the Niners' front office to join him. All this played out against the backdrop of Eddie's plea-bargain in a federal court case involving a riverboat casino licensing scheme. As 1999 closed, the convicted felon's status with the team (he reportedly wanted to regain control, after being forced to step aside during the legal mess) and the status of the new stadium remained in limbo. And the team had become decrepit.

A few end notes: 49ers tickets are about $50, but good luck purchasing one. The games have been sold out since 1981. Allow at least 90 minutes to 3Com Park from either Napa or Santa Rosa, progressively longer from points farther north. And for heaven's sake, bring a jacket and a thermos of something hot.

Oakland Raiders
Network Associates Coliseum,
off I-880, about 5 miles south of I-980
• (888) 44-RAIDE(RS)
• The Ticket, 1050 AM

That wasn't a tremor you felt in June 1995, it was the earth tilting back to its proper axis upon the Raiders' return to Oakland—the first time a pro sports franchise had come back to a city it once fled. To the citizens of Oakland and its working-class satellites such as Hayward and San Leandro, there never was a doubt about the return of their not-so-prodigal son,

Al Davis. Los Angeles just never seemed right for the team that is symbolized by a surly, one-eyed pirate.

So far, however, the homecoming has produced more political contention than playoff contention. The hastily brokered deal that brought the Raiders back to town has left the city of Oakland responsible for unsold "personal seat licenses," and this is a city with little financial cushion. Still, the East Bay fans have waited a long time for the return of "Raidah football," as Davis might say, and they are generally forgiving.

Oakland was one of the eight original American Football League franchises and has proven to be quite successful. The Raiders, as they will tell you themselves at every opportunity, have the best record in all of professional sports since 1963, claiming three Super Bowl victories and 12 AFL/AFC West titles (the team spent 13 years in Los Angeles, 1982-94). The team's pinnacle was 1972 to 1976, when the blustery John Madden coached at least seven Pro Football Hall of Fame players: center Jim Otto, guard Gene Upshaw, tackle Art Shell, wide receiver Fred Biletnikoff, kicker George Blanda, linebacker Ted Hendricks and corner-back Willie Brown (not to be confused with San Francisco's iconoclastic mayor of the same name). The '76 team shook off three consecutive losses in the AFC Championship Game to overwhelm Minnesota 32-14 in Super Bowl XI. The Raiders also captured the Lombardi Trophy in January of 1981 and 1984.

Stars of the 1980s included soft-spoken quarterback Jim Plunkett, relentless defensive end Howie Long and incomparable running back Marcus Allen. Davis' never-ending search for the right head coach continued in 1998, when he brought in young Jon Gruden, an offensive whiz kid from the Philadelphia Eagles. The team finished 8-8 in '98 behind a defense that ranked as one of the league's best before suffering key injuries in the second half of the season, and hovered right around 500 in '99, too. Tim Brown is still one of the NFL's most exciting receivers, and the Raiders have a couple of top-tier defenders in cornerback Charles Woodson and defensive tackle Darrell Russell.

The Raiders' rich on-field history notwithstanding, the best reason to come to Oakland on an autumn Sunday always has been the spontaneous circus that erupts in the parking lot and the cheap seats. It's a freak show of the highest order—not as physically dangerous as the version at the Los Angeles Coliseum, but more entertaining. Expect to see Darth Vaders, Grim Reapers, dangling bronco effigies, and more Harley-Davidsons and pirate tattoos than you can shake a cutlass at. Tickets are $41, $51 and $61.

Finally, take note that the Raiders moved their summer training camp to Napa in 1996. They practice on a field behind the Napa Valley Marriott Hotel at 3425 Solano Avenue, which runs parallel to Calif. Highway 29. Those sessions are closed to the public, but the team has an annual fan day in July—and perhaps a couple of open workouts—at Memorial Stadium, which is near the intersection of Jefferson Street and Pueblo Avenue.

INSIDERS' TIP

Legendary quarterback Joe Montana owns a getaway ranch in Knights Valley, which is sort of a southern extension of Alexander Valley. Don't be shocked to see him shopping for produce at the Palisades Market in Calistoga.

Basketball

Golden State Warriors
The Area in Oakland, off I-880, about 5 miles south of I-980
• (510) 986-2222 • KNBR 680 AM

Careful observers will note that the Warriors and their NBA neighbors, the Sacramento Kings, were absent from the Wine Country, Bay Area, American and world sports landscapes for much of the so-called 1998-99 season—along with the rest of the near-moribund, salary-heavy league. The owners and players had the decency to resolve their bitter labor strife in time to jury-rig a 50-game schedule from January to June of 1999. Roughly 200 free agents hopped from team to team as the post-Michael Jordan epoch got started. The Warriors joined the fray.

Golden State rid itself of Latrell Sprewell, the troubled superstar guard. The Warriors added veterans John Starks, Terry Cummings and Jason Caffey, and had high hopes for first-round draft choice Antawn Jamison.

Born in Philadelphia in the 1940s, they moved west, becoming the San Francisco Warriors from 1962 to 1971, before floating across the bay to Oakland to become Golden State. They played a few games in San Diego early on, and they played all their 1996-97 home games in San Jose while the Coliseum Arena was being renovated. Now they are back in Oakland and looking to overcome a string of aggravating seasons.

The team that brought Wilt Chamberlain from Philadelphia in 1962 has won only one NBA title on the West Coast. That came in 1975, when superstar Rick Barry and a gang of overachievers shocked the Washington Bullets in a four-game sweep. Big-time performers such as Nate Thurmond and Cazzie Russell came before 1974-75, Bernard King and World B. Free after, but no other Warriors team has gone all the way. Golden State's frustration during the 1980s is summed up by the trade that sent work-horse center Robert Parish to Boston for the draft pick used on Joe Barry Carroll.

Things seemed to be looking up under coach Don Nelson in the early 1990s, but the situation blew up when Nelson feuded with star forward Chris Webber in 1994-95. Webber demanded a trade, and the Warriors obliged. Three months later Nelson was gone too, and the team was left to pick up the pieces. Can Golden State's fortunes turn? The team may have taken a step in the right direction when owner Christopher Cohan hired respected coach P.J. Carlesimo in 1997. Cohan's move proved less than brilliant as the team struggled to an ugly 19-63 record, a statistic bound to be rendered academic when Sprewell grabbed Carlesimo by the throat during a December practice session and was suspended without pay for the remainder of the season. The news dominated all accounts of the Warriors' progress, or lack of it. Warriors tickets and range from $10 to $100.

Sacramento Kings
ARCO Arena,
near the northeast corner of I-5 and I-80
• (916) 928-6900 •KHTK 1140 AM

Game after game, ARCO Arena is filled to the rafters with screaming, maniacal Kings fans. Finally, they've got something to shout about. In their first 13 seasons in Sacramento the Kings never had a winning season. But the love of hoops was unconditional here. Sellouts are practically a Sacramento city ordinance.

Existing franchises in various sports, including the Raiders and the A's, certainly have taken notice, making overtures to Sacramento in the

> **INSIDERS' TIP**
>
> **St. Louis Rams head coach Dick Vermeil was born and raised in Calistoga. In fact, the Vermeil House, at 913 Washington Street, is a designated historical site that has been converted into a medical facility.**

recent past regarding possible moves. (Sacramento has been the Kings' home since 1985, but they've moved before—from Rochester, Cincinnati and Kansas City.) Los Angeles-based developer Jim Thomas has headed a four-man ownership group since 1992, and he would like to add a championship one day. It's not as outlandish as it once sounded. Chris Webber, a powerful rebounder and scorer, has blossomed at the other end of Jason Williams' improbable no-look passes. With Vlade Divac and Nick Anderson adding veteran leadership, the Kings have become part of the NBA elite.

ARCO Arena is just north of Sacramento. From the Wine Country, take I-80 through Sacramento and turn off on I-5 north. Take the Del Paso Road exit and follow the signs. Tickets range from $12 to $60 per game, though all but the cheapest seats are snapped up by season-ticket holders. In fact, if you're after Kings tickets you are encouraged either to book weeks in advance or befriend a lonely corporate CEO.

Hockey

San Jose Sharks
San Jose Arena, off I-880
Ticket Master • (415) 421-8497,
(408) 287-4275 • KARA 105.7 FM

The Sharks made a reputation as giant-killers as they knocked off high-ranked opponents, Detroit and then Calgary, in the opening rounds of the 1994 and 1995 NHL playoffs. But the problem for San Jose has been getting to the playoffs. The Sharks have been known as the bottom feeders of the Western Conference, though Coach Darryl Sutter's 1999-2000 squad was eminently respectable.

San Jose Arena is a tidy venue smack dab in the middle of a tidy city, and professional hockey has been an incongruous hit in Silicon Valley. To get to the arena, exit Interstate 880 at Coleman Avenue, turn left on Coleman, right on Julian and follow the parking signs. The Sharks began play in 1991, and the arena opened two years later. Recently, general manager Dean Lombardi has assembled a solid cast that includes right wing Owen Nolan and center Vincent Damphousse.

Be advised that San Jose is about 40 miles

Rohnert Park Stadium is home of the Sonoma County Crushers, part of the independent Western Baseball League.

south of San Francisco or Oakland, so getting there and back from the Wine Country takes an investment of a full day or a long evening. Sharks tickets range from $17 for the most distant upper-reserved seats to $83 for sideline club seats. Many others are in the $35 to $45 range.

Soccer

San Jose Earthquakes
Spartan Stadium, off I-280
• (408) 985-GOAL • KLIV 1590 AM

When Major League Soccer officially set up shop in spring of 1996, the fledgling league chose San Jose as the site of its inaugural game. The city had everything MLS was looking for: an established soccer tradition, a first-rate stadium and a well-run organization headed by transplanted Englishman Peter Bridgwater. More than 31,000 fans crammed into Spartan Stadium on April 6, 1996, and the Clash (as they were then known) did not disappoint, leaving with a 1-0 victory over D.C. United.

Hope springs eternal in the heart of Silicon Valley for a team led by defender John Doyle and goalkeeper Joe Cannon. Midfielder Eddie Lewis, 24, was named to the U.S. National Team for '99 while gifted forward Ronald

Cerritos played for El Salvador. In 2000 they will mesh under the tutelage of Bay Area favorite Lother Osiander.

Spartan Stadium is on the San Jose State University campus, accessible by Interstate 280 in the heart of San Jose. Exit at Seventh Street, turn right on Seventh and proceed about 1½ miles to the stadium. (And please note the distance caveat stated at the end of the Sharks' summary.) Adult tickets range from $13 for behind-the-goal seats to $20 for the "premier" category. (Gold Club seats at midfield are sold out.) There are discounts for kids younger than 14 and seniors older than 60, beginning at $7 for the cheap seats. The Major League Soccer schedule runs from March through October.

Golf

Transamerica Senior Golf Championship
Silverado Country Club and Resort,
1600 Atlas Peak Rd., Napa
• (707) 252-8687, (800) 286-GOLF

The PGA Senior Tour returned to Napa's Silverado Resort in October 1999 for the Transamerica, a tournament that in 11 years has raised more than $1.5 million for Napa Valley charities such as the Queen of the Valley Hospital Foundation and local Boys and Girls Clubs. The splendid 6632-yard, par 72 course, with its 1857 Colonial clubhouse, consistently lures the biggest names on the Senior Tour. Recent participants include Arnold Palmer, Lee Trevino, Chi Chi Rodriguez, Dick Stockton and Tom Weiskopf.

The 1998 version featured Jim Colbert's emotional comeback from prostate cancer surgery in 1997. Colbert scored a 5-under-par 67 on the final day and won the tournament by one stroke. His $150,000 winner's share made him the all-time leader in the Senior PGA money list. Bruce Sleisher won in '99.

The weeklong event includes two practice rounds (free to attend the first day, $5 the second), a two-day Pro-Am competition ($13 each day to attend) and three rounds of serious golf ($18 the first day, $20 for each of the latter two). You also can choose from a series of packages that include subsequent admission to the tournament grounds and clubhouse. They run from $13 to $105. All of the noted prices are at the gate; you can save by ordering early. Parking at the Transamerica runs $4 for a daily pass or $10 for a tournament pass. Silverado is northeast of downtown Napa, off Calif. Highway 121.

Motor Sports

Don't be surprised if the still air of your summer evening is suddenly torn apart by the growl of a 750-horsepower engine, the scent of ripening grapes replaced by a whiff of high-octane fuel. Love 'em or hate 'em, racing machines are here to stay in Wine Country. This section is divided by venue.

Calistoga Speedway
Napa County Fairgrounds, 1435 N. Oak St., Calistoga • (707) 942-5111

Calistoga is a gathering point for devotees of sprint cars, those miniature, winged beasts that evolved from old Indy 500 roadsters. Pound for pound, sprint cars pack as much power as modern-day Indy cars, and they seem to be as loud. Two features that separate sprint cars from the pack are the wings and the tires. Each vehicle has a billboard-size wing on top of its roll cage and a smaller one on the nose. They produce downward force, which helps the car grip the track; the larger one also happens to provide handy space for advertising. Sprint cars have fatter tires on the outside wheels to help

them roll into corners. In fact, it is a rarity for any two tires on one car to be of the same size.

Calistoga Speedway's half-mile dirt track hosts approximately seven sprint-car nights a year: four sanctioned by the Northern Auto Racing Club and a three-day event put on by the World of Outlaws. The NARC nights tend to be in early May, Memorial Day weekend and Fourth of July weekend. The World of Outlaws event is Labor Day weekend. A typical program might include four 10-lap heat races, a feature-inversion dash, a 12-lap semi-main event and a 25-lap feature event. Tickets run about $15 for NARC races and $80 for the Outlaws' three-day package.

Sears Point Raceway
Calif. Hwys. 37 and 121
• (800) 870-RACE

Quick: Which event drew the largest crowd in the history of Northern California sports? It wasn't the 49ers vs. Dallas in the 1994 NFC Championship Game or one of the A's-Giants World Series contests in 1989. It was the NASCAR Winston Cup stock car race that drew 102,000 in May 1996. That event was staged at Sears Point.

If it's nitro-burning, rubber-ripping and asphalt-grabbing, chances are you'll find it here. This might be the world's busiest raceway, with an average of 340 days a year of activity including 50 of 52 weekends. Much of that is devoted to the resident Russell Racing School, but there is plenty of competition among a variety of internally combusting machines.

Besides the twisting, 12-turn, 2.52-mile road course and the quarter-mile drag strip, Sears Point offers 700,000 square feet of coexisting shop space and posh, tower VIP seats. The facility is in a beautiful corner of lush rolling hills at the southern tip of Sonoma County. If you just want a look, it's open to the public free of charge on weekdays. If you want to get truly revved, race tickets range from $15 to $100, with many in the $15 to 25 range.

Petaluma Speedway
Petaluma Fairgrounds,100 Fairgrounds Dr.
• (707) 762-7223

Check the notes about sprint cars listed in the Calistoga Speedway section and apply them here. NARC stages two events on Petaluma's three-eighths-mile, semi-banked track over the July 4th weekend and in early October. The fairgrounds are just west of U.S. Highway 101 on E. Washington Street. If you have to ask how far away it is, maybe this sport isn't for you. A 1996 survey showed that sprint-car fans traveled an average of 82 miles to each event.

Running

Sutter Home Napa Valley Marathon
Calistoga to Napa • (707) 255-2609

Hey, if you're gonna torture yourself, you might as well do it in Eden. This is an unbeatable course: 26.2 miles due south along the Silverado Trail, hills hugging the left side of the road and a yellow sea of blooming mustard to the right. Only the last half-mile, the approach to the finish line at Vintage High School, is within any city limits. And after three moderate hills in the first 6 miles, the course offers a gently rolling descent.

The Napa Valley Marathon usually takes place the first Sunday in March. The 2000 edition will be the 22nd annual. You can park at Vintage High and take a shuttle bus to the start line (just south of Calistoga on the Silverado Trail) but be punctual—the last bus leaves at 5:30 AM. Weather can vary, of course, but bet on lifting fog and temperatures in the mid-40s at start time (7 AM), progressing to warm sunshine later in the morning. Early entry costs $50, and it jumps to $65 on pre-race Saturday. For $20 you can run unofficially, which means you can use aid stations and medical services, but you don't get the glory of running through the finish chute.

The Relay
Calistoga to Santa Cruz • (415) 508-9700

The marathon doesn't present enough of a challenge for you? Try The Relay, a 194-mile trek that winds through seven counties and 36 cities from Calistoga to Santa Cruz, past cow pastures and redwoods and across the Golden Gate Bridge. The first Relay attracted exactly nine teams in 1995, but it has mushroomed to thousands of runners since then.

Everything about this race is unique, except for sore feet and sweaty bodies. Start times are staggered at the Calistoga Mineral plant. Teams of 12 competitors split up 36 3-to-7-mile legs, with vans leapfrogging runners to their next start position. The race heads south on the Silverado Trail, with com-

petitors running through the night and the first finishers reaching the Pacific early the next morning. Several Silicon Valley companies have gotten involved, presenting more peculiarities. This was the first race in which runners wore bar codes and got scanned at checkpoints. The Relay's home page (www.TheRelay.com) even offers a three-dimensional preview of each leg.

The Relay is run under a full moon in September or October. The entry fee is $40 per runner, climbing to $50 in August. Individuals looking for a team have two options: Find one yourself at the website, or mark the appropriate box on your application and organizers will place you.

Bicycle Road Races

Cherry Pie Criterium
Napa Valley Corporate Park, Napa • (707) 224-2369

The carbo-loading comes after the race at this event. Besides the $1,500 or so in prize money—including $500 for the Pro I-II division—the top three finishers in each class are awarded fresh cherry pies. The 2000 Cherry Pie is the 25th annual. The 1-mile course, which includes one modest hill, is bounded by Napa Valley Corporate Drive, Napa Valley Corporate Way and Trefethen Way. The simplest way to find the start/finish line is to look for the famous Grape Crusher statue south of Napa. Between 300 and 350 racers split up into 11 divisions, including a recumbent category. It is run the second or third Sunday in February.

Napa Grand Prix
First and Main Sts., Napa • (707) 963-7736

This criterium (a timed road race, with the winner determined by number of laps completed) got its start only recently—in 1994—but its following is on the upswing. Hoping for a breeze off the Napa River in early August, the restaurants of downtown Napa put extra tables on the sidewalk so their customers can sip cool drinks and watch the colors go blurring by. The Master's race is a U.S. Cycling Federation district championship, and there are several other divisions including a 90-minute Pro race that draws about 80 riders. The

INSIDERS' TIP

If you're going to the Oakland Coliseum or the Arena for a game, consider taking BART, the Bay Area Rapid Transit system. You can park in Richmond, at the northwest tip of what is commonly called the East Bay, and take a train to the Coliseum's doorstep. Call (415) 992-2278 for schedules and directions.

Serious runners can compete in Wine Country's organized races.

0.7-mile course is bounded by First, School, Second, and Main streets.

Petaluma Criterium
Oakmead Business Park, Petaluma
• (707) 778-1360

Here is another opportunity for brightly decorated cyclists to peacefully invade an otherwise drab corporate park. This one is at Oakmead Business Park on the southeast end of town, just off Lakeville Highway (a.k.a. Calif. Highway 116). The 2000 Petaluma Criterium will be the twelfth. The course is 0.7 miles, and all races are one hour except for the Pro, which is 90 minutes and offers $1,000 in prize money. Cash also is awarded to the cycling clubs with the highest cumulative point totals, even if their members fail to win any individual titles. The race usually is the second Sunday in June, and the entrance fee is between $15 and $20. Expect 300 to 350 riders and glorious weather.

Wine Country Cycling Classic
Graton and Santa Rosa • (707) 528-3283

What started as the Santa Rosa Criterium in 1984 has become a two-day road event, the largest of its kind in Northern California. The Classic takes place in late March or early April and includes a total field of nearly 1,500 riders. The first day features the Graton Road Race, staged on an 11-mile course that presents four short, rolling climbs and one certified calf-burner. The Pro division race is 88 miles long and pays about $4,000. Graton is 3.5 miles north of Petaluma, just west of Calif. 116.

The Kendall-Jackson Winery Criterium is run on the second day, and it is the main event. As many as 5,000 spokeheads turn out to watch the action on a flat, fast 0.7-mile course in downtown Santa Rosa. The racing is only part of a day of festivities that includes a live band and a team of aerial bike tricksters. The Senior I/Pro division competes for 90 minutes and splits about $3,500. The starting/finish line is on Sonoma Avenue. Take the Downtown Santa Rosa exit from U.S. 101 and head east on Third Street to Santa Rosa Avenue. Turn right and proceed two blocks. Dave Walters, who organizes the Classic, also stages a weekly criterium every Tuesday night from April through

August. The first race starts at 6 PM at Corporate Center Industrial Park. Call for directions.

Arm Wrestling

World's Wristwrestling Championship
McNear's Mystic Theater,
23 Petaluma Blvd. N., Petaluma
• (707) 765-2121

Dave Devoto is one of arm wrestling's pioneers, and he stages this biceps bash on the second Saturday of every October. (The 2000 edition will be the 39th annual.) Men, women, right-handers, left-handers, even masters—18 separate divisions in all—show up armed only with their arms, eager to capture part of the $5,000 pot. There is a weigh-in Friday night, continued Saturday morning from 8 to 10:30 AM. Then come two periods of action: elimination rounds from 1 to 5 PM and the final rounds from 8 to 10:30 PM. Admission is $10 and the auditorium will be packed, so get there early if you want to sit close enough to get hit with a droplet of sweat. Just take the Petaluma Boulevard North exit off of U.S. 101.

Horse Jumping

Napa Valley Fairgrounds
1435 N. Oak St., Calistoga
• (707) 942-5111

Carousel Show Management stages hunter-jumper horse shows here in mid-July and early October. The five-day event in July includes the Napa Valley Classic, probably the biggest one-day event of its kind in this part of California. Local merchants set up wine- and food-tasting stalls outside the jumping area. Admission is $25, and some $10,000 is generated for the Hospice of Napa Valley. The October show is a four-day event that includes the Northern California Hunter Jumper Association medal finals. There are separate awards for juniors, amateurs and ponies. Admission is free.

Sonoma County Fairgrounds
Calif. Hwy. 12, east of U.S. Hwy. 101,
Santa Rosa • (707) 545-4200

Carousel also organizes two three-day events at the Sonoma County Fairgrounds, which are off Calif. Highway 12, not more than a mile east of U.S. 101. The first show is in May, the second over Labor Day weekend. The latter includes the Carousel medal finals and an evening event under the lights. There is no charge for either show.

Horse Racing

Sonoma County Fairgrounds
Calif. Hwy. 12, east of U.S. Hwy. 101,
Santa Rosa • (707) 545-4200

If the hoofbeat of the thoroughbreds should happen to draw your attention in midsummer, heed the call to the colors. What you'll find at the Sonoma County Fair from late July through early August is one of the country's most entertaining 12-day horse racing meets. Top jockeys such as Russell Baze, Dennis Carr and Rafael Meza guide the trainees of Jerry Hollendorfer, Brent Sumja, Lloyd Mason and others as thousands cheer home the world's greatest four-legged athletes. Wagering on the competition is optional. First post is 1:15 PM.

The Jockey Club
1350 Bennett Valley Rd.
Santa Rosa • (707) 524-6340

Officially dubbed "The Jockey Club Off-Track Wagering at the Sonoma County Fairgrounds," this is where Wine Country's wise guys and other hip handicappers amuse themselves when the shed rows across the street aren't booked with blood stock. It's a year-round off-track concession offering races live via satellite TV from major courses in California (e.g. Golden Gate Fields, Bay Meadows, Santa Anita, Hollywood Park, Del Mar), New York and Florida.

Three bucks gets you through the door and into a well-kept room stocked with eight projection big-screen TVs, 70 monitors, a full bar and complete food and beverage services. Friendly clerks will take your wagers, or you may purchase a voucher and have at the auto-tote self-serve screens yourself. Either way, remember: There's a winner in each race.

College Sports

With only three four-year colleges inside its borders, the expansive Wine Country isn't exactly a hotbed of collegiate sports. Again, the Bay Area might be the place to turn if you really feel like waving a pom-pom and belting out fight songs. Here is a brief look at your options.

Sonoma State University
1801 E. Cotati Ave., Rohnert Park
• (707) 664-2701

With a couple of players in the NFL, including Pro Bowl guard Larry Allen of the Dallas

Top jockeys and their four-legged athletes compete at the Sonoma County Fairgrounds in July and August.

Cowboys, the NCAA Division II Cossacks had reached a respected place among small football programs. That came to an end in 1997, when the university dropped football in the face of formidable travel expenses.

Sonoma State still has plenty of athletics, including seven women's and five men's teams (the student body is 60 percent female). Soccer is king and queen there: The women, who made it to the Division II championship game in 1998, have enjoyed great success in the '90s, winning six straight Northern California Athletic Conference titles from 1990 to 1995 and a national championship in 1990. The men won five of seven NCAC titles between 1990 and 1996. The Cossacks jumped to the California Collegiate Athletic Association in the 1998-99 sports year.

Pacific Union College
1 Angwin Ave., Angwin • (707) 965-6344

Tiny PUC has to scramble to come up with funding for sports, but the NAIA Division II school does what it can. It fields men's and/or women's teams in soccer, volleyball, tennis, cross-country, basketball, golf and softball, with all but tennis staged on campus. The Pioneers have produced recent California Pacific Conference champions in women's basketball and men's golf.

University of California
2223 Fulton St., Berkeley
• (800) GO-BEARS

Known primarily for its academics and tradition of radical politics, Cal also has a rich sports heritage, with Rose Bowl victories dating back to 1921 (28-0 over Ohio State). The football program, which produced such stars as Craig Morton, Steve Bartkowski, Wesley Walker and Chuck Muncie in the 1960s and '70s, has seen better days. Coach Bruce Snyder took the Bears to strong conference finishes and a Citrus Bowl victory in the early 90s, but since then the program has floundered.

Bears basketball experienced a recent renaissance, begun by phenomenal point guard Jason Kidd (now an NBA star) in the early 1990s. In 1996-97, first-year coach Ben Braun took over a team in disarray (and headed for NCAA probation, thanks to the misdeeds of his predecessor Todd Bozeman), lost leading scorer Ed Gray at the end of the Pac-10 schedule and still managed to invade the NCAA tourney's Sweet Sixteen. There, the Golden Bears fell in a close game to North Carolina.

Ironically, Braun's team signaled another resurgence in late '98 by extending its record to 9-1 for the 1998-99 season with a 78-71 victory over the Tar Heels. That squad was denied Big Dance access, but showed the selection committee by winning the lower-visibility NIT tournament. The Bears came back to earth in 1999–2000.

Stanford University
Stanford Ticket Office, Stanford
• (415) 723-1021, (800) BEAT-CAL

Stanford is acclaimed for its squeaky-clean (well, at least by today's standards) sports programs, but it still manages to attract professional-caliber talent. Historically, the Cardinal (singular, please) has been something of a quarterback factory, producing NFL passers from Frankie Albert to John Brodie to Jim Plunkett to John Elway. Lately, the basketball team has ascended under professorial coach Mike Montgomery. In 1998, Arthur Lee, Mark Madsen and a group of no-names made it to the Final Four, where they lost their semifinal game in overtime to eventual champion Kentucky. That run led to a preseason No. 1 ranking in more than one poll for 1998-99. The 1999-2000 school year was even dizzier, as Madsen led the hoops teams to national contention while Tyrone Willingham's football team earned a Rose Bowl berth.

In the mid-'90s, Tara VanDerveer's women's basketball program earned most of the acclaim. The Cardinal women, building on the legacy of Jennifer Azzi and showcasing the graceful Kate Starbird (Class of '96) were an annual powerhouse that captured two Division I women's hoops titles early in the decade. VanDerveer's leave of absence to coach the U.S. Women's Olympic team to a gold medal is considered by many to be the reason for the program's recent slippage.

Kidstuff

Let's face it, munching crackers in a succession of tasting rooms while the grown-ups sip wine and toss around lofty adjectives isn't most kids' idea of a memorable vacation. The bed and breakfast inns discourage them, and few of the four-star restaurants serve corn dogs.

But worry not, you don't have to change your plans and head to Orlando. If the adults are even the slightest bit flexible, any family can find common ground in Wine Country. That might not be the first impression you get from perusing this chapter. Why? Because most of the reliable kid pleasers are just as popular with adults and are profiled accordingly in other sections of the book. For example, our Attractions chapter is rife with amusements for the prepubescent set, from the river ship *Grand Romance* in Napa to Ripley's Memorial Museum in Santa Rosa to the Old Faithful Geyser in Calistoga.

Our Parks and Recreation chapter has more great outdoors than you can shake a 9-year-old at, plus fun diversions like horseback riding, swimming and bowling. Add to those the wet activities in our On the Water chapter, and don't forget the professional and minor league athletic events you'll find if you turn to the Spectator Sports section.

But even after all that, we were left with a few places and events that begged for inclusion. Here they are—family-oriented attractions, including a handy selection of book and toy stores. It's everything you need to prevent boredom, even among an age group that prides itself on being bored.

LOOK FOR:
• Napa County
• Sonoma County
• Mendocino County
• Lake County
• Outside the Wine Country

Napa County

Napa Skate Park
Pearl and Clinton Sts., Napa
• **(707) 257-9529**

If they're bouncing off the walls, just put a skateboard under their feet and give 'em a gentle nudge. The skate park is just about what you'd expect: a cemented city block with an assortment of hills, dips, ramps and pathways. This is a free, do-it-yourself attraction. Bring your own board, supervise your own children, bandage your own knees. Roller skates and roller blades are welcome too.

John F. Kennedy Memorial Regional Park
Streblow Dr. off Calif. Hwy. 121, Napa
• **(707) 257-9529**

The largest of Napa's munici-pal parks at 340 acres, Kennedy has four group picnic areas, hiking and jogging trails, volleyball courts, a lighted baseball diamond and a multi-use ball field. It also has a duck pond and playground for the really young ones, plus a boat ramp for family outings. It's a tranquil, breezy setting adjacent to the Napa River.

Paradise Miniature Golf
640 Third St., Napa
• **(707) 258-1695**

What would a family road trip be without a few rounds of minia-ture golf? Paradise is in the heart of Napa (which some would say is in the heart of Paradise). It has a 19-hole course and a snack bar with candy and soft drinks. A couple of favorites: the 5th hole, with its grand loop-the-loop and, best of all, the 17th—the Valley Fog Hole—which tests your bad-weather vision as well as your hand-eye coordination. The cost is $3.50 for adults, $2 for kids 12 and younger and $3 for members of the "senior tour." Paradise is open from 3 to 7 PM Monday through Friday and 11 AM to 7 PM on Saturday and Sunday during the summer; it's open weekends only in the off-season.

Carolyn Parr Nature Museum
3107 Browns Valley Rd., Napa
• (707) 255-6465

This modest facility a mile west of Calif. Highway 29 is sponsored by the Napa Valley Naturalists. People come here to see the museum's dioramas, which show five habitats: grassland, chaparral, marshland, riparian and woodland/forest. Inside each diorama are examples of native plants and animal specimens, from raccoons and wood ducks to king snakes and badgers. There is an extensive raptor display and a special kids' section with hands-on items like pelts and skulls. Adults enjoy the Carolyn Parr museum too, but the small scale seems ideally suited to children. Admission is free. The museum is open from 1 to 4 PM Saturday and Sunday, and for group tours by appointment (50 cents per head). It is at the entrance to Westwood Hills Park, a 111-acre green space with picnic facilities and a self-guided nature trail.

Learning Faire
964 Pearl St., Napa
• (707) 253-1024

This Napa toy store, which recently celebrated its 20-year anniversary under continuous ownership, prides itself on selectivity. All products are prescreened for safety, and they sell nothing that promotes violence. Learning Faire stocks Brio, Thomas wooden trains and Legos, plenty of other toys and lots of games, puzzles, crafts, books, cassettes, and CDs. There are hands-on stations and the occasional market-research play day—when manufacturer reps bring new toys for kids to sample.

Fun & Games
3646 Bel Aire Plaza, Napa
• (707) 257-1468

Tradition is important to the folks at Fun & Games. They stock no video games, no electronic games and no weaponry. Instead you'll find marbles, Wiffle bats and a colorful variety of yo-yos. (The store even hosts yo-yo events that draw nationally prominent, um, yo-yoers.) Fun & Games focuses on a handful of children's book publishers, including Scholastic and Ran-

dom House. You'll find puzzles, timers and games sitting out, waiting for tiny hands. And they have plenty of travel games, perfect for the drive home to Phoenix.

The Toy Cellar
Vintage 1870, 6525 Washington St., Yountville • (707) 944-2144

Sprawling Vintage 1870 tends to be a lot more popular with moms than juniors. The antidote? Let them roam around The Toy Cellar with its books and Brio trains, its Beanie Babies and Playmobil, its Steiff bears and model rockets, its LGB German trains and old-fashioned metal jack-in-the-boxes. Meanwhile, Dad can pop down to the wine cellar (see our Shopping chapter).

Crane Park
Crane Ave. and Grayson Ave., St. Helena
• (707) 963-5706

St. Helena families and kids of every stripe gather at this well-kept sanctuary. The 10-acre park has two baseball diamonds, horseshoe pits, lighted bocce courts and tennis courts, substantial picnic set-ups, a playground and volleyball pits. On summer Fridays the Farmers Market is here.

Sonoma County

Southern Sonoma

The Clubhouse Family Fun Center
19171 Sonoma Hwy., Sonoma
• (707) 996-3616

When's the last time you paid $4 for 18 holes of golf? If you think miniature golf is a breeze of a game, just watch as your 10-year-old marks down all the low scores and comes in with a free game for whacking his ball on the 18th just right. The course is laid out to look like historic Sonoma, with ponds, fountains and a lifelike City Hall. Not just for kids, it's a great place for dating teens. The Clubhouse also features a wide variety of the latest video games as well as sports games like air hockey, basketball and football video games. To put an extra spin on a great family day, have a hot dog at the pond-side picnic area and talk about that 10-inch putt that just missed. The course and game room are open Monday through Thursday from noon to 8 PM, Friday and Saturday to 10 PM and Sunday from 10 AM to 9 PM. The rate for anyone older than 5 is $4 a game; kids younger than 5 play free. Special packages are available for family groups and birthday parties.

Train Town
20264 Broadway, Sonoma
• (707) 938-3912

It's difficult to say who gets the most fun out of this train ride, kids or adults. The whole layout is so cleverly crafted that it's a marvel of dedication to the art of the train buff. The miniature train travels through scenic landscapes of trees, lakes, bridges, a 140-foot-long tunnel and a small-scale replica of a turn-of-the-century Sonoma Valley town called Lakeville. While adults may feel they have arrived in Lilliput, kids seem right in tune with the tiny country they travel through. Midway along, the best part for many kids is the petting zoo. For five minutes the train stops and everyone hauls out to pet llamas, horses and miniature goats and to feed the ducks and geese. Back at the station there's a carousel ride ($1) and some interesting mechanical exhibits (see our Attractions chapter). Trains operate 10 AM to 5 PM every day in summer. Winter hours are 10 AM to 5 PM Friday through Sunday. At other times of the year, Engineer Kermit makes his own decisions on operating hours—it often depends on school schedules and rain—and will stick the "Open" sign out when he's there. Trains leave every 30 minutes. Adult fare is $3.75; kids and seniors go for $2.75. Did we mention the merry-go-round, at $1 a spin? Riders up!

Morton's Warm Springs
1651 Warm Springs Rd., Kenwood
• (707) 833-5511

One of the last of the natural mineral-water swimming holes, Morton's has three beautiful pools—for toddlers, for kids and for the family. More fun can be had at the volleyball courts, horseshoe pits, baseball field and game room with all the latest video games. There are 11 naturally landscaped picnic areas (one by a stream) with barbecue pits and shaded tables. Morton's is well-known locally as a family gathering place and for hosting family and corporate picnics of up to 2,400 people. Parking is available at no extra charge. The snack bar is conveniently close to the pools with ice-cold drinks and a wide selection of hot dogs, hamburgers, chips and all those picnic eats that make a family day so much fun. Morton's Warm Springs is open from the first weekend in May through most of September, from 10 AM to 7:30 PM on weekends and from 10:30 AM to 6 PM on weekdays. The pool is open a half-hour later. Weekday admission is $4.50 for adults and $4 for children; on weekends, it's $6 for adults and $5 for children for a full day of activity.

Early Work
141 Kentucky St., Petaluma
• (707) 765-1993

Early Work was formerly a shop for teachers looking for educational materials, but it is now open to the public. It's a great favorite with children because of its selection of creative toys and learning materials. There's something for everyone here, from age 1 to 100. Toys and books cover the areas of art, science, math and language. There's a story time and event schedule that changes from month to month—call the store for times.

Jungle Vibes
163 Kentucky St., Petaluma
• (707) 762-6583

They call it a nature and science store, but it's really an adventure where nature and science meet world culture. Forget the plane fare —at this unique Petaluma store walking in the door is like entering another country. Imagine strolling from vendor to vendor amid gondolas and giant baskets heaped high with handmade textiles and artifacts. The sound of foreign tongues and the smell of strange new fruits converge. A taste of adventure and multicultural exploration goes a long way in

INSIDERS' TIP

Napa County offers a number of unique summer camps, some run by local recreation departments and others run privately. Napa's Community Resources Department (707-257-9529) can give you a rundown of public options. Some of the more interesting private camps include Napa Valley Music Associates' MidSummer MusiCamp (707-252-8671), featuring group voice technique, music theory and stretching for musicians; Congregation Beth Sholom's Camp Sholom Chaverim, with programs such as "The Yemenite Connection" and "The Art of Jewish Cooking"; and the English Pro Soccer Camp taught by Les Carroll, the men's soccer coach at Napa Valley College.

KIDSTUFF

KIDSTUFF

Kids try their luck fishing at Bodega Bay.

Photo: Tina Luster-Hoban

our busy lives, and Jungle Vibes is set to help the community explore the world, using nature and science toys and books to complement an authentic collection of ethnic arts and sounds. This is the place to expand your child's world.

Victoria's Fashion Stables
4193 Old Adobe Rd., Petaluma
• (707) 769-8820

It's a place with good stuff for good kids—small, medium, or large.

For the little ones, there's a petting zoo along with pony rides. This isn't your average petting zoo, though. You'll start by seeing clucking chickens and waddling ducks, proceed to greeting pygmy goats, potbellied pigs, and baby horses and then go on to a lesson in how to milk a cow. Pony rides are suitable for even very small children: someone will walk along beside the horse and even hold the little one on if necessary. A half-hour of pony riding will cost $15, or the pony ride can be combined with the petting zoo for $15. Older children will enjoy horseback riding. These are well-mannered horses, not simply trained to ride in-line. The price of trail rides, English or Western, is $15 for a half-hour, up to $50 for two hours. Those who have paid for rides or the zoo can picnic at no extra charge (barbecue

grills are available). The stables are open every day except Tuesday. Appointments are preferred though drop-ins can usually be accommodated. Every October, there's a pumpkin patch here. Victoria's also operates a day use and overnight campground, with fishing nearby. Wait, there's more: a horse and carriage service for weddings.

Wildlife Natural History Museum
201 Fair St., Petaluma
• (707) 778-4787

This museum is part of Petaluma High School and is operated entirely by students under the supervision of a science teacher. It's the largest museum on a high school campus in the United States, with 9,000 square feet of exhibit space and a $3 million inventory that includes 100 live animals. Stuffed animals cover the range of Asia, Africa and North America. Live animals include chinchillas, iguanas, pythons and other snakes. There's also a saltwater tide pool for kids to enjoy. Almost 8,000 school kids come to see the museum each school year. Unfortunately, the budget to allow for public viewing is small, and the museum is open to the public only on the first and third Saturdays of the month during the school year. Admission for kids younger than 12 is $1; anyone older pays $2.

Cal Skate
**6100 Commerce Blvd.,
Rohnert Park**
• **(707) 585-0500**

Although much of the roller-skating schedule is devoted to adults or classes, there is plenty of open skating. Call for the schedule. Adult prices are usually $4 to $6.

Scandia Family Fun Center
**5301 Redwood Dr.,
Rohnert Park**
• **(707) 584-1361**

There's fun for everyone here: miniature golf, batting cages, go-carts, a video arcade, an Indy raceway, Tidal Wave bumper boats and a snack bar. It opens every day at 10 AM and stays open until 11 PM on weekdays and midnight on weekends. Prices vary by attraction.

A boy enjoys the bumper boats at Scandia Fun Center in Rohnert Park

Photo: Tina Luster-Hoban

KIDSTUFF

Toobtown
6591 Commerce Blvd., Rohnert Park
• **(707) 588-8100**

This one is for children 12 and younger. Toobtown offers unlimited play in a four-story tube structure, plus a dinosaur-bounce and fun in the gym, three bumper boat rides in a pond, and lots of rides on horses and tortoises and spaceships. It's for children as young as 8 months, all of whom must be accompanied by an adult. Socks are required by the dress code. Hours are 10 AM to 8 PM Sunday through Thursday, 10 AM to 9 PM on Friday and Saturday. Weekday prices are $4.95; it's $6.95 on the weekend. Kids younger than 2 can play free.

Copperfield's Books
2316 Montgomery Dr., Santa Rosa
• **(707) 578-8938**
650 Fourth St., Santa Rosa
• **(707) 576-7681**

Voted best kids' bookstore by an independent Sonoma County readers' poll, Copperfield's keeps up a steady stream of events to get kids interested in reading. Book promotions are unusual: For the *Cat in the Hat* program, kids had a chance to get their picture taken with the Cat himself. Family Fun Night brought out Curious George and provided an opportunity to help the man in the yellow hat find his curious companion. Occasional get-togethers with balloons and storytelling give book reading a party atmosphere. (See the Bookstores section of our Shopping chapter for more on Copperfield's.)

Gingerbread
2417 Magowan Dr., Santa Rosa
• **(707) 546-9100**

For children, this is an enchanting book and toy store, located in Montgomery Village shopping center and filled with bears, books, a stuffed animal named Muffy and more. From time to time, an actors' group sends out costumed characters (like Raggedy Ann and Andy, Winnie the Pooh and even Dr. Seuss characters) to dance and play with the children.

Howarth Park
630 Summerfield Rd., Santa Rosa
• **(707) 443-3770**

One of 27 parks in Santa Rosa, Howarth is the big one, a 152-acre retreat into the world of nature. There's a 25-acre lake where families can rent canoes, rowboats, paddleboats and sailboats and even take sailing lessons. Kids and parents also can fish for trout, bluegill and bass throughout the year. In another part of the park, a simulated steam train follows a quarter-mile track over a bridge and through a tunnel. But wait, there's more: a carousel, pony rides and Old Man Olson's farm, where kids can pet a variety of barnyard animals. Bring a picnic and have a great day! The park is open from 6 AM to 9 PM in summer and 6 AM to 6 PM in winter. Boat rentals (fishing is optional and subject to state regulations) and amusement rides are in operation Tuesday through Sunday from 11 AM to 5 PM during summer and on weekends in spring and fall.

Petrified Forest
4100 Petrified Forest Rd., Santa Rosa
• (707) 942-6667

The trees died a few million years ago, but they remain alive forever as stone sculptures of what they used to be. Paths wind in and out through the fossilized forest (see our Attractions chapter). Visitors can take a quarter-mile loop that requires about 20 minutes to stroll. Summer hours are 10 AM to 4:30 PM. Admission is $4 for adults, $3 for kids ages 12 through 17, $1 for kids 6 through 11 and $3 for seniors 60 and older. Almost as interesting as the forest is the museum and gift shop, where you can buy all kinds of good stuff—stones you've never seen before and pieces of wood turned to stone. There's also a good selection of books.

Redwood Empire Ice Arena
1667 West Steele Ln., Santa Rosa
• (707) 546-7147

Charles Schulz, famous for his *Peanuts* cartoons, grew up in Minnesota and never lost his love for ice skating. The rink he built in Santa Rosa is a beautiful venue compared to the outdoor rinks he knew in his youth. A full range of skating is offered, with mornings reserved for programs and classes (many world champions have trained here). The arena is open daily, but hours vary. Skating, including skate rental, is $7.50 for adults and teens and $6.50 for those

younger than 12. Aside from the ice arena, there's a wonderful Peanuts Gallery gift shop that's appealing to all ages (see our Shopping chapter). You can also buy skates here, both ice and roller. (For more information on the arena, see our Attractions chapter.)

riley street art supplies
103 Maxwell Ct., Santa Rosa
• (707) 526-2416

This is a great place to pick up childrens' craft supplies, including face-painting kits, tempera paints, tattoo books, how-to-draw books and build-your-own foam dinosaur kits. For one week each July (exact dates vary), a kids' art camp is held at the store from 9 AM to 1 PM at a cost of $120 per child. Youngsters get professional instruction in whatever medium is suitable for their age. This is a premier shopping spot for professional artists and craftspeople.

Santa Rosa Junior College Planetarium
2001 Lark Hall, 1501 Mendocino Ave., Santa Rosa • (707) 527-4371

Star-studded shows feature various astronomical phenomena, with the night sky projected (with special effects) onto the dome, using state-of-the-art equipment. Offered only during the school year, shows are scheduled at 7 and 8:30 PM on Fridays and Saturdays, and at 1:30 and 3 PM on Sundays. Cost is $4 for adult general admission and $2 for students and seniors, all on a first-come, first-served basis. Children younger than 5 are not admitted.

Smith's Mount St. Helena Trout Farm and Hatchery
18401 Ida Clayton Rd., Calistoga
• (707) 987-3651

Smith's has been raising trout for private ponds for almost 60 years now. On weekends they open up their ¾-acre lake to the public, and locals have learned that it's one of the best diversions in the area for children. The propri-

INSIDERS' TIP

If you are set on wine tasting but have a twinge of remorse for your captive children, we can suggest three Napa Valley wineries that the young ones might actually halfway enjoy. Sterling Vineyards is popular because of the gondola ride to the top of the knoll; they also serve soft drinks in their tasting room. St. Supéry Vineyards & Winery is fun for all because of its interactive wine appreciation displays. (What kid could resist "smell-o-vision"?) And the boat fountains fronting Niebaum-Coppola Estate seem to be especially popular with toddlers. You can find more information on all three in our Wineries chapter.

etors provide poles and bait, and they even clean and bag the trout for you afterward. All you do is bait, cast and reel. You pay only for the fish you take—$3 to $5, depending on size. From Calif. Highway128 in Knights Valley, just north of Calistoga, go 7 miles north at the big sign for Smith's. On Saturdays and Sundays from February through October, the fun lasts from 10 AM to 5 PM.

Northern Sonoma

Windsor Waterworks & Slides
5225 Conde Ln., Windsor
• **(707) 838-7360**

The excitement begins 42 feet up, where you can pair up with a friend or go it alone on the big double-tube river ride. Or maybe you'd rather plunge down the speed slide for the thrill of a young lifetime. Want more? Try King Richard's run, a giant of a slide, with double tubes that propel you through a tunnel of fun. The height requirement for those thrill rides is 45 inches. But the little ones (at least 36 inches tall) haven't been forgotten. There's a special body flume just for them. Between rides, there's time to swim, play volleyball, pitch horseshoes or take a whack at ping-pong. Bring a picnic, or grab a pizza pocket or hot dog at Friar Tuck's. It's open 11 AM to 7 PM from May through September (weekends only until June 15). Adults and teens pay $13.25 for full use of the park, kids ages 4 to 12 are $12.25, and those younger than 4 are free. There is another option: an afternoon splash special running from 4 to 7 PM is only $9.75 per person.

The Toyworks
103-B Plaza St., Healdsburg
• **(707) 433-4743**

A store of educational toys, Toyworks claims 13,000 different items, from European toys, Lego blocks and science and nature items to educational books and Lionel trains. Store hours are 10 AM to 6 PM Monday through Saturday and Sunday from 11 AM to 5 PM.

Lake Sonoma Fish Hatchery
3333 Skaggs Springs Rd., Geyserville
• **(707) 433-9483**

Here's a chance to peek in on all phases of fish life, depending on the season. In summer you'll see the small, young fish; later in the season, from late October through March, you'll be able to watch the coho salmon and steelheads returning to spawn, and climbing the fish ladder. The coho

salmon will die after spawning, but the steelheads will live to return to the sea. Once the eggs have been laid and fertilized, the fish hatchery starts collecting the eggs once a week—each Thursday at 10:30 AM. Summer hours here are 9 AM to 5 PM daily; winter hours are 9 AM to 4 PM, Wednesday through Sunday. There is no charge. Visitors also will enjoy a display of Native American artifacts, plus information on local geology.

West County/Russian River

Pet-a-Llama Ranch
5505 Lone Pine Rd., Sebastopol
• **(707) 823-9395**

You only need to look into a llama's soulful, gentle eyes and stroke its long, softly curving banana ears, to fall in love. The llama's long eyelashes are to be envied; their arched necks give them dignity. The place to get acquainted with these exotic animals is at Pet-a-Llama Ranch, where two dozen of them live and entertain visitors. School groups come during the week to learn about the animals' habits, to get up close and personal with them and give them a snack. Saturday and Sunday, though, is open house from 12 noon to 4 PM from April to December. Kids will get a kick out of feeding them (it's 50¢) and listening to the manager of the ranch tell what llama life is all about: where they come from, what they eat and how they're used as pack animals in their native South America.

J's Amusements
16101 Neeley Rd., Guerneville
• **(707) 869-3102**

Rides including the tilt-a-whirl, go-carts, Roundup, bumper cars, water slides and a roller coaster are featured at this amusement park. No admission fee is charged. You pay as you enjoy the individual rides—most are $1.50, bumper cars cost $2.25 and $6 gets you unlimited use of the water slide. Summer hours (mid-June to mid-September) are 11 AM to 11 PM. In winter the park is open on weekends from 11 AM to 10 PM Saturday and 11 AM until 6 PM on Sunday.

Mendocino County

Pomo Visitor Center
Marine Dr., Lake Mendocino, Ukiah
• **(707) 485-8285**

The round shape of the center is modeled on the Pomo tribe's ceremonial dance house,

KIDSTUFF

where cultural knowledge was passed down through the generations. Kids will be intrigued with the games the Pomo played, will learn how clam shells were used as money and will have the chance to hold animal skins in the wild animal exhibit. The gift shop, operated by the Pomo, has a fascinating collection of items made by local Native Americans. Admission is free. The museum is open from 9 AM to 5 PM daily, June through October (see our Attractions chapter).

Mendocino Parks and Recreation Department
213 E. Laurel St., Fort Bragg
• (707) 964-9446

This county recreation program provides fun for kids the whole summer long. An indoor swimming pool is available for recreational swimming and for swim classes. Day use of the pool is $1.75 for kids, $2.75 for adults, $2.25 for seniors, and $7 for a family. A multi-use gymnasium provides a wide variety of other athletic activities including roller skating, available at $2.25 (75 cents for skates). Basketball and other athletic activities for youngsters (and adults) generally cost $1.25. Schedules vary by week and month, so it is necessary to call or drop by for activity information. A complete schedule is available by mail.

Skunk Train
Laurel St. Depot, Fort Bragg
• (707) 964-6371

The train gives a sharp whistle, there's a blast of steam, and the engine starts chugging out of the station into the forest. The "Skunk" got its name from the odor of earlier gas engines, but today the train is moved by steam (or sometimes diesel fuel). It will take you all the way to Willits, but when you're travelling with kids, a more intelligent choice might be the trip to Northspur, at the halfway mark. There you can find food treats, cold juices and soft drinks, then take the return trip on the next train. Fare for the full round trip is $35 for adults and $18 for children ages 3 to 17. The half-day trip is $27 for adults and teens, $14 for children. Reservations are recommended. (For more on the Skunk Train, see our Attractions chapter.)

Triangle Tattoo Museum
356-B N. Main St., Fort Bragg
• (707) 964-8814

Here are some amazing examples of skin art among various peoples of the world, and an

opportunity to see the tools used and learn how tattooing is done. (See our Attractions chapter for more information.) The museum is open noon to 6 PM from Sunday through Thursday, noon to 8 PM on Friday and Saturday. Admission is free, and tours are given upon request.

Lake County

McLaughlin Gold Mine Tour
26775 Morgan Valley Rd., near Lower Lake
• (707) 263-9544, (800) 525-3743

The Homestake Mining Company is done digging here in the southeastern extreme of the county, but this is where it processes the ore it takes from the surrounding area. The Lake County Marketing Program takes reservations for the tours, which depart at 10 AM on the second and fourth Friday and Saturday of each month, Memorial Day weekend through September (unless it's raining). The tour starts with a scale model of the mine, then it's into the van to drive around the processing area and up to the rim of the open pit, an 800-foot-deep pockmark that happens to rest on the spot of an extinct volcano. Homestake is still in the process of crushing and grinding some 10 million tons of rock that remain in the stockpile. The tour is free and lasts about three hours. Wear comfortable shoes and bring a bag lunch if you want to.

Outrageous Waters
Calif. Hwy. 53 & Old State Hwy. 53,
Clearlake • (707) 995-1402

The newest way to beat the heat in Lake County is to make the long slide into a pool at this water park. Next to the slides is a fun center with volleyball courts and a video arcade. Coming soon: race cars and batting cages. Outrageous Waters also has a food concession, storage lockers and a kiddie pool for those not ready to take the plunge. The park is open from noon to 7 PM daily in the summer, and on Wednesday through Sunday in the off season. Admission is $12.95 for adults, $8.95 for children shorter than 48 inches (infants 3 and under are free) and $3.95 for seniors 55 and older. ID-bearing Lake County residents get a discount, and the whole world gets one after 4:30 PM.

Lakeside County Park
Park Dr. near St. Francis Dr., Lakeport
• (707) 262-1618

Lake County's biggest neighborhood park (53 acres) has a lot to offer: three baseball diamonds, two volleyball courts, a picnic area and a playground. Of course, Clear Lake is right there, so it's possible the kids won't see dry land until it's time to leave. The park has two boat ramps as well.

Highland Springs Disc Golf Course
Highland Springs Park, Highland Springs Rd. off Calif. 29, Lakeport
• **(707) 263-2295**

Hey kids, want to play a trick on Mom and Dad? Tell them they deserve a break, and you want to treat them to nine holes of golf. Then when you get to the park, bust out a Frisbee! The golf course makes up about 15 acres of Highland Springs Park's 2,600 acres, and it is dotted with trees and other "hazards." (It even borders a lake, so watch those slices.) It's a do-it-yourself activity so be sure to bring a disc. The park is open from 6 AM to 9 PM daily.

The Book Stop, Nature & Discovery Shop
305 N. Main St., Lakeport
• **(707) 263-5787**

Lake County's most comprehensive bookstore (see our Shopping chapter) is also a haven for tykes of all ages. One of the store's five rooms is the Nature and Discovery Shop, which celebrated its grand opening last June. The bustling shop offers videos, science-oriented material, physics-based games, puppets and stuffed animals, puzzles, magnetic games, toy airplanes, posters and prints, paper dolls, children's literature and, perhaps most crucial, the larg-

est selection of Beanie Babies in Lake County. The Book Stop almost always has a few hands-on demonstrations to keep the kids from tearing up those valuable first editions.

Outside the Wine Country

Six Flags Marine World
Marine World Parkway, Vallejo, Calif.
• **(707) 643-ORCA**

Yes, it falls outside our "official" boundaries, but rare is the Wine Country parent who hasn't succumbed to the splashy fun of Marine World. Now run by the Six Flags Corporation, the park has occupied its present 160-acre spot since 1986. It's one of those places that is impossible to conquer in a day, though you can certainly try. The long bill of shows includes performances by whales and dolphins, sea lions, tigers, lions and humans on water skis. The ongoing attractions are too numerous to mention—among them are Shark Experience, Walrus Experience, Butterfly World, Elephant Encounter, the Primate Play Area and the Animal Nursery. And don't miss a recent addition: a 10-story roller coaster called Roar. One-day tickets are $34 for adults and teens, $24 for children 4 through 12 and $25 for seniors 60 or older. Two-day passes are available at significant discounts. Parking is $4 per vehicle. From Napa, go south on Calif. 29, then east on Calif. Highway 37 for just more than a mile. Days and hours of operation vary by season, so call ahead.

KIDSTUFF

Daytrippin'

LOOK FOR:
• Point Reyes
  National Seashore
• The Big Trees
• Lake Tahoe

Why anyone would care to spend a day outside of Wine Country, we can't imagine. On the other hand, we thoroughly respect your right of wanderlust. California brims with the magnificent and the quaint, and much of it lies within a few hours' drive of Napa or Santa Rosa. Sausalito is reliably pleasant. Berkeley is still funky. The gold country of the Sierra foothills is rich in history. All of them are suitable destinations, and so are the three areas outlined below.

Depending on where you start, the spots we're recommending may be considered day trips, but it's more likely you'll need to view them as overnight or weekend getaways. And don't forget to toss handfuls of baguette from your car every mile or two, so that you can be sure to find your way back to Wine Country.

Point Reyes National Seashore

Just southwest of Wine Country is a windswept triangle of coastal beauty known as Point Reyes. Walk above steep, unstable cliffs (not too close to the edge, please), look for shells on lonely beaches, roll down lofty dunes, explore tidal marshes and climb into foggy forest. You're equally likely to bump into a tule elk, a sea lion or a cow.

Dividing Point Reyes from the bulk of Marin County is the long, skinny arm of Tomales Bay—and the infamous **San Andreas Fault**, the active demarcation line between the Pacific and North American tectonic plates. Point Reyes is moving away from the rest of the mainland, heading toward Alaska at the rate of two inches a year.

To get to the park, take Petaluma-Point Reyes Road southwest from Petaluma about 20 miles. A good place to start your excursion in the 71,000-acre park is the **Bear Valley Visitor Center**, a big barn of a building just off Calif. Highway 1 near Olema. Close to the center you'll encounter **Morgan Horse Ranch**, **Kule Loklo**, and several hiking trails. Morgan Ranch is the only working horse-breeding farm in the national park system. Kule Loklo is a re-creation of a Miwok village, with traditional domed shelters. If you visit in July you might get to witness the annual Native American Celebration, during which Miwok-descended basket makers, stone carvers, singers and dancers bring the exhibit to life.

There is an abundance of things to do in Point Reyes. **Limantour Estero** is an estuary where most of the bird watchers head; **McClures Beach** has excellent tide pools; the windy **Great Beach**, one of the longest in the state, gets high marks from beachcombers; and **Drakes Beach** (which, like Drakes Bay and Drakes Estero, is named for Sir Francis Drake, the English privateer who supposedly landed here in 1579) is a Northern California rarity: a safe swimming beach. **Drakes Beach Cafe** is the only food concession in the park.

Of course, there are plenty of hiking routes, including 70 miles of trails in a big chunk of park set aside as a wilderness area. Probably foremost among attractions is **Point Reyes Lighthouse**, built about 1870 to help prevent the many shipwrecks that had plagued the treacherous, rocky shoreline for centuries. The lighthouse is accessed via a 307-step descent. It's not only an interesting structure in its own right but also one of California's best spots for whale watching. Peak season is Christmas through the end of January, when it's not uncommon to see 100 or more plumes in a day. During this busy migration period, the Park Service runs a shuttle from Drakes Beach to the lighthouse.

In the southern end of the park, near the time-warped town of Bolinas, is the **Point Reyes Bird Observatory**, the first of its kind in the country when it was founded in 1965. You couldn't select a more appropriate spot for an aviary. It is said Point Reyes has the greatest diversity of bird species in the continental United States, with some 350 species regularly showing up in the Audubon Society's annual Christmas bird count. The observatory offers classes, interpretive exhibits and a nature trail.

Even the villages are pretty here. **Point Reyes Station** and **Inverness**, in particular, have remained undisturbed by the masses of visitors. Note that the local microclimate is highly unpredictable—except at the actual point, which is the foggiest place on the West Coast. For more up-to-date information, look for a copy of *Coastal Traveler*, a free quarterly published by the *Point Reyes Light*, the area's Pulitzer Prize-winning newspaper, or call the national seashore at (415) 663-1092.

The Big Trees

You hear a lot about those redwood forests of California, but where exactly do they begin and end? You can find redwoods outside Monterey, and several Wine Country state parks are devoted to the giants (see our Parks and Recreation chapter). Santa Rosa refers to itself as capital of the Redwood Empire. But if you really want to behold the specimens that have inspired poetry and major awe (and more than a little avarice) during the last 200 years, you have to drive north into Humboldt County. There you will find the last large stands of California coast redwood.

Sequoia sempervirens covered some 2 million acres when Archibald Menzies first gave them botanical classification in 1794. The state government created several parks around individual groves in the 1920s, but by 1965 logging had reduced the redwood ecosystem to about 300,000 acres. This prompted the U.S. government to consolidate various state, federal and private holdings into **Redwood National Park** in 1968.

More land was added to the park in 1978, after bitter wrangling between environmental and pro-industry groups and deterioration of virgin growth due to upstream logging along Redwood Creek. The 110,000-acre national park is the destination of many visitors, along with three remaining state parks: **Jedediah Smith Redwoods**, **Del Norte Coast Redwoods** and **Prairie Creek Redwoods**. All four parks are adjacent and, in fact, co-managed by the National Park Service and the California Department of Parks and Recreation. The national park is a World Heritage Site, the only one on the Pacific coast of the United States. Prairie Creek, meanwhile, is home to the last herds of **Roosevelt elk** in California.

Farther south, between Garberville and Ferndale, is the famed **Avenue of the Giants**, a 33-mile stretch of roadway that parallels U.S. Highway 101 and offers up the most majestic succession of trees on the planet. The Avenue follows the Eel River and cuts through 51,000-acre **Humboldt Redwoods State Park**, the largest state park in Northern California. Along the road you'll encounter a hollow redwood (**Chimney Tree**), a redwood trunk made into a domicile (**One-Log House**) and a redwood you can bisect without leaving the car (**Shrine Drive Thru Tree**, one of the state's oldest surviving tourist attractions).

What are the groves like? It's hard to describe them without sounding as if you've been puffing Humboldt County's No. 1 cash crop. The feeling of serenity and mysticism that grips you in these misty groves cannot be duplicated. The crunchy forest bed, packed with needles, is soft and inviting, and the 10-foot ferns are colorfully primeval. The hills are carved by countless streams. The trees themselves are ancient. Their bark is resistant to fire and insects alike, so they tend to stick around awhile if they can avoid the axe.

DAYTRIPPIN'

INSIDERS' TIP

"Tahoe" is a Washoe Indian word for "lake," but the magnificent body of water on the California-Nevada border has gone by many other names since the arrival of Europeans. First it was Mountain Lake, then Lake Bonpland. And from 1852 to 1945 it was called Lake Bigler, after John Bigler, a California governor who had Confederate ties during the Civil War.

The oldest dated coast redwood is 2,200 years old. And big? Three of the six tallest trees in the world, including the grand-champion, 368-foot **Howard Libby Redwood** are in the national park. Redwood trunks can rise 100 feet before the first branch makes an appearance. Remember that the reason these trees can grow so high is the large amount of moisture they receive. The weather tends to range from damp to downpour, with an occasional crystal-clear day to keep you guessing.

All the attractions mentioned here are accessed via U.S. 101 between Garberville and Crescent City, just south of the Oregon border. From Wine Country, simply continue north on U.S. 101 through Mendocino County; Garberville is about 10 miles past the county line. Admission to the state parks is $6, which will get you into all of them. There is no charge to enter the national park. Camping and hiking options abound. For more information, call the northern parks at (707) 464-6101 or Humboldt Redwoods State Park at (707) 946-2409.

Photo: Destination Sonoma County

These mighty redwoods are in Sonoma County, but there are larger redwood forests to the north.

Lake Tahoe

Nature has lavished on **Lake Tahoe** the bluest waters, the greatest proliferation of stately pines, the most handsome mountains and the most brilliant cloud-studded skies you'll find anywhere—all that and keno, too! Mark Twain was the first travel writer to tour the Lake of the Sky. His awestruck descriptions have since been quoted by 1,000 or more equally dumbfounded travel writers who can scarcely describe the indescribable.

Photos simply don't capture this cobalt-blue beauty, nor do paintings. The colors are right, but oddly, they seem too perfect, too vivid. Tahoe lies half in California and half in Nevada (the South Shore is a two-hour drive from Sacramento, on U.S. Highway 50), which gives impetus for travel to a swarm of **weekend gamblers**. They head for our neighbor state and hope Lady Luck will smooch the slot machine they've selected; that some of the more colorful chips will pass across the green felt to their waiting wallets.

But Tahoe's best bet is the lake itself. Twelve miles wide and 22 miles long, it provides a backdrop for all the water-oriented fun one would expect from the largest alpine lake in North America (in the Western Hemisphere, only Lake Titicaca is larger). Look out across the waters, and you'll see colorful hot-air balloons rising from a barge in the middle of the lake just as the sun makes its appearance over the edge of the Sierra Nevada Mountains.

Two-masted **sailboats** cut a leisurely path across the waves, while **yachts** hurry on their way. Couples in **canoes** or orange **kayaks** paddle through the shallow waters. Anglers, waiting patiently for the trout to find them, sit in their **fishing boats**, unimpressed by the brave soul hovering above them, dangling from a rainbow-hued **parasail.**

At 99.9 percent pure—the same as distilled water—Lake Tahoe is as clean as it is beautiful. Fortunately, the Sierra Club and other environmental groups are fighting to keep it that way. All of this is available at a price, mainly from the beaches of the city of **South Lake Tahoe** or at **Kings Beach** on the north shore. In addition, the *M.S. Dixie II* takes passengers on two cruises a day—an afternoon run that crosses the lake to **Emerald Bay** (with its turquoise waters), and a morning cruise that features a big breakfast while following the shoreline. Prices are $16 for a basic cruise, $18 for a brunch cruise and $28 for a dinner cruise.

For a look at the lake as a whole, nothing beats the spectacular 72-mile perimeter drive. It will take about five hours (with scenic stops) on a good weather day. Plan to begin your drive early from any Tahoe community. In summer, pack or buy a picnic lunch for a brief sojourn in an adjacent park. In winter, include a midday pit stop at a ski area. Options exist for numerous side trips while traveling the highway that circles North America's second-deepest lake (maximum depth: 1,645 feet). If all the water were somehow released from the lake—and if water behaved very differently than it does in real life—it would cover the entire state of California to a depth of 8 inches.

Heading clockwise from South Lake Tahoe, you'll soon find yourself climbing a steep grade to a point overlooking the breathtaking vistas of **Emerald Bay State Park**. Below is the 39-room **Vikingsholm Castle**, a 19th-century mansion built by Laura Knight, who fell in love with Norway and sent craftsmen there to copy museum pieces for her home. Tours are available to those who walk the half-mile down the hill, which is the only visitor access except by boat. Vistas along the entire west shore are so stunning, you'll be hauling your Nikon out of the car every few minutes. Heading northeast, you'll pass what has essentially always been the residential zone of Tahoe. San Francisco's early social elite spent their summers here, and millionaires put up huge estates. More recently, one of them was used as a film site for *The Godfather*.

Tahoe's oldest permanent settlement is **Tahoe City**, on the northwest shores of the lake. Three shopping complexes and several condominium projects give this town a year-round population of 2,000. Near the site of the bridge over the **Truckee River** (called Fanny Bridge because of the people hanging over its floodgates), there's a wonderful collection of Indian lore at the **Gatekeeper's Museum**. Tahoe City is also the take-off point for three-hour **rafting trips** down the Truckee River, and it is a favored location for fishermen who head out to deep water with a guide in search of Mackinaw and cutthroat trout.

The lake's north shore abounds with interesting geological formations—immense boulders and tiny carnelian stones. Along the north shore you'll cross the state line into Nevada, where gambling is legal. One of its more famous casinos, the **Cal-Neva**, once belonged to Frank Sinatra. Those were the days when Hollywood luminaries filled the lobby. At the northeast corner of the lake, you'll find **Incline Village**, with its shopping center, fine art galleries, craft shops, restaurants and, for culture vultures, drama, opera, Shakespeare and mime, courtesy of the North Tahoe Fine Arts Council.

South of Incline Village lies one of Tahoe's best beaches—**Sand Harbor State Beach**, strewn with giant boulders, the refuse of Tahoe's ice age. Paths climb to the top of one of the granite outcroppings, allowing a view down into turquoise waters so clear that submerged boulders as high as a house can be seen in full detail. Facilities for picnicking and barbecuing in a wooded setting are unusually pleasant. Also on the west shore you'll find **Ponderosa Ranch**, developed at the time the TV show *Bonanza* was popular. Some consider it corny, but kids have plenty of room to run around, and anyone who used to watch the show will recognize Ben Cartwright's office and accouterments.

Most of Tahoe's east shore is privately owned, but there is a small area (recognizable by a proliferation of parked cars) where sun worshippers thread their way down a footpath through the forest and spread out nude on the massive rocks to achieve that all-over tan. **Zephyr Cove**, meanwhile, is where you set sail on the *M.S. Dixie*. It's near the state line.

INSIDERS' TIP

The coast redwood is the tallest tree in the world, but is it the largest living thing? No. Scientists now believe that a 106-acre stand of aspens in Utah is actually 47,000 trees connected by one root system. In fact, the redwood is not even the biggest individual tree. Its close cousin, the giant sequoia, is not quite as tall, but is more massive because of its thick, dense trunk.

DAYTRIPPIN'

Emerald Bay is a popular destination for boaters on Lake Tahoe.

And there are other options for side trips. At Incline Village, for example, there's a junction with Nev. Hwy. 27 that will take you to **Reno** or to **Virginia City**, a lively ghost town recalling days when silver taken from its mines built San Francisco and made millionaires whose names are still familiar. Its wooden plank streets and weathered buildings are surprisingly authentic, though the usual tourist shops line the street as well. (Look to the buildings' upper stories for a true feeling of the Old West.) Reno, famous as the "biggest little city in the world," is rife with sleek, splashy gambling casinos. The city has achieved a modest fame among nearby California cities for its inexpensive hotel rooms. Recently it has also become home to the National Bowling Association, which is quartered in a massive complex of bowling lanes and offices.

In winter, some of the best skiing in the world takes place at South Lake Tahoe—specifically at **Heavenly Valley**. If you're not on hand during the winter months, take advantage of the tram anyway; ride to the top of the mountain and take a stroll along the path that rides the rim. A park ranger is on hand to lead the way.

DAYTRIPPIN'

Real Estate

LOOK FOR:
• **Napa County**
• **Sonoma County**
• **Mendocino County**
• **Lake County**

What is the real estate market like in the Wine Country? That's like asking: What is the wine like? Some of it's good, some not so good. There are bargains and rip-offs, exclusive clusters and little-known treats. And in most cases, it's all a matter of taste.

The point is that the real estate business is complicated enough within a single city. When you're talking about a huge, four-county area like ours, the subject rejects any sort of blanket statement. Therefore, we offer separate introductions for each county, followed by listings of real estate companies and publications.

Our goal with this chapter is to give you a basic, working idea of the market in each area of our four-county coverage region. Thus, we'll quote some average prices and provide some broad descriptions. Take this information as a starting point on your real estate search, but be sure to rely on your real estate agent for the most up-to-date prices and details.

If you are not from California, you should know some things about Golden State property transactions before you go hunting for domiciles. First of all, things are complicated here. The standard real estate purchase contract runs eight tightly packed pages, and the buyers and sellers don't normally get together to sign papers in one sitting as they do in some parts of the country. Also, California is very strict about disclosures—an obvious boon for buyers and a cautionary note for sellers.

Napa County

Napa Valley is a long, flat plain. But if you plot real estate prices along the floor of the valley, it looks more like a tilted hill. In fact, it looks not unlike the ol' Prudential rock. The bargain prices are in American Canyon, just south of Napa. There are many good deals within the Napa city limits too, though the town has its tony neighborhoods. And as you head north on Calif. Highway 29, you can practically hear the meter running on home costs. Yountville is more expensive than Napa, the Oakville-Rutherford area is more expensive than Yountville and St. Helena is the most expensive town in the valley. The price tags drop again in Calistoga, down to about the Yountville level.

Along the way, you will find every sort of residence imaginable: new tract homes, flourishing Victorians, modest 1940s bungalows, mountaintop castles and prefab structures. (In places like Calistoga, you'll see them all side-by-side.) And if you are visiting from outside California, you probably will consider everything overpriced. Make no mistake about it, you do pay for quality of life here. If you fall in love with the Wine Country's postcard scenery, robust lifestyle and small-town sense of community, you won't be the first. More and more people want to relocate here, retire here or commute from here (to the Bay Area), yet the supply of homes is tightly limited.

The whole of Napa County is a designated agricultural preserve, a decision ratified by the county Board of Supervisors in 1968. The California Chapter of the American Planning Association has called the move revolutionary. The designation put development decisions in the hands of the board and set a 20-acre minimum for any new subdivision of land—a dimension that later increased to 40 acres, and more recently to 160.

The voters took the plan a step further with Measure J in 1990, giving themselves the power to vote down any exceptions to the rule regarding minimum subdivision acreage. In effect, there is a virtual moratorium on subdivision within the county. Around Napa, for example, the only new development is in North Napa and the Big Ranch Road area. The Napa Yacht Club offered growth space for many years, but it is just about sold out. It's a frustrating situation for developers, but most residents are pleased with the valley's farsightedness. The Ag Preserve designation protects the vineyards and keeps the scenery uncluttered, and those are the twin engines that drive Napa's megadollar tourist economy.

Despite limited availability caused by building restrictions, the Napa County real estate market was relatively stagnant until a couple of years ago. Many houses sat on the market for months, and it was not uncommon for list prices to drop by 20 percent. Now the Napa County Association of Realtors notes a strong upswing. Sellers are compromising less and receiving multiple offers, occasionally allowing them to sell for more than the original asking price. None of this is good news for buyers, of course.

Before getting into specific areas, we can make a couple of generalizations for the valley. First, a dictum that applies here and just about everywhere else in the world: Property value tends to be directly related to elevation. In other words, the rich folks live on the hilltops. It must have something to do with the days when people disposed of their garbage by throwing it out the window. Second, the really ritzy places tend to be large holdings in the country.

In Napa, most of the Victorian splendor is in Old Town—the letter streets south of Lincoln Avenue between California Boulevard and Jefferson Street—and the Napa Abajo/Fuller Park area. Fuller Park, in fact, is a Historical Preservation District. As such, it is eligible to receive economic incentives from the city for refurbishment, and this is certain to raise property values. The boundaries of the preservation district are ragged, but you can more or less think of it as bordered by Jefferson, Third, Brown and Pine streets.

Another desirable locale, and much more expensive, is Silverado Country Club, where the massive homes (2,000 to 5,000 square feet) go for $380,000 to $950,000. Silverado condominiums fetch an average of nearly $350,000. All of that said, most of the action in Napa is taking place north of town and in Browns Valley, a west-side neighborhood. These are bedroom communities that people see as good values. A new three-bedroom, two-bath home in north Napa, probably just smaller than 1,500 square feet, will go for $200,000 or more.

St. Helena is the town that best typifies the Wine Country dream: charming, early-century stone-front buildings, modest scale, vineyard views and well-kept flower gardens. Accordingly, the prices tend to be sky high here, especially on the west side of town. Calistoga offers more of a mixed bag, but it does have some wonderfully restored old houses, especially on Cedar and Myrtle streets just northwest of Lincoln. Again, you must remember that country estates are considered the true gems, especially if they have significant acreage.

Here are average prices for homes (condos included) sold in various Napa County towns in the first six months of 1999: Yountville, $303,000; St. Helena, $400,000; Calistoga, $324,000. Figures were unavailable for Angwin, but local Realtors suggest a range that is just below St. Helena's, with many properties offering income units (rented to Pacific Union College students). Valley vineyards have been more than viable lately, and working grape land costs anywhere from $50,000 to $100,000 an acre.

Rentals

There are a lot of rentals to choose from in Napa—apartments, duplex bungalows, split-up Victorians, condominiums, the works—but slim pickings elsewhere in the county. A two-bedroom apartment in Napa should cost $600 to $900 per month, while a three-bedroom house is more like $1,100 to $1,300. North of Napa there aren't many apartments you would consider exclusive or chic. Prospective renters often must choose between houses and small, undistinguished apartments. The former include some attrac-

INSIDERS' TIP

Many houses in Calistoga advertise hot-water wells. They're great for backyard Jacuzzis, but experienced residents tend not to use them for interior plumbing. The sulfuric mineral water is very corrosive.

tive properties, but they don't come cheap. A two-bedroom, one-bath rental in Calistoga might cost $900, while a one-bedroom apartment lists for $600.

Property Rentals Only Inc.
2005 Delpha Dr., Napa • (707) 252-6147

You can usually find 25 to 50 rental listings posted outside the Property Rentals Only office. If anything piques your interest, the company will hand you an application; you can then take your stack of paperwork, drive by selected properties and mark those that you feel may be appropriate. The majority of PRO's buildings are in Napa, but they handle Yountville, St. Helena and Calistoga too. All they charge is a $20 fee for a credit check. If you're in a rush, file this hotline number: (707) 252-0749.

Real Estate Companies

Prudential California Realty
2015 Redwood Rd., Napa • 259-4900

Prudential has been in Napa Valley for more than 10 years, and broker Ed Wickman now oversees this redefined office. (His wife, Sally, manages the place.) With more than 20 Realtors, Prudential California covers all of Napa County and all sorts of property. It also has a full-time commercial department, not to mention three outposts in neighboring Solano County.

Century 21 Alpha Realty
1290 Jefferson St., Napa • (707) 255-8711

With 15 Realtors working the county, Century 21 has been one of the valley's premier offices since the early 1970s. Helen Johnson's crew focuses primarily on residential property, but also ventures into commercial space, acreage and investment property. More services in the Century 21 portfolio: property management and real estate license training.

Coldwell Banker
1775 Lincoln Ave., Napa • (707) 258-5200
1239 Main St., St. Helena • (707) 963-1152
6505 Washington St., Yountville
• (707) 944-0421

This is the county's biggest real estate office based on several parameters, not the least of which is its 69 Realtors (56 in the Napa office alone). The company covers the entire county and all variety of property, though it is particularly strong in the realms of vineyard

and residential holdings. The latter extends to houses, condos, mobile homes, farms and ranches. (The St. Helena office is known for properties valued at $500,000 or more.) Coldwell Banker also has the advantage of "preview" listings: expensive pieces that are advertised nationally or even internationally.

Continental Real Estate
743 First St., Napa • (707) 257-1177

Shane (one name suffices, á la Cher) is the sole proprietor of this business, and she's a busy gal. She made more than 60 sales totaling in excess of $12 million in 1998, making her the most productive Realtor in the county, according to independent research. Do-it-all Continental covers the whole valley but concentrates on Napa city. Shane also offers notary, appraisal and consulting services.

RE/MAX Napa Valley
780 Trancas St., Napa • (707) 255-0845

There is plenty of experience at work here. RE/MAX has 28 agents, with a grand total of more than 400 years of combined experience, working the length of the valley. They handle various residential and commercial properties, including large developments and subdivisions. Still, they stress that no job is too small.

Silverado Realty
1561 Third St., Ste. B, Napa
• (707) 252-4755

Silverado does country, residential and income property in Napa, including Silverado Country Club. The country club alone has plenty of houses and condos from which to choose. The office started in 1970 and has two Realtors.

Morgan Lane
1932 Sierra Ave., Napa • 252-2177
6795 Washington St., Yountville
• (707) 944-8500
1346 Main St., St. Helena • (707) 963-5226

This company doesn't want to exclude anyone, but it is clearly known for its high-end listings of vineyard acreage and estate homes. (If you want a serious case of house envy, gaze at their property board.) Morgan Lane has 33 Realtors in Yountville, St. Helena and Sonoma, covering all of Napa and Sonoma valleys. The company also is an official affiliate of Sotheby's, and as such has access to high rollers from San Francisco to Singapore and readers of publications such as *The New York Times* and *The Wall Street Journal*.

Santa Rosa's Chamber Plaza provides visitors and locals with information about the business community.

Arroyo Real Estate
1540 Railroad Ave., St. Helena
• (707) 963-1342

This is a small company that goes for luxury. Arroyo's three Realtors are long-time residents of Napa Valley. The firm's realm stretches from Yountville to the north end of the county, and the listings are exclusive—fine country homes, vineyard estates and similarly desirable acreage.

Frank Howard Allen
1316 Main St., St. Helena • (707) 963-5266

One of Sonoma's most respected real estate offices moved into Napa Valley in 1998. They'll help you locate your dream home in either county. The St. Helena site has five Realtors, including a woman who once was mayor of the town (plus her son and daughter-in-law). Frank Howard Allen handles a mix of residential, vineyard and undeveloped land.

Up Valley Associates
1126 Adams St., St. Helena
• (707) 963-1222

Up Valley has four brokers and two agents who cover the entire county, though they focus on, well, the name tells the story. The company does a little bit of everything. Most of the Realtors have been with the office since it adopted its name in 1979. As one of them said, "We're all really old." In other words, they can offer you a wealth of helpful experience.

California Properties
13 Angwin Plaza, Angwin
• (707) 965-2485

Connections? What can you say about a company whose lineup includes the former proprietor of historic Alta Vineyards and the director of the St. Helena Hospital Men's Chorus? California Properties, which started in St. Helena in 1983, has four Realtors who serve most of Napa County. They stick primarily to residential property but also handle a few vineyard sales.

Beck & Taylor
1406 Lincoln Ave., Calistoga
• (707) 942-5500

Robert Beck's small shop is a general brokerage, but it has some specialties that set it apart in Calistoga. Beck & Taylor handles substantial property management and commercial space. In addition, one of its Realtors concentrates on the sale and purchase of bed and breakfast inns around Northern California. The company generally covers the entire Napa Valley.

Calistoga Realty Co.
1473-C Lincoln Ave., Calistoga
• (707) 942-9422

This is Calistoga's largest real estate company, with four licensed Realtors and an office manager. They handle Napa Valley down to Yountville plus Knights Valley and a few other corners of Sonoma County. Calistoga Realty carries more listings than anyone in the immediate area, primarily residential and small land parcels.

Real Estate Publications

Wine Country Weekly Real Estate Reader
1921 Jefferson St., Napa • (707) 258-6150

This is far more than a series of property listings. The *Reader's* editorial format offers a comprehensive look at the four-county real estate market, highlighted by San Francisco attorney Alan Seher's regular column on new tax laws. The paper is distributed throughout the Wine Country, not to mention real estate offices, BART stations (rapid transit outposts) and supermarkets in 10 Bay Area counties. Every week it focuses on a particular area and analyzes how recent home sales there compare to the previous year. It also lists every open house in the Wine Country and includes 10 pages of classified ads. The *Reader's* sharpest focus is on estate vineyards, wineries and farm and ranch property.

Distinctive Properties of Napa Valley
P.O. Box 2849, Yountville
• (707) 257-0803

When it comes to depth of listings, *Distinctive Properties* is the bible of Napa Valley. Make that the bibles: There are two versions of the publication. One is a monthly printed in black and white (inside, anyway) on newspaper stock. The monthly lists 500 to 600 different properties from the southern to northern tip of the valley, with a handy price index on page 6. The other edition is a slick, color quarterly that focuses on estates, vineyards and executive homes that go for $300,000 or more. Both publications are free, distributed throughout Napa and Sonoma valleys and around the Bay Area. David Barker has published *Distinctive Properties* since 1987.

The Real Estate Book of Napa County
4086 Byway E., Napa • (707) 253-1284

This is a small, free booklet that has been publicizing a wide range of Napa and Lake county properties for about six years. *The Real Estate Book* is distributed mainly in those two counties, and to a lesser extent in Sonoma, Solano and Marin counties. Each issue includes listings from anywhere between 30 and 75 different real estate companies.

Sonoma County

Sonoma County has a lot going for it. The proximity of the ocean gives it moderate summers and winters. Its mountains are low and pleasantly rolling; its valleys are laced with neat rows of vines. In springtime, wild mustard turns the vineyard floors yellow, while the hills shine green. It's a dreamer's paradise. But paradise is not inexpensive, and real estate prices are likely to be higher in Sonoma County than in most of the rest of the nation. For anyone contemplating the purchase of a home in Sonoma County, it's valuable to understand the forces dictating prices. To start with, a good deal of migration is from San Francisco Bay Area cities. Living in harried city conditions, folks think of how nice it would be to have a life in the country that remains close to the amenities of city living. For these people, the maxim is "the closer the better," and this makes the southern part of Sonoma County extremely appealing, just 45 minutes from the Golden Gate. This doesn't necessarily pigeonhole the cities as "bedroom communities" (though there is a good deal of commuting). It's more a matter of reaching out for the best of two worlds.

Because of this geographical desirability, Petaluma, the city of Sonoma and Sonoma Valley, in particular, are affected by their position. Median real estate prices in these two towns are likely to be in the $260,000 neighborhood, higher than in towns farther north on the U.S. Highway 101 corridor. Another factor has affected home prices in Petaluma. A surge of rapid growth took place when industries based in adjacent Marin County (which has the highest cost of living in Northern California) found many employees lived in lower-cost Petaluma. Following the lead of those economy-minded workers, the industries themselves began moving to Petaluma.

The resulting population growth has had its effect on home prices, but affordability is not a lost commodity in the cities of Petaluma and Santa Rosa. A new wave of savvy builders has closed the gap of affordability with cleverly designed condominiums that manage to give the feel of luxury and space while maintaining a price tag in the $200,000 range. New homes are going up adjacent to cities in unincorporated county lands, where taxes are lower. Sonoma County's only sizable city is Santa Rosa, with a population of 125,700. Here, as in most cities, home seekers will find sections of high-priced, handsome Victorian homes, a score of new modern housing developments (some still in progress) and a scattering of more affordable homes as low as $125,000. In general, median prices in the northwest sector of Santa Rosa are about $175,000; in the southeast, $200,000; in the southwest, $145,000; and $235,000 in the northeast.

In towns to the north on the U.S. 101 corridor, magnificent homes of vineyard owners dot the hillsides in a sort of baronial splendor, and in forested villages just above Sonoma there are pockets of luxurious homes where millionaires live. But in the main, real estate prices are lower than in the southern part of the county. An interesting real estate situation exists in the town of Windsor. Until the late '80s, it was a sleepy village, not going much of anywhere until it was "discovered" by housing developers. They just kept building and building. As a result, almost everything in the town is of recent origin. Now incorporated, this is the fastest growing city in Sonoma County. Median home prices in Windsor are about $212,000.

The small city of Sebastopol on the edge of Apple Country is, in a way, an anomaly in the county—an area where many homes are set on large acreage. People who live here like the idea of country living with amenities such as extra guest houses and plenty of room for dogs to run and horses to graze. Because of the super-large lot sizes, Sebastopol has among the highest housing costs in the county. Estate-size lots, rambling homes and mini-ranches will often push or top the $1 million mark. Own a horse and hope to emulate a country gentry member? You're talking anywhere from $600,000 to $8 million.

There is little residential property along the Sonoma Coast, except in small villages or sprawling developments such as Sea Ranch, where people build second homes and may later turn them into primary residences. Sea Ranch building sites range from a quarter-acre to 3 or more acres. They are in the range of $80,000 to $200,000 in the meadow, with oceanfront lots going for as high as $600,000. For people who love the ocean, life along the Sonoma Coast is indeed soul-satisfying. Fortunately, it can also be rented. (See Rentals, below.)

One thing is certain: Wherever you choose to settle down in Sonoma County, there is no dearth of well-qualified Realtors and brokers to clear a path for you. The firms we have selected to highlight for this guide are among the best. But there are 100 or more other excellent agents and brokers who are familiar with their territory. The publications listed will help you find one that suits you.

Before we get into our listings of the listers—the specific real estate companies—we remind you that local chambers of commerce are also helpful clearinghouses of information. Often, you can get more specifics about locations and individual agencies through them. The Sonoma Valley Chamber of Commerce is at 645 Broadway, Sonoma. Call (707) 996-1033 for assistance. Also, the North Coast Builders Exchange in Santa Rosa, (707) 542-9502, can help with information for individuals hiring contractors or building custom homes.

Rentals

Average rental price in 1998 for apartments and duplexes in Sonoma County was $550 to $850. Average rental for two- to three-bedroom homes was $900 to $1,600. To a great extent, this variation has to do with location. Small villages, Cloverdale for example, offer rentals as low as $550, but they are often far from sources for employment. In Santa Rosa, where good jobs can be found, a recent-vintage, three-bedroom house will rent at $1,300 minimum, while a two-bedroom, undistinguished house in the older section of town rents at $800. In the city of Sonoma, the favorable climate and pleasant ambiance have attracted retired folks from city life. They come with their retirement funds and live in homes that cost upwards of $300,000. The rental picture reflects those real estate values. One solution is to live in the unincorporated community at the edge of the city. This is an older section—houses tend to be modest, though many have been remodeled into very pleasant cottages that rent for $750 or more.

Sonoma Management
662 Broadway, Sonoma • (707) 938-3177

Robert and Sylvia Bernard have operated this full-service rental agency since 1982, serving those moving to Sonoma from all walks of life. The office is in a historical home built more than 100 years ago. The Bernards provide listings throughout Sonoma Valley with no fee charged to the renter-client.

The Rental Connection
1220 Fourth St., Santa Rosa
• (707) 575-9652

Owner Cathy J. Romero provides a rental listing service that covers all of Sonoma County. Prospective renters pay a $50 service fee that gives them one month of access to a comprehensive list of rental properties tailored to their needs. The listings divide the county into 17 areas to offer comprehensive coverage in a convenient format.

West County Property Management
6380 Vine Hill School Rd., Sebastopol
• (707) 823-5700

Jim and Lynn Eis provide long-term rental services at no cost to the client. Rentals range from an average of $550 to $1,500 per month and are normally on a month-to-month basis with security deposits.

D&G Property Management
14080 Mill St., Guerneville
• (707) 869-0623

This firm offers permanent rentals in western Sonoma County. Studio apartments start at $500. You can expect to pay $750 for a two-bedroom, one-bath unit, but a four-bedroom home might go as high as $1,400. Although much of D&G's clientele is looking for residential property, the company also offers business and commercial sites.

Vacation Rentals

If you are interested in a short-term rental for a va-

cation stay, Sonoma County has agencies that can help. **Russian River Vacation Homes, Russian River Getaways, Sea Coast Hide-a-Ways,** and **Rams Head Realty** all offer vacation rentals. See our Hotels and Motels chapter for more details on these and other Wine Country agencies specializing in vacation homes.

Real Estate Companies

The Prudential California Realty
13716 Arnold Dr., Glen Ellen
• (707) 939-2030
456 S., E St., Santa Rosa • (707) 524-6111
7300 Healdsburg Ave., Sebastopol
• (707) 829-2011
6601 Commerce Blvd., Rohnert Park
• (707) 584-7500

An award-winning team of seasoned pros covers everything from mobile homes to ranches and wineries in Sonoma County. Additional offices serve Northern California, but the Prudential is hooked into a network that is not just national but worldwide. Comprehensive relocation services can help you make the transition wherever you come from.

Frank Howard Allen Realtors
462 W. Napa, Sonoma • (707) 939-2000
9200 Sonoma Hwy., Kenwood
• (707) 833-2881
905 E. Washington, Petaluma
• (707) 762-7766
2245 Montgomery Dr., Santa Rosa
• (707) 523-3000
16203-A First St., Guerneville
• (707) 869-3865

Frank Howard Allen Realtors has 11 corporate-owned offices and three independently owned firms operating as licensees. They handle all types of real estate, including residential, commercial, vacation and business properties. In Napa and Sonoma counties, they specialize in wineries and vineyards. The Sonoma offices boast about one-third of the company's nearly $1 billion in total annual sales. In business more than 85 years, this is one of the Bay Area's largest independent, locally owned and operated real estate firms. Special relocation services can

REAL ESTATE

be arranged and coordinated from Frank Howard Allen's administrative offices in Novato.

Coldwell Banker
800 Broadway, Sonoma • (707) 996-3232
333 S. McDowell Blvd., Petaluma
• (707) 762-6611
50 Enterprise Dr., Rohnert Park
• (707) 524-8500
790 Sonoma Ave., Santa Rosa
• (707) 527-5600
412 Healdsburg Ave., Healdsburg
• (707) 433-1497
555 Calif. Hwy. 1, Bodega Bay
• (707) 875-2200

Claiming to be the nation's largest full-service real estate company, Coldwell Banker in Sonoma County handles all types of properties including homes, ranches, mobile homes, and land and investment property. A free national relocation service is offered, and a buyer-seller coupon booklet gives discounts at Sears on home improvement items. Ask for their *Best Buyer Guidebook* to help find and finance your dream home. All Coldwell Banker offices are independently owned and operated.

RE/MAX
369 W. Napa St., Sonoma
• (707) 935-3450
775 Baywood Dr., Suite 100, Petaluma •
(707) 769-1400
5550 State Farm Dr.,
Rohnert Park • (707) 588-5888
320 College Ave., Santa Rosa
• (707) 524-3500

With 30 associates in the four offices listed, RE/MAX has experts in transactions involving dwellings, business property, commercial developments and agricultural real estate. Each RE/MAX office is independently owned and operated, assuring the dedicated service of personnel with local knowledge about the areas they cover. These offices specialize in southern Sonoma County properties.

Century 21
561 Broadway, Sonoma • (707) 938-5830
616 Petaluma Blvd. S., Petaluma
• (707) 762-2787
1057 College Ave., Santa Rosa
• (707) 544-9656
107 North St., Healdsburg
• (707) 433-4404
114 Lake St., Cloverdale • (707) 894-5232

If you're attracted to a name you've seen elsewhere, Century 21 has a presence on the real estate scene that's recognized nationwide for its reliability and attention to clients. With offices covering strategic points in Sonoma County, Century 21 specialists offer knowledge of local residential markets. They try to tune into individual needs in a real estate area that is unusually diverse.

Griewe Real Estate
141 E. Napa St., Sonoma • (707) 938-0916

This independently owned firm started business in 1990 under the ownership of Jim and Linda Griewe and serves all of Sonoma Valley. With three additional full-time professional associates, Griewe Real Estate is intimately familiar with the area and has a reputation for excellence and integrity. Griewe sale signs hang in front of many homes in the Sonoma Valley, but they also deal in vineyard properties. Services include multiple-listing service, computer search programs and relocation services.

Morgan Lane
500 Broadway, Sonoma • (707) 935-5777

With 10 agents throughout Sonoma County, Morgan Lane covers properties throughout Wine Country, as far north as Boonville in Mendocino County. (See previous listing under Napa County Real Estate Companies.)

Coralee Barkela & Company
9212 Sonoma Hwy., Kenwood
• (707) 833-6700

Coralee Barkela has been a top real estate professional in Sonoma County since the early 1970s, and in 1997 she opened her own office. With the help of five agents, this company covers all of Sonoma County.

Highly knowledgeable about grape culture and wine making, she concentrates heavily on ranches and vineyards as well as high-quality residential properties.

Pacific Union Residential Brokerage
640 Broadway, Sonoma
• (707) 939-9500

Originally a Bay Area company specializing in commercial and estate-type property sales, Pacific Union now serves residential clients throughout the Sonoma Valley. The agents are all highly seasoned professionals, most of them brokers in their own right, with an average of 12 years of experience. Relocation services are offered.

Broadway Realty
654 Broadway, Sonoma • (707) 996-1072

Robert and Sylvia Bernard, longtime owners of Sonoma Management (see previous listing in Rentals), expanded to join 35-year veterans Mori & Perkins Real Estate and form a company that encompasses both enterprises. This is a real family business—Bill Mori is Sylvia's uncle, and the property where the Broadway offices are located has been in the family since Sylvia's grandfather bought it 60 years ago. These are people who know Sonoma very well, with some 50 years of experience all told, and they serve a diverse clientele throughout the Sonoma Valley. They are capable of selling everything from residences to vineyard acreage in an area they know thoroughly.

Mid-Towne Realty, Inc.
709 Healdsburg Ave., Healdsburg
• (707) 433-6555

This local, professional and independent firm has been in business for more than 30 years. In addition to serving clientele in the Healdsburg community, the office also handles Russian River properties, both for sales and rentals. Relocation services are provided to purchasers from other areas.

North County Properties
21069 Geyserville Ave., Geyserville
• (707) 857-1728

Karen and Doug Waelde, a husband and wife team, have been in the real estate business for 17 years in Healdsburg and (for the last four years) in Geyserville, a favorable location between two beautiful wine appellations—Dry Creek Valley and Alexander Valley. They cover the area between Santa Rosa and Cloverdale, including the town of Windsor. It's a piece of countryside they know as well as they know their own back yard. The Waeldes are there to negotiate purchase and sale of residential property, vacation property (second homes), farms, ranches, mini-ranches (from 2 to 200 acres) and vineyards, and they are particularly pleased to offer expertise to first-time buyers.

Sea Ranch Realty
Sea Ranch Lodge, Sea Ranch
• (707) 785-2494, (800) SEA RANCH

Sea Ranch is a private community that extends 10 miles along the Sonoma Coast. Sea Ranch Realty provides information on existing home sales or building opportunities. Offices are right on site at the lodge, and the company offers homes on ocean bluffs or grassy meadows.

Real Estate Publications

For more information about the Sonoma County real estate market, check the real estate section in the Friday edition of *The Sonoma Index-Tribune*, or the *Santa Rosa Press-Democrat's* Sunday real estate section. You can also pick up the following free publications at area grocery stores, drug stores or newspaper racks.

Distinctive Properties

Sponsored by the participating real estate firms that advertise, this publication comes out every other month in black-and-white, with a color version published quarterly. It covers only Sonoma and Napa counties. Distribution is primarily in supermarkets, but locations that display free literature are also used as outlets. Range of properties included varies from mobile homes to million-dollar estates.

The Press Democrat Real Estate Network—The Redwood Empire's Guide to Homes and Property

This publication, issued every other month, covers all counties of Wine Country. Primarily black-and-white, with a few color photos, it presents advertising by individual real estate firms. Distribution is free at magazine racks at supermarkets, drug stores and individual real estate offices. Primarily, properties are listed by individual real estate firms, but the magazine additionally provides maps and graphs and an indexed location guide. Residential property listings range from $95,000 fixer-uppers to $2.5 million spreads.

The Prudential California Realty: A Presentation of Wine Country Properties

This colorful quarterly presentation covers Sonoma Valley and the four Prudential California Realty offices. In addition to availability at Prudential offices, the magazine-format publication can be found at wineries, supermarkets and drug store racks. All types of property, including commercial, are covered in a wide price range. One issue, for example, listed a French-Norman country estate, along with a listing for low-cost condominium units priced at $125,000.

Real Estate in the Wine Country

This glossy real estate magazine, published weekly, colorfully and effectively presents properties in all four counties of Wine Country. It's available at supermarkets, drug stores and any available public-literature distribution point. Individual real estate firms advertise in the publication and present a full range of properties from mobile homes and residential ranches to acreage and vineyards. Residential properties range from fixer-uppers starting in the low $100,000 category to estates costing $850,000 and up.

Mendocino County

The rugged Mendocino coast stretches 120 miles along the Pacific from its southern point at Gualala to the King Mountain range on the north. Each of the small towns and hamlets that dot the coastline has its own unique identity and charm. And each has a different set of real estate values.

In general, if you long for a view of the sea, it will cost you. But what it costs depends on where you want to settle in. Fort Bragg with a population of about 6,000, is basically a lumbering and fishing community, though tourism is becoming a factor. Most of Fort Bragg's homes are long-established, but there is some new construction going on. A new housing development is slowly making an appearance, with the builder preferring to work on contract, one home at a time. Average price of single-family dwellings in the area is $200,000, though ocean views can go as high as $450,000.

Eight miles south in tiny Mendocino (population 1,200), the cost of housing rises steeply. A two-bedroom home in the village, without a view of the water, will likely be priced at $325,000. Add an ocean view, and the price would rise to $500,000 on average—these addresses top out in the millions.

In the inland valleys, a few modest-sized towns and hamlets cling to U.S. 101—Hopland, Ukiah, Willits. The landscape is agricultural, and it is prime grape-growing territory. Nestled in the valley below the spectacular coastal range is Ukiah, county seat and Mendocino's largest city (population 15,000). It's a blend of businesses, recreational opportunities, affordable housing, verdant vineyards and orchards, and untamed wilderness. The city's west side includes hundreds of historic homes and buildings shaded by a lush canopy of mature trees. Norman Crampton's *100 Best Small Towns* in 1993 named Ukiah the No. 1 small town in California.

Overall, housing in the Ukiah area presents the best of two worlds. In town one is close to everything—quiet, family-oriented neighborhoods are the city's primary feature. Just minutes from the city limits is the Yokayo Valley countryside. Dotted with orchards and vineyards, rolling green hills and stands of oak and redwood, one can get away from it all and still be a quick 10-minute drive from the town's amenities. Average price for a three-bedroom home is $150,000, average home rental runs $900 a month and apartments rent for $500 on average.

The town of Willits, 25 miles north of Ukiah, is at a latitude where motorists will notice a change in topography and vegetation. The scrub oaks characteristic of the southern part of the county begin a gradual change to the thick redwood forests that stretch to the Oregon border, and the coastal range between Willits and the ocean is densely wooded. Through these deep and mountainous forests pioneer railroad men carved out a path for the California Western Railroad in 1885. Today that railroad, known as the "Skunk," is still carrying freight and has become a popular attraction for passengers and rail buffs (see our Attractions chapter). Known mainly as a railroad hub and lumber community, Willits offers modest home prices, running from $85,000 to $200,000 for a three-bedroom home.

You'll find other information about the Mendocino market in the real estate pages of the *Fort Bragg Advocate-News*. Chambers of commerce often prove to be valuable resources as well. The Greater Ukiah Chamber of Commerce is at 200 S. School Street. Call (707) 462-4705 for assistance.

Rentals

Frontier Realty Property Management
218 S. Humboldt St., Willits
• **(707) 459-1525**

The oldest property management firm in Willits, Frontier has been in business since 1977. They serve Willits and Mendocino County only.

Vacation Rentals

If your stay will be short and oriented toward fun, or if you want a change of pace, you may want to rent a vacation home. **Pacific Resorts Realty** and **Mendocino Coast Reservations** offer vacation rentals. Details about these and other vacation rental agencies in Wine Country can be found in our Hotels and Motels chapter.

Real Estate Companies

Wally Johnson Realty
3800 Eastside Calpella Rd., Ukiah
- **(707) 485-8700**

Realtor Wally Johnson has served the Ukiah area since 1990, dealing in homes, income property, lots and land sales as well as quality manufactured homes. He is a member of the Mendocino County Board of Realtors.

E.S. Wolf & Company
514 South School St., Ukiah • (707) 463-2719

This broker deals entirely in large properties—ranch lands, vineyards and large estates. It is also the exclusive Mendocino representative for Sotheby's International Realty, handling the local end of that firm's national and international dealings.

Pacific Properties
36 South St., Willits
- **(707) 459-6175**

This is the largest independently owned and operated real estate office in Willits, with six agents specializing in residential and county properties. They also represent Brooktrails, a housing development where the price of homes runs from $105,000 to $200,00.

Mendo Realty
690 S. Main St., Fort Bragg
- **(707) 964-5302**
1061 Main St., Mendocino
- **(707) 937-5822**

The Mendocino coast's oldest real estate firm, Mendo Realty covers the coast from Gualala to Westport. Most of their representatives have a lengthy tenure at this location. With such, they have accumulated firsthand knowledge of area history and trends in residential properties as well as commercial, business, ranch and timber acreage.

These lucky residents have a wonderful view of both the Russian River and the Pacific Ocean.

Sea Cottage Real Estate
45120 Main St., Mendocino
- **(707) 937-0423, (800) 707-0423**

The first certified residential specialist on the Mendocino coast, this firm has been in business since 1979. With six agents, Sea Cottage covers the entire Mendocino coast.

Lake County

Mount St. Helena is only 4,300 feet high, but when it comes to the real estate landscape, it might as well be Everest. The southern slopes of the mountain fall away to Napa Valley and its $200,000 average home. The northern slopes level off into Lake County, where bargains abound.

Lake and Napa counties are roughly the same size, yet Lake's population is only about 50,000—smaller than the city of Napa. It is a truly rural environment—ranchland sprinkled

REAL ESTATE

with pickup trucks, Kountry Kafes and the occasional double-wide trailer. Lake's relative isolation has kept housing prices cheap, and the urban nomads are starting to trickle in. In fact, this is the fastest-growing county north of the Golden Gate, at least on a percentage basis. And while the real estate markets of Napa and Sonoma are just beginning to see brighter days, Lake County has seen steady turnover for several years.

There is very little here in the way of subdivided development. About the only major subdivision is the gated community of Hidden Valley Lake, and it has room to nearly double its current configuration. Middletown, the community closest to Napa Valley, is in high demand. It's already getting hard to find anything between Middletown and the county line. And like just about anywhere else in the Wine Country, it is the country estates that fetch the highest selling prices.

A typical three-bedroom, two-bath house, say 1,300 to 1,500 square feet, might cost $100,000 to $120,000 on Cobb Mountain but only $70,000 to $80,000 (do not adjust your dial) in Clearlake. The same house could cost $105,000 to $110,000 if it sat next to Hidden Valley Lake, or $120,000 to $200,000 if it rested on a few acres in the country. And here are some average home sale prices around Clear Lake in the first half of 1998, to give you an idea of the market: Lakeport, $97,000; Kelseyville, $105,000; The Rivieras (overlooking Soda Bay), $98,000; Lucerne and Nice, $80,000. Land prices vary wildly. A bid of $60,000 could get you two acres or 20, depending on views and grape-growing potential.

Rentals

Demand for rentals exceeds supply in Lake County, as there are very few apartments outside of senior or low-income housing. It is getting more expensive to rent a house, but rates are still reasonable. Three-bedroom, two-bath homes top out at about $850 per month. A two-bedroom apartment might go for $500.

Real Estate Companies

Neft & Neft Realtors
21162 Calif. Hwy. 29, Middletown
• **(707) 987-3630, (800) 200-0374**

David Neft is a genetically programmed Realtor, having inherited the business from his property-handling parents in 1978. His office has four Realtors and listings throughout the county, though it concentrates on Middletown, Cobb Mountain and Hidden Valley Lake. Neft & Neft has always been known for facilitating the first-home American dream, but it is branching out to include sales of commercial vineyards and acreage.

House of Realty
19851 Hartman Rd., Middletown
• **(707) 987-3800**

This office has been tackling the southern Lake County real estate market since 1984. Its five Realtors concentrate on Cobb, Middletown and Hidden Valley Lakes.

Century 21
14260 Lakeshore Dr., Clearlake
• **(707) 994-6141**
1175 N. Main St., Lakeport
• **(707) 263-4235**

Each of Century 21's two Lake County offices has been in place for 20 years or more, so they have plenty of experience around the lake and throughout the county. There are about 10 Realtors in the two locations, and they handle everything from residential property to exclusive acreage.

Shore Line Realty
13725 E. Hwy. 20, Clearlake Oaks
• **(707) 998-1137**
1556 New Long Valley Rd., Spring Valley
• **(707) 998-2211**
9945 E. Hwy. 20, Glenhaven
• **(707) 998-3366**
3183 St. Francis Dr., Lakeport
• **(707) 279-9069**

Shore Line's broker and six agents together have more than 100 years of experience as licensed Realtors. The business itself has been operating in Lake County since 1981. They do all types of property, but offer several specialties within the office—such as commercial and income-producing property (lakefront resorts included), and vineyards or undeveloped hillside.

Coldwell Banker
190 S. Main St., Lakeport • **(707) 262-1000**
21037 Calistoga Rd., Suite 8, Middletown
• **(707) 994-3740**

Coldwell Banker's 14 Realtors handle all of Lake County. The office trades heavily in residential property but also has a commercial division called T&C Properties—a sideline that makes use of broker Robert Dunk's accounting background.

CPS Country Air
808 Lakeport Blvd., Lakeport
• **(707) 263-2620**
9730 Soda Bay Rd., The Rivieras
• **(707) 277-9255**
Calif. Hwy. 175 and Golf Rd., Cobb Mountain • **(707) 928-5113**

With three offices and 18 certified Realtors, CPS enjoys Lake County's largest market share. The office specializes in residential sales and covers the entire county. They manage rental property, too.

Noble Realty
6222 E. Calif. Hwy. 20, Lucerne
• **(707) 274-1050**

14892 Lakeshore Dr., Clearlake
• **(707) 994-8291**
12858 E. Calif. Hwy. 20, Clearlake Oaks
• **(707) 998-1155**
9733 Soda Bay Rd., The Rivieras
• **(707) 277-7477**
200 Lakeport Blvd., Lakeport
• **(707) 263-1818**
3654 E. Calif. Hwy. 20, Nice
• **(707) 274-5576**
375 E. Calif. Hwy. 20, Upper Lake
• **(707) 275-2060**

If you look at volume of sales in Lake County during the last decade or so, Noble probably rests at the top of the heap. The company has 22 Realtors and several satellite offices around Clear Lake, but the main office is in Lucerne. Noble handles the entire county and all sorts of property, with its largest share in land, including vineyards. May Noble started the business in 1968.

Retirement

LOOK FOR:
- Senior Services
- Senior Centers
- Retirement Housing Options
- Educational Opportunities
- Volunteer Opportunities

For city dwellers who have lived out middle-age in the thick of metropolitan life—fighting traffic, scurrying among high-rise office buildings, battling big-city fatigue—Wine Country looks like heaven itself.

These folks come up from San Francisco for a weekend, or fly in from places like Chicago or Minneapolis or Cleveland for the week, to sample a lifestyle that seems, well, soul-satisfying. And in the back of their minds is a nagging notion that won't go away: "I could be happy retiring here."

So Wine Country has become a happy haven for retirees, those young-at-heart oldsters who are aging with grace and style. They're a lively lot, this new breed of senior citizens. Instead of orthopedic shoes, they're filling closets with footwear appropriate for hiking, tennis, golf, biking, boating and walking. In their former lives they were businesspeople, teachers, salespeople, lawyers and homemakers. Now they've turned the rooms that were formerly for children into offices, darkrooms, hobby centers and exercise rooms. They're signing up for classes for everything from painting to winetasting. And more than anything else, they have become volunteers—those essential citizens who move the wheels of progress in learning centers, churches, libraries and civic organizations.

In short, Wine Country is a place well geared to the 65-plus segment of our population (and those other lucky dogs who have been able to hang up the work togs at a younger age). In this chapter, you'll find living accommodations and lifestyle options for the affluent, the middle-of-the-roaders and those of lower income (though Wine Country can never really be considered inexpensive). Residential developments restricted to the older-than-55 crowd are an option seized by many, with some featuring a club-like style of living. Adult-only mobile-home parks offer a popular choice, and in some areas, city government has provided cozy, subsidized cottages for low-income seniors, though this option usually entails a waiting list. For older folks who want to (or must) cut down on the working side, there are complexes of apartments that offer individual living with one to three meals a day. And for some who need watchful care, Wine Country has that covered too.

We start the information rolling with listings of area senior services, which have grown right alongside the growth of the Wine Country's senior population.

Senior Services

Our world is filled with slogans designed to express connection. "Reach out and touch someone," "You're in good hands," and others of similar tone give a wonderful sense of reassurance. But when it comes right down to it, just where do we turn? Here are a few connections that should make it easier for seniors to find their way around in new territory.

INSIDERS' TIP

The California Department of Fish and Game offers a reduced-fee sport-fishing license for those age 65 and older.

Napa County

The Volunteer Center of Napa County
1820 Jefferson St., Napa
• (707) 252-6222, (707) 963-3922

The Volunteer Center does all sorts of good work in the county, and its Senior Services Program, funded by the Area Agency on Aging (serving Napa and Solano counties) and the United Way, is foremost on the list. Especially valuable is the *Senior Guide* it publishes each year. It's a well-organized 15-page catalog of write-ups and phone numbers, with suggestions on topics ranging from health services and home care to housing and transportation.

Comprehensive Services for Older Adults
2261 Elm St., Napa
• (707) 253-4625, (800) 498-9455

This program, administered by the Napa County Health and Human Services Agency, offers in-home care to the aged, blind and disabled who can't afford to fend for themselves. The manifold services include household tasks and shopping, non-medical personal care when needed to assure safety, alcohol and drug counseling, adult protective services and psychiatric case management for seniors 62 or older who suffer from mental illness and/or Alzheimer's disease. Comprehensive Services also assists with procurement of food stamps and Medi-Cal (state-subsidized medical insurance) benefits.

Senior Class
Queen of the Valley Hospital, 1000 Trancas St., Napa • (707) 253-9000

Queen of the Valley has targeted older adults for health promotion and education with this membership program since 1986. Members are offered a variety of classes, lectures and health screenings, conducted by the hospital's able team of healthcare professionals. It's $15 to join and $10 a year thereafter, though nobody is turned away. (For more on Queen of the Valley, see our Healthcare chapter.)

Napa Valley Dining Club
1755 Industrial Way, Napa
• (707) 253-6112, (800) 788-0124

This service cooks up hot, nutritious meals for people 60 years or older on a donation basis. When needed, the club will even transport guests to one of six Napa County sites or deliver food to homes. Call one day in advance for reservations.

Napa Valley Committee on Aging
1500 Jefferson St., Napa
• (707) 224-5121

This is a referral service for seniors seeking in-home care or housekeeping. The committee also offers handyman service for minor home repairs. (The fee is negotiable.)

Garden Haven
2447 Old Sonoma Rd., Napa
• (707) 253-3425

Even the most devoted caregiver needs an occasional break, and here is a day center you can trust to watch over your elderly relative or friend, especially if they suffer from Alzheimer's or dementia. Activities include music, exercise regimens, crafts, cooking and gardening. Wheelchairs are welcome. The center is open Monday, Tuesday, Thursday and Friday from 10 AM to 3 PM. The cost is $12.50 per day.

Senior Employment
601 Sacramento St., Ste. 1401, Vallejo
• (707) 553-9058

People 55 and older who are mentally and physically fit, and who are looking for a little extra cash, are encouraged to get in touch with the Area Agency on Aging Serving Napa/Solano Counties. They'll help you find part-time employment.

> **INSIDERS' TIP**
> Another strong point at Silverado Orchards retirement community in St. Helena: free transportation every Monday, Wednesday and Friday, or as needed for emergencies.

Sonoma County

Council on Aging
730 Bennett Valley Rd., Santa Rosa
• (707) 525-0143

This is the overall program that provides many of the benefits that are incorporated in member organizations such as the senior centers listed subsequently. Council on Aging provides dining rooms with a hot, healthy noontime meal at 10 locations in Sonoma County. Under the Meals on Wheels program, a hot meal is delivered seven days a week to the homes of temporarily or chronically homebound seniors. Legal consultation services are provided, as well as money management programs, health insurance counseling and door-to-door transportation for seniors with doctor visits. An excellent Senior Resource Guide has been made available by the council, available at senior centers or by calling the listed number.

American Association of Retired Persons
P.O. Box 662, Santa Rosa 95402
• (707) 527-7282
1094 Petaluma Blvd., Petaluma
• (707) 769-8560
5901 Redwood Hwy., Windsor
• (707) 838-6936

AARP is a senior advocacy organization for people who have reached 50 years of age. Its mission is to promote the welfare and status of the country's elder population, and some of this work is carried on through chapters such as the Sonoma County chapters listed here. The agenda is likely to be the same for the different chapters—there's always a monthly meeting (call the numbers listed to find out which day and time), educational opportunities, insurance advantages and travel information. Meetings usually include speakers involved with state or local government, health organizations, Medicare or widowhood. Some chapters organize social activities. The Santa Rosa chapter, for instance, has an annual picnic in July, featuring hot dogs and a potluck assortment of foods furnished by members. A nominal membership fee is charged ($3 to $5 per year), but anyone older than 50 is welcome to attend meetings.

AARP Senior Community Service Employment Program
2050 W. Steele Ln., Ste. E-1, Santa Rosa
• (707) 525-9190

Partially government-sponsored, this is an AARP program to help low-income seniors get back into the work force through on-the-job training with organizations such as the American Red Cross and Goodwill Industries. It is also an employment office that can find jobs in the private sector after training.

AARP 55 Alive/Mature Driving
980 Ninth St., Ste. 700, Sacramento 95814
• (916) 446-2277

This drivers' educational program for those older than 55 is available through three locations in Sonoma County: Sonoma Vintage House in Sonoma, (707) 996-0311; Lucchesi Park Senior Center in Petaluma, (707) 778-4339; and Sebastopol Burbank Senior Center, (707) 829-2440. There is an $8 charge for the two-day course.

North Bay HI-CAP
55 Maria Dr., Ste. 837, Petaluma
• (800) 303-4477

The North Bay Health Insurance Counseling and Advocacy Program (HI-CAP) covers six counties north of the Golden Gate Bridge (including all four in Wine Country). The center offers one-on-one counseling by trained volunteers registered by the California Department of Aging. They provide independent, unbiased information on health insurance, including Medicare and supplemental programs. They also help clients sort out their medical finances and make sure they are being billed appropriately for Medicare. There is no charge for this service.

Petaluma Ecumenical Project
1400 Caulfield Ln., Petaluma
• (707) 762-2336

In 1977 three local ministers came together to find a way to provide low-cost housing for seniors. With community backing, the Petaluma Ecumenical Project sought out suitable building sites and developed architectural plans. The group has built and manages nine projects and is now supported by 11 churches and AARP contributions.

Jewish Seniors Program
3855 Montgomery Dr., Santa Rosa
• (707) 528-4222

The wide spectrum of entertainment and educational opportunities offered through this program includes musical events, folk dancing, autobiographical writing, book discussion, parties and trips. Want to learn Yiddish? That's an option too! The group welcomes participants from all denominations.

Sons In Retirement
Sonoma • (707) 938-2643

To join, you must simply be older than 60 and retired. Members meet once a month for lunch and to hear a speaker. Other than that there are few requirements, although you're expected to make all the meetings: If you miss three in a row without good reason, you're dropped from the rolls. Sonoma County has five groups of 125 each, offering various forms of entertainment—golf, bowling and photography groups and travel excursions, to mention a few. Bus tours to Reno or Lake Tahoe are frequent, and trips as far afield as Yellowstone and Canada are possible. SIR headquarters is in Sacramento. In Sonoma County there's a waiting list to join.

Mendocino County

Linkages Multipurpose Senior Services Program
487 N. State St., Ukiah • (707) 468-9347

The Linkages Multipurpose Senior Services Program is a nonprofit community agency that strives to meet the needs of people with disabilities so that they can remain in their own homes and live an independent life of dignity. Some of the home-care services that MSSP helps obtain include personal care, home repairs, house cleaning, shopping, transportation and home-delivered meals. The agency serves Ukiah, Willits, Hopland, Potter Valley and the Fort Bragg/Mendocino area, plus Lake County.

Lake County

Community Care
14642 Lakeshore Dr., Clearlake
• (707) 995-7010

Community Care helps anyone older than 18 with disability or illness, but it is seniors who have come to rely on the program most. A nonprofit agency funded by a variety of sources, Community Care seeks to arrange affordable, competent help for people trying to live independently at home. At no charge, the agency's Multipurpose Senior Services Program serves frail elderly people (65 or older) who are Medi-Cal recipients.

Senior Health
922 Bevins Ct., Lakeport
• (707) 263-2241, (707) 994-9433

This function of the Lake County Health Department offers free general health assessments for area seniors, including a nutritional analysis. The department also screens for blood pressure and hearing, and will run blood tests for a small fee.

Senior Centers

They're social centers, educational resources, service sources and just plain fun places for seniors with leisure time. Most of the centers publish newsletters so everyone can find out what's in store. All have an extensive, varied program of activities, and all offer services such as blood pressure and hearing testing, legal counsel and tax assistance on a regular basis.

Napa County

Senior Citizens Center
1500 Jefferson St., Napa
• (707) 255-1800

Older residents get one-stop shopping at this office. Nearly 60 clubs and organizations—including the Senior Friendship Club and Napa Grange—use the center as a meeting place. It's open Monday through Friday, from 8 AM to 4 PM. Activities range from dances, bingo and potluck dinners to arts and crafts and pancake breakfasts. Friday mornings welcome a diversity of guest speakers for Senior Seminars. Call for a monthly schedule of events.

Berryessa Senior Citizens
4380 Spanish Flat Loop Rd., Berryessa
• (707) 966-0206

The highlands surrounding Lake Berryessa sound like a nice place for retired folks ....and, well, they are. The center has a strong lineup of health, educational, social and recreational programs. If you call for a monthly schedule, you'll discover potluck meals, bingo, crafts, Adventure College classes, trips, dances and more.

Sonoma County

Southern Sonoma

Vintage House
264 First St. E., Sonoma
• (707) 996-0311

Staffed largely by senior volunteers, Vintage House is open Monday through Friday, serving more than 1,000 individuals each month with up to 70 classes and activities, most of them free or low-cost. Among the choices you'll find art classes, line dancing, tap dancing, international folk dance instruction, canasta, bridge in several forms, exercise classes and classes in French, Italian and Spanish at levels for beginner, intermediate and advanced speakers. A choral group, the Vintage House Singers, is coached by a professional music director and performs twice a year. The Department of Motor Vehicles has a representative show up each month to administer driving tests, and

RETIREMENT

the tax man cometh during his season. Lunch is served each day in the dining room for a small fee.

Lucchesi Park Senior Center
211 Novak Dr., Petaluma
• **(707) 778-4399**

This facility largely houses the recreational part of Petaluma's senior program. The local meal program has been separated and is now administered by Petaluma People Services Center. Dancing is very popular here. Line dancing events draw 25 to 40 participants each week, and ballroom dancing attracts 100 or more. Group exercise goes over big, along with the computer classes, art instruction and creative writing classes. Many daytrips and extended trips are sponsored.

Rohnert Park Senior Center
6800 Hunter Dr., Rohnert Park
• **(707) 585-6780**

Active seniors as well as disabled persons who can manage on their own are welcome here to chat, play cards and watch the once-a-month movie. General activities include line dancing, duplicate bridge, basketry, Spanish classes, a craft shop, and a billiards table. Every other month an early-evening dance brings out a lively crowd. According to the director, seniors often claim this is the best center around, and it draws older folks from as far away as Ukiah. A noon meal is served.

Santa Rosa Multi-Purpose Senior Center
704 Bennett Valley Rd., Santa Rosa
• **(707) 545-8608**

Dancing is big here—afternoon ballroom dancing twice a week, line dancing and tap dancing. Bingo, bridge, whist, chess and pinochle games are lively, and there are two billiards tables. Watercolor and acrylic painting classes are a big draw, and there's creative writing, a poetry group and Spanish instruction. The drama group puts on shows, and a choral

A retired couple takes a leisurely stroll on a poppy-edged path.

group attracts those who like to belt out a tune. Once a month the Friendship Club organizes a potluck lunch. A movie is shown each Sunday, and for the energetic, a bike group sets out on Saturdays. No meals are served here. However, the Council on Aging uses the center kitchen to prepare meals for delivery to the homebound.

Northern Sonoma

Windsor Senior Center
9231 Foxwood Dr., Windsor
• **(707) 838-1250**

This center is surrounded by roses—45 varieties in a lovely garden. In the artistic category, classes are available in oil and pastel painting and sculpture. Card players have a choice of pinochle or bridge, and seniors can learn to play the guitar, study genealogy or join in a quilting bee. A program called Step Into Life offers encouragement for "women in transition." For the athletic, the bocce ball court is an attraction, as is the horseshoe pit. But most popular of all is the swimming pool: Windsor tends to be hot in summer, and the pool is a terrific place to cool off. It is outfitted for the disabled, who can be lowered from wheelchair to water by a special lift device.

Healdsburg Senior Center
133 Matheson St., Healdsburg
• **(707) 431-3324**

Lunch is served here Monday through Friday, and a bus service is available to bring seniors to the center as well as to take them to shopping areas and other destinations around town. Crafts are popular here, with a group meeting once a week to work on a variety of handcrafts including the art of flower arranging. An unusually talented group of woodworkers has attained several awards for items created at the center. Bingo brings the lucky and unlucky to play each Thursday. Department of Motor Vehicles testing also is provided on a regular basis.

Cloverdale Senior Multi-Purpose Center
Second and Commercial Sts., Cloverdale
• **(707) 894-4826**

Weekly blood-pressure screenings, visits by an optometrist and hearing-aid maintenance are among the services offered in Cloverdale. Line dancing is offered one day each week, and an instructor comes in to help seniors create an autobiographical record of their lives. A newsletter keeps seniors apprised of coming attractions at the center, where lunch is served every weekday.

INSIDERS' TIP

In addition to the many umbrella organizations in Napa County, take note of these specific self-help societies: Alzheimer's Support Group, (707) 257-7885; Arthritis Support Group, (707) 255-3002; Stroke Support Group, (707) 257-4957; Visually Impaired Support Group, (707) 253-0290; Widowed Persons Association of California, (707) 226-7683 or (707) 944-2030.

West County/Russian River

Sebastopol Burbank Senior Center
167 N. High St., Sebastopol
• **(707) 829-2440**

This center receives laudable backing from the community, and several stores and bakeries bring in day-old products to distribute among the members. In addition, lunch is served in the dining room each weekday, and home-delivered meals are dispatched to those who cannot come in. Card games and bingo are regular sources of entertainment, and every

once in a while, there's a special program by a harp and flute duo. Through a coalition of other senior service groups, a lively travel program has been developed in Sebastopol. Not only do seniors make short local trips—say, to Lake Tahoe, the San Francisco Zoo, the Golden Gate Bridge and the Sonoma County Fair—but they have also have taken journeys as far afield as Alaska and the Panama Canal.

Russian River Community Senior Center
15010 Armstrong Woods Rd., Guerneville
• **(707) 869-0618**

.   Both on-site lunch and Meals on Wheels are provided from this center, and because this is a rural area, limited transportation is provided. Afternoon field trips and picnics are ideally suited to this vacation spot with its many scenic locales. Writing autobiographies and practicing t'ai chi are among indoor activities.

Mendocino County

U.S. Highway 101

Ukiah Senior Center
499 Leslie St., Ukiah
• **(707) 462-4343**

A lot happens here—it would be hard not to have fun. There's line dancing, ballroom dancing and dancing classes, plus a Saturday night dance to practice your lessons. You can play bingo, pinochle, bridge, Scrabble or chess, learn to knit or crochet or practice t'ai chi. The exercise class is on Tuesday, Wednesday and Thursday. Legal help, tax assistance and health screenings are available. Oh yes, lunch is served in the dining room each weekday.

Willits Senior Center
1501 Baechtell Rd., Willits
• **(707) 459-6826**

A noon meal is served at the center and delivered to shut-ins. Seniors enjoy movies and bingo twice a week and a dance once a month. Breakfast is served once a month, and special weekend dinners are staged monthly. A worthy program at Willits is Extra Hands—a plan to hire people to do chores like gardening, cleaning house and shopping for seniors who find these activities difficult. Drivers are provided to take people to medical appointments. The center is fortunate: there are 100 volunteers to help. Some funds are created by a thrift shop run by the seniors themselves. Says the director, "They have made the shop look like a real department store."

Mendocino Coast

South Coast Senior Citizens
140 Main St., Point Arena
• (707) 882-2137

Arts and crafts occupy part of the daily schedule in Point Arena. An abalone breakfast is served on the second Sunday a month, and a spaghetti dinner is served on the fourth Friday. Monthly bus trips are scheduled to visit various spots and happenings. In November, the seniors create a haunted house as a fund-raiser. The dining room here provides a noon meal twice a week and provides transportation so seniors can get to the center. Delivered meals also are provided on the same days.

Fort Bragg Senior Center
490 N. Harold St., Fort Bragg
• (707) 964-0443

Seniors enjoy bingo twice a week and can take a course in writing provided by the College of the Redwoods staff. From time to time a four-week improvisation class gives seniors a chance to practice acting, and occasionally a professional writer comes to tell seniors how they can learn to write and sell their output. A hot meal is served here each weekday from 11:30 AM to 12:30 PM, with transportation provided.

Lake County

Highlands Senior Service Center
14773 Lakeshore Dr., Clearlake
• (707) 994-3051

Highlands does a little bit of everything. It provides free legal assistance, money management advice and medical transportation at 16

cents per mile. (They'll haul you as far as 300 miles.) The center also screens and hires people to provide in-home support services such as shopping, maintenance and things of that nature. It also stages a blood pressure clinic on the second Monday and last Wednesday of each month. Meals are in the dining room at noon, for a suggested donation of $2.50; Highlands' Meals on Wheels program caters to the homebound.

Live Oaks Senior Center
12519 Oaks Plaza, Clearlake Oaks
• (707) 998-1950

Experienced folks are treated well in Clearlake Oaks. This center is open daily from 8 AM to 2 PM, with lunch served about noon. They do blood-pressure testing every Tuesday, a birthday lunch one Friday a month (presents included) and a health clinic on the third Wednesday of each month. Live Oaks also offers HMO information and counseling, loans equipment to the handicapped and even sells fishing licenses to low-income, high-energy seniors.

Lakeport Senior Center
527 Konocti Ave., Lakeport
• (707) 263-4218

Drawing much of its funding from the Older Americans Act of 1965, this center keeps things peppy. The agenda includes bingo every Wednesday, exercise classes and crafts. You can even kick up your heels for line dancing. The hearing-aid technician comes once a week, the podiatrist once a month. The center also serves Sunday breakfast monthly.

Upper Lake Senior Outreach
9410 Mendenhall Ave., Upper Lake
• (707) 275-3513

Here's a portion of what the elderly can expect in Upper Lake: information referral, shopping assistance, employment screening and escorts (not that kind). The center directs people to food sources if necessary and sets up a health clinic every Thursday. A small group of interfaith volunteers helps out with driving duty and chores.

Retirement Housing Options

In the city of Sonoma, more than one-third of the population is older than 60, and the situation is similar in most of southern Sonoma County. This means a wide assortment of housing arrangements for retired folks in that area.

Many retirees, of course, are simply absorbed into the general population. However, some choose to buy a home in one of the many active adult communities, which are not much different from any other residential area except that residents must have reached a certain age to

Photo: Tina Luster-Hoban

The Riverwalk Bridge in Petaluma provides a perfect path for walking.

live there. Usually there is a club-house and limited activities for homeowners. But mainly, there are no children. Among the most popular of these communities in Sonoma are Temelec, Chantarelle and Creekside. By far, the largest of these adult communities is Oakmont. It lies between Valley of the Moon and Santa Rosa but is actually within the Santa Rosa city limits. Its population runs to 5,000, with amenities including two golf courses, bowling greens, several activity rooms and a sizable shopping center within the complex. It is possible to rent as well as buy at Oakmont.

Other popular options in Sonoma are adult mobile-home communities that limit residency to those over 55. These are generally operated by an on-site manager. They are practical, fairly inexpensive and surprisingly spacious and appealing. A few worthy of mention are Pueblo Serena, Seven Flags and De Anza Moon Valley. Residents own their own home but pay a monthly rental fee to the landowner for the lot. In Sonoma, this lot-rental fee has been regulated by city government and is rather low. A point of caution, however: In negotiating for the purchase of a home, it is wise to inquire as to whether you're permitted to rent out your home in case you choose to be absent for a length of time.

Although southern Sonoma County remains the setting for a large portion of Wine Country's adult mobile-home parks, they also are popular in other areas, partially because they are an inexpensive alternate to home ownership. Many are subject to rent control, which is adjusted annually by city government, and buyers should keep in mind that if rent control should cease, their home may be sitting on expensive property, making it difficult to sell and not so easy to move elsewhere.

With Wine Country in general showing every sign of becoming Northern California's retirement zone, senior housing facilities across the region are expanding to meet the demand. This is particularly true in the area of independent-living apartment complexes that provide housekeeping, meals and laundry services, while allowing for complete freedom of movement and individuality. Following are listings for this type of retirement-living option (with a couple of other independent-living choices thrown in) within our four-county area.

Napa County

Silverado Orchards
601 Pope St., St. Helena
• (707) 963-3688

In a quiet, green setting between St. Helena proper and the Silverado Trail is this popular retirement community. Silverado Orchards has 80 units all together—small studios, deluxe studios, one-bedroom apartments and a couple of two-bedroom units. It's an active population that takes advantage of the immediate area's nice walking routes, plus twice-a-week exercise classes. They get a wealth of musical presentations in the multi-purpose room. Because the proprietors are Seventh Day Adventists (the community itself is strictly nondenominational), residents can choose vegetarian meals if so desired.

Woodbridge Village
727 Hunt Ave., St. Helena
• **(707) 963-3231**

In 1992 this HUD-supported retirement complex won an award for best landscaping in St. Helena. The park-like grounds have only improved since then, the managers say, thanks in part to some resident green thumbs. Woodbridge is a series of tidy one-bedroom, one-bathroom apartments, most of them grouped into fourplexes. Vineyards remain on one side of the property. HUD defines a senior as anyone age 62 or older.

Rancho de Calistoga
2412 Foothill Blvd., Calistoga
• **(707) 942-6971**

Yes, it's a mobile-home park, but if all of them looked like this, they would have a very different reputation. Centuries-old oak trees tower over the big lawn area out front, and the whole community is full of flowering plants. Rancho de Calistoga has a total of 184 lots. It also has a clubhouse, recreation building, pool and spa. Oh, and activities? They include bingo twice a month, bridge, poker, exercise classes, quilting, potlucks and Wednesday-morning brunch. The park is meant for seniors 55 and older.

Sonoma County

Westlake Wine Country House
800 Oregon St., Sonoma
• **(707) 996-7101**

Billed as a "luxury congregate retirement facility," Westlake Wine Country offers one- and two-bedroom suites, fully carpeted (bring your own furniture), with a small kitchen, private deck or balcony and three meals a day in a rather elegant dining room. Having guests? You can use one of the smaller dining rooms suitable for up to a dozen. You can also rent rooms for your guests in the complex for a nominal fee. The Westlake van takes residents to shopping or medical appointments, or you can use a parking space for your own car.

Westlake Springs
4855 Snyder Lane, Rohnert Park
• **(707) 585-7878**

Although the Springs enjoys country views of rolling green farmlands, the property is near shopping, one block from a large medical complex and a short putt to the nearest golf course. This complex is owned by the same company as Sonoma's Westlake Wine Country (see previous listing), with accommodations slightly upgraded in price and style. You can participate in a wide range of activities, both in-house and away—wine-and-cheese socials, book reviews, college courses, pool tournaments, movies, swimming, library visits, exercise and game-room fun. The complex consists of 176 apartments and 190 residents.

Valley Orchards Retirement Community
2100 E. Washington St., Petaluma
• **(707) 778-6030**

No medical or nursing service is provided here, the manager says, "but from time to time the resident may contract for outside assistance for bathing or personal care, which makes it a good bit cheaper than assisted living." Valley Orchards provides three meals a day, utilities, cable TV, transportation three days a week, housekeeping once a week, bathroom and bedroom laundry, 24-hour emergency assistance and yard maintenance. Valley Orchard's 104 units are split between large studios and one- and two-bedroom apartments.

Friends House
684 Benicia Dr., Santa Rosa
• **(707) 538-0152**

A Quaker institution, Friends House is composed of four interrelated programs for the older person: independent-living apartments and houses, an adult day-care center, an assisted-living facility, and a skilled-nursing facility. A large part of the 6-acre Friends House site contains 60 garden apartments. People live in their own homes with their own belongings and garden space. One- and two-bedroom apartments are available, and recently some three-bedroom, two-bath homes were added to accommodate couples who want more space within the Friends House community. New residents must pay an entrance fee, and a monthly assessment covers housekeeping services. There is a charge for food service in the dining room. Cultural activities and visits to symphony performances, art galleries, libraries and sporting events are offered.

The Lodge at Paulin Creek
2375 Range Ave., Santa Rosa
• **(707) 575-3722**

The Lodge is set in park-like grounds with inviting courtyards. Apartments are sunny and bright, with the charm of designer fabrics, art reproductions and handmade quilts. They range from studios to three-bedroom, two-bath units. Some dining options are offered—you can either be served graciously in the dining room or serve yourself casually from the salad and hot entree buffet. Amenities include a pool, fitness trail, billiards room, an opportunity to garden and a calendar of day trips.

Mendocino County

Redwood Meadows
1475 Baechtel Rd., Willits
• (707) 459-1616

In a lovely setting with walkways and green belts, Redwood Meadows is a senior apartment community open to active, independent seniors older than 55. The community center houses a game room, craft room and television lounge. Because it is right next door to the Willits Senior Center (see previous listing), the amenities of that group are easily accessible. Meals are not served, but the dining room is a center for potlucks, parties, movies, lectures and other social events. Small pets are allowed.

The Woods
43300 Little River Airport Rd., Little River
• (707) 937-0294

Quality manufactured homes nestled among redwoods, pines and rhododendrons make up this residential community for seniors. Currently there are 88 homes, and a total of 111 are planned. The Woods is on 37 sunbelt acres connected by winding roads that lead walkers to a heated indoor pool and spa or the clubhouse, library or art room. State park beaches and golf courses are minutes away. Assisted-living facilities are also available.

Redwood Coast Seniors
489 N. Harold St., Fort Bragg
• (707) 964-0443

This organization maintains a list of Fort Bragg senior Housing. Entries are all clean, well-maintained apartments or detached houses, with rents on a sliding scale according to income.

Lake County

Autumn Village
14930 Burns Valley Rd., Clearlake
• (707) 995-1650

This community is divided into two complexes, with 40 one-bedroom apartments on one end and 22 on the other. Autumn Village

has a reputation for tidy grounds and well-maintained units. It features bingo on Saturday, movies each Wednesday evening and a potluck dinner on the third Thursday of the month. On Monday morning from 9 to 11 AM, many of the women get together for crafts, sewing and chit-chat.

Highlands Village
6215 Old Hwy. 53, Clearlake
• (707) 994-7538

A HUD-subsidized establishment, Highlands Village is open to seniors 62 and older who are eligible for public assistance. Dotted with gardens, the complex has 39 units, 38 of which are one-bedroom apartments. (Four are units for the disabled.) The laundry and recreation rooms are centrally located. Highlands Village has a tenants' association that schedules dinners, bingo every Tuesday and numerous other activities.

Educational Opportunities

Several agencies and area schools offer opportunities for inquisitive, mature men and women to prove there is no age limit to new intellectual experiences. In addition to the resources listed, many senior centers throughout Wine Country offer classes in writing, foreign languages, computer skills and other subjects.

Napa County

- Napa Valley College Community Education, 2277 Napa-Vallejo Highway, Napa, (707) 253-3070
- North Bay Driving School, 1878 El Centro Avenue, Napa, (707) 252-2066
- Pacific Union College Extension, Angwin, (707) 965-6311, (800) 862-7080

Sonoma County

- Petaluma Adult Education Center, 11 Fifth Street, Petaluma, (707) 778-4633
- Sonoma State University Gerontology Program, 1801 E. Cotati Avenue, Rohnert Park, (707) 664-2411
- Lewis Adult Education Center, 2230 Lomitas Avenue, Santa Rosa, (707) 528-5421
- Santa Rosa Junior College, 1501 Mendocino Avenue, Santa Rosa, (707) 527-4011

RETIREMENT

- New Vista Adult Education School, 6980 Analy Avenue, Sebastopol, (707) 824-6455

Lake County

- Yuba College, 7105 S. Center Drive, Clearlake, (707) 995-7900
- Konocti Adult School, 14110 Lakeshore Drive, Clearlake, (707) 994-7142

Volunteer Opportunities

A number of programs are available that put to use the skills, talents and personalities of older individuals who choose to work full- or part-time for little or no remuneration. Here are a handful of options.

Retired and Senior Volunteer Program
264 First St. E., Sonoma
- **(707) 996-4644**
17A Fourth St., Petaluma
- **(707) 762-0111**
1316 Maurice Ave., Rohnert Park
- **(707) 795-3990**
1041 Fourth St., Santa Rosa
- **(707) 573-3399**

RSVP provides volunteer opportunities in more than 400 community agencies for people older than 60. This is an umbrella agency through which most volunteers work, whether they restock library shelves or send out mailing for Pets Lifeline.

Service Corps of Retired Executives
777 Sonoma Ave., Ste. 115-B, Santa Rosa
- **(707) 571-8342**

Members of SCORE are retired business executives who volunteer their time and expertise without charge to advise and help people who are running or starting a new business. Sponsored by the Small Business Administration, it's open to any retired executive in any field of business.

Foster Grandparent Program
15000 Arnold Dr., Eldridge
- **(707) 938-6201**
413 N. State St., Ukiah • (707) 462-1954

This is a nationwide volunteer program for those 60 years or older who choose to make a lasting connection with children with special needs (whether mental or physical) and become a permanent mentor. Forty hours of orientation are required to acquaint the grandparent with the facility and the child, but the rewards go both ways. The child forms a permanent loving attachment, and the grandparent/senior learns to know the child as a person in a close-knit relationship. It's not an easy commitment. The pair spends four hours a day together, five days a week. There is a modest stipend that goes with the work, plus transportation and lunch.

Education and Child Care

Education

LOOK FOR:
- Public Schools
- Private Schools
- Two-Year Colleges
- Four-Year Colleges and Universities
- Other Institutes of Higher Learning
- Child Care

You might not realize just how undeveloped our four-county area is until you take a look at higher education. Within a 7,000-square-mile expanse, you find only three four-year universities: one state school, a brand-new campus specializing in engineering and a small, private Adventist college on top of a mountain.

Yet you can't say the Wine Country undervalues education. The public school systems here are considered solid. The rates of high school seniors matriculating to universities, though they vary from district to district, tend to be higher than national and state averages. But there simply aren't enough potential students to justify a large number of local four-year colleges.

We profile those universities later in this chapter, after we examine the public school systems, private schools of various philosophy and grade range, and two-year junior colleges. Within each category, the breakdown is county by county. At the close we briefly cover child-care options—perhaps the most important section for those who are visiting the Wine Country for a short time.

Public Schools

Napa County

Anyone who questions Napa County's commitment to education would do well to look at the winter-spring social calendar. That time of year is dominated by charitable events devoted to private or public schools. One Upvalley nursery school alone reported a haul of more than $40,000 from its dazzling 1999 fundraiser.

But if there is a strong commitment to Napa Valley's schools, there is widespread disagreement on at least one issue: bilingual education. As with many areas of California, a large immigrant population—in this case, almost wholly from Mexico—mingles with those of us who migrated earlier. In 1999 there were 19,104 pupils in Napa County public schools, dispersed among five districts: Calistoga Joint Union, Napa Valley Unified, St. Helena Unified, Howell Mountain and Pope Valley. About 16 percent of those students showed limited proficiency with English, and the language in which they should be instructed has been hotly debated.

Muddying the issue in 1997 was Proposition 227 and its wake of legal challenges. Two schools with highly regarded dual-immersion programs—

where all students spend periods of time learning in both English and Spanish—suddenly were faced with the prospect of English-only instruction. One of them, Westwood Elementary School in Napa, signed over its program to the private Edison project, removing it from Prop. 227 jurisdiction. The other, St. Helena Elementary School, became one of many facilities statewide to wait in limbo for court resolution.

In the meantime, Napa County's charted performance remains relatively strong. SAT I scores were well above the state average in 1998-99. Countywide, 95 percent of high-school students received their diplomas in 1998-99, while nearly 50 percent went on to attend some form of college.

Within the five districts are many specific success stories. Ten Napa County campuses received California Distinguished School Awards after evaluations of their curricula, test scores, school environments, parent participation and special programs. Capell Elementary School scored in the 80th percentile or better in three disciplines (reading, math and language) on the 1999 STAR tests; two alternative schools, Bel Aire and Pueblo Vista, did nearly as well. St. Helena High School's SAT scores and graduate rate are among the best in the state. In 1991-92 the Western Association of Schools and Colleges conferred a six-year accreditation on Vintage High School, a rare term bestowed in recognition of excellence.

Finally there is New Technology High School, a Napa facility where students spend most of their time online or in-lab, with minimal teacher supervision. New Tech was named a U.S. Department of Education Demonstration School for its technological advances. It graduated its first senior class of future Silicon Valley moguls in 1998.

Sonoma County

This county's schools consistently rank in the top third of the state, although they're funded at less than the state average. Thirty-eight of the county's schools have been named California Distinguished Schools, and four have been recognized as National Blue Ribbon schools. Within Sonoma County's 40 school districts, 154 schools serve students from kindergarten through 12th grade. There are 91 elementary schools, 18 junior high schools, 15 high schools, 23 special alternative schools and seven charter schools. Enrollment runs around 70,000 each year, which represents approximately 90 percent of the county's student population.

The growth in diversity among Sonoma County students is significant. Today, local schools are educating the most culturally, socially, academically and linguistically diverse youth population in the county's history. More than 10 percent of the county's students are limited in their ability to speak English, 11 percent receive special education services, 7 percent are enrolled in programs for gifted students and 5 percent attend alternative programs such as independent study, home study or continuation school.

Many educational options are offered because the school system recognizes an obligation to offer opportunities for success for all kids. The majority of efforts in this direction are aimed at secondary school students, who are more likely to get lost in the system because of larger student populations at the higher grade levels. For those who can't keep up, for example, a smaller, more personalized environment is arranged. This independent study, like home study, demands that at least one parent be a stay-at-home presence. Students meet with teachers at specified intervals to review their progress.

Teenage parents also are offered a safety net. In the Petaluma School District, for instance, teens can leave infants and toddlers in a district-operated child-care center for the morning while they pursue their academic studies. The public school system also is working to address the needs of teens who have problems with alcohol or other drugs. Through programs such as Clean and Sober, the dropout rate for Sonoma County, at 2.8 percent, is considerably lower than the state average of 4.4 percent, and it continues to go down.

While attending to the needs of students with special needs, Sonoma County schools also consistently score in the top third of the state for every grade level and subject tested through the California Assessment Program. Average SAT scores for the county are significantly higher than state and national averages. In 1999 Sonoma County high schools graduated 3,430 students, and more than 1,300 of them completed the requirements for admission into California's university and state college systems.

And things just keep getting better. New magnet programs are under consideration. Local districts are consistently tracking forward with school improvements, made possible by the passage of several multimillion-dollar community bond issues. New schools are being built, and older schools are being modernized and retrofitted for earthquake security. New libraries are being installed, and a system amphitheater is being built so students can perform outdoor plays.

Mendocino County

The size of this county is so immense and the geography so diverse—with its various communities separated by forests, mountains and slow-driving winding roads—that schools within the system operate almost independently of each other, relying on guidelines from the central offices of the county superintendent of schools. There are 12 districts that include 27 elementary schools, 15 middle schools, and 21 high schools (including continuation high schools). There are also six charter schools in the county.

Still, academic standards are high, with most schools posting average SAT scores at or slightly above national levels. About 35 percent of students go on to college, generally of the two-year community type. Special emphasis is put on vocational job training, with programs specifically aimed at jobs like firefighting (Mendocino County is heavily forested) and agriculture (since the area is mostly rural). This sort of training starts as early as grade 9 for those who have no plans to go on to college and can benefit from learning a vocation.

There are other special programs. Preschool classes are offered, as well as classes for those for whom English is a second language. In addition, a staff member regularly makes the county circuit (racking up 100,000 miles a year) to assist with home-study programs and teach life skills to disadvantaged young people. The high school in Ukiah, the county seat, has classes at Juvenile Hall for young people who have run afoul of the law, as well as a Clean and Sober program for students with alcohol or drug problems.

Athletic programs are available, usually including basketball, baseball, softball, soccer, track, volleyball, cheerleading and sometimes swimming, golf and tennis. Fort Bragg High School is proud of its exemplary drama program that has given students an opportunity to work with acting and stage management. It has been extremely popular. Mendocino High School has an outstanding program called Windows to the Future, initiated in 1991, that links traditional studies in arts and sciences with computer technology. And here's a major advantage to having a widely scattered county population: Class sizes in Mendocino County schools are generally small, often having fewer than 20 students per teacher.

Lake County

In rural counties such as Lake, a school is more than a place to send your child for six hours a day. It's often the center of the community—a meeting hall and polling place and local playground, especially in unincorporated areas. (Lake County has only two incorporated cities.) The homecoming parade goes right down the center of town, and the big football game draws distant neighbors who don't get enough opportunities to bump into one another.

Lake County is divided into seven school districts: Kelseyville Unified, Konocti Unified, Lakeport Unified, Middletown Unified, Lucerne Elementary, Upper Lake Union Elementary and Upper Lake Union High School. Between them, they served 9,534 students in 1998-99. Transportation is a challenge in Lake, with some pupils riding buses for hours each day. The transportation must be subsidized, of course, and that cuts into teacher salaries. The county's wage schedule is below the state average; then again, low housing costs certainly offset the difference.

Five Lake County schools—Lucerne Elementary, Riviera Elementary, Middletown Middle (it only sounds redundant),

INSIDERS' TIP

Choosing one child-care center over another can be a daunting affair. One way to start is to ask a prospective facility for its nine-digit community-care license number. If the center does not have such a license, issued by the State of California, go somewhere else.

Kelseyville High and Middletown High—have been recognized in recent years as Distinguished Schools by the state of California. Middletown Middle School has a "Mac Lab" for its students' regular use and has developed a Student Court program in collaboration with the California State Bar Association. Kelseyville High School is in the top 10 percent in the state in placing students in vocational education classes. And several of the districts now employ the Success for All reading system. Devised at Johns Hopkins University, it's an intensive program that is particularly effective in teaching disadvantaged children.

SAT scores tend to be in the range of the state average. One immediate goal of the Lake County Office of Education is to wire all of its campuses to the Internet.

Private Schools

A wide variety of private schooling options exists in Wine Country. Individual school listings follow the geographical order for each county explained in How to Use This Book.

Napa County

Justin-Siena High School
4026 Maher St., Napa • (707) 255-0950

Justin High School for boys was founded by the Christian Brothers of the San Francisco District in 1966, Siena High School for girls by the Dominican Sisters of San Rafael that same year. In 1972 the two schools merged to form Justin-Siena, a private, Catholic, coeducational high school that now serves about 615 students in grades 9 through 12. Justin-Siena is widely regarded as one of the finest secondary educational facilities in Northern California. Ninety-seven percent of graduates go on to college, two-thirds of those to four-year institutions. The high school has a strong college preparatory curriculum and Honors programs in English, science, math and foreign languages.

The student body tends to be active outside the classroom. The sports program has been quite successful; the school won 13 league championships in 1997-98, and the golf team won the Northern California championship. Justin-Siena also requires 100 hours of community service for graduation, including an annual Just-In Service day that involves all students and staff in a full day of activity. What else? How about two gymnasiums and more than 120 computers with Internet access. In addition to a classical liberal arts curriculum, the school offers courses in drama, photography, jazz band, dance, choral, history of film and literature, and environmental ecology.

Kolbe Academy
1600 F St., Napa • (707) 255-6412

"Absurdly simple" is how Kolbe's administrators describe the school's philosophy. It's a small Ignatian school (a total of 20 to 30 students in grades 1 through 12) that, unlike most modern Jesuit institutions, returns to the methods and objectives of Ignatius of Loyola, who founded the order in the 1600s. Kolbe has three main goals: to help the student to speak, to write and to act, and these are accomplished through a regimen of imitation and repetition. Oral presentations play a large role in the educational process here. Every Friday, for example, students deliver five-minute presentations; audience members, in turn, are graded on the questions they ask. There is a heavy emphasis on drama as well. Every pupil at the academy gets into character at some point.

The Oxbow School
530 Third St., Napa • (707) 255-6000

Further evidence of Napa's quest for consideration as a world-class arts hub is the Oxbow School, recently founded by Ann Hatch (who previously founded the Capp Street Project artist-in-residence program in San Francisco) and wine luminary Robert Mondavi. Set on 3 acres within a looping bend of the Napa River, the school offers a one-semester fine arts program for high school juniors or second-semester seniors. Students live in dormitories and earn marks through the portfolios they assemble. The focus is on studio art in four domains: drawing and painting, print-making, sculpture and new media (which include photography, video and digital art). The Oxbow School takes only 48 students per semester. Admission is competitive and expensive ($12,500 for the 1999-2000 school year), though a need-blind admissions policy welcomes students regardless of their ability to pay.

Napa Adventist Junior Academy
2201 Pine St., Napa • (707) 255-5233

As it celebrates its 50th anniversary, Napa Adventist Junior Academy (NAJA) has a lot to be proud of. Take the award-winning music program, for instance. Children learn the Kodaly Program in grades 1 through 4. Grades 4 through 6 have recorded a pair of compact discs—one Christian, the other Christmas songs—and grades 7 through 10 often perform at music festivals. The entire school is wired for the Internet, and the older kids play a variety of after-school sports. (NAJA, which resides on a 10-acre campus, is kindergarten through 10th grade—the traditional Adventist structure.) The approximately 200 students come from as far away as Vacaville and Sonoma, eager to reap the Christian education that the school promises.

St. John's Lutheran School
3521 Linda Vista Ave., Napa
• **(707) 226-7970**

This Christian-based school (in the Lutheran Church's Missouri Synod) was founded in 1937. It now sits in a pleasant grove of cedars north of Redwood Road. The approximately 275 students, ranging from preschoolers to 8th graders, are encouraged to develop beliefs and behavior consistent with Lutheran teachings, and to pass each grade with the requisite skills in communication, critical thinking and analysis. St. John's offers some sports activities, a bit of arts and crafts and after-school care.

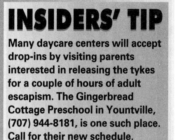

INSIDERS' TIP

Many daycare centers will accept drop-ins by visiting parents interested in releasing the tykes for a couple of hours of adult escapism. The Gingerbread Cottage Preschool in Yountville, (707) 944-8181, is one such place. Call for their new schedule.

Casa Montessori School
780 Lincoln Ave., Napa • (707) 224-1944

"Respect" is the buzzword at this small (approximately 60 pupils) Napa school. Everyone must be treated with courtesy, and that goes for students as well as teachers. It is an ungraded elementary school, which means the kids progress at their own rate. The scope is preschool (age 3) through 6th grade, but students can go far beyond that level if abilities dictate. In fact, administrators stress that most Casa students function about two years above the norm. How does the school do it? Part of the answer is self-correcting material—books, puzzles and games that allow youngsters to work independently.

St. Apollinaris Elementary School
3700 Lassen St., Napa • (707) 224-6525

Napa County's largest Catholic elementary/middle school (kindergarten through 8th grade) is in north Napa, near Trower Avenue. The academic program is rigorous, and there is a lineup of after-school sports for the more than

300 students who attend. The school was founded in 1959.

Foothills Adventist Elementary School
711 Sunnyside Rd., St. Helena
• **(707) 963-3546**

In 1902 the Elmshaven Seventh-Day Adventist Church built a one-room schoolhouse for its pupils. That school, Foothills Elementary, now supports more than 175 students (grades K through 8) and is sponsored by four Adventist churches. Foothills balances religious training with lessons in reading, writing, math, social studies, science, technology, physical education and music. Most noteworthy is the school's outdoor education programs. Describing the world of nature as "God's second book," Foothills offers memorable field trips. Primary kids might spend a day combing tide pools in Point Reyes or climbing Mount St. Helena. The middle school pupils, meanwhile, might go to Catalina Island Marine Institute for five days of oceanography and marine studies, or to the Marin Headlands Institute for a week of ecological training.

St. Helena Montessori School
1328 Spring St., St. Helena
• **(707) 963-1527**

This is Napa County's only Catholic Montessori facility, though it isn't affiliated with any one church. It's part of the Association Montessori Internationale, and its teachers must be accredited by that Amsterdam-based organization (founded by Dr. Maria Montessori in 1929). The school has about 75 pupils ranging from 2½ to 12 years (6th grade), and they are continually challenged to expand their abilities, though in a generally noncompetitive atmosphere. The youngest ones do tumbling and gymnastics, the elementary schoolers receive training in computers and foreign language, and all are exposed to the Orff-Schulwerk systematic music program.

St. Helena Catholic School
1255 Oak Ave., St. Helena
• **(707) 963-4677**

This school has been providing a Catholic education to Napa Valley residents since 1963. The sisters still aim for a well-rounded educa-

The Everett B. Person Theatre is a popular arts venue on the Sonoma State University campus in Rohnert Park

tion for their economically and ethnically diverse student body. With 130 to 135 kids spread between kindergarten and 8th grade, multi-age classrooms are the norm (except for the kindergartners). The Boys and Girls Club of St. Helena meets on campus in the afternoon, making it easy for Catholic School kids to take part.

Sonoma County

Old Adobe School
252 W. Spain St., Sonoma
• (707) 938-4510

As the name suggests, Old Adobe School was founded in a historic adobe building believed to have been built by Gen. Mariano Vallejo 200 years ago. It has since been moved to its present location on the grounds of the First Congregational Church. The school was started by John Larson, a single parent who saw a need for a school that could offer children quality instruction, an unpressured environment, and high regard for the individual child.

Old Adobe is private, nonprofit and has no religious affiliations. It is managed by a board consisting of parents, teachers, the school director and involved community members. It includes preschool as well as kindergarten (ages 2 through

6), with extended day care available for both classes. While separate age levels are given different instruction, there is frequent opportunity for children to interact with older or younger students during outside time and music time. The teaching philosophy can be summed up by a conversation between Alice in Wonderland and the Cheshire Cat. "Could you please tell me which is the right way to go?" asked Alice. "That depends entirely on where you want to get to," replied the cat. Each child is encouraged to develop and express his total self, learning, discovering and creating while growing. Cooperation rather than competition is stressed.

St. Francis Solano School
342 W. Napa St., Sonoma
• (707) 996-4994

St. Francis Solano School is something of an institution in Sonoma. The school traces its roots to Presentation Academy, founded in 1882 as an adjunct of the Sisters of Presentation Convent in Sonoma. Many years after the convent school had closed for lack of financial support, wine patriarch Samuele Sebastiani funded a new school for the St. Francis parish. Today, St. Francis Solano School is housed in its 1945 building next to the church. In 1996-97 the school underwent a $1.2 million remodeling to meet city requirements for earthquake safety and to reshape and modernize classrooms and offices.

The school is currently a diocesan school, and enrollment is around 350 students in kindergarten through 8th grade. Uniforms are required. Significant parental commitment (of both the financial and the hands-on varieties) is required, and upper-grade students are required to perform service hours. The school's reputation for academic excellence is well-established, with its middle school students consistently winning national and state honors in competitions. Other values emphasized at St. Francis Solano include community service, the gospel message, social justice and moral values.

The Presentation School
276 E. Napa St., Sonoma
• (707) 996-2496

Believing Sonoma Valley needed more educational opportunities, The Presentation School was founded in 1997 by local families, headed by Nancy and Don Sebastiani of the well-known winery family. The K-8 school opened in temporary quarters at the Sonoma Community Center with an enrollment of 150 students. Presentation School takes its name from Sonoma's original Presentation Academy, established in 1882 by the Sisters of Presentation from San Francisco. An independent Catholic school, Presentation's philosophy is, through education, "to build community, to proclaim the gospel message and to reach out to the world in service." Its core curriculum, in addition to traditional subjects, includes religious studies, language arts, music and physical education. With a limit of 20 students per grade, Presentation School offers "individualized instruction in a challenging, enriching and nurturing environment." Students are required to wear uniforms.

St. Vincent de Paul High School
849 Keokuk St. (at Magnolia), Petaluma
• (707) 763-1032

This Catholic high school run by the St. Vincent de Paul parish takes pride in its prep school academic environment. It has won top national awards for physics and biology instruction, and 95 percent of the school's graduates go on to college. With an enrollment of slightly more than 400, the school places an emphasis on Christian values and academic excellence and attracts students, both Catholic and non-Catholic, from all over southern and central Sonoma County. St. Vincent's also has a full interscholastic athletic program for boys and girls and has won many league championships in

the last decade in volleyball, football and baseball. Students are not required to wear uniforms. The parish also runs a small K-8 grade school.

Adobe Christian Preschool/Daycare
2875 Adobe Rd., Petaluma
• (707) 763-2012

Adobe school offers preschool and daycare for children from 2 to 5 years old, in a strong Christian environment. The curriculum stresses language development through the study of Bible literature and exploration of science and nature through gardening, animal care and nature study. There is also music, gymnastics and computer play. The philosophy of the school is to enable each child to experience the joy of playing, working and learning with other children. Child care is available from 6:30 AM to 6 PM.

Ursuline High School
90 Ursuline Rd., Santa Rosa
• (707) 524-1130

This Catholic school was started in 1880 in downtown Santa Rosa, but has been in its present location since 1957. The current population is more than 400 girls, who are required to wear uniforms. It's a college preparatory school—99 percent of the students go on to post-secondary school, and 85 percent of those graduate from four-year colleges across the country. SAT scores average 590 in verbal and 570 in math—higher than both state and national averages.

Aside from strong academic requirements, students must also perform community service. Seniors must plan a special project that puts them in the community researching needs, coming up with solutions, then implementing them with the help of a local mentor. Before graduation the student must appear before a board to describe the project, its goals and the steps planned to accomplish those goals. This is a determining factor in graduation. As a result of the program, many Ursuline students go on to become strong community leaders. The boys' school, Cardinal Newman High School, is just down the road, and although Ursuline freshmen and sophomores do not commingle, the girls in their junior and senior years share social activities with the boys of Cardinal Newman.

Cardinal Newman High School
50 Ursuline Rd., Santa Rosa
• (707) 546-6470

Students here adhere to the principle of education for "mind, body and spirit." Unlike

Ursuline High School, its girls' school counterpart, Cardinal Newman does not require uniforms for its 450 male students, but it does promote the same ideal of service to the community. Cardinal Newman is well-known for its emphasis on sports, and the Santa Rosa school has had great success in basketball and football. However, there are plenty of other sports to choose from—baseball, wrestling, swimming, water polo, tennis, soccer, cross-country skiing and track, to name a few. The school has a tradition of academic excellence, with more than 95 percent of students enrolling in four-year universities or two-year community colleges upon graduation.

St. Luke Lutheran School
905 Mendocino Ave., Santa Rosa
• (707) 545-0526

St. Luke's student body is drawn from throughout the Sonoma County area. It serves the educational needs of children from preschool through 8th grade in a nurturing environment geared to touch and change young lives spiritually, academically, emotionally, socially and intellectually. It is the goal of faculty to provide a positive atmosphere in which students develop self-discipline, experience their special status as God's own and are accepted by their teachers and peers. Any necessary discipline is approached in a dignified manner.

Stuart School
431 Humboldt St., Santa Rosa
• (707) 528-0721

Believing that "success is the strongest foundation for academic growth," Stuart School works with children from pre-kindergarten through 8th grade, and has done so since 1977. The downtown location is convenient for working parents and gives students opportunities for library and museum visits, and athletic activities in the nearby park. The faculty has extensive credentials, and they stress fundamental education built on phonics, vocabulary, reading, composition, science, math—and yes, recess! Believing that active kids are better students, every class has plenty of moving-around time.

Jacquelyn Giovanniello, who started the school in 1977 with her husband Ralph, holds a bachelor of music degree, two master's degrees, and a Ph.D. in Education. She was named Outstanding Educator for 1995-96 by the California League of Middle Schools. Ralph has served as superintendent in three school districts.

Merryhill Country School
4044 Mayette Ave. (Infants through junior kindergarten), Santa Rosa • (707) 575-7660
4580 Bennett View Dr. (K-6), Santa Rosa
• (707) 575-0910

The preschool program at Merryhill encourages youngsters to develop in a creative and stimulating environment. Focus is on activity-based learning, which includes counting, sorting and graphing and play-time learning with paints, puppets and music. The program for kindergarten through 6th grade is a strong, skills-based curriculum in literature, math, science, the visual arts, computer skills and Spanish. Parent involvement is considered one of the significant reasons that children succeed. The school is supervised from 6:30 AM to 6 PM daily.

The Bridge School
1625 Franklin Ave., Santa Rosa
• (707) 575-7959

In a nurturing and educationally stimulating environment, this school's goal is to bridge social development with academic growth. To that end, three programs are offered: Full Day Extended Care allows kids to experience this fun world from 7:30 AM to 5:30 PM Monday through Friday; Program Two offers either morning or afternoon half-day care; and Program Three is a flexible two- or three-day half-day program. Director Julie Day has a B.A. in child development, and her focus emphasizes the importance of allowing children room for individual creativity within a safe and nurturing environment. She has created parenting clubs and informative newsletters in an attempt to bridge the programs between school and family. Her combination of professional expertise and warm heart give The Bridge its unique difference.

INSIDERS' TIP

Isn't it time you thought about enrolling your 10-year-old in college? Sonoma State University's EXCEL program offers a variety of interesting, one-day Saturday classes for kids of various age groups (typically, grades 4-6 or 6-10). A recent example: Junior prosecutors and defenders develop their cases and present evidence at A Day in Court. EXCEL programs run in spring and summer only. For more information, call Sonoma State's Extended Education office at (707) 664-2394.

Little Angels Children's Center
4305 Hoen Ave., Santa Rosa
- **(707) 579-4305**

Offering both day care and preschool, the objectives at Little Angels are to help children acquire readiness skills, increase their ability to express themselves, learn to get along with others through work and play and accept responsibilities within a group setting. Although the school is owned and operated without church support, there are Bible stories, songs and prayers, with child participation. Other than that, the philosophy is to harness children's eagerness, curiosity and ability to grow in a stimulating environment.

Mendocino County

Mariposa School
3800 Low Gap Rd., Ukiah
- **(707) 462-1016**

With a successful record covering 27 years of hands-on education for children from first through fifth grade, Mariposa School follows a tradition of social and academic learning in multi-age classrooms. In a nurturing environment, youngsters pursue an academic program that integrates art, music, drama, Spanish and development of social skills. The country setting itself is beautiful—a place where children can play and learn amid oak woodlands.

Cozy Corner Children's Center
530 S. Main St., Ukiah
- **(707) 462-1251**

Children in this school are mainly ages 2 through 5, though children up to age 12 are welcome. Half-day or full-day sessions are available, and drop-ins are accepted. The strong point here is the loving and nurturing environment, but teachers work with the youngsters on academic readiness as well with a hands-on approach to learning to use the five senses. A dandy creative play area is augmented by a computer room to advance technological skills. The school usually has about 25 youngsters attending.

Melville Montessori School
400 E. Valley St., Willits
- **(707) 459-3100**

Although this is a Montessori school, it operates more on the American Montessori plan, according to Athena Melville, a founder of the school in 1980. Its program is more holistic, covering every aspect of the child, not just the intellect. Emphasis is on impressive and expres-sive areas. The philosophy mixes dance, singing, making music and having fun with concentration on history, English, science, the humanities and mathematics. Melville likes the idea of children teaching younger children, saying both older and younger students learn from the practice. Each Monday is "suggestion pig" day, when they break out the pig and see what suggestions have been dropped in by students. (Rulings are on a majority basis.) With fewer than 24 students total in kindergarten through grade 12, the pupil-teacher ratio remains low at about 12 students per teacher. The school invites visitors on a drop-in basis, from 9 AM to 3 PM on school days.

Deep Valley Christian School
8555 Uva Dr., Redwood Valley
- **(707) 485-8778**

Not sponsored by any specific religious organization, Deep Valley Christian School is committed to developing the best in every child, utilizing a back-to-basics curriculum that emphasizes individual responsibility. The student population runs to about 350 (grades K through 12 are represented), with average SAT scores well above state and national levels. Situated in beautiful Redwood Valley, a region of vineyards and oaks, the school is growing so rapidly that new buildings are being added to house a science lab, computer lab and gym. The athletic program includes both junior varsity and varsity football teams, volleyball, basketball and track. A great deal of pride is also taken in the music program at Deep Valley—especially the band. There are about 30 students to a class at the high-school level, and the school receives the strong support of parents, who are required to put 25 hours of volunteer time into school activities each year.

Lake County

Zemorah Christian Academy
16174 Main St., Lower Lake
- **(707) 994-4206**

Zemorah is Christian, but nondenominational. If you agree with the mission statement, you're free to sign up your kids. The K-through-12 school seeks to build "godly Christian character traits" such as discipline, honesty and kindness. It also has a strong phonics program—kindergartners are usually reading within nine weeks. Zemorah has music and drama programs and a full computer network. (The kids start learning the keyboard in 1st grade.)

Hilltop Christian Academy
40th St. and Snook Ave., Clearlake
• **(707) 994-3122**

This accredited, 12-grade facility is part of the School of Tomorrow, a national aggregation of 7,000 institutions. In 1997 the School of Tomorrow recognized Hilltop as a Quality School, its second-highest commendation. Hilltop teaches all the basics—math, English, etc.—with Biblical concepts. The student body is between 65 and 70.

Westlake Seventh Day Adventist Christian School
6585 Westlake Rd., Lakeport
• **(707) 263-4607**

This small Adventist school is in a perfectly peaceful setting, amidst oak trees at the Nice-Lucerne Cutoff. There are only two teachers and 20 to 40 students, but that doesn't negate extracurricular activities. The lower grades might make pizza or cookies one day, and the upper grades have been known to hold a three-day "outdoor school" in Southern California. Westlake, founded in 1942, serves grades 1 through 8.

Two-Year Colleges

Napa County

Napa Valley College
2277 Napa-Vallejo Hwy. (Calif. Hwy. 221), Napa
• **(707) 253-3000, (800) 826-1077**

Napa Valley College dates back to 1942 and has occupied its current site—180 tree-lined acres near the Napa River—since 1965. It's a two-year community college with about 9,000 students and associate degree programs in a spectrum of fields, including business administration, healthcare and, not surprisingly, viticulture and wine technology. On-campus facilities include a Child and Family Studies and Services complex and an Olympic-sized swimming pool. The school has an Upper Valley

Campus on the outskirts of St. Helena and a Small Business Development Center in Napa. It also shares a guaranteed transfer agreement with the University of California at Davis, Sacramento State University and Sonoma State University. And in case you were interested, it's the sister college of Launceston College in Tasmania.

Sonoma County

Santa Rosa Junior College
1501 Mendocino Ave., Santa Rosa
• **(707) 527-4011**

The scholarship program that blesses Santa Rosa Junior College is unique in all of America because of an association with the county-based Exchange Bank. In 1948 the bank's president, Frank P. Doyle, set up a trust that in the 1950-51 school year paid out $19,475 in scholarships to 95 students. In 1998-99, Doyle Scholarship money totaled $3.5 million for about 4,000 students, with some students receiving up to $1,750. Located on more than 100 acres, the college has a full-time enrollment of almost 7,000. Emphasis centers on general education, transfer education for students headed to four-year institutions and occupational education in the fields of dental hygiene, radiologic technology, respiratory therapy and many other areas.

The college's athletic teams (nicknamed the Bear Cubs) are part of the Bay Valley Conference, with the exception of the football team, which plays in the NorCal Conference. Intercollegiate competition for men and women is offered in baseball, basketball, cross-country, football, golf, gymnastics, soccer, swimming, tennis, track and field, volleyball, water polo and wrestling. A recent addition to Santa Rosa Junior College is an 87-seat planetarium. It has a dome 40 feet in diameter and 27 feet high. (See our Attractions chapter for information on this and other museums at the college; see our Arts and Culture chapter for information on theater troupes

INSIDERS' TIP
TrustLine is a powerful new resource for those wanting to hire a nanny or license-exempt child-care provider. All child-care providers listed with TrustLine have submitted their fingerprints to the California Department of Justice and have no disqualifying child-abuse reports or criminal convictions, and they are all in good standing with the Immigration and Naturalization Service. It costs the provider $90 to be registered. Nannies and babysitters placed through an employment agency must be listed on the TrustLine registry. For more information, call (415) 882-0234.

and events at the school.) An additional 40-acre campus in east Petaluma offers occupational training, national park ranger training, police and fire technology and public safety.

Empire College
3033 Cleveland Ave., Santa Rosa
• (707) 546-4000

Empire College offers four specialized associate degrees—in accounting, office technology, legal office administration, and medical assistance. It also offers certificates to those studying to become legal secretaries, medical administrative/clinical assistants, medical transcriptionists, bookkeepers, and travel and tourism agents. A state-accredited college, Empire has operated since 1961 and now has some 500 students.

Mendocino County

Mendocino College
1000 Hensley Creek Rd., Ukiah
• (707) 463-3073

The campus of Mendocino College occupies 126 acres and serves a rural area that encompasses 3,200 square miles. The school has additional educational centers at Willits and at Lakeport in Lake County. Founded in 1972 as a junior college, Mendocino provides the first two years of study for a four-year degree, or confers an associate degree with vocational training in a wide variety of fields. There are programs in horticulture, agriculture, administration of justice, business administration, computer and information sciences, premedicine and pre-nursing, to name a few.

Construction projects have been ongoing since 1985, when the Lowery Library building was completed and the college moved into its permanent facility. Other campus buildings include the classroom/office building, horticulture center, and a child-care center. One of the most stunning new buildings is the Center for Performing Arts, with its 400-seat theater and recording studio that houses programs in theater arts, music, arts and textiles. The physical education program and the college's sports activities take place in an $8.2-million complex.

INSIDERS' TIP

A basic familiarity with Spanish is more important than ever in California, especially in businesses that employ a lot of Latino immigrants (restaurants, agriculture, construction-based businesses). If you're seeking to improve your *lengua española*, you might call Spanish For Business at (707) 257-1809. It's a Napa-based company that teaches Spanish in small groups.

Both the Willits and Lake County centers provide administrative services and classrooms, plus counseling and financial aid assistance. Mendocino College has an additional facility at Point Arena, 50 miles southwest of Ukiah, which serves as a field laboratory for science classes in marine biology, geology and meteorology.

College of the Redwoods
1211 Del Mar Dr., Fort Bragg
• (707) 962-2600

The main campus of College of the Redwoods is at Eureka in Humboldt County. This is a two-year community college offering associate degrees, career training and enrichment classes to residents of the north coast of California. Students receive top academic instruction in science, mathematics and humanities courses, which transfer to Humboldt State University and other colleges and universities across the nation.

The Fort Bragg campus is beautiful, with low-lying buildings of natural-finish wood, an unobstructed view of the ocean and a student population of 1,200. In addition to courses offered at the main campus, the Fort Bragg center offers courses in marine science. The Fort Bragg school is also well-known for courses in fine woodworking—they have a one-year program (though many sign up for a second year); its worldwide fame is such that students come from all over the world to study cabinetry and furniture-making. The college also offers a program that links art with computer technology to provide for study in photo transfer work and graphics communication. College of the Redwoods has no athletic program.

Lake County

Yuba College
15880 Dam Rd., Clearlake
• (707) 995-7900

Since 1972 Lake County has been home to the secondary campus of Yuba College, a community college based in Marysville (to the east in Yuba County). The Clearlake campus offers a dozen different degree certificates, specializing in business and vocational fields such as welding, food services, computers and income tax preparation. It also has the only program in Northern California to study water and wastewater treatment. Yuba College has between 1,200 and 1,500 students in Lake County, some 300 of whom attend full-time during the day. The faculty is composed of six full-time and numerous part-time teachers drawn from the business community. The school is currently trying to raise funds for a Performing Arts Center to enhance the 11-acre campus.

Mendocino College (Lake Center)
1005 Parallel Dr., Lakeport
• (707) 263-4944

Mendocino College, centered in Ukiah, also has a satellite at a leased facility in downtown Lakeport (see previous listing for Mendocino College in this chapter). It used to be that you couldn't get your two-year degree without attending at least some classes at the main campus, but that is no more. The Lake Center now offers most, but not all, of the certificate programs found in Ukiah, including business office technology (with subcategories in legal assistance and medical assistance), small business management, child development and psychology. Students get library services through an arrangement with the Lake County Library, and would-be astronomers make use of the Lake County Observatory/Planetarium on Mount Konocti. The college has about 1,000 students in Lakeport, counting both full- and part-time attendees.

Four-year Colleges and Universities

Napa County

Pacific Union College
1 Angwin Ave., Angwin
• (707) 965-6311

PUC is a small (just more than 1,600 students), private, Seventh-day Adventist college surrounded by 1,800 acres of crops and forest on the top of Howell Mountain, where it has been since 1906. The views are fabulous, and the education is highly regarded. *U.S. News & World Report* ranked the school the top liberal arts college in California in 1998, and *The Right College* places it in the top 10 in the nation for the percentage of male graduates that enter medical school. The student-faculty ratio is an appealing 12-to-1.

Pacific Union is most definitely a unique experience. The student body is ethnically diverse, the cafeteria is vegetarian (in line with Seventh-day Adventist practice), and the Abroad Program offers overseas study, including full-year programs in Argentina, Austria, France, Kenya and Spain. Service is a big part of a PUC student's commitment. Many strike out on yearlong missions, and even more are actively involved with local homeless shelters, prison ministries and the like. The college offers associate, bachelor's and master's degrees in 19 academic departments. The 50-plus areas of study include all the usual subjects, plus things like digital media technology, fashion merchandising and medical technology. Pacific Union is on the quarter system.

Sonoma County

University of Northern California
101 S. San Antonio Rd., Petaluma
• (707) 765-6400

This new university, established in 1993, welcomes students from around the world. It aspires to become a premier engineering and scientific university with substantial programs in the liberal arts. Students enjoy small classes with ample individual attention from professors dedicated to quality teaching. At this writing, there are about 50 full-time equivalent students at the university, more than half of which are in graduate studies. Interdisciplinary studies are encouraged, and all academic programs emphasize the importance of effective communication for success in the modern world. The university focuses on programs in biological technology, and its early degree programs include the B.E., M.S. and Ph.D. in Biomedical Engineering and the B.A. in Engineering and in Languages and Linguistics. The idyllic 194-acre campus, with spectacular views of unspoiled scenery, provides an ideal environment for learning.

Sonoma State University
1801 E. Cotati Ave., Rohnert Park
• (707) 664-2880

This university was established on 270 acres of farmland in 1960 to fill an educational void in the North Bay counties. Today it offers undergraduate liberal arts and science curricula and 13 master's degree programs to a student population of about 7,000. Its computer engineering graduates walk directly into high-paying jobs, and similar results are expected for those completing the new wine business pro-

Photo: Tina Luster-Hoban

Sonoma State University in Rohnert Park is the cornerstone of higher education in this area.

gram. The school's Sonoma Plan is considered a model nursing program throughout America.

Performing arts get top billing at the campus, with plays from the pens of local writers and international favorites performed year round, along with dance recitals and musical concerts (see our Arts and Culture chapter). Sonoma State ranks high in sports among the 23 campuses of the state system, with championships in men's and women's soccer, volleyball, women's basketball and baseball during the 1997-98 school year. In all, the university has 16 intercollegiate teams. Its outdoor swimming pool is open to faculty, staff and students and has access for the disabled.

Other Institutes of Higher Learning

Napa County

The Culinary Institute of America at Greystone
2555 Main St., St. Helena • (707) 967-1100

Executives of the Culinary Institute of America, that factory of chefs in Hyde Park, New York, looked at some 50 potential sites

when they decided to establish a West Coast center for continuing education. Their logical choice was Greystone, the majestic winery built in 1888 and used by the Christian Brothers to make sparkling wine from 1950 to 1989. After a massive gift from the Heublein Corporation (then owners of the property) and a $14 million renovation, the CIA opened for business in Napa Valley in August 1995.

It remains the only center in the world dedicated exclusively to continuing education for professionals in the food, wine, health and hospitality fields. Inside, the facilities are almost as impressive as the 22-inch-thick tufa stone walls that frame Greystone's exterior. The third story is an immense teaching kitchen with 15,000 square feet of undivided floor space, 35-foot ceilings and clusters of exquisite Bonnet stoves. In the middle of the space is a dining area where students sample the various assignments they and their cohorts have handed in.

The building also houses the EcoLab Theater, a 125-seat amphitheater used for cooking demonstrations and lectures; the Wine Spectator Greystone Restaurant (see our Restaurants chapter for more on that); The Campus Store with its preponderance of cooking equipment, books and uniforms; and the DeBaun Food and Wine Museum, which displays a changing collection of wine-related artifacts. Outside the old winery are garlic and onion beds, seven ter-races of herbs, an edible flower and herbal tea garden and, off-site, 15 acres of Merlot grapes and an organic fruit and vegetable garden.

Courses vary in length from three days to the 30-week, two-semester Baking and Pastry Arts Certification Program. (The average class dura-tion is one week.) Examples of recent courses include Soups, Stocks, Sauces and Salsas; Food and Beverage Cost Control; Food and Wine Dy-namics; and the annual Food Writers' Workshop. The faculty is drawn from three sources: the small but talented core of resident instructors, visiting teachers from Hyde Park and guest instructors. The latter have included everyone from Tra Vigne's Michael Chiarello to Rick Bayless, owner and chef of Topolobampo and the Frontera Grill in Chicago, to Jeff Dawson, garden director for Fetzer Vineyards.

Sonoma County

Western Institute of Science and Health
130 Avram Ave., Rohnert Park
• **(707) 664-9267**

The Western Institute of Science and Health offers an Associate of Science program for physi-cal therapist assistants and helps its students find employment in hospitals, outpatient clin-ics, public schools and home-health agencies. The Institute teaches students, through aca-demic courses and clinical internship experi-ences, how to effectively treat patients who suffer from physical impairment. Graduates must pass a state examination given by the Physical Therapy Examination Committee be-fore they may practice in California.

Mendocino County

Dharma Realm Buddhist University
City of Ten Thousand Buddhas,
2001 Talmage Rd., Ukiah
• **(707) 468-9112**

State-approved Dharma Realm University offers year-round education to qualified stu-dents, with programs leading to bachelor's, master's and doctoral certificates. The empha-sis is on Buddhist study and practice, including loyalty, felicity, humaneness and righteousness. Students are given the opportunity to develop their innate wholesome wisdom. At the same time, high standards of academic excellence are maintained. Degrees are currently offered in

Buddhist studies and practice, translation and Buddhist education. Full scholarships are avail-able to qualified students.

Child Care

Sometimes it seems there are more child-care centers than children out there. In any case, there are dozens from which to choose, no matter where you're located in Wine Coun-try. And each differs from the next in small ways. Some centers are church-affiliated, oth-ers purely secular; some are in charming, turn-of-the-century Victorians, others in office com-plexes; some provide transportation, others leave that to you; some accept infants, others don't; some are low-tech, others have comput-ers the kids can tinker with; some aren't really "centers" at all, but licensed homes.

Each county has at least one organization that will help you sort out all the factors, free of charge. They are able to quote prices, describe individual providers and refer you to ones in which you might be interested. Here we list those, by county.

Napa County

Community Resources for Children
5 Financial Plaza, Ste. 224, Napa
• **(707) 253-0376 (general information),**
  (707) 253-0366 (referrals)

This nonprofit agency, funded primarily by the California Department of Education but supplemented by federal and private contribu-tions, is an important friend to Napa County families. Community Resources for Children (CRC) is contacted most often for its free re-ferrals to child-care centers and in-home pro-viders. It does a lot more than that, though. It gives financial assistance to qualifying fami-lies, trains prospective child-care providers, ad-vocates for children and families in the com-munity, provides low-cost car seats to eligible families and maintains a lending library of toys, videos, books and educational resources. CRC can help you find a continuing day-care center or a one-day baby sitter. *Se habla español.*

Sonoma County

Community Child Care Council
396 Tesconi Ct., Santa Rosa
• **(707) 544-3077**

This service (known as 4Cs) helps parents

find a suitable system of child care by providing names of licensed centers or homes near the parents' home or workplace. To assure that parents get the best from their search, 4Cs provides a list of questions parents should ask when they call—such as what educational training is offered, whether the staff has CPR training and any special programs offered. Another list indicates things parents should look for when they visit the facility. No recommendations are offered, but lists of licensed care centers and homes are extensive.

If parents prefer someone unlicensed to come into their home, such as a nanny or au pair, 4Cs will give advice on that as well. Other possibilities that 4Cs can help with include co-op, parent participation preschool planning and organizing play groups in which parents and children meet in one another's homes on a rotating basis.

River Child Care Services
16315 First St., Guerneville
• (707) 869-3613

This service covers the area along the Russian River and West County as far as the coast, providing information on choosing childcare and offering lists of licensed providers and home-based care. In addition to long-term regular care, they also can advise on babysitting services. The organization can provide parents with important information about prospective providers, such as methods of discipline used (spanking is not allowed), what happens if the provider is ill or the child is ill, and where meals are eaten.

River Child Care Services offers a list of workers interested in caring for children on a family-by-family basis. However, a referral does not imply a recommendation or a guarantee of quality. A brochure they publish gives some good hints on interviewing candidates by phone.

Mendocino and Lake Counties

North Coast Opportunities, Inc.
413 N. State St., Ukiah
• (707) 462-1954
1450 S. Main St., Willits
• (707) 459-2019
155 Cypress St., Ft. Bragg
• (707) 964-3080
14560 Lakeshore Dr., Clearlake
•(707) 994-4647
850 Lakeport Blvd., Lakeport
• (707) 263-4688
9470 Mendenhall Ave., Upper Lake
• (707) 275-9474

This valuable, not-for-profit organization is dedicated to offering referrals and resources to families in the largely rural and dispersed counties of Mendocino and Lake. Anyone who calls is given a free referral to one or more state-licensed child-care facilities. North Coast Opportunities also offers child-care subsidies, support services for both parents and providers, and a helpful food and nutrition program. If you have a general question about the service, call the Parent-Child Information Center at (707) 462-1954.

Healthcare

LOOK FOR:
- Walk-In/Prompt-Care Centers
- Hospitals
- Hospice Care
- Alternative Healthcare

Considering that most of our Wine Country region is rural, the population relatively sparse and the towns small to midsize, healthcare is amazingly accessible and excellent in quality. Beyond that, you'll find hospital staff members are "small-town friendly," devoid of the harried rush found in some big-city hospitals.

On the local level, zealous hospital benefactors have pitched in to provide state-of-the-art equipment and medical instruments. And to top it off, some of Northern California's finest doctors have gravitated by choice to this laid-back land, providing the kind of technically current surgical and medical expertise that normally exists in metropolitan areas.

Emergency service is available throughout much of the area. So . . . if you should be unfortunate enough to get sick in our territory, rest assured you'll be treated well by experts.

Walk-In/Prompt-Care Centers

Napa County

ExpressCare
Queen of the Valley Hospital,
1000 Trancas St., Napa
- **(707) 257-4008**

This walk-in center, an adjunct of Queen of the Valley's emergency room, is open from 9 AM to 9 PM daily and can address a variety of non-lethal illnesses, allergies and injuries. (As the ExpressCare brochure says, "There is no such thing as a little emergency.") Board-certified physicians are on hand to treat you, and they will make referrals or deliver follow-up care if needed.

Upper Napa Valley Urgent Care
1370 Railroad Ave., St. Helena
- **(707) 963-4399**

Upvalley residents gained a little peace of mind when this clinic opened in St. Helena in 1999. Urgent Care treats all non-life-threatening ailments, including pain, migraine headaches, asthma, rashes, in-

fections, allergies and Homer Simpson-style, self-inflicted boo-boos. No appointment is necessary. The hours are generally Monday, Wednesday and Friday from 11 AM to 6 PM; Tuesday and Thursday from 9 AM to 6 PM; Saturday from 11 AM to 4 PM and Sunday from 11 AM to 3 PM.

Sonoma County

Sutter Medical Center
Urgent Care Center
3325 Chanate Rd., Santa Rosa
- **(707) 576-4100**

An urgent-care center operates as a separate unit of Sutter Medical Center, just outside the emergency department. Minor, non-life-threatening injuries and ailments can be

INSIDERS' TIP

Sutter Lakeside Hospital serves a modest population but a huge geographic area. In an effort to cut down the hospital's response time, a heliport was added in 1983. Now seriously injured patients can be airlifted straight to Lakeport.

treated at this walk-in clinic at a lower cost than in the emergency room. It's open seven days a week, Mondays through Fridays from 1 PM to 9 PM, Saturdays and Sundays 8:30 AM to 5 PM. (Meanwhile, Sutter's emergency room is open seven days a week, 24 hours a day.)

Lake County

Lower Lake Clinic
9245 Calif. Hwy. 53,
Lower Lake • (707) 994-0400

This facility is affiliated with Redbud Community Hospital. The walk-in clinic has a staff of nurse practitioners and a rotation of doctors to dispense prescriptions and medical advice. It's open from 9 AM to 4:30 PM Monday through Friday, excluding a noon to 1:30 PM lunch break.

Sutter Lakeside Hospital
Urgent Care Center
5176 Hill Rd. E., Lakeport
• (707) 262-5008

Sutter Lakeside has an urgent care center available for those who need non-emergency treatment, but have no primary care physician. There are two ways to end up here: make an appointment, or go to the emergency room and get screened by a trained nurse who refers you here. The urgent care center is open 9 AM to 9 PM daily.

Hospitals

Napa County

Queen of the Valley Hospital
1000 Trancas St., Napa • (707) 252-4411

Queen of the Valley might be best known as the hospital that posts a hotel-trained concierge in the front lobby. It's a well-respected facility with 162 beds. QVH has a community cancer center, a high-end imaging department, home-care services, maternity services (including an intensive-care nursery), occupational health services, a regional heart center where open-heart surgeries are performed and a respiratory-care department. Queen of the Valley is the designated trauma center for Napa County. It has a 24-hour emergency room and offers the Queen's Carriage, a van that serves outpatients from Yountville to American Canyon.

A couple of QVH services stand out. The Acute Rehabilitation Center offers comprehensive physical, occupational and speech thera-pies for people who have experienced trauma (such as a stroke or spinal cord injury). And the hospital's community pharmaceutical services provide infusion capability, clinical monitoring and computerized pumps for patients at home. Queen of the Valley is part of the St. Joseph Health System, which emphasizes dignity, service, justice and excellence.

St. Helena Hospital
650 Sanitarium Rd., Deer Park
• (707) 963-3611,
TTY/TDD: (707) 963-6527

We know, the address conjures up lightning storms and strange goings-on in the basement, but don't be alarmed. This full-service community hospital, off the Silverado Trail about 3 miles northeast of St. Helena, dates back to the 1800s, when a sanitarium was a health resort.

St. Helena Hospital has 192 licensed beds and 36 beds for residential health-enhancement programs. It also has a wide range of specialties, including cardiac surgery, cardiovascular rehabilitation, pulmonary rehabilitation, mental health services, oncology, obstetrics, pain rehabilitation and preventive medicine. And it not only offers many services but also performs them well. The Joint Commission on Accreditation of Healthcare Organizations gave the facility a score of 96 out of 100.

A member of the Adventist Health network of facilities, St. Helena is known for its sleep disorders clinic and, especially, its cardiovascular lab—a major heart center for Northern California. If you want a state-of-the-art, peephole view of someone's arteries, this lab is the place to go. Add to the mix hospice services (through a joint venture with Queen of the Valley Hospital) and extensive adult mental health services, both inpatient and day treatment. The hospital's Health Center offers community classes on relevant fitness topics such as smoking cessation and weight loss.

Finally, St. Helena has a Women's Center in downtown St. Helena, providing mammography, bone density testing, a health resource library and a wide range of health education classes and support groups. The Women's Center is at 1299 Pine Street; call (707) 963-1912.

Sonoma County

Sonoma Valley Hospital
347 Andrieux St., Sonoma
• (707) 935-5000

When Sonoma Valley Hospital was created

in 1944, the vision was to combine the best of medicine with a warm and caring staff. Since that date, tremendous advances in research and diagnosis have changed the face of medicine. But Sonoma Valley Hospital remains a warm, caring, family-oriented hospital with the same small-town spirit that permeates the community from which it draws its patients.

Today's 83-bed facility serves 40,000 people in Sonoma Valley. The credentialed medical staff totals 136 active, consulting and courtesy physicians involved in 25 different disciplines. The intensive care unit has six private rooms staffed by experienced critical-care nurses. A full range of cardiopulmonary testing equipment is available, along with cardiac rehab programs. A Birth Center provides a comfortable, homey place where labor, delivery, recovery and postpartum phases all take place in one room with the family at hand. Recently a state-of-the-art system was installed linking doctors instantly to patient information and test results.

Besides serving as an acute-care hospital, Sonoma Valley has also evolved over the years as a resource for keeping local residents healthy with fitness activities, screening clinics and education programs.

Petaluma Valley Hospital
400 N. McDowell Blvd., Petaluma
• **(707) 778-1111**

With 86 beds and 30 medical specialties from cardiology to urology, this is a busy place. The attractive two-story, 19-year-old hospital is also a genuine community resource. There's a full-service emergency department with a physician on duty 24 hours a day and a helipad for emergency helicopter air transport. The pharmacy is open and staffed seven days a week, 24 hours a day. Other features available to the community include home healthcare, a hospice and an electronic telecommunications system called Lifeline that provides 24-hour emergency access to anyone who might need quick response at home.

Petaluma Valley has a number of educational programs that offer assistance in quitting smoking and living with cancer. The hospital also offers consultation for diabetics. Other services include counseling on nutrition, food

allergies, dialysis and pregnancy. Visitors are welcome to tour Petaluma Valley Hospital.

Santa Rosa Memorial Hospital
1165 Montgomery Dr., Santa Rosa
• **(707) 546-3210**

Memorial Hospital opened its doors in 1950 under the guidance of the Sisters of St. Joseph, founders of eight other hospitals on the West Coast since 1920. All services and programs are guided by the healing mission of the Sisters—service, excellence, justice and dignity for all members of the community.

In addition to cutting-edge surgical facilities and medical equipment, 225-bed Memorial Hospital has some unique services including the Mobile Health Clinic, which serves children 16 and younger from low-income families that have difficulty locating affordable healthcare. Care is provided by medical professionals who speak English and Spanish. The hospital has also set up a clinic for students at Elsie Allen High School—one of only 50 such school-based clinics in California—to treat minor illnesses or injuries, administer immunizations and provide counseling for emotional problems.

The Family Birthing Center is beautiful—a setting to remember for a lifetime—its soothing decor of pastel colors and wallcoverings inspired by impressionist painters. Windows open onto a garden patio where new mothers and the family can stroll. Top-notch medical equipment helps ensure safe delivery, with operating rooms available should Caesarean delivery be necessary. (It's a wonder that the Sonoma County birth rate hasn't risen sharply!)

INSIDERS' TIP

Need some information on a medical condition affecting you or a family member? The Redwood Health Library, a community service of Petaluma Valley Hospital, is a consumer health library—a medical library designed for public use. At 314 Western Avenue in Petaluma, (707) 778-9114, it is the only resource of its kind in Sonoma County.

Warrack Hospital
2449 Summerfield Rd., Santa Rosa
• **(707) 542-9030**

Built in 1960, Warrack is a 79-bed hospital with four operating rooms. Its primary services cover intensive and coronary care, pediatric surgery and diagnostic imaging. Emergency care is available 24 hours a day, with a physician always on duty. Warrack is one of the few certified diabetic counseling centers in the state, with educational programs to help patients adjust to living with the condition. Special programs are offered on diabetes and pregnancy. Warrack also has a physician referral service, giving names of physicians who are still accepting new patients.

Sutter Medical Center of Santa Rosa
3325 Chanate Rd., Santa Rosa
• (707) 576-4000

This hospital was established in 1866 and has provided advanced health-care services for Sonoma County and the adjoining communities for 132 years.

As a teaching institution affiliated with the University of California at San Francisco School of Medicine, Community Hospital is regionally recognized for its wide range of specialty services, including a high-risk maternity department, newborn intensive care unit and an emergency trauma care program. It offers other special services too. Need health information? A free call to (800) 500-0114 will connect you with a registered nurse who can give advice or refer you to a physician.

The Emergency/Trauma department provides specialized care for head injuries 24 hours a day, utilizing the most advanced diagnostic equipment and life-support technology in the area. It's the only hospital in the region with on-site magnetic resonance imaging (MRI) available around the clock.

North Coast Health Care Center
1287 Fulton Rd., Santa Rosa
• (707) 543-2400

Operating in six locations (five in Santa Rosa and one in Petaluma), the North Coast clinics offer a wide range of services, both inpatient and outpatient. Two locations have hospital facilities for medical and surgical patients, with a specialty of orthopedic surgery. Some of the other services in its six facilities include physical and speech therapy, and rehabilitation from brain injuries, strokes, spinal cord injuries and comas. Home healthcare and pre-employment physicals are also offered.

Healdsburg General Hospital
1375 University Ave., Healdsburg
• (707) 431-6500

Today's Healdsburg General is a far cry from the World War I-era, wood-frame building that burned to the ground in the 1930s. Amazingly,

there was no loss of life, although patients had to be carried one-by-one down flights of stairs from surgery. Rebuilt during World War II when medical staff was virtually unavailable, the hospital was mainly operated by the director of nursing, who coped with staff shortages by hiring schoolgirls to do nursing chores while she slept on a gurney (on call) at night.

Today's hospital is a beautiful modern facility boasting 43 beds, 275 employees, 50 physicians and 48 volunteers. Hospital services include a 24-hour emergency room, orthopedic services, a homey family birthing center, same-day surgery center and an outpatient mental health program for seniors.

Palm Drive Hospital
501 Petaluma Ave.,
Sebastopol
• (707) 823-8511

A small hospital with 55 beds and one operating room, Palm Drive offers an unusual specialty—a Sleep Center that monitors the sleep patterns of insomniacs and helps find remedies. It is one of the few small hospitals with such a program. Another popular program is an occupational medicine center for those with work-related injuries. It offers therapy to help the injured get back on the job. The hospital also has an excellent orthopedic center. Home healthcare services include respiratory therapy, and the emergency room is open 24 hours a day.

INSIDERS' TIP

If you are a Kaiser Permanente subscriber staying in the Napa area, note that the hospital group has a facility in Vallejo, only 15 miles away. They'll take your calls at (707) 258-2500.

Mendocino County

Ukiah Valley Medical Center
275 Hospital Dr., Ukiah
• (707) 462-3111

A member of the Adventist Health Corporation, this 116-bed hospital has offered a full spectrum of outpatient treatment and surgery since its inception in 1956, when it was known as Hillside Hospital. In 1979 it joined the 18-hospital Adventist Health group. This affiliation provides the advantage of being connected to a network of locations so that patients can be transferred quickly, by helicopter if necessary, to whichever Adventist Health hospital specializes in treating the particular problem.

The Adventist's university at Loma Linda is famed for being on the cutting edge of cardiac expertise, knowledge and treatment.

HEALTHCARE

Hence, Ukiah Valley offers a high-quality cardiac specialty department.

Frank R. Howard Memorial Hospital
Madrone and Manzanita Sts., Willits
• **(707) 459-6801**

Affiliated with the Adventist Health group since 1986, Frank R. Howard Memorial Hospital has been a part of the Willits community for 72 years. Willits is a small community (population 4,100) and also serves as a gateway to wide-open spaces to the north. That means the hospital serves a population in a wide area of wilderness and ranch and forest land as far north as the Oregon border. There is 24-hour emergency service. While the hospital is small (just 28 beds), its connection with the Adventist group gives it wide latitude in serving patients through larger hospitals in the group.

Redwood Coast Medical Services
46900 Ocean Dr., Gualala
• **(707) 884-4005**

In a town too small to accommodate a hospital, this federally qualified medical-service facility fills a gap with medical specialists that include an ophthalmologist, cardiologist, oncologist and orthopedist. Doctors are on duty 24 hours a day to treat injuries and medical emergencies for visitors and residents alike, and can be reached for services after Redwood Coast closes.

Mendocino Coast District Hospital
700 River Dr., Fort Bragg
• **(707) 961-1234**

Its garden setting makes this lone hospital on the Mendocino coast very attractive. Created by the cities of the coastal community in 1971, it still maintains an attitude that locals call "neighbors taking care of neighbors." Patients from large cities often remark on this small-town support and warmth, and on how amazingly caring the hospital personnel can be. With 54 beds, two operating rooms and an outpatient surgery area, services offered include critical-care facilities, laboratory services, radiology and cardiopulmonary care. A very active ambulance service travels to coastal areas as far away as Westport, 16 miles north.

Lake County

Redbud Community Hospital
18th Ave. and Calif. Hwy. 53, Clearlake
• **(707) 994-6486**

Squeezed, as many smaller hospitals are these days, by spiraling insurance and equipment costs, Redbud Community (established 1968) became part of the large Adventist Health network (see previous listings for St. Helena Hospital, Ukiah Valley Medical Center and Frank R. Howard Memorial Hospital). Anything but a hostile takeover, the deal was approved by 89 percent of Clearlake voters in 1996.

Redbud's makeup changed little in the process. It is still a 40-bed facility with 180 full-time employees, a volunteer staff of about 40 and 75 doctors—25 to 30 of them on active duty at any given time. The hospital has 24-hour emergency care and offers services such as nuclear medicine, mammography, cardio-pulmonary care, imaging techniques (such as ultrasound), obstetrics and gynecology, an intensive care unit and extensive outpatient service.

Sutter Lakeside Hospital
5176 Hill Rd. E., Lakeport
• **(707) 262-5000**

Lakeside Community Hospital was Lake County's first major infirmary, established as a 30-bed unit in 1945. The private facility was donated to the community by the family of Dr. Neal Woods in 1966, when it was deeded to the nonprofit Lakeside Community Hospital corporation. In 1978 the hospital moved from its original structure to a 32,000-square-foot facility on adjoining property, toting all its supplies and equipment—not to mention 14 patients—up the hill. Lakeside added a new wing in 1986, and in 1992 it joined Sutter Health, a nonprofit organization operating across Northern California.

Today the hospital provides a broad range of services, including an emergency department that, combined with the urgent care center, treats 25,000 patients a year; an intensive care unit; a full array of medical imaging

---

INSIDERS' TIP

St. Helena Hospital was founded as St. Helena Sanitarium in 1878. The founder was Merritt Kellogg —Seventh-Day Adventist, holistic-health maniac and half-brother of cereal mogul Will Keith Kellogg. For an outrageously fictionalized account of Merritt's spa endeavors, rent *The Road to Wellville*, a movie starring John Cusack and Anthony Hopkins.

Photo: Tina Luster-Hoban

Queen of the Valley Hospital provides quality medical and emergency care for visitors and residents of Napa.

diagnostics, including CAT scans, MRIs and mammography; a cardiac rehabilitation center; home medical services and an obstetric wing. Sutter Lakeside also has added four outpatient centers offering obstetric and gynecological, internal medicine, pediatric and family care services. Despite the arrangement with Sutter Health, a local board of directors plots the hospital's course.

Hospice Care

Napa County

Hospice of Napa Valley
5 Financial Plaza, Ste. 201, Napa
• **(707) 258-9080, (800) 451-4664**

If the time comes to end the aggressive search for a cure and to focus instead on comfort and symptom alleviation as death approaches, hospice care is the appropriate choice. Hospice of Napa Valley, a nonprofit organization and a joint community service of St. Helena Hospital and Queen of the Valley Hospital, has been serving the county since 1979.

The hospice's provisions include round-the-clock, on-call nursing, short-term respite to reduce caregiver stress, medical equipment, oxygen and intermittent visits from team members. That team includes a medical director, the patient's physician, registered nurses, medical social workers, home health aides, chaplains, bereavement counselors and volunteers. Hospice of Napa Valley accepts patients regardless of ability to pay. Grief education and counseling services are also available to community members.

Sonoma County

Hospice of Petaluma
416 Payran St., Petaluma
• **(707) 778-6242**

Memorial Hospice
558 B St., Santa Rosa
• **(707) 568-1094**

Working in tandem, these agencies exist to provide support and care for persons facing life-threatening illness so that they may live as fully and comfortably as possible. Hospice of Petaluma (working with Memorial Hospice of Santa Rosa) benefits the community served by Petaluma Valley Hospital and Santa Rosa Memorial hospitals. A counseling and social work staff offers emotional support, counseling and information about community resources. A hospice chaplain provides spiritual support. Nursing services include expert pain and symptom management, home visits, and 24-hour on-call family assistance. Trained volunteers also lend support and provide companionship for family members. After the fact, there also is grief counseling, support and education.

Lake County

Hospice Services of Lake County
1717 S. Main St., Lakeport
• **(707) 263-6222**

Lake County citizens suffering from heart disease, cancer, AIDS and end-stage Alzheimer's have been turning to this state-licensed hospice since 1979. It's a nonprofit organization committed to the medical, nursing, psychological, emotional and spiritual needs of the terminally ill and their families. The goal is to keep subjects at home and to provide comfort care rather than a curative treatment approach to the disease, when that is what the patient wishes.

The patient's personal physician must authorize hospice care. Bereavement counselors offer grief support before the death and for up to one year afterward at no charge. The organization denies care to no one, regardless of a patient's ability to pay.

Alternative Healthcare

Alternative forms of treatment and prevention proliferate and thrive around here. Why? First of all, this is the Wine Country, where health and quality of life are paramount. And second, this is California, where people tend to be open-minded in their decision-making.

So if you harbor a general mistrust of hospitals and M.D.s, or if you're simply in search of a less confrontational cure for what ails you, you're in luck. Within a short drive you can find homeopaths and naturopaths, Ayurvedics and herbalists, acupuncturists and acupressurists, chiropractors and yoga gurus, reflexologists and hypnotists and practitioners of reiki, rolfing and biofeedback. You can even find a few shaman healers if you try hard enough. The Sonoma

County phone book alone lists 55 acupuncturists, 46 hypnotists, 10 homeopaths and about a million chiropractors. If you want to verify a license, you might call the Medical Board of California at (916) 263-2635.

Now get out there and heal.

Safety in Numbers

Call 911 during any medical emergency. If an ambulance is not what you need, consider one of the following numbers. In the first group are lines that apply throughout the Wine Country. They are followed by county-specific numbers.

Throughout Wine Country

Poison Control Center
• (800) 523-2222
National HIV and AIDS Information
Service
• English: (800) 273-2437;
Spanish: (800) 344-7432;
TDD: (800) 243-7889
Crisis Line for the Handicapped
• (800) 426-4263
California Smokers Helpline
• (800) 766-2888
Centers for Disease Control and
Prevention (Sexually Transmitted
Disease Hotline)
• (800) 227-8922
Medical Board of California
(Central Complaint Unit)
• (800) 633-2322
Mental Health Referral Service
• (800) 843-7274
Dental Referral • (800) DENTIST

Napa County

Suicide Prevention
• Napa/Yountville: (707) 255-2555;
Calistoga/St. Helena: (707) 963-2555
Napa County Health and Human
Services Department • (707) 253-6052
Napa Valley AIDS Project • (707) 258-2437
Napa County Alcohol and Drug
Services • (707) 253-4412
Napa Emergency Women's Services
• (707) 255-6397
Napa Walk-In Center (short-term
crisis counseling) • (707) 224-4309

Sonoma County

Sonoma County Department
of Health Services and Center for
HIV Prevention and Care
• (707) 524-7373
Suicide Prevention • (707) 576-8181
Crisis Line for the Handicapped
• (800) 426-4263
Department of Alcohol and Drug
Programs • (800) 879-2772

Mendocino County

Mendocino County Health
Department •(800) 734-7793
Mendocino County Suicide
Prevention • (800) 575-43599
Community Care AIDS Project
of Mendocino and Lake Counties
• (707) 995-1606

Lake County

Lake County Health Department
• Clearlake: (707) 994-9433;
Lakeport: (707) 263-2241
Lake County Mental Health
Department (Suicide Prevention)
• (800) 222-8220
Community Care AIDS Project of Lake
and Mendocino Counties
• (707) 995-1606

Media

LOOK FOR:
- Daily Newspapers
- Other Newspapers
- Magazines
- Other Publications
- Radio Stations
- Television

California's Wine Country likes to bill itself as a collection of small, unhurried towns with an air of big-city sophistication. The image is true—to a degree. The wine industry and the spas have brought a certain refinement to the area. The tourists and settlers attracted by the Napa lifestyle come in all flavors, but they tend to be educated, experienced and relatively affluent.

One realm to which this worldliness does not extend is the media. To be sure, Wine Country has access to major information sources. You can subscribe to the *San Francisco Chronicle*, the nation's 10th-largest newspaper, practically anywhere in the four-county region. You can pick up the *New York Times* in many tourist-oriented towns. And thanks to cable TV, even Kalihari bushmen, it seems, can tune in to CNN every night.

But the homegrown media are humble and sparse. We have few daily papers and fewer TV stations, despite the large geographic area we are addressing. The diversity of radio programming is limited. (If you prefer religious, country-western or Mexican salsa stations, you're in luck.)

Still, you don't hear too many complaints. Why not? Because a lot of Wine Country residents don't want to be directly plugged in to the rest of the world. It isn't stubborn insularity so much as basic contentedness. That's why small-town papers are so important in the Wine Country. The people who subscribe to *The Ferndale Enterprise* or the *Middletown Times Star* or the *Sonoma Index-Tribune* would just as soon get detailed news of plans to build a community swimming pool as the scoop on Bill Clinton's latest scandal. And like we said, those nationally and globally focused sources are there when you need them—like when you're on vacation.

One final note: We included some tourist-oriented publications on this list, but real estate publications are included in the Real Estate chapter.

Daily Newspapers

Napa County

The Napa Valley Register
1615 Second St., Napa
- **(707) 226-3711**

Napa County's only daily dates back to 1863, though it has gone through a few changes of ownership since Abe Lincoln's administration. The paper is now a member of the Pulitzer Community of Newspapers. It had been the second-largest community paper in the Scripps chain (after Tucson's *Arizona Daily Star*) before Pulitzer gobbled up that group. Current paid circulation is about 20,500.

The Register ably handles the entire county, nodding to St. Helena and Calistoga in its "Upvalley" section. The paper uses wire-service reports but does a lot of local reporting, such as a multifaceted 1997 series about the valley's farmworkers that garnered much acclaim. Particularly popular is Kevin Courtney, who has been writing an everyman Sunday column for more than 25 years. Less popular, though not for lack of effort, is a smart alecky Wednesday column penned by a certain *Insid-*

ers' Guide co-author. The editorial page is always interesting.

The Register is an afternoon paper during the week, switching to morning delivery on Saturday and Sunday. Also worth noting here is its monthly news-rack supplement: *Inside Napa Valley*, a tourist-aimed tabloid with better-than-expected features on art, food, wine and coming events. The supplement is free.

Sonoma County

The Press Democrat
427 Mendocino Ave., Santa Rosa
• (707) 546-2020

For a wide segment of Sonoma County's population, as well as for readers in adjoining counties of Wine Country, the morning daily *Press Democrat* serves as the only newspaper they feel they need to read. With a daily circulation of about 95,000 (105,000 on Sundays) it is highly successful at combining solid national and international coverage with state news and a generous scoop of local affairs.

The *P.D.*, as locals call it, is owned by *The New York Times* now but has been serving the Sonoma County area since 1857. Although the paper's name includes the word Democrat, editor Bruce Kyse says the editorial stance is really middle-of-the-road, based on a policy of looking at issues as they develop instead of from a liberal or conservative position.

One of the paper's best-read features is the real estate section, with on-the-mark reports and charts backed up by the inside knowledge of Realtor John Favre, who also writes a column each month covering real estate trends and offering predictions. For newcomers to Santa Rosa and the county, it should be required reading for insightful knowledge of the market.

A strong sports section features popular columnists such as Bob Padecky and Lowell Cohn. On the entertainment scene, local residents keep abreast of what's going on about town through a lively entertainment section called "On Q." Gaye LeBaron's column also offers colorful, behind-the-scenes coverage of Santa Rosa people, places and happenings.

Mendocino County

Ukiah Daily Journal
590 S. School St., Ukiah
• (707) 468-0123

This newspaper's roots go back to 1860,

when it was called the *Redwood Journal*. Former editor Robb Hicken plowed his way through 137 years of back issues to come up with a complete history of the paper, and in mid-1997 he published a three-page supplement to the *Daily Journal* to give readers a look at what was important news for Ukiah in other times. (A few copies are still available.) With a circulation of 8,000, the *Daily Journal*, now edited by K.C. Meadows, covers local and county news that the metropolitan dailies don't. Coverage includes sports, society news, club activities, high school events and news from Mendocino College on Ukiah's foothills.

Other Newspapers

Napa County

Napa County Record/Positive Living
1320 Second St., Napa
• (707) 252-8877

The *Record* started as a monthly paper in 1946, went weekly, and in 1996 switched back to monthly, where it now comfortably abides. Distributed free on the last Friday of every month, it's a family-oriented community paper that covers topics such as business, automobiles, and hunting and fishing. *Positive Living* has two special editions: a program-style section dedicated to Symphony on the River (see our Festivals and Events chapter) and a seniors section that prints in February, July and October (the last one focusing on the local Senior Games). *Positive Living* sponsors an internship at New Technology High School, allowing students to lay out a page in the paper each month during the school year.

St. Helena Star
1328 Main St., St. Helena
• (707) 963-2731

St. Helena's well-preserved Victorian charm even extends to its newspaper, the *Star*, which has been a family-owned broadsheet weekly since it was founded in 1874. The paper attempts to stay within the city limits, plus Angwin and its Howell Mountain environs.

The weekly paper astutely covers the important local issues—growth, tourism, elections—and its wine coverage is getting more comprehensive. (There is a special wine edition every October.) George Starke, whose column concentrates on the human side of the wine industry, has ruffled a few feathers by breaking news on the buying and selling of vineyards. But even the editors will admit that the feature best known for reeling in readers is the precious Police Log. You don't really know St. Helena until you have studied this compendium of barking dogs, double-parked cars and nosy neighbors.

The Weekly Calistogan
1328 Main St., St. Helena
• (707) 963-2731

This might be the only newspaper in the nation whose motto is longer than some of its features. And we quote: "Published at the Head of the Napa Valley, a Beautiful and Fertile Section of Country, Possessing a Climate that for Health and Comfort is Not Surpassed on Earth." Amen.

The Calistogan is co-owned with the *St. Helena Star* and, like that paper, comes out each Thursday. When publisher Paul Krsek shut down the *Weekly Calistogan* office and moved the staff to St. Helena (to share space with the *St. Helena Star*) in 1999, locals worried they were about to lose an institution founded in 1877. Krsek insists he is committed to Calistoga, but it's safe to say the role of the *Calistogan* is in flux. In the meantime, Randy Johnson's coverage of the local sports scene is about as thorough as you'll find in a small-town paper.

Sonoma County

The Sonoma Index-Tribune
117 W. Napa St., Sonoma
• (707) 938-2111

Established in 1879, the twice-weekly *Sonoma Index-Tribune* has been in the same family since 1884. Current publisher Robert Lynch leads the family's third generation to own and operate the paper. His son, Bill, is editor and CEO. Bill's brother, Jim, is the chief financial officer.

The paper publishes every Tuesday and Friday, with a paid circulation of 12,500. The *Index-Tribune* is an award-winning community newspaper covering all aspects of local news: schools, city government, the fire and water boards, the wine business, prep and youth sports, adult recreational sports leagues, even bake sales and spaghetti dinners. If something is happening in Sonoma Valley, you'll find it in the *Index-Tribune*. The Friday issue also includes the latest in local entertainment and covers the local theater scene.

In May 1997, the *Index-Tribune* received five awards for excellence in the annual California Newspaper Publishers Association Better Newspapers Contest, including a coveted honor in the general excellence category.

Four times a year, the newspaper publishes *Sonoma Valley Magazine* as a supplement to the newspaper. It includes a variety of features and special stories on local people and institutions. The newspaper also publishes a monthly tourist newspaper, *The Sonoma Valley Visitor News*, which is distributed free through wineries, hotels and visitor locations.

The newspaper's editorial policy leans toward community "boosterism," and the paper often leads the charge in support of local school bond elections and fund-raising for local service projects. In mid-1997 the *Index-Tribune* published an illustrated, hardcover history of the community called *The Sonoma Valley Story*. It covers the history of the community from before the Spanish missionaries arrived up to the present day.

Petaluma Post
P.O. Box 493, Petaluma
• (707) 762-0203

David Bennet has published this monthly tabloid newspaper since 1988 and, toward the middle of each month, distributes 20,000 copies throughout southern Sonoma County and adjoining northwest Marin County.

The paper runs 24 to 32 pages and can be picked up free at any of 350 locations. "Light and bright" is his aim, Bennet says. He wants people to be happy they live in this beautiful place, and wants to give people who are visiting plenty of information about the area's people and events. There is no hard news, just news of the availability of pleasant pursuits and the people who make up this corner of Wine Country.

Argus Courier
830 Petaluma Blvd., Petaluma
• (707) 762-4541

Published each Wednesday, this publication (currently owned by the Pulitzer chain) has been in business since 1855, making it the oldest paper in Sonoma County. Publisher David Ferro and managing editor Chris Samson print strictly Petaluma community news and information on arts and entertainment. Circulation is 8,500. About 12,000 non-subscribing Petalumans receive a free weekly shopper each Wednesday.

The Community Voice
320 Professional Center Dr., Ste. 100,
Rohnert Park • (707) 584-2222

The Community Voice, published every

Wednesday, is the local newspaper for residents of Rohnert Park and Cotati. It tells them what is going on in their schools and neighborhoods. Columnists write up the little news about anniversaries, birthdays and other small-town happenings. The paper's well-designed sports section covers local recreational activities—especially youth sports—with the intensity that city papers use to cover the major leagues.

The newspaper works closely with the Rohnert Park and Cotati chambers of commerce, is involved in promoting local business and beats the drum for many local events and institutions, including the local professional baseball team, the Crushers (see our Spectator Sports chapter). There is also a reporter covering Sonoma State University. The newspaper publishes an annual "Key to the City" section, a summary and directory of dining, entertainment, recreation, sports and commerce in the area.

Sonoma County Independent
540 Mendocino Ave., Santa Rosa
• (707) 527-1200

Established in 1979, this free weekly tabloid comes out each Thursday, with numerous distribution points in Sonoma County. Editor Greg Cahill sees to it that the 48 pages are chock-full of news stories relating to civic issues that concern Sonoma County residents ("Meet the Feisty Nun Who Rocked the Diocese of Santa Rosa" was a recent headline), as well as rundowns on arts, eats and entertainment (profiles of musicians and artists, movie reviews). On top of all this, there's great photography.

Sonoma County Herald-Recorder
1818 Fourth St., Santa Rosa
• (707) 545-1166

Published Monday, Wednesday and Friday, with a readership of 2,500, the *Herald-Recorder* covers real estate, business and legal news, with statistical information from the Recorder's Office and County Clerk plus news affecting local attorneys and real estate interests. The publisher is Christine Griego; the editor is Erik Cummins. The paper has been published since 1899.

Sonoma-Marin Farm News
870 Piner Rd., Santa Rosa
• (707) 544-5575

The Farm Bureau has been distributing its monthly agricultural newspaper to the ranchers of Sonoma County and adjoining Marin County for 22 years. Editor Laurie Ferguson focuses on different laws and regulations that affect farm lands and disseminates informa-tion on wetlands and tree ordinances that apply to vineyards and dairy and cattle ranches. There is also general farming and viticulture news. Circulation is 3,200.

The Business Journal
5464 Skylane Blvd., Ste. B, Santa Rosa
• (707) 579-2900

Editors Ken Clark and Randy Sloan publish strictly business news, focusing particularly on new business startups, expansions of existing firms and information on relocations. Circulation is more than 10,000. Usually the 26 to 45 pages will include a profile of a top-level executive telling about his company—its history and anticipation of future progress. *The Business Journal* is published every other Monday and covers Sonoma, Marin, and Napa counties. They also print a monthly 20-page wine industry *Business Journal*, and the *680 Business Journal* for Contra Costa and Alameda counties.

Healdsburg Tribune
5 Mitchell Ln., Healdsburg
• (707) 433-4451

The front-page banner announces: "Our 135th Year." The Tribune has had different owners over the years but has never interrupted printing. The present editor, Kathryn Roth, puts out a well-rounded weekly, small-town paper, covering all the news of Healdsburg and Geyserville: community affairs and events, legal matters and local personalities. The paper also prints occasional special sections. One of the most popular is the annual "Heroes" page, which features a local resident who's been singled out by the newspapers' readers for serving above and beyond the call of duty. It is usually someone less than extraordinary—maybe a man who collects tin cans and sells them for the benefit of the local food bank. Roth also edits *The Windsor Times*. This, too, is strictly locally oriented and, like the *Healdsburg Tribune*, prints on Wednesdays. Together, the newspapers' circulation is 8,200.

Cloverdale Reveille
207 N. Cloverdale Blvd., Cloverdale
• (707) 894-3339

This community newspaper is published on Wednesdays and covers community and school news. Records stacked away in old files indicate the *Reveille* was first published in 1879. Present circulation is 2,400. Editor Bonny Hanchette is proud of the role of small newspapers in relaying local news to readers. "It's a special field I think will continue," she says.

MEDIA

Bodega Bay Navigator
1580 Eastshore Rd., Bodega Bay
• (707) 875-3574

A weekly newspaper established in 1986, with a circulation of 1,400, the *Bodega Bay Navigator* comes out on Thursdays and is distributed throughout Sebastopol, Russian River and Bodega Bay. Publisher and editor Joel Hack focuses on both community news and global issues, and has printed some controversial or unusual stories that other small papers often shy away from. For example, the *Navigator* has published stories on teen pregnancy services, violence and the plight of the Navajo nation.

Sonoma West Times & News
130 S. Main St., Suite 114, Sebastopol
• (707) 823-7845

Locally owned and intimately focused, this paper picks up where the *Sebastopol Times* and *Russian River News* left off. Publisher Rollie Atkinson says the *Time & News* is "about our families, our towns, about the guy next door." Those towns are primarily Sebastopol, Bodega Bay, and Guerneville. Look for the paper each Wednesday.

Mendocino County

Fort Bragg Advocate-News
450 N. Franklin St., Fort Bragg
• (707) 964-5642
Mendocino Beacon
45066 Ukiah St., Mendocino
• (707) 937-5874

Sharon Brewer is publisher and Katherine Lee the managing editor for both these once-a-week papers. Both papers trace their histories to the heydays of the lumbering industry that gave birth to the towns. The *Fort Bragg Advocate-News* was founded in 1889, *The Mendocino Beacon-News* in 1877. At that time news was of forests and shipping and sawmills. Today the slant is local with a strong appeal to tourists. The *Advocate* is based in Fort Bragg, which has a population of 6,000; the *Beacon* serves Mendocino, with its population of 1,000. Each covers news of the community, the arts, school affairs and local personalities. One of the most popular features in both papers is the calendar of events.

Independent Coast-Observer
Box 1200, Gualala 95445 • (707) 884-3501

Stephen McLaughlin edits this weekly paper, covering the coastal area from Jenner to Elk. This is strictly a visitors' publication, offering news of upcoming events, art exhibits (with a rundown on some of the artists) and reviews of musical groups performing in Mendocino and elsewhere in the area. There are 3,000 copies printed each week and distributed to restaurants along the coast. A free supplement, *Destination Mendonoma*, is published once a year, in May.

Anderson Valley Advertiser
12451 Anderson Valley Rd., Boonville
• (707) 895-3016

Described by Editor Bruce Anderson as "left-wing and populist," this weekly comes out on Wednesdays and covers news of Anderson Valley, an area largely devoted to farming and vineyards. But Anderson also gives in-depth coverage to political matters in the valley, particularly to the activities of the board of supervisors, and often challenges political policies. Because some of his views incite strong reactions, he claims to get more mail than the big daily newspapers in the area. Circulation of this paper is 3,000.

Lake County

Middletown Times Star
21168 Calistoga St., Middletown
• (707) 987-3602

This weekly paper ignores those faraway urban metropolises—and by that we mean Santa Rosa and Napa. The *Times Star* has no *Associated Press* wire and no grand yearnings. The 128-year-old publication covers the issues important to economically hard-put Middletown and southern Lake County—things like tourism, logging, agriculture and the Geysers. It publishes every Thursday, and many of the locals turn immediately to Sharon Dawson's humor column. Also popular: the event listings and the wide variety of opinions on the editorial page.

Clear Lake Observer-American
14913-B Lakeshore Dr., Clearlake
• (707) 994-6444

This is a paper that gets high marks for its strictly local news. In fact, the California Newspaper Publishers Association gave it a general excellence award in 1996, calling it the best biweekly paper in the state.

The *Observer-American*, published Wednesday and Saturday, covers Clearlake, Clearlake Oaks, Lower Lake and Middletown, paying practically no attention to the "civilized" world.

It has been providing solid, balanced reporting for about 60 years, going after nuts-and-bolts issues such as Lake County's water and sewer systems. Case in point: A few years ago, rumors circulated that raw sewage was being dumped into Clear Lake. The paper investigated and found that the runoff in question was actually percolating from local ponds. It was, they discovered, cleaner than the lake water.

Lake County Record-Bee
2150 N. Main St., Lakeport
• (707) 263-5636

The *Lake County Bee* was founded in 1873, the *Lakeport Press and Record* in 1925. Those two oldtimers have since been merged into the *Record-Bee*, which publishes five times a week (Tuesday through Saturday). Though traditionally devoted to the immediate community, the paper recently adopted an "updated" look that placed a greater emphasis on state and national news. The *Record-Bee* is owned by Lake Publishing, which also owns the *Clear Lake Observer-American*.

Lake Currents
P.O. Box 3595, Clearlake 95422
• (707) 994-7308

This grass-roots monthly is dedicated to sustainable living—a rubric that includes arts and cultural events, environmental concerns, education, agriculture and thoughtful business development. Distributed primarily via mailing list and coffee house, *Lake Currents* asks for donations but has no formal fee structure.

Magazines

Appellation
1040 Main St., Napa
• (707) 255-2525

Appellation lived for years as a simple, tabloid-format insert in the *Napa Valley Register*, but has evolved into a handsome, four-color, bimonthly publication with a circulation of about 80,000.

This magazine is hard to pigeonhole, except to say that it portrays all facets of what we might ambitiously call The Good Life. Now published by Earls Communications and

directed by editor-in-chief Colleen Daly, *Appellation's* pages are filled with food (including recipes and restaurant reviews), wine, travel destinations, jaunty personalities and general finery. The magazine's roots are firmly planted in Napa and Sonoma valleys, but it has dispatched photographers and writers all over the globe to portray people who know how to have a swell time with a bottle of wine.

The current departments include a serious wine column called "By the Glass"; "Mixed Case," with topics ranging from the world's only wine university (in France) to California's youngest winemaker; and "Unfiltered," wine-related musings by guest journalists and novelists. Also contributing behind the scenes is Alexis Bespaloff, author of the best-selling *Complete Guide to Wine*. Note that *Appellation's* newsstand edition includes one of the best Wine Country maps you'll find.

Sonoma Business
50 Old Courthouse Sq., Ste. 105,
Santa Rosa • (707) 575-8282

James Dunn edits this glossy monthly magazine, impressive with its well-designed cover and artistic inside pages. Dunn says what this magazine has that's different from other business journals is high-quality writing and long, in-depth, multi-interview analyses of industries in Sonoma County. The businesses they cover include technology and the Internet, real estate and investing, service professions and both viniculture and viticulture, and there are profiles of newsmakers. An annual issue prints the top 500 industries in the county, ranked by gross revenues. Dunn says that issue is used by the entire local business community to find out which companies are the big moneymakers. The magazine's wine issue doubles as the official program of the Sonoma County Harvest Fair. Circulation is more than 7,000.

Other Publications

Lake County Visitor
P.O. Box 2692,
Clearlake 95422
• (707) 995-1725

This tabloid-sized publication comes out once a year, right around New Year's Day. Published by

INSIDERS' TIP

Because of the paucity of local radio stations and, especially, the hilly, signal-blocking terrain, more and more Wine Country residents are plugging into cable radio. The DMX system has 30 "canned" offerings of various stripes (everything from Tejano to rap), plus 10 regional radio stations. The cost: about $10 per month. Call your cable company for more information.

Shelley Graphics, it's basically a countywide tourist guide that includes a calendar of events and suggestions for things to do and see. You can find it at the Lake County Visitors Center and the various chambers of commerce.

Weddings & Honeymoons in the Vineyards of Northern California
J.R. Publications, 4928 Rincon Ave., Santa Rosa
• (707) 827-6966

Anyone planning to marry in Wine Country should waste no time in getting a copy of *Weddings & Honeymoons in the Vineyards of Northern California*, a resource book written by Judith Rivers and published by J.R. Publications. Everything you'll need to know about wedding locations is provided in this book. Included are questions you should ask each of the vendors you plan to hire, lists of clergy and loads of helpful hints. The book can be found at area bookstores (see the Bookstores section of our Shopping chapter), or call (707) 570-0820 to order directly. To find out more about other J.R. Publications titles, call the number listed.

INSIDERS' TIP

The Napa Valley Register prints its community calendar on Thursday and Sunday. The calendar lists upcoming musical performances, lectures and fund-raisers.

Radio Stations

KVON-1440 AM

Between bouts of revelry, even Napa Valley tourists sometimes crave a direct line to the outside world. They often turn to Napa's KVON for news, opinion and information. This has been a full-time news and talk station since the early 1980s, making it one of the most established info stations in Northern California. KVON is a past recipient of the National Association of Broadcasters' "Crystal Award."

KVYN-99.3 FM

This Napa station is self-described as Hot Adult Contemporary. It's an upbeat mix of pop, rock, dance, alternative and ballads, mostly from the '80s and '90s. KVYN is music-intensive but, as an affiliate of ABC News, it has its talkative side too. The station offers local news, sports and weather to residents and tourists.

KXBX-1270 AM

This is a mature station, both in terms of its own age (it has been around since the 1940s) and the lifestyle of its listeners. KXBX plays

adult standards and offers plenty of talk programming, including a call-in health show with a local pharmacist and a Saturday-morning food-and-travel show. The station's main morning guy, Bill Moen, was a San Francisco institution for 32 years.

KXBX-98.3 FM

An adult contemporary station out of Lakeport, KXBX is the most listened to frequency in Lake County. It has been broadcasting since the early 1980s. The station is heavily into promotion and giveaways, and it sponsors a 10-week summer concert series in Lakeport. It's the sister station of KXBX-AM.

Station List

Adult Contemporary

KHGB-95.9 FM
KSAY-98.5 FM
KVYN-99.3 FM
KWNE-94.5 FM
KXBX-98.3 FM
KZST-100.1 FM

Christian

KCDS-89.9 FM
KLVR-91.9 FM
KPRA-89.5 FM

Country

KFGY-92.9 FM
KRPQ-104.9 FM
KUKI-103.3 FM

Jazz

KJZY-93.7 FM

News, Talk, Sports

KDAC-1230 AM
KFOG-104 FM
KMPO-1300 AM
KSRO-1350 AM
KVON-1440 AM

Oldies, Standards

KFMB-92.7 FM
KTOB-1490 AM
KXBX-1270 AM

Public Radio

KRCB-91.1 FM
KZYX-90.7 FM

Rock

KFXS-101.7 FM, 1250 AM
KGRP-100.9 FM (Classic rock)
KLLK-96.7 FM (Alternative)
KMGG-97.7 FM (Rock oldies)
KNTI-99.5 FM (Classic rock)

Spanish

KMXN-1150 AM
KRSS-1460 AM

Television

Station List

ABC - KGO Channel 7 (Napa, Sonoma, Mendocino, Lake);
CBS - KPIX Channel 5 (Napa, Sonoma, Mendocino, Lake); KOVR Channel 14 (Lake)
NBC - KRON Channel 4 (Napa, Sonoma, Mendocino, Lake); KCRA Channel 3 (Lake)
FOX - KTVU Channel 2 (Napa, Sonoma, Mendocino, Lake); KTXL Channel 12 (Lake)
PBS - KQED Channel 9 (Napa, Sonoma, Mendocino, Lake); KRCB Channel 22 (Sonoma);
UPN - KBHK Channel 44 (Napa, Sonoma, Mendocino) and Channel 11 (Lake)
Independents - KFTY Channel 50 (Sonoma, Mendocino)

Local Broadcast Channels

KFTY Channel 50 (Independent)
533 Mendocino Ave., Santa Rosa
• (707) 526-5050

Started in 1981 by Wichard Brown, then owner of the *Marin Independent Journal*, this station is now owned by Ackerley Broadcast Group, a Seattle-based advertising, sports and entertainment conglomerate. KFTY serves the six counties just north of San Francisco (or, as they term it, "north of the Gate"). General programming includes news, movies, sitcoms and public interest programs, with a special 30-minute North Bay news program Monday through Friday at 7 PM and a one-hour news program at 10 PM.

This station is intensely community-oriented and sponsors the Luther Burbank Rose Parade (see our Festivals and Annual Events chapter) each spring, along with a health, fitness and safety series at the end of June.

KRCB Channel 22 (Public TV)
5850 Labath Ave., Rohnert Park
• (707) 585-8522

This public television station was started in December 1984, and now reaches the counties of Sonoma, Napa, Mendocino and Lake, plus portions of Alameda, Marin, Solano, and Contra Costa counties. It even broadcasts to San Francisco.

Programming is typical public television fare: *Sesame Street*, *Nova*, *This Old House*, news programs, a *North Bay Journal* featuring regional business news and *Expressions*, which features local artists. It has pledge drives and an auction in November (its affiliate, KRCB-91.1 FM, is also listener-supported).

Cable Television Providers

Napa County

AT&T Cable Services
2260 Brown St., Napa
• (800) 436-1999

AT&T, which bought out TCI in this area, offers dazzling, if somewhat expensive, cable service. All of the company's packages come with TV Guide on-screen, music channels and pay-per-view, and all of them are digitally transmitted. Digital Standard offers 18 special-interest channels such as Turner Classic Movies, CNN and ESPN for $42.99 per month.

Add two premium movie channels (HBO, Show-time, Cinemax or Movie Channel) for an extra $12, or three movie channels for an extra $17.

Century Communications
211 Wapoo Ave., Calistoga
• (707) 963-7121

Napa County residents got a dose of good

The Sonoma Index-Tribune *has been owned by the same family since 1884.*

news/bad news in 1997 when Century announced the addition of The Disney Channel to its basic package—along with a small rate hike. Basic cable is 34 stations (sorry, urbanites, no Bravo or Comedy Central), with five more Century Select channels (including most of the Turner stations) and five premium channels also available.

Sonoma County

Century Communications
1001 Broadway, Sonoma
• **(707) 996-8482**
595 Martin Ave., Rohnert Park
• **(707) 584-4617**

Century Communications was founded in 1973 and currently provides basic cable and Century Select channels in more than 325 cities in 27 states. In Sonoma County, basic service provides 34 channels, with five additional hookup options.

Mendocino County

Century Communications
1060 N. State St., Ukiah
• **(707) 462-8737**
1260 N. Main St., Fort Bragg
•**(707) 964-6613**

Century Communications in Mendocino

County provides 36 channels with its basic service package. It's the usual cable fare as you know it, with SportsChannel, HBO, and pay-per-view movies.

Lake County

Mediacom
13221 E. Calif. Hwy. 20, Clearlake Oaks
• **(707) 998-1516, (800) 832-4440**

Mediacom is the name in cable for almost all of Lake County. The company offers 21 channels for $17.89 a month in its Limited Basic package—primarily local network and independent stations, plus C-SPAN and The Weather Channel. For $31.49 per month you can upgrade to the Basic Plus package, a 48-channel stable that adds standbys such as-the Discovery Channel, Arts & Entertainment, ESPN, Cable News Network, Nickelodeon and the Nashville Network. Four premium channels also are available. Mediacom offers several FM radio stations free to its cable TV customers.

Worship

Every now and again some wise guy offers a variation on a witticism we've heard too many times before: "Give the United States a good shake-up, and everything loose will land in California."

We might not like the word "loose," but we are proud of the climate of open-mindedness that has brought a wonderful diversity to California. It manifests itself in many ways—including the way we worship. Here in Wine Country, where a certain sense of innovative spontaneity dominates the culture, an amazingly eclectic assortment of houses of worship has taken root and prospered. In Sonoma County alone, with a thinly spread population of about 400,000 (no larger than a good-sized American city), the Yellow Pages list 78 different faiths.

That would be in line with figures gathered at the turn of the century, when it was revealed that Sonoma County had more churches than any other county in the state except San Francisco. The zeal of the early religious organizers and preachers sustained the pioneers and laid a firm foundation for the church building of the future. Although the earliest religious activity had been the domain of the Spanish missionaries—particularly under the direction of Fr. Jose Altimira, who established the mission in Sonoma—that system broke down when the young republic of Mexico secularized the missions in the 1830s, leaving a religious vacuum (see our History chapter). But when the first families started to move into the Sonoma and Napa valleys early in the 1860s to establish farms and businesses, organized religion moved apace. Some of the churches built in those times remain. Many have been designated historic landmarks, their congregations dedicated to keeping the coffers filled and the weather-beaten structures painted.

LOOK FOR:
• Napa County
• Sonoma County
• Mendocino County
• Lake County

Napa County

The story of spirituality in Napa County—or, more accurately, of European-rooted religion—is sprinkled with visionaries, hard knocks and roustabouts. Fittingly, the tale more or less begins with the Gold Rush. Among the starry-eyed prospectors who gravitated to California in 1849 was James Milton Small, an ordained minister of the Cumberland Presbyterian Church. In the fall of 1850, Small gave up on gold and moved to Napa to save souls, preaching to early settlers in the dining room of a boarding house.

Three years later the national Presbyterian Board of Missionaries sent the Rev. J.C. Herron from Philadelphia to the Napa Valley. He sermonized in the old Court House, a trying experience according to the record of an original church member: "The inside appearance of the Court-room was rather sorry for a place of worship, especially when Court had been held there the preceding day. . . . No carpets and no curtains, no paint, no finish of any kind had been wasted on this public hall. No lamps, or even candle-sticks were there . . . The upper part of the building was used for public offices, and a jail; and it was not at all an uncommon thing for the nervous and timid ones of the congregation, during service, to be annoyed by the rattling of chains and other discordant sounds proceeding from the prisoners' apartments."

It was in reaction to such conditions that the Presbyterians build the first church in Napa city in 1855, at a time when white settlers were true pioneers. After the congregation moved its facilities a couple of years later, the old edifice was reduced to service as a paint shop. In 1858 it was purchased by a group of black Methodists, who splintered from their white congregation, moved the structure to Washington Street and called it the African Methodist Church. That church is gone, but a bell purchased for $600 by the main Presbyterian congregation in 1868 announces the hour of prayer even today, at the First Presbyterian Church at 1333 Third Street in Napa. (It was "warranted for one year.") Rev. Richard Wylie was the pastor of First Presbyterian when that bell was acquired, and he remained in the pulpit until 1921—a remarkable tenure of 54 years, minus a couple of years he spent in Europe recuperating from illness. One of Wylie's successors, Rev. Lee Vernon, had a 16-year run (1937-1953), during which he was well-known for broadcasting "Religious News of the Week" for KVON on Sunday afternoons.

Soon after the original Napa temple had been raised, the Presbyterians built a church in St. Helena. On July 26, 1873, somebody tried to burn it down, fastening bags saturated with coal oil up the length of the belfry rope and setting them ablaze. The fire was discovered and dampened before any real damage was done, but the relief was short-lived: The building was destroyed by fire in February 1874. Two years before that, a Presbyterian church had been erected in Calistoga.

Rev. S.D. Simonds is said to have been the first Methodist Episcopal preacher to reside in Napa Valley. That was about 1851. A year later Rev. Asa White delivered a sermon in a grove of redwood trees known as Paradise Park. The grove was part of the Tucker farm, about halfway between St. Helena and Calistoga, and it became the site of the first church in Napa Valley in 1853. The 700-square-foot temple was called the White Church—either because of its color (it is reported to have been the only painted edifice in the valley) or in honor of Asa. The White Church burned down in the early 1900s.

The Methodists built a separate church in Napa in 1856. The Rev. James Corwin, besides his evangelical duties, happened to be engineer at a sawmill north of St. Helena. The owner of the mill, Erwin Kellogg, donated use of his facility long enough for the Rev. Corwin to cut the logs and have them hauled to Napa for the new church. The Methodists also laid the foundation for a church in Calistoga in 1868, but construction didn't go much further. The railroad wanted the land, you see, and there wasn't much the railroad didn't get. Sam Brannan donated another site to the congregation, and the church, Calistoga's first, was completed in 1869. It also served as the local primary school for a year.

The Napa Collegiate Institute, a private Methodist college, was founded in Napa in 1860. The name was changed to Napa College in 1890, and by 1896 financial difficulties had forced the California Conference to move the school to Santa Clara. There it was known as the University of the Pacific, forerunner to the school of the same name that now is located in Stockton.

In 1917 a new Methodist church was opened in Napa. During the dedication service, it was reported that $31,000 had been raised for building the church—$5,000 short of the total cost. Addressing the congregation, Bishop Adna Leonard said, "A collection is now in order. This is a courteous congregation. I am going to ask you to remain until the benediction is reached." Leonard's lock-the-doors-until-we're-solvent strategy worked. He marked pledges on a blackboard until the goal of $36,000 was attained. That building stands today, a registered landmark of English Gothic architecture. The downstairs pews actually date to 1895. The organ, fashioned by the Wicks Organ Company of Highland, Illinois, is only 20 years old, but is worth noting. It was tonally designed for the building and made to fit within the existing organ chamber. As for the trees in the parking lot, they were planted by Boy Scout Troop No. 2 many years ago.

The Christian Church appeared in the valley in 1853, when J.P. McCorkle preached under a madrone tree in Yountville. His flock founded a church in Browns Valley in 1865, then moved to Napa in 1870, setting up shop in the building that previously had housed the town's first newspaper, the *Napa Reporter*. Later that year they purchased land at the corner of Pearl and Randolph streets and built a proper church. (The American Legion Post is there now.)

The Roman Catholics held occasional services in Margaret McEnerny's boarding house on Main Street in Napa in the mid-1850s. (The priest would ride over from the Sonoma Mission.) When the attending Mass outgrew Mrs. McEnerny's parlor, services were moved to a warehouse next door, then to the second floor of a building on the southwest corner of First and Main streets. Finally Napa merchant George Cornwell, a non-Catholic, donated land on Main Street, and St. John the Baptist Church was erected in 1858. It's not the St. John's you see today,

WORSHIP

Photo: Bill Hoban

St. Anthony's Catholic Church is a familiar Mendocino sight for visitors and locals.

however. Father Slattery built a beautiful Gothic church in 1881, and that is where noted French-born, English-adopted author Hilaire Belloc was married in 1897, having followed his heart across the Atlantic. Unfortunately, that church was leveled in the 1960s. The current edifice was built in 1957.

One of the most colorful religious figures of early Napa Valley was Father Peter Deyaert, a Belgian priest whose far-flung parish covered Napa and Lake counties, and portions of Solano and Sonoma. A contemporary, Frank Leach, described him thus: "Father Deyaert . . . was exceedingly popular with all classes. He was fond of outdoor life, especially in trampling the neighboring hills and shooting quail. . . . He would frequently go into saloons, not to scold or preach to those who happened to be in there, but simply to be social." For many years, Father Deyaert's grave was in the St. John's schoolyard.

The first Catholic Church in St. Helena was built in 1866; actually, it was the remodeled home of a Mrs. Sheehan at Oak Avenue and Tainter Street. When the local parishioners got a new church in 1878, they paid $72 for the old bell from the Napa Courthouse. It became the first bell in St. Helena. Separate Catholic parishes were formed in Calistoga in 1915 and Yountville in 1920.

The Seventh-day Adventist Church held its first meetings in 1873, in tents at the site of what is today known as Fuller Park in Napa, and a church was dedicated in the winter of 1873-74. That building still stands, after many alterations, on the corner of Church and Second streets, though the Adventists moved out in 1958. Also in 1873, the Seventh-day Adventists held a bustling one-week Camp Meeting, only their second in California, in a shady grove at the confluence of Conn Creek and the Napa River, about a mile northeast of Yountville. Sixty-three tents were neatly arranged around thoroughfares—Present Truth Street, Law and Order Street, etc. On Sunday nearly 1,500 people pushed in and out of the big evangelistic tent, and afterwards 29 were baptized in the river. One of them was Moses J. Church, who founded the city of Fresno and was a seminal figure in the irrigation of the San Joaquin Valley.

In 1877, Dr. Merritt Kellogg was busy laying the groundwork for what would become the St. Helena Sanitarium. One of his builders, Frank Lamb, remembered hearing Ellen White remark at an Adventist meeting in Oakland, "We are going to have a health institution on the Pacific coast." The famed mystic (her visions in the 1860s called Adventists to adopt the message of

WORSHIP

health reform) didn't know exactly where, but "we had to go across water to get to it." Kellogg, in need of funding, immediately invited White and her husband to St. Helena for a view of his site. White said she had seen the terrain in her visions; this must be the place. She purchased 8½ acres next to Kellogg's and helped turn the area into an Adventist stronghold.

The history of Calistoga, meanwhile, is inexorably entwined with the Church of Jesus Christ of Latter-Day Saints, for Sam Brannan, that iconoclastic founding father and California's first millionaire, was a Mormon. After sailing around the Cape with a church group in the 1840s, Brannan hung onto the collected tithings. He wanted San Francisco to be the center of Mormon culture, not Salt Lake City. Brigham Young saw otherwise, and he eventually excommunicated Brannan for absconding with those funds. (He just as easily could have done it in response to Sam's legendary drinking and philandering.)

The first LDS church in the valley was in St. Helena, adjacent to where that town's current Mormon church stands on Spring Street. One curious note concerning the denomination: Lilburn Boggs, who issued the infamous Mormon Extermination Order as governor of Missouri, is buried at Tulocay Cemetery in Napa.

Other early arrivals included Christ (Episcopal) Church, organized in 1858. One of the church's earliest rectors was Rev. William Goodwin, inventor of the dry plate used in early photographic processes. Goodwin, it's said, helped make a multi-millionaire out of George Eastman.

It wasn't just proper townsfolk who received the Lord's word, either. The Oat Hill Quicksilver Mine, in the rocky mountains east of Calistoga, offered its diggers weekly church and Sunday school. Nor was worship confined to English speakers. Second-language services are a common occurrence today, but they aren't a recent invention. St. John Evangelical Lutheran Church gave sermons in German in the early 1900s. And even before that, in 1879, Napa was one of only two California cities to have a Chinese mission. Five evenings a week, local Chinese laborers were given instruction in English and Christianity, first in the chapel of the sponsoring Presbyterian Church, then in an old brick building on Franklin Street that was rented for $50 a year.

By 1963 Napa County counted some 37 separate churches representing 20 denominations. Today it's more like 50 churches and 27 denominations, not to mention the many spiritual individualists who defy traditional classification.

Sonoma County

A zealous young Spanish priest, Father Jose Altimira, was the first to bring Christianity to these parts. He came to what is now Sonoma County in 1823 to establish the Mission San Francisco de Solano, northernmost in a chain of missions spaced along California's coast. Despite the overthrow of the Spanish rulers in Mexico, Altimira was nothing if not enthusiastic, and he convinced his colleagues in the church that the area would be a better climate than San Francisco for the Native American converts.

Altimira's mission building was not impressive—a flimsy wooden structure that was swept twice by fire before achieving its present, fireproof adobe state. The Catholic Church's plan was that missions would be conveyed to the Native Americans they converted and trained, and within six years, Altimira claimed 1,000 converts.

The mission would not last (a decree soon was issued by the Mexican government that all church properties were to be "secularized," or confiscated), but the influences of this early presence of organized religion are still evident today.

Other church activity began to stir in the established city of Sonoma around 1859, about the time Congregationalists established Cumberland Presbyterian College, a learning center where services were also sometimes held. But some distance from the village there lived a rancher named Edwin Sutherland who decided he would start his own

INSIDERS' TIP

Two of the most interesting religious structures in Calistoga are of the Eastern Orthodox faith. At the corner of Cedar and Berry streets, the Saint Simeon Russian Orthodox Church features the traditional onion dome. And the Holy Assumption Monastery on Washington Street is a replica of the old Russian chapel at Fort Ross, built entirely of wood. Don't be surprised if a bearded monk steps out to greet you in the peaceful courtyard.

Saddle of Faith

One of the most persistent of the rugged western individualists was the circuit-riding preacher.

It was said that whenever a new territory was opened up, the first to arrive were the whiskey seller and the missionary. Often the circuit-rider's pulpit was under a tree or in a saloon, for a church was definitely not one of the first structures in a new settlement. The God of the American West, it was said, did his good work from the saddle. The territories these men served were sometimes as wide as the West itself. Methodist bishop John Asbury traveled 270,000 miles in ministering to his western flock. Father Francis de Smet covered more than 180,000 miles.

One of the first circuit riders to approach Sonoma County was Isaiah L. Hopkins, a Southern Methodist who served his apprenticeship as a junior preacher riding what was known as the Bodega Circuit. His territory is an example of the dedication required — it included Petaluma, Santa Rosa, Healdsburg, Mark West and Macedonia, and on as far as Sebastopol. In 1857 it was reported of Hopkins' work that "many souls were converted and brought into the Church." He received $75 for his services that year.

"A wine producing community such as Sonoma County was by no means favorable for the morals of the youth who lived there," proclaimed Presbyterian circuit-rider C.H. Crawford. "The greatest drawback to church work I found was rum power. Men were bold and impudent under the influence of 'Old Tanglefoot.'" Sunday was the drinking and gambling day of the week. Naturally, there were those who did not drink, and God-fearing families who conducted themselves morally in immoral surroundings. But it required the courage of a grizzly bear and plenty of divine grace to stand up and say it.

Besides strong drink, the circuit-riders fought irreverence. According to an account of the day, itinerant preacher Brother Iry Taylor walked past a saloon one Sunday morning and found a man by the name of "Kentuck" mocking a church service. To Taylor's horrified eyes, four young men came forward and knelt at the bench and received crackers and whiskey, in mockery of the communion.

These were no namby-pamby preachers, but men of strong opinion, strongly

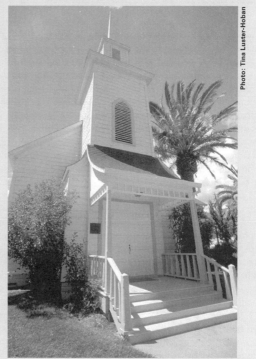

Photo: Tina Luster-Hoban

WORSHIP

Before the erection of places like the United Methodist Church in St. Helena, the circuit riders preached throughout the area.

(Continued on next page)

voiced. Circuit-riding Brother John McCorkle of the Christian Church ("Bro Mac") usually preached his sermons under an oak tree to an audience that might include gamblers and prostitutes as well as professionals. He was a fiery speaker, able to rouse a crowd, and people loved to gather around. No preacher, however, attained the notoriety of Episcopalian Reverend D'Estaing, who preached his sermons with a gun on his hip (much to the chagrin of his flock), convinced Santa Rosa was dangerous territory. Attendance dissipated, and Rev. D'Estaing was defrocked by the Diocese. Rumors persisted that he may have actually shot someone.

Many preachers were indistinguishable from the gamblers they spoke to — a long black coat, white shirt and string tie were the trademark of both. Sometimes they appeared in the jeans of the sturdy farm folk they came to enlighten. It was said of Bro Mac, who preached to crowds while dressed in homespun Kentucky trousers, that his audience "was made up of every walk of life — the rancher, the coquette, gamblers and horse racers." He was a compelling speaker who seldom made speaking errors although he was said to be illiterate.

Another wandering preacher was described as long-legged, cadaverous and melancholy, wearing a black, wide-brimmed, low-crowned hat. He sported a scraggly beard of the variety known as a Galway choker. He carried a large Bible under one arm and used the other to wave a horsewhip. In one boot was a Bowie knife; a rimfire revolver was hidden in the other. It was all, he said, "to discourage over-familiarity."

Whatever role these free spirits played in the epic drama of the taming of the West, they were tough of fiber and filled with the vigorous juice of life. They were nonconformists bringing the good news to an often bad-tempered lot.

WORSHIP

church under the protecting branches of a large live oak tree on his property. He had five children, his sister across the road had six, and with the children of a few neighbors he established the Big Tree Sunday School in his own back yard.

Sutherland had a strong bass voice and his wife was a soprano, and thus a small choir was formed to augment the teaching. One can only imagine the inspiration of hearing those hymns wafting across the meadow on a summer breeze. Still, a church must be for all seasons, not just for balmy Sunday mornings. Within three years preliminary efforts were being launched to leave the Big Tree Sunday School behind and form a church in the village. It would be called the First Congregational Church of Sonoma. That church still stands today, though in a different location, at 252 W. Spain Street. The choir there is said to be one of the best in Sonoma. Still, one wonders if music could ever sound quite the same as it did on those Sunday mornings under the live oak.

Conducting church services outside was actually not uncommon in those days of circuit-riding preachers. As early as 1852, on a ranch 6 miles from what would in time become Santa Rosa, an organized congregation of Baptists formed under the direction of circuit-riding Rev. Stephen Riley, using the home of rancher Martin Hudson as a Sunday morning place of worship. When the congregation grew too large for the Hudson home, preacher and flock moved outdoors to the banks of a river, under the spreading branches of a large live oak. Being bombarded by winter rains and interrupted by wandering cattle, however, helped take the luster off outdoor worship, and the congregation raised enough money to build a proper church, the Lebanon Baptist, which eventually merged with the First Baptist Church.

It was here that the First Baptist Church shot into the spotlight when it was revealed it had been built out of one single tree—a 3,000-year-old redwood 275 feet high and 18 feet in diameter—cut on a ranch near Guerneville. The congregation had been unaware of the church's unique status until 1900, when a member, attorney Thomas Butts, told his story. He had been employed by a mill in Guernevillle at the time the tree was cut down. The mill owner knew it was to be used to build a church, and under his watchful eye every step of the milling process was personally monitored to be certain the wood wasn't mingled with other lumber. Butts himself planed the wood and was instructed to keep it separated. Thus it was that one tall tree built a church, thanks to the foresight of a mill owner whose goal was to publicize California's redwoods and advertise his own services.

In 1939 Robert Ripley, a church member, featured the church in his "Believe It Or Not" column and gave it instant fame. Today the Church Of One Tree, at 492 Sonoma Avenue in Santa Rosa, houses the Robert Ripley Museum (see our Attractions chapter). Although the church started as a Baptist church, it became a church for many faiths, and on a given Sunday as many as 5,000 people worshipped there—there were 10 services offered each week. Finally it was necessary to break up the flock. Two of today's Baptist congregations in Santa Rosa, the Community Baptist Church at 1620 Sonoma Avenue and the First Baptist Church at 3300 Sonoma Avenue, trace their roots to the church Ripley attended.

Fame of a different sort was achieved by members of a Petaluma Baptist church who installed a certain church bell, the legend of which still lingers. Having learned of a bell for sale in San Francisco, a committee was dispatched to purchase what was said to be the sweetest-sounding instrument in the land. On arrival they learned the bell had been used by vigilantes during Gold Rush days whenever they hanged another lawless rascal, but the group bought it anyway for $550. It is said the bell's tolling could be heard for 12 miles.

The sexton took to ringing the bell whenever the Union Army had a victory—a source of annoyance to Southern sympathizers who had paid liberally for its purchase. One morning in 1864, the bell was removed, but by nightfall 40 members of the opposing party found it and hoisted it again to the church tower with the American flag flying above it. The next morning, the bell sounded only once and never rang clear again. It had cracked during the changing of hands.

The 1870s and '80s saw tremendous expansion of church activity in Sonoma County. Like mushrooms on a wet morning, denominations sprang up everywhere—Methodists, Baptists, Presbyterians, Episcopalians and a sizable number of fundamentalist groups.

In the early days of frontier religion, most congregations were served by a circuit rider, a pastor who tended many flocks and spent most of his life on horseback. Pity the Rev. Isaac Owen, a Methodist minister whose circuit included 10 congregations from Sonoma to Bodega and everything else up to the Russian River. One of the most renowned preachers of Sonoma County was the Rev. James Woods, who established a Presbyterian church in Healdsburg in 1858. His first congregation included Cyrus Alexander, who owned the entire valley north of Healdsburg and was himself a minister. In fact, it was Alexander who proposed that if the church could raise $1,000 he would put up $800 to secure the Methodist property on the plaza, which was up for sale. The lot was eventually purchased and the church was renovated and occupied.

It remained there until 1932, when the Presbyterians and Methodists decided to join forces; one church had the building, the other had a large congregation. Together they created the Federated Church, which stands today at 555 Monte Vista Avenue in Healdsburg. At about the same time, the Church of Christ established a congregation in Healdsburg, followed by the Seventh-day Adventists and the Episcopalians.

In Cloverdale, a First Congregational Church was established by the American Home Mission Society in 1868. The Catholics started making a place for themselves in Cloverdale as early as 1870, holding Mass in the Cloverdale Hotel, a hostelry of some 30 rooms. Various priests served the church, coming from other parishes. In 1879 a Scotsman named Peter Donohue established a railroad line and took considerable interest in building a Catholic church. The original church cost about $4,000 and was a rustic frame building. In 1962 the new Cloverdale St. Peter's was built at 491 S. Franklin Street. The church has changed considerably from the days when missionaries came barefooted to say Mass; nowadays, three Masses are said each Sunday and two daily.

In Santa Rosa, the first semblance of a Catholic church (a wooden building with eight pews) was established in 1860 on a lot donated by one of Gen. Vallejo's relatives, Julio Carrillo. For the next 15 years, St. Rose parish was served by a priest who came up from Marin County once a month for Mass. Finally, in 1876, a new parish was formed to include Sebastopol, Healdsburg, Cloverdale and Guerneville. The parish's most popular priest was Fr. John Conway, loved for his sense of humor. He stayed for 37 years.

Today, St. Rose parish is considered the mother church in Santa Rosa, with a seating capacity of 500. The church that was built in 1900, while Fr. Conway was there, still stands as a

Photo: Tina Luster-Hoban

The Church of the Oaks, a historic building, is still in use in Cotati.

historical monument, but it is empty and unused, declared unsafe in earthquake conditions. Still grand, it is now surrounded by a new church that wraps around it like a boomerang. The new building at 398 10th Street is stunning, with walls of colored glass. From inside, many portraits of Christ become brilliant when the sun shines through the windows.

Churches that once fell neatly into a half-dozen denominations—mainly Methodist, Baptist, Catholic—have now splintered into dozens of churches. It started during the Civil War when Southern Methodists and Southern Baptists started their own congregations to denote their sympathies with the South. Today there are American Baptists, Independent Baptists, Fundamental Baptists and GARBC Baptists. We have various branches of Presbyterians including Korean Western. We have Buddhist and Soto Zen centers, and we have Pentecostal, Orthodox Eastern, New Age churches and a group called Metropolitan Community, plus a Church of God of Prophecy and the Foursquare Gospel.

If it is a similar upwelling of faith and devotion that resides in all these houses of worship, rest assured that the North Coast allows each of its citizens a unique way of describing it

Mendocino County

It was a rough bunch of citizens who came to populate the Mendocino Coast in 1854. Lumber was a booming industry that needed lots of workers, and single men by the hundreds poured in from everywhere to work in the mills. After a hard day's work battling logs, lumberjacks were looking for entertainment, and they found it on the east end of Mendocino, a wild, wide-open district that gained the name Fury Town for its typical mood on a Saturday night. Saloons and bawdy houses lined the streets. "Big River Bits" (the local name for $20 gold pieces) were stacked on gambling tables.

This was a hard-living breed, and any parson who sought to bring religion to them necessarily possessed a rare courage and tenacity. In 1854 the first Protestant services in this infant village on Big River were conducted in the cookhouse of the Mendocino Lumber Company. The first ministers who came to preach in Mendocino on an itinerant basis were Methodists, and it was four years before visiting ministers of any other persuasion showed up. When no preacher was available, Mendocino pioneer Peter Kelley, who was an ordained minister from Prince Edward Island, took over.

By 1859 eight determined members from the community applied to the Presbyterian denomination for status as an established congregation, and a mere nine years later they had built a church. It was a lovely little white church, in the Gothic style, designed by the same architect who designed the State Capitol in Sacramento. Today the Mendocino Presbyterian Church is one of the first structures to catch your eye as you enter the village of Mendocino.

It was often rough going for the little congregation. Harmony did not always prevail. One account tells of a confrontation in which the president of the Board of Trustees punched the pastor in the nose. Rugged pioneer personalities sometimes clashed. At one point a schism split the congregation, and attendance declined to the point that the Presbytery considered dissolving it. But the group rode out the rough times, and in 1967 the church celebrated its first 100 years.

Now a California historic landmark, the church also is listed in the Federal Registry of Historic Places. From its original eight charter members, it has grown to a membership of 230—this oldest of California's still-active Presbyterian churches is still vigorous and young. Guided tours are conducted on Saturdays between 10 AM and noon, from July 4 through Labor Day.

Perhaps the first church to be established in Fort Bragg was the First Baptist Church at the corner of East Pine and North Franklin streets. Like most early churches, the congregation first met at a home in nearby Casper, beginning in 1878. By 1887 a formal church with a handsome, tall steeple was under construction on land donated by the Fort Bragg Lumber Company.

That church is still there, though it would be hard to identify it. In 1911 the building was put on rollers, pushed farther back on the lot, and turned to face east instead of south. A new church was built right on top of the old. The original church now serves as a social room and Sunday school. One of the grand features of this early church was a beautiful, 1,200-pound bell, purchased in England and shipped around Cape Horn. It was said the bell rang so clear you could hear it all the way to Casper on a windy day. But by 1932 the clapper had worn out and had to be replaced—unfortunately by a clapper so heavy it cracked the bell. Another clapper, furnished by the fire department, would fit only upside down. At last the bell came down and was set behind the church, where weeds soon overgrew it. Rescued by a church member who was a Daughter of the Golden West, it is now proudly displayed in front of the church with a plaque on it. The present church holds 300 people and is a rare example of a Protestant church built in the California Mission style.

Another of Fort Bragg's oldest churches is the Episcopal St. Michels and All Angels at 201 Fir Street. It was built in 1911 at the instigation of a number of women in town who had become seriously annoyed by the proliferation of saloons and brothels. They advised their husbands it was time to build a church, and this one, with pews for 200 worshippers, was built of local heart-redwood at a cost of $3,600. One of its unique features is a dramatic rose window created by Charles Stevenson, a local artist of some acclaim. The window features a portrait of St. Michael with his hands outstretched. The window is so beautiful that it's kept lighted at night for the pleasure of the people in the community.

The First Methodist Church at 270 N. Pine Street in Ukiah originally served two congregations—one dating to 1850, the other to 1857. In 1926 they united and built a new church. When fire ravaged that building, they put another right on top of it—a brick building with grounds that spread out over a full city block. (They're still finding rubble from the old church under the sanctuary.) Its steeple is the first thing you see on the horizon as you come into town on U.S. 101.

From the beginning, the great fame of this church came from the vesper chimes played high in the steeple. Every day someone mounted the stairs to play the chimes at 5 PM, a welcome signal to office workers across town that it was time to go home. The chimes wore out (as chimes will), but have been replaced by a programmed version that again rings out at 5.

Perhaps the most beautiful of Mendocino's spiritual centers is the Sagely City of Ten Thousand Buddhas, set among 488 acres of groves and meadows in the beautiful Ukiah Valley at Talmage. The grounds include more then 70 buildings, set on approximately 80 landscaped acres, and among them is the Dharma Realm Buddhist University (see our Education and Child Care chapter). An atmosphere of quiet peace pervades the City of Ten Thousand Buddhas. Everyone shares a common goal: the sincere pursuit of spiritual truth and value, along with a

WORSHIP

desire to become wiser and more compassionate. All residents, whether students, faculty, administrators or staff workers observe a basic ethical code that prohibits killing, stealing, sexual misconduct, false speech (lying, lewd speech, cruel words and gossip) and intoxicants. They strive to free their thoughts, words and deeds from any fighting, greed, selfishness, self-seeking ambition and lying.

The Dharma Realm Buddhist Association was incorporated in the United States in 1959 to bring the teachings of the Buddha. In 1966 the Most Venerable Master Hsuan Hua set up a center for Buddhist study in San Francisco. It has been moved to the Ukiah Valley to become one of California's foremost Buddhist centers. Serious-minded individuals from all walks of life may attend intensive recitation or bowing sessions and meditation retreats. The Dharma Realm Buddhist Association offers daily and weekly lectures and ceremonies, classes, vegetarian meals and celebrations of Buddhist holidays.

Lake County

Even in the 1990s, Lake County is a bucolic and loosely populated domain. Back in the pioneer days it could be downright primitive. Spreading the gospel in such conditions was hard and time-consuming work, performed (as in other Wine Country locales) by "circuit rider" ministers who got to know every pothole and muddy quagmire in the land (see this chapter's Close-up, "Saddle of Faith"). At the same time, the rural nature of the area made a house of worship that much more important to the community. The church was a place for weddings, christenings, baptisms, funerals, political meetings, puppet shows and coffee socials. The young people's society encouraged chaperoned courting and, in effect, shaped the county by bringing together important families.

The first denomination to organize within the bounds of the county was the Methodist Episcopal Church. The California Conference of the M.E. Church established a Clear Lake Circuit in 1857, and followers met in the schoolhouse in Big Valley. The first Methodist church was constructed in Lakeport in 1870. Big Valley finally got its Methodist church in 1897, but services were discontinued 19 years later. John Hendricks, who owned the surrounding land, bought the church, tore it down and built a granary in its stead. In Upper Lake, Methodist camp meetings sometimes lasted two weeks. Interested parties would flock to the area in ranch wagons and cook beef or mutton in a barbecue pit. The ministers often wound up with 50 to 60 converts.

Another early Methodist church, this one in Scotts Valley, had an unusual floor plan: All seats faced toward, and the rostrum and pulpit away from, the entrance. "This was quite a shock to anyone coming to church here for the first time," wrote Alice W. Deacon in her book *Scottslandia*. "One had to go past the pulpit and down the aisles with the eyes of everyone upon him. This convenient arrangement saved everyone from looking back to see who each arrival was."

The Methodists also built a wooden church in the southern part of the county in 1871, when the village of Guennoc was relocated and redubbed Middletown. When they replaced the Church of the Pioneers in 1890, the old structure was set on rollers and moved by horsepower to the edge of town. The procession took a week. In 1918 a fire wiped out practically all of Middletown—but not the old church, by then a private residence. The neglected building was finally done in by a storm in 1948. Its 1890 replacement, made of stone, survives today.

Holy Mass was celebrated for the first time in Lake County in 1862 or 1863, by a predominately Irish gathering in a schoolhouse in Big Valley. In 1867 the Catholic church established a mission farm in Big Valley, under the guidance of Father Luciano Osuna. It was called St. Turibius Mission, though it's not known whether the site was named for the Bishop of Astorga, Spain, circa 450, or the Archbishop of Lima, Peru, who helped spread Catholicism during the Spanish conquest in the early 1600s.

In any case, the mission held 160 acres of fertile valley land on the south shore of Clear Lake, and that soon grew to 225 acres (at least 80 of which were under cultivation). There was an Indian rancheria with a schoolhouse and wooden living quarters, and the tribal people were paid for their work. Father Luciano was able to convert nearly the entire tribe of Pomos living around Clear Lake. He baptized 567 people between 1867 and 1878; most of them were Indians, and a few were Russian. The U.S. government made the Indian school at St. Turibius a contract day school from 1888 to 1900. In 1915 the church at the mission was moved to the Finley Rancheria, which had just been created by the U.S. Indian Bureau.

The conversion of natives has remained an interesting sidelight to worship in Lake County. The American Indian Full Gospel Assembly Church was built about 1945 by making an addition to Harry's Garage on the Big Valley Rancheria. Average attendance was about 40. Eight years later the Big Valley Pomo Indian Association granted the church a plot of land for a new structure. It's now known as the Big Valley Community Church.

Jumping back in time again, Catholic churches were soon erected in Kelseyville (St. Peter's in 1870), Lakeport (Immaculate Conception of the Blessed Virgin Mary, 1871), Lower Lake (St. Joseph's, 1881) and Sulphur Banks (St. Anthony's, 1909). St. Joseph's was equipped with an exquisite, hand-carved altar, fashioned in Napa Valley by Swiss and Italian craftsmen. St. Anthony's was erected to serve the mine workers at Sulphur Banks. The bricks used in construction, almost certainly tainted with mercury, were obtained from old mine furnaces at $5 a load. St. Peter's still stands in Kelseyville. They added an entrance room, tower and steeple in 1913 and wrapped the bottom portion of the building in a concrete block skirt between 1955 and 1960, but some of what you see is more than a century old.

When the Catholics needed a new Lakeport church in 1916, they bought the property of the dilapidated Benvenue Hotel on Main Street, between Seventh and Ninth streets. The fathers lived in the old hotel while constructing the church, which was in the Mission style with a stucco exterior.

Siblings John and Lee Gard owned most of Kelseyville, and they were friends of all denominations. John donated land for the Catholic and Methodist churches, Lee for the Presbyterian. The First Presbyterian Church of Clear Lake opened in Kelseyville in 1874. "It was pronounced bold by friends, hazardous by the indifferent and a failure in advance by the critical," wrote Slocum, Bowen & Co. in their *History of Lake County* (1881). The Presbyterians abandoned the brick, semi-Gothic church when they moved to a new location in 1883.

The Episcopal Church established Trinity Mission in Lakeport in 1876. The missionaries held regular services at Lakeport, rotated among three other sites in the county and made occasional trips to Ukiah. Meanwhile, the American Sunday School Union appointed Rev. Will E. Read as its Missionary for the Northern District of California in July, 1880. Read commenced his work in Lake County about a year later. He stayed through the summer of 1881 to organize Sunday schools, supply literature and offer moral support. In Slocum's history, he's described as "an earnest, eloquent preacher, a zealous, indefatigable worker."

Often, the problem in Lake County has been getting enough bodies in the pews each Sunday. A note in the Methodist Church record from 1906 states, "A siege of measles in early summer followed by a long spell of excessive heat have caused some falling off in attendance during the summer." In 1922 the Methodist, Presbyterian and Christian churches in Kelseyville were all in dire financial straits. When a minister wasn't available at one of the churches, the congregation simply attended another. So Rev. Story, a Methodist, with the help of the high school principal, initiated a federation called the Kelseyville United Community Church. Two years later the Methodists withdrew, but in 1929 their church and manse were destroyed by a fire. The Presbyterians were without a minister at the time, so they invited Rev. John Anderson and his Methodist flock to share their sanctuary (the then-new stucco building now known as Social Hall). On New Year's Day, 1930, the two denominations reunited as the Kelseyville Federated Church. The federation lasted until 1948, and church membership grew during that time.

As a final note, on May 15, 1971, the Middletown Methodists opened the cornerstone of their Church of the Pioneers. Trustees chiseled away at the stone and mortar to reveal a 1-foot by 8-inch by 4-inch copper box. It was a time capsule, and inside was a copy of the *Middletown Independent* dated October 7, 1893. The hold was enlarged to accommodate a larger, stainless steel box filled with contemporary items. If you're around in 2071 (the 200th anniversary of the church), you can make your way to Middletown and watch it unsealed.

Index

955 Ukiah Street Restaurant 138–139

A

A&M Market 304
A'Roma Roasters and Coffeehouse 143
AARP (American Association of Retired Persons) 348
Above the Clouds 83–84
Abrams House Inn 88
Admiral William Standley State Recreation Area 282
Adobe Drug 257
Adventures Aloft 211
Aerostat Adventures 212
Agape Christian Book Store 259
Agate Cove Inn 93
Air Flambuoyant 212
Airport Cinema 8 146
airports 19–24
Albion River Inn & Restaurant 67–68, 137
Alcatraz Island 46
Alexander Valley 6
Alexis Baking Company 114
Alinder Gallery 275
All Seasons Cafe 120
Ambrose Bierce House, The 79
Amelia Claire 242
American Photo Impressions 276
Amtrak 24
Ana's Cantina 142
Anchor Charters 208
Anchor Lodge Motel 68
Anchorage Inn 71
Anderson Creek Inn 90
Anderson Marsh State Historic Park 210
Anderson Valley Brewing Company 126–127
Anderson Valley Historical Museum 207
Andrews Hall 262
Annadel State Park 279, 292–293
Annie's Jughandle Beach Inn 95
annual events 215-235
Antique Fair 253
Antique Harvest & Robert's Relics 255
Antique Marketplace & Annex 254
Antique Society 255
Antique Tours 26
antiques 252–256
Applewood Inn & Restaurant 90, 136
Arbor Guest House 75
Arbor House Inn 96
Arena Theater 146
Argus Courier 382
arm wrestling 316
Armida Winery 182
Armstrong Redwoods State Reserve 281
Armstrong Woods Pack Station 294
Arrowood Vineyards & Winery 178
Arroyo Real Estate 336
Art and All That Jazz 248
art galleries 270–276
Art in the Redwoods 228
Artesa Winery 158

Artful Eye, The 243, 245
arts 260–276
Atlas Peak Grill 114
attractions 194–214
Auberge du Soleil 98, 118
Austin Creek State Recreation Area 281–282
Autumn Village 355
Avalon Players 262
Avenue of the Giants 329

B

Baechtel Creek Inn 67
Bale Grist Mill State Historic Park 195–196
Bale Mill Classic Country Furniture 242–243
Balloons Above the Valley 211
balloons and gliders 211–212
Barbara Friday Weekend Wear 238
bars and clubs 141–145
Bartholomew Park Winery 175
baseball 307–309
basketball 310–311
Bay Hill Mansion 88
Bay View Restaurant 135
Beach Blanket Babylon 48
beaches. *See* coast
Beaded Nomad, The 239
Bear Creek Campground 112
Bear Flag Inn 82
Bear Moon Clothing 244
Bear Republic Brewing Company 125–126, 144
Beaucanon Winery 168
Beaulieu Vineyard 164
Beauty Store & More 238
Beazley House, The 75
Beck & Taylor 336–337
bed and breakfast inns 73–96
Bell Haven Resort 70
Belle de Jour Inn 86
Beltane Ranch 84
Belvedere Winery 182
Benziger Family Winery 178
Beringer Vineyards 171
Beringer, Jacob and Frederick 32
Berry's Saw Mill 206
Bicycle Factory, The 293
Bicycle Rack, The 293
bicycle rentals 293
Bicycle Trax 293
bicycling 292–293
    road races 314–316
Big River Lodge 103
Biscuits and Blues 48
Bistro Don Giovanni 114
Bistro Jeanty 116
Bistro Ralph 132, 134
Black Bart Festival 221
Blackberry Festival 228
Blair House 93
Blessing of the Balloons 216
Blue Abbey, The 254

Blue Lakes 303
Blue Violet Mansion, The 74
Blue Wing Inn 201
Bodega Bay Lodge Resort 66
Bodega Bay RV Park 107
Bodega Bay Surf Shack 304
Boggs Mountain 285, 296
Bonaventura Balloon Company 211–212
Book Loft 259
Book Nook, the 259
Book Stop, Nature & Discovery Shop, The 327
Book Stop, The 259
Book Warehouse 257
Bookends Book Store 256
bookstores 256–259
Bookwinkle's Children's Books 259
Bookworm, The 258
Boonville Airport 22
Bothe-Napa Valley State Park 106, 278
Boulevard Bowl 293
Boutique Mystique 238
bowling 293–294
Brannan Cottage Inn 82
Brannan's Grill 122
Brannon, Sam 30
Brava Terrace 118
Breakers Inn 67
brewpubs 124–127
Bridge School, The 364
Bright Lights Candle Company 251–252
Brix 116
Broadway Realty 341
Brookside Vineyard Bed & Breakfast 76
Buena Vista Winery 175
Burgundy House Inn 77–78
bus lines 24

C

cab companies 27
Cafe at Sonoma Mission Inn 128
Cafe Beaujolais 138
Cafe Sarafornia 122
Cal Skate 323
California Carnivores 248
California Properties 336
California Wine Tours 26–27
Calistoga Bookstore, The 257
Calistoga Inn & Restaurant 60–61, 122, 142
Calistoga Pottery 243
Calistoga Realty Co. 337
Calistoga Roastery 122
Calistoga Spa Hot Springs 100
Calistoga Speedway 313
Calistoga Village Inn & Spa 101
Calistoga Wine Stop 192
Calla Lily Fine Linens 241–242
Camellia Inn 86
Cameo Cinema 145
camping 105–112
Candy Cellar, The 243
Cannery, The 46
Cantina, The 143
Canyon Road Winery 185
Cardinal Newman High School 363–364
Carillo, Joaquin 38
Carneros Creek 157
Carolyn Parr Nature Museum 320
Carriage House Restaurant, The 142
Carriage Occasions 214
Caspar Headlands State Beach and Reserve 284

Caspar Inn, The 145
Cat & The Fiddle 253
Catahoula Restaurant & Saloon 122–123
Catch a Canoe & Bicycles Too 293
Catfish Books 259
Cavanagh Inn 84–85
Cazanoma Lodge 67
Cedar Gables Inn 74–75
Cedar Rouch 295–296
Celadon 114
Century 21 335, 340, 344
Century Communications 387–388
Chandelle of Sonoma 178
Chanterell 114–115
Chanticleer Antiques 254
Chardonnay Lodge 57
Charles Krug Winery 171
Chaslor Guest Ranch and Stables 294
Chateau Montelena 174–175
Chateau Souverain 185–186
Chateau Souverain, The Cafe at the Winery 134
Chateau St. Jean 179
Chateau, The 57–58
Chelsea Antiques 253–254
Cherry Pie Criterium 314
Cheshire Bookshop 259
Chez Peyo Country French Restaurant 135
child care 370–371
children's attractions 319–327
Chimney Rock Winery 159
Chimney Tree 329
Chinatown 46
Chocolate Cabernet Fantasy 216
Christopher Queen Galleries 275
Christopher's Inn 79
Churchill Manor Bed & Breakfast Inn 74
Cinnabar Theater 270
Cinnamon Bear Bed & Breakfast 78–79
City Lights Books 48
Classic Duck, The 238
Clear Lake 303
Clear Lake State Park 111, 285–286
Clearlake Cinema 146
Cline Cellars 175–176
Clo's Ice Creamery 143
Clos du Bois 185
Clos du Val 158–159
Clos Pegase Winery 174, 273
Clothes Time 238
Clover Cinemas 146
Cloverdale Municipal Airport 22
Club Rumors 143
coast 298–300
Coast Cinemas 146
Cobb Village Inn Motel 69
Cobbie Shoe Shop 238
Coddingtown Regional Mall 238
Coldwell Banker 335, 340, 344–345
College of the Redwoods 367
college sports 316–318
Comfort Inn 61
Community Voice, The 382–383
Compadres Mexican Bar & Grill 116–117
Company's Comin' 238
Conn Creek Winery 168
Continental Lanes 293
Continental Real Estate 335
Copperfield's Books 256, 258, 323
Copperfield's Cafe 142–143
Coralee Barkela & Company 340
Corsentino Winery 160

Cotati Accordion Festival 227–228
Cotati Chamber of Commerce 14
Cottage Grove Inn 82
Cottage, The 83
Country Inn at Fort Bragg 95
Country Meadow Inn 85–86
Country Pine Antiques 253
Courtyard, The 250
Cow Mountain Recreation Area 286, 296
Cozy Corner Children's Center 365
CPS Country Air 345
Crane Creek Regional Park 279
Crane Park 320
Crazy Creek Soaring 212
Crown Books 258
Culinary Institute of America at Greystone 369–370
Cuvaison Winery 174

D

D&G Property Management 339
D. Gutierrez Gallery 276
dance organizations/venues 267–268, 270
Davis Bynum Winery 182–183
Days Inn 67, 70
daytrips 328–332
De Loach Vineyards 181–182
Dean & DeLuca 192, 240
Decker's 256
Deep Valley Christian School 365
Deja-Vu Hat Co. 251
Della Santina's 129
Depot Hotel Cucina Rustica 129
Depot Park Museum 196–197
Destination: Napa Valley Tours 214
Dharma Realm Buddhist University 370
di Rosa Preserve 271
Dickens Street Faire 235
Diner, The 117
Discovery Inn 67
Disney's Water Sports 306
Distinctive Properties of Napa Valley 337
Dixie Jazz Festival 227
Domaine Carneros 157
Domaine Chandon 117, 160
Don's Bait & Tackle 304
Doran Park 107, 280
Double Decker Lanes 293
Doubletree Hotel 64
Downtown Joe's 141
Dr. Wilkinson's Hot Springs 99
Dreamweavers Theater 261
Dry Creek General Store 134
Dry Creek Valley 6
Dry Creek Vineyard 184
Dunnewood Vineyards and Winery 189
Dutch Henry 173

E

E.S. Wolf & Company 343
Early Work 321
Ed's Market 304
Edgewater Resort and RV Park 111
education 357–370
Egghead's Restaurant 139–140
El Bonita Motel 59
El Dorado Hotel 62
El Paseo de Sonoma (Pinelli Building) 201
El Pueblo Inn 62
Elk Cove Inn 92

Elms, The 80
Embassy Suites Napa Valley 57
Empire College 367
Enoteca Wine Shop 192–193
Equus 131
Erika Hills 253
Evans Airport Service 22–23
Executive Limousine 26
Exploratorium 48
ExpressCare 372

F

Faerie Ring Campground 108
Fairfield Osborn Preserve 279
Fairmont Hotel 48
Farm Trails 246–247
Farmhouse Inn, The 89, 136
Featherbed Railroad Company 96
Fensalden Inn 92–93
Fern Grove Cottages 90
Ferrari Carrano Vineyard & Winery 184
Fetzer Cycles 293
Fetzer Valley Oaks Bed & Breakfast 90
Fetzer Vineyards 188–189
Fiddles & Cameras 251
Fideaux 242
Fieldstone Winery 186
Fiesta Patrias 230
Fior d'Italia 49
Fisherman's Wharf 45–46
fishing 304, 306
Flag Store, The 244
Flamino Resort Hotel & Fitness Center 64
flora and fauna 53–55
Flying Carpets 241
Folie á Deux Winery 172
football 309–310
Foothill Cafe 115
Foothill House 82–83
Foothills Adventist Elementary School 361
Footlighters Little Theater 209
Foppiano Vineyards 183
For the Shell of It 251
Forbestown Inn 95–96
Ford House Museum 208
Forestville 7
Forks Theater 146
Fort Bragg Cyclery 293
Fort Bragg Door to Door 27
Fort Bragg Leisure Time RV Park 110
Fort Ross Book & Gift Shop 258
Fort Ross Lodge 66
Fort Ross State Historic Park 205–206
Fountaingrove Inn 64
Franciscan Oakville Estates 168
Frank Howard Allen Realtors 336, 339–340
Frank R. Howard Memorial Hospital 376
Freemark Abbey Winery 172
French Laundry, The 117
Friends House 354
Frontier Realty Property Management 342
Fuchsiarama 238
Fuller Grove 112
Fun & Games 320

G

Gables Inn, The 85
Gaige House Inn 84
Gallery Bookshop & Bookwinkle's Children's Books

259
Gallery on Main Street, The 272–273
Garden Court Cafe & Bakery 130
Garden Grill 139
Garden Haven 347
Garner's Resort 111, 304
General's Daughter, The 127–128
George Alexander House 86
Getaway Adventures & Bike Shop 214
Getaway Bike Shop 293
Geyser Peak Winery 186–187
Geyserville Inn 65–66
Ghirardelli Square 46
Gillwoods Restaurant 118
Gingerbread 323
Gingerbread Storybooks and Whimsy 238
Glass Mountain Inn 78
Glen Ellen 5
Glen Ellen Inn Restaurant 130
Glen Ellen Tasting Room 178–179
Glendeven 91
Glenelly Inn 84
Gloria Ferrer Champagne Caves 176
Gloriana Theater 266–267
Golden Gate Park 48
Golden Goose, The 250–251
Golden Haven Hot Springs 100–101
Golden State Warriors 310–311
golf 287–292, 312–313
Goltermann Gardens & Country Inn 85
Goodtime Bicycle Company, The 293
Goosecross Cellars 160
Gottschalks 238
Grace Hudson Museum and Sun House 206–207, 249
Graeser Winery 174
Grape Leaf Inn 86
Gravenstein Apple Fair 228
Great Highway 48
Great Rubber Ducky Race 222
Green Valley Cafe 118–119
Greenwood Creek State Beach 283
Greenwood Pier Cafe 144
Greenwood Ridge Vineyards 189–190
Greenwood State Park Visitors Center 205
Grey Whale Bar & Cafe 139
Grey Whale Inn, The 95
Greyhound Bus Lines 24
Grgich Hills Cellar 164, 168
Griewe Real Estate 340
Grille at Sonoma Mission Inn 128–129
Groezinger, Gottlieb 32
Gualala Arts Center 275
Gualala Point Regional Park 108, 280–281
Gualala River 301
Guenoc and Langtry Estate 191
Guest House Museum 209
Gundlach Bundschu Winery 176

H

Hakusan Sake Gardens 194
Handley Cellars 190
Hanna Winery 187
Hans Fahden Vineyards 175
Haraszthy, Count Agoston 36
Harbin Hot Springs 104
Harbor House 92
Harbor Lite Lodge 68
Harvest Inn 59
Harvest Market 251
Haydon Street Inn 86–87

Headlands Coffee House 145
Heald, Harmon 37
Healdsburg Classics 254–255
Healdsburg General Hospital 375
Healdsburg Inn on the Plaza 87
Healdsburg Municipal Airport 22
Healdsburg Museum 205
Healdsburg Tribune 383
healthcare 372-79
Hearth Song 248
Heaven on Wheels 27
Heitz Wine Cellar 169–170
Held-Poage Memorial Home and Library 207
Helen Putnam Regional Park 279
Hemphill's Lounge 142
Hendy Woods State Park 109, 283
Hennessey House, The 75
Hennessey, Lake 302
Henry Joseph Gallery 271
Heritage House 103, 138
Hess Collection Winery, The 271
Hess Collection, The 158
Hi-Seas Inn 69
Hidden Gardens Tour 220
Hidden Valley Lake Country Club 292
Hideaway Cottages 80
High Tide Surf Shop 304, 306
Highland Springs Disc Golf Course 327
Highland Springs Loop 292
Highlands Senior Service Center 352
Highlands Village 355
Hill House of Mendocino 68
Hillscrest B&B 83
Hilltop Christian Academy 366
Hispanic Chamber of Commerce/Sonoma County 14
history 28–44
hockey 311–312
Hoffman House 134
Holdenried Farms 252
Holiday Harbor RV Park 111
Home Sweet Home 238
Honor Mansion 87
Hop Kiln Winery 183
Hope-Bosworth House 87–88
Hope-Merrill House 88
Hopland Antiques 255
horse jumping 316
horse racing 316
horseback riding 294
hospices 378
hospitals 373–376, 378
Hot Pepper Jelly Company 251
Hotel D'Amici 61
Hotel La Rose 65
Hotel St. Helena 60
hotels/motels 56–71
House of Realty 344
Howarth Park 323–324
Hoyman Browe Studio 249
Humboldt Redwoods State Park 329
hunting 294–296
Husch Vineyards 190
Hyde Street Pier 46
Hydro Bar & Grill 123, 142

I

I. Wolk Gallery 272
Images Fine Art 271–272
Indian Springs 99–100
Indian Valley Reservoir 303

INDEX

Ink House, The 78
Inn at Occidental, The 89
Inn at Schoolhouse Creek 93
Inn at Southbridge, The 59–60
Inn at the Tides 66
Inn of the Beginning 143
Inn on Randolph 75
Inti 239
Irish Cottage, The 245, 248, 255
Irish Pedlar Antiques 252
Irish Shop, The 251

J

J's Amusements 325
J's Garden 252
J.M. Rosen's 130
Jack London Bookstore 257
Jack London State Historic Park 202
Jackson State Forest 110, 284, 296
Japanese Cultural Festival 216
Jarvis Conservatory 267–268
Jasper O'Farrell's 144
Jepson Vineyards 188–189
Jesse Peter Native American Art Museum 203
Jessel Miller Gallery 271
JHM Stamps & Collectibles 239
Jimtown Store 255
Joan & David 237
Jockey Club, The 316
John Ash & Co. 131
John Dougherty House 93
John F. Kennedy Memorial Regional Park 319
John Muir Inn, The 58
Johnson's Alexander Valley Wines 187
Joshua Grindle Inn 93–94
Jug Handle State Reserve 284
Jungle Vibes 321–322
Just D-Vine Limousine Service 27
Justin-Siena High School 360

K

Kelley House Museum 208
Kelly's Kamp 111
Kelsey, Andrew 42
Kelseyville Motel 71
Kendall-Jackson Winery Wine Country Store 183
Kentucky Street Antiques 254
Kenwood Inn, The 101–102
Kenwood Restaurant 130
Kenwood Vineyards 179–180
King's Sport and Tackle Shop 306
Kits Corner Store & Gas 304
Kodiak Jack's 143
Kolbe Academy 360
Konocti Adult School 356
Konocti Harbor Resort & Spa 104, 145
Korbel Champagne Cellars 188
Kornell Rombauer Cellars 173
Kragen Auto Parks 238
Kristalberg Bed & Breakfast 96
Kruse Rhododendron State Reserve 280
Kule Loklo 328
Kunde Estate Winery 180

L

La Belle Epoque 75–76
La Boucane 115
La Case Restaurante 129

La Chaumiere 80
La Famigilia di Robert Mondavi 160
La Fleur Bed and Breakfast Inn 78
La Gare French Restaurant 132
La Residence 77
La Villeta de Sonoma 245
Lake Berryessa 5
Lake County
  attractions 209–210
  bars and clubs 145
  bed and breakfast inns 95–96
  camping 110–112
  children's attractions 326–327
  golf 291–292
  hospitals 376, 378
  hotels/motels 69–71
  movie theaters 146
  real estate 342–345
  restaurants 140
  schools 359-366
  spas/resorts 104
  telephone numbers 15
  theater 267
  visual arts 276
  walk-in clinics 373
  wineries 155, 191–192
  worship 398–399
Lake County Museum 210
Lake County Outdoor Passion Play 222
Lake County Repertory Theater 267
Lake Mendocino Recreation Area 282
Lake Point Lodge 70
Lake Sonoma Fish Hatchery 325
Lake Sonoma Wildlife Area 296
Lake Sonoma Winery 184
Lake Sonoma—Liberty Glen 107
Lakeport Auto Movies 146
Lakeport Cinema 5 146
Lakeport Community Players 267
Lakeport Tackle 304
lakes 302–303
Lakeshore Bowl 294
Lakeside Cinema 5 146
Lakeside County Park 326–327
Lakeside Village Bookstore 258
Lambert Bridge Winery 184–185
Lampson Field 22
Landmark Vineyards 180–181
Langtry, Lillie 43–44
Lark in the Morning Musique 250
Lavender Hill Spa 213
Learning Faire 320
Leaves of Grass Bookstore 259
Ledford House Restaurant, The 137–138
Lee Youngman Galleries 273
Legacy Gift Shop, The 245
Lehman's Lollipop Farm 252
Levi's 237
Levin & Company 258
Lewis Adult Education Center 355
Li'l Stinker Antiques 255
Liberty Glen 107
limousine services 26–27
Lincoln Avenue Spa 212–213
Lisa Hemenway's Restaurant 132
Little Angels Children's Center 365
Little Caesars 238
Little River Airport 22
Little River Inn 103, 138, 291
Live Oaks Senior Center 352
Llano House Antiques 255

Loch Lomond Park 110
Lodge at Noyo River 95
Lodge at Paulin Creek, The 354–355
London Fog 237
London, Jack 37
Lone Dog Fine Art & Antiques 253
Los Arroyos Golf Course 289
Los Posadas State Forest 292
Lotus Thai Restaurant 132
Louis M. Martini Winery 170
Lower Hunting Creek 106
Lower Lake Clinic 373
Lower Lake Schoolhouse and Museum 209–210
Lucas Wharf & Bar 134–135
Lucchesi Park Senior Center 350
Luther Burbank Center for the Arts 264–265
Luther Burbank Gold Ridge 205
Luther Burbank Home and Gardens 203

M

M&M Campgrounds 111
MacCallum House Restaurant Grey Whale
    Bar & Cafe 139
Mackerricher State Park 110, 284–285
Madrona Manor 87, 134
magazines 385
Magliulo's Restaurant and Pensione 128
Magnum Cinema, The 145
MaiFest 218–219
Mailliard Redwoods State Reserve 282–283
Main Street Books 256
Main Street Station 144
Maison Fleurie 77
malls 237–239
Manchester State Beach 283
Manchester State Park 109–110
Manor Oaks Overnighter Park 108
Margaret's Antiques 253
Marianne's Antiques 254
Mario's Bohemian Cigar Store 49
Marioni's 128
Mariposa School 365
Mark West Vineyards & Winery 188
Marketplace, The 217
Markham Vineyards 171–172
Marlana River Designs 249
Marlowe's 141
Marryhill Country School 364
Martini & Prati Wines 182
Marty's Top o' the Hill 144
Mary's Pizza Shack 129–130
Matanzas Creek Winery 181
Mayo Family Wineries 179
McLaughlin Gold Mine Tour 326
McNear's Restaurant 130–131
Meadowood Napa Valley 98
Mediacom 388
Melitta Station Inn 85
Melting Pot, The 250
Melville Montessori School 365
Memorial Hospice 378
Mendo Realty 343
Mendocino Art Center 275
Mendocino Book Company, The 259
Mendocino Bounty 249
Mendocino Brewing Company 126
Mendocino Coast Botanical Gardens 208–209, 251
Mendocino Coast District Hospital 376
Mendocino College 367, 368
Mendocino County
    attractions 206–209
    bars and clubs 144–145
    bed and breakfast inns 90–95
    camping 108–110
    children's attractions 325–326
    coast 299–300
    golf 291
    hospitals 375–376
    hotels/motels 67–69
    movie theaters 146
    real estate 342–343
    restaurants 136–140
    schools 365
    spas/resorts 102–104
    theater 265–267
    vacation rentals 71–72
    visual arts 275
    wineries 152, 154–155, 188–191
    worship 396–398
Mendocino County Museum 207
Mendocino Headlands State Park 284
Mendocino Hotel, Restaurant & Garden Room 68,
    138
Mendocino National Forest 286, 296
Mendocino Theater Company 266
Merryvale Vineyards 170–171
Mervyn's 238
Michelle Marie's Patisserie 238
Mid-Towne Realty, Inc. 341
Middle Creek Campground 112
Middletown County Park Community Pool 297
Middletown Times Star 384
Midnight Sun Inn 87
Mieggs, Harry 41
Milagros 244
Milano Winery 189
Milat Vineyards 169
Mill Creek Vineyards 183
Mission San Francisco Solano 197
Mistral 132
Mixx 132
Model Bakery 119
Molly's Brown's Saloon 144
Mom's Apple Pie 135
Montgomery Village 238
Montgomery Woods State Reserve 282
Monticello Vineyards 158
Moonlight Bar & Grill, The 143
Moore's Flour Mill 249
Moose's 48
Moosse Cafe, The 139
Morgan Lane 335, 340
Morton's Warm Springs 321
Mosswood 240
Mostly Mozart 226
motor sports 313–314
Mount View Hotel 61
Mount View Spa 212
Mountain Home Ranch 61–62
Mountain House Winery and Lodge 88
Movado 237
movie theaters 145–146
Mumm Napa Valley 164, 272
Murphy's Irish Pub 142
music organizations/venues 267–268, 270
Mustard Magic 216
Mustard on the Silverado Trail 217
Mustards Grill 117
Mystic Theatre & Dance Hall 143

N

Nance's Hot Spring 99
Napa Adventist Junior Academy 360–361
Napa Bowl 293
Napa CineDome 8 145
Napa Country Inn 57
Napa County
  area overview 4–5
  attractions 194–196, 198–201
  balloons and gliders 211–212
  bars and clubs 141–142
  bed and breakfast inns 74–80, 82–83
  camping 105–106
  children's attractions 319–320
  emergency numbers 379
  golf 287–289
  history 28–33
  hospitals 373
  hotels/motels 57–62
  lakes 302
  map 10
  movie theaters 145
  music/dance organizations and venues 267–268
  parks 278
  private schools 360
  public schools 357–358
  public transportation 24
  real estate 333–337
  restaurants 114–120, 122–123, 127
  rivers 300–301
  spas/resorts 97–101
  telephone numbers 14
  theater 261–262
  tours 213–214
  trivia 11
  visual arts 271–273
  walk-in clinics 372
  wine shops 192–193
  Wine Train 198–201
  wineries 149–150, 157–161, 163–164, 168–174
  worship 389–392
Napa County Airport 22
Napa Emergency Women's Services 379
Napa Firefighters Museum 195
Napa Grand Prix 314–315
Napa Premium Outlets 237
Napa River 300–301
Napa Skate Park 319
Napa Soda Springs 30–31
Napa Town Center 237
Napa Valley Art Association 271
Napa Valley Balloons, Inc. 211
Napa Valley Bike Tours & Rentals 213, 293
Napa Valley Classic Irish Festival 217
Napa Valley College 261, 268, 355, 366
Napa Valley Crown Limousine 26
Napa Valley Dining Club 347
Napa Valley Grapevine Wreath Company 240
Napa Valley Holidays 213
Napa Valley Keyboards 239
Napa Valley Lodge 58–59
Napa Valley Marriott 57
Napa Valley Museum 195
Napa Valley Olive Oil Co. 240–241
Napa Valley Open Studios Tour 232
Napa Valley Opera House 265
Napa Valley Ovens 123 .
Napa Valley Railway Inn 58
Napa Valley Symphony 268
Napa Valley Tours and Trail Hikes 213–214

Napa Valley Trail Rides 294
Napa Valley Travelodge 57
Napa Valley Wine Auction 222–223
Napa Valley Wine Festival 233
Napa Valley Wine Train 198–201
Napa Walk-In Center 379
Napa-Sonoma Marshes Wildlife Area 295
Navarro River 301
Navarro River Redwoods 283
Navarro Vineyards 190
Neft & Neft Realtors 344
Negri's 136
Neighborhood, The 252–253
New Vista Adult Education School 356
newspapers 380–385
Nicholson House 94
Niebaum-Coppola Estate Winery 163–164
nightlife 141–146
Nob Hill 45
Noble Realty 345
North Bay HI-CAP 348
North Beach 46, 48
North Coast Brewing Company 127
North Coast Health Care Center 375
North Coast Opportunities, Inc. 371
North County Properties 341
North State Cafe 137
Northcoast Artists Gallery 275
Northwestern Pacific Railroad 205
Noyo Bowl 293

O

Oak Knoll Inn 77
Oakland Athletics 308
Oakland International Airport 20–21
Oakland Raiders 309–310
Oakville Grocery Co. 248
Oakville Ranch Winery 163
Oat Hill Mine Trail 285
ocean. See coast
Odyssey Limousine 27
Old Adobe Bar and Grille 115
Old Adobe Fiesta 228
Old Adobe School 362
Old Faithful Geyser of California 196
Old Mill Days 232
Old Stewart House Inn 95
Old World Inn, The 76
Old-Fashioned Fourth of July Celebration 225
Old-Time Fiddle Contest 216
Oldie's And Things 255
Olive Press, The 245
Omelette Express 131–132
On the Waterfront 306
One Man's Junk, Another Man's Gold 256
One-Log House 329
Open Door Book Store 256
Orr Hot Springs 102
Outrageous Waters 326
Overland Sheepskin Company 240
Ox Roast 223
Oxbow School, The 360

P

Pacific Café 46
Pacific Heights 48
Pacific Limousine 27
Pacific Properties 343
Pacific Resorts Realty 72, 342

INDEX

Pacific Theatres 16 146
Pacific Union College 317, 355, 368
Pacific Union Residential Brokerage 340
Pacifico Restaurante Mexicano 123
Paint Your World 239–240
Pairs Parkside Cafe 119
Palisades Mountain Sport 293
Palm Drive Hospital 375
Panache 251
Pangaea Cafe 137
Paradise Miniature Golf 319–320
Paradise Ridge Winery 181
Parducci Wine Cellars 189
Park Place Restaurant 140
parks 277–286
Parrett Field 22
Patterson's Pub 144–145
Paul Bunyan Days 230
Paul M. Dimmick Wayside State Camp 109
Paulin Hall Auditorium 268
Pear Blossom Festival 219–220
Pedal 'Round the Puddle 231–232
Pedroncelli Winery 187
Peju Province Winery 163
Perry's 48
Pet-a-Llama Ranch 325
Petaluma 5–6, 35–36
Petaluma Adobe State Historic Park 202
Petaluma Criterium 315
Petaluma Ecumenical Project 348
Petaluma Historical Museum 202
Petaluma Marsh Wildlife Area 296
Petaluma Municipal Airport 22
Petaluma Speedway 313–314
Petaluma Valley Hospital 374
Petaluma Village Premium Outlets 237
Petrified Forest, The 204, 324
Pezzi King Vineyards 185
Photo Finish, The 218
Piatti Restaurant 117–118, 142
Piccolino's Italian Café 116, 142
Pillsbury, Lake 303
Pine Acres Resort 71, 111–112
Pine Beach Inn & Suites 69
Pine Ridge Winery 159
Pinoli Ranch Country Inn 90–91
Pinot Blanc 119
Pioneer Christmas Grist Mill State Park 234–235
planetariums 324
Pleasure Cove Resort 105–106
Ployez Winery 191
Point Arena 9
Point Arena Lighthouse and Museum 207–208
Ponderosa Ranch 331
Powerhouse Brewing Company, The 144
Prager Winery & Port Works 170
Precision Hairstyling 238
Presentation School, The 363
Preston Vineyards 185
Property Rentals Only Inc. 335
Prudential California Realty, The 335, 339
public transportation 24–26
publications 385–386
Punch Line 48
Pure Luxury 26
Putah Creek Resort 99
Pygmalion House 85

Q

Quail Meadows Campground 108–109

Quality Inn 62, 64
Queen of the Valley Hospital 373
Quivira Vineyards 185

R

R.S. Basso Home 242
Rabbit Ridge Vineyards 183
Rachel's Inn 91
radio stations 386–387
RadioShack 238
Ragle Ranch Regional Park 281
Railroad Square Basement Antiques 254
Rainbow Cattle Company 144
RAKU Ceramics Collection 272
Raley's Towne Center 237–238
Rams Head Realty 71–72, 339
Rancho Caymus 59
Rancho de Calistoga 354
Rasmussen Art Gallery 273
Raven Film Center, The 146
Ravenswood Winery 176
Raymond Vineyard & Cellar 168–169
RE/MAX 335, 340
Readers' Books 257
real estate 333–345. *See also* rentals; vacation rentals
Real Goods Solar Living Center 206
Real Goods Store 249
recreation 287-297. *See also* arts; attractions; daytrips;
        individual sports; nightlife
Red Hen Antiques 253
Red Hot 'n' Roll 222
Redbud Community Hospital 376
Redwood Coast Medical Services 376
Redwood Coast Seniors 355
Redwood Empire District Fair 228
Redwood Empire Ice Arena 204, 324
Redwood Meadows 355
Redwood National Park 329
Redwood Valley Cellars 189
Reebok 237
Relay, The 314
religion. *See* worship
Remick Ridge Vineyards 181
Ren Brown Collection, The 274–275
Rendezvous Restaurant 145
Rendezvous, The 140
Rental Connection, The 339
rentals 334–335, 338–339, 342, 344
resorts. *See* spas/resorts
Restaurant at Meadowood, The 118
Restaurant, The 139
restaurants 113–140
retirement 346-356. *See also* senior citizens
Ridenhour Ranch House Inn 89–90
riley street art supplies 324
Rincon Cyclery 293
Rio Theater 146
Ristorante Piatti 129
River Bend Campground 108
River Child Care Services 371
River House 130
River's End Restaurant 135
Riverfront Antique Center 252
Rivership Grand Romance 195
RMS Distillery 194–195
Robert Louis Stevenson State Park 278
Robert Mondavi Winery 161, 268
Robert Sinskey Vineyards 160
Robinson & Co. 248
Roche Winery 176–177

Rodney Strong Vineyards 183–184
Roederer Estate 190–191
Rolf Nord Kriken 276
Roman Spa 100
Rombauer Vineyards 172
Roots of Motive Power Festival 229–230
Ross Dress for Less 238
Royal Coach Limousine Service 26
Royal Oak Vintner's Court, The 116
running 314
Russian Gulch State Park 110, 284
Russian River 301
Russian River Getaways 71, 339
Russian River Heritage Christmas 235
Russian River Vacation Homes 71, 339
Rutherford Hill Winery 168

S

Sacramento International Airport 21
Sacramento Kings 311
Safari West 204
Saks Fifth Avenue 237
Salt Point Lodge 66
Salt Point State Park 107, 280
Salute to the Arts 225
Salvador Vallejo Adobe (Swiss Hotel) 201
San Francisco 45–49
San Francisco 49ers 309
San Francisco Giants 307–308
San Francisco International Airport 20
San Jose Earthquakes 312
San Jose Sharks 311–312
Sandpiper House Inn 92
Santa Rosa 6, 35
Santa Rosa Airporter 23
Santa Rosa Courtyard by Marriott 65
Santa Rosa Junior College 265, 324, 355, 366–367
Santa Rosa Memorial Hospital 374
Santa Rosa Multi-Purpose Senior Center 350
Santa Rosa Players 264
Santa Rosa Plaza 238
Santa Rosa Symphony 270
Santa's Arrival 234
Scandia Family Fun Center 323
Scarlett's Country Inn 79
Scharffenberger Cellars 190
School Bell Antiques 255
Schoolhouse Canyon Campground 108
Schooner Gulch 283
Schram, Jacob 32
Schramsberg Vineyards and Cellars 173
Schug-Carneros Estate Winery 177
Scott Courtyard 80
Sea Coast Hide-a-Ways 71, 339
Sea Cottage Real Estate 343
Sea Gull Inn 94
Sea Ranch Lodge 66–67, 275
Sea Ranch Realty 341
Sea Rock Inn 94
Seabird Lodge 69
Seafoam Lodge 91–92
Sears 238
Sears Point Raceway 197, 313
Sebastiani Theatre 145
Sebastiani Vineyards 177
Sebastopol Antique Mall 255
Sebastopol Cinemas 146
Seguin Moreau Napa Cooperage 194
senior centers 349–352
senior citizens 355–356 *See also* retirement
Senior Citizens Center 349

Senior Class 347
senior services 346–349
Shackford's 239
Shady Oaks Country Inn 78
Sharpsteen Museum, The 196
Shaw's Shady Acres 110–111
Sheepdog Trials 220–221
Sheepshearing at the Adobe 219
shopping 236–260
Shore Line Realty 344
Showley's at Miramonte 119
Sicilian Country Steakhouse 140
Sign of the Bear 244
Silver Oaks Cellars 160–161
Silver Rose Inn & Spa 99
Silverado Country Club & Resort 97–98, 141–142, 287
Silverado Museum 195
Silverado Orchards 353–354
Silverado Realty 335
Silverado Vineyards 159
Simi Winery 187
Sinkyone Wilderness State Park 285
Six Flags Marine World 327
Sixth Street Antiques 254
Skunk Train 209, 326
Smalltown Christmas, A 235
Smith Redwoods State Reserve 282
Smith's Mount St. Helena Trout Farm and Hatchery 324–325
Smothers Winery and Remick Ridge Vineyards 181
SNOOPY'S Gallery and Gift Shop 245
soccer 312
Sonoma Airporter 23–24
Sonoma Barracks 197, 201
Sonoma Bookends Bookstore 257
Sonoma Cattle Co. 294
Sonoma Cheese Factory 244
Sonoma Cinemas 145
Sonoma Coast State Beach 280
Sonoma County
    attractions 196–197, 201–206
    bars and clubs 142–144
    bed and breakfast inns 83–90
    camping 106–108
    children's attractions 320–325
    golf 289–291
    historic Sonoma 197, 201
    hospitals 373–375
    hotels/motels 62, 64–67
    lakes 302
    movie theaters 145–146
    music/dance organizations and venues 268, 270
    Petaluma 5–6
    real estate 337–342
    restaurants 127–132, 134–136
    schools 358–359, 362–365
    spas/resorts 101–102
    theater 262, 264–265
    tours 214
    vacation rentals 71–72
    visual arts 273–275
    walk-in clinics 372–373
    wineries 150–152, 175–188
    worship 392, 394–396
Sonoma County Airport 21
Sonoma County Hilton 64
Sonoma County Museum 203–204
Sonoma County Repertory Theatre 265
Sonoma Hotel 62
Sonoma Management 339
Sonoma Mission Inn & Spa 101
Sonoma Museum of Visual Art 274

Sonoma Outfitters 245
Sonoma Plaza 197
Sonoma Rock & Mineral 244
Sonoma Sky Park 22
Sonoma State University 264, 273, 316–317, 355, 368–369
Sonoma Theatre 145
Sonoma Valley Airport 22
Sonoma Valley Chorale 268, 270
Sonoma Valley Cyclery 293
Sonoma Valley Harvest Wine Auction 229
Sonoma Valley Hospital 373–374
Sonoma Valley Regional Park 278
Sonoma, Lake 302
Sons In Retirement 348–349
Soo Yuan 123
South Coast Senior Citizens 352
Southwest Art in the Wine Country 232
Spanish Flat Resort 106
spas 212–213
spas/resorts 97–104
spectator sports. See individual sports
Spirits In Stone 273
Spoke Folk Cyclery 293
sports. See bicycling; college sports; spectator sports
Sports Bowl 294
Sports Ltd. 293
Spreckels Performing Arts Center 264
Spring Lake Park 106–107, 279
Sprits in Stone 243–244
St. Apollinaris Elementary School 361
St. Clement Vineyards 172
St. Francis Solano School 362–363
St. Francis Winery and Vineyards 181
St. Helena Catholic School 361–362
St. Helena Community Pool 297
St. Helena Cyclery 293
St. Helena Hospital 373
St. Helena Montessori School 361
St. Helena Olive Oil Co. 240
St. Helena Premium Outlets 237
St. Helena St. Helena Antiques 253
St. Helena Wine Merchants 192
St. John's Lutheran School 361
St. Luke Lutheran School 364
St. Mary's Mardi Gras 217
St. Supéry Vineyards & Winery 163
St. Vincent de Paul High School 363
Stag's Leap Wine Cellars 159
Standish-Hickey State Recreation Area 282
Stanford Inn by the Sea—Big River Lodge 103
Stanford University 318
Starlite Motel 71
Steele Wines 192
Steltzner Vineyards 159
Sterling Vineyards 173–174
Stevenson Manor Inn 61
Stevenson, Robert Louis Stevenson 31–32
Stevenswood Lodge 92
Stillwater Cove Regional Park 280
Stone, Charles 42
Stonegate Winery 173
Stuart School 364
Sugarloaf Ridge State Park 106, 278–279
Sunflower Chinese Restaurant 140
Sunset Campground 112
Super 8 Motel 71
Surfwood 142
Surrey Inn 69
Sutter Home Winery 170
Sutter Lakeside Hospital 376, 378
Sutter Lakeside Hospital Urgent Care Center 373

Sutter Medical Center of Santa Rosa 375
Sutter Medical Center Urgent Care Center 372–373
Sweeney's Sports 304
Sweetriver Saloon 143
Sweetwater Spa & Inn 68, 103–104
swimming 296–297
Swiss Hotel, The 128
Symphony on the River 229

T

Tahoe City 331
Tally Ho II Old Fish House 306
Tamale Malone's Irish Cantina & Grille 144
Tanglewood House 84
Tantau 242
Tapioca Tiger 242
taxi services 27
Taylor & Norton Wine Merchants 193
Taylor's Refresher 119–120
Tee Room Restaurant 140
television stations 387–388
tennis 297
Terra 120
Thatcher Inn 90, 137
theater 261–262, 264–267
Third Street AleWorks 124–125
Thistle Dew Inn 83
Tides Wharf & Restaurant, The 135
Tivoli 241
Tomatina 120
Toobtown 323
Topolos 136
Topolos at Russian River Vineyards, Winery & Restaurant 188
Toscano Hotel 201
Touch of Class Limousine Service, A 27
tours 213–214
Tower Records 49
Town of Windsor Parks and Recreation 297
Town of Yountville Recreation 297
Toy Cellar, The 320
Toyon Books 258
Toyworks, The 325
Tra Vigne 120
Tradewinds 143
Traditions 248
Train Town 197, 321
Transamerica Senior Golf Championship 312–313
travel 16–26
Travelodge 69–70
Travelodge/Vineyard Valley Inn Motel 65
Trefethen Vineyards 158
Trentadue Winery 187
Triangle Tattoo Museum 209, 326
Triple-S-Ranch 61, 123
Trojan Horse Inn 83
Trubody Ranch 77
Tucker Farm Center 261–262
Turnbull Wine Cellars 161, 163
Twisted Vines 131
Tylart Shop 238–239

U

UA Cinema 6 146
UA Coddingtown Cinemas 146
UA Empire Cinemas 145
UA Movies 5 146
Ukiah 8
Ukiah 6 Theater 146
Ukiah Chamber of Commerce 15

INDEX

Ukiah Municipal Airport 22
Ukiah Municipal Golf Course 291
Ukiah Playhouse 265
Ukiah Senior Center 351
Ukiah Valley Medical Center 375–376
Union Hotel Restaurant 135–136
Union Square 46
University of California 317–318
University of Northern California 368
Up Valley Associates 336
Upper Lake Senior Outreach 352
Upper Napa Valley Urgent Care 372
Uptown Cinema 145
Ursuline High School 363

V

V. Sattui Winery 169
vacation rentals 71–72
Vallejo, Mariano 33
Vallejo, Salvador 42
Valley Oaks Deli 136–137
Valley Orchards Retirement Community 354
Van Damme State Park 110, 283–284, 293
Vanderbilt and Company 241
Vasquez House 201
Vella Cheese Company 244
Velvet Rabbit 249–250
Viansa Winery and Italian Marketplace 177–178
Vichy Springs Resort 102–103
Victoria's Fashion Stables 322
Victorian Farmhouse, The 92
Victorian Garden Inn 83
Vikingsholm Castle 331
Villa Ca-Toga Tour 220
Villa Messina 87
Villa Mt. Eden winery 168
Village Park Campground 108
Vincent Arroyo Winery 174
VINE, The 24
Vintage 1870 237
Vintage 1870 Wine Cellar, The 192
Vintage Aircraft Co. 197
Vintage Bank Antiques 254
Vintage House 349–350
Vintage Inn 58
Vintage Plaza Antiques 254
Vintage Towers Inn 88
Vintners Inn 65
Violette's at the Mansion 142
Vista Manor Inn 69
visual arts 270–276
Viva Sonoma 244
Volpi's Ristorante 131
Volunteer Wheels 25

W

W.C. "Bob" Trowbridge Canoe Trips 304
walk-in clinics 372–373
Wally Johnson Realty 343
Wappo Bar & Bistro 127
Warehouse Repertory Theatre 267
Warrack Hospital 374–375
Washington Square Cinema 5 145
watercrafts 304, 306
Wayside Inn, The 82
Wellington Vineyards 179
Wermuth Winery 172–173
West Coast Seaplane Splash-In 230
West County Museum 205

West County Property Management 339
Western Institute of Science and Health 370
Westlake Seventh Day Adventist Christian School 366
Westlake Springs 354
Westlake Wine Country House 354
Westport-Union Landing State Beach 285
Westshore County Park Swimming Pool 297
Westside Regional Park 280
Wet Pleasure Jet Ski & Watercraft Rentals, A 304
Wexford & Woods 243
Whale Festivals 218
Whale Watch Inn 91
Wharf Master's Inn 91
Wharf Restaurant 139
Whistle Stop Antiques 254
Whistlestop Antiques 255–256
White Sulphur Springs Resort & Spa 98–99
Whitegate Inn 94–95
Wikiup Golf Course 290
Wildhurst Vineyards 191
Wildlife Natural History Museum 322
WilkesSport 242
Willits Celtic Renaissance 221–222
Willits Community Theatre 265–266
Willits KOA 109
Willits Senior Center 351–352
Windsor Chamber of Commerce 14
Windsor Golf Club 290
Windsor Vineyards Tasting Room 184
Windsor Waterworks & Slides 204–205, 325
Windsorland RV Trailer Park 107
Windwalker Board Sports and School of Windsurfing 306
wine 32–33, 153–54
Wine & Dine Tours 213
Wine Country Cycling Classic 315–316
Wine Country Inn, The 59
Wine Country Kennel Club 223
Wine Exchange of Sonoma, The 193
Wine Rack Shop, The 193
wine shops 192–193
Wine Spectator Greystone Restaurant 120
Wine Valley Lodge 57
Wine Way Inn 79–80
wineries 157–192
Winesong 230
winetasting 155, 157, 165–167
Wisteria Garden Bed & Breakfast 80, 82
Wok Wiz 46
Woodbridge Village 354
Wooden Duck Antique Shop 255
Woods, The 355
Wordsworth Books 257–258
World's Wristwrestling Championship 316
worship 389–399

Y

Yokayo Bowl 293
Yorkville Vineyards & Cellars 191
Yoshi-Shige 116
Yount, George 28–29
Yountville Inn 58
Yuba College 356, 367–368

Z

ZD Wines 164
Zemorah Christian Academy 365
Zino's Ristorante 129